AMERICAN FICTION SERIES

GENERAL EDITOR

HARRY HAYDEN CLARK, *University of Wisconsin*

AMERICAN FICTION SERIES

Unabridged reprints of historically important but now inaccessible novels, mainly of the earlier periods, under the general editorship of Harry Hayden Clark, professor of English, University of Wisconsin. The individual volumes are edited by American scholars, who have supplied Introductions, Chronologies, and Bibliographies.

NOW PUBLISHED

MODERN CHIVALRY, BY HUGH HENRY BRACKENRIDGE
Edited by Claude M. Newlin, Michigan State College

ORMOND, BY CHARLES BROCKDEN BROWN
Edited by Ernest Marchand, Stanford University

SATANSTOE, BY JAMES FENIMORE COOPER
Edited by Robert E. Spiller, Swarthmore College, and Joseph D. Coppock, Hendrix College

HORSE-SHOE ROBINSON, BY JOHN PENDLETON KENNEDY
Edited by Ernest E. Leisy, Southern Methodist University

THE YEMASSEE, BY WILLIAM GILMORE SIMMS
Edited by Alexander Cowie, Wesleyan University

J. P. Kennedy

HORSE-SHOE ROBINSON

BY

JOHN PENDLETON KENNEDY

EDITED, WITH INTRODUCTION,
CHRONOLOGY, AND BIBLIOGRAPHY
BY

ERNEST E. LEISY
SOUTHERN METHODIST UNIVERSITY

A. F. S.

AMERICAN BOOK COMPANY
NEW YORK CINCINNATI CHICAGO BOSTON
ATLANTA DALLAS SAN FRANCISCO

Kennedy's Horse-Shoe Robinson

E. P. 1

Made in U. S. A.

PREFACE

The novel, which is at present the chief literary type of expression in America, has undergone in its comparatively brief history many changes of fashion. One theme, however, that of the nation's birth, has interested readers in all periods. In the 1830's so strong was the feeling for manifest destiny that it amounted to a movement in which romancers attempted to show what contribution their particular region had made to the national independence. John Pendleton Kennedy, though not a "professional" novelist, appears in retrospect the most readable of those who then essayed historical fiction. As his best novel, *Horse-Shoe Robinson,* is now available only in a considerably abridged and bowdlerized form it has seemed advisable to republish it. The text followed is that of the second copyright edition of 1852, rather than that of 1835, because it was the last revised by its author. This revised text differs from the first chiefly in matters of punctuation, commas replacing dashes, explicit phrases taking the place of indefinite ones, legal terminology being simplified, and profanity here and there being toned down. Approximately fifty sentences were modified, but nowhere did the author materially change the thought.

It is a pleasure to express thanks to Professor Jay B. Hubbell, to Dr. Edd W. Parks, and to the general editor, Professor Harry H. Clark, for assistance kindly given in editing this volume.

E. E. L.

Dallas, Texas

CONTENTS

Preface v
Introduction ix
A Kennedy Chronology xxvii
Selected Bibliography xxix
HORSE-SHOE ROBINSON, by John Pendleton Kennedy
Note on the Text 2
The Dedication to Irving 3
Kennedy's Introduction 5
Kennedy's Preface to First Edition 11
Complete Text of *Horse-Shoe Robinson* . . . 13–550

ILLUSTRATIONS

Portrait of Kennedy . . . . frontispiece
Letter to William Gilmore Simms . following page xxiv
Inscription to Commodore M. C. Perry . . facing page 1
Title Page of 1852 Edition . . . . page 1
Map of Horse-Shoe Robinson Country . . facing page 16
An Illustration by Darley . . . . . . facing page 48

INTRODUCTION

When the two volumes of *Horse-Shoe Robinson* appeared from the press of a Philadelphia publisher in 1835, no less a critic than Edgar Allan Poe said, "We feel little afraid of hazarding our critical reputation when we assert that they will place Mr. Kennedy at once in the very first rank of American novelists."[1] Poe was right, even though his obligations to Kennedy might be thought to account for his partisanship.[2] This first romance by a new writer "at once took firm hold upon the public fancy,"[3] and passed into a second, and then a third edition. Kennedy's name was linked with Cooper's;[4] and a writer in the *New York Review* went so far as to declare, "We know of no author on this side of the Atlantic who possesses superior advantages, or who would work for eminence with better assurance of success."[5] The writers of fiction then before the public included, besides Fenimore Cooper, the fiery John Neal, the versatile Paulding, Timothy Flint, Lydia Child, Catherine Sedgwick, and one or two others. In this very year Simms had made a strong bid for recognition with *The Yemassee* and Caruthers published *The Cavaliers of Virginia*. So well, however, had Kennedy treated subject and scene that *Horse-Shoe Robinson* enjoyed "and justly a popularity second to that of no other Southern novel of the time."[6]

1. *Southern Literary Messenger*, I, 522 (May, 1835); reprinted in *The Complete Works of Edgar Allan Poe*, edited by Harrison, VIII, 4.

2. Kennedy was one of the judges who awarded Poe the prize for his story "MS. Found in a Bottle." Kennedy helped Poe to place some of his stories, and introduced him to T. W. White, the editor of the *Southern Literary Messenger*, who invited Poe in 1835 to become his assistant, and subsequently editor.

3. *Southern Quarterly Review*, XXII, 203 (July, 1852).

4. *Southern Literary Journal*, I, 206 (Nov., 1835). "Horse-Shoe Robinson reminds us of Cooper's Leatherstocking, and is, we think, nearly, if not quite, equal to that striking original."

5. *New York Review*, X, 150–151 (1842).

6. Killis Campbell, "The Kennedy Papers," *Sewanee Review*, XXV, 1 (1917). Cf. Carl Holliday, *A History of Southern Literature* (1906), p. 176.

I

Kennedy's life was in mid-career when *Horse-Shoe Robinson* was published. He was forty years of age. Three years before, he had drawn in *Swallow Barn* a picture of the old gentry in Virginia. With rare sympathy and understanding he delineated those happy regional qualities which were even then fading from life in the Old Dominion.[7] He was to bring out three years later his only other novel, *Rob of the Bowl,* a romance of colonial Maryland, his native state. His extensive public services were in the main to come later.

Kennedy's preparation for authorship like Washington Irving's, had been partly classical, partly eighteenth century.[8] It consisted also of much outdoor life. As the son of a distinguished family in Baltimore, his was a youth of considerable social activity. Early he began to write ephemera; among these "effusions" he later remembered a farce, acted by his playfellows, and letters in the manner of Sterne, whom he then greatly admired.[9] He frequented the theatre, where he was particularly impressed by the acting of Jefferson, Cooke, and Kean; and he developed a fondness for music that was to be lifelong. From a debating society he acquired discipline in writing as well as respect for the opinions of others. Judge Hollingsworth of the Baltimore Court took a strong fancy to the young man, and stimulated his wit and respect for scholarship.[10] This influence, together with that of his study of the classics, and of his debating society, he says, "floated me to the eddy [the law] upon which I was destined to swim."[11] The outbreak of the War of 1812, however, offered

7. See the Introduction in J. B. Hubbell's edition of *Swallow Barn,* New York, 1929.

8. "I studied Greek a whole winter, by rising before daylight; I read Locke, Hume, Robertson — all the essayists and poets, and many of the metaphysicians; studied Burke, Taylor, Barrow; worked at chemistry, geometry, and the higher mathematics, although I never loved them; made copious notes on all the subjects which came within my study; sketched, painted (very badly), read French, Spanish, and began German; copied large portions of Pope's translations from Homer, and wrote critical notes upon them as I went along." — Kennedy's Diary, quoted by H. T. Tuckerman, *The Life of John Pendleton Kennedy* (New York, 1871), p. 41.

9. *Ibid.*, p. 48. 10. *Ibid.*, p. 58–60. 11. *Ibid.*, p. 63.

the young graduate of Baltimore College the excitement of military service, for which he now volunteered. Participation in the skirmish at Bladensburg nursed his ideas of romance and kindled in him chivalric ideas of love. Besides, active familiarity with maneuvers and experiences in camp gave him that close acquaintance with military life which he was to use so vividly in *Horse-Shoe Robinson*.

The profession of the law claimed Kennedy's first allegiance. His pleasant association with men like Luther Martin, William Pinkney, Generals Harper and Winder, and, on occasion, with William Wirt, impressed him with the social prestige of the profession. But, like others of his day, he found the dry details of law irksome, and turned in preference "to the humanizing generalities of literature, with unabated relish; he wrote, and read history, poetry and fiction, as soon as he had disposed of a case or got through a document."[12] While his friend Pennington was engaged upon a chancery bill, Kennedy and another co-resident of bachelor's hall, Cruse, were preparing a forthcoming number of *The Red Book*. Thus, like Irving and Paulding with their *Salmagundi* papers, these young Baltimoreans entertained their young friends with their lucubrations.

More serious tasks now confronted Kennedy. He found himself in the Maryland legislature for three successive years, 1820–1823. While there he advocated internal improvements, opposed imprisonment for debt, and came out openly against slavery.[13] He encountered opposition in connection with each of these measures, but his policies were in line with national progress. He became a friend and admirer of Henry Clay, and an opponent of Andrew Jackson. President Monroe appointed him secretary of the legation to Chile, but this honor he declined. He married, but within the year suffered the loss of his wife. Five years later, in 1829, he married Elizabeth Gray, daughter of a wealthy cotton-spinner of Ellicott Mills, just outside Baltimore.

Professor Parrington has suggested that this second marriage was the turning-point in Kennedy's life, that from now on the

12. *Ibid.*, p. 108.

13. Frank Meriwether's paternalistic scheme of gradual emancipation as outlined in *Swallow Barn*, Chapter XLVI, is essentially Kennedy's view, a view not materially altered in the carefully revised later edition.

erstwhile Jeffersonian embraced the tenets of capitalism.[14] It is apparent, however, that Kennedy had already shown protectionist leanings,[15] and what seems a change was merely the strengthening of earlier tendencies. The drift of the times was away from an agrarian economy and toward an industrial order, and nowhere was this change more noticeable than in Baltimore. In 1830 Kennedy wrote a defense of the tariff as against Churchill C. Cambreleng's *Report on Commerce and Navigation.* This paper was widely circulated, and Kennedy was appointed the following year one of a committee to draft a statement of the protectionist view for a national convention of manufacturers. In 1838 he was sent to Congress, the first Whig so honored in his district. After two years in Congress he published *Annals of Quodlibet,* " the most vivacious criticism of Jacksonianism in our political library."[16] The narrative recorded ludicrous events in a small town under a Democratic régime just before the election of William Henry Harrison to the presidency. The principal concern of the inhabitants was the establishment of a bank, on a highly speculative foundation; when the directors could no longer hoodwink the public the cashier absconded to Europe, and the downfall of the scheme was attributed to the Whigs. It was a clever satire on the agrarian opposition to the rising money power and gave Kennedy a position of eminence in his party. When President Tyler abandoned the Whigs for the Locofocos, three years later, Kennedy was selected by his colleagues in Congress to draft a manifesto condemning the course of the Chief Executive. *A Defense of the Whigs* (1843), a careful review of the history of the two parties, was Kennedy's response.

When the problem of secession from the Union came up,

14. V. L. Parrington, *The Romantic Revolution in America, 1800–1860* (1927), p. 49. Edward Gray, Kennedy's wealthy father-in-law, and he had common interests other than financial. Both loved books of romance and both had enthusiasm for the American Revolution. Gray, an Irish immigrant, had admired Washington from afar, and on his arrival in Philadelphia had become intimately associated with his hero and with Hamilton in a business way. By thrift and indefatigable industry he had overcome several financial reverses, and thanks to protectionist policies was now a flourishing manufacturer. See Tuckermann, *op. cit.*, p. 247.

15. Note for example his attitude on measures while in the Maryland legislature, mentioned above.

16. Parrington, *op. cit.*, p. 56.

Kennedy took the national view, though it was not easy to part from his Southern friends.[17] On the question of sovereignty he took the position that

> no state conquered a sovereignty for itself in the War of the Revolution; but that the thirteen Colonies combined to overthrow the British sovereignty . . . and after that, by a united consent and agreement parcelled out to the states just so much power as the united body thought fit to give them; that, therefore, if there were any sovereignty in each state it was derivative and came by grant, and was not original or inherent in each state; that it did not exist before the union of the Revolution but was derived from that union.[18]

During the fifties Kennedy sought to conciliate extremists by writing to men of influence both in the North and in the South. Through impassioned pleas in the newspapers he further tried to stem the tide of rebellion before it should be too late. But his efforts were in vain. In the third year of the conflict he began a series of letters to the editor of the *National Intelligencer* in which he tried to persuade the belligerent parties to arbitrate their differences. These papers were published in book form as *Mr. Ambrose's Letters on the Rebellion*.[19] When the war was over Kennedy was among the first to work for reconciliation.

Kennedy was a man of eminent respectability. His journals attest the significance and scope of his social sympathies. "It seems to have been an absolute necessity of his nature," says his biographer,[20] "to hold intimate relations with his fellowmen, to exchange views, to cherish friendships, to 'flit the time gently as they did in the golden age.'" The Baltimore of his day had

17. *Ibid.*, p. 46. Kennedy was "an American Victorian of the Cobden-Bright school, standing midway between the northern radical and the Southern Fire-Eater."

18. Kennedy's notebook, quoted by E. M. Gwathmey, *John Pendleton Kennedy* (New York, 1931), p. 51.

19. *Mr. Ambrose's Letters on the Rebellion* (1865) traced the origin of secession to "a few Quixotes in politics" (p. 6) and a "system of traditionary dialectics [which] had bred a class of hair-splitting *doctrinaires*" (p. 7). Dreams of a Southern empire fostered the war of opinion into a bloody battle. After vindicating the benignity of the Federal Government, the author appeals to those "with vision undisturbed by passion" to "give an example of that noble patriotism which accounts our country dearer than all human blessings and its service only subordinate to that we owe the Creator" (p. 85).

20. Tuckerman, *op. cit.*, p. 344.

two literary clubs, one of which Kennedy headed.[21] His relations with literary men were extensive and most agreeable in character. "He constantly assisted and encouraged poor authors partly because he loved their vocation and, in no small degree, because he felt that his own prosperous circumstances gave them a claim upon his kindness."[22] He was the patron of Poe, a warm friend of Irving and Willis, and was on terms of friendly intercourse with Cooper, Longfellow, Lowell, Holmes, Paulding, Prescott, Simms, Cooke, and Bayard Taylor in this country, and with Thackeray, Dickens, Landor, Lever, Rogers, and G. P. R. James among the English writers of the day. It is significant, however, that their letters deal with social amenities and not with literary matters.

Kennedy's social sympathies are reflected in his work. For him a circle is "unsurpassed" where "the wise and the gay, the beautiful and the rarely gifted unite in a splendid little constellation, in which wealth throws its sunbeam glitter over the wings of love."[23] In *Swallow Barn* the substantial planter in his mansion on the James is little vexed with life's crosses. In *Horse-Shoe Robinson* a similarly wealthy, easygoing, contemplative Virginian has troubles galore, but the hero possesses "a handsome fortune" which he combines with the heroine's at the conclusion of their vicissitudes. In *Rob of the Bowl* the wily buccaneer loses his life but endows the young couple with his wealth at the end.

Upholder of the doctrine of property that Kennedy was, he

21. Hervey Allen, *Israfel* (1926), p. 353. Kennedy headed the old "Tusculum" Club to which William Gwynn and others belonged. It was more literary, and the other club more journalistic. Mary Phillips, *Edgar Allan Poe, the Man* (1926), p. 339, mentions other members as John Neal, Francis Scott Key, Jared Sparks, Samuel Woodworth, William Wirt. James Wynne (*Harper's Magazine*, XXV, 335) saw most of Kennedy at "The Monday Club" which "met alternately at the houses of various members . . . and was almost certain to command the presence of any distinguished stranger who chanced to be in town." It was "composed of four doctors of law, four doctors of divinity, four doctors of medicine and four gentlemen distinguished for literary attainments." On Baltimore's literary life see John E. Uhler, *Literary Taste and Culture in Baltimore* (Johns Hopkins, 1922).

22. Tuckerman, *op. cit.*, p. 363.

23. *Horse-Shoe Robinson*, p. 87, below. See also p. 84 in which Philip Lindsay is the exponent "of a refined and polished civilization, which no after day in the history of this empire has yet surpassed — perhaps not equalled."

yet had a strong belief in natural goodness. A sturdy common sense manifests itself in his warm-hearted creations. In Horse-Shoe he remarks a "real delicacy of mind that lies at the bottom of a kind nature, and inhabits the shaggy breast of the rustic, at least full as often as it lodges in the heart of the trim worldling."[24] A kind of fatalism underlies human conduct. "What is destiny but these under-currents that come whencesoever they list, unheeded at first, and irresistible ever afterwards!"[25] Good and evil are inextricably bound up with each other. "There is some good things in this world that's good," says Kennedy's sergeant, "and some that's bad. But I have always found that good and bad is so mixed up and jumbled together, that you don't often get much of one without a little of the other."[26] A lifelong member of the Presbyterian church,[27] Kennedy believed that good breeding and Christian charity carried their own reward.[28] His characters are ever deferent to religion, but he never obtrudes religious views into fiction as does Fenimore Cooper. In this respect as in others he deserves credit for his moderation and restraint in a period when few works of fiction were tempered by a sense of humor.

When Kennedy began to write fiction in *Swallow Barn* (1832), he wrote in the manner of Queen Anne's day. Popular taste in America at the time followed the tradition, established by Irving, of gentility, grace, quietude of thought, and gentle

24. *Horse-Shoe Robinson*, p. 55.

25. *Ibid.*, p 87.

26. *Ibid.*, p. 206.

27. During his youth Kennedy "was in the habit of appropriating a portion of every Sunday to religious studies, which consisted, in part, in writing extracts from the Scriptures, and the finest passages I found in theological writers" (Tuckerman, *op. cit.*, p. 47). Kennedy's religious views were never narrowly pietistic, however. On his sixty-fifth birthday he recorded as usual his humble thankfulness for life, and added: "I endeavor to avoid the uncharitableness of sectarian opinion, and maintain an equal mind toward the various forms in which an earnest piety shapes the divisions of the world of believers, — tolerating honest differences as the right of all sincere thinkers, and looking only to the kindly nature of Christian principle as it influences the personal lives and conduct of men, as the substantial and true test of a sound religion" (Tuckerman, *op. cit.*, p. 354).

28. *Horse-Shoe Robinson*, p. 385. "It is an honest and virtuous cause that takes me away," says Mildred, "and I will attempt it with a valiant spirit. It cannot but come to good." The chief vice of James Curry, the villain, is his overweening ambition (*ibid.*, p. 235). Cf. also Chapter IV in *Swallow Barn* for gentility as an attribute of the good life.

humor. From his youth Kennedy had known the country life of Virginia, where is laid the scene of *Swallow Barn.* He had on many an occasion enjoyed there the generous hospitality of relatives. That free-handed living, as it existed in the first quarter of the nineteenth century, he now gathered in happy retrospect. He pictured with felicity local types like the Virginia gentleman of the old school; the country lawyer, eccentric, convivial, oracular; and various characters, like the hoyden Bel Tracy and the drunken blacksmith Mike Brown, which served for relief. He learned also how to make plausible the details of a love suit; to describe picturesque landmarks like the old mill, or interesting woodland vistas; all those touches which offered a social tableau he observed sympathetically. But there was no real story, unless the slender thread of a friendly litigation between neighbors, which terminated in a successful love-affair, be regarded as having narrative interest. What Kennedy had yet to learn was the management of the sustained narrative of a full-fledged romance.[29] This he was to discover in his next work, *Horse-Shoe Robinson,* a historical novel of the American Revolution.

II

The historical novel helped to remove the stigma which once clung to prose fiction in America. In the guise of presenting patriotic information it ingratiated itself with readers who normally winced at fiction. Its comparative freedom from rules fitted it to be a popular medium of imaginative expression in the New World. As a consequence it developed during the period of national expansiveness, following the second War with Great Britain, into the favorite literary form. It enjoyed a second period of popular favor in the eighteen-nineties and following.

29. Parrington, *op. cit.,* pp. 50–51. "His literary development was an evolution from a sketchy and humorous Addisonian, with its echoes of the eighteenth century, to the full Victorian romantic. . . . His three best-known books, written between the ages of thirty-six and forty-five, are unlike enough to have been written by different men. *Swallow Barn,* like the youthful sketches of *The Red Book,* is Irvingesque, and the Irving influence crops out again in a late book *Quodlibet;* but *Horseshoe Robinson* is substantial Revolutionary romance, done in a sober narrative with touches of realism; and *Rob of the Bowl* is light and whimsical cavalier romance, all atmosphere and small talk, utterly unlike Irving."

Many of these novels are now forgotten, and some deservedly so, but the *genre* persists.[30]

Its origin the historical novel in America owed to the influence of Sir Walter Scott. A forerunner like *The First Settlers of Virginia* (1805) by John Davis merely indicated what confusion existed about writing historical romance before the great Scotchman evolved his formula. Scott

> recombined, according to formulas of his own, many elements present in the fiction of his day,—the tendency to localized or national tales with that interest in humble personages on whom local characteristics are most deeply impressed, which appears most plainly in Miss Edgeworth's Irish stories; the interest in romantic landscape and word-painting of natural scenery which found its most striking expression in Mrs. Radcliffe's theatrical yet impressive scenes; the tale of adventure reinforced by the revived interest in travel and antiquarian taste for old buildings and trappings; and the eagerness for an imaginative interpretation of history which had expressed itself in many would-be historical tales.[31]

In *The Spy* (1821) Cooper led the way in adapting the method of Scott to American materials, in this case to events of the Revolutionary struggle. But Cooper lacked the historical acumen of Scott, as is well demonstrated in *Lionel Lincoln* (1825). He thought also that our annals were bare.[32] His novels, therefore, are primarily romances of adventure. He could draw memorably historical types like the scout, the Indian, the sailor, but his attempts to picture well-known historical figures, Washington, John Paul Jones, Montcalm, were feeble and shadowy. His immediate contemporaries, John Neal, Lydia Child, Catherine Sedgwick, James McHenry, James K. Paulding, experimented variously in grafting upon the stock of historical fiction, the Gothic romance, the sentimental-didactic tale, and social satire. But they did it with the awkwardness of amateurs.

By the eighteen-thirties, however, novel writing in America

30. For a survey of the subject consult Ernest E. Leisy, *The American Historical Novel before 1860* (unpublished University of Illinois dissertation, 1923).

31. L. D. Loshe, *The Early American Novel* (1907), pp. 83–84.

32. See Preface to *Red Rover* (1828); *The Travelling Bachelor*, II (1828), p. 103; *Heidenmauer* (1832), Chapter V; *Home as Found*, I (1838), p. iv. See also *Notions of the Americans* in R. E. Spiller's *James Fenimore Cooper* (American Writers Series, 1936), pp. 3 ff.

had attained a modicum of self-assurance.[33] The nation's semicentennial had been duly acclaimed. Local histories had been written. Novelists now sought to introduce the traditions and usages of one section to another. Thus William A. Caruthers introduced life in the Old Dominion in *The Cavaliers of Virginia* (1832) and in *The Knights of the Horse-shoe* (1845); William Gilmore Simms presented frontier life in Carolina in *The Yemassee* (1835), and laid *Beauchampe* (1842) in Kentucky, *Guy Rivers* (1834) in Georgia, *Richard Hurdis* (1838) in Alabama, and *Border Beagles* (1840) in Mississippi; D. P. Thompson gave the piquant provincialism of Vermont in *The Green Mountain Boys* (1839); Charles Fenno Hoffman pictured romance in the Mohawk valley in *Greyslaer* (1840), and Cooper, after his European sojourn, concluded to fall in line with the novel of local tradition in his Littlepage Manuscripts (1845–1846). Hand in hand with this cultivation of local history went the development of realism. It was the artistic counterpart of a search for the verities which underlay the spiritual welter of the period. The temperance agitation, the Mormon movement, the experiment at Brook Farm, to name but a few, were indicative of a widespread ferment. The seaboard squabbled with the interior over internal improvements; East and West were sometimes in antagonism concerning public lands; North and South were at odds over nullification. Coincident with these came a quickening of the creative spirit which attempted in various writings of the period to get at truth and reality. As novelists modified the Scott-Cooper pattern to allow for regional peculiarities, they achieved more vigorous and consequently more memorable work than the imitators. For instance, the scout of Simms or of Thompson was sharply distinguished from a Highland outlaw of Scott. He lived as a vivid person because of his distinctly local attributes.

33. *New York Review, op. cit.*, p. 151. "The task of the novel writer of today is much more arduous than . . . thirty years ago. There are as many good critics of novels now as there were readers of them formerly. The public taste has grown nice."

III

The story of *Horse-Shoe Robinson* is laid in Virginia and the Carolinas during the closing years of the War of Independence. In the early part of the conflict active warfare had been largely in the North. Lexington, Bunker Hill, Boston, Saratoga, New York, Princeton, Monmouth, Philadelphia had each been the center of vigorous fighting. In the South, Charleston had suffered in 1776 a ten-hour bombardment of the fort on Sullivan's Island, but this attack by Clinton had been unsuccessful, and for two years the Carolinas were not molested again.

When the British forces made little headway in subduing the colonies to the North, they changed their strategy, and determined to resume activity in the South. For this purpose Colonel Campbell and Admiral Parker were dispatched to Savannah, and finding the city defended by only nine hundred men, were able to secure its surrender at the close of 1778. Early the following year Augusta was captured, and Georgia was in the hands of the British. While the Virginia and Carolina coasts were harassed by British seacraft, officers went into the Carolinas to rally the Tories. British sympathizers were numerous in South Carolina, and, with the aid of some of the ablest British officers, gave the champions of independence in the South a severe test of endurance.

Early in 1780 Clinton brought a large force from New York to Charleston. For forty days he besieged the city. At length, on May 12, he secured its surrender, and with it as a base he proceeded to overrun the colony. The Tories now took heart, and with the aid of the British, struck blow for blow in internecine warfare. Tarleton's Legion of regulars and Tories terrorized the countryside with their vindictive bush-fighting. The humble followers of Marion, Sumter, and Pickens engaged in partisan reprisals, and ultimately subdued their enemies.

In the ranks were many who like Horse-Shoe Robinson served their country with quiet heroism. The incident in Chapter XXII in which Ensign St. Jermyn and his four men were taken prisoner by Horse-Shoe with the aid of fourteen year old Andy Ramsay had its counterpart in the careers of Marion and others.

Back and forth went the fortunes of war. In June four hundred Carolinians defeated thirteen hundred Tories at Ramsour's Mills. Sumter routed the regulars at Hanging Rock; and at Musgrove's Mills the patriots were also successful. But in August, at the battle of Camden, Gates's army was badly defeated by Cornwallis.

The battle of King's Mountain, in which Major Ferguson was slain and his force of eleven hundred Tories were taken prisoners, was a major achievement of the war. Chapter LVII vividly and accurately describes the assault. When a month later, Tarleton attacked Sumter at Blackstocks, he was repulsed with great loss, and prospects began to brighten for the colonials. In January of 1781 the continentals under General Greene, who now took command of the veterans that had fought gallantly at Camden, dealt Tarleton a crushing blow in the battle of the Cowpens, near King's Mountain. Shortly after followed the engagements at Guilford Court House, Hobkirk's Hill, Ninety-Six, Eutaw Springs; and then on October 19 occurred the surrender of Cornwallis at Yorktown, Virginia.

The fratricidal nature of the Revolutionary struggle was not generally understood until novelists like Cooper, Kennedy, and Simms emphasized it. Whig historians had developed the legend of a spontaneous uprising against the mother country and concealed or ignored evidence to the contrary.[34] But in *The Spy*, in *Horse-Shoe Robinson*, and in *The Partisan* it was apparent that the struggle was in reality a civil war. Characters like Wat Adair and Hugh Habershaw consistently plotted against their neighbors on either side. This irregular warfare which received scant attention from the historians was brought out importantly in these novels. "But for the partisan warfare," wrote Simms, "the regular armies would have taken the field in vain."[35] Francis Marion, the "Swamp Fox," was particularly expert in the stratagem of partisan warfare. With but a few dozen men

34. See C. F. Adams, *Studies Military and Diplomatic* (1911); S. G. Fisher, "The Legendary and Myth-making Process in Histories of the American Revolution," *Proceedings of the American Philosophical Society*, LI, No. 204 (April-June, 1912); Charles Kendall Adams, "Some Neglected Aspects of the Revolutionary War," *Atlantic Monthly*, LXXXII, 174.

35. W. G. Simms, *The Partisan*, rev. ed., 1854, p. viii.

at most he darted in and out of the morasses of the Pedee and the Black rivers to strike at the foe, and as quickly vanished unperceived. Often without food, shelter, or sufficient clothing, he distinguished himself by his bravery, resourcefulness, and unselfish personal character. His camp life and methods of warfare are well illustrated in Chapter XLI.

IV

Against this historical background of Virginia and the Carolinas, Kennedy placed, with careful attention to local detail, such diverse characters as the studiously inclined lord of the manor, with Tory leanings; his patriotic daughter, the victim of a scheming loyalist; a rustic maiden and her frontier lover; a miller with stanch Presbyterian principles; British officers, some shadowy, others highly individualized like Ferguson "the heathen Tory"; patriot leaders like Marion and Sumter, dashing out of woodland retreats; Tarleton and his troops in thieving and burning reprisals; and aged non-combatants facing ruin.

Early in the story the character who promised to be the hero was made captive and naturally assumed a rôle of subordinate interest.[36] From this point the author concentrated on the titular hero, a resourceful blacksmith, and set him to "squiring" the captive's beloved through the tightening net of a Tory admirer.

Horse-Shoe Robinson, like Leather-Stocking, was one of those primitive characters born of peculiar local influences. Though illiterate, he possessed admirable mother-wit and manly probity. He differed from Leather-Stocking and similar types east and west in his intense patriotism, his companionable temper, and his imperturbable good humor. He is not so poetical as his prototype, but more social and joyous. Kennedy claims to have met the original on one of his horseback journeys to the western section of South Carolina. When years later the tale was read to its surprised hero, he is said to have replied, "It's

36. In this he is not unlike his namesake in Scott's *The Heart of Midlothian* (1818). *American Quarterly Review,* XVIII, 241: Butler is like one of Scott's heroes — a mere creature for the development of others' energies — a slave of circumstances. Habershaw is a kind of Tory Capt. Bobadil.

all true and right — in its right place — excepting about them women, which I disremember." [37]

The heroine, though a product of the contemporary school of sensibility, shows more resolution than most of her prototypes. As she is a young woman of considerable intellectual force, her distress is really moving. The death of John Ramsay, likewise, is well motivated, and enlists more sympathy than usually attended the removal of a secondary figure. On the whole the romance element owes little to Scott. So well are the minor figures drawn that they rather suggest Shakespeare, Habershaw being a kind of Dogberry. The few historical figures — Marion, Tarleton, Cornwallis, Ferguson — are skilfully introduced, though they appear but briefly. There is an air of veracity in the accounts of the bush-fighting. Although Kennedy cherished poetic justice as keenly as his contemporaries, he was too much a realist [38] to allow his partisans to escape without hurt.

Not a little of the charm of *Horse-Shoe Robinson* is owing to the author's acute delineation of landscape.[39] For some time American writers had complained that they could not write romance without ivied walls or snowy summits old in story.[40] The endless expanse of forest had fascinated Chateaubriand; and Coleridge and Southey had dreamt of a pantisocracy on the banks of the Susquehanna; Charles Brockden Brown had pictured native scenery in *Edgar Huntly;* but not until Irving

37. Introduction to 1852 edition of *Horse-Shoe Robinson* (p. 10, below). But see John R. Moore, " Kennedy's Horse-Shoe Robinson: Fact or Fiction? " *American Literature,* IV, 160–166 (1932), which suggests that Kennedy fictionalized from general observation. Moore overlooks the evidence about Mike Brown, the sergeant and blacksmith in *Swallow Barn,* which tends to substantiate his views. The well-known figure of Davy Crockett may also have had something to contribute to the picture. Kennedy quotes one of Crockett's phrases in a letter he wrote while composing *Horse-Shoe Robinson* (Tuckerman, *op. cit.,* p. 135).

38. His general attitude toward his material is reflected in the heading of Chapter XXII: " An adventure wherein it is apparent that the actions of real life are full as marvellous as the inventions of romance."

39. Gwathmey, *op. cit.,* p. 91: " Kennedy's greatest talent as a writer lay in his power of description."

40. The lack of historic background felt by early writers of American fiction has been summarized by various scholars. See G. H. Orians, " The Romance Ferment after Waverly," *American Literature,* III, 408–431 (1932). For a recent comprehensive survey see William Ellery Sedgwick, " The Materials for an American Literature: A Critical Problem of the Early Nineteenth Century," *Harvard Studies and Notes in Philology and Literature,* XVII, 141–162 (1935).

supplied a sense of beauty to what had been regarded as the unpicturesque Hudson, and not until Cooper invested the wilderness with romantic charm did writers feel that the American scene could be worthily presented in a work of fiction. Kennedy's localism was definitely Irvingesque.[41]

The style, too, in many respects suggests Irving. It is studded with references to the classics, Shakespeare, the Bible, and old ballads; at the same time it is more colloquial than that of most of his contemporaries.[42] Its genial humor, its old-fashioned prolixity, its urbane overtones are, like Irving's, the style of a gentleman. Poe called it a style that is "simple and forcible," yet "richly figurative and poetical," "altogether devoid of affectation . . . a style of writing above all others to be desired, and above all others difficult of attainment."[43] When compared with the tendency of Cooper or Bird toward melodrama, Kennedy's exercise of a sense of restraint is noticeable. His avoidance of stereotyped adjectives adds to the authenticity of the narrative. His descriptive and dramatic talent, coupled with his intimate acquaintance with the locality and with the stalwart hero in homespun, resulted in making *Horse-Shoe Robinson* a considerably more vivid and realistic novel than was generally current at the time.

The success of Kennedy with *Horse-Shoe Robinson* may have suggested to Simms the writing of *The Partisan,* which used the same materials.[44] A comparison of the two books is in order. As a native South Carolinian Simms read in local chronicles the details of partisan warfare. The cypress swamps he knew at first hand. He borrowed from Scott, Godwin, and Cooper sundry conventions for his plot, and before the close of the year

41. Cf. V. L. Parrington, *op. cit.*, p. 49. "Like Irving, Kennedy was a devout romantic, with a love of the old-time picturesque. He was a child of the break-up of the eighteenth century and an ebullient romanticism that permeated writing thereafter; but where Irving wanted the English romantic, Kennedy was content to remain native." *Horse-Shoe Robinson* was dedicated to Irving (p. 3, below).

42. In his youth Kennedy filled his notebooks with elaborately colloquial sentences from *Tristram Shandy*. Tuckerman, *op. cit.*, p. 48.

43. *Southern Literary Messenger,* I, 524 (May, 1835); cf. *Southern Literary Journal,* I, 206 (Nov., 1835): "The style of the work is easy and graceful without parade . . . elevating the standard of fictitious composition in our country."

44. William P. Trent, *William Gilmore Simms* (Boston, 1892), p. 94.

The Partisan (1835) was off the press. Naturally the book showed the signs of haste. *The Partisan* was in places more exciting than *Horse-Shoe Robinson,* but it was also more melodramatic. Its plot, which began with suddenness, showed no sense of development, nor of climax; it closed abruptly some time after the defeat of Gates at Camden, instead of with the more dramatic American success at King's Mountain.[45]

Though the stories have largely the same material, Simms prefers to portray types and Kennedy individuals. *The Partisan* is more fantastic. It exhibits, for example, the strange conduct of a hag and her half-breed son, a low-country type, and a maniac, whose appearances are as unexpected as Brown's Wieland. The gourmand Porgy in the role of a Sancho is more startling than Horse-Shoe. Other elements are paralleled in *Old Mortality*. Simms's true strength lies rather in his description of the swamp fights. He makes the celerity and prowess of Marion an excellent foil for the obstinacy and self-conceit of Gates, the new commander of the regular army.

Simms presented in a more favorable light than Kennedy the patriotic ardor of South Carolina.[46] It is valuable to have in a historical novel such familiarity with local history as Simms possessed, as well as such ardor. But his novel is the less effective of the two because his imagination less fully illumined the bare transcript of history.

45. Simms explained the foreshortening of his plot on the ground that before he had progressed far with his story he found his material sufficiently ample to design a trilogy (*The Partisan,* rev. ed., 1854, introduction). Simms ultimately wrote a series of seven Revolutionary tales, of which *Eutaw, The Forayers,* and *Woodcraft* are better constructed.

46. He admitted that her numerical force had been lessened by the loyalist Scotch, German, and Quaker settlements of the interior. He explained that the shelter sought in Florida by refugee Tories from all States had made her the harboring place for swarms of outlaws. But he denied a luke-warm attitude toward independence. On the contrary, the British, he asserted, were so provoked with the ingratitude of a favorite colony of the crown that they sent their ablest generals to that section, with the result that every Carolinian was in the field, on one side or the other. In this connection see also Simms's review of *Horse-Shoe Robinson, Southern Quarterly Review,* XXII, 203–220 (July, 1852). Poe, however, says: "It is well known that throughout the whole war this state evinced more disaffection to the confederated government than any other of the Union, with the exception perhaps of the neighboring state of Georgia" (*Southern Literary Messenger,* I, 522).

Text of letter from John Pendleton Kennedy to William Gilmore Simms. Simms's dedication of his Count Julian *(1845) to Kennedy called forth this letter, reproduced in facsimile on following pages, by courtesy of Mr. W. T. H. Howe.*

Baltimore, Mar. 18, 1846

My dear Sir

Messrs Taylor & Co, the Publishers, sent me, a few days ago, a copy of Count Julian, in which I find you have done me the honor of a dedication. I very gratefully acknowledge this kind remembrance, and attach the more value to it as it comes from "a brother in the art" whose good opinion affords so fair a motive for self-gratulation. Laudari laudato has been long admitted as an established excuse for some little glorification of ourselves, — though I hope you will acquit me of any very earnest opinion that my *labors* (holiday sports rather) in our common field have entitled me to the rank which your dedication would seem to infer. I am no better than a laggard in the glorious path where you have become a leader, yet still have enough of the esprit du corps about me to take pleasure in the contemplation of your distinguished career. You may always count upon me as one to vindicate your claim to the high reputation you have earned in the literature of our country; and, if nothing more, you will, at least, find me a good bottle-holder whenever you may have occasion to enter the ring.

I shall go at Count Julian with an eager appetite, having before me the double incentive of pleasure and duty — the romance itself, and the regard I entertain for its author — to say nothing of the natural affection due to so well-born and promising a foster child.

With sincere esteem I am

My dear Sir

Very truly

Your friend

J. P. Kennedy

Wm Gilmore Simms Esq.

Woodland S. C.

Baltimore Mar. 18. 1846

My dear Sir

Messrs Taylor & Co, the publishers, sent me, a few days ago, a copy of Count Julian, in which I find you have done me the honor of a dedication I very gratefully acknowledge this kind remembrance, and attach the more value to it as it comes from "a brother in the art" whose good opinion affords so fair a motive for self-gratulation Laudari laudato has been long admitted as an established excuse for some little glorification of ourselves, - though I hope you will acquit me of any very earnest opinion that my labors (holiday sports rather) in our common field have entitled me to the rank which your dedication would seem to infer. I am no better than a laggard in the glorious path where you have become a leader, yet still have enough of the esprit du corps about me to take pleasure in the contemplation of your distinguished career. You may always count upon me as one to vindicate your claim to the high reputation you have earned in the literature of our country; and, if nothing more, you will, at least, find me a good bottle-holder whenever you may have occasion to enter the ring.

I shall go at Count Julian with an eager appetite, having before me the double incentive of pleasure and duty — the romance itself, and the regard I entertain for its author — to say nothing of the natural affection due to so well-born and promising a foster child.

With sincere esteem I am

my dear Sir

very truly

yours friend

J. P. Kennedy

Wm Gilmore Simms Esq

Woodland S.C.

V

Horse-Shoe Robinson was written in the form conventional in the romance of the eighteen-thirties. The balance between gentry and commoners, between the main characters, who succeed, and the secondary lovers who produce pathos is well maintained. Kennedy had no elaborate literary theories. In fact, beyond regarding himself as "an admirer of the picturesque in characters and manners" he is strangely silent about literary matters.[47] Writing was to him a gentleman's avocation. The dedications to his books call it an "idle craft." Social interests were of first importance. Nevertheless, he had a theory of writing history, which was best expressed in the following statements:

> That which makes history the richest of philosophies and the most genial pursuit of humanity is the spirit that is breathed into it by the thoughts and feelings of former generations, interpreted in actions and incidents that disclose the passions, motives, and ambitions of men, and open to us a view of the actual life of our forefathers. When we contemplate the people of a past age employed in their own occupations, observe their habits and manners, comprehend their policy and their methods of pursuing it, our imagination is quick to clothe them with the flesh and blood of human brotherhood, and to bring them into full sympathy with our individual nature. History then becomes a world of living figures, — a theatre that presents to us a majestic drama, varied by alternate scenes of the grandest achievements and the most touching episodes of human existence.
>
> In the composing of this drama the author has need to seek his material in many a tangled thicket as well as in many an open field. Facts accidentally encountered, which singly have but little perceptible significance, are sometimes strangely discovered to illustrate incidents long obscured and incapable of explanation. They are like the lost links of a chain, which being found, supply the means of giving cohesion and completeness to the heretofore useless fragments. The scholar's experience is full of these reunions of illustrative incidents gathered from regions far apart in space, and often in time.

47. *Swallow Barn*, Hubbell ed., p. 9. In Chapter XXVI he adds: "If perchance my story should not advance according to the regular rules of historico-dramatic composition to its proper conclusion, I do not hold myself accountable for any misadventure on that score. I sketch with a careless hand; and must leave the interest I excite — if such a thing may be — to the due development of the facts as they come within my knowledge."

The historian's skill is challenged to its highest task in the effort to draw together those tissues of personal and local adventure which, at first without seeming or suspected dependence, prove, when brought into their proper relationship with each other, to be unerring exponents of events of highest concern.[48]

Perhaps the outstanding fault of Kennedy's book was his inability to realize this ideal fully.[49] But if he did not wholly succeed in blending fact and fiction, he was measurably more successful than any of his predecessors. He resorted to the strong arm of coincidence more than necessary; and he could not avoid the pitfall of melodrama, though he exercised more restraint in these matters than other writers of the time. His narrative, in common with theirs is prolix, but that is in a manner the secret of his illusion. He injected into novel-writing a dramatic method to take the place of a method too largely expository. His romance marked a definite advance in realism. His zest in characterization and his genial manner in writing were badly needed in the American novel of his day, and his *Horse-Shoe Robinson* is still worth reading. It is as Poe said, " A book of no ordinary character." [50]

48. J. P. Kennedy, " A Legend of Maryland," *Atlantic Monthly*, VI, 29 (July, 1860). Note the similarity between the above passage and Macaulay's essay on " History," which reflects the influence of Scott.

49. J. R. Moore, *op. cit.*, p. 166: " The outstanding fault of the book has been the author's attempt to intersperse fact and fiction without actually blending them."

50. *Works of Edgar Allan Poe*, Harrison ed., VIII, p. 7.

A KENNEDY CHRONOLOGY

1795. John Pendleton Kennedy was born October 25, in Baltimore, Maryland, the eldest son of a prosperous Scotch-Irish merchant, John Kennedy, and a (West) Virginia beauty, Nancy Pendleton. Attended Mr. Priestley's excellent school (later called Sinclair's Academy). William Sinclair, assistant to Mr. Priestley, had a marked influence on Kennedy. Classical training; belonged to debating society.

1809. Father's business failure caused family to move to Virginia. Kennedy's horseback rides to Martinsburg, Bower, and Berkeley Springs furnished pictures for his books later.

1812. Kennedy took the degree of Bachelor of Arts at Baltimore College.

1812–13. Studied law in office of Uncle Edmund Pendleton. Enlisted as private of the United Volunteers of Fifth Regiment, Maryland Militia, under command of Colonel Joseph Sterrett; marched to the defense of Washington and saw action in the skirmish at Bladensburg and North Point.

1816. Read law in the office of Walter Dorsey, and was admitted to the Bar. Member of Baltimore's gay society, intimate with Pennington, Dulany, and Cruse.

1818–19. Kennedy and Peter Hoffman Cruse published *The Red Book* (2 vols.) at intervals of about a fortnight.

1820–23. Served in Maryland Legislature.

1824. Declined appointment of Secretary of Legation to Chile. Married to Mary Tennant, who died in October.

1829. Married Elizabeth Gray of Ellicott Mills, Maryland, daughter of a wealthy cotton-spinner, and lived with her happily forty-one years.

1830. Reviewed in *National Intelligencer* Cambreleng's Report on Commerce and Navigation, combating its anti-protective arguments.

1832. Published *Swallow-Barn* under the *nom-de-plume* of Mark Littleton.

1833. Served as one of three judges in short story contest won by Edgar Allan Poe with "MS. Found in a Bottle."

1835. Published *Horse-Shoe Robinson: A Tale of the Tory Ascendency.*

1838. Published *Rob of the Bowl: A Legend of St. Inigoes,* a romance of colonial Maryland.

1838. Elected to Congress as a Whig; re-elected in 1840 and 1842. Chairman of Committee on Commerce.

1840. Published *Annals of Quodlibet,* a satire of Jacksonian democracy.

1841. Advocated an appropriation to test the merits of the Morse telegraph.

1843. *A Defense of the Whigs,* denounced Tyler's defection.

1846. Speaker of the Maryland House of Delegates.

1849. Published *Memoirs of the Life of William Wirt* (2 vols.).

1850. Elected Provost of the University of Maryland.

1852. Appointed Secretary of the Navy; urged Perry's Japan Expedition and Dr. Kane's second Arctic voyage.

1853. Elected member of the American Philosophical Society.

1860. Opposed secession.

1863. Elected Fellow of the Academy of Arts and Sciences. Received honorary degree of Doctor of Laws from Harvard University, July 16.

1865. Published *Letters of Mr. Paul Ambrose on the Great Rebellion in the United States.*

1866. Appointed U. S. Commissioner to the Paris Exhibition. Last of three trips to Europe. President, Board of Trustees of Peabody Institute, Baltimore.

1870. Died, August 18, at Newport, Rhode Island. Buried in Baltimore.

SELECTED BIBLIOGRAPHY

I. Text

The Works of John Pendleton Kennedy. 1854. 3 vols.

The Collected Works of John Pendleton Kennedy. 1871. 10 vols. (Includes Life by H. T. Tuckerman. The individual works of Kennedy published during his lifetime that are not listed here will be found listed in the Chronology, above.)

Horse-Shoe Robinson: A Tale of the Tory Ascendency. Philadelphia: 1835. 2 vols. 2nd edition, 1835. London: 1835, 1839.

Horse-Shoe Robinson. New York: 1852. Philadelphia: 1860, 1865. New York: 1833, 1896 (abridged for schools), 1907. Leipzig: 1853–1856.

Horse-Shoe Robinson. Dramatized by Clarence Dance and given in National Theater, New York, Nov. 23, 1836, and Park Theater, New York, March 19, 1841; also by C. W. Tayleure, Holliday Street Theater, Baltimore, April, 1856, with James K. Hackett in title rôle. (See Montrose J. Moses, *Representative Plays by American Dramatists,* 1925, II, 765–823.)

Occasional Addresses; and the Letters of Mr. Ambrose on the Rebellion . . . , 1872.

At Home and Abroad: A Series of Essays: with a Journal in Europe in 1867–8 . . . , 1872.

II. Biography

[Anonymous.] "Hon. John P. Kennedy," *American Whig Review,* XIII, 13–14 (January, 1851). (Brief outline of career; inaccurate as to dates.)

Gwathmey, Edward M. *John Pendleton Kennedy.* New York: 1931. (A brief biography which aims to stress the literary side of Kennedy, but offers substantially little not found in Tuckerman.)

Hubbell, Jay B. Introduction to *Swallow Barn* in American Author's Series. New York: 1929. (A careful biographical sketch, relating Kennedy to Poe and Thackeray, and based in part on material in the author's *Virginia Life in Fiction,* 1922.)

Kennedy, John Pendleton. Diary in Manuscript at Peabody Library, Baltimore. 17 vols: 2 vols. for years 1829–39; 15 vols. for years 1847–69.

Latrobe, John H. B. "John Pendleton Kennedy," in *Appleton's Cyclopedia of American Biography,* III, 517. New York: 1887–1889.

Link, Samuel Albert. *Pioneers of Southern Literature.* I, 223–247. Nashville and Dallas: 1899, 1903. (Contains nothing not found in Tuckerman.)

Moses, Montrose J. *The Literature of the South,* 247–252. New York: 1910.

Tuckerman, Henry Theodore. *The Life of John Pendleton Kennedy.* New York: 1871. (The authorized Life; quotes copiously from letters and journals, but not sequentially.)

Williams, Mary Wilhelmina. "John Pendleton Kennedy," in *Dictionary of American Biography,* X, 333–334.

III. Criticism

[Anonymous.] "Kennedy's Novels," *New York Review,* X, 144–152 (January, 1842). (A favorable early review of *Swallow Barn, Horse-Shoe Robinson, Rob of the Bowl, and Quodlibet.*)

[Anonymous.] *American Monthly Magazine,* II, 255; V, 466.

[Anonymous.] *American Quarterly Review,* XVIII, 240–242 (1835). (A generally favorable notice.)

[Anonymous.] Review of *Horse-Shoe Robinson, Knickerbocker Magazine,* VI, 71 (July, 1835). (A two-paragraph notice.)

Campbell, Killis. "The Kennedy Papers," *Sewanee Review,* XXV, 1–19, 193–208, 348–360 (January–July, 1917). (Kennedy's letters to Irving, to Southern writers, and to English literary men.)

Charvat, William. *Origins of American Critical Thought, 1810–1835.* University of Pennsylvania: 1936. (Suggests Kennedy was a disciple of Fielding in emphasis upon manners, customs, and character.)

Cooke, John Esten. "The Author of Swallow Barn," *Appleton's Journal,* X, 205–206 (August 16, 1873). (Reminiscent comment by a cousin, chiefly on Kennedy as a *raconteur.*)

Duyckinck, E. A. and G. L. *Cyclopædia of American Literature,* II (1855), 219–223.

[Everett, A. H.] *Swallow Barn*. A review. *North American Review*, XXXVI, 519–544 (April, 1833). (Discerning, though a large portion is quoted from the book.)

Gaines, Francis P. *The Southern Plantation*. Columbia University: 1924. (Less useful to readers of *Horse-Shoe Robinson* than of *Swallow Barn*.)

Griswold, R. W. *The Prose Writers of America*. Fourth ed., revised, 1846, pp. 341–353.

Leisy, Ernest E. *The American Historical Novel before 1860*. 1923. (Unpublished University of Illinois dissertation which relates Kennedy to other writers of historical fiction.)

Moore, J. R. "Horse-Shoe Robinson: Fact or Fiction?" *American Literature*, IV, 160–166 (May, 1932).

Orrick, Jesse Lewis. "John Pendleton Kennedy," in *The Library of Southern Literature*, VII (1913), 2897–2926.

Parks, Edd W., editor. *Southern Poets*. American Writers Series. New York: 1936. (Useful for Southern background in social, religious, and literary theory, and has a full annotated bibliography as a guide for study.)

Parrington, Vernon L. *The Romantic Revolution in America, 1800–1860*. New York: 1927, 46–56. (Excellent; relates Kennedy's works to his Whig principles.)

Poe, Edgar Allan. Review of *Horse-Shoe Robinson, Southern Literary Messenger*, I, 522–536 (May, 1835). (A discerning early review.)

[Simms, William Gilmore.] Review of *Horse-Shoe Robinson, Southern Quarterly Review*, XXII, 203–220 (July, 1852). (A correction of Kennedy's historical view of South Carolina.)

Townsend, H. G. *Philosophic Ideas in the United States*. New York: 1934.

Trent, William P. *William Gilmore Simms*. Boston: 1892.

Uhler, John E. "Kennedy's Novels and his Posthumous Works," *American Literature*, III, 471–479 (January, 1932).

—— *Literary Taste and Culture in Baltimore*. (Unpublished Johns Hopkins University dissertation, 1927.)

Van Doren, Carl. *The American Novel*. New York: 1921, pp. 59–60. (Also in *The Cambridge History of American Literature*, I, 311–312.)

Winthrop, Robert C. Tributes to the Memory of John Pendleton Kennedy, *Proceedings of the Massachusetts Historical Society*, XI, 354–369 (Sept. 8, 1870).

[Wynne, John.] "John P. Kennedy," *Harper's Magazine*, XXV, 335–340 (Aug., 1862). (A Baltimore friend comments on Kennedy's life and writings.)

IV. Bibliography

Van Doren, Carl. *Cambridge History of American Literature*, I (1917), 535–536.

To Commodore M. C. Perry

with the regards of

his friend

John P. Kennedy

Washington Nov. 14. 1852.

A pleasant & prosperous voyage to Japan and the thank's of the country when you return!

Kennedy was Secretary of the Navy under President Fillmore from July, 1852, to March, 1853. Among his services was the organization of the naval expedition to Japan under command of Commodore Matthew C. Perry. A few days before the expedition sailed, Kennedy inscribed as above a copy of Horse-Shoe Robinson, *wishing Perry "A pleasant and prosperous voyage to Japan and the thanks of the country when you return." Reproduction by courtesy of Mr. W. T. H. Howe.*

(*Facsimile of 1852 title page*)

HORSE-SHOE ROBINSON:

A Tale

OF THE

TORY ASCENDENCY.

BY JOHN P. KENNEDY,

AUTHOR OF "SWALLOW BARN

"I say the tale as 'twas said to me."
Lay of the Last Minstrel.

Revised Edition.

NEW YORK:
GEORGE P. PUTNAM, 10 PARK PLACE.

1852.

NOTE ON THE TEXT

The text followed in this edition of Horse-Shoe Robinson *is that of the second copyright edition, 1852. It has seemed advisable to republish this edition, rather than that of 1835, because it was the last revision of the work by its author. This revised text differs from the first chiefly in matters of punctuation (commas replacing dashes), explicit phrases taking the place of indefinite ones, legal terminology being simplified, and profanity here and there being toned down. Approximately fifty sentences were modified, but nowhere did the author materially change the thought. The oddities and eccentricities of the 1852 text have been followed in this reprint. The only other edition of this novel now in print abridges the text by one third.*

TO WASHINGTON IRVING, ESQ.

DEAR IRVING: —

With some little misgiving upon the score of having wasted time and paper both, which might have been better employed, I feel a real consolation in turning to you, as having, by your success, furnished our idle craft an argument to justify our vocation.

You have convinced our wise ones at home that a man may sometimes write a volume without losing his character — and have shown to the incredulous abroad, that an American book may be richly worth the reading.

In grateful acknowledgment of these services, as well as to indulge the expression of a sincere private regard, I have ventured to inscribe your name upon the front of the imperfect work which is now submitted to the public.

Very truly, yours, &c.,

JOHN P. KENNEDY.

Baltimore, May 1, 1835.

INTRODUCTION

In the winter of eighteen hundred and eighteen–nineteen, I had occasion to visit the western section of South Carolina. The public conveyances had taken me to Augusta, in Georgia. There I purchased a horse, a most trusty companion, with whom I had many pleasant experiences: a sorrel, yet retained by me in admiring memory. A valise strapped behind my saddle, with a great coat spread upon that, furnished all that I required of personal accommodation. My blood beat temperately with the pulse of youth and health. I breathed the most delicious air in the world. My travel tended to the region of the most beautiful scenery. The weather of early January was as balmy as October; a light warm haze mellowed the atmosphere, and cast the softest and richest hues over the landscape. I retraced my steps from Augusta to Edgefield, which I had passed in the stage coach. From Edgefield I went to Abbeville, and thence to Pendleton. I was now in the old district of Ninety Six, just at the foot of the mountains. My course was still westward. I journeyed alone, or rather, I ought to say, in good company, for my horse and I had established a confidential friendship, and we amused ourselves with a great deal of pleasant conversation — in our way. Besides, my fancy was busy, and made the wayside quite populous — with people of its own: there were but few of any other kind.

In the course of my journey I met an incident, which I have preserved in my journal. The reader of the tale which occupies this volume has some interest in it.

" Upon a day," as the old ballads have it, one of the best days of this exquisite climate, my road threaded the defiles of some of the grandest mountains of the country. Huge ramparts of rock toppled over my path, and little streams leaped, in beautiful cascades, from ledge to ledge, and brawled along the channels, which often supplied the only footway for my horse, and, gliding through tangled screens of rhododendron, laurel, arbor vitæ, and other evergreens, plunged into rivers, whose waters exceed anything I had ever conceived of limpid purity. It may be poetical to talk of liquid crystal, but no crystal has the absolute perfection of the transparency of these streams. The more distant mountain sides, where the opening valley offered them to my view, were fortified with stupendous walls, or banks of solid and unbroken rock, rising in successive benches one above another, with masses of dark pine between; the highest forming a crest to the mountain, cutting the sky in sharp profile, with images of castellated towers, battlements, and buttresses, around whose summits the inhabiting buzzard, with broad extended wings, floated and rocked in air and swept in majestic circles.

The few inhabitants of this region were principally the tenants of the bounty lands, which the State of South Carolina had conferred upon the soldiers of the Revolution; and their settlements, made upon the rich bottoms of the river valleys, were separated from each other by large tracts of forest.

I had much perplexity in some portions of this day's journey in finding my way through the almost pathless forest which lay between two of these settlements. That of which I was in quest was situated upon the Seneca, a tributary of the Savanna river, here called Tooloolee. It was near sundown, when I emerged from the wilderness upon a wagon road, very uncertain of my whereabout, and entertaining some rather anxious misgivings as to my portion for the night.

I had seen no one for the last five or six hours, and upon falling into the road I did not know whether I was to take the right or the left hand — a very material problem for my solution just then.

During this suspense, a lad, apparently not above ten years of age, mounted bare back on a fine horse, suddenly emerged from the wood about fifty paces ahead of me, and galloped along the road in the same direction that I had myself resolved to take. I quickened my speed to overtake him, but from the rapidity of his movement, I found myself, at the end of a mile, not as near him as I was at the beginning. Some open country in front, however, showed me that I was approaching a settlement. Almost at the moment of making this discovery, I observed that the lad was lying on the ground by the road-side. I hastened to him, dismounted, and found him sadly in want of assistance. His horse had run off with him, thrown him, and dislocated, as it afterwards appeared, his shoulder-joint.

Whilst I was busy in rendering such aid as I could afford, I was joined by a gentleman of venerable aspect, the father of the youth, who came from a dwelling-house near at hand, which, in the engrossment of my occupation, I had not observed. We lifted the boy in our arms and bore him into the house.

I was now in comfortable quarters for the night. The gentleman was Colonel T——, as I was made aware by his introduction, and the kindly welcome he offered me, and I very soon found myself established upon the footing of a favored guest. The boy was laid upon a bed in the room where we sat, suffering great pain, and in want of immediate attention. I entered into the family consultation on the case. Never have I regretted the want of an acquisition, as I then regretted that I had no skill in surgery. I was utterly incompetent to make a suggestion worth considering. The mother of the family happened to be absent that night; and, next to the physician, the mother is the best adviser. There was an elder son, about my own age, who was playing a fiddle when we came in; and there was a sister younger than he, and brothers and sisters still younger. But we were all alike incapable. The poor boy's case might be critical, and the nearest physician, Dr. Anderson, resided at Pendleton, thirty miles off. This is one of the conditions of frontier settlement which is not always thought of.

In the difficulty of the juncture, a thought occurred to Colonel T., which was immediately made available. "I think I will send for Horse-Shoe Robinson," he said, with a manifest lighting up of the countenance, as if he had hit upon a happy expedient. "Get a horse, my son," he continued, addressing one of the boys, "and ride over to the old man, and tell him what has happened to your brother; and say, he will oblige me if he will come here directly." At the same time, a servant was ordered to ride to Pendleton, and to bring over Dr. Anderson.

In the absence of the first messenger the lad grew easier, and it became apparent that his hurt was not likely to turn out seriously. Colonel T., assured by this, drew his chair up to the fire beside me, and with many expressions of friendly interest inquired into the course of my journey, and into the numberless matters that may be supposed to interest a frontier settler in his intercourse with one just from the world of busy life. It happened that I knew an old friend of his, General ——, a gentleman highly distinguished in professional and political service, to whose youth Colonel T. had been a most timely patron. This circumstance created a new pledge in my favor, and, I believe, influenced the old gentleman in a final resolve to send that night for his wife, who was some seven or eight miles off, and whom he had been disinclined to put to the discomfort of such a journey in the dark, ever since it was ascertained that the boy's case was not dangerous. I am pretty sure this influenced him, as I heard him privately instructing a servant to go for the lady, and to tell her that the boy's injury was not very severe, and "that there was a gentleman there who was well acquainted with General ——." I observed, hanging in a little black frame over the fireplace, a miniature engraved portrait of the general, which was the only specimen of the fine arts in the house — perhaps in the settlement. It was my recognition of this likeness that led, I fear, to the weary night ride of the good lady.

In less than an hour the broad light of the hearth — for the apartment was only lit up by blazing pine faggots, which, from time to time, were thrown upon the fire — fell upon a goodly figure. There was first a sound of hoofs coming through the dark — a halt at the door — a full, round, clear voice heard on the porch — then the entrance into the apartment of a woodland hero. That fine rich voice again, in salutation, so gentle and so manly! This was our expected counsellor, Horse-Shoe Robinson. What a man I saw! With near seventy years upon his poll, time seemed to have broken its billows over his front only as the ocean breaks over a rock. There he stood — tall, broad, brawny, and erect. The sharp light gilded his massive frame and weather-beaten face with a pictorial effect that would have rejoiced an artist. His homely dress, his free stride, as he advanced to the fire; his face radiant with kindness; the natural gracefulness of his motion; all afforded a ready index to his character. Horse Shoe, it was evident, was a man to confide in.

"I hear your boy's got flung from his horse, Colonel," he said, as he advanced to the bed-side. "Do you think he is much hurt?" "Not so badly as we thought at first, Mr. Robinson," was the reply. "I am much obliged to you for coming over to-night. It is a great comfort to have your advice in such times."

"These little shavers are so venturesome — with horses in particular," said the visitor; "it's Providence, Colonel, takes care of 'em. Let me look at you, my son," he continued, as he removed the bed-clothes, and began to handle the shoulder of the boy. "He's got it out of joint," he added, after a moment. "Get me a basin of hot water and a cloth, Colonel. I think I can soon set matters right."

It was not long before the water was placed beside him, and Robinson went to work with the earnestness of a practised surgeon. After applying wet cloths for some time to the injured part, he took the shoulder in his broad hand, and with a sudden movement, which was followed by a shriek from the boy, he brought the dislocated bone into its proper position. "It doesn't hurt," he said, laughingly: "you are only pretending. How do you feel now?"

The patient smiled, as he replied, "Well enough now; but I reckon you was joking if you said that it didn't hurt."

Horse Shoe came to the fireside, and took a chair, saying, "I larnt that, Colonel, in the campaigns. A man picks up some good everywhere, if he's a mind to; that's my observation."

This case being disposed of, Horse Shoe determined to remain all night with the familly. We had supper, and, after that, formed a little party around the hearth. Colonel T. took occasion to tell me something about Horse Shoe; and the Colonel's eldest son gave me my cue, by which he intimated I might draw out the old soldier to relate some stories of the war.

"Ask him," said the young man, "how he got away from Charleston after the surrender; and then get him to tell you how he took the five Scotchmen prisoners."

We were all in good humor. The boy was quite easy, and everything was going on well, and we had determined to sit up until Mrs. T. should arrive, which could not be before midnight. Horse Shoe was very obliging, and as I expressed a great interest in his adventures, he yielded himself to my leading, and I got out of him a rich stock of adventure, of which his life was full. The two famous passages to which I had been asked to question him — the escape from Charleston, and the capture of the Scotch soldiers — the reader will find preserved in the narrative upon which he is about to enter, almost in the very words of my authority. I have — perhaps with too much scruple — retained Horse Shoe's peculiar vocabulary and rustic, doric form of speech — holding these as somewhat necessary exponents of his character. A more truthful man than he, I am convinced, did not survive the war to tell its story. Truth was the predominant expression of his face and gesture — the truth that belongs to natural and unconscious bravery, united with a frank and modest spirit. He seemed to set no especial value upon his own exploits, but to relate them as items of personal history, with as little comment or emphasis as if they concerned any one more than himself.

It was long after midnight before our party broke up; and when I got to my bed it was to dream of Horse Shoe and his adventures. I made a record of what he told me, whilst the memory of it was still fresh, and often afterwards reverted to it, when accident or intentional research brought into my view events connected with the times and scenes to which his story had reference.

The reader will thus see how I came into possession of the leading incidents upon which this "Tale of the Tory Ascendency" in South Carolina is founded.

It was first published in 1835. Horse-Shoe Robinson was then a very old man. He had removed into Alabama, and lived, I am told, upon the banks of the Tuskaloosa. I commissioned a friend to send him a copy of the book. The report brought me was, that the old man had listened very attentively to the reading of it, and took great interest in it.

"What do you say to all this?" was the question addressed to him, after the reading was finished. His reply is a voucher, which I desire to preserve: "It is all true and right — in its right place — excepting about them women, which I disremember. That mought be true, too; but my memory is treacherous — I disremember."

April 12, 1852

PREFACE TO THE FIRST EDITION

THE events narrated in the following pages, came to my knowledge in the progress of my researches into the personal history of some of the characters who figure in the story. I thought them worth being embodied into a regular narrative, for two reasons: —

First, because they intrinsically possess an interest that may amuse the lovers of adventure, and

Second, because they serve to illustrate the temper and character of the War of our Revolution.

As yet, only the political and documentary history of that war has been written. Its romantic or picturesque features have been left for that industrious tribe of chroniclers, of which I hold myself to be an unworthy member, and who have of late, as the public is aware, set about the business in good earnest. It shall go hard with us if we do not soon bring to light every remnant of tradition that the war has left!

An opinion has heretofore prevailed that the Revolution was too recent an affair for our story-telling craft to lay hands upon it. But this objection, ever since the fiftieth anniversary, has been nullified by common consent, — that being deemed the fair poetical limit which converts tradition into truth, and takes away all right of contradiction from a surviving actor in the scene. The pension roll is manifestly growing thinner, and the widows — married young after the peace — make a decided majority on the list. These are the second-hand retailers of the marvels of the war; and it is observed that, like wine which has descended to the heir, the events have lost none of their flavor or value by the transmission. This is all so much clear gain to our fraternity; and it is obvious, therefore, that we must thrive.

My reader will perceive that I have been scrupulous to preserve the utmost historical accuracy in my narrative: and I hope, when he has finished the perusal, that he may find reason to award me the commendation of having afforded him some pleasure, by the sketch I have attempted of the condition of things in the south during the very interesting period of the "Tory Ascendency."

THE AUTHOR.

May 1, 1835.

CHAPTER I

A TOPOGRAPHICAL DISCOURSE

THE belt of mountains which traverses the state of Virginia diagonally, from north-east to south-west, it will be seen by an inspection of the map, is composed of a series of parallel ranges, presenting a conformation somewhat similar to that which may be observed in miniature on the sea-beach, amongst the minute lines of sand hillocks left by the retreating tide. This belt may be said to commence with the Blue Ridge, or more accurately speaking, with that inferior chain of highlands that runs parallel to this mountain almost immediately along its eastern base. From this region westward the highlands increase in elevation, the valleys become narrower, steeper and cooler, and the landscape progressively assumes the wilder features which belong to what is distinctly meant by "the mountain country."

The loftiest heights in this series are found in the Alleghany, nearly one hundred and fifty miles westward from the first thread of the belt; and as the principal rivers which flow towards the Chesapeake find their sources in this overtopping line of mountain, it may be imagined that many scenes of surpassing beauty exist in those abrupt solitudes where the rivers have had to contend with the sturdy hills that nature had thrown across their passage to the sea.

The multiplication of the facilities of travel which the spirit of improvement has, of late years, afforded to this region; the healthfulness, or, — to use a term more germain to its excellence, — the voluptuousness of the climate, and the extraordinary abundance of waters of the rarest virtue, both for bathing and drinking, have all contributed, very recently, to render the mountains of Virginia notorious and popular amongst that daintily observant crowd of well-conditioned people who yearly migrate in quest of health, or of a refuge from the heats of summer, or who, perchance, wander in pursuit of those associations of hill and dale which are supposed to repair a jaded imagination, and to render it romantic and fruitful.

The traveller of either of these descriptions, who holds his journey westward, will find himself impelled to halt at Charlottesville, as a pleasant resting-place in the lap of the first mountains, where he may stop to reinforce his strength for the prosecution of the rugged task that awaits him. His delay here will not be unprofitable. This neat little village is not less recommended to notice by its position in the midst of a cultivated and plentiful country, than by its contiguity to the seats of three Presidents of the Union; and, especially, by its immediate proximity to Monticello, whose burnished dome twinkles through the crown of forest that adorns the very apex of its mountain pyramid, and which, as it has now grown to be the Mecca of many a pilgrim, will of itself furnish a sufficient inducement for our traveller's tarrying. An equal attraction will be found in the University of Virginia, which, at the distance of one mile, in the opposite direction from that leading to Monticello, rears its gorgeous and fantastic piles of massive and motley architecture — a lively and faithful symbol (I speak it reverently) of the ambitious, parti-colored and gallican taste of its illustrious founder.

From Charlottesville, proceeding southwardly, in the direction of Nelson and Amherst, the road lies generally over an undulating country, formed by the succession of hills constituting the subordinate chain of mountains which I have described as first in the belt. These hills derive a beautiful feature from the manner in which they are commanded, — to use a military phrase, — by the Blue Ridge, which, for the whole distance, rests against the western horizon, and heaves up its frequent pinnacles amongst the clouds, clothed in all the variegated tints that belong to the scale of vision, from the sombre green and purple of the nearer masses, to the light and almost indistinguishable azure of its remotest summits.

The constant interruption of some gushing rivulet, which hurries from the neighboring mountain into the close vales that intercept the road, communicates a trait of peculiar interest to this journey, affording that pleasant surprise of new and unexpected scenery, which, more than any other concomitant of travel, wards off the sense of fatigue. These streams have worn deep channels through the hills, and constantly seem to solicit the road into narrow passes and romantic dells, where fearful crags are seen toppling over the head of the traveller, and sparkling waters tinkle at his feet; and where the richest and rarest trees of the forest seem to have chosen their several stations, on mossy bank or cloven rock, in obedience to some master mind intent upon the most tasteful and striking combination of these natural elements.

A part of the country embraced in this description, has obtained the local designation of the South Garden, perhaps from its succession of fertile fields and fragrant meadows, which are shut in by the walls of mountain on either hand; whilst a still more remote but adjacent district of more rugged features, bears the appellation of the Cove, the name being suggested by the narrow and encompassing character of the sharp and precipitous hills that hem in and overshadow a rough and brattling mountain torrent, which is marked on the map as the Cove creek.

At the period to which my story refers, the population of this central district of Virginia, exhibited but few of the characteristics which are found to distinguish the present race of inhabitants. A rich soil, a pure atmosphere, and great abundance of wood and water, to say nothing of the sylvan beauties of the mountain, possessed a great attraction for the wealthy proprietors of the low country; and the land was, therefore, generally parcelled out in large estates held by opulent owners, whose husbandry did not fail, at least, to accumulate in profusion the comforts of life, and afford full scope to that prodigal hospitality, which, at that period even more than at present, was the boast of the state. The laws of primogeniture exercised their due influence on the national habits; and the odious division of property amongst undeserving younger brothers, whom our modern philosophy would fain persuade us have as much merit, and as little capacity to thrive in the world as their elders, had not yet formed part of the household thoughts of these many-acred squires. From Charlottesville, therefore, both north and south, from the Potomac to the James river, there extended a chain of posts, occupied by lordly and open-hearted gentlemen, — a kind of civil cordon of bluff free-livers who were but little versed in the mystery of "bringing the two ends of the year together."

Since that period, well-a-day! the hand of the reaper has put in his sickle upon divided fields; crowded progenies have grown up under these paternal roof-trees; daughters have married and brought in strange names; the subsistence of one has been spread into the garner of ten; the villages have grown populous; the University has lifted up its didactic head; and everywhere over this abode of ancient wealth, the hum of industry is heard in the carol of the ploughman, the echo of the wagoner's whip, the rude song of the boatman, and in the clatter of the mill. Such are the mischievous interpolations of the republican system!

My reader, after this topographical sketch and the political reflections with which I have accompanied it, is doubtless well-prepared for the introduction of the worthy personages with whom I am about to make him acquainted.

CHAPTER II

WHEREIN THE READER IS INTRODUCED TO TWO WORTHIES WITH WHOM HE IS LIKELY TO FORM AN INTIMATE ACQUAINTANCE

It was about two o'clock in the afternoon of a day towards the end of July, 1780, when Captain Arthur Butler, now holding a brevet, some ten days old, of major in the continental army, and Galbraith Robinson were seen descending the long hill which separates the South Garden from the Cove. They had just left the rich and mellow scenery of the former district, and were now passing into the picturesque valley of the latter. It was evident from the travel-worn appearance of their horses, as well as from their equipments, that they had journeyed many a mile before they had reached this spot; and it might also have been perceived that the shifting beauties of the landscape were not totally disregarded by Butler, at least, — as he was seen to halt on the summit of the hill, turn and gaze back upon the wood-embowered fields that lay beneath his eye, and by lively gestures to direct the notice of his companion to the same quarter. Often, too, as they moved slowly downward, he reined up his steed to contemplate more at leisure the close, forest-shaded ravine before them, through which the Cove creek held its noisy way. It was not so obvious that his companion responded to the earnest emotions which this wild and beautiful scenery excited in his mind.

Arthur Butler was now in the possession of the vigor of early manhood, with apparently some eight and twenty years upon his head. His frame was well proportioned, light and active. His face, though distinguished by a smooth and almost beardless cheek, still presented an outline of decided manly beauty. The sun and wind had tanned his complexion, except where a rich volume of black hair upon his brow had preserved the original fairness of a high, broad forehead. A hazel eye sparkled under the shade of a dark lash, and indicated, by its alternate playfulness and decision, an adventurous as well as a cheerful spirit. His whole bearing, visage and figure, seemed to speak of one familiar with enterprise and fond of danger: — they denoted gentle breeding predominating over a life of toil and privation.

MAP OF HORSE-SHOE ROBINSON COUNTRY

Notwithstanding his profession, which was seen in his erect and peremptory carriage, his dress, at this time, was, with some slight exceptions, merely civil. And here, touching this matter of dress, I have a prefatory word to say to my reader. Although custom, or the fashion of the story-telling craft, may require that I should satisfy the antiquarian in this important circumstance of apparel of the days gone by, yet, on the present occasion, I shall be somewhat chary of my lore in that behalf; — seeing that any man who is curious on the score of the costume of the revolution time, may be fully satisfied by studying those most graphic "counterfeit presentments" of sundry historical passages of that day, wherewith Colonel Trumbull has furnished this age, for the edification of posterity, in the great rotunda of the Capitol of the United States. And I confess, too, I have another reason for my present reluctance, — as I feel some faint misgiving lest my principal actor might run the risk of making a sorry figure with the living generation, were I to introduce him upon the stage in a coat, whose technical description, after the manner of a botanical formula, might be comprised in the following summary: — long-waisted — wide-skirted — narrow-collared — broad-backed — big-buttoned — and large-lapelled; — and then to add to this, what would be equally outlandish, yellow small-clothes, and dark-topped boots, attached by a leather strap to the buttons at the knee, — without which said boots, no gentlemen in 1780 ventured to mount on horseback.

But when I say that Captain Butler travelled on his present journey, habited in the civil costume of a gentleman of the time, I do not mean to exclude a round hat pretty much of the fashion of the present day — though then but little used except amongst military men — with a white cockade to show his party; nor do I wish to be considered as derogating from that peaceful character when I add that his saddle-bow was fortified by a brace of horseman's pistols, stowed away in large holsters, covered with bear skin; — for, in those days, when hostile banners were unfurled, and men challenged each other upon the highways, these pistols were a part of the countenance (to use an excellent old phrase) of a gentleman.

Galbraith Robinson was a man of altogether rougher mould. Nature had carved out, in his person, an athlete whom the sculptors might have studied to improve the Hercules. Every lineament of his body indicated strength. His stature was rather above six feet; his chest broad; his limbs sinewy, and remarkable for their symmetry. There seemed to be no useless flesh upon his frame to soften the prominent surface of his muscles; and his ample thigh, as he sat upon horseback, showed the working of its texture at each step, as if part of the animal on which he rode. His was one of those iron forms that might be imagined almost bullet proof. With all these advantages of person, there was a radiant, broad, good nature upon his face; and the glance of a large, clear, blue eye told of arch thoughts, and of shrewd, homely wisdom. A ruddy complexion accorded well with his sprightly, but massive features, of which the prevailing expression was such as silently invited friendship and trust. If to these traits be added an abundant shock of yellow, curly hair, terminating in a luxuriant queue, confined by a narrow strand of leather cord, my reader will have a tolerably correct idea of the person I wish to describe.

Robinson had been a blacksmith at the breaking out of the revolution, and, in truth, could hardly be said to have yet abandoned the craft; although of late, he had been engaged in a course of life which had but little to do with the anvil, except in that metaphorical sense of hammering out and shaping the rough, iron independence of his country. He was the owner of a little farm in the Waxhaw settlement, on the Catawba, and having pitched his habitation upon a promontory, around whose base the Waxhaw creek swept with a regular but narrow circuit, this locality, taken in connexion with his calling, gave rise to a common prefix to his name throughout the neighborhood, and he was therefore almost exclusively distinguished by the sobriquet of Horse Shoe Robinson. This familiar appellative had followed him into the army.

The age of Horse Shoe was some seven or eight years in advance of that of Butler — a circumstance which the worthy senior did not fail to use with some authority in their personal intercourse, holding himself, on that account, to be like Cassius, an elder, if not a better soldier. On the present occasion, his dress was of the plainest and most rustic description: a spherical crowned hat with a broad brim, a coarse grey coatee of mixed cotton and wool, dark linsey-woolsey trowsers adhering closely to his leg, hob-nailed shoes, and a red cotton handkerchief tied carelessly round his neck with a knot upon his bosom. This costume, and a long rifle thrown into the angle of the right arm, with the breech resting on his pommel, and a pouch of deer-skin, with a powder horn attached to it, suspended on his right side, might have warranted a spectator in taking Robinson for a woodsman, or hunter from the neighboring mountains.

Such were the two personages who now came " pricking o'er the hill." The period at which I have presented them to my reader was, perhaps, the most anxious one of the whole struggle for independence. Without falling into a long narrative of events which are familiar, at least to every American, I may recall the fact that Gates had just passed southward, to take command of the army destined to act against Cornwallis. It was now within a few weeks of that decisive battle which sent the hero of Saratoga " bootless home and weather-beaten back," to ponder over the mutations of fortune, and, in the quiet shades of Virginia, to strike the balance of fame between northern glory and southern discomfiture. It may be imagined then, that our travellers were not without some share of that intense interest for the events " upon the gale," which everywhere pervaded the nation. Still, as I have before hinted, Arthur Butler did not journey through this beautiful region without a lively perception of the charms which nature had spread around him. The soil of this district is remarkable for its blood-red hue. The side of every bank glowed in the sun with this bright vermillion tint, and the new-made furrow, wherever the early ploughman had scarred the soil, turned up to view the predominating color. The contrast of this with the luxuriant grass and the yellow stubble, with the grey and mossy rock, and with the deep green shade of the surrounding forest, perpetually solicited the notice of the lover of landscape; and from every height, the eye rested with pleasure upon the rich meadows of the bottom land — upon the varied cornfields spread over the hills; upon the adjacent mountains, with their bald crags peeping through the screen of forest, and especially upon the broad lines of naked earth that, here and there, lighted up and relieved, as a painter would say, with its warm coloring, the heavy masses of shade.

The day was hot, and it was with a grateful sense of refreshment that our wayfarers, no less than their horses, found themselves, as they approached the lowland, gradually penetrating the deep and tangled thicket and the high wood that hung over and darkened the channel of the small stream which rippled through the valley. Their road lay along this stream and frequently crossed it at narrow fords, where the water fell from rock to rock in small cascades, presenting natural basins of the limpid flood, embosomed in laurel and alder, and gurgling that busy music which is one of the most welcome sounds to the ear of a wearied and overheated traveller.

Butler said but little to his companion, except now and then to express a passing emotion of admiration for the natural embellishments of the region; until, at length, the road brought them to a huge mass of rock, from whose base a fountain issued forth over a bed of gravel, and soon lost itself in the brook hard by. A small strip of bark, that some friend of the traveller had placed there, caught the pure water as it was distilled from the rock, and threw it off in a spout, some few inches above the surface of the ground. The earth trodden around this spot showed it to be a customary halting place for those who journeyed on the road.

Here Butler checked his horse, and announced to his comrade his intention to suspend, for a while, the toil of travel.

"There is one thing, Galbraith," said he, as he dismounted, "wherein all philosophers agree — man must eat when he is hungry, and rest when he is weary. We have now been some six hours on horseback, and as this fountain seems to have been put here for our use, it would be sinfully slighting the bounties of providence not to do it the honor of a halt. Get down, man; rummage your havresac, and let us see what you have there."

Robinson was soon upon his feet, and taking the horses a little distance off, he fastened their bridles to the impending branches of a tree; then opening his saddle-bags, he produced a wallet with which he approached the fountain, where Butler had thrown himself at full length upon the grass. Here, as he successively disclosed his stores, he announced his bill of fare, with suitable deliberation between each item, in the following terms:

"I don't march without provisions, you see, captain — or major, I suppose I must call you now. Here's the rear division of a roast pig, and along with it, by way of flankers, two spread eagles (holding up two broiled fowls), and here are four slices from the best end of a ham. Besides these, I can throw in two apple-jacks, a half dozen of rolls, and — "

"Your wallet is as bountiful as a conjurer's bag, sergeant; it is a perfect cornucopia. How did you come by all this provender?"

"It isn't so overmuch, major, when you come to consider," said Robinson. "The old landlady at Charlottesville is none of your heap-up, shake-down, and running-over landladies, and when I signified to her that we mought want a snack upon the road, she as much as gave me to understand that there wa'n't nothing to be had. But I took care to make fair weather with her daughter, as

I always do amongst the creatures, and she let me into the pantry, where I made bold to stow away these few trifling articles, under the denomination of pillage. If you are fond of Indian corn bread, I can give you a pretty good slice of that."

"Pillage, Galbraith! You forget you are not in an enemy's country. I directed you scrupulously to pay for everything you got upon the road. I hope you have not omitted it to-day?"

"Lord, sir! what do these women do for the cause of liberty but cook, and wash, and mend!" exclaimed the sergeant. "I told the old Jezebel to charge it all to the continental congress."

"Out upon it, man! Would you bring us into discredit with our best friends, by your villanous habits of free quarters?"

"I am not the only man, major, that has been spoiled in his religion by these wars. I had both politeness and decency till we got to squabbling over our chimney corners in Carolina. But when a man's conscience begins to get hard, it does it faster than anything in nature: it is, I may say, like the boiling of an egg — it is very clear at first, but as soon as it gets cloudy, one minute more and you may cut it with a knife."

"Well, well! Let us fall to, sergeant; this is no time to argue points of conscience."

"You seem to take no notice of this here bottle of peach brandy, major," said Robinson. "It's a bird that came out of the same nest. To my thinking it's a sort of a file leader to an eatable, if it ar'n't an eatable itself."

"Peace, Galbraith! it is the vice of the army to set too much store by this devil brandy."

The sergeant was outwardly moved by an inward laugh that shook his head and shoulders.

"Do you suppose, major, that Troy town was taken without brandy? It's drilling and countermarching and charging with the bagnet, all three, sir. But before we begin, I will just strip our horses. A flurry of cool air on the saddle spot is the best thing in nature for a tired horse."

Robinson now performed this office for their jaded cattle; and having given them a mouthful of water at the brook, returned to his post, and soon began to despatch, with a laudable alacrity, the heaps of provision before him. Butler partook with a keen appetite of this sylvan repast, and was greatly amused to see with what relish his companion caused slice after slice to vanish, until nothing was left of this large supply but a few fragments.

"You have lost neither stomach nor strength by the troubles, sergeant; the short commons of Charleston would have gone something against the grain with you, if you had stayed for that course of diet."

"It is a little over two months," said Robinson, "since I got away from them devils; and if it hadn't been for these here wings of mine (pointing to his legs), I might have been a caged bird to-day."

"You have never told me the story of your escape," said Butler.

"You were always too busy, or too full of your own thoughts, major, for me to take up your time with such talk," replied the other. "But, if you would like me to tell you all about it, while you are resting yourself here on the ground, and have got nothing better to think about, why, I'll start like old Jack Carter of our mess, by beginning, as he used to say when he had a tough story ahead, right at the beginning."

"Do so, sergeant, and do it discreetly; but first, swallow that mouthful, for you don't speak very clear."

"I'll wash down the gutter, major, according to camp fashion, and then my throat will be as clear as the morning gun after sunrise."

And saying this, the tall soldier helped himself to a hearty draught of cool water mingled in fair proportion with a part of the contents of his flask, and setting the cup down by his side, he commenced as follows: —

"You was with us, major, when Prevost served us that trick in Georgia, last year — kept us, you remember, on the look out for him t'other side of the Savannah, whilst all the time he was whisking of it down to Charleston."

"You call this beginning at the beginning? Faith, you have started a full year before your time. Do you think yourself a Polybius or a Xenophon — who were two famous old fellows, just in your line, sergeant — that you set out with a history of a whole war?"

"I never knew any persons in our line — officers or men — of either of them names," — replied Robinson, — "they were nicknames, perhaps; — but I do know, as well as another, when a thing turns up that is worth notice, major; and this is one of 'em: — and that's the reason why I make mention of it. What I was going to say was this — that it was a sign fit for General Lincoln's consarnment, that these here British should make a push at Charleston on the tenth of May, 1779, and get beaten, and that exactly in one year and two days afterwards, they should make another push and win the town. Now, what was it a sign of, but that they and the tories was more industrious that year than we were?"

"Granted," said Butler, "now to your story, Mister Philosopher!"

"In what month was it you left us?" inquired the sergeant gravely.

"In March," answered Butler.

"General Lincoln sent you off, as we were told, on some business with the continental congress: to get us more troops, if I am right. It was a pity to throw away a good army on such a place — for it wa'n't worth defending at last. From the time that you set out, they began to shut us in, every day a little closer. First, they closed a door on one side, and then on t'other: till, at last they sent a sort of flash-o'-lightning fellow — this here Colonel Tarleton — up to Monk's corner, which, you know, was our back door, and he shut that up and double bolted it, by giving Huger a most tremenjious lathering. Now, when we were shut in, we had nothing to do but look out. I'll tell you an observation I made, at that time."

"Well."

"Why, when a man has got to fight, it's a natural sort of thing enough; — but when he has got nothing to eat, it's an onnatural state. I have hearn of men who should have said they would rather fight than eat: — if they told truth they would have made honest fellows for our garrison at Charlestown. First, our vegetables — after that devil took up his quarters at Monk's corner — began to give out: then, our meat; and, finally, we had nothing left but rice, which I consider neither fish, flesh, nor good salt herring" ——

"You had good spirits, though, sergeant."

"If you mean rum or brandy, major, we hadn't much of that; — but if you mean jokes and laughs, it must be hard times that will stop them in camp. — I'll tell you one of them, that made a great hurra on both sides, where we got the better of a Scotch regiment that was plaguing us from outside the town. They thought they would make themselves merry with our starvation — so, they throwed a bomb shell into our lines, that, as it came along through the air, we saw had some devilment in it, from the streak it made in daylight; and, sure enough, when we come to look at it on the ground, we found it filled with rice and molasses — just to show that these Scotchmen were laughing at us for having nothing to eat. Well, what do we do but fill another shell with brimstone and hogslard, and just drop it handsomely amongst the lads from the land o'cakes? Gad, sir, it soon got to the hearing of the English regiment, and such a shouting as they sot up from their lines against the Scotchmen! That's what I call giving as good as they saunt, major — ha ha ha! "

" It wasn't a bad repartee, Galbraith," said Butler, joining in the laugh. " But go on with your siege."

" We got taken, at last," proceeded Horse Shoe, " and surrendered on the 12th of May. Do you know that they condescended to let us go through the motions of marching outside the lines? Still it was a sorry day to see our colors tied as fast to their sticks as if a stocking had been drawn over them. After that, we were marched to the barracks and put into close confinement."

" Yes, I have heard that; and with heavy hearts — and a dreary prospect before you, sergeant."

" I shouldn't have minded it much, Major Butler, it was the fortune of war. But they insulted us as soon as they got our arms from us. It was a blasted cowardly trick in them to endeavor to wean us from our cause, which they tried every day; it was seduction, I may say. First, they told us that Colonel Pinckney and some other officers had gone over; but that was too onprobable a piece of rascality, — we didn't believe one word on't. So, one morning Colonel Pinckney axed that we mought be drawed up in a line in front of the barracks; and there he made us a speech. We were as silent as so many men on a surprise party. The colonel said — yes, sir, and right in their very teeth — that it was an infamious, audacious calamy: that whenever he desarted the cause of liberty, he hoped they would take him, as they had done some Roman officer or other — I think one Officious, as I understood the colonel — you've hearn of him, may be — and tie his limbs to wild horses, and set them adrift, at full speed, taking all his joints apart, so that not one traitorious limb should be left to keep company with another. It was a mighty severe punishment, whoever he mought'a been. The British officers began to frown — and I saw one chap put his hand upon his sword. It would have done you good to witness the look the colonel gave him, as he put his own hand to his thigh to feel if his sword was there — he so naturally forgot he was a prisoner. They made him stop speaking howsever, because they gave out that it was perditious language; and so, they dismissed us — but we let them have three cheers to show that we were in heart."

"It was like Pinckney," said Butler; "I'll warrant him a true man, Galbraith."

"I'll thribble that warrant," replied Galbraith, "and afterwards make it nine. I wish you could have hearn him. I always thought a bugle horn the best music in the world, till that day. But that day Colonel Charles Cotesworth Pinckney's voice was sweeter than shawns and trumpets, as the preacher says, and bugles to boot. I have hearn people tell of speeches working like a fiddle on a man's nerves, major: but, for my part, I think they sometimes work like a battery of field-pieces, or a whole regimental band on a parade day. Howsever, I was going on to tell you, Colonel Pinckney put a stop to all this parleying with our poor fellows; and knowing, major, that you was likely to be coming this way, he axed me if I thought I could give the guard the slip, and make off with a letter to meet you. Well, I studied over the thing for a while, and then told him a neck was but a neck any how, and that I could try; and so, when his letter was ready, he gave it to me, telling me to hide it so that, if I was sarched, it couldn't be found on my person. Do you see that foot?" added Horse Shoe, smiling, "it isn't so small but that I could put a letter between the inside sole and the out, longways, or even crossways, for the matter of that, and that, without so much as turning down a corner. Correspondent and accordingly I stitched it in. The colonel then told me to watch my chance and make off to you in the Jarseys, as fast as I could. He told me, besides, that I was to stay with you, because you was likely to have business for me to do."

"That's true, good sergeant."

"There came on a darkish, drizzly evening; and a little before roll call, at sun set, I borrowed an old forage cloak from Corporal Green — you mought have remembered him — and out I went towards the lines, and sauntered along the edge of the town, till I came to one of your pipe-smoking, gin-drinking Hessians, keeping sentry near the road that leads out towards Ashley ferry: — a fellow that had no more watch in him — bless your soul! — as these Dutchmen hav'n't — than a duck on a rainy day. So, said I, coming up boldly to him, 'Hans, wie gehet es' — 'Geh zum Teufel,' says he, laughing — for he knowed me. That was all the Dutch I could speak, except I was able to say it was going to rain, so I told him — 'Es will regnen' — which he knowed as well as I did, for it was raining all the time. I had a little more palaver with Hans, and, at last, he got up on his feet and set to walking up and down. By this time the drums beat for evening quarters, and I bid Hans good night; but, instead of going away, I squatted behind the Dutchman's sentry box; — and, presently, the rain came down by the bucket full; it got very dark and Hans was snug under cover. The grand rounds was coming; I could hear the tramp of feet, and as no time was to be lost, I made a long step and a short story of it, by just slipping over the lines and setting out to seek my fortune."

"Well done, sergeant! You were ever good at these pranks."

"But that wasn't all," continued Robinson. "As the prime file leader of mischief would have it, outside of the lines I meets a cart with a man to drive it, and two soldiers on foot, by way of guard.

"The first I was aware of it, was a hallo, and then a bagnet to my breast. I didn't ask for countersigns, for I didn't mean to trade in words that night; but, just seizing hold of the muzzle of the piece, I twisted it out of the fellow's hand, and made him a present of the butt-end across his pate. I didn't want to hurt him, you see, for it wa'n't his fault that he stopped me. A back-hander brought down the other, and the third man drove off his cart, as if he had some suspicion that his comrades were on their backs in the mud. I didn't mean to trouble a peaceable man with my compliments, but on the contrary, as the preacher says, I went on my way rejoicing."

"You were very considerate, sergeant; I entirely approve of your moderation. As you are a brave man, and have a natural liking for danger, this was a night that, doubtless, afforded you great satisfaction."

"When danger stares you in the face," replied Horse Shoe, "the best way is not to see it. It is only in not seeing of it, that a brave man differs from a coward: that's my opinion. Well, after that I had a hard time of it. I was afraid to keep up the Neck road, upon account of the sodgers that was upon it; so I determined to cross the Ashley, and make for the Orangeburg district. When I came to the ferry, I was a little dubious about taking one of the skiffs that was hauled up, for fear of making a noise; so I slipped off my shoe that had your letter, and put it betwixt my teeth and swum the river. I must have made some splashing in the water — although I tried to muffle my oars, too, for first, I heard a challenge from the ferry-house, and then the crack of a musket: but it was so dark you couldn't see an egg on your own nose. There was a little flustering of lights on the shore, and a turnout of the guard, may be; but, I suppose, they thought it was a sturgeon, or some such beast, and so made no more of it; and I got safe to the other bank."

"Faithfully and bravely, sergeant!"

"For the first three or four days the chances were all against me. The whole country was full of tories, and it wasn't safe to meet a man on the road: you couldn't tell whether he was friend or enemy. I durstn't show my face in day-time at all, but lay close in the swamps; and when it began to grow dark, I stole out, like a wolf, and travelled across the fields, and along the byways."

"You had a good stomach to bear it, sergeant."

"A good stomach enough, but not much in it. I'll tell you another observation I made; when a man travels all night long on an empty stomach, he ought either to fill it next morning or make it smaller."

"And how is that to be managed, friend Horse Shoe?"

"Indian fashion," replied the sergeant. "Buckle your belt a little tighter every two or three hours. A man may shrivel his guts up to the size of a pipe stem. But I found a better way to get along than by taking in my belt"——

"Now, for another stratagem!"

"I commonly, about dark crept as near to a farm house as I mought venture to go; and, putting on a poor mouth, told the folks I had a touch of the small-pox, and was dying for a little food. They were Christians enough to give me a dish of bread and milk, or something of that sort, and cowards enough to keep so much out of the way, as not to get a chance to look me in the face. They laid provisions on the ground, and then walked away while I came up to get them. Though I didn't think much of the fashion I was waited on, and had sometimes to quarrel with a bull-dog for my supper, I don't believe I ever ate with a better appetite in my life. The first bread of freedom, no matter how coarse, a man eats after his escape from prison, is the sweetest morsel in nature. And I do think it is a little pleasanter when he eats it at the risk of his life."

Butler nodded his head.

"Well, after this," continued Horse Shoe, "I had like to have lost all by another mishap. My course was for the upper country, because the nearer I got to my own home the better I was acquainted with the people. That scrummaging character, Tarleton, you may have hearn, scampered off, as soon as ever Charlestown was taken, after Colonel Abraham Buford, who was on his way down to the city when the news was fotch him of our surrender. Buford accordingly came to the right about, to get out of harm's way as fast as he could, and Tarleton followed close on his heels. Think of that devil, major, trying to catch a man a hundred miles away! It was a brazen hearted thing! considering, besides, that Buford had a good regiment with him. When nobody thought it anything more than a brag, sure enough, he overhauls Buford yonder at the Waxhaws — onawares, you may say — and there he tore him all to pieces. They say it was a bloody cruel sight, to see how these English troopers did mangle the poor fellows. I doubt there wasn't fair play. But, major, that Tarleton rides well and is a proper soldier, take him man to man. It so happened that as I was making along towards Catawba, who should I come plump upon, but Tarleton and his lads, with their prisoners, all halting beside a little run to get water!"

"Again in trouble, sergeant! Truly you have had full measure of adventures!"

"I was pretty near nonplushed, major," said Horse Shoe, with a broad laugh, "but I thought of a stratagem. I let fall my under jaw, and sot my eyes as wild as a madman, and twisted my whole face out of joint — and began to clap my hands, and hurra for the red coats, like a natural fool. So, when Tarleton and two or three of his people came to take notice of me, they put me down for a poor idiot that had been turned adrift."

"Did they hold any discourse with you?"

"A good deal; and, just to try me, they flogged me with the flats of their swords; but I laughed and made merry when they hurt me worst, and told them I thanked them for their politeness. There were some of our people amongst the prisoners, that I knew, and I was mortally afeard they would let on, but they didn't. Especially, there was Seth Cuthbert, from Tryon, who had both of his hands chopped off in the fray at the Waxhaws; he was riding double behind a trooper, and he held up the stumps just to let me see how barbarously he was mangled. I was dubious they would see that he knowed me, but he took care of that. Bless your soul, major! he saw my drift in the first shot of his eye. Thinking that they mought take it into their noddles to carry me along with them back, I played the quarest trick that

I suppose ever a man thought of; it makes me laugh now to tell it. I made a spring that fetched me right upon the crupper of Colonel Tartleton's horse, which sot him to kicking and flirting at a merry rate; and, whilst the creature was floundering as if a hornet had stung him, I took the colonel's cap and put it upon my own head, and gave him mine. And after I had vagaried in this sort of way for a little while, I let the horse fling me on the ground. You would have thought the devils would have died a laughing. And the colonel himself, although at first he was very angry, couldn't help laughing likewise. He said that I was as strange a fool as he ever saw, and that it would be a pity to hurt me. So he threw me a shilling, and, whilst they were all in good humor, I trudged away."

"It was a bold experiment, and might be practised a thousand times without success. If I did not know you, Robinson, to be a man of truth, as well as courage, I should scarce believe this tale. If any one, hereafter, should tell your story, he will be accounted a fiction-monger."

"I do not boast, Major Butler; and, as to my story, I care very little who tells it. Every trick is good in war. I can change my face and voice both, so that my best friends shouldn't know me: and, in these times, I am willing to change every thing but my coat, and even that, if I have a witness to my heart, and it will serve a turn to help the country. Am I not right?"

"No man ever blames another for that, sergeant, and if ever you should be put to the trial, you will find friends enough to vouch for your honesty."

"When I got away from Tarleton it wasn't long before I reached my own cabin. There I mustered my horse and gun, and some decent clothes; and after a good sleep, and a belly full of food, I started for the north, as fast as I could, with my letter. I put it into your own hands, and you know the rest."

"This will be a good tale for a winter night," said Butler, "to be told hereafter, in a snug chimney corner, to your wife and children, when peace, as I trust it may, will make you happy in the possession of both. Your embassy has had marvellous good luck so far. I hope it may prove a happy omen for our future enterprise. Now it is my turn, Galbraith, to tell you something of our plans. Colonel Pinckney has apprised me of the state of things in the upper country. Our good friend Clark there mediates an attempt to regain Augusta and Ninety-six; and we have reason to believe that some levies will be made by our confederates in

Virginia and elsewhere. My business is to co-operate in this undertaking; and as it was essential I should have the guidance of some man acquainted with that country — some good soldier, true and trusty — the colonel has selected you to accompany me. These red coats have already got possession of all the strongholds; and the tories, you know, swarm in the country, like the locusts of Egypt. I stand in need, sergeant, of a friend with a discreet head and a strong arm. I could not have picked out of the army a better man than Sergeant Galbraith Robinson. Besides, Horse Shoe," he added, putting his hand gently upon the sergeant's shoulder, " old acquaintance has bred an affection between us."

" I am a man that can eat my allowance, major," said Robinson, with an awkward diffidence at hearing the encomium just passed upon him, " and that's a matter that doesn't turn to much profit in an empty country. But I think I may make bold to promise, that you are not like to suffer, if a word or a blow from me would do you any good."

" Your belt may be serviceable in two ways in this expedition, Horse Shoe: it may be buckled closer in scant times, and will carry a sword in dangerous ones."

" May I ask, major," inquired Horse Shoe, " since you have got to talking of our business, what has brought us so high up the country, along here? It seems to me that the lower road would have been nearer."

" Suppose I say, Galbraith," replied Butler, with animation, " that there is a bird nestles in these woods, I was fond of hearing sing, would it be unsoldierlike, think you, to make a harder ride and a larger circuit for that gratification? "

" Oh! I understand, major," said Horse Shoe, laughing, " whether it be peace or whether it be war, these women keep the upper hand of us men. For my part, I think it's more natural to think of them in war than in peace. For, you see, the creatures are so helpless, that if a man don't take care of them, who would? And then, when a woman's frightened, as she must be in these times, she clings so naturally to a man! It stands to reason! "

" You will keep my counsel, Galbraith," interrupted Butler. " I have a reason which, perhaps, you may know by and by, why you should not speak of any thing you may see or hear. And now, as we have spent a good hour in refreshment, sergeant, make our horses ready. We'll take the road again."

Robinson promised caution in all matters that might be committed to his charge, and now set himself about saddling the horses for the journey. Whilst he was engaged in this occupation, Butler was startled to hear the sergeant abruptly cry out — "You devil, Captain Peter Clinch! what are you about?" and, looking hastily around, saw no one but the trusty squire himself, who was now sedately intent upon thrusting the bit into his horse's mouth, — a liberty which the animal seemed to resent by sundry manifestations of waywardness.

"To whom are you talking, Galbraith?"

"Only to this here contrary, obstropolous beast, major."

"What name did you call him by?" inquired Butler.

"Ha, ha, ha! was it that you was listening too?" said Horse Shoe. "I have christened him Captain Peter — sometimes Captain Peter Clinch. I'll tell you why. I am a little malicious touching the name of my horse. After the surrender of Charlestown, our regiment was put in the charge of a provost marshal, by the name of Captain Clinch, and his first name was Peter. He was a rough, ugly, wire-haired fellow, with no better bowels than a barrel of vinegar. He gave us all sorts of ill usage, knowing that we wa'n't allowed to give him the kind of payment that such an oncomfortable fellow desarved to get. If ever I had met him again, major, *setters parbus* — as Lieutenant Hopkins used to say — which is lingo, I take it, for a fair field, I would'a cudgelled his pate for him, to the satisfaction of all good fellows. Well, when I got home, I gave his name to my beast, just for the pleasure of thinking of that hang-gallows thief, every time I had occasion to give the creetur a dig in the ribs, or lay a blow across his withers! And yet he is a most an excellent horse, major, and a hundred times more of a gentleman than his namesake, — though he is a little hard-headed too — but that he larnt from me. It really seems to me that the dumb beast thinks his name a disgrace, as he has good right, but has got used to it. And, besides, I hear that the cross-grained, growling dog of a captain has been killed in a scuffle since I left Charlestown, so now I consider my horse a sort of tombstone with the ugly sinner's name on it; and as I straddle it every day you see, that's another satisfaction."

"Well, sergeant, there are few men enjoy their revenge more good-humoredly than you. So, come, straddle your tombstone again, and make the bones beneath it jog."

In good glee, our travellers now betook themselves once more to the road.

CHAPTER III

AN INCIDENT THAT SAVORS OF ROMANCE

By the time the sun had fallen to the level of the summits of the Blue Ridge, Butler and Robinson had progressed so far in their journey, as to find themselves in the vicinity of the Rockfish river — a rapid mountain stream, that traverses the southern confine of Albemarle, and which, at that period, separated this county from Amherst. Their path had led them, by a short circuit, out of the ravine of Cove creek, along upon the ridges of the neighboring hills; and they were now descending from this elevation, into the valley of the Rockfish, near to the point where the Cove creek forms its junction with this river. The hill was covered with a stately forest, and a broad, winding road had been cut down the steep side, in such a manner as to present a high bank on one hand, and an abrupt sheer descent on the other. From this road might be seen, at intervals, glimmering through the screen of underwood, the waters of the small river below; whilst, at the same time, the circuitous course of the descending track left but few paces of its length visible from any one point, except where, now and then, it came boldly forth to the verge of some wild crag, from which glimpses were to be obtained of its frequent traverses towards the deep and romantic dell that received the mingled tribute of the two streams.

Here, as our travellers journeyed downward, their attention was awakened by the cry of hounds in pursuit of game. These sounds came from the wood on the crest of the hill above them; and the clamorous earnestness with which they assailed the ear, and roused the far echo of the highlands, showed the object of chase to have been suddenly surprised and hotly followed. The outcry was heard, for some moments, pursuing a direction towards the river, when, suddenly from the midst of the forest, the sharp twang of a rifle-shot showed that some hunter was on the watch to profit by the discovery of the dogs.

Robinson, as soon as he heard the report, urged his horse forward with speed, to the first turn of the road below; dismounted, and, throwing his rifle into the palm of his left hand, stood ready to give his fire wherever he might find occasion. Butler followed, and reined up close beside his companion.

"There is game afoot," said Galbraith, "and if that shot has not done its business, it may be my turn to try a hand."

These words were hardly spoken, when a wounded buck rushed to the brink of the bank, some twelve or fifteen feet above the heads of the travellers, and regardless of the presence of enemies, made one frantic bound forward into the air, and fell dead almost at Robinson's feet. So effectually had the work of death been done upon the poor animal, that he seemed to have expired, in the convulsion of this last leap, before he reached the ground; his antlers were driven into the clay; his eyes were fixed, and not a struggle followed.

"It was a home-shot that brought this poor fugitive to the earth," said Butler, as he stood gazing at the piteous spectacle before him, "and sped by a practised hand."

"I don't count him a good man, major," said Galbraith, with professional indifference, "who would mangle his meat by random firing. Now, this buck was taken sideways, as he leaped above the tops of the bushes, which is the ticklishest of all the ways of shooting a deer. The man that plucked this fellow, I'll warrant, can plant his ball just where he likes: right under the arm is the place for certainty; and the thing couldn't have been prettier done if the man had had a rest and a standing shot."

During this short interval, the hounds had arrived on the spot where the buck lay bleeding, and these, after a few minutes, were followed by two hunters of very dissimilar appearance, who came on foot, slowly leading their horses up the hill.

The first was a tall, gaunt woodman, of a sallow complexion, jet black eyes, and round head of smooth black hair. His dress was simply a coarse linen shirt and trowsers, the heat of the day being such as to allow him to dispense with coat and waistcoat. He carried, in one hand, a battered straw hat, and in the other, trailed a long rifle. His feet were covered with a pair of moccasins of brown leather, and the ordinary hunting equipments were suspended about his person.

The second was a youth apparently about sixteen, dressed in a suit of green summer-cloth, neatly and fancifully adapted to his figure, which was graceful and boyish. The jacket was short, and gathered into a small skirt behind; and both this and the pantaloons were garnished with a profusion of black cord and small black buttons. A highly polished leather belt was buckled around his waist; a cap of green cloth rested, somewhat conceitedly, amongst the rich locks of a head of light, curly hair that fell, with girlish beauty, over a fair brow, and gave softness to a countenance of pure white and red; and a neat foot showed to advantage in a laced boot. The whole appearance of the youth was of one of an amiable and docile bearing, and the small rifle or carbine which he bore in his hand, as well as the dainty accoutrements that belonged to it, amongst which was a diminutive bugle, looked more like the toys of a pampered boy, than any apparatus of service.

No sooner had these two approached near enough to Butler and his attendant for recognition, than the youth, quitting the hold of his horse, sprang forward with a joyous alacrity and seized Butler by the hand.

"Captain Butler," he cried with great animation, "how glad I am you have come! And how fortunate it is that I should meet you! Get down from your horse, I have something to tell you. Here, Stephen Foster, take this gentleman's horse."

"You are a fine fellow, Harry," said Butler, dismounting. "That smiling face of yours is full of pleasant news; it assures me that all are well at the Dove Cote." Then having given his horse in charge to Robinson, and walked a few paces apart with his young friend, he enquired, in a low and anxious tone, "Mildred, my dear Henry, what of your sister Mildred? Has she received my letter? Does she expect me? Is your father — "

"Now, captain," interrupted the other — "but heigh! don't the newspapers say you are brevetted? I am a pretty fellow to forget that! Well then, Major Butler, let me answer one question at a time. In the first place, sister Mildred is as well as any girl can be, that has a whole bushel of crosses to keep her out of spirits. Poor thing, she frets so, about you and my father. In the second place, she received your letter a week ago, and has had me patrolling this ridge every day since, just to keep a look-out for you; and, for the sake of company, I have had Stephen Foster hunting here all the time — more for an excuse than anything else, because on this side of the river the drives are not the best for deer — a man might be here a fortnight and not get a shot. Sister Mildred wanted me, if I should see you first, just to whisper to you that it is impossible to do anything with my father, especially at this time, for he has one of these English officers staying at the Dove Cote now, who, I am afraid, and so is sister Mildred, has come to do some mischief. Mildred says I must make some appointment with you to see her privately. I thought of Mrs.

Dimock's, but this Englishman has a servant staying over there, and may be it wouldn't do. So, major, you will have to ride down to the big chestnut, on the bank of the river, just under the rock that we call the Fawn's Tower — you know where that is? it isn't more than two miles from here."

"I know it well, Henry, I will wait there patiently," replied Butler, as he now returned to his horse.

"Haven't we been in luck," said Henry, "to get so fine a buck at last? This fellow has eight branches. It is Stephen's rifle that has done it."

The woodman, during this conversation, had taken possession of his spoil, and was now busily engaged with his knife in cutting open and preparing the animal for transportation, according to the usages of woodcraft, whilst Robinson stood by, admiring the dexterity with which this office was performed. When the buck was, at last, thrown by Stephen across his horse, Henry gave him orders to ride forward.

"You will carry our game to your own house, Stephen; and don't forget, to-morrow, to let us have the saddle at the Dove Cote. And Stephen, you need not say that we have found any acquaintances upon the road, you understand?"

The man bowed his head, in token of obedience, and getting upon his long-backed steed, behind the buck, was soon lost to view in the windings of the hill.

"Sister Mildred is sometimes downright melancholy," said the young hunter, after he had remounted, and now rode beside Butler. "She is troubled about you, and is always telling me of some unpleasant dream. I almost think she is over-fanciful; and then she reads everything about the army, and talks almost like a man about soldiering. Do you know she is making a soldier of me? I am constantly reading military books, and practising drill, and laying out fortifications, just as if I was going into camp. My father doesn't know a word of it; his time is taken up with these English officers, writing to them, and every now and then there are some of them at our house. Mildred knows them — a famous spy she would make! Isn't she an excellent girl, Major Butler?"

"You and I should guard her, Henry, with more care than we guard our lives," replied Butler, with a serious emphasis.

"I hope," returned Henry, "she will be in better spirits after she sees you."

"I would to heaven," said Butler, "that we all had more reason to be of good cheer, than we are likely to have. It is as cloudy a day, Henry, as you may ever behold again, should you live, as I pray you may, to the ripest old age."

Henry looked up towards the west.

"There are clouds upon the sky," he said, "and the sun has dropped below them; but there is a streak of yellow light, near to the line of the mountain, that our wise people say is a sign that the sun will rise in beauty to-morrow."

"There is a light beyond the mountain," replied Butler, half speaking to himself, "and it is the best, the only sign I see of a clear to-morrow. I wish, Henry, it were a brighter beam."

"Don't you know Gates has passed South?" said Henry, "and has some pretty fellows with him, they say. And ar'n't we all mustering here — every man most? Ask Stephen Foster what I am?"

"And what will he tell me?"

"Why, that I am his deputy-corporal in the mounted riflemen; Stephen is the lieutenant."

"Oh, I crave your favor, brother officer, good master deputy-corporal, Henry Lindsay! and does your father allow you to ride in the ranks of the friends of liberty?"

"Sister Mildred persuaded him that as I am a mere lad, as she says, — look at me, major, — a pretty well grown lad, I take it, there is no harm in my playing soldier. So I ride always with Stephen Foster, and Mildred got me this light rifle-carbine. Now, major, I fancy I am pretty nearly as good a marksman as rides in the corps. Who is this with you?" asked Henry, looking back at Robinson, who loitered some distance in the rear purposely to avoid what might be deemed an intrusion upon the private conference of the two friends.

"That is a famous soldier, Henry; he was at the siege of Charleston, and last year at Savannah. He has had some hard blows, and can tell you more of war than you have ever read in all your studies."

"He wears a curious uniform," said Henry, "for a regular soldier. What is his name?"

"Galbraith Robinson — or Horse Shoe Robinson — to give him his most popular distinction. But it would be well to keep his name secret."

"I have heard of Horse Shoe," said Henry, with an expression of great interest. "So, this is the man himself? From all reports he is as brave as" —

"As who?" asked Butler, smiling at the tone of wonder with which Henry spoke.

"As Caius Marcius Coriolanus, who, I make no doubt, major, was about the bravest man in the books."

Butler laughed, and applauded the young martialist for his discrimination.

The road from the foot of the hill pursued the left, or northern, bank of the Rockfish, which shot along, with a rapid flood, over the rocks that lay scattered in its bed; and the gush of whose flight fell upon the ear like the loud tones of the wind. From either margin it was shaded by huge sycamores, whose tops, at this twilight hour, were marked in broad lines upon the fading sky, and whose wide spreading boughs met, from side to side, over the middle of the stream, throwing a deeper night upon the clear and transparent waters. The valley was closely bound by high precipitous hills, whose steep crags and narrow passes seemed to echo and prolong the gush of the stream, that was now mingled with the occasional lowing of cattle, the shriek of the owl, and the frequent hoarse scream of the whip-poor-will.

When our party had advanced about a mile along this road, Henry Lindsay took his bugle and blew a blast which seemed to dance in its reverberations from one side of the river to the other.

"Mildred knows my signal," said he; "that is the scout's warning: cavalry approaches: dress your line: prepare to receive a general officer."

"Henry, pray drop your military phrase, and tell me what this means?" said Butler.

"Ride on till you arrive beneath the Fawn's Tower. Wait for me there. I will give you a signal when I approach: and trust me for a faithful messenger. The river is deep at the rock, but you will find a boat fastened to this bank. When you hear my signal come across. Mr. Dimock's is only another mile; and, I'll warrant, the old lady will make you comfortable. Love, they say, major," added Henry, sportively, "is meat and drink, and a blanket to boot; but for all that, Mrs. Dimock's will not be amiss — especially for Horse Shoe, who, I take it, will have the roughest time of the party. If love is a blanket, Mr. Robinson," Henry continued, addressing himself to that worthy, "it doesn't cover two, you know."

"To my thinking, young sir," replied Horse Shoe, with a laugh, "it wouldn't fold so cleverly in a knapsack."

"Now that I have given my orders," said Henry, "and done my

duty, I must leave you, for my road lies across the ford here. Where are my hounds? Hylas, Bell, Blanche, you puppies, where are you?"

Here Henry blew another note, which was immediately responded to by the hounds; and, plunging into the rapid and narrow stream, followed by the dogs, who swam close behind him, he was seen, the next moment, through the twilight, galloping up the opposite hill, as he called out his "good night" to his friends.

As soon as Henry had disappeared, the other two pricked their steeds forward at a faster pace. The rapid flow of the river, as they advanced along its bank, began to change into a more quiet current, as if some obstruction below had dammed up the water, rendering it deep and still. Upon this tranquil mirror the pale crescent of the moon and the faintly peeping stars were reflected; and the flight of the fire-fly was traced, by his own light and its redoubled image, upon the same surface.

The high toppling cliff of the Fawn's Tower, that jutted forth like a parapet above the road, soon arrested the attention of Butler; and at its base the great chestnut flung abroad his "vast magnificence of leaves," almost in emulation of the aspiring crag.

"We have reached our appointed ground," said Butler. "I shall want my cloak, Galbraith; the dews begin to chill my limbs."

They dismounted, and Butler threw his cloak around his shoulders. Then, in a thoughtful, musing state of mind, he strolled slowly along the bank of the river, till he was temporarily lost to view in the thick shades and sombre scenery around him. Robinson, having secured the horses, sat himself down at the foot of the chestnut, unwilling to interrupt, by conversation, the anxious state of feeling which he had the shrewdness to perceive predominated in Butler's mind.

CHAPTER IV

A MEETING OF LOVERS — SOME INSIGHT INTO THE FUTURE

THE twilight had subsided and given place to a beautiful night. The moon had risen above the tree tops, and now threw her level rays upon the broad face of the massive pile of rocks forming the Fawn's Tower, and lit up with a silvery splendor, the foliage that clothed the steep cliff and the almost perpendicular hill in its neighborhood. On the opposite side of the river, a line of beech and sycamore trees, that grew almost at the water's edge, threw a dark shadow upon the bank. Through these, at intervals, the bright moonlight fell upon the earth, and upon the quiet and deep stream. The woods were vocal with the whispering noises that give discord to the nights of summer; yet, was there a stillness in the scene which invited grave thoughts, and recalled to Butler's mind some painful emotions that belonged to his present condition.

" How complicated and severe are those trials " — such was the current of his meditations — " which mingle private grief with public misfortune: that double current of ill which runs, on one side, to the overthrow of a nation's happiness, and, on the other, to the prostration of the individual who labors in the cause! What a struggle have I to encounter between my duty to my country and my regard for those tender relations that still more engross my affections, nor less earnestly appeal to my manhood for defence! Upon the common quarrel I have already staked my life and fortune, and find myself wrapt up in its most perilous obligations. That cause has enough in it to employ and perplex the strongest mind, and to invoke the full devotion of a head and heart that are exempt from all other solicitude: yet am I embarrassed with personal cares that are woven into the very web of my existence; that have planted themselves beside the fountain of my affections, and which, if they be rudely torn from me, would leave behind — but a miserable and hopeless wreck. My own Mildred! to what sad trials have I brought your affection; and how nobly hast thou met them!

" Man lives in the contentious crowd; he struggles for the palm that thousands may award, and far-speeding renown may rend the air with the loud huzza of praise. His is the strife of the theatre where the world are spectators; and multitudes shall glorify his success, or lament his fall, or cheer him in the pangs of death. But woman, gentle, silent, sequestered — thy triumphs are only for the heart that loves thee — thy deepest griefs have no comforter but the secret communion of thine own pillow! "

Whilst Butler, who had now returned beneath the cliff of the Fawn's Tower, was absorbed in this silent musing, his comrade was no less occupied with his own cares. The sergeant had acquired much of that forecast, in regard to small comforts, which becomes, in some degree, an instinct in those whose profession exposes them to the assaults of wind and weather. Tobacco, in his reckoning, was one of the most indispensable muniments of war; and he was, accordingly, seldom without a good stock of this commodity. A corn cob, at any time, furnished him the means of carving the bowl of a pipe; whilst, in his pocket, he carried a slender tube of reed which, being united to the bowl, formed a smoking apparatus, still familiar to the people of this country, and which, to use the sergeant's own phrase, " couldn't be touched for sweetness by the best pipe the very Queen of the Dutch herself ever smoked; and that " — he was in the habit of adding — " must be, as I take it, about the tenderest thing for a whiff that the Dutchman knowed how to make."

A flint and steel — part also of his gear — now served to ignite his tobacco, and he had been, for some time past, sedately scanning the length and breadth of his own fancies, which were, doubtless, rendered the more sublime by the mistiness which a rich volume of smoke had shed across his vision and infused into the atmosphere around his brain.

" Twelve shillings and nine pence," were the first words which became audible to Butler in the depth of his revery. " That, major," said the sergeant, who had been rummaging his pocket, and counting over a handful of coin, " is exactly the amount I have spent since this time last night. I paid it to the old lady of the Swan, at Charlottesville, taking a sixpence for mending your bridle rein. Since you must make me paymaster for our march, I am obliged to square accounts every night. My noddle wont hold two days' reckoning. It gets scrimped and flustered with so many numberings, that I lose the count clean out."

" It is of little consequence, Galbraith," replied Butler, seeking to avoid his companion's interruption.

" Squaring up, and smoothing off, and bringing out this and that shilling straight to a penny, don't come natural to me," continued Robinson, too intent upon his reckoning to observe the disinclination of Butler to a parley, "money matters are not in my line. I take to them as disunderstandingly as Gill Bentley did to the company's books, when they made him Orderly on the Waccamaw picquet. For Gill, in the first place, couldn't write, and, in the next place, if he could'a done that, he never larnt to read, so you may suppose what a beautiful puzzleification he had of it to keep the guard roster straight."

"Sergeant, look if yonder boat is loose; I shall want it presently," said Butler, still giving no ear to his comrade's gossip.

"It is tied by an easy knot to the root of the tree," said Robinson, as he returned from the examination.

"Thank you," added Butler with more than usual abstractedness.

"Something, major, seems to press upon your spirits to-night," said the sergeant, in the kindest tones of inquiry. "If I could lend a hand to put any thing, that mought happen to have got crooked, into its right place again, you know, Major Butler, I wouldn't be slow to do it, when you say the word."

"I would trust my life to you, Galbraith, sooner than to any man living," replied the other, with an affectionate emphasis: — "But you mistake me, I am not heavy of heart, though a little anxious, sergeant, at what has brought me here, comrade," he added as he approached the sergeant, upon whose broad shoulder he familiarly laid his hand, with a smile; "you will keep a fellow soldier's counsel?"

"As I keep my heart in my body," interrupted Galbraith.

"I am sure of it; even as you keep your faith to your country, my true and worthy brother," added Butler with animation, "and that is with no less honesty than a good man serves his God. Then, Galbraith, bear it in mind, I have come here for the sake of a short meeting with one that I love, as you would have a good soldier love the lady of his soul. You will hereafter speak of nothing that may fall within your notice. It concerns me deeply that this meeting should be secret."

"Major, I will have neither eyes nor ears, if it consarns you to keep any thing that mought chance to come to my knowledge, private."

"It is not for myself, sergeant, I bespeak this caution; I have nothing to conceal from you; but there is a lady who is much interested in our circumspection. I have given you a long and solitary ride on her account, and may hereafter ask other service from you. You shall not find it more irksome, Galbraith, to stand by a comrade in love, than you have ever found it in war, and that, I know, you think not much."

"The war comes naturally enough to my hand," replied Galbraith, "but as for the love part, major, excepting so far as carrying a message, or, in case of a runaway, keeping off a gang of pestifarious intermeddlers, or watching, for a night or so, under a tree, or any thing, indeed, in the riding and running, or watching, or scrimmaging line — I say, excepting these, my sarvice moughtn't turn to much account. I can't even play a fiddle at a wedding, and I've not the best tongue for making headway amongst the women. Howsomdever, major, you may set me down for a volunteer on the first forlorn hope you may have occasion for."

"Mr. Lindsay lives on the hill across the river. There are reasons why I cannot go to his house; and his daughter, Galbraith, is an especial friend to us and to our cause."

"I begin to see into it," interrupted the sergeant, laughing, "you have a notion of showing the old gentleman the same trick you played off upon Lord Howe's provost marshal, when you was lieutenant at Valley Forge, touching your stealing away his prisoner, Captain Roberts. That was a night affair, too. Well, the best wife a man can have, major, is the woman that takes to him through fire and water. There was Colonel Gardiner, that stole his wife just in that way, against all opposition of both father and mother, and a better woman never stitched up a seam, to my knowledge and belief."

"I have no thought of such an enterprise, sergeant," said Butler; "our purpose, for the present, must be confined to a short visit. We are houseless adventurers, Galbraith, and have little to offer to sweetheart or wife that might please a woman's fancy."

"When a woman loves a man, especially a sodger," replied the sergeant, "she sets as little store by house and home as the best of us. Still, it is a wise thing to give the creatures the chance of peace, before you get to tangling them with families. Hark, I hear something like footsteps on t'other side of the river! Mister Henry must be on his march."

After an interval, a low whistle issued from the opposite bank, and, in a moment, Butler was in the skiff, pushing his way through the sparkling waters.

As the small boat, in which he stood upright, shot from the bright moonlight into the shade of the opposite side, he could obscurely discern Mildred Lindsay leaning on her brother's arm, as they both stood under the thick foliage of a large beech. And scarcely had the bow struck upon the pebbly margin, before he bounded from it up the bank, and was, in the next instant, locked in the embrace of one whose affection he valued above all earthly possessions.

When that short interval had passed away, in which neither Mildred nor Arthur could utter speech; during which the lady leant her head upon her lover's bosom, in that fond familiarity which plighted faith is allowed to justify in the most modest maiden, sobbing the while in the intensity of her emotions, she then at last, as she slowly regained her self-possession, said, in a soft and melancholy voice, in which there was nevertheless a tone of playfulness:

"I am a foolish girl, Arthur. I can boast like a blustering coward, when there is nothing to fear; and yet I weep, like a true woman, at the first trial of my courage."

"Ah, my dear Mildred, you are a brave girl," replied Butler, as he held both of her hands and looked fondly into her face, "and a true and a tried girl. You have come kindly to me, and ever, like a blessed and gentle spirit of good, are prompt to attend me through every mischance. It is a long and weary time, love, since last we met."

"It is very, very long, Arthur."

"And we are still as far off, Mildred, from our wishes as at first we were."

"Even so," said Mildred sorrowfully. "A year of pain drags heavily by, and brings no hope. Oh, Arthur, what have I suffered in the thought that your life is so beset with dangers! I muse upon them with a childish fear, that was not so before our last meeting. They rise to disturb my daily fancies, and night finds them inhabiting my pillow. I was so thankful, that you escaped that dreary siege of Charleston!"

"Many a poor and gallant fellow soldier there bit his lip with a chafed and peevish temper," said Butler; "but the day will come, Mildred, when we may yet carry a prouder head to the field of our country's honor."

"And your share," interrupted Mildred, "will ever be to march in the front rank. In spite of all your perils past, your hard service, which has known no holiday, your fatigues, that I have sometimes feared would break down your health, and in spite too, of the claims, Arthur, that your poor Mildred has upon you, you are even now again bound upon some bold adventure, that must separate us, ah, perhaps, for ever! Our fate has malice in it. Ever beginning some fresh exploit!"

"You would not have your soldier bear himself otherwise than as a true knight, who would win and wear his lady-love by good set blows when there was need for them?"

"If I were the genius that conjured up this war, I would give my own true knight a breathing space. He should pipe and dance between whiles," replied Mildred sportively.

"He that puts his sickle into this field amongst the reapers," said Butler, with a thoughtful earnestness, "should not look back from his work."

"No, no, though my heart break while I say it — for, in truth, I am very melancholy, notwithstanding I force a beggar's smile upon my cheek; no, I would not have you stay or stand, Arthur, until you have seen this wretched quarrel at an end. I praised your first resolve — loved you for it — applauded and cheered you; I will not selfishly now, for the sake of my weak, womanish apprehension, say one word to withhold your arm."

"And you are still," said Butler, "that same resolute enthusiast that I found in the young and eloquent beauty who captivated my worthless heart, when the war first drew the wild spirits of the country together under our free banner?"

"The same foolish, conceited, heady, prattling truant, Arthur, that first took a silly liking to your pompous strut, and made a hero to her imagination out of a boasting ensign — the same in all my follies, and in all my faults — only altered in one quality."

"And pray, what is that one quality?"

"I will not tell you," said Mildred carelessly. "'Twould make you vainer than you are."

"It is not well to hide a kind thought from me, Mildred."

"Indeed it is not, Arthur. And so, I will muster courage to speak it," said the confiding girl with vivacity, after a short pause during which she hung fondly upon her lover's arm; and then suddenly changing her mood, she proceeded in a tone of deep and serious enthusiasm, "it is, that since that short, eventful and most solemn meeting, I have loved you, Arthur, with feelings that I did not know until then were mine. My busy fancy has followed you in all your wanderings — painted with stronger hues than nature gives to any real scene the difficulties and disasters that might cross your path — noted the seasons with a nervous acuteness of remark, from very faint-heartedness at the thought that they might blight your health or bring you some discomfort. I have pored over the accounts of battles, the march of armies, the tales of prisoners relating the secrets of their prisons; studied the plans of generals and statesmen, as the newspapers or common rumor brought them to my knowledge, with an interest that has made those around me say I was sadly changed. It was all because I had grown cowardly and feared even my own shadow. Oh, Arthur, I am not indeed what I was."

The solemnity, force and feeling with which Mildred gave utterance to these words, strangely contrasted with the light and gay tone in which she had commenced; but her thoughts had now fallen into a current that bore her forward into one of those bursts of excited emotion, which were characteristic of her temper, and which threw a peculiar energy and eloquence into her manner. Butler, struck by the rising warmth of her enunciation, and swayed in part by the painful reflections to which her topic gave rise, replied, in a state of feeling scarcely less solemn than her own —

"Ah, Mildred," and as he spoke, he parted her hair upon her pale forehead and kissed it, "dearest girl, the unknown time to come has no cup of suffering for me that I would not hold a cheap purchase for one moment like this. Even a year of painful absence past, and a still more solicitous one to come, may be gallantly and cheerfully borne when blessed with the fleeting interval of this night. To hear your faith, which though I never dwelt upon it but with a confidence that I have held it most profane to doubt, still, to hear it avowed from your own lips, now again and again, repeating what you have often breathed before, and in letter after letter, written down, it falls upon my heart, Mildred, like some good gift from heaven, specially sent to revive and quicken my resolution in all the toils and labors that yet await me. There must be good in store for such a heart as thine; and, trusting to this faith, I will look to the future with a buoyant temper."

"The future," said Mildred, as she lifted her eyes to the pale moon that now sheeted with its light her whole figure, as she and her lover strayed beyond the shade of the beech, "I almost shudder when I hear that word. We live but in the present; that, Arthur, is, at least, our own, poor as we are in almost all beside. That future is a perplexed and tangled riddle — a dreadful uncertainty, in the contemplation of which I grow superstitious. Such ill omens are about us! My father's inexorable will, so headstrong, so unconscious of the pain it gives me; his rooted, yes, his fatal aversion to you; my thraldom here, where, like a poor bird checked by a cord, I chafe myself by fluttering on the verge of my prison bounds; and then, the awful perils that continually impend over *your* head — all these are more than weak imaginings; they are the realities of my daily life, and give me, what I am almost ashamed to confess, a sad and boding spirit."

"Nay, nay, dearest Mildred! Away with all these unreasonable reckonings!" replied Butler, with a manner that too plainly betrayed the counterfeit of mirth. "Seclusion has dealt unworthily with you. It has almost turned thee into a downright sentimental woman. I will have none of this stepping to the verge of melancholy. You were accustomed to cheer me with sunny and warm counsel; and you must not forget it was yourself who taught me to strike aside the waves of fortune with a glad temper. The fates can have no spite against one so good as thou art! Time may bear us along like a rough trotting horse; and our journey may have its dark night, its quagmires, and its jack-o'-lanterns, but there will come a ruddy morning at last — a smoother road, and an easier gait; and thou, my girl, shalt again instruct me how to win a triumph over the ills of life."

"And we will be happy, Arthur, because all around us will be so," added Mildred, catching the current of Butler's thoughts, with that ready versatility which eminently showed the earnestness and devotion of her feelings — "Ah, may heaven grant this boon, and bring these dreams to life! I think, Arthur, I should be happier now, if I could but be near you in your wanderings. Gladly would I follow you through all the dangers of the war."

"That were indeed, love, a trial past your faculty to endure. No, no, Mildred, she who would be a soldier's wife, should learn the soldier's philosophy — to look with a resigned submission on the present events, and trust to heaven for the future. Your share in this struggle is to commune with your own heart in solitude, and teach it patience. Right nobly have you thus far borne that grievous burden! The sacrifice that you have made — its ever present and unmitigated weight, silently and sleeplessly inflicting its slow pains upon your free and generous spirit; that, Mildred, is the chief and most galling of my cares."

"This weary war, this weary war," breathed Mildred, in a pensive under key, "when will it be done!"

"The longest troubles have their end," replied Butler, "and men, at last, spent with the vexations of their own mischief, fly, by a selfish instinct, into the bosom of peace. God will prosper our enterprise, and bring our battered ship into a fortunate haven."

"How little like it seems it now!" returned Mildred. "The general sorrow, alone, might well weigh down the stoutest heart. That cause which you have made mine, Arthur, to which you have bestowed your life, and which, for *your* sake," she added proudly, "should have this feeble arm of mine, could it avail, is it not even now trembling on the verge of ruin? Have not your letters, one after another, told me of the sad train in which misfortunes have thickened upon the whole people? of defeat, both north and south, and, at this very time, of disgraceful mutiny of whole regiments under the very eye of Washington — that Washington who loves his country and her soldiers as a husband loves his bride, and a father his children. Have not those, to whom we all looked for champions, turned into mere laggards in the war for freedom? Oh, Arthur, do you not remember that these are the thoughts, the very words, which were penned by your own hand, for my especial meditation? How can I but fear that the good end is still far off? How can I but feel some weight upon my heart?"

"You have grown overwise, Mildred, in these ruminations. I am to blame for this, that in my peevish humor, vexed with the crosses of the day, I should have written on such topics to one so sensitive as yourself."

"Still it is true, Arthur, all report confirms it."

"These things do not become your entertainment, Mildred. Leave the public care to us. There are bold hearts, love, and strong arms yet to spare for this quarrel. We have not yet so exhausted our mines of strength, but that much rough ore still lies unturned to the sun, and many an uncouth lump of metal remains to be fashioned for serviceable use. History tells of many a rebound from despondency, so sudden and unreckoned, that the wisest men could see in it no other spring than the decree of God. He will fight the battle of the weak, and set the right upon a sure foundation."

"The country rings," said Mildred, again taking the more cheerful hue of her lover's hopes, and following out, with an affectionate sympathy, his tone of thought, "with anticipation of victory from Gates's southern march."

"That may turn out to be a broken reed," interrupted Butler, as if thinking aloud, and struck by Mildred's reference to a subject that had already engrossed his thoughts; "they may be deceived. Washington would have put a different man upon that service.

I would have a leader in such a war, wary, watchful, humble—diffident as well as brave. I fear Gates is not so."

"Then, I trust, Arthur," exclaimed Mildred, with anxious alacrity, "that your present expedition does not connect you with his fortunes!"

"I neither follow his colors nor partake of his counsels," replied Butler. "Still my motions may not be exempt from the influence of his failure or success. The enemy, you are aware, has possessed himself of every post of value in South Carolina and Georgia. I go commissioned to advise with discreet and prudent men upon the means to shake off this odious domination. So far only, and remotely, too, I am a fellow-laborer with Gates. There are gallant spirits now afoot, Mildred, to strip these masters of their power. My office is to aid their enterprise."

"If you needs must go, Arthur, I have no word to say. You will leave behind you an aching heart, that morning, noon, and night, wearies heaven with its prayers for your safety. Alas, I have no other aid to give! How soon—how soon," she said, with a voice that faltered with the question, "does your duty compel you to leave me?"

"To-morrow's sunrise, love, must find me forth upon my way."

"To-morrow, Arthur? so quickly to part!"

"I dare not linger; not even for the rich blessing of thy presence."

"And the utmost length of your journey?"

"Indeed, I know not. At present my farthest aim is Ninety-six and Augusta. It much depends upon the pleasure of our proud and wilful masters."

Mildred stood for some moments looking upon the ground in profound silence. Her bosom heaved with a sad emotion.

"It is a dangerous duty," said she, at last. "I cannot speak my apprehension at the thought of your risks amongst the fierce and treacherous men that overrun the country to which you travel."

"These perils are exaggerated by distance," returned Butler. "A thousand expedients of protection and defence occur when present, which the absent cannot fancy. It is a light service, Mildred, and may more securely be performed with a gay heart than with a sad one. I pray you, do not suffer that active imagination of yours to invest the every day adventures of your poor soldier with a romantic interest of which they are not worthy. I neither slay giants, nor disenchant ladies, nor yoke

An illustration for Horse-Shoe Robinson *by F. O. C. Darley.*

captive griffins together. No, no, I shall outrun some over-fed clown, and outwit some simple boobies; and, perhaps, soil my boots in a great slough, and then hasten back, love, to boast of my marvels to the credulous ear of my own sweet girl, who, I warrant, will think me a most preposterous hero."

"How can you laugh, Arthur? And yet I would not have you catch my foolish sadness, either."

"I have with me, besides, Mildred, a friend good at need; one Galbraith Robinson, a practised and valiant soldier, who sits on yonder bank. He is to be the companion of my journey; he is shrewd, vigilant and cautious, an inhabitant, moreover, of the district to which I am bound; his wisdom can do much for my success. Then I travel, too, in peaceful guise. My business is more concerned with negotiation than with battle."

"It is a waylaid path, Arthur," said Mildred, in the same faint voice with which she had spoken before.

"Never take it so heavily, my love!" exclaimed Butler, familiarly seizing her hand, whose trembling now betrayed her agitation, — "it is the mere sport of the war to be upon a running service, where a light stratagem or so will baffle a set of dull-pated clodpoles! I scarcely deem it a venture, to dodge through a forest, where every man flies from his neighbor out of mutual distrust. These fellows have brought themselves upon such bad terms with their own consciences, that they start like thieves at the waving of a bulrush."

"They would be the more cruel," replied Mildred, "if some ill luck should throw you into their power. If that should happen," she added, and for a while she hesitated to speak, as a tear fell upon Butler's hand — "If that should happen, I cannot bear the thought."

"They dare offer me no wrong, Mildred. The chances of battle are sufficiently various to compel even the victors to pursue the policy of humanity to prisoners. The conqueror of to-day may himself be a captive to-morrow, and a bloody reprisal would await his barbarity. Again, let me remind you, these are not fit topics for your meditation."

"They are topics for my heart, Arthur, and will not be driven from it. If your lot should put you in the power of the enemy, the name of Mildred Lindsay, and the relation you bear her, whispered in their ears, may, perhaps, unlock their charity. My father has many friends in those ranks, and it may be that I am not unknown to some of them: oh, remember that!"

"You have little need to teach me to think or speak of Mildred Lindsay," said Butler, eagerly. "I cannot forget that name. But I may well doubt its charm upon the savage bulldogs who are now baiting our citizens in Carolina; those ruthless partizans who are poisoning the fountains of contentment at every fire-side. It is not a name to conjure evil spirits with."

"Major Butler," said Henry, who during this long interval had been strolling backward and forward, like a sentinel, at some distance from his sister and her lover, and who, with the military punctilio of a soldier on duty, forbore even to listen to what he could not have helped overhearing, if it had not been for humming a tune — "Major, I don't like to make or meddle with things that don't belong to me — but you and Mildred have been talking long enough to settle the course of a whole campaign. And as my father thinks he can't be too careful of Mildred, and doesn't like her walking about after night-fall, I shouldn't be surprised if a messenger were despatched for us — only I think that man Tyrrel is hatching some plot with him to-night, and may keep him longer in talk than usual."

"Who is Tyrrel?" inquired Butler.

"One that I wish had been in his grave before he had ever seen my father," answered Mildred with a bitter vehemence. "He is a wicked emissary of the royal party sent here to entrap my dear father into their toils. Such as it has ever been his fate to be cursed with from the beginning of the war; but this Tyrrel, the most hateful of them all."

"Alas, alas, your poor father! Mildred, what deep sorrow do I feel that he and I should be so estranged. I could love him, counsel with him, honor him, with a devotion that should outrun your fondest wish. His generous nature has been played upon, cheated, abused; and I, in whom fortune and inclination should have raised him a friend, have been made the victim of his perverted passion."

"True, true," exclaimed Mildred, bursting into tears, and resting her head against her lover's breast, "I can find courage to bear all but this — I am most unhappy;" and for some moments she sobbed audibly.

"The thought has sometimes crossed me," said Butler, "that I would go to your father and tell him all. It offends my self-respect to be obliged to practise concealment towards one who should have a right to know all that concerns a daughter so dear to him. Even now, if I may persuade you to it, I will go hand in hand with you, and, with humble reverence, place myself before him and divulge all that has passed between us."

"No, no, Arthur, no," ejaculated Mildred with the most earnest determination. "It will not come to good. You do not understand my father's feelings. The very sight of you would rouse him into frenzy; there is no name which might fall upon his ear with deeper offence than yours. Not yet, Arthur, the time has not yet come."

"I have been patient," said Butler, "patient, Mildred, for your sake."

"To try him now," continued Mildred, whose feelings still ran, with a heady impetuosity, upon this newly-awakened and engrossing topic; "now, in the very depth of his bitterest aversion to what he terms an impious rebellion, and whilst his heart is yet moved with an almost preternatural hate against all who uphold the cause, and to you, especially, above whose head there hovers, in his belief, some horrid impending curse that shall bring desolation upon him and all who claim an interest in his blood — no, no, it must not be!"

"Another year of pent-up vexation, self-reproach and anxious concealment must then glide by, and perhaps another," said Butler. "Well, I must be content to bear it, though, in the mean time, my heart bleeds for you, Mildred; it is a painful trial."

"For good or for evil our vow is now registered in heaven," replied Mildred, "and we must abide the end."

"I would not have it other than it is, dearest girl, except this stern resolve of your father — not for the world's wealth," said Butler warmly. "But you spoke of this Tyrrel — what manner of man is he? How might I know him?"

"To know him would answer no good end, Arthur. His soul is absorbed in stratagem, and my dear father is its prey. I too am grievously tormented by him; but it is no matter, I need not vex your ear with the tale of his annoyance."

"Indeed!" exclaimed Butler with a sudden expression of resentment.

"All that concerns my father, concerns me," said Mildred. "It is my evil destiny, Arthur, to be compelled to endure the associations of men, whose principles, habits, purposes, are all at war with my own. Alas, such are now my father's constant companions! This man Tyrrel, whose very name is a cheat put on, I doubt not, to conceal him from observation — goes farther than the rest in the boldness of his practice. I have some misgiving that he is better acquainted with the interest you take in me, than we might suspect possible to a stranger. I fear him. And then, Arthur, it is my peculiar misery that he has lately set up a disgusting pretension to my regard. Oh! I could give him, if my sex had strength to strike, the dagger, sooner than squander upon him one kind word. Yet am I obliged by circumstance to observe a strained courtesy towards him, which, frugal as it is, makes me an unwilling hypocrite to my own heart."

"Tyrrel," ejaculated Butler, "Tyrrel! I have heard no such name abroad!" then, muttering a deep curse, as he bit his lip with passion, he added, "Oh, that I could face this man, or penetrate his foul purpose! How is it likely I might meet him?"

"You shall have no temptation to a quarrel," said Mildred; "your quick resentment would but give activity to his venom. For the sake of my peace, Arthur, and of your own, inquire no further. Time may disclose more than rash pursuit."

"Leave that to sister Mildred and myself, major," said Henry, who listened with great interest to this conversation, "I have *my* eye upon him — let that satisfy you; and when sister Mildred puts up the game, depend upon it, I will bring him down."

"Thanks, thanks, dear Henry! I can trust you for a ready friend, and will even follow your good advice. A more favorable season for this concern may soon arrive; meantime, I will bear this hint in mind."

Again Henry made an appeal to the lovers to bring their conference to an end. It was a sorrowful moment, the events of which were brief, earnest and impassioned, and such as a dull scribbler, like myself, might easily mar in the telling; yet they were such as zealous and eager natures, who have loved with an intense and absorbing love, and who have parted in times of awful danger and uncertainty, may perchance be able to picture to themselves, when they recall the most impressive incident of their lives to memory. I will only say, that, in that dark shade where the beech tree spread his canopy of leaves over the cool bank, and marked his shadow's profile on the green sward — that grassy sward, on which "the constant moon" lit up the dewy lamps, hung by the spider on blade and leaf; and in that silent time, when the distant waterfall came far-sounding on the ear, when sleepless insects chirped in the thicket, and dogs, at some remote homestead, howled buglelike to the moon; and in that chill hour, when Mildred drew her kerchief close around her dew-besprinkled shoulders, whilst Arthur, fondly and affectionately, half enveloped her in the folds of a military cloak, as he whispered words of tender parting in her ear, and imprinted a kiss upon her cheek; and when, moreover, Henry's teeth chattered like a frozen warder's, then it was, and there, that this enthusiastic girl again pledged her unalterable devotion to the man of her waking thoughts and nightly dreams, come weal, come woe, whatever might betide; and the soldier paid back the pledge with new ardor and endearment, in the strong language that came unstudied from the heart, meaning all that he said, and rife with a feeling beyond the reach of words. And, after "mony a locked and fond embrace," full tearfully, and lingeringly, and, in phrase oft repeated, the two bade "farewell," and invoked God's blessing each upon the other, and then, not without looking back, and breathing a fresh prayer of blessings, they separated on their dreary way, Mildred retiring, as she had come, on the arm of her brother, and Butler, springing hurriedly into the skiff and directing its swift passage to the middle of the stream, where, after a pause to enable him to discern the last footsteps of his mistress, as her form glided into the obscure distance, he sighed a low "God bless her," then resumed his oar, and sturdily drove his boat against the "opponent bank."

CHAPTER V

A COMFORTABLE INN, AND A GOOD LANDLADY — THE MISFORTUNES OF HEROES DO NOT ALWAYS DESTROY THE APPETITE

As soon as Butler landed from the skiff, he threw his cloak into the hands of the sergeant; then, with a disturbed haste, sprang upon his horse, and, commanding Robinson to follow, galloped along the road down the river as fast as the nature of the ground and the obscurity of the hour would allow. A brief space brought them to the spot where the road crossed the stream, immediately in the vicinity of the widow Dimock's little inn, which might here be discerned ensconced beneath the cover of the opposite hill. The low-browed wooden building, quietly stationed some thirty paces off the road, was so adumbrated in the shelter of a huge willow, that the journeyer, at such an hour as this, might perchance pass the spot unconsciously by, were it not for an insulated and somewhat haggard sign-post that, like a hospitable seeker of strangers, stood hard by the road side, and there displayed a shattered emblem in the guise of a large blue ball, a little decayed by wind and weather, which said Blue Ball, without superscription or device, was universally interpreted to mean "entertainment for man and horse, by the widow Dimock." The moonlight fell with a broad lustre upon the sign post and its pendent globe; and our travellers, besides, could descry, through the drapery of the willow, a window, of some rear building of the inn, richly illuminated by what, from the redness of the light, might be conjectured to be a bundle of blazing faggots.

As the horses had, immediately upon entering the ford, compelled their masters to a halt, whilst they thrust their noses into the water and drank with the greediness of a long and neglected thirst, it was with no equivocal self-gratulation that Robinson directed his eye to the presignifications of good cheer which were now before him. Butler had spoken "never a word," and the sergeant's habits of subordination, as well as an honest sympathy in what he guessed to be the griefs of his superior officer, had constrained him to a respectful silence. The sergeant, however, was full of thoughts which, more than once during the gallop from the Fawn's Tower, he was on the point of uttering by way of consolation to Butler, and which nothing prevented but that real delicacy of mind that lies at the bottom of a kind nature, and inhabits the shaggy breast of the rustic, at least full as often as it lodges in the heart of the trim worldling. The present halt seemed, in Horse Shoe's reckoning, not only to furnish a pretext to speak, but, in some degree, to render it a duty; and, in truth, an additional very stimulating subject presented itself to our good squire, in his instantaneous conviction that the glare from the tavern window had its origin in some active operation which, at this late hour, might be going on at the kitchen chimney; to understand the full pungency of which consideration, it is necessary to inform my reader, that Robinson had, for some time past, been yielding himself to certain doubts, whether his friend and himself might not arrive at the inn at too late an hour to hope for much despatch in the preparation for supper. In this state of feeling, partly bent to cheer the spirits of Butler, and partly to express his satisfaction at the prospect of his own comfort, he broke forth in the following terms —

"God bless all widows that set themselves down by the roadside, is my worst wish! and, in particular, I pray for good luck to the widow Dimock, for an orderly sort of body, which I have no doubt she is; and keeps good hours — to judge by the shine of the kitchen fire which is blazing yonder in the rear — and which, to tell truth, major, I began to be afeard would be as dead, by this time o' night, as the day the hearth-stone was first laid. She desarves to be spoken of as a praiseworthy woman. And, moreover, I should say she has popped her house down in a most legible situation, touching our day's march, by which I mean it isn't one step too near a reasonable bed hour. I count it lucky, major, on your account; and although it isn't for me to give advice in woman affairs — for I know the creatures do try the grit and edge of a man amazingly sometimes — yet, if I mought say what was running in my head fit for a gentleman and an officer like you to do in such a tribulation, it would be this: drop thinking and chawing over your troubles, and take them with a light heart, as things that's not to be mended by a solemncolly long-facedness. A good victual's meal and a fair night's rest would make another man of you. That's my observation; and I remember once to hear you say the same yourself, upon occasion of your losing the baggage wagons last fall on the Beaufort convoy. You ha'n't forgot it, major?"

"Thank you, thank you, sergeant. Your counsel is kindly offered and wisely said, and I will follow it. But it is a little hard, fellow soldier," added Butler, with something like an approach to jocularity, "it's a little hard to have one's misfortunes cast in his teeth by a comrade."

"I thought it would make you laugh, major!" replied Robinson, with a good-natured solicitude, "for it wan't in the possibilities of a mortal earthly man to save the baggage; and, I remember, you laughed then, as well as the rest of us, when them pestifarious, filching sheep stealers made off with our dinners: nobody ever blamed you for it."

"Ah, Galbraith, you are a good friend, and you shall say what you please to me," said Butler, with a returning cheerfulness; "sorrow is a dull companion to him who feeds it, and an impertinent one to everybody beside. So, ride forward, and we will endeavor to console ourselves with the good cheer of the widow. And, hark, Galbraith, this Mistress Dimock is an especial friend of mine: pray you, let her see, by your considerateness towards her, that you are aware of that — for my sake, good Horse Shoe."

The two soldiers soon reached the inn, and, having dismounted, Butler aroused the attention of the inmates by a few strokes upon the door with his riding rod.

The reply to this summons was a shrill invitation, in a feminine voice, to "walk in;" and no sooner had Butler thrown open the door and advanced a few paces into the passage, than the head of an elderly female was seen thrust through the partially expanded doorway of the adjoining room. Another instant, and the dusky figure of Mistress Dimock herelf was visible to our travellers.

"What would you be pleased to have, sir?" inquired the dame, with evident distrust at this untimely approach of strangers.

"Accommodation for the night, and whatever you have good to offer a friend, Mistress Dimock."

"Who are you that ride so late?" again interrogated the hostess; "I am cowardly, sir, and cautious, and have reason to be careful who comes into my house; a poor unprotected woman, good man."

"A light, mother," said Butler, "and you shall know us better. We are travellers and want food and rest, and would have both with as little trouble to you as possible; a light will show you an old friend."

"Wait a moment," returned the dame; and then added, as she

observed Butler walk into a room on the left, "Take care, sir, it is risking a fall to grope in the dark in a strange house."

"The house is not so strange to me as you suppose. Unless you have moved your furniture I can find the green settee beyond the cupboard," said Butler, familiarly striding across the room, and throwing himself into the old commodity he had named.

The landlady, without heeding this evidence of the conversancy of his visitor with the localities of the little parlor, had hastily retreated, and, in a moment afterwards, returned with a light, which, as she held it above her head, while she peered through a pair of spectacles, threw its full effulgence upon the face of her guest.

"Dear me, good lack!" she exclaimed, after a moment's gazing; "Arthur Butler, o' my conscience! And is it you, Mr. Butler?" Then, putting the candle upon the table, she seized both of his hands and gave them a long and hearty shake. "That Nancy Dimock shouldn't know your voice, of all others! Where have you been, and where are you going? Mercy on me! what makes you so late? And why didn't you let me know you were coming? I could have made you so much more comfortable. You are chilled with the night air; and hungry, no doubt. And you look pale, poor fellow! You surely couldn't have been at the Dove Cote?" which last interrogatory was expressed with a look of earnest and anxious inquiry.

"No, not there," replied Butler, almost in a whisper; "alas, my kind dame, not there," he added, with a melancholy smile, as he held the hand of the hostess and shook his head; "my fortune has in no jot improved since I left you almost a year ago. I broke from you hastily then to resume my share in the war, and I have had nothing but hard blows ever since. The tide, Mistress Dimock, sets sadly against us."

"Never let your heart fail you," exclaimed the landlady; "it isn't in the nature of things for the luck to be for ever on the shady side. Besides, take the good and bad together, you have not been so hardly dealt by, Captain Butler."

"Major Butler, madam, of the second Carolina continental reg'lar infantry," interrupted Robinson, who had stood by all this time unnoticed, "*Major* Butler; the captain has been promoted, by occasion of the wiping out of a few friends from the upper side of the adjutant's roll, in the scrimmage of Fort Moultrie. He is what we call, in common parley, brevetted."

This annunciation was made by the sergeant with due solemnity, accompanied by an attempt at a bow, which was abundantly stiff and ungraceful.

"My friend Sergeant Robinson," said Butler; "I commend him, Mistress Dimock, to your especial favor, both for a trusty comrade, and a most satisfactory and sufficient trencher man."

"You are welcome and free to the best that's in the house, sergeant," said the landlady, courtesying; "and I wish, for your sake, it was as good as your appetite, which ought to be of the best. Mr. Arthur Butler's word is all in all under this roof; and, whether he be captain or major, I promise you, makes no difference with me. Bless me! when I first saw you, major, you was only an ensign; then, whisk and away! and back you come a pretty lieutenant, about my house: and then a captain, forsooth! and now, on the track of that, a major. It is up-up-up the ladder, till you will come, one of these days, to be a general; and too proud, I misdoubt, to look at such a little old woman as me! hegh, hegh, hegh! a pinch of snuff, Mr. Arthur." And here the good dame prolonged her phthisicky laugh for some moments, as she presented a bog of Scotch snuff to her guest. "But I'll engage promotion never yet made the appetite of a travelling man smaller than before; so, gentlemen, you will excuse me while I look after your supper."

"The sooner the better, ma'am," said Robinson; "your night air is a sort of a whetstone to the stomach: but first, ma'am, I would be obligated to you, if you would let me see the ostler."

"Hut, tut! and have I been drivelling here all this time," exclaimed the dame, "without once spending a thought upon your cattle! Tony, Tony, To-ny, I say," almost shrieked the hostess, as she retreated along the passage towards the region of the kitchen, and then back again to the front door. "Are you asleep? Look to the gentlemen's horses; lead them to the stable, and don't spare to rub them down; and give them as much as they can eat. Where are you, old man?"

"What's the use of all this fuss, Missus Dimock? Arn't I here on the spot, with the cretur's in my hand?" grumbled out an old, stunted negro, who answered to the appellation of ostler: "Arn't I getting the baggage off, as fast as I can onbuckle the straps?—I don't want nobody to tell me when I ought to step out. If a hos could talk, he ain't got nothing new to say to me. Get out, you varmints," he shouted, with a sudden vivacity of utterance, at three or four dogs that were barking around him: "Consarn you! What you making such a conbobberation about? You all throat when you see gentmen coming to the house; better wait tell you see a thief; bound, you silent enough then, with your tail twixt your legs! Blossom, ya sacy slut, keep quiet, I tell you!"

In the course of this din and objurgation, the old negro succeeded in disburdening the horses of their furniture, and was about to lead them to the stable, when Robinson came to give him some directions.

"Mind what you are after with them there cattle. Give them not a mouthful for a good hour, and plenty of fodder about their feet; I'll look at them myself before you shut up. Throw a handful of salt into the trough, Tony, and above all things, don't let me catch you splashing water over their backs; none of that; do you hear?"

"Haw, haw, haw!" chuckled Tony; "think I don't know how to take care of a hos, mass! Been too use to creturs, ever sense so high. Bless the gentman! one of the best things on arth, when you're feared your hos is too much blowed, is to put a sprinkling of salt in a bucket o' water, and just stir a leetle Indian meal in with it; it sort of freshes the cretur up like, and is onaccountable good in hot weather, when you ain't got no time to feed. But cold water across the lines! oh, oh, I too cute in hos larning for that! Look at the top of my head — gray as a fox!"

"Skip then, or I'll open upon you like a pack of hounds," said Robinson, as he turned on his heel to re-enter the house, "I'll look in after supper."

"Never mind me," replied Tony, as he led the horses off, "I have tended Captain Butler's hos afore this, and he wan't never onsatisfied with me."

These cares being disposed of, Horse Shoe returned to the parlor. The tidy display of some plain furniture, and the scrupulous attention to cleanliness in every part of the room, afforded an intelligent commentary upon the exact, orderly and decent character of the Widow Dimock. The dame herself was a pattern of useful thrift. Her short figure, as she now bustled to and fro, through the apartment, was arrayed in that respectable, motherly costume which befitted her years; and which was proper to the period of my story, when the luxury of dress was more expensive than at present, and when a correspondent degree of care was used to preserve it in repair. Evidences of this laudable economy were seen in the neatness with which a ruffle was darned, or a weak point fortified by a nicely adjusted patch, presenting, in some respect, a token both of the commendable pride of the wearer, and of the straitness of the national means, since the prevalence of war for five years had not only reduced the wealth of individuals and rendered frugality indispensable, but had, also, literally deprived the country of its necessary supply of commodities; thus putting the opulent and the needy, to a certain extent, upon the same footing. On the present occasion, our good landlady was arrayed in a gown of sober-colored chintz, gathered into plaits in the skirt, whilst the body fitted closely over a pair of long-waisted stays, having tight sleeves that reached to the elbow. The stature of the dame was increased a full inch by a pair of high-heeled, parti-colored shoes, remarkable for their sharp toes; and a frilled muslin cap, with lappets that reached under the chin, towered sufficiently high to contribute, also, something considerable to the elevation of the tripping little figure of its wearer.

In such guise did Mistress Dimock appear, as she busied herself in preparing needful refreshment for the travellers; and for some time the house exhibited all that stir which belongs to this important care when despatched in a retired country inn.

By degrees, the table began to show the bounties of the kitchen. A savory dish of fried bacon, the fumes of which had been, for a quarter of an hour, gently stimulating the appetite of the guests, now made its appearance, in company with a pair of broiled pullets; and these were followed by a detachment of brown-crested hoecakes — the peculiar favorite of the province; an abundance of rich milk, eggs, butter, and other rural knick-nackeries, such as no hungry man ever surveys with indifference. These were successively deposited upon a homespun table cloth, whose whiteness rivalled the new snow, with an accuracy of adjustment that, by its delay, produced the most visible effects upon the sergeant, who, during the spreading of the board, sat silently by, watching, with an eager and gloating earnestness, the slow process, ever and anon uttering a short hem, and turning about restlessly on his chair.

I may pause here, after the fashion of our worthy friend Horse Shoe, to make an observation. There is nothing that works so kindly upon the imagination of a traveller, if he be in any doubt as to his appetite, as the display of such a table. My particularity of detail, on the present occasion, will, therefore, be excused by my reader, when I inform him that Butler had arrived at the inn in that depressed tone of spirits which seemed to defy refreshment; and that, notwithstanding this impediment, he played no insignificant part afterwards at supper; a circumstance mainly attributable to that gentle but irresistible solicitation, which the actual sight and fragrance of the board addressed to his dormant physical susceptibility. I might, indeed, have pretermitted the supper altogether, were there not a philosophical truth at the bottom of the matter, worthy of the notice of the speculative and curious reader; namely, that where a man's heart is a little teased with love, and his temper fretted by crossings, and his body jolted by travel; especially, when he has been wandering through the night air, with owls hooting in his ears; and a thin drapery of melancholy has been flung, like cobwebs, across his spirits, then it is my doctrine, that a clean table, a good-humored landlady and an odorous steaming-up of good things, in a snug, cheerful little parlor, are certain to beget in him a complete change of mood, and to give him, instead, a happy train of thoughts and a hearty relish for his food. Such was precisely Butler's condition.

He and the sergeant now sat down at the table, and each drew the attention of the other by the unexpected vigor of their assaults upon the dainties before them; Robinson surprised to find the major so suddenly revived, and Butler no less unprepared to see a man, who had achieved such wonders at dinner, now successively demolish what might be deemed a stout allowance for a well fed lion.

"It almost seems to go against the credit of my house," said the hostess, "to set gentlefolks down at my table without a cup of tea; but so it is; we must get used to be stripped of all the old-fashioned comforts. It is almost treason for an honest woman to have such an article in her house now, even if it could be fairly come by. Still, I'll engage I am tory enough yet to like the smell of hyson. They have no mercy upon us old women, major; they should have a care, or they will drive us into the arms of the enemy."

"Faith then, ma'am," interrupted Horse Shoe bluntly, as he threw his eye over his shoulder at the landlady, who had broken into a laugh at her own sally of humor, "it would be no wonder if you were soon driven back again."

"Shame on you, Mr. Sergeant Robinson," retorted the dame, laughing again, "I didn't expect to hear such a speech from you; that's a very sorry compliment to a poor country woman.

If the men on our side think so little of us as you do, it would be no wonder if we all desert to King George: but Major Arthur Butler, I am sure, will tell you that we old bodies can sometimes make ourselves very useful — gainsay it who will."

"You seem to be rather hard, Galbraith," said Butler, "on my good friend Mistress Dimock. I am sure, madam, the sergeant has only been unlucky in making himself understood; for I know him to be a man of gallantry to your sex, and to cherish an especial liking for the female friends of our cause, amongst whom, Mistress Dimock, I can certify he is prepared to set a high value upon yourself. The sergeant was only endeavoring to provoke your good humor. Try this honey, Galbraith; Mistress Dimock is famous for her beehives; and perhaps it will give a sweeter edge to your tongue."

"I spoke, major," replied Robinson, awkwardly endeavoring to extricate himself under this joint rebuke, and, at the same time, plunging a spoon into the dish to which Butler had invited his notice, "consarning the difficulty of having ladies — whether old or young make no difference, it wa'n't respecting the age of Mistress Dimock, nor her beauty, by no means, that I said what I did say; but it was consarning of the difficulty of having the women with them in their marches and their countermarches. What could such tender creatures have done at such a place as the sieging of Charlestown? Certain, this is most elegant honey!" he added, by way of parenthesis, as he devoured a large slice of bread, well covered with a fragment of honeycomb, as if anxious to gain time to collect his ideas; for, with all Horse Shoe's bluntness, he was essentially a diffident man. "It is my opinion, ma'am, the best thing the women can do in these here wars, is to knit; and leave the fighting of it out, to us who hav'n't faces to be spoiled by bad weather and tough times."

"I don't want to have art nor part in these quarrels," replied the widow. "The saints above are witnesses, I think it unnatural enough to see a peaceable country, and a quiet honest people, vexed and harried, and run down with all this trooping of horses, and parading of armies, and clattering of drums, amongst the hills that never heard any thing worse than the lowing of a heifer before. But still, I wish well to liberty; and if it must be fought for, why, I am even content to take my share of the suffering, in my own lonesome way; and they that bear the heat of the day, and their friends, shall always be served in my house with the best that's in it, and at the most reasonable rates. Even if they come without money, I am not the woman to turn them off with an empty stomach; I mean them of the right side."

"Well, that's as sensible a speech, Mistress Dimock," said Horse Shoe, quickly seizing the occasion to make amends to the landlady for his former bluntness, "and as much to the purpose, and spoken with as much wisdom and circumscription, as mought come out of the mouth of e'er a lady in the land — high born or low born — I don't care where the other comes from. And it does a man's heart good to hear the womankind holding out such presentments. It's encouraging on the face of it."

During this conversation the supper was finished, and Mrs. Dimock had now seated herself, with her elbows upon the table, so placed as to allow her to prop her chin upon her hands, in which position she fell into an earnest but quiet, under-toned confabulation with Butler, who partook of it with the more interest, as it related to the concerns of the family at the Dove Cote.

"Mr. Lindsay, poor man," said the dame, in the course of this conference, "is wofully beset. It almost looks as if he was haunted by an evil spirit, sure enough, which folks used to say of him after his wife's death — and which, to tell you the truth, our young lady Mildred has sometimes more than half hinted to me; he is so run at, and perplexed, and misguided by strangers that can have no good intention in coming to see him. There is Mr. Tyrrel, over at the Dove Cote at this very time, on his third visit, major, in less now than two months past; yes, let me see, he brought the news here of the recapitulation — I think you military call it — though, heaven knows, I have but a poor head for these bloodthirsty words — I mean the taking of Charleston; three times has he been here, counting from that day. Where he comes from, and who are his kith and kin, I am sure I don't know."

"Tyrrel, ha! yes, I have heard of him to-night, for the first time," said Butler.

"He must be a rich man," continued the hostess, "for he travels with two white servants, and always pays his way in gold. One of his men is now in the house; and, between you and me, major, this man is a very inquisitive sort of person, and would hardly be taken for a serving man; and he is a cautious fellow too, although there is a good deal of swagger and bullying about him, which might deceive one at first sight."

"Here, in the house to-night?" inquired Butler.

"Speak low, major, the man is now walking the porch before our windows."

"What does Mildred say of this Tyrrel?" asked Butler.

"Has she been here lately?"

"The good lady never stirs from home whilst Tyrrel is at the Dove Cote; for fear, I believe, that he will follow her, for they do whisper about in the neighborhood — though I don't say it to alarm you, Mr. Arthur, that this man is of the high quality, a nobleman, some say, and that he has come here a-courting. Only think of the assurance of the man! But if he was a prince, and every hair of his head strung with diamonds, and Miss Mildred was as free as the day you first saw her, I can say with safety he would find but cold comfort in that game; for she despises him, major, both for himself and for his tory principles. She does hate him with a good will. No, no, her heart and soul are both where they ought to be, for all her father, poor man, and this rich gentleman! Oh, it is a cruel thing that you and our pretty lady cannot live quietly together; but Mr. Lindsay is past talking to about it. I declare I think his mind is touched: I positively believe it would kill him if he knew all that has passed in this house; but he is, in the main, a good man, and a kind father, and is very much to be pitied. I see you are sad and sorrowful, Mr. Arthur: I didn't mean to distress you with my prating. You tell me, you think you may travel as far as Georgie."

"Even so far, good dame, if some accident should not shorten my career. These are doubtful times, and my path is as uncertain as the chances of war. It may be long before I return."

"I grieve night and day, and my heart bleeds for Miss Mildred, for she is so good, so constant, so brave, too, for a woman," said the widow with unaffected emotion. "Well-a-day! what woes these wars have brought upon us! You told her your plans, Mr. Arthur?"

"Our interview was short and painful," replied Butler. "I scarcely know what I said to her. But, one thing I entreat of you: my letters will be directed to your charge; you will contrive to have them promptly and secretly delivered: oblige me still in that, good mother. Henry will often visit you."

"And a brave and considerate young man he is, major; I'll

be surety for his making of an honorable and a real gentleman. Do you join the army in Carolina?"

"Perhaps not. My route lies into the mountains, our troops struggle for a footing in the low country."

"If I may make bold, Major Butler, to drop a word of advice into your ear, which, seeing that I'm an older man than you," interrupted the sergeant, in an admonitory whisper, "I think I have got good right to do, why I would just say that there may be no great disconvenience in talking before friends; but sometimes silence brings more profit than words. So, I vote that we leave off telling the course of our march till such time as it is done, and all is safe. There will be briers enough in our way, without taking the trouble to sow them by the roadside. The man that stands a little aside from that window, out on the porch, throws his shadow across the sill oftener than is honest, according to my reckoning. You said, ma'am," continued Horse Shoe, addresssing the widow, "that the fellow in the porch yon is Mr. Tyrrel's man."

"He walks later than usual to-night," replied Mrs. Dimock, "for though he can't be called a man of regular hours, yet, unless he can find an idler to keep him company, he is accustomed to be in his bed before this."

"He is after no good, depend upon that," said Horse Shoe. "I have twice seen the light upon his face behind the shutter: so, true man or spy, it's my admonishment not to speak above the purring of a cat."

"You are right, Galbraith," said Butler. "We have many reasons to distrust him; and it is at least safest to keep our affairs private."

"If I thought he was prying," continued Galbraith, "which I do measurably insinuate and believe, I would take the freedom to give him the benefit of a drilling on good manners. Ha, major! as I have a hand, he is reconnoitring us now at this identical time! Didn't you see him pass up and down before the door, and look in as greedily as if our faces were picture-books for him to read? I will have a word with him, and, wise or simple, I will get his calibre before I am done with him. Never let on, major; stay where you are. I promised to look after our horses."

The hostess and her guest now continued their communion; in which we leave them, whilst we follow Horse Shoe towards the stable.

CHAPTER VI

> There're two at fisty-cuffs about it;
> Sir, I may say at dagger's drawing,
> But that I cannot say, because they have none.
>
> MAYOR OF QUINBOROUGH.

WHEN Horse Shoe left the apartment, he discovered the person, whose demeanor had excited his suspicion, leaning against a post of the porch, in front of the house. The moonlight, as it partially fell upon this man's figure, disclosed a frame of sufficient mould to raise a surmise, that, in whatever form of communication the sergeant might accost him, he was not likely to find a very tractable subject to his hand. Robinson, however, without troubling himself with the contemplation of such a contingency, determined to delay his visit to the stable long enough to allow himself the expression of a word of warning or rebuke, to indicate to the stranger the necessity for restraining his curiosity in regard to the guests of the inn. With this view he halted upon the porch, while he scanned the person before him, and directed an earnest gaze into his face. The stranger, slightly discomfited by this eager scrutiny, turned his back upon his visitor, and, with an air of idle musing, threw his eyes towards the heavens, in which position he remained until summoned by the familiar accost of Horse Shoe.

"Well! and what do you make of the moon? As sharp an eye as you have in your head, neighbor, I'm thinking it will do you no great sarvice there. You're good at your spying trade; but you will get nothing out of her; she keeps her secrets."

Startled by this abrupt greeting, which was made in a tone halfway between jest and earnest, the stranger quickly confronted his challenger, and bestowed upon him a keen and inquiring inspection; then breaking into a laugh, he replied with a free and impudent swagger—

"You are mistaken, Master Jack Pudding. What says the proverb? Wit's in the wane when the moon's at full. Now, our mistress has let me into a secret. She tells me that you will not lose your wits, when she comes to her growth. The reason why? first, because she never troubles herself with so small a stock as yours, and second, because your thick skull is moon-proof; so you're safe, friend."

"A word in your ear," said Horse Shoe; "*you* are not safe, friend, if you are cotched again peeping through the chinks of the window, or sneaking upon the dark side of the doorway, to pick up a crumb of talk from people that are not axing your company. Keep that in your memory."

"It's a base lie, Mr. Bumpkin, if you mean to insinuate that I did either."

"Oh, quiet and easy, good man! No flusterifications here! I am civil and peaceable. Take my advice, and chaw your cud in silence, and go to bed at a reasonable hour, without minding what folks have to say who come to the widow Dimock's. It only run in my head to give you a polite sort of a warning. So, good night; I have got business at the stable."

Before the other could reply, Robinson strode away to look after the accommodations of the horses.

"The devil take this impertinent ox-driver!" muttered the man to himself, after the sergeant had left him; "I have half a mind to take his carcase in hand, just to give it the benefit of a good, wholesome manipulation. A queer fellow, too — a joker! A civil, peaceable man! — the hyperbolical rogue! Well, I'll see him out, and, laugh or fight, he shan't want a man to stand up to him!"

Having by this train of reflection brought himself into a mood which might be said to hover upon the isthmus between anger and mirth, ready to fall to either side as the provocation might serve, the stranger sauntered slowly towards the stable, with a hundred odd fancies as to the character of the man he sought running through his mind. Upon his arrival there he found that Horse Shoe was occupied in the interior of the building, and being still in a state of uncertainty as to the manner in which it was proper he should greet our redoubtable friend, he took a seat on a small bench at the door, resolved to wait for that worthy's reappearance. This delay had a soothing effect upon his temper, for as he debated the subject over in his mind, certain considerations of policy seemed to indicate to him the necessity of making himself better acquainted with the business and quality of the individual whom he came to meet.

After a few moments, Horse Shoe was seen with old Tony at the stable door, where, notwithstanding the unexpected presence of the man to whom he had so lately offered his unwelcome advice, and upon whom he now conferred not the slightest notice, he continued uninterruptedly, and with deliberate composure, to give his orders upon what, at that moment, doubtless, he deemed matter of much graver importance than any concern he might have in the visit of his new acquaintance.

"Do what I tell you, Tony; get a piece of linen, rub it well over with tallow, and bring it here along with a cup of vinegar. The beast's back is cut with the saddle, and you must wash the sore first with the vinegar, and then lay on the patch. Go, old fellow, and Mrs. Dimock, may be, can give you a strip of woollen cloth to sarve as a pad."

With these instructions the negro retired towards the house.

"I see you understand your business," said the stranger. "You look to your horse's back at the end of a day's journey, and you know how to manage a sore spot. Vinegar is the thing! You have had a long ride?"

"How do you know that?" inquired Horse Shoe.

"Know it! any man might guess as much by the way you shovelled down your supper. I happened by chance to pass your window, and seeing you at it, faith! for the soul of me I couldn't help taking a few turns more, just to watch the end of it. Ha! ha! ha! give me the fellow that does honor to his stomach! And your dolt head must be taking offence at my looking at you! Why, man, your appetite was a most beautiful rarity; I wouldn't have lost the sport of it for the pleasure of the best supper I ever ate myself."

"Indeed!" said Robinson, drily.

"Pease upon the trencher!" exclaimed the other, with the air of a pot companion; "that's the true music for good fellows of your kidney! But it isn't every where that you will find such bountiful quarters as you get here at the Blue Ball; in that cursed southern country a man like you would breed a famine, if you even do not find one ready made to your hand when you get there."

"Where mought you be from?" asked the sergeant, with great gravity, without responding to the merriment of his visitor, and purposely refraining from the answer which he saw it was the other's drift to obtain relative to the course of his travel.

"It was natural enough that you should have mistaken my object," continued the stranger, heedless of Horse Shoe's abrupt question, "and have suspected me for wanting to hear some of your rigmarole; but there you did me wrong. I forgive you for that, and, to tell you the truth, I hate your —— "

"That's not to the purpose," said Horse Shoe; "I axed you a civil question, and maybe, that's more than you have a right to. You can answer it or let it alone. I want to know where mought you be from?"

"Since you are bent upon it, then," replied the other, suddenly changing his tone, and speaking with a saucy emphasis, "I'll answer your question, when you tell me what *mought* be your right to know."

"It's the custom of our country," rejoined Horse Shoe, "I don't know what it may be in yourn, to larn a little about the business of every man we meet; but we do it by fair, out-and-out question and answer — all above board, and we hold in despise all sorts of contwistifications, either by laying of tongue-traps, or listening under eaves of houses."

"Well, most wise and shrewd master, what do you call my country? Ha! ha! ha! I would be sworn you think you have found some mare's nest! If it were not that your clown pate is somewhat addled by over feeding, I would hold your speech to be impertinent. My country, I'd have your sagacity to understand —— "

"Tut, man, it ar'n't worth the trouble of talking about it! I never saw one of your people that I didn't know him by the first word that came out of his lips. You are an Englishman, and a red coat into the bargain, as we call them in these parts. You have been a sodger. Now, never bounce at that, man! There's no great harm in belonging to that craft. They listed you, as likely as not, when you was flusticated with liquor, and you took your pay; there was a bargain, and it was your business to stand to it. But I have got a piece of wisdom to whisper to you, insomuch as you are not in the most agreeablest part of the world to men of your colors, it would be best to be a little more shy against giving offence. You said some saucy things to me just now, but I don't grudge your talking, because you see, I am an onaccountable hard sort of person to be instigated by speeching."

"Verily, you are a most comical piece of dulness," said the other, in a spirit of raillery. "In what school did you learn your philosophy, friend? You have been brought up to the wholesome tail of the plough, I should say — an ancient and reputable occupation."

"When I obsarved, just now," replied Robinson, somewhat sternly, "that I couldn't be instigated, I meant to be comprehended as laying down a kind of general doctrine that I was a man not given to quarrels; but still, if I suspicioned a bamboozlement, which I am not far from at this present speaking, if it but come up to the conflagrating of only the tenth part of the wink of an eye, in a project to play me off, fore God, I confess myself to be as weak in the flesh as e'er a rumbunctious fellow you mought meet on the road."

"Friend," said the other, "I do not understand thy lingo. It has a most clodpolish smack. It is neither grammar, English, nor sense."

"Then, you are a damned, onmannerly rascal," said Horse Shoe, "and that's grammar, English, and sense, all three."

"Ha, you are at that! Now, my lubberly booby, I understand you," returned the other, springing to his feet. "Do you know to whom you are speaking?"

"Better than you think for," replied the sergeant, placing himself in an erect position to receive what hc had a right to expect, the threatened assault of his adversary, "I know you, and guess your arrand here."

"You do?" returned the other sharply. "You have been juggling with me, sir. You are not the gudgeon I took you for. It has suited your purpose to play the clown, eh? Well, sir, and pray, what do you guess?"

"Nothing good of you, considering how things go here. Suppose I was to say you was, at this self-same identical time, a sodger of the king's? I have you there!"

The stranger turned on his heel and retreated a few paces, evidently perplexed at the new view in which the sergeant suddenly rose to his apprehension. His curiosity and his interest were both excited to gain a more distinct insight into a man whom he had mistaken for a mere simpleton, but whose hints showed him to be shrewdly conversant with the personal concerns of one, whom, apparently, he had seen to-night for the first time in his life. With this anxiety upon his mind, he again approached the sergeant, as he replied to the last question.

"Well, and if I were? It is a character of which I should have no reason to be ashamed."

"That's well said!" exclaimed Horse Shoe. "Up and speak out, and never be above owning the truth; that's the best sign that can be of a man. Although it mought be somewhat dangerous, just hereabouts, to confess yourself a sodger of King George — let me tell you, that, being against you, I am not the person to mislest you on that head, by spreading the news abroad, or setting a few dozen of whigs upon your scent, which is a thing easily done. If your business here is peaceable and lawful, and you don't let your tongue brawl against quiet and orderly people, you are free to come and go for me."

"Thank you, sir; but look you; it isn't my way to answer questions about my own business, and I scorn to ask any man's leave to come and go where and when my occasions call me."

"If it isn't your way to answer questions about your own business," replied Horse Shoe, "it oughtn't to be your way to ax them about other people's; but that don't disturb me; it is the rule of the war to question all comers and goers that we happen to fall in with, specially now, when there's a set of your devils scampering and raging about in Carolina, hardly a summer day's ride off this province, burning houses and killing cattle, and turning everything topsy-turvy, with a pack of rascally tories to back them. In such times all sorts of tricks are played, such as putting on coats that don't belong to a man, and deceiving honest people by lies, and what not."

"You are a stranger to me," said the other; "but let me tell you, without circumlocution or periphrase, I am a free born subject of the king, and I see no reason why, because some of his people have turned rebels a true man, who travels his highway, should be obliged to give an account of himself to every inquisitive fellow who chooses to challenge it. Suppose I tell you that you meddle with matters that don't concern you?"

"Then you mought chance to get your head in your hand, that's all. And, hark, if it wan't that I am rather good-natured, I mought happen to handle you a little rough for that nicknaming of the friends of liberty, by calling them rebels. It doesn't suit such six-pence-a-day fellows as you, who march right or left at the bidding of your master, to rob a church or root up an honest man's peaceful hearth, without so much as daring to have a thought about the righteousness of the matter — it doesn't suit such to be befouling them that fight for church and fireside both, with your scurvy, balderdash names."

"Well, egad! you are a fine bold fellow who speaks his thoughts, that's not to be denied!" said the stranger, again suddenly changing his mood, and resorting to his free and easy address. "You suit these times devilish well. I can't find it in my heart to quarrel with you. We have both been somewhat rough in speech, and so, the account is square. But now tell me, after all, are you sure you have guessed me right? How do you know I am not one of these very rebels myself?"

"For two good and point-blank reasons. First, you dar'n't deny that you have pocketed the king's money and worn his coat — that's one. And, second, you are now here under the orders of one of his officers."

"No, no, good friend," said the man, with a voice of less boldness than heretofore, "you are mistaken for once in your life. So far what you say, I don't deny — I am in the service of a gentleman, who for some private affairs of his own has come on a visit to this part of the province, and I admit I have been in the old country."

"I am not mistaken, good friend," drawled out Robinson, affectedly. "You come from the south. I can tell men's fortunes without looking into the palms of their hands."

"You are wrong again," said the other tartly, as he grew angry at being thus badgered by his opponent, "I come from the north."

"That's true and it's false both," returned Robinson. "From the north, I grant you — to the south with Sir Henry, and from the south up here. You will find I can conjure a little, friend."

"The devil take your conjuring!" exclaimed the other, as he bit his lip and strode restlessly backward and forward; which perplexity being observed by the sergeant, he did not fail to aggravate it by breaking into a hoarse laugh, as he said——

"It wa'n't worth your while to try to deceive me. I knowed you by manifold and simultaneous signs. Him that sets about scouting after other people's secrets, ought to be wary enough to larn to keep his own. But don't take it so to heart, neighbor, there's no occasion for oneasiness — I have no mind to harm you."

"Master bully," said the stranger, planting himself immediately in front of the sergeant, "in England, where I was bred, we play at cudgels, and sometimes give broken heads; and some of us are gifted with heavy fists, wherewith we occasionally contrive to box a rude fellow who pries too much into our affairs."

"In our country," replied Horse Shoe, "we generally like to get a share of whatever new is stirring, and, though we don't practise much with cudgels, yet, to sarve a turn, we do, now and then, break a head or so; and, consarning that fist work you happened to touch upon, we have no condesentious scruples against a fair rap or two over the knowledge-box, and the tripping-up of a fractious chap's heels, in the way of a sort of a rough-and-tumble, which, may be, you understand. You have been long enough here, mayhap, to find that out."

"Then, it is likely, it would please you to have a chance at such a game? I count myself a pretty tolerable hand at the play," said the stranger, with a composure corresponding to that exhibited by Horse Shoe.

"Ho, ho! I don't want to hurt you, man," replied the Sergeant. "You will get yourself into trouble. You are hot-headeder than is good for your health."

"As the game was mentioned, I thought you might have a fancy to play it."

"To be sure I would," said Horse Shoe, "rather than disappoint you in any reasonable longing. For the sake of quiet — being a peaceable man, I will take the trouble to oblige you. Where, do you think, would be the likeliest spot to have it?"

"We may readily find a piece of ground at hand," replied the other. "It is a good moonlight play, and we may not be interrupted if we get a little distance off before the negro comes back. Toe to toe, and face to face, suits me best with both friend and foe."

"A mule to drive and a fool to hold back, are two of the contrariest things I know," said Robinson, "and so, seeing that you are in arnest about it, let us go at it without more ado upon the first good bit of grass we can pop upon along the river."

In this temper the two antagonists left the vicinity of the stable, and walked some hundred paces down along the bank of the stream. The man with whom Horse Shoe was about to hold this strange encounter, and who now walked quietly by his side, had the erect and soldierly port of a grenadier. He was square-shouldered, compact and muscular, and the firmness of his gait, his long and easy stride, and the free swing of his arm as he moved onward in the moonlight, showed Robinson that he was to engage with an adversary of no common capacity. There was, perhaps, on the other side, some abatement in this man's self-confidence, when the same light disclosed to his deliberate inspection the brawny proportions of the sergeant, which, in the engrossment of the topics bandied about in the late dialogue, he had not so accurately regarded.

When they had walked the distance I have mentioned, they had little difficulty to select a space of level ground with a sufficient mould for the purpose of the proposed trial of strength.

"Here's as pretty a spot as we mought find on the river," said Robinson, "and so get ready, friend. Before we begin, I have a word to say. This here bout is not a thing of my seeking, and I take it to be close akin to downright tom-foolery, for grown up men to set about thumping and hammering each other, upon account of a brag of who's best man, or such like, when the whole univarse is full of occasions for scuffles, and stands in need of able-bodied fellows, to argufy the pints of right and wrong, that can't be settled by preachers, or books, or lawyers. I look upon this here coming out to fight no better than a bit of arrant nonsense. But, as you will have it, it's no consarn of mine to stop you."

"You are welcome to do your worst," replied the other, "and the less preaching you make with it, the more saving of time."

"My worst," interrupted Horse Shoe, "is almost more than I have the conscience to do to any man who isn't a downright flagratious enemy; and, once more, I would advise you to think before you draw me into a fray; you are flustrated, and sot upon a quarrel, and mayhap, you conjecture that by drawing me out from behind my retrenchments, by which is signified my good nature, and forcing me to deploy into line and open field, you'll get the advantage of an old sodger over me; but there, Mr. Dragoon, you are mistaken. In close garrison or open field, in siege or sally, crossing a defile or reconnoitring on a broad road, I am not apt to lose my temper, or strike without seeing where my blow is to hit. Now, that is all I have to say: so, come on."

"You are not what you seem," said the antagonist, in a state of wonder at the strain of the sergeant's composed and deliberate speech, and at the familiarity which this effusion manifested with the details of military life. "In the devil's name, who are you? But, don't fancy I pause to begin our fight, for any other reason than that I may know who I contend with. On the honor of a soldier, I promise you, I will hold you to your game — man, or imp of hell — I care not. Again, who in the devil are you?"

"You have hit it," replied Horse Shoe. "My name is Brimstone, I am first cousin to Belzebub."

"You have served?"

"I have."

"And belong to the army yet?"

"True again; and I am as tough a sodger, and may be I mought say, as old a sodger as yourself."

"Your hand, fellow soldier. I mistook you from the beginning. You continentals — that's the newfangled word — are stout fellows, and have a good knack at the trick of war, though you wear rough coats, and are savagely unrudimented in polite learning. No matter what colors a man fights under, long usage makes a good comrade of him; and, by my faith! I am not amongst the last to do him honor, even though we stand in opposite ranks. As you say, most sapient Brimstone, we are not much better than a pair of fools for this conspiracy to knock about each other's pates, here at midnight; but you have my pledge to it, and so, we will go at it, if it be only to win a relish for our beds; I will teach you, to-night, some skill in the art of mensuration. You shall measure two full ells upon this green sod."

"There's my hand," said Horse Shoe; "now, if I am flung, I promise you I won't be angry. If I sarve you in the same fashion, you must larn to bear it."

"With all my heart. So here I stand upon my guard. Begin."

"Let me feel your weight," said Robinson, laughing, as he put one hand upon his adversary's shoulder, and the other against his side. "Hark you, master, I feel something hard here about your ribs; you have pistols under your coat, friend. For the sake of fair play and keeping rid of foul blood, you had best lay them aside before we strike. Anger comes up onawares."

"I never part from my weapons," replied the other, stepping back and releasing himself from Robinson's grasp. "We are strangers; I must know the company I am in, before I dismiss such old cronies as these. They have got me out of a scrape before this."

"We took hands just now," said Robinson, angrily. "When I give my hand, it is tantamount to a book oath that I mean fair, round dealing with the man who takes it. I told you, besides, I was a sodger — that ought to have contented you — and you mought sarch my breast, inside and out, you'd seen in it nothing but honest meanings. There's something of a suspectable rascality, after that, in talking about pistols hid under the flaps of the coat. It's altogether onmanful, and, what's more, onsodgerly. You are a deceit, and an astonishment, and a hissing, all three, James Curry, and no better, to my comprehension, than a coward. I know you of old, although, mayhap, you disremember me. I have hearn said, by more than one, that you was a double-faced, savage-hearted, disregardless beast, that snashed his teeth where he darsn't bite, and bullied them that hadn't the heart to fight: I have hearn that of you, and, as I live, I believe it. Now, look out for your bull head, for I will cuff you in spite of your pistols."

With these words, Horse Shoe gave his adversary some half dozen overpowering blows, in such quick succession as utterly defied and broke down the other's guard; and then, seizing him by the breast, he threw the tall and stalwart form of Curry at full length upon the ground.

"There's your two ells for you! there's the art of menstirration, you disgrace to the tail of a drum," exclaimed Horse Shoe, with accumulating wrath, as the prostrate man strove to extricate himself from the lion grasp that held him. In this strife, Curry several times made an effort to get his hand upon his pistol, in which he was constantly foiled by the superior vigor of the sergeant.

"No, no," continued the latter, as he became aware of this attempt, "James Curry, you shall never lay hold upon your firearms whilst I have the handling of you. Give them up, you twisting prevaricationer; give them up, you disgracer of powder and lead; and larn this from a rebel, that I don't blow out your brains, only because I wouldn't accommodate the devil by flinging such a lump of petrifaction into his clutches. There, man," he added, as he threw the pistols far from him into the river, his exasperation, at the same time, moderating to a lower temperature, "get upon your feet; and now, you may go hunt for your cronies in yonder running stream. You may count it a marcy that I haven't tossed you after them, to wash the cowardly blood off your face. Now that you are upon your legs, I tell you here, in the moonlight, man to man, with nobody by to hold back your hand, that you are a lying, deceitful skulker, that loves the dark side of a wall better than the light, and steals the secrets of honest folks, and hasn't the heart to stand up fairly to the man that tells you of it. Swallow that, James Curry, and see how it will lay upon your stomach."

"I will seek a time!" exclaimed Curry, "to right myself with your heart's blood."

"Pshaw! man," replied Horse Shoe, "don't talk about heart's blood. The next time we come into a field together, ax for Galbraith Robinson, commonly called Horse Shoe Robinson.

Find me out, that's all. We may take a frolic together then, and I give you my allowance to wear your pistols in your belt."

"We may find a field yet, Horse Shoe Robinson," returned Curry, "and I'll not fail of my appointment. Our game will be played with broadswords."

"If it should so turn out, James, that you and me are to work through a campaign in the same quarter of the world, as we have done afore, James, I expect, I'll take the chance of some holiday to pay my respects to you. I won't trouble you to ride far to find me; and then, it may be broadsword or pistol, rifle or bagnet, I'm not overscrumptious which. Only promise I shall see you when I send for you."

"It's a bargain, Galbraith Robinson! Strong as you think yourself in your cursed rough-and-tumble horseplay, I am soldier enough for you any day. I only ask that the time may come quickly."

"You have no objection to give us a hand to clinch that bargain, James?" asked Horse Shoe. "There's my paw; take it, man, I scorn to bear malice after the hot blood cools."

"I take it with more pleasure now," said Curry, hastily seizing the hand, "than I gave mine to you before to-night, because it is a pledge that suits my humor. A good seat in a saddle, four strong legs below me, and a sharp blade, I hold myself a match for the best man that ever picked a flint in your lines."

"Now, friend Curry," exclaimed the sergeant, "good night! Go look for your pop-guns in the river; and if you find them, hold them as a keepsake to remember Horse Shoe Robinson. Good night."

Robinson left his adversary, and returned to the inn, ruminating, as he walked, over the strange incident in which he had just been engaged. For a while his thoughts wore a grave complexion; but, as his careless good humor gradually broke forth through the thin mist that enveloped it, he was found, before he reached the porch, laughing, with a quiet chuckle, at the conceit which rose upon his mind, as he said, half-audibly, "Odd sport for a summer night! Howsever, every one to his liking, as the old woman said; but to my thinking, he mought have done better if he had gone to sleep at a proper hour, like a moralised and sober Christian."

When he entered the parlor, he found Butler and the landlady waiting for him.

"It is late, sergeant," said the Major. "You have forgotten

the hour; and I began to fear you had more to say to your friend, there, than suited the time of night."

"All is right, by your smiling," added the landlady; "and that's more than I expected at the time you walked out of the room. I couldn't go to my bed, till I was sure you and my lodger had no disagreeable words; for, to tell you the truth, I am greatly afraid of his hot and hasty temper."

"There is nothing hot or hasty about him, ma'am," replied Robinson; "he is about as peaceable a man as you mought expect to meet in such times as these. I only told him a little scrap of news, and you would have thought he would have hugged me for it, ha, ha, ha."

"We are to sleep in the same room, sergeant," said Butler, "and our good hostess will show us the way to it."

The dame, upon this hint, took a candle, and conducted her guests to a chamber in the upper story, where, after wishing them "a good night," she courtesied respectfully, and left them to their repose.

"Tell me, sergeant, what you made out of that fellow," said Butler, as he undressed himself. "I see that you have had some passage with him; and, from your tarrying so long, I began to be a little apprehensive of rough work between you. What passed, and what have you learned?"

"Enough, major, to make us more circumscriptious against scouts, and spies, and stratagems. When I was a prisoner at Charlestown, there was an amazing well-built fellow, a dragoon, that had been out with Tarleton; but, when I saw him, he was a sort of rithmatical account-keeper and letter-scribbler for that young fighting-cock, the Earl of Caithness, him that was aidegong to Sir Henry Clinton. Well, this fellow had a tolerable bad name, as being a chap that the devil had spiled, in spite of all the good that had been pumped into him at school; for, as I have hearn, he was come of gentle people, had a first rate edication, and I reckon, now, major, he talks as well as a book, whereupon I have an observation."

"Keep that until to-morrow, sergeant," interrupted Butler, "and go on with what you had to tell me."

"You must be a little sleepy, major: however, this fellow, they say, was cotched cheating with cards one day, when he was playing a game of five shilling loo with the King or the Queen, or some of the dukes or colonels in the guards — for he wa'n't above any thing rascally. So, it was buzzed about, as you may suppose when a man goes to cheating one of them big fish — and the King gave him his choice to enlist, or go to the hulks; and he, being no fool, listed, as a matter of course. In that way he got over here; and, as I tell you, was a sort of sarvent to that young Earl. He sometimes came about our quarters to list prisoners and make Tories of 'em, for his own people kept him to do all that sort of dirty work, upon account of the glibness of his tongue. He was a remarkable saucy fellow, and got nothing but ill-will from the prisoners — though, I make no doubt, the man is a tolerable sodger on sarvice. Now, after telling you all this, major, you must know that the identical, same, particular man that we saw looking through the porch window at us to-night" —

"Is the man you have been describing? Is it possible? Are you sure of it?"

"I knowed him the minute I clapped eyes on him: his name is James Curry: but, as I didn't stay long at Charlestown, and hadn't any thing to do with him in particular, it seems he didn't remember me."

"You conversed with him?"

"Most sartainly I did. I wanted to gather a little consarning of his visit up here: but the fellow's been so battered about in the wars, that he knows how to hold his tongue. I had some mischief in me, and did want to make him just angry enough to set his speech loose; and, besides, I felt a little against him upon account of his misdoings with our people in Carolina, and so, I said some rough things to him; and, as my discourse ar'n't none of the squarest in pint of grammar and topographical circumlocution — as Lieutenant Hopkins used to say — why he set me down for a piece of an idiot, and began to hoax and bamboozle me. I put that matter straight for him very soon, by just letting him say so much and no more. And then, as I was a peaceable man, major, he seemed to see that I didn't want to have no quarrel with him, which made him push it at me rather too hard, and all my civility ended in my giving him what he wanted at first — a tolerable, regular thrashing."

The sergeant continued to relate to Butler the details of this adventure, which he did with more prolixity than the weariness of his listener was able to endure; for the major, having in the progress of the narrative got into bed, and having, in the increasing oscitancy of his faculties, exhausted every expression of assent by which one who listens to a tale is accustomed to notify his attention — he at length dropped into a profound sleep, leaving the sergeant to conclude at his leisure.

When Robinson perceived this, he had nothing left but to betake himself, with all expedition, to his own rest; whereupon he threw off his coat, and taking the coverings of the bed appropriated to his use, spread them upon the floor, as he pronounced an anathema against sleeping on feathers, (for it must be observed, that our good hostess, at that early day, was liable to the same censure of an unnatural attachment to feather beds in summer, which may, at the present time,* be made against almost every country inn in the United States,) and then extinguishing the candle, he stretched himself upon the planks, as he remarked to his unconscious companion, "that he was brought up on a hard floor;" and after one or two rolls, he fell into that deep oblivion of cares, by which nature re-summons and supplies the strength which toil, watching and anxiety wear down.

The speed of Horse Shoe's journey through this pleasant valley of sleep might be measured somewhat in the same manner that the route of a mail stage may sometimes be traced through a mountain defile, by the notes of the coachman's horn; it was defined by the succession of varying intonations through which he ascended the gamut, beginning with a low but audible breathing, and rising through the several stages of an incipient snore, a short quick bark, and up to a snort that constituted the greatest altitude of the ascent. Occasionally a half articulated interjection escaped him, and words that showed in what current his dreams were sailing: "No pistols! Look in the water, James! Ha ha!" These utterings were accompanied with contortions of body that more than once awaked the sleeper; but, at last, the huge bulk of Horse Shoe grew motionless in a deep and strong sleep.

The next morning, at early dawn, our travellers resumed their journey, which I will leave them to prosecute, whilst I conduct my reader to the affairs and interests that dwell about the Dove Cote.

* This stricture, true in 1835, the date of the first edition of these volumes, has, I am happy to notice, lost much of its point in the lapse of sixteen years.

[Kennedy's note.]

CHAPTER VII

SOME ACCOUNT OF PHILIP LINDSAY — SENSIBILITY AND RETIREMENT APT TO ENGENDER A PERNICIOUS PHILOSOPHY

THE thread which I have now to take up and weave into this history requires that my narrative should go back for some years. It briefly concerns the earlier fortunes of Philip Lindsay.

His father emigrated from England, and was established in Virginia about the year 1735, as a secretary to the governor of the province. He was a gentleman of good name and fortune. Philip was born within a year after this emigration. As America was then comparatively a wilderness, and afforded but few facilities for the education of youth, the son of the secretary was sent at an early age to England, where he remained, with the exception of an occasional visit to his parents, under the guardianship of a near relative, until he had completed, not only his college course, but also his studies in the Temple — an almost indispensable requirement of that day for young gentlemen of condition.

His studies in the Temple had been productive of one result, which Lord Coke, if I remember, considers idiosyncratic in the younger votaries of the law — he had fallen in love with an heiress. The natural consequence was a tedious year, after his return home, spent at the seat of the provincial government, and a most energetic and persevering interchange of letters with the lady, whom my authority allows me to name Gertrude Marshall. This was followed by another voyage across the Atlantic, and finally, as might be predicted, by a wedding with all proper observance and parental sanction. Lindsay then returned, a happier and more tranquil man, to Virginia, where he fulfilled the duties of more than one public station of dignity and trust.

In due course of time he fell heir to his father's wealth, which with the estate of his wife made him one of the most opulent and considerable gentlemen of the Old Dominion.

He had but two children — Mildred and Henry — with four

years difference between their ages. These were nurtured with all the care and indulgent bounty natural to parents whose affections are concentrated upon so small a family circle.

Lindsay's character was grave and thoughtful, and inclined him to avoid the contests of ambition and collision with the world. A delicate taste, a nice judgment, and a fondness for inquiry made him a student and an ardent lover of books. The ply of his mind was towards metaphysics; he delved into the obsolete subtleties of the old schools of philosophy, and found amusement, if not instruction, in those frivolous but ingenious speculations which have overshadowed even the best wisdom of the schoolmen with the hues of a solemn and absurd pedantry. He dreamed in the reveries of Plato, and pursued them through the aberrations of the Coryphæans. He delighted in the visions of Pythagoras, and in the intellectual revels of Epicurus. He found attraction in the Gnostic mysteries, and still more in the phantasmagoria of Judicial Astrology. His library furnished a curious index to this unhealthy appetite for the marvellous and the mystical. The writings of Cornelius Agrippa, Raymond Lully, and Martin Delvio, and others of less celebrity in this circle of imposture, were found associated with truer philosophies and more approved and authentic teachers.

These studies, although pursued with an acknowledgment of their false and dangerous tendency, nevertheless had their influence upon Lindsay's imagination. There are few men in whom the mastery of reason is so absolute as to be able totally to subdue the occasional uprising of that element of superstition which is found more or less vigorous in every mind. A nervous temperament, which is almost characteristic of minds of an imaginative cast, is often distressingly liable to this influence, in spite of the strongest resolves of the will and the most earnest convictions of the judgment. If those who possess this temperament would confess, they might certify to many extraordinary anxieties and troubles of spirit, which it would pain them to have the world believe.

Lindsay's pursuits had impressed his understanding with some sentiment of respect for that old belief in the supernatural, and had, perhaps, even warmed up his faith to a secret credulity in these awful agencies of the spiritual world, or at least to an unsatisfied doubt as to their existence. Many men of sober brow and renown for wisdom are unwilling to acknowledge the extent of their own credulity on the same topic.

His relations to the government, his education, pursuits and temper, as might be expected, had deeply imbued Lindsay with the politics of the tory party, and taught him to regard with distrust, and even with abhorrence, the revolutionary principles which were getting in vogue. In this sentiment he visited with a dislike that did not correspond with the more usual development of his character, all those who were in any degree suspected of aiding or abetting the prevailing political heresy of the times.

About two years after the birth of Mildred, he had purchased a tract of land in the then new and frontier country lying upon the Rockfish river. Many families of note in the low country had possessed themselves of estates at the foot of the Blue Ridge, in this neighborhood, and were already making establishments there. Mr. Lindsay, attracted by the romantic character of the scenery, the freshness of the soil, and the healthfulness of the climate, following the example of others, had laid off the grounds of his new estate with great taste, and had soon built, upon a beautiful site, a neat and comfortable rustic dwelling, with such accommodation as might render it a convenient and pleasant retreat during the hot months of the summer.

The occupation which this new establishment afforded his family; the scope which its improvement gave to their taste; and the charms that intrinsically belonged to it, by degrees communicated to his household an absorbing interest in its embellishment. His wife cherished this enterprise with a peculiar ardor. The plans of improvement were hers; the garden, the lawns, the groves, the walks — all the little appendages which an assiduous taste might invent, or a comfort-seeking fancy might imagine necessary, were taken under her charge; and one beauty quickly following upon another, from day to day, evinced the dominion which a refined art may exercise with advantage over nature. It was a quiet, calm, and happy spot, where many conveniences were congregated together, and where, for a portion of every succeeding year, this little family nestled, as it were, in the enjoyment of voluptuous ease. From this idea, and especially as it was allied with some of the tenderest associations connected with the infancy of Mildred, it was called by the fanciful and kindly name of "The Dove Cote."

The education of Mildred and Henry became a delightful household care. Tutors were supplied, and the parents gave themselves up to the task of supervision with a fond industry. They now removed earlier to the Dove Cote with every returning spring, and remained there later in the autumn. The neighborhood furnished an intelligent and hospitable society; and the great western wilderness smiled with the contentment of a refined and polished civilization, which no after day in the history of this empire has yet surpassed — perhaps, not equalled. It is not to be wondered at, that a mind so framed as Lindsay's, and a family so devoted, should find an exquisite enjoyment in such a spot.

Whilst this epoch of happiness was in progression, the political heaven began to be darkened with clouds. The troubles came on with harsh portents; war rumbled in the distance, and, at length, broke out in thunder. Mildred had, in the meantime, grown up to the verge of womanhood, — a fair, ruddy, light-haired beauty, of exceeding graceful proportions, and full of the most interesting impulses. Henry trod closely upon her heels, and was now shooting through the rapid stages of boyhood. Both had entwined themselves around their parents' affections, like fibres that conveyed to them their chief nourishment; and the children were linked to each other even, if that were possible, by a stronger band.

The war threw Lindsay into a perilous predicament. His estates were large, and his principles exposed him to the sequestration which was rigidly enforced against the royalist party. To avoid this blow, or, at least, to mitigate its severity, he conveyed the estate of the Dove Cote to Mildred; assigning, as his reason for doing so, that, as it was purchased with moneys belonging to his wife, he consulted and executed her wish, in transferring the absolute ownership of it to his daughter. The rest of his property was converted into money, and invested in funds in Great Britain. As soon as this arrangement was made, about the second year of the war, the Dove Cote became the permanent residence of the family; Lindsay preferring to remain here rather than to retire to England, hoping to escape the keen notice of the dominant party, and to find, in this classic and philosophical privacy, an oblivion of the rude cares that beset the pillow of every man who mingled in the strife of the day.

He was destined to a grievous disappointment. His wife, to whom he was romantically attached, was snatched from him by death, just at this interesting period. This blow, for a time, almost unseated his reason. The natural calm of such a mind as Lindsay's is not apt to show paroxysms in grief. Its sorrow was too still and deep for show. The flight of years, however, brought healing on their wings; and Mildred and Henry gradually relumed their father's countenance with flashes of cheerful thought, that daily grew broader and more abiding; till, at last, sense and duty completed their triumph, and once more gave Lindsay to his family, unburdened of his grief, or, if not unburdened, conversing with it only in the secret hours of self-communion.

His hopes of ease and retirement were disappointed in another way. The sequesterment of the Dove Cote was not sufficient to shut out the noise nor the intrigues of the war. His reputation, as a man of education, of wealth, of good sense, and especially as a man of aristocratic pretensions, irresistibly drew him into the agitated vortex of politics. His house was open to the visits of the tory leaders, no less than to those of the other side; and, although this intercourse could not be openly maintained without risk, yet pretexts were not wanting, occasionally, to bring the officers and gentlemen in the British interest to the Dove Cote. They came stealthily and in disguise, and they did not fail to involve him in the insidious schemes and base plottings by which a wary foe generally endeavors to smoothe the way of invasion. The temporary importance which these connections conferred, and the assiduous appeal which it was the policy of the enemy to make to his loyalty, wrought upon the vanity of the scholar, and brought him, by degrees, from the mere toleration of an intercourse that he at first sincerely sought to avoid, into a participation of the plans of those who courted his fellowship. Still, however, this was grudgingly given — as much from the inaptitude of his character, as from a secret consciousness, at bottom, that it was contrary to the purpose that had induced him to seek the shelter of the woods. Unless, therefore, the spur was frequently applied to the side of his reluctant resolution, his zeal was apt to weary in its pace, or, to change my figure for one equally appropriate, to melt away in the sunny indolence of his temper.

I have said that, during the tenderer years of the children, and up to the period of the loss of their mother, they had received the most unremitting attention from their parents. The bereavement of his wife, the deep gloom that followed this event, and the now engrossing character of the war, had in some degree relaxed Lindsay's vigilance over their nurture, although it had in no wise abated his affection for them; on the contrary, perhaps this was more concentrated than ever. Mildred had grown up to the blossom-time of life, in the possession of every personal attraction. From the fanciful ideas of education adopted by her father, or rather from the sedulous care with which he experimented upon her capacity, and devoted himself to the task of directing and waiting upon the expansion of her intellect, she had made acquirements much beyond her years, and altogether of a character unusual to her sex. An ardent and persevering temper had imparted a singular enthusiasm to her pursuits; and her air, though not devoid of playfulness, might be said to be habitually abstracted and self-communing.

As the war advanced, her temper and situation both enlisted her as a partisan in the questions which it brought into discussion; and, whilst her father's opinions were abhorrent to this struggle for independence, she, on the other hand, unknown to him, was casting her thoughts, feelings, affections, and hopes upon the broad waters of rebellion; and, if not expecting them to return to her, after many days, with increase of good, certainly believing that she was mingling them with those of patriots who were predestined to the brightest meed of glory.

A father is not apt to reason with a daughter; the passions and prejudices of a parent are generally received as principles by the child; and most fathers, counting upon this instinct, deem it enough to make known the bent merely of their own opinions, without caring to argue them. This mistake will serve to explain the wide difference which is sometimes seen between the most tenderly attached parent and child, in those deeper sentiments that do not belong to the every-day concerns of life. Whilst, therefore, Mr. Lindsay took no heed how the seed of doctrine fructified and grew in the soil where he desired to plant it, it in truth fell upon ungenial ground, and either was blown away by the wind, or perished for want of appropriate nourishment.

As the crisis became more momentous, and the discussion of national rights more rife, Mildred's predilections ran stronger on the republican side; and, at the opening of my story, she was a sincere and enthusiastic friend of American independence, — a character (however it may be misdoubted by my female readers of the present day, nursed as they are in a lady-like apathy to all concerns of government, and little aware, in the lazy lap of peace, how vividly their own quick sensibilities may be enlisted by the strife of men) neither rare nor inefficient amongst the matrons and maidens of the year seventy-six, some of whom — now more than fifty years gone by — are embalmed in the richest spices and holiest ointment of our country's memory.

It is, however, due to truth to say, that Mildred's eager attachment to this cause was not altogether the free motion of patriotism. How often does some little under-current of passion, some slight and amiable prepossession, modest and unobserved, rise to the surface of our feelings, and there give its direction to the stream upon which floats all our philosophy! What is destiny but these under-currents that come whencesoever they list, unheeded at first, irresistible ever afterwards!

My reader must be told that, before the war broke out, this enthusiastic girl had flitted across the path of Arthur Butler, then a youth of rare faculty and promise, who combined with a gentle and modest demeanor an earnest devotion to his country, sustained by a chivalrous tone of honor that had in it all the fanciful disinterestedness of boyhood. It will not, therefore, appear wonderful that, amongst the golden opinions the young man was storing up in all quarters, some fragments of this grace should have made a lodgment in the heart of Mildred Lindsay.

Butler was a native of one of the lower districts of South Carolina, and was already the possessor, by inheritance, of what was then called a handsome fortune. He first met Mildred, under the safe-conduct of her parents, at Annapolis in Maryland, at that time the seat of opulence and fashion. There the wise and the gay, the beautiful and the rarely-gifted united in a splendid little constellation, in which wealth threw its sun-beam glitter over the wings of love, and learning and eloquence were warmed by the smiles of fair women: there gallant men gave the fascinations of wit to a festive circle unsurpassed in the new world, or the old, for its proportion of the graces that embellish, and the endowments that enrich life. In this circle there was no budding beauty of softer charm than the young Mildred, nor was there amongst the gay and bright cavaliers that thronged the "little academy" of Eden, (the governor of the province,) a youth of more favorable omen than Arthur Butler.

The war was at the very threshold, and angry men thought of turning the ploughshare into the sword. Amongst these was Butler; an unsparing denouncer of the policy of Britain, and an unhesitating volunteer in the ranks of her opposers. It was at this eventful time that he met Mildred. I need hardly add that under these inauspicious circumstances they began to love. Every interview afterwards (and they frequently saw each other at Williamsburg and Richmond) only developed more completely the tale of love that nature was telling in the heart of each.

Butler received from Congress an ensign's commission in the

continental army, and was employed for a few months in the recruiting service at Charlottesville. This position favored his views and enabled him to visit at the Dove Cote. His intercourse with Mildred, up to this period, had been allowed by Lindsay to pass without comment: it was regarded but as the customary and common-place civility of polite society. Mildred's parents had no sympathy in her lover's sentiments, and consequently no especial admiration of his character, and they had not yet doubted their daughter's loyalty to be made of less stern materials than their own. Her mother was the first to perceive that the modest maiden awaited the coming of the young soldier with a more anxious forethought than betokened an unoccupied heart. How painfully did this perception break upon her! It opened upon her view a foresight of that unhappy sequence of events that attends the secret struggle between parental authority and filial inclination, when the absorbing interests of true love are concerned: a struggle that so frequently darkens the fate of the noblest natures, and whose history supplies the charm of so many a melancholy and thrilling page. Mrs. Lindsay had an invincible objection to the contemplated alliance, and immediately awakened the attention of her husband to the subject. From this moment Butler's reception at the Dove Cote was cold and formal; and Mr. Lindsay did not delay to express to his daughter a marked aversion to her intimacy with a man so uncongenial to his own taste. I need not dwell upon the succession of incidents that followed: are they not written in every book that tells of young hearts loving in despite of authority? Let it suffice to say that Butler, "many a time and oft," hied stealthily and with a lover's haste to the Dove Cote, where, "under the shade of melancholy boughs," or sometimes of good Mistress Dimock's roof, he found means to meet and exchange vows of constancy with the lady of his love.

Thus passed the first year of the war. The death of Mrs. Lindsay, to which I have before adverted, now occurred. The year of mourning was doubly afflictive to Mildred. Her father's grief hung as heavily upon her as her own, and to this was added a total separation from Butler. He had joined his regiment and was sharing the perils of the northern campaigns, and subsequently of those which ended in the subjugation of Carolina and Georgia. During all this period he was enabled to keep up an uncertain and irregular correspondence with Mildred, and he had once met her in secret, for a few hours only, at Mistress Dimock's, during the autumn immediately preceding the date of the opening of my story.

Mrs. Lindsay, upon her death-bed, had spoken to her husband in the most emphatic terms of admonition against Mildred's possible alliance with Butler, and conjured him to prevent it by whatever means might be in his power. Besides this, she made a will directing the distribution of a large jointure estate in England between her two children, coupling, with the bequest, a condition of forfeiture, if Mildred married without her father's approbation.

I have now to relate an incident in the life of Philip Lindsay, which throws a sombre coloring over most of the future fortunes of Mildred and Arthur, as they are hereafter to be developed in my story.

The lapse of years, Lindsay supposed, would wear out the first favorable impressions made by Arthur Butler upon his daughter. Years had now passed: he knew nothing of the secret correspondence between the parties, and he had hoped that all was forgotten. He could not help, however, perceiving that Mildred had grown reserved, and that her deportment seemed to be controlled by some secret care that sat upon her heart. She was anxious, solicitous, and more inclined, than became her youth, to be alone. Her household affections took a softer tone, like one in grief. These things did not escape her father's eye.

It was on a night in June, a little more than a year before the visit of Butler and Robinson which I have narrated in a former chapter, that the father and daughter had a free communion together, in which it was his purpose to penetrate into the causes of her disturbed spirit. The conference was managed with an affectionate and skilful address on the part of the father, and "sadly borne" by Mildred. It is sufficient to say that it revealed to him a truth of which he was previously but little aware, namely, that neither the family afflictions nor the flight of two years had rooted out the fond predilection of Mildred for Arthur Butler. When this interview ended Mildred retired weeping to her chamber, and Lindsay sat in his study absorbed in meditation. The object in life nearest to his heart was the happiness of his daughter; and for the accomplishment of this what sacrifice would he not make? He minutely recalled to memory all the passages of her past life. What error of education had he committed, that she thus, at womanhood, was found wandering along a path to which he had never led her, which, indeed, he had ever taught her to avoid? What accident of fortune had brought her into this, as he must consider it, unhappy relation? "How careful have I been," he said, "to shut out all the inducements that might give a complexion to her tastes and principles different from my own! How sedulously have I waited upon her footsteps from infancy onward, to shield her from the influences that might mislead her pliant mind! And yet in this, the most determinate act of her life, that which is to give the hue to the whole of her coming fortune, the only truly momentous event in her history — how strangely has it befallen!"

In such a strain did his thoughts pursue this harassing subject. The window of his study was open, and he sat near it, looking out upon the night. The scene around him was of a nature to awaken his imagination and lead his musings towards the preternatural and invisible world. It was past midnight, and the bright moon was just sinking down the western slope of the heavens, journeying through the fantastic and gorgeous clouds, that, as they successively caught her beam, stood like promontories jutting upon a waveless ocean, their rich profiles tipped with burnished silver. The long black shadows of the trees slept in enchanted stillness upon the earth: the night-wind breathed through the foliage, and brought the distant gush of the river fitfully upon his ear. There was a witching harmony and music in the landscape that sorted with the solitary hour, and conjured up thoughts of the world of shadows. Lindsay's mind began to run upon the themes of his favorite studies: the array of familiar spirits rose upon his mental vision; the many recorded instances of what was devoutly believed the interference of the dead in the concerns of the living, came fresh, at this moment, to his memory, and made him shudder at his lonesomeness. Struggling with this conception, it struck him with an awe that he was unable to master: "some invisible counsellor," he muttered, "some mysterious intelligence, now holds my daughter in thrall, and flings his spell upon her existence. The powers that mingle unseen in the affairs of mortals, that guide to good or lead astray, have wafted this helpless bark into the current that sweeps onward, unstayed by man. I cannot contend with destiny. She is thy child, Gertrude," he exclaimed, apostrophizing the spirit of his departed wife. "She is thine, and thou wilt hover near her and protect her from those who contrive against her peace: thou wilt avert the ill and shield thy daughter!"

Excited almost to phrensy, terrified and exhausted in physical energy, Lindsay threw his head upon his hand and rested it against the window-sill. A moment elapsed of almost inspired madness, and when he raised his head and looked outward upon the lawn, he beheld the pale image of the being he had invoked, gliding through the shrubbery at the farthest verge of the level ground. The ghastly visage was bent upon him, the hand steadily pointed towards him, and as the figure slowly passed away the last reverted gaze was directed to him. "Great God!" he ejaculated, "that form — that form!" and fell senseless into his chair.

During the night, Mildred was awakened by a low moan, which led her to visit her father's chamber. He was not there. In great alarm she betook herself to his study, where she found him extended upon a sofa, so enfeebled and bewildered by this recent incident that he was scarcely conscious of her presence.

A few weeks restored Lindsay to his usual health, but it was long before he regained the equanimity of his mind. He had seen enough to confirm his faith in the speculations of that pernicious philosophy which is wrapt up in the studies of which I have before given the outline; and he was, henceforth, oftentimes melancholy, moody, and reserved in spite of all the resolves of duty, and in defiance of a temper naturally placid and kind.

Let us pass from this unpleasant incident to a theme of more cheerful import: the loves of Mildred and Arthur. I have said these two had secret meetings. They were not entirely without a witness. There was a confidant in all their intercourse: no other than Henry Lindsay, who united to the reckless jollity of youth an almost worshipping love of his sister. His thoughts and actions were ever akin to hers. Henry was therefore a safe depository of the precious secret; and as he could not but think Arthur Butler a good and gallant comrade, he determined that his father was altogether on the wrong side in respect to the love affair, and, by a natural sequence, wrong also in his politics.

Henry had several additional reasons for this last opinion. The whole countryside was kindled into a martial flame, and there was nothing to be heard but drums and trumpets. There were rifle-corps raising, and they were all dressed in hunting-shirts, and bugles were blowing, and horses were neighing: how could a gallant of sixteen resist it? Besides, Stephen Foster, the woodman, right under the brow of the Dove Cote, was a lieutenant of mounted riflemen, and had, for some time past, been training Henry in the mystery of his weapon, and had given him divers lessons on the horn to sound the signals, and had enticed him furtively to ride in a platoon on parade, whereof he had dubbed

Henry corporal or deputy corporal. All this worked well for Arthur and Mildred.

Mr. Lindsay was not ignorant of Henry's popularity in the neighborhood, nor how much he was petted by the volunteer soldiery. He did not object to this, as it served to quiet suspicion of his own dislike to the cause, and diverted the observation of the adherents of what he called the rebel government, from his own motions; whilst, at the same time, he deemed it no other than a gewgaw that played upon the boyish fancy of Henry without reaching his principles.

Mildred, on the contrary, did not so regard it. She had inspired Henry with her own sentiments, and now carefully trained him up to feel warmly the interests of the war, and to prepare himself by discipline for the hard life of a soldier. She early awakened in him a wish to render service in the field, and a resolution to accomplish it as soon as the occasion might arrive. Amongst other things, too, she taught him to love Arthur Butler and keep his counsel.

CHAPTER VIII

THE MANSION OF A GENTLEMAN AND A SCHOLAR

THE site of the Dove Cote was eminently picturesque. It was an area of level ground, containing, perhaps, two acres, on the summit of a hill that, on one side, overhung the Rockfish river, and on the other rose by a gentle sweep from the champaign country below. This summit might have been as much as two hundred feet above the bed of the stream, and was faced on that side by a bold, rocky precipice, not absolutely perpendicular, but broken into stages or platforms, where grassy mould had accumulated, and where the sweet-brier and the laurel, and clusters of the azalea, shot up in profuse luxuriance. The fissures of the crag had also collected their handful of soil and gave nourishment to struggling vines, and everywhere the ash or pine, and not infrequently the dogwood, took possession of such spots upon the rocky wall, as these adventurous and cliff-loving trees had found congenial to their nature. The opposite or northern bank of the river had an equal elevation, and jutted forward so near to the other as to leave between them a cleft, which suggested the idea of some sudden abruption of the earth in those early paroxysms that geologists have deemed necessary to account for some of the features of our continent. Below was heard the ceaseless brattle of the waters, as they ran over and amongst the rocks which probably constituted the *debris* formed in the convulsion that opened this chasm. It was along through this obscure dell that the road, with which my reader is acquainted, found place between the margin of the stream and the foot of the rocks. The general aspect of the country was diversified by high knolls and broken masses of mountain land, and the Dove Cote itself occupied a station sufficiently above the surrounding district to give it a prospect, eastward, of several miles in extent. From this point the eye might trace the valley of the Rockfish, by the abrupt hill-sides that hemmed it in, and by the growth of sombre pines that coated the steeps where nothing else could find a foot-hold. Not far below, in this direction, was to be seen the Fawn's tower, a singular pinnacle of rock, which had acquired its name from the protection it was said to have afforded to a young deer against the assault of the hounds; the hard-pressed animal, as the tradition relates, having gained this insulated point by a bound that baffled the most adventurous of his pursuers, and admiration of the successful boldness of the leap having won from the huntsman the favor that spared his life.

With the exception of a large chestnut near the edge of the cliff, and of some venerable oaks, that had counted centuries before the white man rested his limbs beneath their shade, the native growth of the forest had been removed by Lindsay from the summit I have described, and he had substituted for the wild garniture of nature a few of the choicest trees of the neighboring woods. Here he had planted the elm, the holly and the linden tree, the cedar and the arbor vitæ. This platform was semicircular, and was bounded by a terrace or walk of gravel that swept around its circumference. The space inclosed was covered with a natural grass, which the frequent use of the scythe had brought to the resemblance of velvet; and the lower side of the terrace was guarded by a hedge-row of cedar. Over this green wall, as the spectator walked forth in fair summer time, might he look out upon the distant woods and meadows; and there he might behold the high-road showing itself, at distant intervals, upon the hill-sides; and in the bottom lands, that lay open to the sun through the forest-bound valleys, might he see herds of grazing cattle, or fields of yellow grain, or, perchance, the slow moving wain burdened with hay, or slower moving plough.

The mansion itself partook of the character of the place. It was perched — to use a phrase peculiarly applicable to its position — almost immediately at that point where the terrace made an angle with the cliff, being defended by a stone parapet, through which an iron wicket opened upon a flight of rough-hewn steps, that terminated in a pathway leading down to the river.

The main building was of stone, consisting of one lofty story, and capped with a steep roof, which curved so far over the front as to furnish a broad rustic porch that rested almost upon the ground. The slim pillars of this porch were concealed by lattice-work, which was overgrown with creeping vines; and the windows of the contiguous rooms, on either side of a spacious hall, opened to the floor, and looked out upon the lawn and upon the quiet landscape far beyond. One of these apartments was also accessible through the eastern gable, by a private doorway shaded by a light veranda, and was appropriated by Lindsay to his library. This portal seemed almost to hang over the rock, having but the breadth of the terrace between it and the declivity, and showing no other foreground than the parapet, which was here a necessary defence against the cliff, and from which the romantic dell of the river was seen in all its wildness.

There were other portions of the mansion constructed in the same style of architecture, united to this in such a manner as to afford an uninterrupted communication, and to furnish a range of chambers for the use of the family. A rustic effect was everywhere preserved. Stacks of chimneys shot up in grotesque array; and heavy, old-fashioned windows looked quaintly down from the peaked roof. Choice exotics, planted in boxes, were tastefully arranged upon the lawn; cages with singing-birds were suspended against the wall; and the whole mass of building, extending along the verge of the cliff, so as to occupy the entire diameter of the semicircle, perhaps one hundred and fifty feet, sorted by its simplicity of costume, if I may so speak, and by its tidy beauty, with the close-shaven grass-plot and its trim shades.

Above the whole, flinging their broad and gnarled arms amongst the chimney tops, and forming a pleasing contrast with the artificial embellishments of this spot, some ancient oaks, in primeval magnificence, reared their time-honored trunks, and no less sheltered the habitation from the noon-tide heats, than they afforded an asylum to the ringdove and his mate, or to the countless travellers of the air that here stopped for rest or food.

Such was the general aspect of the Dove Cote; a spot where a philosopher might glide through life in unbroken contemplation; where a wearied statesman might betaken himself to reassemble the scattered forces of intellect for new enterprises; where the artist might repair to study with advantage the living graces of God's own painting; and where young beauty might bud and bloom amongst the most delicate and graceful forms of earth.

The interior of the dwelling was capacious and comfortable. Its furniture, suitable to the estate of the owner, was plain, and adapted to a munificent rather than to an ostentatious hospitality. It was only in the library that evidence might be seen of large expense. Here, the books were ranged from the floor to the ceiling, with scarcely an interval, except where a few choice paintings had found space, or the bust of some ancient worthy. One or two ponderous lounging chairs stood in the apartment;

and the footstep of the visitor was dulled into silence by the soft nap of (what, in that day, was a rare and costly luxury) a Turkey carpet. This was in all respects an apartment of ease, and it was provided with every incentive to beguile a student into silent and luxurious communion with the spirit of the sages around him, — whose subtlest thoughts and holiest breathings, whose most volatile fancies, had been caught up, fixed, and turned into tangible substance, more indestructible than adamant, by the magic of letters.

I have trespassed on the patience of my reader to give him a somewhat minute description of the Dove Cote, principally because I hope thereby to open his mind to a more adequate conception of the character of Philip Lindsay. By looking at a man in his own dwelling, and observing his domestic habits, I will venture to affirm, it shall scarcely in any instance fail to be true, that, if there be seen a tasteful arrangement of matters necessary to his comfort; if his household be well ordered, and his walks clean and well rolled, and his grassplots neat; and if there be no slovenly inattention to repairs, but thrift against waste, and plenty for all; and, if to these be added habits of early rising and comely attire — and, above all, if there be books, many books, well turned and carefully tended — that man is one to warm up at the coming of a gentleman; to open his doors to him; to take him to his heart, and to do him the kindnesses of life. He is a man to hate what is base, and to stand apart from the mass, as one who will not have his virtue tainted. He is a man, moreover, whose worldly craft may be so smothered and suppressed, in the predominance of the household affections, that the skilful and designing, alas, may ever practise with success their plans against him.

CHAPTER IX

AN INTRIGUE

I MUST now introduce my reader to the library described in the last chapter, where, beside a small table covered with papers, and lighted by two tall candles, sate Philip Lindsay, with a perplexed and thoughtful brow. Opposite to him, in an easy chair, reclined his guest, Mr. Tyrrel; a man whose appearance might entitle him to claim something like thirty-five years; and whose shrewd and intellectual expression of countenance, to which an air of decision was given by what might be called an intense eye, denoted a person conversant with the business of life; whilst an easy and flexible address no less distinctly announced him one habituated to the most polished society. The time of this meeting corresponded with that of the interview of Arthur and Mildred, beneath the Fawn's Tower.

It is necessary only to premise that these two had frequently conferred together, within the last two or three days, upon the subject with which they were now engaged.

"Sir Henry Clinton does me too much honor by this confidence," said Lindsay. "He overrates my influence amongst the gentlemen of the province. Truly, Mr. Tyrrel, I am well persuaded that neither my precept nor my example would weigh a feather in the scale against the heady course of this rebellion."

"We are seldom competent to judge of the weight of our own influence," said Tyrrel. "I might scarce expect you to speak otherwise than you do. But I, who have the opportunity to know, take upon myself to say that many gentlemen of note in this province, who are at present constrained by the fear of the new government, look with anxiety to you. They repose faith in your discretion, and would follow your lead. If an excuse be necessary, you might afford them some pretext of pastime to visit the Dove Cote. Here you might concert your plan to co-operate with our friends in the south."

"'Tis a rash thought," replied Lindsay. "This little nook of woodland quiet has never yet been disturbed with the debates of men who meditated the spilling of blood. God forbid that these peaceful walls should hereafter echo back the words that speak of such a purpose."

"It is to spare the shedding of blood, Mr. Lindsay, and to bring speedy peace to a distracted country that we invoke you and other friends to counsel. A single battle may decide the question of mastery over the province. We are well assured that the moment Lord Cornwallis reaches the Roanoke"—

"Cornwallis has yet to win the ground he stands upon," interrupted Lindsay: "there may be many a deadly blow struck before he slakes his thirst in the waters of that river: many a proud head may be low before that day."

"Think you, sir," said Tyrrel, rising as he spoke, "that this patched and ragged levy — this ague-stricken army that is now creeping through the pines of North Carolina, under the command of that pompous pretender, Gates, are the men to dispute with his majesty's forces their right to any inch of soil they choose to occupy? It will be a merry day when we meet them, Mr. Lindsay. We have hitherto delayed our campaign until the harvest was gathered: that is now done, and we shall speedily bring this hero of Saratoga to his reckoning. Then, following at the heels of the runagates, his Lordship, you may be prepared to hear, within two months from this day, will be within friendly hail of the Dove Cote."

"You speak like a boastful soldier, Mr. Tyrrel. It is not unlikely that his lordship may foil Gates and turn him back; such I learn to be the apprehension of the more sagacious amongst the continental officers themselves; but whether that mischance is to favor your incursion into this province may be worth a soberer study than, I doubt, you have given the question. The path of invasion is ever a difficult road when it leads against a united people. You mistake both the disposition and the means of these republicans. They have bold partisans in the field, and eloquent leaders in their senates. The nature of the strife sorts well with their quick and earnest tempers; and by this man's-play of war we breed up soldiers who delight in the game. Rebellion has long since marched beyond the middle ground, and has no thought of retreat. What was at first the mere overflow of popular passion has been hardened into principle, like a fiery stream of lava which first rolls in a flood, and then turns into stone. The delusion of republicanism, like all delusions, is embraced with more enthusiasm than men ever embrace truth. We deem too lightly of these men and their cause, and we have already, more than once, suffered for the error. When they expelled Dunmore they committed treason against the British crown; and they are wise enough to know that that cup, once tasted, must be drained to the bottom: they have, therefore, imbrued their hands the deeper in rebellion. They have raised their idol of democracy high, and have fenced it about with the penalties of confiscation and death to those who refuse to bow before it: and now they stand pledged to the prosecution of their unnatural war, by such a bond of fate as unites mariners who have rashly ventured forth upon a raging sea, in a bark of doubtful strength; their minds braced up, by the thought of instant perdition, to the daring effort necessary to reach their haven."

"That haven shall they never reach," cried Tyrrel impatiently. "Let them invoke the aid of their patron devils! We have a spell shall conjure them back again to their own hell, else there is no virtue in the forged steel which these rebels have felt before."

"The battle is not always to the strong," said Lindsay, "nor is the craft of soldiership without its chances."

"If we had listened, my friend," said Tyrrel, "to musty proverbs, Charleston would have this day been in the secure and peaceful possession of the enemy. All that you say against our present scheme was heretofore urged, though not with such authority, perhaps, against the invasion of Carolina. And yet how prettily have we gainsaid the prophets! Look at their principal town surrendered — all the country strongholds delivered up — the people flocking to our standard for protection — and the whole province lifting up a voice of gratitude for the deliverance we have wrought them. They are even now arming themselves in our behalf, whilst the shattered fragments of the rebel force are flying to the swamps and their mountain fastnesses. Why should not the same game be as well played in Virginia? Trust me, Mr. Lindsay, your caution somewhat overleaps that wholesome moderation, which I do not deny is necessary to check a too sanguine reckoning. Come, good sir, lend us a more auspicious counsel. Sir Henry relies much upon your wisdom, and will not, with good heart, forego your service."

"Sir Henry has sadly disturbed my repose," returned Lindsay. "To tell the truth, I have no stomach for this business. Here, I am native to the province: I have found old friends separated from me; early associations torn up by the roots; and the elements which fed my strongest personal attachments poisoned, by this accursed spirit of revolution. I would hide my head from the storm and die in these shades in peace."

"It is not for Mr. Philip Lindsay, nor such as he," replied Tyrrel, "to desert his sovereign in his hour of need."

"God forgive me for the thought, Mr. Tyrrel, but it remains yet to be proved who most faithfully serve their sovereign; they who counsel peace, or they who push war to its fatal extremes. There lives not a man within the realm of England, to whom I would yield in devotion to the glory of our country. Once make it clear to my judgment that we may hope to regain the lost allegiance of this province by the sacrifice of life and fortune, and, dearly as I cherish the welfare of those around me, I will obey the first summons to the field, and peril this worthless existence of mine in bloody fight. Yea, if need be, I will, with my own hand, apply the torch to this peaceful abode, and give it over a smoking ruin to the cause."

"I know you too well," replied Tyrrel, "to doubt the sincerity of your words. But is it not obvious that the war must inevitably tend to this field? Having gained the Carolinas, should we turn our backs as soon as we have reached the confines of Virginia? On the contrary, does not every obligation of honor impel us to maintain and protect our friends here? The conquest of Virginia is an easier enterprise than you deem it. If the continentals can muster ten thousand men, we, assuredly, may double that number, counting our provincials levied in the south. We have money and all the means of war, whilst this crippled Congress has drained from the people their last groat; their wretched troops will disband from mere want of supplies. They may expect no aid from the north; for there Sir Henry will furnish them sufficient motive to stay at home! We come animated by victories, full of mettle and vigor; they meet us broken by defeats, dejected and torn to pieces by mutiny. Never did treason or rebellion array itself with more certainty of punishment than this!"

"I have read," said Lindsay, "how John Hampden resisted the exaction of twenty shillings of ship money, and for that pittance dared the displeasure of Charles and his Star Chamber: how he voted the impeachment of the judges who were supple enough to warrant the imposition: how, in this cause, he drew the sword and threw away the scabbard: how he brought Strafford to the block for levying war against the commons of England: and through all that disastrous time, have I read that Charles promised the cavaliers splendid victories, and derided the feeble means of those who were in arms against him; yet Hampden shrunk not from the struggle. To me it seems there is a strange resemblance between the congress now sitting at Philadelphia and the parliament of 1640; and this George Washington might claim kindred with John Hampden. I will not seek for further likenesses."

"If I read that history right," replied Tyrrel, "Hampden met his reward at Chalgrove, and Cromwell turned his crop-eared parliament out of doors. We may, perhaps, find a Chalgrove on this continent; — and Sir Henry Clinton will most probably save the wiseacres at Philadelphia from the intrusion of an upstart Cromwell."

"It would be too bold in us to count on that, Mr. Tyrrel. I am the enemy of these men and their purpose, but I cannot deem otherwise of them than as misguided subjects of the king, frenzied by the imagination of grievances. They are men of good intellects and honest hearts, misled by passion. I would that we could give their tempers time to cool. I would, even now, preach moderation and compromise to his majesty's ministers."

"The die is long since cast," said Tyrrel, "and all that remains now is to take the hazard of the throw. At this moment, whilst we debate, friend and foe are whetting their swords for a deadly encounter on the fields of Carolina. It is too late to talk of other arbitrement. Assuredly, my good friend, our destiny directs us to this province: and the time has come when you must decide what course you will take. It has been our earnest wish — Sir Henry's letters, there upon the table, anxiously unfold it — to have you up and active in the cause. Why will you disappoint so fair a hope?"

"Alas! Mr. Tyrrel, — it is a thorny path you would have me tread. Think you I am the man to win my way through these intricacies? I that live in the shelter of these woods by sufferance merely — an unmolested outlaw, to speak soberly, whom these fanatics of liberty have forborne for the sake of past acquaintance and present peaceful habits? Am I not girded round about with the hot champions of independence? Look amongst these hills — there is not a cabin, not a woodman's hut, no, nor stately dwelling, whose roof defends one friend to the royal cause, but my own. My lips are sealed; my very thoughts are guarded, lest I give room to think I mean to fly from my neutrality. These papers that lie upon that table might cost me my life:

your presence here, were your purpose known, might consign me to captivity or exile: — one random word spoken might give me over to the censures of the power that holds its usurped domination in the province. What aid may be expected from one so guarded, fettered, watched and powerless?"

"And can you patiently," exclaimed Tyrrel, "bow to this oppression? You, a native born freeman of the province — a Briton, nursed in the sunny light of liberty! Shall your freedom of speech be circumscribed, your footsteps be followed by spies and traitors, your very inmost thoughts be read and brought up to the censure of the judgment seat? Shall these things be, and the blood still continue to run coolly and temperately through your veins! There are ills, Mr. Lindsay, which even your calm philosophy may not master. But, perhaps, I have mistaken your temper: these evidences, at least, shall not put you in peril," he said, as he took up the letters from the table and held them over the candle, and then threw the flaming mass upon the hearth. "That fear, I hope, is removed; and as for my presence here, one word briefly spoken, and it shall not longer jeopard your safety."

Lindsay looked fixedly at his companion as he destroyed the papers, and then said with a stern emphasis —

"Your duty, sir, is in the field. You have been bred to a profession that teaches you blind obedience to orders. It is not your part to weigh the right of the cause, nor to falter in the execution of any foul purpose of blood, so that it come under the name of honorable warfare. Therefore I excuse this unbecoming warmth: but do not presume upon the hazardous nature of your calling, and fancy that it implies more fidelity to the king than the allegiance of his more peaceful subjects. It is a thought unworthy of you that fear of disaster to myself — be it tenfold more imminent than it has yet been — should arrest my step in that path where my country's honor, or my sovereign's command, bids me advance."

"Worthy and excellent friend," said Tyrrel, taking Lindsay's hand, "I have done you wrong. I am rash and headlong in my temper, and my tongue often speaks what my heart disavows. I am little better than a boy, Mr. Lindsay, and a foolish one; I humbly crave your pardon."

"Speak on," said Lindsay.

"Then briefly this. Your situation is all that you have described it. Sir Henry is aware of the trial he imposes upon you.

He would have you act with the caution which your wisdom dictates; and if it should become necessary to speak that word which is to bring the wrath of the rebels upon your head, remember there is sanctuary and defence under the broad banner of England. Who so welcome there as Philip Lindsay? Even at this moment our councils should be tempered by your presence, and it becomes almost a patriotic duty to pluck you from the seclusion of the Dove Cote, and give you a share in the stirring events of the day. Sir, the country has a claim upon your services, scarce compatible with the idle contemplation of this momentous trial of strength."

Lindsay had advanced to the window, where he remained looking over the moon-lit scene. His companion stood close beside him, and after a short interval took his arm, when they stepped forth upon the porch, and sauntered backward and forward, as Tyrrel continued.

"The government would not be unmindful of the benefits you might confer. There are offices of trust and dignity to be filled in this province when it shall be restored to its allegiance. The highest post would not be unfitly bestowed, if it should be assigned to you. Sir Henry Clinton bids me speak of that, as of a subject that has already occupied his thoughts. It would give grace and dignity to our resumed authority, to have it illustrated by the accomplished scholar and discreet statesman, who has, before this, discharged important and difficult trusts with a fidelity that has won all men's esteem. And then, my dear sir," he added after a pause, "who may say that it shall not be Sir Philip Lindsay, or even something yet higher? — a coronet would not be an honor unsuited even to the wilds of Virginia. His majesty is not slow to discern worth, nor backward to raise it to its proper station. These are toys and baubles to you, Mr. Lindsay, but they are still worth the seeking. You have a son to follow you."

"Ah! there, Mr. Tyrrel, you touch me more nearly than you imagine. You remind me by this language that I have also a daughter. As to Henry, he has a temper and a capacity to make his own way through the world. I fear not for him — nor would I seek for honors to add to his name. But my Mildred! You know not what emotions the thought of her, in these troubles, costs me. Who shall guard and defend her, whilst I pursue this way-laid road of ambition? What sanctuary would she find under a war-encircled banner, should misfortune assail me, and adversity separate us? Alas, alas! — that is the spell that, like a net cast over my limbs, makes me feeble and submissive."

"I have not been without my solicitude, Mr. Lindsay, on that subject," said Tyrrel. "You yesterday did me the honor to say that my proposal in regard to Miss Lindsay was not distasteful to you. Could my ardent wish but be accomplished, she should be placed in safety, assured of ample and kind protection. If, haply, her thoughts should incline to a favorable reception of my offer, which I would fain persuade myself her reverence for you may render not altogether improbable, when she knows that you deem well of my suit, we might remove her to Charleston, where, secure amidst assiduous friends, she would pass the brief interval of alarm, and leave you free to act on this theatre as your honor and duty may impel you."

"Mildred will not leave me," said Lindsay; "my dear daughter would suffer a thousand deaths in the anxiety of such a separation."

"Then why not accompany her to Charleston?" asked Tyrrel. "Your presence there would be equally efficient as at headquarters — perhaps more so."

"There are other obstacles, Mr. Tyrrel. You talk of Mildred as if her heart were to be disposed of at my bidding. You do not know her. I have long struggled to subdue an attachment that has bound her to our worst enemy, I fear with little success. I have trusted to time to wear out what I deemed a mere girlish liking; but it seems to me the traces fade but slowly from her heart."

"I know of whom you speak," said Tyrrel — "that harebrained enthusiast Butler. It is a freakish and transient passion, and cannot but fall into forgetfulness. Miss Lindsay has from circumstances been but little conversant with the world, and, like an inexperienced girl, has fostered in solitude a romantic affection. That alone should be a motive to remove her into a busier scene. Besides, this Butler will be himself forced to give over his hopeless aim — if he has not done so before this: measures are already taken, and I do not scruple to tell you, at my instance — to confiscate his lands in Carolina to his majesty's use. The close of this war will find him penniless, and not unlikely, my dear sir, I myself may be the possessor of his inheritance — I have some pledge of the pre-emption of these lands at a small fee."

"It will win you no favor with Mildred," said Lindsay, "to tell her that you succeed by such a title to this man's wealth.

She is a wayward girl, and is not used to crosses. Her devotion to her purpose, as it sometimes excites my admiration, gives me, in the present case, cause of profound alarm."

"You have spoken to her on this subject?"

"I have not," replied Lindsay, "and almost fear to broach it. I can, therefore, give you no encouragement. Some little time hence — perhaps to-morrow — I may sound her feelings. But remember, as her father, I claim no right beyond that of advice. I shall think myself fortunate if, by giving a new direction to the current of her affections, I can divert her mind from the thoughts of an alliance to me the most hateful — to her full of future misery. A maiden's fancies are scarcely intelligible even to a father."

"These subjects require meditation," said Tyrrel. "I will not press them further upon your thoughts to-night."

"Heaven guide us in the way of safety and happiness!" said Lindsay, almost in a whisper. "Good night, my friend."

When Tyrrel was left alone he strolled forward to the terrace, and passing round to that end which overhung the cliff, near the door that opened from the library, he leaned his breast upon the parapet and looked down upon the wild and beautiful scenery of the valley. The night was calm and full of splendor. The tops of the trees that grew in the ravine, almost perpendicularly beneath his eye, here and there caught the bright moon-beam where it glowed like silver, and the shades, rendered deeper by the contrast, seemed to brood over a black and impenetrable abyss. Occasional glimpses were seen of the river below, as it sparkled along such portions of its channel as were not hidden in darkness. The coolness of the hour and the solitude of the spot were not ungrateful to the mood of Tyrrel's mind, whilst the monotonous music of the river fell pleasantly upon his ear. He was not unheedful of these charms in the scene, though his thoughts were busily employed with a subject foreign to their contemplation.

"Have I advanced," was the tenor of his present self-communion, "the purpose I have so much at heart, by this night's conference? Could I but engage Lindsay in the issues of this war, so commit him in its purposes and its plots as to render his further residence at the Dove Cote insecure, then would I already have half-compassed my point. Where could he remove but to Charleston? And there, amidst the blandishments of friends and the allurements of gay society, I might make sure of Mildred. There, cut off from all means of hearing of this Butler, and swayed, as she must necessarily be, by the current of loyal feelings, she would learn to detest his foul rebellion, and soon lose her favor for the rebel. Then, too, the confiscation of his lands — but I am not so sure of that! — she is rich and would make a merit of sharing her fortune with a man whose brave resistance of oppression — for so, doubtless, Butler persuades her it is — has cost him his wealth: the confiscation should not seem, at least, to be my doing. Well, well, let her be brought to Charleston. Any change were better than to remain here, where anxiety and suspense and solitude nurse and soften her woman's affections, and teach her to fancy her lover whatsoever her imagination delights to think on. Then may not the chances of war assist me? This Butler, all men say, is brave and adventurous. He should be shortlived. Whatever ill may befall him cannot but work good to me. Yet Lindsay has such a sickly caution — such scruple against involving himself in the scheme — I could almost find it in my heart to have it told amongst his neighbors that he is in correspondence with the enemy. Ha, that would be a bright device! — inform against myself! No, no, I will not abuse his generous nature. Let him come fairly into the fold, and I will guard his gentle lambkin like a very shepherd. Then if we make him governor of the province — that will work well. Mildred will thank me for my zeal in that good purpose, at least, and I will marry her and possess her estate, if it be only to enable her to be grateful to me. 'Twill be a brave reward, and bravely shall it be won."

As Tyrrel ruminated over these topics, in the strain indicated by this sketch, the noise of footsteps ascending the rugged stairway of the cliff, and the opening of the iron wicket, but a short distance from where he leaned over the parapet, roused his attention, and put an end to this insidious and selfish communion with his own heart.

The cause of this interruption was soon apparent. Henry and Mildred entered through the gate, and hurried along the path to that part of the terrace where Tyrrel stood. The shade of the house concealed him from their view until they were within a few paces. "Ha, Miss Lindsay! You are a late rambler," he said, in a tone of gallantry. "The dampness of the valley, at this hour, is not altogether safe; the ague is a sore enemy to romance; beware of it."

"I am not afraid of the night," replied Mildred, as she increased the rapidity of her gait; then, turning immediately upon the porch, she almost ran, leaving Henry and Tyrell in pursuit, until she reached the farthest window which was heard descending the moment she passed through it into the parlor. When Tyrrel and Henry entered the same apartment, she had disappeared.

" My sister is not well this evening," said Henry. " We strolled too late upon the river bank."

" It was still an over-hasty retreat," muttered Tyrrel to himself. " It bodes not well for me. I will wager, Henry," he said, raising his voice, " that I can guess what you and your sister have been talking about."

" Let me hear," said Henry.

" First," replied Tyrrel, " she repeated some verses from Shakspeare about the moonlight sleeping on the bank — this is just the night for poetry — and then you both fell to talking sentiment, and then, I'll be bound, you had a ghost story, and by that time, you found you had got too far from the house and were a little frightened, and so came back as fast as you could."

" You are wrong," said Henry. " I have been telling sister Mildred how to bob for eels. Did you know that an eel will never pass a streak of moonlight for fear of being found out by the watchers? "

" Indeed I did not."

" Well, sister Mildred is wiser than you are; and as I have taught you that, I will go to bed."

Tyrrel was again left to resume his meditations, and to hatch his plots for invading the peace of the Dove Cote, on his pillow. To that sleepless pillow he now betook himself.

CHAPTER X

TYRREL RETREATS

The next morning Tyrrel rose with the sun. He had passed a restless night, and now sought refreshment in the early breeze. With this purpose he descended to the river, and strayed along the dewy pathway which crept through the shrubbery on the right bank in the direction of the Fawn's Tower. He had not wandered far before he perceived a horseman moving along the road upon the opposite side.

"Halloo, James Curry! — which way? — What news have you?"

"I seek you, sir, I was on my way to the Dove Cote," replied the horseman, who at the same time turned his horse's head to the river, and, spurring the animal forward, plunged into the stream, which was here still and deep enough to reach above his saddle flaps. After some floundering, the horse and rider gained the margin, where Tyrrel awaited them! The vigor of the animal, as well as the practised hand that held the rein, was shown in the boldness of the attempt to climb the steep bank and break through the briers and bushes that here guarded it. As soon as Curry reached the level ground, he dismounted.

"In God's name, man, what is the matter with your face?" asked Tyrrel.

"It is of that, amongst other things, that I came to speak to you," was the reply; "I have news for you."

"Speak, without prelude. Tell me."

"Major Butler slept last night at Mrs. Dimock's."

"And is there still?"

"No sir. He started at early dawn this morning."

"To join Gates?"

"I think not. He talked of going to Ninety-Six — perhaps to Georgia."

"So, ho! The hawk hovers over that field! Does he travel alone?"

"He has a giant in his company, a great ploughman by the name of Horse Shoe Robinson. A quarrelsome rascal; he would needs pick a quarrel with me last night. And in the skirmish I got this face."

"Did I not command you to bear yourself peaceably? Fool! will you risk our lives with your infernal broils? Now, I would wager you told the fellow your name."

"Little need of that, sir. He told it to me: said he knew me before. The fellow, for all his rough coat, is a regular trained soldier in the rebel service, and has met me somewhere — Heaven knows! — I don't remember him; yet he isn't a man to see once and forget again."

"And me, did he speak of me?"

"He knew that I was in the employ of an English gentleman who was here at the Dove Cote. I have nothing especial to complain of in the man. He speaks soldierly enough; he said he would take no advantage of me for being here as long as our visit was peaceable."

"Humph! And you believed him. And you must fight with him, like a brawling knave. When will you get an ounce of wit into that fool's head! What time of day was it when this Butler arrived?"

"Long after night-fall."

"Did you understand any thing of the purpose of his visit?"

"He talked much with Mistress Dimock, and I think their conversation related to the lady at the Dove Cote. I could hear but a few scattered words."

"Away. — Here (throwing his purse to the horseman), pay up your score at the inn, and at your greatest haste attend me on the river bank, immediately below Mr. Lindsay's house. Ask Mrs. Dimock to have a breakfast prepared for me. — Away, I will expect you in half an hour."

Curry mounted his horse, and choosing a more convenient ford than that which he had passed (for the jutting rocks, on this side, prevented his reaching Mrs. Dimock's without recrossing the river to the road), he soon regained the track, and was seen, almost at high speed, sweeping around the base of the Fawn's Tower.

Tyrrel returned hastily to the Dove Cote, and, seeking his valet, gave orders to have his portmanteau packed, his horse saddled and to be in waiting for him at the foot of the hill. These commands were speedily obeyed, and everything was in readiness for his journey before any of the family had made their appearance in the breakfast room.

Whilst Tyrrel meditated writing a line to explain to Lindsay his present sudden movement, and had drawn near a table for that purpose, he was saluted by the voice of Henry, who had entered the apartment, and stolen unobserved almost immediately behind his chair.

"Booted and spurred, Mr. Tyrrel!" said Henry. "You are for a ride. Will you take a fowling-piece? There are pheasants over upon the hills."

"Oh, ho! Master Henry, you are up! I am glad of it. I was just writing a word to say that business calls me away this morning. Is your father yet abed?"

"He is sound asleep," said Henry; "I will wake him."

"No, my lad. You must not do that. Say I have received news this morning that has called me suddenly to my friends. I will return before long. Is your sister stirring?"

"She was in the garden but a moment since," replied Henry; and the young man left the room, to which he returned after a short space. "Sister Mildred is engaged in her chamber, and begs you will excuse her," said he, as he again entered the door.

"Tush, Henry, I didn't tell you to interrupt your sister. Make her my most respectful adieu. Don't forget it. I have all my way to win," he said to himself, "and a rough road to travel, I fear."

Tyrrel now left the house and descended to the river, accompanied by Henry, who sought in vain to know why he departed in such haste as not to stay for breakfast. James Curry waited below; and, when Henry saw his father's guest mount in his saddle and cross the ford, attended by his two servants, he turned about and clambered up the hill again, half singing and half saying to himself,—"I'm glad he's gone, I'm glad he's gone," accompanied with a trolling chorus, expressive of the satisfaction of his feelings at the moment. "He'd a got a flea in his ear, if he had stay'd. I should like to know what Major Butler would say to Mr. Tyrrel, if he was to meet him. Zooks! may be Butler will see him this very morning at Mrs. Dimock's. Now, I wonder! Shall I whisper that to sister Mildred? She would be glad, for one, I'll be bound! May be, they might have a fight. And if they do, let Mr Tyrrel look out! He never had his bread so buttered in his life, as it would be then."

In such a strain of cogitation and conjecture, Henry reached the parlor, where he found Mildred. The melancholy that hung upon her spirits, the evening before, seemed to have been dispelled by the repose of the night, and was doubtless relieved, in part, by the intelligence that Tyrrel had quitted the Dove Cote.

"Come, sister," said Henry, throwing his arm round her waist, and almost dancing, as he forced her through the open window, "come, it will be a good while before father is ready for his breakfast. Let us look at your flowers; I have something to tell you."

"You are quite an important personage, this morning," replied Mildred, moving off toward the lawn with her brother. "Your face looks as wise as a book of proverbs."

It was some time before the brother and sister returned to the parlour, and when they did so, their father had not yet appeared. The delay was unusual; for Lindsay generally rose at an early hour, and frequently walked abroad before his morning meal. When he at last entered the room, there was an expression of care upon his brow and thought that made him haggard. Mildred, as was her custom, approached him with a kiss, and, taking both of his hands, as she looked up in his face, she said, with some earnestness, —

"You are not well, my dear father."

Lindsay paused a moment, while he gazed affectionately upon her, and then pressing her to his bosom, uttered in a low voice, with a smile, —

"God bless my dear child! How carefully does she read my looks! Come hither, Henry," he continued, as he gave his son one hand, and still held Mildred with the other, and then turned his eyes alternately upon each. "Now, tell me, which of you love me best? Who has waited most patiently for mc this morning? I see by that glance of your blue eye, master Henry, that you have been chiding your lazy father for lying so long abed. Now, I dare say, if the truth were known, you have had your rifle ready to go out and shoot squirrels an hour ago. I beg your pardon, Mr. Sportsman — not to shoot the squirrel, but to shoot at him. Or, perhaps, you mean to bring us a deer to-day; you know you have promised to do that every morning for a week."

"You shall eat a slice from as fine a saddle of venison to-day, father, as you ever saw smoke over a chafing-dish."

"In good truth, shall I, boy? You are a brave promiser! You remember your own adage, — Brag was a good dog, but Holdfast was better."

"In right down earnest, father, you shall. You needn't laugh. Now, you're thinking I have the deer to shoot; there's your mistake. The saddle is this minute lying on the dresser in the kitchen. He was a running buck yesterday; and I could tell where the powder and ball came from (here Henry made the motion of opening a hunting pouch at his side) that put an end to his capers."

"He is a monstrous braggart; is he not, Mildred?" said Lindsay, directing a look of incredulity at his daughter.

"What Henry tells you is true," replied Mildred. "Stephen Foster was here at sun-rise with a part of a buck, which he says was shot yesterday."

"Indeed! Then it is to Stephen's rifle we are indebted. You kill your bucks by proxy, master."

"I'll bet," said Henry, "that Stephen Foster hasn't the impudence to charge one penny for that venison. And why? Because, by the laws of chace, one-half belongs to me."

"Oh, I understand," interrupted Lindsay, with affected gravity; "it is a matter of great doubt which of you shot it. You both fired at once; or, perhaps, Stephen first, and you afterwards; and the poor animal dropped the moment you took your aim, — even before your piece went off. You know your aim, Harry, is deadly, — much worse than your bullet."

"There is no doubt who killed him," said Henry; "for Stephen was on that side of the hill, and I was a little below him, and the buck ran right to Stephen, who, of course, gave him the first shot. But there was I, father, just ready, if Stephen had missed, to bring old Velvet-Horns to the ground, before he could have leaped a rod."

"But, unluckily, Stephen's first shot killed him?"

"I don't know that," replied Henry. "Another person's knife might have done the business; for the deer jumped down the bank into the road, and there" —

Mildred cast a sidelong look of caution at her brother, to warn him against alluding to a third person, whom it was not discreet to mention.

"And there," said Henry, taking the sign, "when I got up to him he was stone dead. I would almost think a deer couldn't be shot dead so suddenly. But Stephen can pitch his lead, as he calls it, just where he likes."

"Well, it isn't fair to inquire who killed him," said Lindsay. "One hunter often turns the game to the other's rifle. And, at all events, your dogs, Henry, I dare say, did as much as either of you."

"Hylas was just at his heels when he was shot," replied Henry; "and a better dog there isn't in Amherst, or Albemarle to boot."

"Well, well! Let us to breakfast. Where is our guest? Tyrrel is surely out before this."

"He has been gone from the Dove Cote more than an hour," said Henry. "He told me to say, that some sudden news took him off in haste. I would have waked you, but he forbade it. His man, Curry, who was waiting for him at the ford, I dare say, brought him some dispatches."

"It was very sudden," said Lindsay, musing; "the great game will be shortly played."

"My dear father, you have not your usual look of health," said Mildred again. "I fear something disturbs you."

"A slight cold, only, from exposure to the night air, perhaps. You did not see Tyrrel this morning, Mildred?"

"I did not wish to see him, father. I was up when he set out, but I was not in his way."

"Fie, girl, you almost speak crossly! Tyrrel, I must think, is not a man to win his way with ladies. But he is a loyal subject to his king. I can tell you, Mildred, loyalty is a virtue of good associations in these times."

"It is the last virtue, my dear father, that a woman ever writes down in the list of noble qualities. We generally forget it altogether. History is so full of the glory of disloyal heroes, that the indiscriminate and persevering loyalty of brave men has come to be but little noticed. Brutus was disloyal, and so was Tell; and the English barons, of whom you boast so much, when you call them sturdy, were disloyal; and Washington — who knows, my dear father, but that he may be written down by some future nation, (and she laid an emphasis on this word,) as another name to give credit to this word, disloyal."

"Thou art a shrewd orator, Mildred," exclaimed her father, as he sought to change the subject, "and I doubt not, if heaven had made you man, you would now be flattering these rebels by persuading them they were all born for heroes. We may thank the gods that they have given you the petticoat instead of the soldier's cloak, and placed you at the head of a breakfast table instead of a regiment."

"I do not think," replied Mildred smiling, "that I should altogether disgrace the cloak now, woman as I am, if the occasion required me to put it on."

"Pray drop this subject, my dear child; you know it makes

me sad. My family, I fear, are foredoomed to some strange mishap from these civil broils. Attend me presently in the library, I have matters to communicate that concern you. Henry, my boy," Lindsay continued, as he rose from his breakfast, "pay Stephen Foster the full value of the venison; as a sportsman you have a right perhaps to your share of the game, but a gentleman shows his courtesy by waiving such claim; he should suffer no friend to be his creditor, even in opinion. Stephen may not expect to be paid; no matter, it concerns your own character to be liberal."

"I have promised Stephen a new rifle," replied Henry, "since they have elected him lieutenant of the Amherst Rangers he wants something better than his old deer gun."

"I positively forbid it," interrupted Lindsay hastily, returning towards the middle of the room from the door through which he was about to depart. "What! would you purchase weapons for these clowns to enable them to shoot down his majesty's liege subjects? to make war upon their rightful king, against his laws and throne? to threaten your life, your sister's and mine, unless we bowed to this impious idol of democracy, which they have set up — this Washington?"

"My dear, dear father," interposed Mildred as she came up to him and flung her arms about his neck. "Consider, Henry is a thoughtless boy, and does not look to consequences."

"Heaven bless you both, my children! I beg your pardons. I am over captious. Henry, pay Stephen for the venison, and give him something better than a rifle. Mildred, I will see you presently."

When Lindsay had left the parlor Mildred besought her brother, in the most earnest terms, to be more guarded against giving expression to any sentiment which might bring their father's thoughts to the existing war. Her own observation had informed her of the nature of the struggle that agitated his mind, and her effort was continually directed to calm and soothe his feelings by the most unremitting affection, and thus to foster his resolution against taking any part in those schemes in which, she shrewdly guessed, it was the purpose of the emissaries of the royal party to involve him.

Her attachment to Arthur Butler she feared to mention to her father, whilst her self-respect and her conviction of her duty to a parent who loved her with unbounded devotion, would not allow her altogether to conceal it. Upon this subject, Lindsay had sufficiently read her heart to know much more about it than she chose to confess; and it did not fail to kindle up in his mind a feverish excitement, that occasionally broke forth in even a petulant reproof, and to furnish the only occasion that had ever arisen of serious displeasure against his daughter. The unhappy association between this incident in the life of Mildred, and the current of a feeling which had its foundation in a weak piece of superstition, to which I have alluded in a former chapter, gave to the idea of Mildred's marriage with Butler a fatal complexion in Lindsay's thoughts. "For what purpose," he asked himself, "but to avert this ill-omened event could I have had such an extraordinary warning?" It had occurred to him that the surest method of protecting his family against this misfortune would be to throw Mildred into other associations, and encourage the growth of other attachments, such as might be expected to grow up in her heart out of the kindness of new friendships. He had even meditated removing her to England, but that plan became so repulsive to him when he found the mention of it distasteful to his children, and it suited so little his own fondness for the retirement he had already cultivated, that he had abandoned it almost as soon as it occurred to him. His next alternative was to favor — though he did so with no great zeal — the proposal lately made by Tyrrel. He little knew the character of the woman he had to deal with. Never was more devotion enshrined in a woman's heart than in Mildred's. Never was more fixed and steady purpose to encounter all hazards and hold cheap all dangers more deeply rooted in man's or woman's resolution, than was Mildred's to cherish the love and follow the fortunes of Arthur Butler.

This conflict between love and filial duty sadly perplexed the daughter's peace; and not less disturbing was the strife between parental affection and the supposed mandate of fate, in the breast of the father.

Henry protested his sorrow for his recent indiscretion and promised more caution for the future, and then recurring to what more immediately concerned his sister's interest, he said, "I do much wonder what Tyrrel's man had to say this morning; it took our good gentleman away so suddenly. I can't help thinking it has something to do with Butler and Horse Shoe. They must have been seen by Curry at Mrs. Dimock's, and old Tony knows the major very well, and has told his name. Besides, do you know, sister, I think Curry is a spy? Else, why should he be left at Mrs. Dimock's always? There was room enough here for both of Mr. Tyrrel's servants. I have a thought that I will reconnoitre: I will ride over to the Blue Ball, and see what I can learn."

"Do, my good brother," replied Mildred, "and in the meantime I must go to my father, who has something disagreeable to tell me — so I fear — concerning that busy plotter who has just left us. My spirits grow heavy at the thought of it. Ah, Henry, if I could but speak out, and unpack my heart, what a load would I throw off! How does it grieve me to have a secret that I dare not tell my dear father! Thank heaven, brother, your heart and mine have not yet had a secret that they could not whisper to each other!"

"Give care the whip, sister," said Henry, like a young gallant, "it belongs to the bat family and should not fly in day-time. Farewell for the next two hours!" and saying these words the sprightly youth kissed his hand, and, with an alert step, left the room.

Mildred now retired to prepare for the interview with her father.

CHAPTER XI

A SCENE BETWEEN A FATHER AND DAUGHTER

WHEN Mildred entered the library Lindsay was already there. He stood before one of the ranges of book shelves, and held a volume in his hand which, for a moment after his daughter's entrance, seemed to engross his attention. Mildred was sufficiently astute to perceive that by this device he struggled to compose his mind for an interview of which she more than guessed the import. She was of a constitution not easily to be driven from her self-possession; but the consciousness of her father's embarrassment, and some perplexity in her own feelings at this moment, produced by a sense of the difficult part she had to perform, slightly discomposed her; there was something like alarm in her step, and also in the expression of her features, as she almost stealthily seated herself in one of the large lounging chairs. For a moment she unconsciously employed herself in stripping a little flower that she held in her hand of its leaves, and looked silently upon the floor; at length, in a low accent, she said, "Father, I am here at your bidding." Lindsay turned quickly round, and, throwing down the volume he had been perusing, approached his daughter with a smile that seemed rather unnaturally to play over his grave and almost melancholy countenance, and it was with a forced attempt at pleasantry he said, as he took her hand: —

"Now, I dare say, you think you have done something very wrong, and that I have brought you here to give you a lecture."

"I hope, father, I have done nothing wrong," was Mildred's grave and almost tremulous reply.

"Thou art a good child, Mildred," said Lindsay, drawing a chair close beside hers, and then, in a more serious tone, he continued, "you are entirely sure, my daughter, that I love you, and devoutly seek your happiness?"

"Dear father, you frighten me by this solemn air. Why ask me such a question?"

"Pardon me, my girl, but my feelings are full with subjects of serious import, and I would have you believe that what I have now to say springs from an earnest solicitude for your welfare."

"You have always shown it, father."

"I come to speak to you, without reserve, of Tyrrel," resumed Lindsay; "and you will not respond to my confidence, unless you answer me in the very truth of your heart. This gentleman, Mr. Tyrrel, has twice avowed to me of late an earnest attachment to you, and has sought my leave to prosecute his suit. Such things are not apt to escape a woman's notice, and you have doubtless had some hint of his predilection before he disclosed it to me."

All the woman's bashfulness disappeared with this announcement. Mildred grew erect in her seat, and as the native pride of her character beamed forth from every feature of her face, she replied —

"He has never, father, vouchsafed to give me such a proof of his good opinion. Mr. Tyrrel is content to make his bargain with you: he is well aware that whatever hope he may be idle enough to cherish, must depend more on your command than on my regard."

"He has never spoken to you, Mildred?" asked Lindsay, without making any comment on the indignant reception his daughter had given to his disclosure. "Never a word? Bethink you, my daughter, of all that has lately passed between you. A maiden is apt to misconstrue attentions. Can you remember nothing beyond the mere civilities of custom?"

"I can think of nothing in the conduct of Mr. Tyrrel but his devotion to the purpose of embroiling my dear father in his miserable politics. I can remember nothing of him but his low voice and noiseless step, his mysterious insinuations, his midnight sittings, his fulsome flattery of your services in the royal cause, the base means by which he has robbed you of your rest and taken the color from your cheek. I thought him too busy in distracting your peace to cast a thought upon me. But to speak to me, father, of attachment," she said, rising and taking a station so near Lindsay's chair as to be able to lean her arm upon his shoulder, "to breathe one word of a wish to win my esteem, that he dared not do."

"You speak under the impulse of some unnecessarily excited feeling, daughter. You apply terms and impute motives that sound too harsh from your lips, when the subject of them is a brave and faithful gentleman. Mr. Tyrrel deserves nothing at our hands but kindness."

"Alas, my dear father, alas, that you should think so!"

"What have you discovered, Mildred, or heard, that you should deem so injuriously of this man? Who has conjured up this unreasonable aversion in your mind against him?"

"I am indebted to no sources of information but my own senses," replied Mildred; "I want no monitor to tell me that he is not to be trusted. He is not what he seems."

"True, he is not what he seems, but better. Tyrrel appears here but as a simple gentleman, wearing, for obvious reasons, an assumed name. The letters he has brought me avouch him to be a man of rank and family, high in the confidence of the officers of the king, and holding a reputable commission in the army: a man of note, worthy to be trusted with grave enterprises, distinguished for sagacity, bravery, and honor, of moral virtues which would dignify any station, and, as you cannot but acknowledge from your own observation, filled with the courtesy and grace of a gentleman. Fie, daughter! it is sinful to derogate from the character of an honorable man."

"Wearing an assumed name, father, and acting a part, here, at the Dove Cote! Is it necessary for his purpose that, under this roof, he should appear in masquerade? May I know whether he treats with you for my hand in his real or assumed character — does he permit me to know who he is?"

"All in good time, Mildred. Content you, girl, that he has sufficiently certified himself to me. These are perilous times, and Tyrrel is obliged to practise much address to find his way along our roads. You are aware it would not be discreet to have him known even to our servants. But the time will come when you shall know him as himself, and then, if I mistake not, your generous nature will be ashamed to have wronged him by unworthy suspicions."

"Believe me, father," exclaimed Mildred, rising to a tone of animation that awakened the natural eloquence of her feelings, and gave them vent in language which more resembled the display of a practised orator than the declamation of a girl, "believe me, he imposes on you. His purposes are intensely selfish. If he has obtained an authority to treat with you or others under an assumed name, it has only been to further his personal ends. Already has he succeeded in plunging you, against your will, into the depth of this quarrel. Your time, my dear father, which once glided as softly and as happily as yon sparkling waters through our valley, is now consumed in deliberations that wear out your spirits: your books are abandoned for the study of secret schemes of politics: you are perplexed and anxious at every account that reaches us of victory or defeat. It was not so, until you saw Tyrrel: your nights, that once knew a long and healthful sleep, are now divided by short and unrefreshing slumbers: you complain of unpleasant dreams and you foretell some constantly coming disaster. Indeed, dearest father, you are not what you were. You wrong yourself by these cares, and you do not know how anxiously my brother Henry and myself watch, in secret, this unhappy change in your nature. How can I think with patience of this Tyrrel when I see these things?"

"The times, Mildred, leave me no choice. When a nation struggles to throw off the rule of lawful authority, the friends of peace and order should remember that the riotous passions of the refractory people are not to be subdued without personal sacrifices."

"You promised yourself, father, here at the Dove Cote to live beyond the sphere of these excitements. And, as I well remember, you often, as the war raged, threw yourself upon your knees, and taught us, — your children, — to kneel by your side, and we put up our joint expressions of gratitude to God, that, at least, this little asylum was undisturbed by the angry passions of man."

"We did, we did, my dearest child. But I should think it sinful to pray for the same quiet when my services might be useful to restore harmony to a distracted and misguided country."

"Do you now think," asked Mildred, "that your efforts are or can be of any avail to produce peace?"

"The blessing of heaven has descended upon the arms of our sovereign," replied Lindsay. "The southern provinces are subdued, and are fast returning to their allegiance. The hopes of England brighten, and a speedy close of this unnatural rebellion is at hand."

"There are many valleys, father, amongst these mountains, and the wide forests shade a solitude where large and populous nations may be hid almost from human search. They who possess the valleys and the wilderness, I have heard it said by wise men, will for ever choose their own rulers."

"Mildred, you are a dutiful daughter, and are not wont to oppose your father's wishes. I could desire to see you, with that shrewd apprehension of yours, that quick insight, and that thoughtful mind, thoughtful beyond the quality of your sex, less favorably bent towards the enterprise of these rebel subjects. I do utterly loathe them and their cause, and could wish that child of mine abated in no one jot of my aversion to them."

"Heaven, father, and your good tutoring have made me what I am," returned Mildred, calmly; "I am but a woman, and speak with a weak judgment and little knowledge. To my unlearned mind it seems that the government of every nation should be what the people wish it. There are good men here, father, amongst your friends — men, who, I am sure, have all kindness in their hearts, who say that this country has suffered grievous wrongs from the insolence of the king's representatives. They have proclaimed this in a paper which I have heard even you say was temperate and thoughtful: and you know nearly the whole land has roused itself to say that paper was good. Can so many men be wrong?"

"You are a girl," replied Lindsay, "and a subtile one; you are tainted with the common heresy. But what else might I expect! There are few *men* who can think out of fashion. When the multitude is supposed to speak, that is warrant enough for the opinions of the majority. But it is no matter, this is not a woman's theme, and is foreign to our present conference. I came to talk with you about Tyrrel. Upon that subject I will use no persuasions, express no wish, not in the slightest point essay to influence your choice. When he disclosed his purpose to me, I told him it was a question solely at your disposal. Thus much it is my duty to say, that should his suit be favored" —

"From the bottom of my heart, father," interrupted Mildred eagerly, and with increasing earnestness. "I abhor the thought. Be assured that if age, poverty, and deformity were showered upon me at once, if friends abandoned me, if my reason were blighted, and I was doomed to wander barefooted amongst thorns and briers, I would not exchange that lot, to be his wife amidst tenfold his honors and wealth. I never can listen to his hateful proposal: there is that in my condition which would make it wicked. Pray, dearest father, as you love your daughter, do not speak of it to me again."

"Resume your calmness, child: your earnestness on this subject afflicts me; it has a fearful omen in it. It tells of a heart fatally devoted to one whom, of all men, I have greatest reason to hate. This unhappy, lingering passion for the sworn enemy of his king and country, little becomes my daughter, or her regard for me. It may rouse me, Mildred, to some unkind wish against thee. Oh, I could curse myself that I ever threw you in the way of this insidious rebel, Butler. Nay you need not conceal your tears; well do they deserve to flow for this persevering transgression against the peace of your father's house. It requires but little skill to read the whole history of your heart."

Lindsay now walked to and fro across the apartment, under the influence of emotions which he was afraid to trust himself to utter. At length resuming his expostulation, in a somewhat moderate tone, he continued:

"Will no lapse of time wear away this abhorred image from your memory? Are you madly bent on bringing down misery on your head? I do not speak of my own suffering. Will you for ever nurse a hopeless attachment for a man whom, it must be apparent to yourself, you can never meet again? Whom if the perils of the field, the avenging bullet of some loyal subject, do not bring him merited punishment, the halter may reward, or, in his most fortunate destiny, disgrace, poverty, and shame pursue. Are you for ever to love that man?"

Mildred stood before her father as he brought this appeal to a close; her eyes filled with tears, her breast heaving as if it would burst; and summoning up all her courage for her reply, when this last question was asked, she looked with an expression of almost angry defiance in his face, as she answered "For ever, for ever," and hastily left the room.

The firm tone in which Mildred spoke these last words, her proud and almost haughty bearing, so unlike anything Lindsay had ever seen before, and her abrupt departure from his presence, gave a check to the current of his thoughts that raised the most painful emotions. For an instant a blush of resentment rose into his cheeks, and he felt tempted to call his daughter back that he might express this sentiment: it was but of a moment's duration, however, and grief, at what he felt was the first altercation he had ever had with his child, succeeded, and stifled all other emotions. He flung himself into the chair, and, dropping his forehead upon his hand, gave way to the full tide of his feelings. His spirits gradually became more composed, and he was able to survey with a somewhat temperate judgment the scene that had just passed. His manner, he thought, might have been too peremptory — perhaps it was harsh, and had offended his daughter's pride: he should have been more conciliatory in his speech. "The old," he said, "are not fit counsellors to the young; we forget the warmth of their passions, and would reason when they only feel. How small a share has prudence in the concerns of the heart!"

But then this unexpected fervor of devotion to Butler — that alarmed him, and he bit his lip, as he felt his anger rising with the thought. "Her repugnance to Tyrrel, her prompt rejection of his suit, her indignant contempt for the man, even that I could bear with patience," he exclaimed. "I seek not to trammel her will by any authority of mine. But this Butler! Oh! there is the beginning of the curse upon my house! there is the fate against which I have been so solemnly warned! That man who had been the author of this unhappiness, and whose alliance with my name has been denounced by the awful visitation of the dead, — that Mildred should cherish his regard, is misery. It cannot and shall not be!"

These and many such reflections passed through Lindsay's mind, and had roused his feelings to a tone of exacerbation against Arthur Butler, far surpassing any displeasure he had ever before indulged against this individual. In the height of this self-communion he was interrupted by the return of Mildred to the apartment, almost as abruptly as she had quitted it. She approached his chair, knelt, laid her head upon his lap, and wept aloud.

"Why, my dear father," she said, at length, looking up in his face while the tears rolled down her cheeks, "why do you address language to me that makes me forget the duty I owe you? If you knew my heart, you would spare and pity my feelings. Pardon me, dear father, if my conduct has offended you. I knew not what I spoke; I am wretched, and cannot answer for my words. Do not think I would wound your affection by unkindness; but indeed, indeed, I cannot hear you speak of Tyrrel without agony."

"Rise, daughter," said Lindsay, almost lifting her up, "I do not chide you for your repugnance to Tyrrel. You mistake me if you think I would dictate to your affections: my grief has a deeper source. This Arthur Butler" —

"Spare that name, father!" interrupted Mildred, retiring to a seat near the window and covering her face with her hands.

"Curse him!" exclaimed Lindsay. "May all the plagues that torment the human bosom fall upon him! Mark me, daughter, I trust I am not an unreasonable father; I know I am not an unkind one; there are few requests that you could make which I would not freely grant. But to hear with patience the name of that man on your lips, to think of him as allied to you by any sympathy, as sharing any portion of your esteem — him, a rebel traitor who has raised his sacrilegious hand against his king, who has sold his name to infamy, who has contributed to fill these peaceful provinces with discord, and to subvert the happiness of this land, which heaven had appointed to be an asylum where man, disgusted with the lusts, rapine, and murder of his fellow, might betake himself as a child to the bosom of his parent — I cannot endure the thought of him! Never again, Mildred, I charge you, never allude to him again!"

"If I could but tell you all!" interrupted Mildred, sobbing, "if I could but patiently have your hearing."

"Never a word of him! as you desire to preserve my affection. I will not hear. Get to your chamber," said Lindsay, almost sternly. "Get to your chamber, this perverse and resolute temper of thine, needs the restraint of solitude."

Mildred rose from her chair and moved towards the door, and as she was about to depart she turned her weeping countenance towards her father.

"Come hither," he said, "thou art a foolish girl, and would bring down wretchedness and woe upon thee. God forgive you! from the bottom of my heart, I forgive you. This thing is not of your own imagining: some malignant spirit has spread his baleful wing above our house. Go, child, forget what has been said, and believe that your father buffets thus harshly with fate for your own welfare. Kiss me, and may heaven shield you against this impending ill!"

"Dear father, hear me," said Mildred, as Lindsay imprinted a kiss upon her forehead.

"Away, away!" interrupted Lindsay, "I would be temperate, nor again forget myself. In all love, Mildred, away."

Mildred left the room, and Lindsay, to restore the equanimity of his temper, which had been so much overthrown by this interview, wandered forth into the valley, whence it was some hours before he returned.

It was not long after the termination of this conference before Henry rode up to the door. The clatter of his horse's hoofs brought Mildred from her chamber into the parlor.

"What! sister, your eyes red with tears?" said Henry. "Who has distressed you?"

"Ah, brother, I have had a weary time in your absence. Our poor father is sadly displeased with me."

"Have you told him all?" asked Henry, with an expression of anxiety.

"He bade me," replied Mildred, "never mention Arthur's name again. He would not hear me speak of Arthur. Have I not reason, dear brother, to be miserable?"

"I love you, Mildred," said Henry, kissing his sister, "and what's more, I love Arthur Butler, and will stand up for him against the world. And I have a good mind to go to my father and tell him I am man enough to think for myself — and more than that — that I, for one, believe these rebels, as he calls them, have the right of it. Why shouldn't I? Can't I shoot a rifle as well as the best of them, and stand by a friend in a quarrel, and make good my words as well as many a man who writes twenty years to his age? Tush! I am tired of this boy-play — shooting with blunted arrows, and riding with my father's hand ever on the neck of my horse, as if I could not hold the reins. Give me sharp steel, Mildred, and throw me on the world, and I'll be bound I make my way as well as another."

"We are surrounded with difficulties, brother," said Mildred, "and have a hard part to perform. We must soothe our dear father's feelings, for he loves us, Henry; and if he could but think as we do, how happy should we be! But there is something fearful in his passions, and it makes me tremble to see them roused."

"This all comes," replied Henry, "from that devil's imp Tyrrel. Oh, I could find it in my heart to trounce that fellow, sister. But you hav'n't asked me about my reconnoitring! I'll tell you. Tyrrel's man, Curry, talked a great deal to old Tony and Mrs. Dimock both, about our friends who went there last night, and found out their names and all about them: and there was some fray between Horse Shoe and Curry, in which, I'll warrant you, Horse Shoe gave him a drubbing; so Tony told me. Well, Butler and Horse Shoe set out this morning at daylight. And Tyrrel went over there to breakfast: and you may suppose he was lucky in not meeting the major, for I am sure there would have been a spot of work if he had. Furthermore, I found out that Tyrrel followed on the same road after Butler, so they may meet yet, you know."

"I pray not," said Mildred.

"Why pray not, sister? I pray they may meet. Let Tyrrel have all the good of it. There, now I believe I have given you all the news, sister, exactly as I picked it up. But here is a trifle I forgot," said Henry, producing a letter addressed to Mildred. "Ah, ha, you brighten up now! This was left by the major with Mrs. Dimock, to be forwarded to you with care and speed."

Mildred tore open the letter, and eagerly perused its contents. They consisted of a few lines hastily penned by Butler, at early dawn, as he was about mounting his horse for the prosecution of his journey. Their purpose was to apprise her of the discovery Robinson had made of the true character of Curry, and also to express his fears that this latter person might disclose to Tyrrel the fact of his, Butler's, visit. He cautioned her to observe the conduct of Tyrrel, and to communicate with him at Gates's head-quarters where he expected to be delayed a few days on his journey: her letter, he said, might be forwarded by some of the parties who at that time were continually passing southward: Henry might look to this; and he concluded by assuring her that he would write as often as he might find means of conveying a packet to the care of good Mistress Dimock, who was sufficiently in the interest of the lovers to keep faithfully any secret which they might confide to her.

This letter served to explain the cause of Tyrrel's sudden departure, and to confirm Mildred in the opinion, which she had before expressed, that this guest of her father was not ignorant of the interest Butler had in her regard. Her determination therefore was to watch his motions narrowly, and to make her lover acquainted with whatever she might discover.

"It is even so," she said musing; "Tyrrel either fears or hates Arthur. I shudder to think that that man should have any motive supplied him to contrive against the peace or safety of one so dear to me. Wretch," she exclaimed, "that he should be insolent enough to hope for my regard! Oh! my father, my father, what a snare has been spread for you by this man! Thank you, brother," she continued, addressing Henry. "You have well executed your mission. Be discreet and ready: I shall have much need of your head and hand both: your heart is mine already, good brother."

"I will ride for you, sister," said Henry, "I will run for you, speak for you, pray for you — if my prayers be worth anything — and strike for you, if need be. If I am but turned of sixteen, I am a man, I trow; and that's more than you are. Good bye! a soldier ought to look after his horse, you know."

"God bless you, dear brother, for an excellent boy," said Mildred smiling, "man I mean — aye and a brave one!"

Henry now walked away, and Mildred betook herself to other cares.

CHAPTER XII

A POLITICAL RETROSPECT. — BUTLER ENTERS SOUTH CAROLINA

It was the misfortune of South Carolina, during the revolutionary war, to possess a numerous party less attached to the union or more tainted with disaffection than the inhabitants of any of the other states. Amongst her citizens the disinclination to sever from the mother country was stronger, the spread of republican principles more limited, and the march of revolution slower, than in either of the other colonies, except, perhaps, in the neighbor state of Georgia, where the people residing along the Savannah river, were so closely allied to the Carolinians in sentiment, habits, and pursuits, as to partake pretty accurately of the same political prejudices, and to unite themselves in parties of the same complexion. Upon the first invasion of Georgia, at the close of the year 1778, the city of Savannah was made an easy conquest, and a mere handful of men, early in 1779, were enabled to penetrate the interior as far as Augusta, and to seize upon that post. The audacity with which Prevost threatened Charleston in the same year, the facility of his march through South Carolina, and the safety which attended his retreat, told a sad tale of the supineness of the people of that province. The reduction of Charleston in the following year, by Sir Henry Clinton, was followed with singular rapidity by the conquest of the whole province. A civil government was erected. The most remote posts in the mountains were at once occupied by British soldiers of provincial troops, mustered under the officers of the royal army. Proclamations were issued to call back the wandering sheep to the royal fold; and they, accordingly, like herds that had been scattered from beneath the eye of the shepherd by some rough incursion of wolves, flocked in as soon as they were aware of the retreat of their enemy. Lord Cornwallis, upon whom the command devolved after the return of Sir Henry Clinton in June to New York, recruited his army from these repentant or unwilling republicans; and the people rejoiced at what they thought the end of strife and the establishment of law. The auxiliaries who had marched from Virginia and North Carolina under Colonel Buford, to assist in the defence of the southern capital, were informed of its surrender as they journeyed thither, and soon found themselves obliged to fly through a country they had come to succor; — and when even at the distance of one hundred and fifty miles from the city, were overtaken by the ruthless troopers of Tarleton, and butchered under circumstances peculiarly deplorable.

In truth, a large proportion of the population of South Carolina seem to have regarded the revolution with disfavor, and they were slow to break their ancient friendship for the land of their forefathers. The colonial government was mild and beneficent in its action upon the province, and the people had a reverence for the mother country deeper and more affectionate than was found elsewhere. They did not resent, because, haply, they did not feel the innovations of right asserted by the British crown, so acutely as some of their neighbors; to them it did not seem to be unreasonable that taxation should be divorced from representation. They did not quarrel with the assumption of Great Britain to regulate their trade for them in such manner as best suited her own views of interest; nor did they see in mere commercial restrictions the justification of civil war and hot rebellion; — because, peradventure, (if I may hazard a reason) being a colony of planters whose products were much in demand in England, neither the regulations of their trade nor the restrictions upon commerce, were likely to be so adjusted as to interfere with the profitable expansion of their labors.

Such might be said to be the more popular sentiment of the State at the time of its subjugation by Sir Henry Clinton and Lord Cornwallis. To this common feeling there were many brilliant exceptions; and the more brilliant because they stood, as it were, apart from the preponderating mass of public judgment. There is no trial of courage which will bear comparison with that of a man whose own opinions stand in opposition, upon fearful question of passion, to those of the "giddy-paced" and excited multitude, and who, nevertheless, carries them "into act." That man who can stand in the breach of universal public censure, with all the fashions of opinion disgracing him in the thoughts of the lookers on, with the tide of obloquy beating against his breast, and the fingers of the mighty, combined many, pointing him to scorn; nay, with the fury of the drunken rabble threatening him with instant death; and, worse than all, having no present friend to whisper a word of defence or palliative, in his behalf, to his revilers, but bravely giving his naked head to the storm, because he knows himself to be virtuous in his purpose; that man shall come forth from this fierce ordeal like tried gold; philosophy shall embalm his name in her richest unction, history shall give him a place on her brightest page, and old, yea, hoary, far-off posterity shall remember him as of yesterday.

There were heroes of this mould in South Carolina, who entered with the best spirit of chivalry into the national quarrel, and brought to it hearts as bold, minds as vigorous, and arms as strong as ever, in any clime, worked out a nation's redemption. These men refused submission to their conquerors, and endured exile, chains, and prisons, rather than the yoke. Some few, still undiscouraged by the portents of the times, retreated into secret places, gathered their few patriot neighbors together, and contrived to keep in awe the soldier-government that now professed to sway the land. They lived on the scant aliment furnished in the woods, slept in the tangled brakes and secret places of the fen, exacted contributions from the adherents of the crown, and by rapid movements of their woodland cavalry and brave blows, accomplished more than thrice their numbers would have achieved in ordinary warfare.

The disaffected abounded in the upper country, and here Cornwallis maintained some strong garrisons. The difficulties that surrounded the republican leaders may well be supposed to have been appalling in this region, where regular posts had been established to furnish to Tories secure points of union, and the certainty of prompt assistance whenever required. Yet notwithstanding the numerical inferiority of the friends of independence, their guarded and proscribed condition, their want of support, and their almost absolute destitution of all the necessaries of military life, the nation was often rejoiced to hear of brilliant passages of arms, where, however unimportant the consequences, the display of soldiership and bravery was of the highest order. In such encounters, or frays, they might almost be called, from the smallness of the numbers concerned and the hand-to-hand mode of fighting which they exhibited, Marion, Sumpter, Horry, Pickens, and many others, had won a fame that in a nation of poetical or legendary associations would have been reduplicated through a thousand channels of immortal verse: but, alas! we have no ballads: and many men, who as well deserve to be remembered as Percy or Douglas, as Adam Bell or Clym of the Clough, have sunk down without even a couplet-epitaph upon the rude stone, that in some unfenced and unreverenced grave-yard still marks the lap of earth whereon their heads were laid.

One feature that belonged to this unhappy state of things in Carolina was the division of families. Kindred were arrayed against each other in deadly feuds, and, not unfrequently, brother took up arms against brother, and sons against their sires. A prevailing spirit of treachery and distrust marked the times. Strangers did not know how far they might trust to the rites of hospitality; and many a man laid his head upon his pillow, uncertain whether his fellow lodger, or he with whom he had broken bread at his last meal, might not invade him in the secret watches of the night and murder him in his slumbers. All went armed, and many slept with pistols or daggers under their pillows. There are tales told of men being summoned to their doors or windows at midnight by the blaze of their farm-yards to which the incendiary torch had been applied, and shot down, in the light of the conflagration, by a concealed hand. Families were obliged to betake themselves to the shelter of the thickets and swamps, when their own homesteads were dangerous places. The enemy wore no colors, and was not to be distinguished from friends either by outward guise or speech. Nothing could be more revolting than to see the symbols of peace thus misleading the confident into the toils of war; nor is it possible to imagine a state of society characterized by a more frightful insecurity.

Such was the condition of the country to which my tale now makes it necessary to introduce my reader. Butler's instructions required that he should report himself to General Gates, and, unless detained for more pressing duty, to proceed with all the circumspection which the enterprise might require, to Colonel Clarke, who, it was known, was at that time in the upland country of South Carolina, raising troops to act against Augusta and other British posts. He accordingly arrived at head-quarters, on the borders of the two Carolinas, in about a week after leaving the Dove Cote. The army of the brave and unfortunate De Kalb, which had been originally destined for the relief of Charleston, had been increased, by reinforcements of militia from Virginia and the adjoining States, to double the computed strength of the British forces; and Gates, on taking command of it, was filled with the most lofty presentiments of victory. Vainglorious and unadvisable, he is said to have pushed forward with an indiscreet haste, and to have thrown himself into difficulties which a wiser man would have avoided. He professed himself to stand in no need of recruits to his army, and Butler, therefore, after the delay of a few days, was left at liberty to pursue his original scheme.

The widespread disaffection of the region through which our adventurers were about to pass, inculcated the necessity of the utmost vigilance to avoid molestation from the numerous parties that were then abroad hastening to the seat of war. Under the almost entire guidance of Robinson, who was familiar with every path in this neighborhood, Butler's plan was to temporize with whatever difficulties might beset his way, and to rely upon his own and his comrade's address for escape.

The sergeant's first object was to conduct his superior to his own dwelling, which was situated on the Catawba, a short distance above the Waxhaws. This was safely accomplished on the second day after they had left Gates. A short delay at this place enabled Butler to exchange the dress he had hitherto worn, for one of a more homely and rustic character, a measure deemed necessary to facilitate his quiet passage through the country. With these precautions he and the trusty sergeant resumed their expedition, and now shaped their course across the region lying between the Catawba and Broad rivers, with the intention of reaching the habitation of Wat Adair, a well known woodsman who lived on the southern side of the latter river, somewhat above its confluence with the Pacolet. The route they had chosen for this purpose consisted of such circuitous and unfrequented paths as were least likely to be infested by the scouts of the enemy, or by questioners who might be too curious regarding the object of their journey.

The second week of August had half elapsed when, towards the evening of a day that had been distinguished for the exhilarating freshness of the atmosphere, such as is peculiar to the highlands of southern latitudes at this season, our travellers found themselves descending through a long and shady defile to the level ground that lay along the margin of the Broad river. The greater part of the day had been spent in threading the mazes of a series of sharp and abrupt hills covered with the native forest, or winding through narrow valleys, amongst tangled thickets of briers and copsewood, by a path scarce wide enough to permit the passage of a single horse. They had now emerged from the wilderness upon a public highway, which extended across the strip of lowland that skirted the river. The proximity of the river itself was indicated by the nature of the ground, that here retained vestiges of occasional inundations, as also by the rank character of the vegetation. The road led through a swamp, which was rendered passable by a causey of timber, and was shaded on either side by a mass of shrubbery, composed of laurel, magnolia, and such other plants as delight in a moist soil, over whose forms a tissue of creeping plants was woven in such profusion as to form a fastness or impregnable retreat for all kinds of noxious animals. Above this wilderness, here and there, might be seen in the depths of the morass, the robust cypress or the lurid pine, high enough for the mast of the largest ship, the ash, and gum, and, towering above all, the majestic poplar, with its branchless trunk bound up in the embraces of a huge serpent-like grapevine.

As soon as Butler found himself extricated from the difficult path that had so much embarrassed his journey, and once more introduced upon a road that allowed him to ride abreast with his companion, he could not help congratulating himself upon the change.

"Well, here at last, Galbraith," he said, "is an end to this bridle path, as you call it. Thank heaven for it! The settlement of the account between this and the plain road would not leave much in our favor: on one side, I should have to set down my being twice unhorsed in riding up perpendicular hills; one plunge up to the belly in the mud of a swamp; a dozen times in danger of strangling from grapevines; and how often torn by briers, I leave you to reckon up by looking at my clothes. And all this is to be cast up against the chance of meeting a few rascally Tories. Faith! upon the whole, it would have been as cheap to fight!"

"Whist, Major, you are a young man, and don't study things as I do. You never catch me without reason on my side. As to standing upon the trifle of a man or two odds in the way of a fight, when there was need of scratching, I wouldn't be so onaccommodating as to ax you to do that. But I had some generalship in view, which I can make appear. This road, which we have just got into, comes up through Winnsborough, which is one of the randyvoos of the Tories: now I thought if we outflanked them by coming through the hills, we mought keep our heads out of a hornets' nest. The best way, Major Butler, to get along through this world is not to be quarrelsome; that's my principle."

"Truly, it comes well from you, sergeant, who within two days past have been in danger of getting your crown cracked at least six times! Were you not yesterday going to beat a man only for asking a harmless question? A rough fellow to-boot, Horse Shoe, who might, from appearance, have turned out a troublesome customer."

"Ho, ho, ho, Major! Do you know who that character was? That was mad Archy Gibbs, from the Broken Bridge, one of the craziest devils after a fracaw on the Catawba; a tearing Tory likewise."

"And was that an argument for wishing to fight him?"

"Why, you see, Major, I've got a principle on that subject. It's an observation I have made, that whenever you come across one of these rampagious fellows, that's always for breeding disturbances, the best way is to be as fractious as themselves. You have hearn of the way of putting out a house on fire by blowing it up with gunpowder?"

"A pretty effectual method, Sergeant."

"Dog won't eat dog," continued Horse Shoe. "Ho, ho! I know these characters; so I always bullies them. When we stopped yesterday at the surveyor's, on Blair's Range, to get a little something to eat, and that bevy of Tories came riding up, with mad Archy at their head, a thought struck me that the fellows mought be dogging us, and that sot me to thinking what answer I should make consarning you, if they were to question me. So, ecod, I made a parson of you, ha, ha, ha! Sure enough, they began as soon as they sot down in the porch, to axing me about my business, and then about yourn. I told them, correspondent and accordingly, that you was a Presbyterian minister, and that I had undertook to show you the way to Chester, where you was going to hold forth. And, thereupon, mad Archy out with one of his tremengious oaths, and swore he would have a sarmint from you, for the good of his blackguards, before they broke up."

"Mad Archy and his blackguards would have profited, no doubt, by my spiritual lessons."

"Rather than let him have anything to say to you," proceeded Robinson, "for you wa'n't prepared, seeing that you didn't hear what was going on, though I spoke loud enough, on purpose, Major, for you to hear us through the window; I up and told Archy, says I, I am a peaceable man, but I'll be d——d if any minister of the gospel shall be insulted whilst I have the care of him; and, furthermore, says I, I didn't come here to interrupt no man; but if you, Archy Gibbs, or any one of your crew, says one ondecent word to the parson, they'll run the risk of being flung sprawling on this here floor, and that's as good as if I had sworn to it; and as for you, Archy, I'll hold you accountable for the good conduct of your whole squad. But, Major, you are about the hardest man to take a wink I ever knowed. There was I a motioning of you, and signifying to get your horse and be off, at least ten minutes before you took the hint."

"I was near spoiling all, Galbraith, for from your familiarity with these fellows I at first thought them friends."

"They were mighty dubious, you may depend. And it was as much as I could do to keep them from breaking in on you. They said it was strange, and so it was, to see a parson riding with pistols; but I told them you was obliged to travel so much after night that it was as much as you could do to keep clear of panthers and wolves; and in fact, major, I had to tell them a monstrous sight of lies, just to keep them in talk whilst you was getting away: it was like a rare guard scrummaging by platoons on a retreat to get the advance off. I was monstrous afeared, major, you wouldn't saddle my horse."

"I understood you at last, Galbraith, and made everything ready for a masterly retreat, and then moved away with a very sober air, leaving you to bring up the rear like a good soldier. And you know, sergeant, I didn't go so far but that I was at hand to give you support, if you had stood in need of it. I wonder now that they let you off so easily."

"They didn't want to have no uproar with me, Major Butler. They knowed me, that although I wa'n't a quarrelsome man, they would'a got some of their necks twisted if I had seen occasion: in particular, I would have taken some of mad Archy's crazy fits out of him — by my hand I would, major! But I'll tell you, — I made one observation, that this here sort of carrying false colors goes against a man's conscience: it doesn't seem natural for a man, that's accustomed and willing to stand by his words, to be heaping one lie upon top of another as fast as he can speak them. It really, Major Butler, does go against my grain."

"That point of conscience," said Butler laughing, "has been duly considered, and, I believe, we are safe in setting it down as entirely lawful to use any deceit of speech to escape from an enemy in time of war. We have a dangerous trade, sergeant, and the moralists indulge us more than they do others: and as I am a minister, you know, you need not be afraid to trust your conscience to my keeping."

"They allow that all's fair in war, I believe. But it don't signify, a man is a good while before he gets used to this flat lying, for I can't call it by any other name."

"If we should be challenged on this road, before we reach Wat Adair's," said Butler, "it is your opinion that we should say we are graziers going to the mountains to buy cattle."

"That's about the best answer I can think of. Though you must be a little careful about that. If you see me put my hand up to my mouth and give a sort of a hem, major, then leave the answer to me. A gang of raw lads might be easily imposed upon, but it wouldn't do if there's an old sodger amongst them; he mought ax some hard questions."

"I know but little of this grazier craft to bear an examination. I fear I should fare badly if one of these bullies should take it into his head to cross-question me."

"If a man takes on too much with you," replied Robinson, "it is well to be a little saucy to him. If he thinks you are for a quarrel, the chances are he won't pester you. But if any of these Tories should only take it into their heads, without our telling them right down in so many words, for I would rather a lie, if it is to come out, should take a roundabout way, that we are sent up here by Cornwallis, or Rawdon, or Leslie, or any of their people to do an arrand, they will be as civil, sir, as your grandmother's cat, for, major, they are a blasted set of cringin' whelps, the best of them, and will take anything that has G. R. marked on it with thanks, even if it was a cat-o'-nine tails, which they desarve every day at rollcall, the sorry devils!"

"I am completely at my wits' end, Galbraith. I have not done much justice to your appointment of me as a parson, and when I come to play the grazier it will be still worse; even in this disguise of a plain countryman I make a poor performer; I fear I shall disgrace the boards."

"If the worst comes to the worst, major, the rule is run or fight. We can manage that, at any rate, for we have had a good deal of both in the last three or four years."

"God knows we have had practice enough, sergeant, to make us perfect in that trick. Let us make our way through this treacherous ground as quickly and as quietly as we can. Get me to Clarke by the shortest route, and keep as much among friends as you know how."

"As to that, Major Butler, it is all a matter of chance, for, to tell you the plain truth, I don't know who to depend upon. A quick eye, a nimble foot, and a ready hand, will be our surest friends. Then with the pistols at your saddle, besides a pair in your pocket, and a dirk for close quarters, and my rifle here for a long shot, major, I am not much doubtful but what we shall hold our own."

"How far are we from Adair's?" asked Butler.

"Not more than a mile," replied Horse Shoe. "You may see the ferry just ahead. Wat lives upon the top of the first hill on the other side."

"Is that fellow to be trusted, sergeant?"

"Better with the help of gold, major, than without it. Wat was never over honest. But it is worth our while to make a friend of him if we can."

Our travellers had now reached the river, which was here a smooth and deep stream, though by no means so broad as to entitle it to the distinction by which, in its lower portion, it has earned its name. It here flowed sluggishly along in deep and melancholy shade.

Butler and his companion were destined to encounter a difficulty at this spot which less hardy travellers would have deemed a serious embarrassment. The boat was not to be seen on either side of the river, having been carried off a few hours before, according to the information given by the inmates of a negro cabin, constituting the family of the ferryman, by a party of soldiers.

Robinson regarded this obstacle with the resignation of a practised philosopher. He nodded his head significantly to his companion upon receiving the intelligence, as he said,

"There is some mischief in the wind. These Tories are always dodging about in gangs; and when they collect the boats on the river, it is either to help them forward on some house-burning and thieving business, or to secure their retreat when they expect to have honest men at their heels. It would be good news to hear that Sumpter was near their cruppers, which, by the by, is not onlikely neither. You would be told of some pretty sport then, major."

"Sumpter's means, sergeant," replied Butler, "I fear, are not equal to his will. There are heavy odds against him, and it isn't often that he can venture from his hiding-place. But what are we to do now, Galbraith?"

"Ha, ha! do as we have often done before this, launch our four-legged ships, and take a wet jacket coolly and dispassionately, as that quare devil Lieutenant Hopkins used to tell us when he was going to make a charge of the bagnet. We hav'n't no time to lose, major, and if we had, I don't think the river would run dry. So, here goes."

With these words Robinson plunged into the stream, and, with his rifle resting across his shoulder, he plied his voyage towards the opposite bank with the same unconcern as if he had journeyed on dry land. As soon as he was fairly afloat he looked back to give a few cautions to Butler.

"Head slantwise up stream, major, lean a little forward, so as to sink your horse's nose nearer to the water, he swims all the better for it. Slacken your reins and give him play. You have it now. It isn't uncomfortable in a day's ride to get a cool seat once in a while. Here we are safe and sound," he continued, as they reached the further margin, "and nothing the worse for the ferrying, excepting it be a trifle of dampness about the breeches."

The two companions now galloped towards the higher grounds of the adjacent country.

By the time that they had gained the summit of a long hill that rose immediately from the plain of the river, Robinson apprised Butler that they were now in the vicinity of Adair's dwelling. The sun had sunk below the horizon, and the varied lustre of early twilight tinged the surrounding scenery with its own beautiful colors. The road, as it wound upwards gradually emerged from the forest upon a tract of open country, given signs of one of those original settlements which, at that day, were sparsely sprinkled through the great wilderness. The space that had been snatched from the ruggedness of nature, for the purpose of husbandry, comprehended some three or four fields of thinly cultivated land. These were yet spotted over with stumps of trees, that seemed to leave but little freedom to the course of the ploughshare, and bespoke a thriftless and slovenly tillage. A piece of half cleared ground, occupying the side of one of the adjacent hills, presented to the eye of our travellers a yet more uncouth spectacle. This spot was still clothed with the native trees of the forest, all of which had been death-stricken by the axe, and now heaved up their withered and sapless branches towards the heavens, without leaf or spray. In the phrase of the woodman, they had been *girdled* some years before, and were destined to await the slow decay of time in their upright attitude. It was a grove of huge skeletons that had already been bleached into an ashy hue by the sun, and whose stiff and dry members rattled in the breeze with a preternatural harshness. Amongst the most hoary of these victims of the axe, the gales of winter had done their work and thrown them to the earth, where the shattered boles and boughs lay as they had fallen, and were slowly reverting into their original dust. Others, whose appointed time had not yet been fulfilled, gave evidence of their struggle with the frequent storm, by their declination from the perpendicular line. Some had been caught in falling by the boughs of a sturdier neighbor, and still leaned their huge bulks upon these supports, awakening the mind of the spectator to the fancy, that they had sunk in some deadly paroxysm into charitable and friendly arms, and, thus locked together, abided their tardy but irrevocable doom. It was a field of the dead; and the more striking in its imagery from the contrast which it furnished to the rich, verdurous, and lively forest that, with all the joyousness of health, encompassed this blighted spot. Its aspect was one of unpleasant desolation; and the traveller of the present day who visits our western wilds, where this slovenly practice is still in use, will never pass through such a precinct without a sense of disgust at the disfiguration of the landscape.

The field thus marred might have contained some fifty acres, and it was now occupied, in the intervals between the lifeless trunks, with a feeble crop of Indian corn, whose husky and parched blades, as they fluttered in the evening wind, added new and appropriate features to the inexpressible raggedness of the scene. The same effect was further aided and preserved by the cumbrous and unseemly worm fence that shot forth its stiff angles around the tract.

On the very apex of the hill up which our travellers were now clambering, was an inclosure of some three or four acres of land, in the middle of which, under the shade of a tuft of trees, stood a group of log cabins so situated as to command a view of nearly every part of the farm. The principal structure was supplied with a rude porch that covered three of its sides; whilst the smoke that curled upwards from a wide-mouthed chimney, and the accompaniment of a bevy of little negroes that were seen scattered amongst the out-houses, gave an air of habitation and life to the place that contrasted well with the stillness of the neighboring wood. A well-beaten path led into a narrow ravine where might be discerned, peeping forth from the weeds, the roof of a spring house; and, in the same neighborhood, a rough garden was observable, in which a bed of broad-leaved cabbages seemed to have their ground disputed by a plentiful crop of burdock, thistles, and other intruders upon a manured soil. In this inclosure, also, the hollyhock and sunflower, rival coxcombs of the vegetable community, gave their broad and garish tribute to the beautifying of the spot.

The road approached within some fifty paces of the front of the cabins, where access was allowed, not by the help of a gate, but only by a kind of ladder or stile formed of rails, which were so arranged as to furnish steps across the barrier of the worm fence at four or five feet from the ground.

"Are you sure of entertainment here, Galbraith?" inquired Butler, as they halted at the stile. "This Wat Adair is not likely to be churlish, I hope?"

"I don't think I am in much humor to be turned away," replied Robinson. "It's my opinion that a man who has rode a whole day has a sort of right to quarters wherever the night finds him — providing he pays for what he gets. But I have no doubt of Wat, Major. Holloa! who's at home? Wat Adair! Wat Adair! Travellers, man! Show yourself."

"Who are you that keep such a racket at the fence there?" demanded a female voice. "What do you mean by such doings before a peaceable house?"

"Keep your dogs silent, ma'am," returned Horse Shoe, in a blunt and loud key, "and you will hear us. If you are Wat Adair's wife you are as good as master of this house. We want a night's lodging and must have it — and besides, we have excellent stomachs, and mean to pay for all we get. Ain't that reason enough to satisfy a sensible woman, Mrs. Adair?"

"If you come to make a disturbance," said a man of a short and sturdy figure, who at this moment stepped out from the house and took a position in front of it, with a rifle in his hand — "if you come here to insult a quiet family you had best turn your horses' heads up the road and jog further."

"We might do that, sir, and fare worse," said Butler, in a conciliatory tone. "You have no need of your gun; we are harmless travellers who have come a long way to get under your roof."

"Where from?" asked the other.

"From below," said Horse Shoe promptly.

"What side do you take?"

"Your side for to-night," returned Robinson again. "Don't

be obstropolous, friend," he continued, at the same time dismounting, "we have come on purpose to pay Wat a visit, and if you ha'n't got no brawlers in the house, you needn't be afraid of us."

By this time the sergeant had crossed the stile and approached the questioner, to whom he offered his hand. The man gazed for a moment upon his visitor, and then asked —

"Isn't this Galbraith Robinson?"

"They call me so," replied Horse Shoe; "and if I ain't mistaken, this is Michael Lynch. You wan't going to shoot at us, Michael?"

"A man must have sharp eyes when he looks in the face of a neighbor now-a-days," said the other. "Come in; Wat's wife will be glad to see you. Wat himself will be home presently. Who have you here, Galbraith?"

"This is Mr. Butler," answered Horse Shoe, as the Major joined them. "He and me are taking a ride across into Georgia, and we thought we would give Wat a call just to hear the news."

"You are apt to fetch more news than you will take away," replied the other; "but there is a good deal doing now in all quarters. Howsever, go into the house, we must give you something to eat and a bed besides."

After putting their horses in charge of a negro who now approached, in the character of an ostler, our adventurers followed Michael Lynch into the house.

CHAPTER XIII

A WOODMAN'S FAMILY

THE apartment into which the travellers were introduced was one of large dimensions, conspicuous for its huge kitchen-like fireplace and ample chimney. The floor, consisting of broad planks, was so much warped as, in several places, to show the ground through the chinks. The furniture was of the rudest form and most homely materials. Three or four rifles were suspended against the walls, together with some trapping implements and various skins of such wild animals of prey and game as abounded in the woods of this region: these were associated with the antlers of the buck, powder-horns, hunting pouches, and a few articles of clothing, — the whole array giving to the room that air of woodland life which denotes the habitation of a hunter, and which so distinctly characterizes the dwellings of our frontier population.

Amongst other articles of household use was a large spinning-wheel that was placed near the door, and beside it stood the dame who had first challenged the visitors. She was a woman who could scarcely be said to have reached the middle period of life, although her wan and somewhat haggard features, and a surly, discontented expression of face, might well induce an observer to attribute more years to her worldly account than she had actually seen. The presence of a rough and untidy cradle and some five or six children, the majority of whom might be below three feet in stature, served in some degree to explain the care-worn and joyless countenance of the hostess. When Butler and his companion were ushered by Lynch into her presence, she gave them no other welcome than a slight nod of the head, and continued to ply her task at the wheel with unremitted assiduity.

In another corner of the room sat a smart-looking young girl who, at this moment, was employed in carding wool. She was a sylvan Hebe, just verging upon womanhood, with a round, active, and graceful figure, which was adorned with that zealous attention to neatness and becoming ornament which, in every station of life, to a certain extent, distinguishes those of the sex who are gifted with beauty. Her cheek had the rich bloom of high health; a full round blue eye seemed habitually to laugh with pleasure; and the same trick of a happy temperament had stamped its mark upon the lines of her mouth. Her accost was altogether different from that of the mistress of the house. She arose from her work immediately upon the entrance of the strangers, courtesied with a modest and silent reserve, and then proceeded to gather up the rolls of carded wool at her feet and to dispose of them in a chest near at hand. Having done this, she left the apartment, not without casting sundry prying glances towards the guests.

Another member of the family was an aged female: she had perhaps seen her eightieth winter. Her attenuated frame seemed to be hovering on the verge of dissolution: a hollow cheek, a sunken, moist eye, and a tremulous palsied motion of the head denoted the melancholy period of dotage; and it was apparent at a glance that this unfortunate being had far outlived both her capacity for enjoyment and the sympathy of her kindred. She now sat in a low elbow-chair, with her head almost in contact with her knees, upon the stone hearth, bending over a small fire of brushwood which had been kindled as well for the purpose of preparing the evening meal as for the comfort of the ancient dame herself — the chilliness of nightfall rendering this additional warmth by no means unpleasant. The beldam silently smoked a short pipe, unmoved by anything that occurred in the apartment, and apparently engrossed with the trivial care of directing the smoke, as she puffed it from her lips, into a current that should take it up the chimney.

Michael Lynch, who acted as landlord in the casual absence of Wat Adair, had no other connexion with the family than that of being joint owner, with the lord of this wild domain, of a small saw-mill in the vicinity, the particular superintendence of which was his especial province. He was, therefore, at particular seasons of the year, an in-dweller at the homestead, and sufficiently in authority to assume a partial direction in the affairs of the house. This man now replaced his rifle upon the pegs appropriated to receive it, and then offered Butler and Robinson chairs, as he said to the mistress of the family: —

"Here's Horse Shoe Robinson, Mrs. Adair; and this other man I think they call Mr. Butler. They've come for a night's lodging. I believe Wat will be right glad to see them."

"You are not often visited with travellers in this part of the country," said Butler, addressing the matron as he drew his chair near to the fire to dry his clothes.

"We have enough of them, such as they are," replied the woman; "and it's a dangerous thing, when there's so many helpless women at home, to be opening the door to all sorts of persons."

"You, at least, run no risk in offering shelter to us this evening," returned Butler; "we are strangers to the quarrel that prevails in your district."

"People puts on so many pretences," said the woman, "that there's no knowing them."

"You have a fine troop of boys and girls," continued Butler, patting the head of one of the boys who had summoned courage to approach him, after various shy reconnoitrings of his person. "Your settlement will require enlargement before long."

"There is more children than is needful," replied the hostess; "they are troublesome brats; but poor people generally have the luck that way."

"Does your husband ever serve with the army, madam?" asked Butler.

The woman stopped spinning for a moment, and turning her face towards Butler with a scowl, muttered,

"How does that matter concern you?"

"Pardon me," replied Butler; "I was recommended to Mr. Adair as a friend, and supposed I might approach his house without suspicion."

"Wat Adair is a fool," said the wife; "who is never content but when he has other people thrusting their spoons into his mess."

"Wat's a wiser man than his wife," interrupted Robinson bluntly, "and takes good care that no man thrusts his spoon into his mess without paying for it. You know Wat and me knows each other of old, Mrs. Adair; and devil a ha'penny did Wat ever lose by good manners yet."

"And who are you to talk, forsooth, Horse Shoe Robinson!" exclaimed the ill-favored dame, tartly. "Who are you to talk of Wat Adair? If he knows you he knows no good of you, I'm sure! I warrant you have come here on honest business now — you and your tramping friend. What do you do up here in the woods, when there is work enough for hearty men below? No good, I will undertake. It is such as you, Horse Shoe Robinson, and your drinking, rioting, broadsword cronies that has given us all our troubles here. You know Wat Adair! "

"A little consideration, good woman! Not so fast; you run yourself out of breath," said Robinson mildly, interrupting this flood of objurgation. "Why, you are as spiteful as a hen with a fresh brood! Remember, Wat and me are old friends. Wat has been at my house both before the war and since, and I have been here — all in friendship you know. And many's the buck I have helped Wat to fetch down. What's the use of tantrums? If we had been thieves, Mrs. Adair, you couldn't have sarved us worse. Why, it's onreasonable in you to fly in a man's face so."

"I'll vouch for Horse Shoe Robinson, Mrs. Peggy Adair," said Lynch. "You oughtn't to think harm of him; and you know it isn't long since we heard Wat talk of him, and say he would like to see him once more! "

"Well, it's my way," replied the hostess, soothed down into a placid mood by this joint expostulation. "We have had cause to be suspicious, and I own I am suspicious. But, Horse Shoe Robinson, I can't say I have anything against you; you and your friend may be welcome for me."

"Heyday! " exclaimed the old crone from the chimney corner. "Who is talking about Horse Shoe Robinson? Is this Horse Shoe? Come here, good man," she said, beckoning with her finger to the sergeant. "Come close and let me look at you. Galbraith Robinson, as I am a sinner! All the way from the Waxhaws. Who'd 'a thought to find you here amongst the Tories? Such a racketing whig as you! Heyday! "

"Whisht, granny! " said Robinson almost in a whisper. "Don't call names."

"We are all Tories here," said the old woman, heedless of the sergeant's caution, "ever since last Thursday, when the handsome English officer was here to see Watty, and to count out his gold like pebble-stones."

"Grandmother, you talk nonsense," said the wife.

"Old Mistress Crosby," interposed Robinson, "is as knowing as she ever was. It's a mark of sense to be able to tell the day of the week when a man changes his coat. But, granny, you oughtn't to talk of Wat's seeing an English officer in his house."

"Golden guineas, honey! " continued the drivelling old woman. "All good gold! And a proud clinking they make in Watty's homespun pocket. A countryman's old leather bag, Galbraith

Robinson, doesn't often scrape acquaintance with the image of the king's head — ha, ha, ha! It makes me laugh to think of it! Ha, ha, ha! Watty's nose cocked up so high too! Who but he, the proud gander! Strutting like quality. Well, well, pride will have a fall, some day, that's the Lord's truth. Both pockets full! " she continued, muttering broken sentences and laughing so violently that the tears ran down her cheeks.

" If you call Wat Adair your friend," interrupted the wife sullenly, and addressing Robinson, " you will show your sense by keeping away from this foolish old woman. She is continually raving with some nonsense that she dreams of nights. You ought to see that she is only half witted. It's sinful to encourage her talking. Grandmother, you had better go to your bed."

" Come this way, deary," said the beldam, addressing an infant that toddled across the floor near to her seat, at the same time extending her shrivelled arm to receive it. " Come to the old body, pretty darling! "

" No," lisped the child with an angry scream, and instantly made its way towards the door.

" Then do you come to me, Peggy," she said, looking up at her granddaughter, the mistress of the family, who was still busy with her wheel. " Wipe my old eye with your handkerchief. Don't you see I have laughed my eyes dim at Watty and his gold? And fill my pipe again, Peggy."

Instead of obeying this command, the mother left her spinning, and ran with some precipitation towards the door to catch up the child, who had staggered to the very verge of the sill, where it paused in imminent peril of falling headlong down the step; and having rescued it from its danger, she returned with the infant in her arms to a chair, where, without scruple at the presence of her visitors, she uncovered her bosom and administered to her offspring that rich and simple bounty which nature has so lavishly provided for the sustenance of our first and tenderest days of helplessness.

" Well-a-day, I see how it is! " muttered the grandmother in an accent of reproof, " that's the way of the world. Love is like a running river, it goes downwards, but doesn't come back to the spring. The poor old granny in the chimney corner is a withered tree up the stream, and the youngest born is a pretty flower on the bank below. Love leaves the old tree and goes to the flower. It went from me to Peggy's mother, and so downwards and downwards, but it never will come back again. The old granny's room is more wanted than her company; she ought to be nailed up in her coffin and put to sleep down, down in the cold ground. Well, well! But Watty's a proud wretch, that for certain! "

In this strain the aged dame continued to pour forth a stream of garrulity exhibiting a mixture of the silly dreamings of dotage, with a curious remainder of the scraps and saws of former experience — a strange compound of futile drivelling and shrewd and quick sagacity.

During the period of the foregoing dialogue, preparations were making for supper. These were conducted principally under the superintendence of our Hebe, who, my reader will recollect, some time since escaped from the room, and who, as Butler learned, in the course of the evening, was a niece of Adair's wife and bore the kindly name of Mary Musgrove. The part which she took in the concerns of the family was in accordance with the simple manners of the time, and such as might be expected from her relationship. She was now seen arranging a broad table, and directing the domestics in the disposition of sundry dishes of venison, bacon, and corn bread, with such other items of fare as belonged to the sequestered and forest-bound region in which Adair resided.

Mary was frequently caught directing her regards towards Butler, whose face was handsome enough to have rendered such a thing quite natural from a young girl: but she seemed to be moved by more than ordinary interest, as the closeness of her scrutiny almost implied a suspicion in her mind of his disguise. In truth there was some incongruity between his manners and the peasant dress he wore, which an eye like Mary's might have detected, notwithstanding the plainness of demeanor which Butler studied to assume.

"We have nothing but corn bread in the house," said Mary in a low tone to her kinswoman, "perhaps the gentlemen (here she directed her eye, for the fiftieth time, to Butler) expected to get wheat. Had I not better pull some roasting-ears from the garden and prepare them? they will not be amiss with our milk and butter."

"Bless you, my dear," said Butler, thrown completely off his guard, and showing more gallantry than belonged to the station he affected. "Give yourself no trouble on my account; we can eat anything. I delight in corn cakes, and will do ample justice to this savory venison. Pray do not concern yourself for us."

"It is easy as running to the garden," said Mary in a sweet and almost laughing tone.

"That's further, my dear," replied Butler, "than I choose you should run at this time of night. It is dark, my pretty girl."

"Gracious!" returned Mary with natural emotion, "do you think I am afraid to go as far as the garden in the dark? We have no witches or fairies in our hills to hurt us: and if we had, I know how to keep them away."

"And how might that be?"

"By saying my prayers, sir. My father taught me, before my head was as high as the back of this chair, a good many prayers: and he told me they would protect me from all sorts of harm, if I only said them in right earnest. And I hear many old people, who ought to know, say the same thing."

"Your father taught you well and wisely," replied Butler; "prayer will guard us against many ills, and chiefly against ourselves. But against the harm that others may do us, we should not forget that a prudence is also a good safeguard. It is always well to avoid a dangerous path."

"But, for all that," said the maiden smiling, "I am not afraid to go as far as the garden."

"If you mean to get the corn," interrupted Mistress Adair, in no very kindly tone, "you had as well go without all this talk. I warrant if you listen to every man who thinks it worth while to jabber in your ear, you will find harm enough, without going far to seek it."

"I thought it was only civil to speak when I was spoken to," replied Mary, with an air of mortification. "But I will be gone this moment:" and with these words the girl went forth upon her errand.

A moment only elapsed when the door was abruptly thrown open, and the tall and swarthy figure of Wat Adair strode into the room. The glare of the blazing faggots of pine which had been thrown on the fire to light up the apartment, fell broadly over his person, and flung a black and uncouth shadow across the floor and upon the opposite wall; thus magnifying his proportions and imparting a picturesque character to his outward man. A thin, dark, weather-beaten countenance, animated by a bright and restless eye, expressed cunning rather than hardihood, and seemed habitually to alternate between the manifestations of waggish vivacity and distrust. The person of this individual might be said, from its want of symmetry and from a certain slovenly and ungraceful stoop in the head and shoulders, to have been protracted, rather than tall. It better deserved the description of sinewy than muscular, and communicated the idea of toughness in a greater degree than strength. His arms and legs were long; and the habit of keeping the knee bent as he walked, suggested a remote resemblance in his gait to that of a panther and other animals of the same species; it seemed to be adapted to a sudden leap or spring.

His dress was a coarse and short hunting-shirt of dingy green, trimmed with a profusion of fringe, and sufficiently open at the collar to disclose his long and gaunt neck: a black leather belt supported a hunting knife and wallet; whilst a pair of rude deer-skin moccasins and a cap manufactured from the skin of some wild animal, and now deprived of its hair by long use, supplied the indispensable gear to either extremity of his person.

Adair's first care was to bestow in their proper places his rifle and powder-horn; then to disburden himself of a number of squirrels which were strung carelessly over his person, and, finally, to throw himself into a chair that occupied one side of the fire-place. The light for a moment blinded him, and it was not until he shaded his brow with his hand and looked across the hearth, that he became aware of the presence of the strangers. His first gaze was directed to Butler, to whom he addressed the common interrogatory, "Travelling in these parts, sir?" and, before time was afforded for a reply to this accost, his eye recognised the sergeant, upon which, starting from his seat, he made up to our sturdy friend, and slapping him familiarly on the back, uttered a chuckling laugh, as he exclaimed:

"Why, Galbraith, is it you, man? To be sure it is! What wind has blown you up here? Have you been running from red coats, or are you hunting of Tories, or are you looking for beeves? Who have you got with you here?"

"Wat, it don't consarn you to know what brought us here — it is only your business to do the best you can for us whilst we are here," replied the sergeant. "This here gentleman is Mr. Butler, a friend of mine that wants to get across into Georgia; and trouble enough we've had to find our way this far, Wat Adair. You've got such an uproarious country, and such a cursed set of quarrelsome devils in it, that a peaceable man is clean out of fashion amongst you. We are as wet as muskrats in swimming the river, and as hungry as wolves in winter."

"And happy," said Butler, "to be at last under the roof of a friend."

"Well, I am glad to see you both," replied Wat. "What put it in my head, Galbraith, I am sure I can't tell, but I was thinking about you this very day; said I to myself, I should just like to see Horse Shoe Robinson, the onconceivable, superfluous, roaring devil! Haw, haw, haw!"

"You were ashamed of your own company, Wat, and wanted to see a decent man once more," replied Horse Shoe, echoing the laugh.

"Mary Musgrove, bustle, girl," said the woodman, as the maiden entered the room with her arms loaded with ears of Indian corn; "bustle, mink! here are two runaways with stomachs like mill-stones to grind your corn. Horse Shoe, get up from that chist, man; I can give you a little drop of liquor, if you will let me rummage there for it. Marcus, boy, go bring us in a jug of cool water. Wife, I'm astonished you didn't think of giving our friends something to drink afore."

"I am sure I don't pretend to know friend from foe," returned the dame; "and it is a bad way to find that out by giving them liquor."

When the boy returned with the water, and the host had helped his guests to a part of the contents of a flask which had been extracted from the chest, Butler took occasion to commend the alacrity of the young servitor.

"This is one of your children, I suppose?"

"A sort of a pet cub," replied the woodman; "just a small specimen of my fetching up: trees squirrels like a dog — got the nose of a hound — can track a raccoon in the dark — and the most meddlesome imp about fire-arms you ever see. Here t'other day got my rifle and shot away half the hair from his sister's head; but I reckon I skinned him for it! You can answer for that, Marcus, you shaver, eh?"

"I expect you did," answered the boy pertly, "but I don't mind a whipping when I've got room to dodge."

"Do you know, Mr. Butler, how I come call that boy Marcus?" said Adair.

"It is one of your family names, perhaps."

"Not a bit. There's nare another boy nor man in this whole country round has such a name — nor woman, neither. It's a totally oncommon name. I called him after that there Frenchman that's come out here to help General Washington — Marcus Lafayette; and I think it sounds mighty well."

Butler laughed, as he replied, "That was a soldierly thought of yours. I think you must call your next Baron, after our old Prussian friend De Kalb."

"Do you hear that, wife?" exclaimed Wat. "Keep that in your head, if it will hold there a twelvemonth. No occasion to wait longer, haw! haw! haw!"

"Wat talks like a natural born fool," retorted the wife. "We have no friends nor enemies on any side. The boy was called Marcus because Watty was headstrong, and not because we cared any more for one general nor another. I dare say there is faults enough on both sides, if the truth was told; and I can't see what people in the woods have to do with all this jarring about liberty and such nonsense."

"Hold your tongue!" said Wat. "Boil your kettle, and give us none of your tinkling brass, as the Bible calls it. You see, Horse Shoe, there's such ridings and burnings, and shooting and murder about here, that these women are scared out of the little wits God has given them; and upon that account we are obliged sometimes to play a little double, just to keep out of harm's way. But I am sure I wish no ill to the Continental army."

"If we thought you did, Wat," replied Robinson, "we would have slept on the hill to-night, rather than set foot across the sill of your door. Howsever, let's say nothing about that; I told Mr. Butler that you would give us the best you had, and so you will. I have known Wat Adair, Mr. Butler, a good many years. We used to call him Wat with the double hand. Show us your fist here, Wat. Look at that, sir! it's broad as a shovel!"

"Cutting of trees," said the woodman, as he spread his large horny-knuckled hand upon the supper table, "and handling of logs, will make any man's paw broad, and mine wa'n't small at first."

"Ha! ha! ha!" ejaculated the sergeant, "you ha'n't forgot Dick Rowley over here on Congaree, Wat, — Walloping Dick, as they nicknamed him — and the scrimmage you had with him when he sot to laughing at you because they accused you for being light-fingered, and your letting him see that you had a heavy hand, by giving him the full weight of it upon his ear that almost drove him through the window of the bar-room at the Cross

Roads? You ha'n't forgot that — and his drawing his knife on you?"

"To be sure I ha'n't. That fellow was about as superfluous a piece of wicked flesh as I say — as a man would meet on a summer's day journey. But for all that, Horse Shoe, he wa'n't going to supererogate me, without getting as good as he sent. When I come across one of your merry fellows that's for playing cantraps on a man, it's my rule to make them pay the piper; and that's a pretty good rule, Horse Shoe, all the world through. But come, here is supper; draw up, Mr. Butler."

Mary Musgrove having completed the arrangement of the board whilst this conversation was in progress, the family now sat down to their repast. It was observable, during the meal, that Mary was very attentive in the discharge of the offices of the table, and especially when they were required by Butler. There was a modest and natural courtesy in her demeanor that attracted the notice of our soldier, and enhanced the kindly impression which the artless girl had made upon him; and it was, accordingly, with a feeling composed, in one degree, of curiosity to learn more of her character, and, in another, of that sort of tenderness which an open-hearted man is apt to entertain towards an ingenuous and pretty female, that he took occasion after supper, when Mary had seated herself on the threshold of the porch, to fall into conversation with her.

"You do not live here, I think I have gathered, but are only on a visit?" was the remark addressed to the maiden.

"No, sir; it is thirty good long miles by the shortest road, from this to my father's house. Mistress Adair is my mother's sister, and that makes her my aunt, you know, sir."

"And your father's name?"

"Allen Musgrove. He has a mill, sir, on the Ennoree."

"You are the miller's daughter, then. Well, that's a pretty title. I suppose they call you so?"

"The men sometimes call me," replied Mary, rising to her feet, and leaning carelessly against one of the upright timbers that supported the porch, "the miller's pretty daughter, but the women call me plain Mary Musgrove."

"Faith, my dear, the men come nearer to the truth than the women."

"They say not," replied the maiden, "I have heard, and sometimes I have read in good books — at least, they called them good books — that you mustn't believe the men."

"And why should you not?"

"I don't well know why not," returned the girl doubtingly; "but I am young, and maybe I shall find it out by and by."

"God forbid," said Butler, "that you should ever gain that experience! But there are many toils spread for the feet of innocence in this world, and it is well to have a discreet eye and good friends."

"I am seventeen, sir," replied Mary, "come next month; and though I have travelled backwards and forwards from here to Ennoree, and once to Camden, which, you know, sir, is a good deal of this world to see, I never knew anybody that thought harm of me. But I don't dispute there are men to be afraid of, and some that nobody could like. And yet I think a good man can be told by his face."

"Are you sure of that?"

"Yes. My father is a good man, and every one says you may see it in his looks."

"I should like to know your father," said Butler.

"I am sure he would be glad to know you, sir."

"Now, my pretty miller's daughter, why do you think so?"

"Because you are a gentleman," replied the girl, courtesying, "for all your homespun clothes."

"Ha! pray how have you found that out?"

"You talk differently from our people, sir. Your words or your voice, I can't rightly tell which, are softer than I have been used to hear. And you don't look, and walk, and behave as if homespun had been all you ever wore."

"And is that all?"

"You stop to consider, as if you were studying what would please other people; and you do not step so heavy, sir; and you do not swear; and you do not seem to like to give trouble. I can't think, sir, that you have been always used to such as are hereabouts. And then there's another reason, sir," added the maiden, almost in a whisper.

"What is that?" asked Butler, smiling.

"Why, sir, when you stooped down to pick up your fork, that fell from the table, I saw a blue ribbon round your neck, and a beautiful gold picture hanging to it. None but gentlemen of quality carry such things about them: and as there is so much contriving and bloody doings going on about here, I was sure you wasn't what you seemed."

"For heaven's sake, my dear," exclaimed Butler, startled by

the disclosure of the maiden's suspicion, which was so naturally accounted for, "keep this to yourself, and the time may come when I shall be able to reward your fidelity. If you have any good will towards me, as I hope you have, tell nobody what you have seen."

"Never fear me, sir," returned the maid. "I wouldn't let on to any one in the house for the world. I am for General Washington and the Congress, which is more than I think the people here are."

"Indeed!" muttered Butler, thoughtfully, and scarce above his breath. "What side does your father take, Mary?"

"My father is an old man, sir. And he reads his Bible, and every night, before we go to bed, he prays aloud before us all, I mean all that belongs to his house, for quiet once more and peace. His petition is that there may be an end of strife, and that the sword and spear may be turned into the pruning-hook and ploughshare — you know the words, sir, perhaps, for they are in the good book, and so he doesn't take any side. But then, the English officers are not far off, and they take his house and use it as they please, so that he has no mind of his own. And almost all the people round us are Tories, and we are afraid of our lives if we do not say whatever they say."

"Alas! that's the misfortune of many more than your father's household. But how comes it that you are a friend of General Washington?"

"Oh, sir, I think he is our friend; and then he is a good man. And I have a better reason still to be on his side," added the maiden tremulously, with her head averted.

"What reason, my good girl?"

"John Ramsay, sir."

"Indeed! a very cogent reason, I doubt not, my pretty maid of the mill. And how does this reason operate?"

"We have a liking, sir," she replied bashfully, but with innocent frankness; "he is for Washington, and we are to be married when the war is over."

"Truly, that is a most excellent reason! Who is John Ramsey?"

"He is a trooper, sir, and out with General Sumpter. We don't see him often now, for he is afraid to come home, excepting when the Tories are away."

"These Tories are very troublesome, Mary," said Butler, laughing; "they annoy us all, on our side of the question. But love John Ramsey, my dear, and don't be ashamed of it, for I'll warrant he is a brave fellow, and deserves a pretty girl with a true heart, for his love to his country."

"That he does!" replied Mary, "for his greatest fault is that he ventures too much. If you should see him, sir, I would like you just to drop him a hint that he ought to take more care of himself. He would mind it from you, but he puts me off with a laugh when I tell him so."

"If I have the schooling of him, he shall be more cautious, for your sake. But the current of true love never did run smooth, Mary; remember that."

"I must go into the house, my aunt Peggy calls me," interrupted the maiden. "I will keep the secret, sir," she added, as she retired from the porch to the household service where her presence was demanded.

"Simple, innocent, and confiding girl," ejaculated Butler, as he now strolled forth under the starlit canopy of night; "how are you contrasted with the rough and savage natures around you! I wear but a thin disguise, when this unpractised country girl is able so soon to penetrate it. And this miniature, too! Oh, Mildred! that the very talisman I bear about me to guard me from evil, should betray me! Well, this discovery admonishes me that I should wear that image nearer to my heart. There," he continued, as he buttoned his waistcoat across his breast; "lie closer and more concealed. I doubt this double-faced woodman, and almost believe in the seeming frivolous dotings of the crone at his fireside. Now, God defend us from treachery and ambuscade!"

Robinson, at this moment, being on his way to the stable, was met by Butler, who half whispered, "Good sergeant, keep your eyes about you, and, mark me, do not omit to take our weapons to our chamber. I have reasons for this caution. I would not trust these people too far."

"Wat dare not play us a trick, major," replied the sergeant. "He knows I would shake the life out of his carcase if I saw him take one step of a traitor. Besides, in this here war time, it's a part of my discipline to be always ready for stolen marches. As you say, major, we will stack arms where we sleep. There is no trust in this dubious country that isn't something the surer with powder and ball to back it."

With this intimation the sergeant continued his walk, and Butler, retiring to the family group, seated himself near the fire.

Wat Adair and his crony, Michael Lynch, had each lighted a pipe, and were now in close conference under the cover of their own smoke, amidst the combined din of romping children and of the noisy spinning-wheel of the wife, which gave life and occupation to the apartment.

"How far do you expect to travel to-morrow?" asked the host, as Butler drew a chair near him.

"That will depend very much," replied Butler, "upon the advice you may give us."

"You wish to get across here into Georgia?" continued Wat.

"By the route least liable to molestation," added the major.

"Let me see, Michael, Grindall's Ford is the best point to make: then there's Christie's, about three miles beyont."

"Just so," replied Lynch; "that will make about twenty-seven and three are thirty miles: an easy day's journey."

"In that case," said Adair, "if you know the road — doesn't Horse Shoe know it, sir?"

"I rather think not," answered Butler.

"Well, it's a little tangled, to be sure; but if you will wait in the morning until I look at my wolf trap, which is only a step off, I will go with you part of the way, just to see you through one or two cross paths: after that all is clear enough. You will have a long day before you, and, with good horses, not much to do."

"Are we likely to meet parties on the road?" asked Butler.

"Oh, Lord, sir, no chance of it," replied the woodman; "everything is drawing so to a head down below at Camden 'twixt Cornwallis and Gates, that we have hardly anything but old women left to keep the country free of Indians."

"And how have you escaped the levy?" inquired the major.

"He, he, he!" chuckled our host; "there's a trick in that. They call me a man of doubtful principles, and neither side are willing to own me," he added, with a tone that seemed to indicate a sense of his own cleverness. "But, bless you, sir, if I chose to speak out, there wouldn't be much doubt in the case. Would there, Michael?"

"Not if you was to be plain in declaring your sentiments," answered Lynch, sedately puffing out a huge cloud of smoke.

"Betwixt you and me, sir," continued Wat, putting his hand up to his mouth, and winking an eye at Butler, "the thing's clear enough. But these are ticklish times, Mr. Butler, and the wise man keepeth his own counsel, as the Scripture says. You understand me, I dare say."

"Perhaps, I do," returned Butler. And here the conversation dropped, Wat and his companion gravely pouring forth volumes of tobacco-fumes in silence, until the sergeant, having made his visit to the stable, now re-entered the room.

"Wat," said Robinson, "show us where we are to sleep. Mr. Butler, to my thinking, it's time to be turning in."

Then throwing his rifle upon one arm, and Butler's holsters over the other, the sergeant waited in the middle of the floor until Mary Musgrove, at the order of Adair, took a candle in her hand, and beckoned our travellers to follow her out at the door. The maiden conducted her charge along the porch to the opposite end of the cabin, where she pointed out their chamber. After bidding their pretty conductress "good night," our travellers prepared themselves for that repose which their wearied frames did not long seek in vain.

CHAPTER XIV

SOMETHING VERY LIKE A DREAM

It was after midnight, and the inmates of the woodman's cabin had been some hours at rest, when Mary Musgrove's sleep was disturbed by strange and unwonted alarms. She was dreaming of Arthur Butler, and a crowd of pleasant visions flitted about her pillow, when, suddenly, clouds darkened the world of her dream, and images of bloodshed caused her to shudder. Horrid shapes appeared to her, marching with stealthy pace through her apartment, and a low and smothered footfall seemed to strike her ear like the ticking of a death-watch. The fright awakened her, but when she came to herself all was still. Her chamber was at the opposite end of the cabin from that where Butler and Robinson slept, and it was separated from the room occupied by Lynch only by a thin partition of boards. The starlight through her window fell upon the floor, just touching, as it passed, the chair over which Mary had hung her clothes, and lighting with a doubtful and spectral light the prominent points of the pile of garments, in such manner as to give it the semblance of some unearthly thing. Mary Musgrave had the superstition common to rustic education, and, as her dream had already filled her mind with apprehensions, she now trembled when her eye fell upon what seemed to her a visitant from another world. For some moments she experienced that most painful of all sufferings, the agony of young and credulous minds when wrought upon by their horror of spectres in the night. Gradually, however, the truth came to her aid, and she saw the dreaded ghost disrobed of his terrors, and changed into a familiar and harmless reality. But this night-fear was scarcely dissipated before she again heard, what in her sleep had conjured up the train of disagreeable images, the noise of footsteps in the adjoining room. In another instant she recognised the sound of voices conversing in a half whisper.

"Michael," said the first voice; "Damn it, man will you never awake? Rouse yourself; it is time to be stirring."

"Wat!" exclaimed the second voice, with a loud yawn, whilst

at the same moment the creaking of the bedstead and a sullen sound upon the floor showed that the speaker had risen from his couch. "Is it you? I have hardly gone to bed, before you are here to rouse me up. What o'clock is it?"

"It is nearly one," replied Wat Adair. "And let me tell you, you have no time to lose. Hugh Habershaw is good ten miles off, and you must be back by day-light."

"You might have given me another hour, I think, if it was only to consider over the right way of setting about this thing. Always look before you leap, that's common sense."

"You were always a heavy-headed devil," said Adair; "and take as much spurring as a spavined horse. What have you to do with considering? Isn't all fixed? Jog, man, jog. You have a beautiful starlight: and I had the crop-ear put up in the stable last night, that no time might be lost; so up, and saddle, and away!"

"Well, you needn't be so d——d busy; don't you see that I am getting ready?"

"Quiet, Mike; you talk too loud. Take your shoes in your hand, you can put them on when you get into the porch."

"There, give me my coat, Wat; and I think I should have no objection to a drop before I set out. It's raw riding of a morning. Now tell me exactly what I am to say to Hugh Habershaw."

"Tell him," replied Wat, "that we have got Horse Shoe Robinson and Major Butler of the Continental army, as snug as a pair of foxes in a bag, and that I will let them run exactly at seven; and —"

"Not to interrupt you, Wat," said the other, "let me ask you a question before you go on. Suppose this shouldn't be the man? Are you sure of it? It would be a d——d unchristian job to give over any other human being to such a set of bloodhounds as Hugh Habershaw and his gang."

"Shaw, Mike; you are a fool! Who, in the name of all the imps, could it be, but Major Butler! Weren't we expecting him along with Horse Shoe, and just at this time?"

"It looks likely enough," replied Lynch. "So go on."

"Tell Hugh to be ready at the Dogwood Spring, at the latest, by eight o'clock. I'll give him a game to play that will supple his joints for him. And mind me, Mike, warn the greasy captain to have his whole squad with him; for Horse Shoe Robinson, you know, is not to be handled by boys; it will be a bull-fight, or I'm mistaken."

"The major seems to have a wicked eye too, Wat," said Lynch. "I shouldn't like much to be in his way, if he was angry; these copperheads are always in a coil ready to strike. But, Wat, how if they don't ride by the Dogwood Spring?"

"Leave that to me; I'll contrive to go as far as the forks of the road with them. And then, if they don't take the right hand fork, why, you may say it's for the want of my not knowing how to tell a lie."

"Now, Wat Adair, I don't like to spoil sport, but, may be, you have never thought whether it would be worth while just to take t'other side, and tell Horse Shoe the whole business. Couldn't we, don't you think, get as much money, and just as honestly, by hoisting colors with Major Butler?"

"But I *have* thought of that, and it won't do, for two reasons. First, these Continentals are on the down-hill, and money is as scarce with them as honesty with the red-coats: and, second, the Tories have got so much the upper hand in the whole country, that I should have my house burnt down and my children thrown into the blaze of it, in less than three days, if I was to let these fellows slip through my fingers."

"Well, I never knew," said Mike Lynch, "any piece of villany that hadn't some good reasons to stand by it, and that's what makes it agreeable to my conscience to take a hand."

"Why, you off-scouring," replied Wat, "it is enough to make Old Scratch laugh, to hear you talk about conscience! There ain't no such a thing going in these days. So be off; I'll look for you at daylight."

"I'll ride, Wat, as if the devil was on my crupper; so good bye!"

The cessation of the voices, the distant tramp of Lynch when he had left the cabin, and the cautious retreat of Wat Adair to his chamber, told to Mary that the affair was settled, and the plan of treachery in full career towards its consummation.

The dialogue that had just passed in the hearing of the maiden, disclosed a plot that deeply agitated and distressed her. What did it become her to do, was the first question that presented itself to her reflection, as soon as she was sufficiently self-possessed to turn her thoughts upon herself. Was it in her power to avert the impending disaster which threatened the lives, perhaps, of those who had sought the hospitality of her kinsman? Perplexed, dismayed, and uncertain how to act, she had recourse to an expedient natural to her education, and such as would appear most obvious to a feeble and guileless female: it was to the simple and faith-inspired expedient of prayer. And now, in artless but sincere language, having first risen up in her bed, and bent her body across her pillow, in the attitude of supplication, she fervently implored the support of Heaven in her present strait, and besought wisdom and strength to conceive and to do that which was needful for the security of the individuals whose peace was threatened by this conspiracy.

"I will arise," she said, as she finished her short and earnest prayer, "with the first light of the dawn, and wait the coming of the strangers from their chamber, and I will then be the first to tell them of the snare that is prepared for them." With this resolve she endeavored to compose herself to rest, but sleep fled her eyelids, and her anxious thoughts dwelt upon and even magnified the threatened perils. It might be too late, she reflected, to wait for the dawn of day; Adair might be before her at the door of the guests and his constant presence might take from her all hope of being able to communicate the important secret to them: it was undoubtedly her surest course to take advantage of the stillness of the night, whilst the household were wrapt in sleep, and apprise the strangers of their danger. But then, how was she to make her way up to their apartment, and arouse them, at this hour, from their slumbers? To what suspicions might the attempt expose her, even from Arthur Butler himself? And, more particularly, what would John Ramsay think of it, if the story should be afterwards told to her disadvantage?

This last was an interrogatory which Mary Musgrove was often found putting to herself, in winding up a self-communion. On the present occasion this appeal to the opinion of John Ramsay had the opposite effect from that which might have been expected from it. It suggested new lights to her mind, and turned her thoughts into another current, and brought that resolution to her aid which her prayer was intended to invoke. What would John Ramsay think — he, the friend of liberty, and of Washington, the compatriot of Butler and Robinson, now toiling with them in the same cause! What would he think, if she, his own Mary (and the maiden rested a moment on this phrase), did *not* do everything in her power to save these soldiers of independence from the blow which treachery was now aiming at them? "John would have good right to be angry with me," she breathed out in a voice that even startled herself, "if I did not give them full warning of what I have heard. This I am sure of, he will believe *my* story whatever others may say."

Innocence and purity of mind are both sword and shield in this world, and no less inspire confidence to defy the malice and uncharitableness of enemies than they strengthen the arm to do what is right. Mary, therefore, resolved to forego all maidenly scruples and bravely to perform her duty, come what might; and having settled upon this conclusion she impatiently awaited the moment when she might venture forth upon her office of humanity. In this situation it was not long before she heard the distant footfall of a horse's gallop along the road, indicating to her the departure of Michael Lynch upon his traitorous embassy.

The time seemed to be propitious, so Mary arose and dressed herself. Then tripping stealthily to the door that opened upon the porch, she undid the bolt. A loud and prolonged creak, from the wooden hinges, caused her to shake from head to foot. She listened for a moment, and, finding that no one stirred, stepped forth with the timid and faltering step which would no less have marked the intent of the burglar, than, as now it did, the frightened motion of a guardian spirit bent upon an errand of good. Midway along the porch she had to pass the window of Adair's apartment: first, the low growl, and then the sudden bark of the watch-dog saluted her ear, and made her blood run cold. The maiden's hand, however, soothed him into silence; but the noise had attracted the notice of Wat Adair, who grumbled out a short curse from within, which was distinctly audible to Mary. She hastily fled to the further end of the porch, and there stood cowering close against the wall, almost as mute and motionless as a statue, scarce daring to breathe, and poised, as in the act to run, with her weight resting on one foot, the other raised from the floor. In this position she remained during a long interval of fear, until, at length, convinced that all was quiet, she again ventured forward. The window of the travellers' chamber looked out from the gable end of the dwelling, and she was now immediately before it. One of the beds of the room, she knew, was placed beside this window, and was occupied by either Butler or Robinson. Tremblingly and mistrustfully, she gave a feeble tap with her hand against the sash. There was no answer: the sleep within was the sleep of tired men, and was not to be broken by the light play of a maiden's fingers. She now picked up a pebble from the ground, and with it again essayed to wake the sleepers. This, too, was unsuccessful. In utter hopelessness of accomplishing her purpose by other means, she ventured upon raising the sash; and having done so, she thrust her head partially into the room as she held up the window-frame with one hand, crying out with an almost choked voice.

"Mr. Butler! Mr. Butler! For mercy, awake!"

There was no other response but the deep breathing of the sleep-subdued inmates.

"Oh! what shall I do?" she exclaimed, as her heart beat with a violent motion. "I might as well call to the dead. Mr. Galbraith Robinson! Ah me, I cannot rouse them without alarming the whole house! Major Butler," she continued, laying a particular stress upon this designation of his rank, "Oh, good sir, awake!"

"What do you want?" muttered Butler in a smothered and sleep-stifled voice, as he turned himself heavily on his pillow, like one moved by a dream.

"Oh, heaven, sir, make no noise! I am ashamed to tell you who I am," said the terrified girl, "but I come for your good — I have something to tell you."

"Away, away!" cried Butler, speaking in his sleep, "I will not be disturbed: I do not fear you. Begone!"

"Oh, sir, hear me," entreated the maiden, "the people in this house know you, and they are contriving evil against you."

"It makes no difference," muttered the only half-awakened soldier. "I will ride where it suits me, if the Tories were as thick as the leaves of the trees."

"There are people gathering to do you harm to-morrow," continued Mary, not suspecting the unconsciousness of the person to whom she addressed herself, "and I only come with a word of warning to you. Do not ride by the Dogwood Spring to-morrow, nor take the right hand road at the first forks: there are wicked men upon that road. Have your eye," she whispered, "upon my uncle Walter. Ride fast and far, before you stop; and pray, sir, as you think fairly of me — Mary Musgrove, sir, — the daughter of Allen Musgrove, the miller — oh, do not tell my name. If you knew John Ramsay, sir, I am certain you would believe me."

The watch-dog had growled once or twice during the period while Mary spoke, and at this moment the door of the principal room of the cabin was heard to move slightly ajar, and the voice of Adair, in a whisper, reached the girl's ear.

"Hist, Michael! In the devil's name what brought you back? Why do you loiter, when time is so precious?"

A long, heavy, and inarticulate exclamation, such as belongs to disturbed sleep, escaped from Butler.

"Father of heaven, I shall let the window fall with fright!" inwardly ejaculated Mary, as she still occupied her uneasy station. "Hush, it is the voice of my uncle."

There was a painful pause.

A heavy rush of wind agitated the trees, and sweeping along the porch caused some horse-gear that was suspended against the wall to vibrate with a rustling noise: the sound pierced Mary's ear like the accents of a ghost, and her strength had well nigh failed her from faint-heartedness.

"I thought it was Michael," said Adair, speaking to some one within, "but it is only the rattling of harness and the dreaming of Drummer. These dogs have a trick of whining and growling in their sleep according to a way of their own. They say a dog sometimes sees a spirit at night. But man or devil it's all one to old Drummer! Sleep quiet, you superfluous, and have done with your snoring!"

With these words, the door was again closed, and Mary, for the moment, was released from suffering.

"Remember," she uttered in the most fear-stricken tone, as she lowered the sash. "Be sure to take the left hand road at the first fork!"

"In God's name, what is it? Where are you?" was the exclamation heard by Mary as the window was closing. She did not halt for further parley or explanation, but now hastily stole back, like a frightened bird towards its thicket. Panting and breathless, she regained her chamber, and with the utmost expedition betook herself again to bed, where, gratified by the consciousness of having done a good action, and fully trusting that her caution would not be disregarded, she gradually dismissed her anxiety, and, before the hour of dawning, had fallen into a gentle though not altogether unperturbed slumber.

CHAPTER XV

HORSE SHOE AND BUTLER RESUME THEIR JOURNEY, WHICH IS DELAYED BY A SAVAGE INCIDENT

MORNING broke, and with the first day-streak Robinson turned out of his bed, leaving Butler so thoroughly bound in the spell of sleep, that he was not even moved by the loud and heavy tramp of the sergeant, as that weighty personage donned his clothes. Horse Shoe's first habit in the morning was to look after Captain Peter, and he accordingly directed his steps toward the rude shed which served as a stable, at the foot of the hill. Here, to his surprise, he discovered that the fence-rails which, the night before, had been set up as a barrier across the vacant doorway, had been let down, and that no horses were to be seen about the premises.

"What hocus-pocus has been here?" said he to himself, as he gazed upon the deserted stable. "Have these rummaging and thieving Tories been out maraudering in the night? or is it only one of Captain Peter's old-sodger tricks, letting down bars and leading the young geldings into mischief? That beast can snuff the scent of a corn field or a pasture ground as far as a crow smells gunpowder. He'd dislocate and corruptify any innocent stable of horses in Carolina!"

In doubt to which of these causes to assign this disappearance of their cavalry, the sergeant ascended the hill hard-by, and directed his eye over the neighboring fields, hoping to discover the deserters in some of the adjacent pastures. But he could get no sight of them. He then returned to the stable and fell to examining the ground about the door, in order to learn something of the departure of the animals by their tricks. These were sufficiently distinct to convince him that Captain Peter, whose shoes had a peculiar mark well known to the sergeant, had eloped during the night, in company with the major's gelding and two others, these being all, as Horse Shoe had observed, that were in the stable at the time he had retired to bed. He forthwith followed the foot-prints which led him into the high road, and thence along it westward for about two hundred paces, where a set of field bars, now thrown down, afforded entrance into the cornfield. At this point the sergeant traced the deviation of three of the horses into the field, whilst the fourth, it was evident, had continued upon the road.

The conclusion which Galbraith drew from this phenomenon was expressed by a wise shake of the head and a profound fit of abstraction. He took his seat upon a projecting rail at the angle of the fence, and began to sum up conjectures in the following phrase:

"The horse that travelled along that road, never travelled of his own free will: that's as clear as preaching. Well, he wa'n't rode by Wat nor by Mike Lynch, or else they are arlier men than I take them to be: but still, I'll take a book oath that creetur went with a bridle across his head, and a pair o' legs astride his back. And whoever held that bridle in his hand, did it for no good! Scampering here and scampering there, and scouring woods in the night too, when the country is as full of Tories as a beggar's coat with ——, it's a dogmatical bad sign, take it which way you will. Them three horses had the majority, and it is the nature of these beasts always to follow the majority: that's an observation I have made; and, in particular, if there's a cornfield, or an oat-patch, or a piece of fresh pasture to be got into, every individual horse is unanimous on the subject."

Whilst the sergeant was engrossed with these reflections, "he was ware," as the old ballads have it, of a man trudging past him along the road. This was no other than Wat Adair, who was striding forward with a long and rapid step, and with all the appearance of one intent upon some pressing business.

"Halloo! who goes there? where away so fast, Wat?" was Robinson's challenge.

"Horse Shoe!" exclaimed Adair, in a key that bespoke surprise, and even alarm,—"Ha, ha, ha!—By the old woman's pipe, you frightened me! I'll swear, Galbraith Robinson, I heard you snoring as I passed by your window three minutes ago."

"I'll swear that's not the truest word you ever spoke in your life, Wat; though true enough for you, mayhap. Do you see how cleverly yon light has broke across the whole sky? When I first turned out this morning it was a little ribbon of day: the burning of a block-house at night, ten miles off, would have made a broader streak. It was your own snoring you heard, Wat; you have only forgot under whose window it was."

"What old witch has been pinching you, Horse Shoe, that *you* are up so early?" asked Adair. "Get back to the house, man,

I will be with you presently; I have my farm to look after, I'll see you presently."

"You seem to me to be in a very onreasonable hurry, Wat, considering that you have the day before you. But, softly, I'll walk with you, if you have no unliking to it."

"No, no, I'm busy, Galbraith; I'm going to look after my traps; I'd rather you'd go back to the house and hurry breakfast. Go! You would only get scratched with briers if you followed me."

"Ha, ha, ha! Wat! Briers, did you say? Look here, man, do you see them there legs? Do they look as if they couldn't laugh at yourn in any sort of scrambling I had a mind to set them to? Tut, I'll go with you just to larn you the march drill."

"Then I'll not budge a foot after the traps."

"You are crusty, Wat Adair; what's the matter with you?"

"Is Major Butler up yet?" asked the woodman thoughtfully.

"*Who* do you say? *Major* Butler."

"*Major!*" cried Adair, with affected surprise.

"Yes, you called him Major Butler?"

"I had some dream, I think, about him: or, didn't you call him so yourself, Horse Shoe?"

"Most ondoubtedly, I did not," replied Robinson seriously.

"Then I dreamt it, Horse Shoe: these dreams sometimes get into the head, like things we have been told. But, Galbraith, tell me the plain up-an-down truth, what brings you and Mr. Butler into these parts? What are you after in Georgia? It does seem strange to find men that are wanted below, straggling here in our woods at such a time as this."

"There are two sorts of men in this world, Wat," said the sergeant, with a smile, "them that axes questions, and them that won't answer questions. Now, which, do you think, I belong to? Why, to the last, you tinker! Where are our horses, Wat? Tell me that. Who let them out of the stable?"

"Perhaps they let themselves out," replied Adair, "they were not haltered."

"You are either knave or fool, Wat. Come here. There are the tracks of the beast that carried the man up this road, who sot loose all the horses that were in that stable."

"Mike Lynch, perhaps," said Adair, with an assumed expression of ignorance. "Where can that fellow have been so early? Oh, I remember, he told me last night that he was going this morning to the blacksmith's. He ought to be back by this time."

"And you are here to larn the news from him?" said the sergeant, eyeing Adair with a suspicious scrutiny.

"You have just hit it, Horse Shoe," returned Wat, laughing. "I did want to know if there were any more squads of troopers foraging about this district: for these cursed fellows whip in upon a man and cut him up blade and ear, without so much as thanks for their pillage, and so I told Mike to inquire of the blacksmith, for he is more like to know than anybody else, whether there was any more of these pestifarious scrummagers abroad."

"And your traps, Wat?"

"That was only a lie, Galbraith — I confess it. I was afeared to make you uneasy by telling you what I was after. But still it wasn't a broad, stark, daylight lie neither; it was only a civil fib, for I was going after my wolf trap before I got my breakfast. But here comes Mike."

At this juncture Lynch was seen emerging from the wood, mounted on a rough, untrimmed pony, which he was urging forward under repeated blows with his stick. The little animal was covered with foam; and, from his travel-worn plight, gave evidence of having been taxed to the utmost of his strength in a severe journey. At some hundred paces, distant, the rider detected the presence of Adair and his companion, and came to a sudden halt. He appeared to deliberate as if with a purpose to escape their notice; but finding that he was already observed by them, he put his horse again in motion, advancing only at a slow walk. Adair hastily quitted Robinson, and, walking forward until he met Lynch, turned about and accompanied him along the road, conversing during this interval in a key too low to be heard by the sergeant.

"Here's Horse Shoe thrusting his head into our affairs. Conjure a lie quickly about your being at the blacksmith's; I told him you were there to hear the news."

"Aye, aye! I understand."

"You saw Hugh?"

"Yes. The gang will be at their post."

"Hush! Be merry; laugh and have a joke — Horse Shoe is very suspicious."

"You have ridden the crop-ear like a stolen horse," continued Adair, as soon as he found himself within the sergeant's hearing. "See what a flurry you have put the dumb beast in. If it had been your own nag, Mike Lynch, I warrant you would have been more tedious with him."

"The crop-ear is not worth the devil's fetching, Wat. He is as lazy as a land-turtle, and too obstinate for any good-tempered man's patience. Look at that stick — I have split it into a broom on the beast."

"You look more like a man at the end of the day than at the beginning of it," said Robinson. "How far had you to ride, Michael?"

"Only over here to the shop of Billy Watson, in the Buzzard's nest," replied Lynch, "which isn't above three miles at the farthest. My saw wanted setting, so I thought I'd make an early job of it, but this beast is so cursed dull I have been good three-quarters of an hour since I left the smith's."

"What news do you bring?" inquired Adair.

"Oh, none worth telling again. That cross-grained, contrary, rough-and-tumble bear gouger, old Hide-and-Seek, went down yesterday with the last squad of Ferguson's new draughts."

"Wild Tom Eskridge," said Wat Adair. "You knowed him, Horse Shoe, a superfluous imp of Satan!" continued the woodman, laying a particular accent on the penultimate of this favorite adjective, which he was accustomed to use as expressive of strong reprobation. So he is cleared out at last! Well, I'm glad on't, for he was the only fellow in these hills I was afeard would give you trouble, Galbraith."

"Superfluous or not," replied the sergeant, pronouncing the word in the same manner as the woodman, and equally ignorant of its meaning, "it will be a bad day for Tom Eskridge, the rank, obstropolous Tory, when he meets me, Wat Adair. I have reason to think that he tried to clap some of Tarleton's dragoons on my back over here at the Waxhaws. There's hemp growing for that scape-grace at this very time."

"You heard of no red coats about the Tiger?" asked Adair.

"Not one," replied Lynch; "the nearest post is Cruger's, in Ninety-Six."

"Then your way, Mr. Robinson, is tolerable for to-day," added Adair: "but war is war, and there is always some risk to be run when men are parading with their rifles in their hands. But see! it is hard upon sunrise. Let us go and give some directions about breakfast. I will send out some of the boys to hunt up the horses; they will be ready by the time we have had something to eat."

Without further delay, Adair strode rapidly up the hill to the dwelling-house, the sergeant and Lynch following as soon as the latter had put his jaded beast in the stable. By the time these were assembled in the porch the family began to show signs of life, and it was a little after sunrise when Butler came forth ready for the prosecution of his journey. A few words were exchanged in private between Lynch and the woodman, and after much idle talk and contrived delay, two lazy and loitering negro boys were sent off in quest of the travellers' horses. Not long after this the animals were seen coursing from one part of the distant field to another, defying all attempts to get them into corner, or to compel them to pass through the place that had been opened in order to drive them towards the stable.

There was an air of concern and silent bewilderment visible upon Butler's features, and an occasional expression of impatience escaped his lips as he watched from the porch the ineffectual efforts of the negroes to force the truant steeds towards the house.

"All in good time," said Adair, answering the thoughts and looks of Butler, rather than his words, "all in good time; they must have their play out. It is a good sign, sir, to see a traveller's horse so capersome of a morning. Wife, make haste with your preparations; Horse Shoe and his friend here mustn't be kept back from their day's journey. Stir yourself, Mary Musgrove!"

"Will the gentlemen stay for breakfast?" inquired Mary, with a doubtful look at Butler.

"Will they? To be sure they will! Would you turn off friends from the door with empty stomachs, you mink, and especially with a whole day's starvation ahead of them?" exclaimed the woodman.

"I thought they had far to ride," replied the girl, "and would choose, rather than wait, to take some cold provision to eat upon the road."

"Tush! Go about your business, niece! The horses are not caught yet, and you may have your bacon fried before they are at the door."

"It shall be ready, then, in a moment," returned Mary, and she betook herself diligently to her task of preparation. During the interval that followed, the maiden several times attempted to gain a moment's speech with Butler, but the presence of Adair or Lynch as frequently forbade even a whisper; and the morning meal was at length set smoking on the table without the arrival of the desired opportunity. The repast was speedily finished, and the horses having surrendered to the emissaries who had been despatched to bring them in, were now in waiting for their masters. Horse Shoe put into the woodman's hand a small sum of money in requital for the entertainment afforded to his comrade and himself, and having arranged their baggage upon the saddles, announced that they were ready to set forward on their journey. Whilst the travellers were passing the farewells customary on such occasions, Mary Musgrove, whose manner during the whole morning gave many indications of a painful secret concern, now threw herself in Butler's way, and as she modestly offered him her hand at parting, and heard the little effusion of gallantry and compliment with which it was natural for a well-bred man and a soldier to speak at such a moment, she took the opportunity to whisper — "The left hand road at the Fork — remember!" and instantly glided away to another part of the house. Butler paused but for an instant, and then hurried forward with the sergeant to their horses.

"Wat, you promised to put us on the track to Grindall's Ford," said Horse Shoe, as he rose into his seat.

"I am ready to go part of the way with you," replied the woodman, "I will see you to the Fork, and after that you must make out for yourselves. Michael, fetch me my rifle."

It was not more than half past six when the party set forth on their journey. Our two travellers rode along at an easy gait, and Wat Adair, throwing his rifle carelessly across his shoulder, stepped out with a long swinging step that kept him, without difficulty, abreast of the horsemen, as they pursued their way over hill and dale.

They had not journeyed half a mile before they reached a point in the woods at which Adair called a halt.

"My trap is but a little off the road," he said, "and I must beg you to stop until I see what luck I have this morning. It's a short business and soon done. This way, Horse Shoe; it is likely I may give you sport this morning."

"Our time is pressing," said Butler. "Pray give us your directions as to the road, and we will leave you."

"You would never find it in these woods," replied Wat; "there are two or three paths leading through here, and the road is a blind one till you come to the fork; the trap is not a hundred yards out of your way."

"Rather than stop to talk about it, Wat," said the sergeant, "we will follow you, so go on."

The woodman now turned into the thickets, and opening his way through the bushes, in a few moments conducted the two soldiers to the foot of a large gum tree.

"By all the crows, I have got my lady!" exclaimed Wat Adair, with a whoop that made the woods ring. "The saucy slut! I have yoked her, Horse Shoe Robinson! There's a picture worth looking at."

"Who?" cried Butler; "of whom are you speaking?"

"Look for yourself, sir," replied the woodman. "There's the mischievous devil; an old she-wolf that I have been hunting these two years. Oh, ho, madam! Your servant!"

Upon looking near the earth, our travellers descried the object of this triumphant burst of joy, in a large wolf that was now struggling to release herself from the thraldom of her position. The trap was ingeniously contrived. It consisted of a long opening into the hollow trunk of the tree, beginning about four feet from the ground, and cut out with an axe down to the root. An aperture had been made at the upper end of the slit about a foot wide, and the wood had been hewed away downwards, in such a manner as to render the slit gradually narrower as it approached the lower extremity, until near the earth it was not more than four inches in width, thus forming a wedge-shaped loophole into the hollow body of the tree. A part of the carcase of a sheep had been placed on the bottom inside, the scent of which had attracted the wolf, and, in her eagerness to possess herself of this treasure she had risen on her hind legs high enough to find the opening sufficiently wide to allow her head to be thrust in, whence, slipping downwards, the slit became so narrow as to prevent her from withdrawing her jaws. The only mode of extrication from this trap was to rear her body to the same height at which she found admission, an expedient which, it seems, required more cunning than this proverbially cunning animal was gifted with. She now stood captive pretty much in the same manner that oxen are commonly secured in their stalls.

For a few moments after the prisoner was first perceived, and during the extravagant yelling of Adair at the success of his stratagem, she made several desperate but ineffectual efforts to withdraw her head; but as soon as Butler and Robinson had dismounted, and, together with their guide, had assembled around her, she desisted from her struggles, and seemed patiently to resign herself to the will of her captor. She stood perfectly still with that passive and even cowardly submission for which, in such circumstances, this animal is remarkable: her hind legs drooped and her tail was thrust between them, whilst not a snarl nor an expression of anger or grief escaped her. Her characteristic sagacity had been completely baffled by the superior wolfish cunning of her ensnarer.

Wat laughed aloud with a coarse and almost fiendish laugh, as he cried out —

"I have cotched the old thief at last, in spite of her cunning! With a warning to boot. Here is a mark I sot upon her last winter," he added, as he raised her fore leg, which was deprived of the foot; "but she would be prowling, the superfluous devil! It is in the nature of these here blood-suckers, to keep a going at their trade, no matter how much they are watched. But I knowed I'd have her one of these days. These varmints have always got to pay, one day or another, for their villanies. Wa'n't she an old fool, Horse Shoe, to walk into this here gum for a piece of dead mutton? Ha, ha, ha! if she had had only the sense to rear up, she might have had the laugh on us! But she hadn't; ha, ha, ha!"

"Well, Wat Adair," said Robinson, "you had a mischievous head when you contrived that trap."

"Feel her ribs, Mr. Butler," cried Wat, not heeding the sergeant; "I know who packed that flesh on her. There isn't a lamb in my flock to-day that wouldn't grin if he was to hear the news."

"Well, what are you going to do with her, Adair?" inquired Butler; "remember you are losing time here."

"Do with her!" ejaculated the woodman; "that's soon told: I will skin the devil alive."

"I hope not," exclaimed Butler. "It would be an unnecessary cruelty. Despatch her on the spot with your rifle."

"I wouldn't waste powder and ball on the varmint," replied Adair. "No, no, the knife, the knife!"

"Then cut her throat and be done with it."

"You are not used to these hellish thieves, sir," said the woodman. "There is nothing that isn't too good for them. By the old sinner, I'll skin her alive! That's the sentence!"

"Once more, I pray not," said Butler imploringly.

"It is past praying for," returned Adair, as he drew forth his knife and began to whet it on a stone. "She shall die by inches, and be damned to her!" he added, as his eye sparkled with savage delight. "Now look and see a wolf punished according to her evil doings."

The woodman stood over his captive and laughed heartily, as he pointed out to his companions the quailing and subdued gestures of his victim, indulging in coarse and vulgar jests whilst he described minutely the plan of torture he was about to execute. When he had done with his ribaldry, he slowly drew the point of his knife down the back-bone of the animal, from the neck to the tail, sundering the skin along the whole length. "That's the way to unbutton her jacket," he said, laughing louder than ever.

"For God's sake, desist!" ejaculated Butler. "For my sake, save the poor animal from this pain! I will pay you thrice the value of the skin."

"Money will not buy her," said Wat, looking up for an instant. "Besides, the skin is spoiled by that gash."

"Here is a guinea, if you will cut her throat," said Butler, "and destroy her at once."

"That would be murder outright," replied Adair; "I never take money to do murder; it goes agin my conscience. No, no, I will undress the old lady, and let her have the benefit of the cool air in this hot weather. And if she should take cold, you know, and fall sick and die of that, why then, Mr. Butler, you can give me the guinea. That will save my conscience," he added, with a grin that expressed a struggle between his avarice and cruelty.

"Come, Galbraith, I will not stay to witness the barbarity of this savage. Mount your horse, and let us take our chance alone through the woods. Fellow, I don't wish your further service."

"Look there now!" said Adair; "where were you born, that you are so mighty nice upon account of a blood-sucking wolf? Man, it's impossible to find your way through this country; and you might, by taking a wrong road, fall in with them that would think nothing of serving you as I serve this beast."

"Wat, curse your onnatural heart," interposed the sergeant. "Stob her at once. It's no use, Mr. Butler," he said, finding that Adair did not heed him, "we can't help ourselves. It's wolf agin wolf."

"I knowed you couldn't, Horse Shoe," cried Wat, with another laugh. "So you may as well stay to see it out."

Butler had now walked to his horse, mounted, and retired

some distance into the wood to avoid further converse with the tormentor of the ensnared beast, and to withdraw himself from a sight so revolting to his feelings. In the meantime, Adair proceeded with his operation with an alacrity that showed the innate cruelty of his temper. He made a cross incision through the skin, from the point of one shoulder to the other, the devoted subject of his torture remaining, all the time, motionless and silent. Having thus severed the skin to suit his purpose, the woodman now, with an affectation of the most dainty precision, flourished his knife over the animal's back, and then burst into a loud laugh.

"I can't help laughing," he exclaimed, "to think what a fine, dangling, holiday coat I am going to make of it. I shall strip her as low as the ribs, and then the flaps will hang handsomely. She will be considered a beauty in the sheep-folds, and then she may borrow a coat, you see, from some lamb; a wolf in sheep's clothing is no uncommon sight in this world."

"Wat Adair," said Horse Shoe, angrily, "I've a mind to take the wolf's part and give you a trouncing. You are the savagest wolf in sheep's clothing yourself that it was ever my luck to see."

"You think so, Horse Shoe!" cried Wat, tauntingly. "You might chance to miss your way to-day, so don't make a fool of yourself! Ill will would only take away from you a finger-post—and it isn't every road through this district that goes free of the Tory rangers."

"Your own day will come yet," replied Horse Shoe, afraid to provoke the woodman too far on account of the dependence of himself and his companion upon Adair's information in regard to the route of their journey. "We have to give and take quarter in this world."

"You see, Horse Shoe," said Adair, beginning to expostulate, "I don't like these varmints, no how; that's the reason why. They are cruel themselves and I like to be cruel to them. It's a downright pleasure to see them winch, for, bless your soul! they don't mind common throat-cutting, no more than a calf. Now here's the way to touch their feelings."

At this moment he applied the point of his knife to separating the hide from the flesh on either side of the spine, and then, in his eagerness to accomplish this object, he placed his knife between his teeth and began to tug at the skin with his hands, accompanying the effort with muttered expressions of delight at the involuntary and but ill-suppressed agonies of the brute. The pain, at length, became too acute for the wolf, with all her characteristic habits of submission, to bear, and, in a desperate struggle that ensued between her and her tormentor, she succeeded, by a convulsive leap, in extricating herself from her place of durance. The energy of her effort of deliverance rescued her from the woodman's hand, and turning short upon her assailant, she fixed her fangs deep into the fleshy part of his thigh, where, as the foam fell from her lips, she held on firmly as if determined to sell her life dearly for the pain she suffered. Adair uttered a groan from the infliction, and, in the hurry of the instant, dropped his knife upon the ground. He was thus compelled to bear the torment of the grip, until he dragged the still pertinaciously-adhering beast a few paces forward, where, grasping up his knife, he planted it, by one deeply driven blow, through and through her heart. She silently fell at his feet, without snarl or bark, releasing her hold only in the impotency of death.

"Curse her!" cried Adair, "the hard-hearted, bloody-minded devil! That's the nature of the beast — cruel and wicked to the last, damn her!" he continued, raving with pain, as he stamped his heel upon her head: "damn her in the wolf's hell to which she has gone!"

Robinson stood by, unaiding, and not displeased to see the summary vengeance thus inflicted by the victim upon the oppressor. This calmness provoked the woodman, who, with that stoicism which belongs to uncivilized life, seemed determined to take away all pretext for the sergeant's exultation, by affecting to make light of the injury he had received.

"I don't mind the scratch of the cursed creature," he said, assuming a badly counterfeited expression of mirth, "but I don't like to be cheated out of the pleasure of tormenting such mischievous varmints. It's well for her that she put me in a passion, or she should have carried a festered carcase that the buzzards might have fed upon before she died. But come — where is Mr. Butler? I want that guinea. Ho, sir!" he continued, bawling to Butler, as he tied up his wound with a strap of buckskin taken from his pouch, "my guinea! I've killed the devil to please you, seeing you would not have it."

Butler now rode up to the spot, and, in answer to this appeal, gave it an angry and indignant refusal.

"Lead us on our way, sir," he added. "We have lost too much time already with your brutal delay. Lead on, sir!"

"You will get soon enough to your journey's end," replied

Adair with a smile, and then sullenly took up his rifle and led the way through the forest.

A full half hour or more was lost by the incident at the trap, and Butler's impatience and displeasure continued to be manifested by the manner with which he urged the woodman forward upon their journey. After regaining the road, and traversing a piece of intricate and tangled woodland, by a bridle-patch into which their guide had conducted them, they soon reached a broader and more beaten highway, along which they rode scarce a mile before they arrived at the Fork.

"I have seen you safe as far as I promised," said the woodman, "and you must now shift for yourselves. You take the right hand road; about ten miles further you will come to another prong, there strike to the left, and if you have luck you will get to the ford before sundown. Three miles further is Christie's. Good bye t' ye! And Horse Shoe, if you should come across another wolf stuck in a tree, skin her, d' ye hear? Ha! ha! ha! Good bye!"

"Ride on!" said Butler to the sergeant, who was about making some reply to Adair; "ride on! Don't heed or answer that fellow, but take the road he directs. He is a beast and scoundrel. Faster, good sergeant, faster!"

As he spoke he set his horse to a gallop. Robinson followed at equal speed, the woodman standing still until the travellers disappeared from his view behind the thick foliage that overhung their path. Having seen them thus secure in his toil, the treacherous guide turned upon his heel, shouldered his rifle, and limped back to his dwelling.

"I have a strange misgiving of that ruffian sergeant," said Butler, after they had proceeded about a quarter of a mile. "My mind is perplexed with some unpleasant doubts. What is your opinion of him?"

"He plays on both sides," replied Horse Shoe, "and knows more of you than by rights he ought. He spoke consarning of you, this morning, as *Major* Butler. It came out of his mouth onawares."

"Ha! Is my name on any part of my baggage or dress?"

"Not that I know of," replied the sergeant; "and if it was, Wat can't read."

"Were you interrupted in your sleep last night, Galbraith? Did you hear noises in our room?"

"Nothing, Major, louder nor the gnawing of a mouse at the

foot of the plank partition. Did you see a spirit that you look so solemn?"

"I did, sergeant!" said Butler, with great earnestness of manner. "I had a dream that had something more than natural in it."

"You amaze me, Major! If you saw anything, why didn't you awake me?"

"I hadn't time before it was gone, and then it was too late. I dreamed, Galbraith, that somehow — for my dream didn't explain how she came in — Mary Musgrove, the young girl we saw ——"

"Ha! ha! ha! Major, that young girl's oversot you! Was that the sperit?"

"Peace, Galbraith, I am in earnest; listen to me. I dreamt Mary Musgrove came into our room and warned us that our lives were in danger; how, I forgot, or perhaps she did not tell, but she spoke of our being waylaid, and, I think, she advised that at this very fork of the road we have just passed, we should take the left hand — the right, according to my dream, she said, led to some spring."

"Perhaps the Dogwood, Major," said Robinson, laughing; "there is such a place, somewhere in these parts."

"The Dogwood! by my life," exclaimed Butler; "she called it the Dogwood spring."

"That's very strange," said Robinson gravely; "that's very strange, unless you have hearn some one talk about the spring before you went to bed last night. For, as sure as you are a gentleman, there is such a spring not far off, although I don't know exactly where."

"And what perplexes me," continued Butler, "is that, this morning, almost in the very words of my dream, Mary Musgrove cautioned me, in a whisper, to take the left road at the fork. How is she connected with my dream? Or could it have been a reality, and was it the girl herself who spoke? I have no recollection of such a word from her before I retired to bed."

"I have hearn of these sort of things before, major, and never could make them out. For my share, I believe in dreams. There is something wrong here," continued the sergeant, after pondering over the matter for a few moments, and shaking his head, "there is something wrong here, Major Butler, as sure as you are born. I wasn't idle in making my own observations: first, I didn't like the crossness of Wat's wife last night; then, the granny there, she raved more like an old witch, with something wicked in her that wouldn't let her be still, than like your decent old bodies when they get childish. What did she mean by her palaver about golden guineas in Wat's pocket, and the English officer? Such notions don't come naturally into the head, without something to go upon. And, moreover, when I turned out this morning, before it was cleverly day, who do you think I saw?"

"Indeed I cannot guess."

"First, Wat walking up the road with a face like a man that had sot a house on fire; and when I stopped him to ax what he was after, down comes Mike Lynch — that peevish bull-dog — from the woods, on a little knot of a pony, pretty nigh at full speed, and covered with lather; and there was a sort of colloguing together, and then a story made up about Mike's being at Billy Watson's, the blacksmith's. It didn't tell well, major, and it sot me to suspicions. The gray of the morning is not the time for blacksmith's work: there's the fire to make up, and what not. Besides, it don't belong to the trade, as I know, here in the country, to be at work so arly. I said nothing; but I made a sort of reckoning in my own mind that they looked like a couple of desarters trying to sham a sentry. Then again, there was our horses turned loose. There is something in these signs, you may depend upon it, Major Butler!"

"That fellow has designs against us, Galbraith," said Butler, musing, and paying but little attention to the surmises of the sergeant, "I can hardly think it was a dream. It may have been Mary Musgrove herself, but how she got there is past my conjecture. I saw nothing, I only heard the warning. And I would be sworn she addressed me as Major Butler. You say Wat Adair gave me the same title?"

"As I am a living man," replied Horse Shoe, "he wanted to deny it; and then he pretended it was a fancy of his own."

"It is very strange, and looks badly," said Butler.

"Never mind, let the worst come to the worst, we have arms and legs both," returned the sergeant."

"I will take the hint for good or for ill," said the major. "Sergeant, strike across into the left hand road; in this I will move no farther."

"That's as wise a thing as we can do," replied Robinson. "If you have doubts of a man, seem to trust him, but take care not to follow his advice. There is another hint I will give you, let us examine our fire-arms to see that we are ready for a battle."

Butler concurring in this precaution, the sergeant dismounted, and having primed his rifle afresh, attempted to fire it into the air, but it merely flashed, without going off. Upon a second trial the result was the same. This induced a further examination, which disclosed the fact that the load which had been put in the day previous had been discharged, and a bullet was now driven home in the place of the powder. It was obvious that this was designed. The machination of an enemy became more apparent when, upon an investigation into the condition of Butler's pistols, they were also found incapable of being used.

"This is some of Michael Lynch's doing whilst we were eating our breakfast," said Horse Shoe, "and it is flat proof of treason in our camp. I should like to go back if it was only for the satisfaction of blowing out Wat's brains. But there is no use in argufying about it. We must set things to rights, and move on with a good look-out ahead."

With the utmost apparent indifference to the dangers that beset them, the sergeant now applied himself to the care of restoring his rifle to a serviceable condition. With the aid of a small tool which he carried for such a use, he opened the breach and removed the ball: Butler's pistols were likewise put in order, and our travellers, being thus restored to an attitude of defence, turned their horses' heads into the thicket upon their left, and proceeded across the space that filled up the angle made by the two branches of the road; and, having gained that branch which they sought, they pressed forward diligently upon their journey.

The path they had to travel was lonely and rugged, and it was but once or twice, during the day, that they met a casual wayfarer traversing the same wild. From such a source, however, they were informed that they were on the most direct road to Grindall's ford, and that the route they had abandoned would have conducted them to the Dogwood spring, a point much out of their proper course, and from which the ford might only have been reached by a difficult and tortuous by-way.

These disclosures opened the eyes of Butler and his companion to the imminent perils that encompassed them, and prompted them to the exercise of the strictest vigilance. Like discreet and trusty soldiers, they pursued their way with the most unwavering courage, confident that the difficulty of retreat was fully equal to that of the advance.

CHAPTER XVI

TORY TROOPERS, A DARK ROAD AND A FRAY

"By the whiskers of the Grand Turk, I have got the four points on you, bully Buff! High, low, jack and the game!" exclaimed Peppercorn.

"You have luck enough to worry out the nine lives of a cat. That's an end to Backbiter, the best horse 'twixt Pedee and the Savannah. So, blast me, if I play any more with you! There, send the cards to hell!" roared out Hugh Habershaw, rising and throwing the pack into the fire.

It was just at the closing in of night, when a party of ruffianly-looking men were assembled beneath a spreading chestnut, that threw forth its aged arms over a small gravelly hillock, in the depths of the forest that skirted the northern bank of the Pacolet, within a short distance of Grindall's fort. The spot had all the qualities of a secret fastness. It was guarded on one side by the small river, and on the other by a complicated screen of underwood, consisting principally of those luxuriantly plaited vines which give so distinct a character to the southern woodland. The shrubbery, immediately along the bank of the river, was sufficiently open to enable a horseman to ride through it down to the road which, at about two hundred paces off, led into the ford.

The group who now occupied this spot consisted of some ten or twelve men under the command of Hugh Habershaw. Their appearance was half rustic and half military; some efforts at soldierly costume were visible in the decoration of an occasional buck-tail set in the caps of several of the party, and, here and there, a piece of yellow cloth forming a band for the hat. Some wore long and ungainly deer-skin pantaloons and moccasins of the same material; and two or three were indued with coats of coarse homespun, awkwardly garnished with the trimmings of a British uniform. All were armed, but in the same irregular fashion. There were rifles to be seen stacked against the trunk of the tree: most of the men wore swords, which were of different lengths and sizes; and some of the gang had a horseman's pistol bestowed conspicuously about their persons. Their horses were attached to the drooping ends of the boughs of the several trees that hemmed in the circle, and were ready for service at the first call. A small fire of brushwood had been kindled near the foot of the chestnut, and its blaze was sufficiently strong to throw a bright glare over the motley and ill-looking crew who were assembled near it. They might well have been taken for a bivouac of banditti of the most undisciplined and savage class. A small party were broiling venison at the fire: the greater number, however, were stretched out upon the ground in idleness, waiting for some expected summons to action. The two I have first noticed, were seated on the butt-end of a fallen trunk, immediately within the light of the fire, and were engaged with a pack of dirty cards, at the then popular game of "all fours."

These two personages were altogether different in exterior from each other. The first of them, known only by the sobriquet of Peppercorn, was a tall, well-proportioned and active man, neatly dressed in the uniform of a British dragoon. His countenance indicated more intelligence than belonged to his companions, and his manners had the flexible, bold, and careless port that generally distinguishes a man who has served much in the army, and become familiar with the varieties of character afforded by such a career. The second was Hugh Habershaw, the captain of the gang. He was a bluff, red-visaged, corpulent man, with a face of gross, unmitigated sensuality. A pale blood-shot eye, which was expressionless, except in a sinister glance, occasioned by a partial squint, a small upturned nose, a mouth with thin and compressed lips inclining downwards at the corners, a double chin, bristling with a wiry and almost white beard, a low forehead, a bald crown, and meagre, reddish whiskers, were the ill-favored traits of his physiognomy. The figure of this person was as uncouth as his countenance. He was rather below the middle height, and appeared still shorter by the stoop of his massive round shoulders, by the ample bulk of his chest, and by the rotundity of his corporation. In consideration of his rank, as the leader of this vagabond squadron, he aimed at more military ornament in his dress than his comrades. A greasy cocked hat, decorated after the fashion described by Grumio, "with the humor of forty fancies pricked in it for a feather," was perched somewhat superciliously upon his poll, and his body was invested in an old and much abused cloth coat of London brown, as it was then called, to the ample shoulders of which had been attached two long, narrow, and threadbare epaulets of tarnished silver lace.

A broad buckskin belt was girded, by the help of a large brass buckle, around his middle, on the outside of his coat, and it served as well to suspend a rusty sabre, as to furnish support to a hunting knife, which was thrust into it in front. His nether person was rendered conspicuous by a pair of dingy small-clothes, and long black boots. Close at the feet of this redoubtable commander lay a fat, surly bulldog, whose snarlish temper seemed to have been fostered and promoted by the peremptory perverseness with which his master claimed for him all the privileges and indulgencies of a pampered favorite.

Such were the unattractive exterior and circumstances of the man who assumed control over the band of ruffians now assembled.

"I wish you and the cards had been broiled on the devil's gridiron before I ever saw you!" continued Habershaw, after he had consigned the pack to the flames. "That such a noble beast as Backbiter should be whipped out of my hand by the turn of a rascally card! Hark'ee, you imp of Satan, you have the knack of winning! your luck, or something else — you understand me — something else, would win the shirt off my back if I was such a fool as to play longer with you. I suspect you are a light-fingered Jack — a light-fingered Jack — d'ye hear that, Master Peppercorn?"

"How now, Bully!" cried Peppercorn; "are you turning boy in your old days, that you must fall to whining because you have lost a turn of play? Is every man a rogue since you have set up the trade? For shame! If I were as hot a fool as you, I would give you steel in your guts. But come, noble Captain, there's my hand. This is no time for us to be catching quarrels; we have other business cut out. As to Backbiter, the rat-tailed and spavined bone-setter, curse me if I would have him as a gift: a noble beast! ha, ha, ha! Take him back, man, take him back! he wasn't worth the cards that won him."

"Silence, you tailor's bastard! Would you breed a mutiny in the camp? Look around you: do you expect me to preserve discipline amongst these wild wood-scourers, with your loud haw-haws, to my very teeth? You make too free, Peppercorn; you make too free! It wouldn't take much to make me strike; damn me, there's fighting blood in me, and you know it. When I am at the head of my men, you must know your distance, sir. Suffice it, I don't approve of this familiarity to the commander of a squad. But it is no matter: I let it pass this time. And, hark in your ear, as you underrate Backbiter, you are a fool, Peppercorn, and know no more of the points of a good horse than you do of the ten commandments. Why, blast you, just to punish you, I'll hold you to the word of a gentleman, and take him back. Now there's an end of it, and let's have no more talking."

"Right, noble Captain!" ejaculated Peppercorn, with a free and swaggering laugh, "right! I will uphold the discipline of the valiant Hugh Habershaw of the Tiger against all the babblers the world over. By the God of war, I marvel that Cruger hasn't forced upon you one of his commissions, before this; the army would be proud of such a master of tactics."

"The time will come, Peppercorn; the time will come, and then I'll teach them the elements of military construction. Mark that word, Peppercorn, there's meaning in it."

"Huzza for Captain Tiger of Habershaw—Habershaw of Tiger, I mean!" cried Peppercorn. "Here's Tiger Habershaw, my boys! Drink to that." And saying these words, the dragoon snatched up a leathern canteen from the ground, and, pouring out some spirits into the cup, drank them off.

The rest of the crew sprang from the grass, and followed the example set them by their comrade, roaring out the pledge until the woods rang with their vociferation.

"Peace! you rapscallions!" screamed the captain. "Have you so little notion where you are, that you bellow like bulls? Is this your discipline, when you should be as silent as cats in a kitchen, hellhound! And you, you coarse-throated devil, Beauty," he said as he kicked his dog, that had contributed to the chorus with a loud sympathetic howl, "you must be breaking the laws of service guard with your infernal roar, like the other fools of the pack. Be still, puppy!"

The clamor upon this rebuke ceased, and the bull-dog crouched again at his master's feet.

"Isn't it time that we were at the ford? Oughtn't our friends to be near at hand?" inquired Peppercorn.

"Black Jack will give us notice," replied Habershaw. "Depend upon him. I have thought of everything like a man that knows his business. I have sent that rascal up the road, with orders to feel the enemy; and I'll undertake he'll clink it back when he once lays eyes on them, as fast as four legs will carry him. But it is always well to be beforehand, Peppercorn. Learn that from me: I never in my campaigns knowed any harm done by being too early. So, Master Orderly, call the roll."

"Ready, sir; always ready when you command," answered

Peppercorn. "Shall I call the ragamuffins by their nicknames, or will you have them handled like Christians."

"On secret service," said Habershaw, "it is always best to use them to their nicknames."

"As when they go horse-stealing, or house-burning, or throat-cutting," interrupted Peppercorn.

"Order, sir, no indecencies! do you hear? Go on with your roll, if you have got it by heart. Be musical, dog!"

"Faith will I, most consummate captain! It is just to my hand: I'll sing you like a bagpipe. I have learnt the roll-call handsomely, and can go through it as if it were a song."

"Begin then: the time is coming when we must move. I think I hear Black Jack's horse breaking through the bushes now."

"Attention, you devil's babies, the whole of you!" shouted Peppercorn. "Horse and gun, every mother's imp of you!"

In a moment the idlers sprang to their weapons and mounted their horses.

"Answer to your names," said the orderly; "and see that you do it discreetly. Pimple!"

"Here," answered one of the disorderly crew, with a laugh.

"Silence in the ranks!" cried Habershaw, "or, by the blood of your bodies, I'll make my whinger acquainted with your hearts!"

"Long Shanks."

"Here! if you mean me," said another.

"Good! Black Jack."

"On patrole," said the captain.

"Red Mug."

"At the book," answered the man in the ranks; and here rose another laugh.

"Red Mug! do you mind me?" said Habershaw, in a threatening tone, as his eye squinted fiercely towards the person addressed.

"Platter Breech."

"I'll stand out against the nickname," said the person intended to be designated, whilst the whole squad began to give symptoms of a mutiny of merriment. "I'll be d——d if I will have it, and that's as good as if I swore to it. I am not going to be cajoled at by the whole company."

"Silence! Blood and butter, you villains!" roared the captain. "Don't you see that you're in line? How often have I told you that it's against discipline to chirp above a whisper when you are drawn out? Take care that I hav'n't to remind you of that again! Andy Clopper, you will keep the denomination I have set upon you. Platter Breech is a good soldier-like name, and you shall die in it, if I bid you. Go on, Orderly — proceed! "

" Marrow Bone."

" Here! "

" Fire Nose."

" Fire Nose yourself, Mister Disorderly! " replied another refractory member, sullenly from the ranks.

" Well, let him pass. That's a cross-grained devil," said the captain, aside to Peppercorn. " I'll bring that chap into order yet, the d——d mutineering back hanger! Pass him."

" Screech Owl."

" Here! "

" That's a decent, good-natured Screech Owl," said Peppercorn. " Clapper Claw! Bow Legs! "

" Both here."

" They are all here, most comfortable Captain, all good fellows and true, and as ready to follow you into the belly of an earthquake as go to supper, it is all the same to them."

" Let them follow where I lead, Peppercorn; that is all I ask," said Habershaw significantly.

" You have forgot one name on your roll, Mister Orderly," said he who had been written down by the name of Fire Nose.

" Whose was that? "

" You forgot Captain Moonface Bragger — captain of the squad."

" Gideon Blake! " shouted Habershaw, with a voice choked by anger, until it resembled the growl of a mastiff, whilst, at the same time, he drew his sword half out of the scabbard. " Howsever, it is very well," he said, restraining his wrath and permitting the blade to drop back into its sheath. " Another time, sir. I have marked you, you limb of a traitor. May all the devils ride over me if I don't drive a bullet through your brain if you ever unfringe my discipline again! Yes, you foul-mouthed half-whig, I have had my suspicions of you before to-day. So look to yourself. A fine state of things when skunks like you can be setting up a mutiny in the service! Take care of yourself, sir, you know me. Now, my lads, to business. Remember the orders I issued at the Dogwood Spring, this morning. This Whig officer must be taken dead or alive, and don't be chicken-hearted about it. Give him the lead — give him the lead! As to the lusty fellow that rides with him — big Horse Shoe — have a care of him; that's a dog that bites without barking. But be on the watch that they don't escape you again. Since we missed them at the spring they have cost us a hard ride to head them here, so let them pay for it. See that they are well into the ford before you show yourselves. Wait for orders from me, and if I fall by the fortune of war, take your orders from Peppercorn. If by chance we should miss them at the river, push for Christie's; Wat has taken care that they shall make for that, to-night. If any of you, by mistake, you understand me, take them prisoners, bring them back to this spot. Now you have heard my orders, that's enough. Keep silent and ready. Mind your discipline. Black Jack is long coming, Orderly; these fellows must travel slow."

"I hear him now," replied Peppercorn.

In the next moment the scout referred to galloped into the circle. His report was hastily made. It announced that the travellers were moving leisurely towards the ford, and that not many minutes could elapse before their arrival. Upon this intelligence Habershaw immediately marched his troop to the road and posted them in the cover of the underwood that skirted the river, at the crossing-place. Here they remained like wild beasts aware of the approach of their prey, and waiting the moment to spring upon them when it might be done with the least chance of successful resistance.

Meantime Butler and Robinson advanced at a wearied pace. The twilight had so far faded as to be only discernible on the western sky. The stars were twinkling through the leaves of the forest, and the light of the firefly spangled the wilderness. The road might be descried, in the most open parts of the wood, for some fifty paces ahead; but where the shrubbery was more dense, it was lost in utter darkness. Our travellers, like most wayfarers towards the end of the day, rode silently along, seldom exchanging a word, and anxiously computing the distance which they had yet to traverse before they reached their appointed place of repose. A sense of danger, and the necessity for vigilance, on the present occasion, made them the more silent.

"I thought I heard a wild sort of yell just now — people laughing a great way off," said Robinson, "but there's such a hooting of owls and piping of frogs that I mought have been mistaken. Halt, Major. Let me listen — there it is again."

"It is the crying of a panther, sergeant; more than a mile from us, by my ear."

"It is mightily like the scream of drunken men," replied the sergeant; " and there, too! I thought I heard the clatter of a hoof."

The travellers again reined up and listened.

" It is more like a deer stalking through the bushes, Galbraith."

" No," exclaimed the sergeant, " that's the gallop of a horse making down the road ahead of us, as sure as you are alive; I heard the shoe strike a stone. You must have hearn it too."

" I wouldn't be sure," answered Butler.

" Look to your pistols, Major, and prime afresh."

" We seem to have ridden a great way," said Butler, as he concluded the inspection of his pistols and now held one of them ready in his hand. " Can we have lost ourselves? Should we not have reached the Pacolet before this? "

" I have seen no road that could take us astray," replied Robinson, " and, by what we were told just before sundown, I should guess that we couldn't be far off the ford. We hav'n't then quite three miles to Christie's. Well, courage, major! supper and bed were never spoiled by the trouble of getting to them."

" Wat Adair, I think, directed us to Christie's? " said Butler.

" He did; and I had a mind to propose to you, since we caught him in a trick this morning, to make for some other house, if such a thing was possible, or else to spend the night in the woods."

" Perhaps it would be wise, sergeant; and if you think so still, I will be ruled by you."

" If we once got by the river-side where our horses mought have water, I almost think I should advise a halt there. Although I have made one observation, Major Butler — that running water is lean fare for a hungry man. Howsever, it won't hurt us, and if you say the word we will stop there."

" Then, sergeant, I do say the word."

" Isn't that the glimmering of a light yonder in the bushes? " inquired Horse Shoe, as he turned his gaze in the direction of the bivouac, " or is it these here lightning bugs that keep so busy shooting about? "

" I thought I saw the light you speak of, Galbraith; but it has disappeared."

" It is there again, major; and I hear the rushing of the river — we are near the ford. Perhaps this light comes from some cabin on the bank."

" God send that it should turn out so, Galbraith! for I am very weary."

" There is some devilment going on in these woods, major. I

saw a figure pass in front of the light through the bushes. I would be willing to swear it was a man on horseback. Perhaps we have, by chance, fallen on some Tory muster; or, what's not so likely, they may be friends. I think I will ride forward and challenge."

"Better pass unobserved, if you can, sergeant," interrupted Butler. "It will not do for us to run the risk of being separated. Here we are at the river; let us cross, and ride some distance; then, if any one follow us, we shall be more certain of his design."

They now cautiously advanced into the river, which, though rapid, was shallow; and having reached the middle of the stream, they halted to allow their horses water.

"Captain Peter is as thirsty as a man in a fever," said Horse Shoe. "He drinks as if he was laying in for a week. Now, major, since we are here in the river, look up the stream. Don't you see, from the image in the water, that there's a fire on the bank? And there, by my soul! there are men on horseback. Look towards the light. Spur, and out on the other side! Quick — quick — they are upon us!"

At the same instant that Horse Shoe spoke, a bullet whistled close by his ear; and, in the next, six or eight men galloped into the river, from different points. This was succeeded by a sharp report of firearms from both parties, and the vigorous charge of Robinson, followed by Butler, through the array of the assailants. They gained the opposite bank, and now directed all their efforts to outrun their pursuers; but in the very crisis of their escape, Butler's horse, bounding under the prick of the spur, staggered a few paces from the river and fell dead. A bullet had lodged in a vital part, and the energy of the brave steed was spent in the effort to bear his master through the stream. Butler fell beneath the stricken animal, from whence he was unable to extricate himself. The sergeant, seeing his comrade's condition, sprang from his horse and ran to his assistance, and, in the same interval, the ruffian followers gained the spot and surrounded their prisoners. An ineffectual struggle ensued over the prostrate horse and rider, in which Robinson bore down more than one of his adversaries, but was obliged, at last, to yield to the overwhelming power that pressed upon him.

"Bury your swords in both of them to the hilts!" shouted Habershaw; "I don't want to have that work to do to-morrow."

"Stand off," cried Gideon Blake, as two or three of the gang sprang forward to execute their captain's order; "stand off! the man is on his back, and he shall not be murdered in cold blood;" and the speaker took a position near Butler, prepared to make good his resolve. The spirit of Blake had its desired effect, and the same assailants now turned upon Robinson.

"Hold!" cried Peppercorn, throwing up his sword and warding off the blows that were aimed by these men at the body of the sergeant. "Hold, you knaves! this is my prisoner. I will deal with him to my liking. Would a dozen of you strike one man when he has surrendered? Back, ye cowards; leave him to me. How now, old Horse Shoe; are you caught, with your gay master here? Come, come, we know you both. So yield with a good grace, lest, peradventure, I might happen to blow out your brains."

"Silence, fellows! You carrion crows!" roared Habershaw. "Remember the discipline I taught you. No disorder, nor confusion, but take the prisoners, since you hav'n't the heart to strike; take them to the rendezvous. And do it quietly — do you hear? Secure the baggage; and about it quickly, you hounds!"

Butler was now lifted from the ground, and, with his companion, was taken into the custody of Blake and one or two of his companions, who seemed to share in his desire to prevent the shedding of blood. The prisoners were each mounted behind one of the troopers, and in this condition conducted across the river. The saddle and other equipments were stripped from the major's dead steed; and Robinson's horse, Captain Peter, was burdened with the load of two wounded men, whose own horses had escaped from them in the fray. In this guise the band of freebooters, with their prisoners and spoils, slowly and confusedly made their way to the appointed place of re-assembling. In a few moments they were ranged beneath the chestnut, waiting for orders from their self-important and vain commander.

CHAPTER XVII

SCENE IN THE BIVOUAC

"BUSTLE, my lads — bustle! These are stirring times," exclaimed Habershaw, riding with an air of great personal consequence into the midst of the troops, as they were gathered, still on horseback, under the chestnut. "We have made a fine night's work of it, and, considering that we fought in the dark against men ready armed for us, this has not been such a light affair. To be sure, in point of numbers, it is a trifle; but the plan, Peppercorn — the plan, and the despatch, and the neatness of the thing — that's what I say I am entitled to credit for. Bless your soul, Peppercorn, these fellows were sure to fall into my trap — there was no getting off. That's the effect of my generalship, you see, Peppercorn. Study it, boy! We could have managed about twenty more of the filthy rebels handsomely; but this will do — this will do. I took, as a commanding officer ought always to do, the full responsibility of the measure, and a good share of the fight. Did I not, Peppercorn? Wasn't I, in your opinion, about the first man in the river?"

"I'll bear witness, valiant and victorious captain," answered the dragoon, "that you fired the first shot; and I am almost willing to make oath that I saw you within at least twenty paces of the enemy, exhorting your men."

"Now lads — wait for the word — dismount!" continued the captain, "and make up your minds to pass the night where you are. Peppercorn, the prisoners I put under your identical charge. Remember that! keep your eyes about you. Set a guard of four men upon them; I will make you accountable." He then added, in a undertone, "Hold them safe until to-morrow, man, and I promise you, you shall have no trouble in watching them after that."

"You shall find them," replied Peppercorn.

"Silence," interrupted the captain; "hear my orders, and give no reply. Now, sir, before you do anything else, call your roll, and report your killed, wounded, and missing."

Upon this order, the dragoon directed the men, after disposing of their horses, to form a line. He then called over the squad by their real names, and immediately afterwards reported to his superior, who, in order to preserve a proper dignified distance, had retreated some paces from the group, the following pithy and soldier-like account: —

"Two men wounded, noble captain, in the late action; two missing; one horse, saddle and bridle lost; one horse and two prisoners taken from the enemy."

"The names of the wounded, sir?"

"Tom Dubbs and Shadrach Green; one slightly scratched, and the other bruised by a kick from the blacksmith."

"The missing, sir?"

"Dick Waters, commonly called Marrow Bone, and Roger Bell, known in your honor's list by the name of Clapper Claw."

"They have skulked," said the captain.

"Marrow Bone is as dead as a door nail, sir," said the orderly with perfect indifference, and standing affectedly erect. "He fell in the river, and the probability is that Clapper Claw keeps him company."

"What!" roared Habershaw, "have the diabolical scoundrels made away with any of my good fellows? Have the precious lives of my brave soldiers been poured out by the d——d rebels? By my hand, they shall feel twisted rope, Peppercorn! — cold iron is too good for them."

"Softly, captain!" said the orderly. "You don't blame the enemy for showing fight? We mustn't quarrel with the chances of war. There is not often a fray without a broken head, captain. We must deal with the prisoners according to the laws of war."

"Of Tory war, Peppercorn, aye, that will I! String the dogs up to the first tree. The devil's pets, why didn't they surrender when we set upon them! To-morrow: let them look out to-morrow. No words, orderly; send out two files to look for the bodies, and to bring in the stray horse if they can find him. A pretty night's work! to lose two good pieces of stuff for a brace of black-hearted whigs!"

The two files were detailed for the duty required, and immediately set out, on foot, towards the scene of the late fray. The rest of the troops were dismissed from the line.

"I would venture to ask, sir," said Butler, addressing the captain, "for a cup of water: I am much hurt."

"Silence, and be d——d to you!" said Habershaw gruffly, "silence, and know your place, sir. You are a prisoner, and a traitor to boot."

"Don't you hear the gentleman say he is hurt?" interposed Robinson. "It's onnatural, and more like a beast than a man to deny a prisoner a little water."

"By my sword, villain, I will cleave your brain for you, if you open that rebel mouth of yours again!"

"Pshaw, pshaw! Captain Habershaw, this will never do," said Peppercorn; "men are men, and must have food and drink. Here, Gideon Blake, give me your flask of liquor and bring me some water from the river. It is my duty, captain, to look after the prisoners."

Gideon Blake, who was a man of less savage temper than most of his associates, obeyed this command with alacrity, and even added a few words of kindness, as he assisted in administering refreshment to the prisoners. This evidence of a gentler nature did not escape the comment of the ruffian captain, who still remembered his old grudge against the trooper.

"Away, sir," he said in a peremptory and angry tone, "away and attend to your own duty. You are ever fond of obliging these beggarly whigs. Hark you, Peppercorn," he added, speaking apart to the dragoon, "take care how you trust this skulking vagabond: he will take bribes from the rebels, and turn his coat whenever there is money in the way. I have my eye upon him."

"If I chose to speak," said Gideon Blake.

"Hold your peace, you grey fox," cried the captain. "Not a word! I know your doublings. Remember you are under martial law, and blast me, if I don't make you feel it! There are more than myself suspect you."

"I should like to know," said Butler, "why I and my companion are molested on our journey. Have we fallen amongst banditti, or do you bear a lawful commission? If you do, sir, let me tell you, you have disgraced it by outrage and violence exercised towards unoffending men, and shall answer for it when the occasion serves. On what pretence have we been arrested?"

"Hark, my young fighting-cock," replied the captain. "You will know your misdemeanors soon enough. And if you would sleep to-night with a whole throat, you will keep your tongue within your teeth. It wouldn't take much to persuade me to give you a little drum-head law. Do you hear that?"

"It is my advice, major," whispered Robinson, "to ax no questions of these blackguards."

"Be it so, sergeant," said Butler, "I am weary and sick."

When other cares were disposed of, and the excited passions of the lawless gang had subsided into a better mood, the dragoon took Butler's cloak from the baggage and spread it upon the ground beneath the shelter of the shrubbery, and the suffering officer was thus furnished a bed that afforded him some small share of comfort, and enabled to take that rest which he so much needed. Robinson seated himself on the ground beside his companion, and in this situation they patiently resigned themselves to whatever fate awaited them.

Soon after this the whole troop were busy in the preparations for refreshment and sleep. The horses were either *hobbled,* by a cord from the fore to the hind foot, and turned loose to seek pasture around the bivouac, or tethered in such parts of the forest as furnished them an opportunity to feed on the shrubbery. The fire was rekindled, and some small remnants of venison roasted before it; and in less than an hour this reckless and ill-governed band was carousing over their cups with all the rude ribaldry that belonged to such natures.

"Come, boys," said Peppercorn, who seemed to take a delight in urging the band into every kind of excess, and who possessed that sort of sway over the whole crew, including their leader no less than the privates, which an expert and ready skill in adapting himself to the humor of the company gave him, and which faculty he now appeared to exercise for the increase of his own influence, "come, boys, laugh while you can — that's my motto. This soldiering is a merry life, fighting, drinking, and joking. By the God of war! I will enlist the whole of you into the regular service — Ferguson or Cruger, which you please, boys! they are both fine fellows and would give purses of gold for such charming, gay, swaggering blades. Fill up your cans and prepare for another bout. I'm not the crusty cur to stint thirsty men. A toast, my gay fellows!"

"Listen to Peppercorn," cried out some three or four voices.

"Here's to the honor of the brave captain Hugh Habershaw, and his glorious dogs that won the battle of Grindall's ford!"

A broad and coarse laugh burst from the captain at the announcement of this toast.

"By my sword!" he exclaimed, "the fight was not a bad fight."

"Can you find a joint of venison, Gideon?" said Peppercorn, aside. "If you can, give it, and a cup of spirits, to the prisoners. Stop, I'll do it myself, you will have the old bull-dog on your back."

And saying this the dragoon rose from his seat, and taking a few fragments of the meat which had been stripped almost to the bone, placed them, together with a canteen, beside Butler.

"Make the best of your time," he said, "you have but short allowance and none of the best. If I can serve you, I will do it with a good heart; so, call on me."

Then turning to the sergeant, who sat nigh, he whispered in his ear, and, with a distinct and somewhat taunting emphasis, inquired,

"Friend Horse Shoe, mayhap thou knowest me?"

"That I do, James Curry," replied the sergeant, "and I have a mean opinion of the company you keep. I don't doubt but you are ashamed to say how you come by them."

"All is fish that comes into the Dutchman's net," said Curry. "To-night I have caught fat game. You are a sturdy fellow, master Blacksmith, and good at a tug, but remember, friend, I owe you a cuff, and if you weren't a prisoner you should have it."

"Show me fair play, James Curry, and you shall have a chance now," said Horse Shoe; "I'll keep my parole to surrender when it is over."

"Silence, fool!" returned Curry, at the same time rudely pinching Robinson's ear. "You will be a better man than I take you to be, if you ever wrestle with me again. I have not forgotten you."

The dragoon now rejoined his comrades.

"Peppercorn," cried Habershaw, "d——n the prisoners, let them fast to-night. The lads want a song. Come, the liquor's getting low, we want noise, we want uproar, lad! Sing, bully, sing!"

"Anything to get rid of the night, noble captain. What shall I give you?"

"The old catch, master Orderly. The Jolly Bottle, the Jolly Bottle," cried Habershaw, pronouncing this word according to ancient usage, with the accent on the last syllable, as if spelt "bottel;" "give us the Jolly Bottle, we all know the chorus of that song. And besides it's the best in your pack."

"Well, listen, my wet fellows!" said Peppercorn, "and pipe lustily in the chorus."

Here the orderly sang, to a familiar old English tune, the

following song, which was perhaps a common camp ditty of the period.

"You may talk as you please of your candle and book,
And prate about virtue, with sanctified look;
Neither priest, book, nor candle, can help you so well
To make friends with the world as the Jolly Bottle."

"Chorus, my lads; out with it!" shouted the singer; and the whole crew set up a hideous yell as they joined him.

"Sing heave and ho, and trombelow,
The Jolly Bottle is the best I trow.

"Then take the bottle, it is well stitched of leather,
And better than doublet keeps out the wind and weather:
Let the bottom look up to the broad arch of blue,
And then catch the drippings, as good fellows do.
With heave and ho, and trombelow,
'Tis sinful to waste good liquor, you know.

"The soldier, he carries his knapsack and gun,
And swears at the weight as he tramps through the sun:
But, devil a loon, did I ever hear tell,
Who swore at the weight of the Jolly Bottle.
So heave and ho, and trombelow,
The Jolly Bottle is a feather, I trow."

Here the song was interrupted by the return of the two files who had been sent to bring in the bodies of the dead. They had found the missing horse, and now led him into the circle laden with the corpses of Bell and Waters. The troopers halted immediately behind the ring of the revellers, and in such a position as to front Peppercorn and the captain, who were thus afforded a full view of the bodies by the blaze of the fire.

"Easy," almost whispered Habershaw, now half intoxicated, to the two troopers, as he lifted his hands and motioned to them to halt; "put them down gently on the ground. Go on, Peppercorn; let the dead help themselves: finish the song! That chorus again, my boys!" And here the last chorus was repeated in the highest key of merriment.

Peppercorn cast an eye at the bodies which, during the interval, had been thrown on the earth, and while the men who had just returned were helping themselves to the drink, he proceeded, in an unaltered voice, with the song.

"When drinkers are dry, and liquor is low,
A fray that takes off a good fellow or so,
Why, what does it do, but help us to bear
The loss of a comrade, in drinking his share?
Then heave and ho, and trombelow,
A fray and a feast are brothers, you know.

"The philosophers say it's a well-settled fact,
That a vessel will leak whose bottom is cracked;
And a belly that's drilled with a bullet, I think,
Is a very bad belly to stow away drink.
So heave and ho, and trombelow,
The dead will be dry to-night, I trow."

"There they are, captain," said one of the returning troopers, after the song, to which he and his companions had stood listening with delighted countenances, was brought to an end, "there they are. We found Dick Waters lying in the road, and when we first came to him he gave a sort of groan, but we didn't lift him until we came back from hunting Roger Bell; by that time the fellow was as dead as a pickled herring. Where do you think we found Clapper Claw? Why, half a mile, almost, down the stream. He was washed along and got jammed up betwixt the roots of a sycamore. We had a long wade after him, and trouble enough to get him — more, I'm thinking, than a dead man is worth. So, give us some more rum; this is ugly work to be done in the dark."

"Scratch a hole for them, lads, under the bushes," said Habershaw: "put a sod blanket over them before morning. That's the fortune of war, as Peppercorn calls it. How are the wounded men getting along?"

"Oh, bravely, captain," replied Shad Green, or, according to his nick-name, Red Mug: "this here physic is a main thing for a scratch."

"Bravely!" echoed Screech Owl, or Tom Dubbs, the same who had been reported by the dragoon as "kicked by the blacksmith;" "we are plastering up sores here with the jolly bottle: —

"Sing heave and ho, and trombelow,
The Jolly Bottle is a feather, I trow."

"What's a cracked crown, so as it holds a man's brains?" continued the the drunken carouser, whilst a laugh deformed his stupid physiognomy.

"How are we off for provisions, quarter-master?" inquired the captain of one of the gang.

"Eaten out of skin, from nose to tail," replied Black Jack.

"Then the squad must forage to-night," continued Habershaw. "We must take a buck, my sweet ones; there are plenty along the river. Get your rifles and prepare lights, and, to keep out of the way of our horses, don't stop short of a mile. Be about it, lads. Black Jack, this is your business."

"True, Captain," replied the person addressed: "I shall have all things ready directly."

It was near midnight when Black Jack, having prepared some faggots of pitch-pine, and selected three or four of the best marksmen, left the bivouac to look for deer. Habershaw himself, though lazy and inordinately impressed with a sense of his own dignity, and now confused with liquor, could not resist the attraction of this sport. He accordingly, not long after the others had departed, took a rifle, and, attended by his bull-dog, whom he never parted from on any occasion, slowly followed in the direction chosen by the hunters.

Those in advance had scarcely walked along the margin of the river a mile before they lighted their faggots, and began to beat the neighboring thickets; and their search was not protracted many minutes when the light of their torches was thrown full upon the eyes of a buck. A shot from one of the marksmen told with unerring precision in the forehead of the animal.

The report and the light brought the corpulent captain into the neighborhood. He had almost walked himself out of breath; and, as he did not very well preserve his perpendicularity, or a straight line of march, he had several times been tripped up by the roots of trees, or by rocks and briers in his path. Exhausted, at length, and puzzled by the stupefaction of his own brain, as well as by the surrounding darkness, he sat down at the foot of a tree, determined to wait the return of the hunting party. His faithful and congenial "Beauty," not less pursy and shot-winded than himself, and not more savage or surly in disposition, now couched upon his haunches immediately between his master's legs; and here this pair of beastly friends remained, silent and mutually soothed by their own companionship. During this interval the person who bore the fire, followed by one of the marksmen, crept slowly onward to the vicinity of the spot where the captain had seated himself. The lapse of time had proved too much for Habershaw's vigilance, and he had, at length, with his head resting against the trunk of the tree, fallen into a drunken slumber. The short crack of a rifle at hand, and the yell of his dog awakened him. He started upon his feet with sudden surprise, and stepping one pace forward, stumbled and fell over the dead body of his favorite Beauty, who lay beneath him weltering in blood. The shot was followed by a rush of the hunter up to the spot: it was Gideon Blake.

"Buck or doe, it is my shot!" cried Gideon, as he halted immediately beside Habershaw.

"May all the devils blast you, Gideon Blake!" thundered out the incensed captain. "You have sought my life, you murdering wolf, and your bullet has killed Beauty."

"I shot at the eyes of what I thought a deer," returned Blake. "You were a fool, Hugh Habershaw, to bring a dog into such a place."

"My poor dog! my brave dog! Beauty was worth ten thousand such bastard villains as you! And to have him killed! May the devil feast upon your soul this night, Gideon Blake! Go! and account for your wickedness. Take that, snake! tiger! black-hearted whig and rebel! and be thankful that you didn't come to your end by the help of hemp!" and in this gust of passion he struck his knife into the bosom of the trooper, who groaned, staggered, and fell.

At this moment the person bearing the fire, hearing the groan of his comrade, rushed up to the spot and seized Habershaw's arm, just as the monster was raising it over the fallen man to repeat the blow.

"Damn him! see what he has done!" exclaimed the captain, as he lifted up the dead body of the dog so as to show in the light the wound inflicted by the ball between the eyes; "this poor, faithful, dumb beast was worth a hundred such hell-hounds as he!"

"I am murdered," said the wounded man; "I am murdered in cold blood."

The noise at this place brought together the rest of the hunters, who were now returning with the buck thrown across a horse that had been led by one of the party. Blake's wound was examined by them, and some linen applied to staunch the blood. The man had fainted, but it was not ascertained whether the stab was mortal. Habershaw stood sullenly looking on during the examination, and, finding that life had not instantly fled, he coolly wiped his knife and restored it to his girdle.

"The fellow has no idea of dying," he said wth a visible concern, "and has got no more than he deserves. He will live to be hung yet. Take him to quarters."

"Make a hurdle for him," said one of the bystanders, and, accordingly, two men cut a few branches from the neighboring wood, and twisting them together, soon constructed a litter upon which they were able to bear the body of the wounded hunter to the rendezvous. The others, scarcely uttering a word as they marched along, followed slowly with the buck, and in half an hour the troop was once more assembled under the chestnut.

For a time there was a sullen and discontented silence amongst the whole crew, that was only broken by the groans of the wounded trooper. Occasionally there was a slight outburst of sedition from several of the troop, as a sharper scream, indicating some sudden increase of pain, from Gideon Blake, assailed their ears. Then there were low and muttered curses pronounced by Habershaw, in a tone that showed his apprehension of some vengeance against himself; and these imprecations were mingled with hints of the disloyalty of the trooper, and charges of a pretended purpose to betray his fellow-soldiers, evidently insinuated by the captain to excuse his act of violence. Then he approached the sick man and felt his pulse, and examined his wound, and pronounced the hurt to be trifling. "It will do him good," he said, with affected unconcern, "and teach him to be more true to his comrades hereafter." But still the fate of the man was manifestly doubtful, and the rising exasperation of the troop became every instant more open. Alarmed and faint-hearted at these symptoms of discontent, Habershaw at last called the men into a circle and made them a speech, in which he expressed his sorrow for the act he had committed, endeavored to excuse himself by the plea of passion at the loss of his dog, and, finally, perceiving that these excuses did not satisfy his hearers, acknowledged his drunken condition and his unconsciousness of the deed he had done until the horrible consequences of it were before his eyes. Here Peppercorn interposed in his favor, alleging that he had examined the wound, and that, in his opinion, the trooper's life was not in danger.

"And as the captain is sorry for it, lads," he concluded, "why, what is to be done but let the thing drop? So, if there's another canteen in the squad, we will wet our whistles, boys, and go to sleep."

This appeal was effectual, and was followed by a hearty cheer.

So, draining the dregs of the last flask, this debauched company retired to rest — Habershaw sneaking away from them with a heart loaded with malice and revenge.

A few men were employed, for a short time, in burying the bodies of the troopers who were killed in the fray; and, excepting the guard, who busied themselves in skinning the buck and broiling some choice slices before the fire, and in watching the prisoners, or attending upon their sick comrade, all were sunk into silence if not repose.

CHAPTER XVIII

THE TROOPERS MOVE WITH THEIR PRISONERS

"Oft he that doth abide,
Is cause of his own paine,
But he that flieth in good tide,
Perhaps may fight again."

OLD PROVERB.

IT was with the most earnest solicitude that Butler and his companion watched the course of events, and became acquainted with the character of the ruffians into whose hands they had fallen. The presence of James Curry in this gang excited a painful consciousness in the mind of the soldier, that he had powerful and secret enemies at work against him, but who they were was an impenetrable mystery. Then the lawless habits of the people who had possession of him, gave rise to the most anxious distrust as to his future fate: he might be murdered in a fit of passion, or tortured with harsh treatment to gratify some concealed malice. His position in the army was, it seemed, known too; and, for aught that he could tell, his mission might be no secret to his captors. Robinson's sagacity entered fully into these misgivings. He had narrowly observed the conduct of the party who had made them prisoners, and with that acute insight which was concealed under a rude and uneducated interior, but which was strongly marked in his actions, he had already determined upon the course which the safety of Butler required him to pursue. According to his view of their present difficulties it was absolutely necessary that he should effect his escape, at whatever personal hazard. Butler, he rightly conjectured, was the principal object of the late ambuscade; that, for some unknown purpose, the possession of this officer became important to those who had procured the attack upon him, and that James Curry had merely hired this gang of desperadoes to secure the prize. Under these circumstances, he concluded that the Major would be so strictly guarded as to forbid all hope of escape, and that any attempt by him to effect it would only be punished by certain death. But, in regard to himself, his calculation was different. "First," said he, "I can master any three of this beggarly crew in an open field and fair fight; and, secondly, when it comes to the chances of a pell-mell, they will not think me of so much account as to risk their necks by a long chase; their whole eyes would ondoubtedly be directed to the Major." The sergeant, therefore, determined to make the attempt, and, in the event of his success, to repair to Sumpter, who he knew frequented some of the fastnesses in this region; or, in the alternative, to rally such friends from the neighboring country as were not yet overawed by the Tory dominion, and bring them speedily to the rescue of Butler. Full of these thoughts, he took occasion during the night, whilst the guard were busy cooking their venison, and whilst they thought him and his comrade wrapt in sleep, to whisper to Butler the resolution he had adopted.

"I will take the first chance to-morrow to make a dash upon these ragamuffins," he said; "and I shall count it hard if I don't get out of their claws. Then, rely upon me, I shall keep near you in spite of these devils. So be prepared, if I once get away, to see me like a witch that travels on a broomstick or creeps through a keyhole. But whisht! the drunken vagabonds mustn't hear us talking."

Butler, after due consideration of the sergeant's plan, thought it, however perilous, the only chance they had of extricating themselves from the dangers with which they were beset, and promised the most ready co-operation; determining also, to let no opportunity slip which might be improved to his own deliverance. "Your good arm and brave heart, Galbraith, never stood you in more urgent stead than they may do to-morrow," was his concluding remark.

When morning broke the light of day fell upon a strange and disordered scene. The drunken and coarse wretches of the night before, now lessened in number and strength by common broil and private quarrel, lay stretched on their beds of leaves. Their motley and ill-assorted weapons lay around in disarray; drinking cups and empty flasks were scattered over the trodden grass, the skin and horns of the buck, and disjointed fragments of raw flesh were seen confusedly cast about beneath the tree, and a conspicuous object in the scene were the clots of blood and gore, both of men and beast, that disfigured the soil. Two new-made graves, or rather mounds, hastily scratched together and imperfectly concealing the limbs of the dead, prominently placed but a few feet from the ring of last night's revelry, told of the disasters of the fight at the ford. The brushwood fire had burned down into a heap of smouldering ashes, and the pale and sickly features of the wounded trooper were to be discerned upon a pallet of leaves, hard by the heap of embers, surrounded by the remnants of bones and roasted meat that had been flung carelessly aside. In a spot of more apparent comfort, sheltered by an overhanging canopy of vines and alder, lay Butler stretched upon his cloak, and, close beside him, the stout frame of Horse Shoe Robinson. In the midst of all these marks of recent riot and carousal, sat two swarthy figures, haggard and wan from night-watching, armed at every point, and keeping strict guard over the prisoners.

The occasional snort and pawing of horses in the neighboring wood showed that these animals were alert at the earliest dawn; whilst among the first who seemed aware of the approach of day, was seen rising from the earth, where it had been flung in stupid torpor for some hours, the bloated and unsightly person of Hugh Habershaw, now much the worse for fatigue and revelry of the preceding night. A savage and surly expression was seated on his brow, and his voice broke forth more than ordinarily harsh and dissonant, as he ordered the troop to rouse and prepare for their march.

The summons was tardily obeyed; and while the yawning members of the squad were lazily moving to their several duties and shaking off the fumes of their late debauch, the captain was observed bending over the prostrate form of Gideon Blake, and directing a few anxious inquiries into his condition. The wounded man was free from pain, but his limbs were stiff, and the region of the stab sore and sensitive to the least touch. The indications, however, were such as to show that his wound was not likely to prove mortal. By the order of Habershaw, a better litter was constructed, and the troopers were directed to bear him, by turns, as far as Christie's, where he was to be left to the nursing of the family. It was a full hour before the horses were saddled, the scattered furniture collected, and the preparations for the march completed. When these were accomplished the prisoners were provided with the two sorriest horses of the troop, and they now set forward at a slow pace, under the escort of four men commanded by James Curry. The two troopers who bore the sick man followed on foot; Habershaw with the remainder, one of whom had appropriated Captain Peter, whilst he led the horses of the dismounted men, brought up the rear.

On the journey there was but little spoken by any member of

the party; the boisterous and rude nature of the men who composed the troop seemed to have been subdued by sleep into a temper of churlish indifference or stolid apathy. Peppercorn, or James Curry, as the reader now recognises him, strictly preserved his guard over the prisoners, manifesting a severity of manner altogether different from the tone of careless revelry which characterized his demeanor on the preceding night. It never relaxed from an official and sullen reserve. A moody frown sat upon his brow, and his communication with the prisoners was confined to short and peremptory commands; whilst, at the same time, he forbade the slightest intercourse with them on the part of any of the guard. During the short progress to Christie's he frequently rode apart with Habershaw; and the conversation which then occupied these two was maintained in a low tone, and with a serious air that denoted some grave matter of deliberation.

It was more than an hour after sunrise when the cavalcade reached the point of their present destination. There were signs of an anxious purpose in the silence of the journey, broken as it was only by low mutterings amongst the men, above which sometimes arose an expression of impatience and discontent, as the subject of their whispered discussions appeared to excite some angry objection from several of the party; and this mystery was not less conspicuous in the formal order of the halt, and in the pause that followed upon their arrival at the habitation.

The house, in front of which they were drawn up, was, according to the prevailing fashion of the time, a one-storied dwelling covering an ample space of ground, built partly of boards and partly of logs, with a long piazza before it, terminating in small rooms, made by inclosing the sides for a few feet at either extremity. Being situated some twenty paces aside from the road, the intervening area was bounded by a fence through which a gate afforded admission. A horse-rack, with a few feeding troughs, was erected near this gate; and a draw-well, in the same vicinity, furnished a ready supply of water. With the exception of a cleared field around the dwelling, the landscape was shaded by the natural forest.

A consultation of some minutes' duration was held between Habershaw and Curry, when the order to dismount was given, accompanied with an intimation of a design to tarry at this place for an hour or two; but the men, at the same time, were directed to leave their saddles upon their horses. One or two were detailed to look after the refreshment of the cattle, whilst the remainder took possession of the principal room. The first demands of the troop were for drink, and this being indulged, the brute feeling of conviviality which in gross natures depends altogether upon sensual excitement, began once more to break down the barriers of discipline, and to mount into clamor.

The scenes of the morning had made a disagreeable impression upon the feelings of Butler and his comrade. The changed tone and the ruffian manners of the band, the pause, and the doubts which seemed to agitate them, boded mischief. The two prisoners, however, almost instinctively adopted the course of conduct which their circumstances required. They concealed all apprehension of harm, and patiently awaited the end. Horse Shoe even took advantage of the rising mirth of the company when drink began to exhilarate them, and affected an easy tone of companionship which was calculated to throw them off their guard. He circulated freely amongst the men, and by private conference with some of the individuals around him, who, attracted by his air of confiding gaiety, seemed inclined to favor his approaches of familiarity, he soon discovered that the gang was divided in sentiment in regard to some important subject touching the proposed treatment of himself and his friend. A party, at least, he was thus made aware, were disposed to take his side in the secret disputes which had been in agitation. He was determined to profit by this dissension, and accordingly applied himself still more assiduously to cultivate the favorable sentiment he found in existence.

Whilst breakfast was in preparation, and Habershaw and Curry were occupied with the wounded man in an adjoining apartment, the sergeant, playing the part of a boon companion, laughed with the rioters, and, uninvited, made himself free of their cups.

"I should like to know," he said to one of the troopers, "why you are giving yourselves all this trouble about a couple of simple travellers that happened to be jogging along the road? If you wanted to make a pitched battle you ought to have sent us word; but if it was only upon a drinking bout you had set your hearts, there was no occasion to be breaking heads for the honor of getting a good fellow in your company, when he would have come of his own accord at the first axing. There was no use in making such a mighty secret about it; for, as we were travelling the same road with you, you had only to show a man the civility of saying you wanted our escort, and you should have had it at a word. Here's to our better acquaintance, friend!"

"You mightn't be so jolly, Horse Shoe Robinson," said Shad

Green — or, according to his nickname, Red Mug, in a whisper; "if some of them that took the trouble to find you, should have their own way. It's a d——d tight pull whether you are to be kept as a prisoner of war, or shoved under ground this morning without tuck of drum. That for your private ear."

"I was born in old Carolina myself," replied Horse Shoe, aside to the speaker; "and I don't believe there is many men to be found in it who would stand by and see the rules and regulations of honorable war blackened and trod down into the dust by any cowardly trick of murder. If it comes to that, many as there are against two, our lives will not go at a cheap price."

"Whisht!" returned the other, "with my allowance, for one, it shan't be. A prisoner's a prisoner, I say; and damnation to the man that would make him out worse."

"They say you are a merry devil, old Horse Shoe," exclaimed he who was called Bow Legs, who now stepped up and slapped the sergeant on the back. "So take a swig, man; fair play is a jewel! — that's my doctrine. Fight when you fight, and drink when you drink — and that's the sign to know a man by."

"There is some good things," said the sergeant, "in this world that's good and some that's bad. But I have always found that good and bad is so mixed up and jumbled together, that you don't often get much of one without a little of the other. A sodger's a sodger, no matter what side he is on; and they are the naturalest people in the world for fellow-feeling. One day a man is up, and then the laugh's on his side; next day he is down, and then the laugh's against him. So, as a sodger has more of these ups and downs than other folks, there's the reason his heart is tenderer towards a comrade than other people's. Here's your health, sir. This is a wicked world, and twisted, in a measure, upside down; and it is well known that evil communications corrupts good manners; but sodgers were made to set the world right again, on its legs, and to presarve good breeding and Christian charity. So there's a sarmon for you, you tinkers!"

"Well done, mister preacher!" vociferated a prominent reveller. "If you will desert and enlist with us you shall be the chaplain of the troop. We want a good swearing, drinking, and tearing blade who can hold a discourse over his liquor, and fence with the devil at long words. You're the very man for it! Huzza for the blacksmith!"

"Huzza for the blacksmith!" shouted several others in the apartment.

Butler, during this scene, had stretched himself out at full length upon a bench, to gain some rest in his present exhausted and uncomfortable condition, and was now partaking of the refreshment of a bowl of milk and some coarse bread, which one of the troopers had brought in.

" What's all this laughing and uproar about? " said Habershaw, entering the room with Curry, just at the moment of the acclamation in favor of the sergeant. " Is this a time for your cursed wide throats to be braying like asses! We have business to do. And you, sir," said he, turning to Butler, " you must be taking up the room of a half dozen men on a bench with your lazy carcase! Up, sir; I allow no lolling and lying about to rascally whigs and rebels. You have cost me the death of a dog that is worth all your filthy whig kindred; and you have made away with two of the best men that ever stept in shoe leather. Sit up, sir, and thank your luck that you haven't your arms pinioned behind you, like a horse thief."

" Insolent coward," said Butler, springing upon his feet; " hired ruffian! you shall in due time be made to pay for the outrage you have inflicted upon me."

" Tie him up! " cried Habershaw; " tie him up! And now I call you all to bear witness that he has brought the sentence upon himself; it shall be done without waiting another moment. Harry Gage, I give the matter over to you. Draw out four men, take them into the yard, and dispatch the prisoners off-hand! shoot the traitors on the spot, before we eat our breakfasts! I was a fool that I didn't settle this at daylight this morning — the rascally filth of the earth! Have no heart about it, men; but make sure work by a short distance. This is no time for whining. When have the Whigs shown mercy to us! "

" It shall be four against four, then! " cried out Shadrach Green, seconded by Andrew Clopper; " and the first shot that is fired shall be into the bowels of Hugh Habershaw! Stand by me, boys! "

In a moment the parties were divided, and had snatched up their weapons, and then stood looking angrily at each other as if daring each to commence the threatened affray.

" Why, how now, devil's imps! " shouted Habershaw. " Have you come to a mutiny? Have you joined the rebels? James Curry, look at this! By the bloody laws of war, I will report every rascal who dares to lift his hand against me! "

" The thing is past talking about," said the first speaker, coolly.

"Hugh Habershaw, neither you nor James Curry shall command the peace if you dare to offer harm to the prisoners. Now, bully, report that as my saying. They are men fairly taken in war, and shall suffer no evil past what the law justifies. Give them up to the officer of the nearest post — that's what we ask — carry them to Innis's camp if you choose; but whilst they are in our keeping there shall be no blood spilled without mixing some of your own with it, Hugh Habershaw."

"Arrest the mutineers!" cried Habershaw, trembling with rage. "Who are my friends in this room? Let them stand by me, and then — blast me if I don't force obedience to my orders!"

"You got off by the skin of your teeth last night," said Green, "when you tried to take the life of Gideon Blake. For that you deserved a bullet through your skull. Take care that you don't get your reckoning this morning, captain and all as you are."

"What in the devil would you have?" inquired Habershaw, stricken into a more cautious tone of speech by the decided bearing of the man opposed to him.

"The safety of the prisoners until they are delivered to the commander of a regular post; we have resolved upon that!" was the reply.

"Curry!" said Habershaw, turning in some perplexity to the dragoon as if for advice.

"Softly, Captain; we had better have a parley here," said Curry, who then added in a whisper: "There's been some damned bobbery kicked up here by the blacksmith. This comes of giving that fellow the privilege of talking."

"A word, men," interposed Horse Shoe, who during this interval had planted himself near Butler, and with him stood ready to act as the emergency might require. "Let me say a word. This James Curry is my man. Give me a broadsword and a pair of pistols, and I will pledge the hand and word of a sodger, upon condition that I am allowed five minutes' parole, to have a pass, here in the yard, with him — it shall be in sight of the whole squad — I pledge the word of a sodger to deliver myself back again to the guard, dead or alive, without offering to take any chance to make off in the meantime. Come, James Curry, your word to the back of that, and then buckle on your sword, man. I heard your whisper."

"Soldiers," said Curry, stepping into the circle which the party had now formed around the room, "let me put in a word as a peace-maker. Captain Habershaw won't be unreasonable. I will vouch for him that he will fulfil your wish regarding the conveying of the prisoners to a regular post. Come, come, let us have no brawling! For shame! put down your guns. There may be reason in what you ask, although it isn't so much against the fashion of the times to shoot a Whig either. But anything for the sake of quiet amongst good fellows. Be considerate, noble captain, and do as the babies wish. As for Horse Shoe's brag — he is an old soldier, and so am I; that's enough. We are not so green as to put a broadsword and a brace of pistols into the hands of a bullying prisoner. No, no, Horse Shoe! try another trick, old boy! Ha, ha, lads! you are a set of fine dashing chaps, and this is only one of your madcap bits of spunk that boils up with your liquor. Take another cup on it, my merry fellows, and all will be as pleasant as the music of a fife. Come, valiant Captain of the Tiger, join us. And as for the prisoners — why let them come in for snacks with us. So there's an end of the business. All is as mild as new milk again."

"Well, well, get your breakfasts," said Habershaw gruffly. "Blast you! I have spoiled you by good treatment, you ungrateful, carnivorous dogs! But, as Peppercorn says, there's an end of it! So go to your feeding, and when that's done we will push for Blackstock's."

The morning meal was soon despatched, and the party reassembled in the room where the late disturbance had taken place. The good-nature of Robinson continued to gain upon those who had first taken up his cause, and even brought him into a more lenient consideration with the others. Amongst the former I have already noted Andrew Clopper, a rough and insubordinate member of the gang, who, vexed by some old grudge against the fat captain, had efficiently sustained Green in the late act of mutiny, and who now, struck with Horse Shoe's bold demeanor towards Curry, began to evince manifest signs of a growing regard for the worthy sergeant. With this man Horse Shoe contrived to hold a short and secret interview that resulted in the quiet transfer of a piece of gold into the freebooter's hand, which was received with a significant nod of assent to whatever proposition accompanied it. When the order of "boot and saddle" was given by Habershaw, the several members of the troop repaired to their horses, where a short time was spent in making ready for the march; after which the whole squad returned to the porch and occupied the few moments of delay in that loud and boisterous carousal which is apt to mark the conduct of such an ill-organized body in the interval immediately preceding the commencement of a day's ride. This was a moment of intense interest to the sergeant, who kept his eyes steadily fixed upon the movements of Clopper, as that individual lingered behind his comrades in the equipment of his horse. This solicitude did not, however, arrest his seeming mirth, as he joined in the rude jests of the company and added some sallies of his own.

"Give me that cup," he said at length, to one of the men, as he pointed to a gourd on a table; "before we start I have a notion to try the strength of a little cold water, just by way of physic, after all the liquor we have been drinking," and, having got the implement in his hand, he walked deliberately to the draw-well, where he dipped up a draught from the bucket that stood on its brink. As he put the water to his lips and turned his back upon the company, he was enabled to take a survey of the horses that were attached to the rack near him: then, suddenly throwing the gourd from him, he sprang towards his own trusty steed, leaped into his saddle at one bound, and sped, like an arrow from a bow, upon the highway. This exploit was so promptly achieved that no one was aware of the sergeant's purpose until he was some twenty paces upon his journey. As soon as the alarm of his flight was spread, some three or four rifles were fired after him in rapid succession, during which he was seen ducking his head and moving it from side to side with a view to baffle the aim of the marksmen. The confusion of the moment in which the volley was given rendered it ineffectual, and the sergeant was already past the first danger of his escape.

"To horse and follow!" resounded from all sides.

"Look to the other prisoner!" roared out Habershaw; "if he raises his head blow out his brains! Follow, boys, follow!"

"Two or three of you come with me," cried Curry, and a couple of files hastened with the dragoon to their horses. Upon arriving at the rack it was discovered that the bridles of the greater part of the troop were tied in hard knots in such a manner as to connect each two or three horses together.

A short delay took place whilst the horsemen were disentangling their reins, and Curry, being the first to extricate his steed, mounted and set off in rapid pursuit. He was immediately followed by two others.

At the end of half an hour the two privates returned and reported that they had been unable to obtain a view of the sergeant or even of Curry. Shortly afterwards the dragoon himself was descried retracing his steps at a moderate trot towards the house. His plight told a tale upon him of discomfiture. One side of his face was bleeding with a recent bruise, his dress disarranged and his back covered with dust. The side of his horse also bore the same taint of the soil.

He rode up to Habershaw — who was already upon the road at the head of the remaining members of the squad, having Butler in charge — and informed him that he had pursued the sergeant at full speed until he came in sight of him, when the fugitive had slackened his gait as if on purpose to allow himself to be overtaken.

"But, the devil grip the fellow!" he added, "he has a broadside like a man-of-war! In my hurry I left my sword behind me, and, when I came up with him, I laid my hand upon his bridle; but, by some sudden sleight which he has taught his horse, he contrived, somehow or other, to upset me — horse and all — down a bank on the road-side. And, when I lay on the ground sprawling, do you think the jolly runagate didn't rein up and give me a broad laugh, and ask me if he could be of any *sarvice* to me? He then bade me good bye, saying he had an engagement that prevented him from favoring me any longer with his company. Gad! it was so civilly done that all I could say was, luck go with you, Mr. Horse Shoe; and, since we are to part company so soon, may the devil pad your saddle for you! I'll do him the justice to say that he's a better horseman than I took him for. I can hardly begrudge a man his liberty who can win it as cleverly as he has done."

"Well, there's no more to be said about it," remarked Habershaw. "He is only game for another day. He is like a bear's cub; which is as much as to signify that he has a hard time before him. He would have only given us trouble; so let him go. Now, boys, away for Blackstock's; I will engage I keep the fox that's left safely enough."

With these words the troop proceeded upon their march.

CHAPTER XIX

Horse Shoe's successful escape from the hands of the Tories, it will be conjectured, had been aided by Clopper. The sergeant had sufficiently assured himself of the present safety of Butler, from the spirit with which a strong party of Habershaw's followers had resisted the bloody purpose of their leader before breakfast; and he had also, by the timely reward secretly conveyed to Clopper, received a pledge from that individual that the same protection should still be accorded to the major, in the event of his own extrication from the gang by the perilous exploit which he then meditated. It is no doubt apparent to the reader, that the favor which saved the lives of the prisoners was won from the captors by the address of Robinson, and that whatever good will was kindled up amongst them, was appropriated principally to the sergeant, Butler having elicited but little consideration from the band, beyond that interest which the roughest men are apt to take in the fortunes of a young and enterprising soldier. Neither the major's manners nor temper were adapted to conciliate any special regard from such natures.

The escape of the sergeant, therefore, although it added nothing to the peril's of Butler's situation, still operated in some degree to his present inconvenience. It caused him to be more rigorously guarded than before, and consequently to be more restricted in his personal comfort. He was hurried forward at a rough and uneasy pace; and both from Habershaw and Curry, and those more immediately of their party, he experienced a surly indifference to the pain that this occasioned him. They seemed to have no regard either to his wants or feelings, and in the passing remarks that fell from them he could gather harsh surmises as to the manner in which he was now likely to be disposed of.

"It is their own fault," said one of them to his companion, as Butler overheard the conversation; "if every prisoner is strung up and shot nowadays. He makes no more of hanging our people than so many wolves; and there was Captain Huck—will any man say that Sumpter hadn't him murdered in cold blood?"

"Yes," added the other, "let a Tory be caught over yonder

amongst the Iredell Whigs, on t'other side of the line, or in Tryon, or down here at the Waxhaws, why, a grey fox in a barn yard with forty dogs would have as good a chance for his life. So, for my share, I am glad to see our folks break up that blasted breed, root and branch."

"Innis has got as keen a nose for a Whig as a blood-hound," said the first speaker, "and won't stop long to consider what's right to be done, if he gets this chap in his clutches; so it is of no great account that we didn't make short work of it this morning."

Such remarks produced a gloomy effect upon Butler's mind. He had witnessed enough, in the scenes of the morning, to convince him that Habershaw had been employed to waylay him and take his life, and that the latter purpose had only failed by the lucky conjuncture of circumstances which led to the mutiny. He was aware, too, that Curry was the prime conductor of the scheme, and drove matters, by a secret influence, as far as he could towards its accomplishment, whilst with a professional hardihood and most hypocritical bearing he affected to be indifferent to the issue. This fellow's malice was the more venomous from his address, and the gay, swaggering, remorseless levity with which he could mask the most atrocious designs: nothing could baffle his equanimity; and he seemed to be provided, at all times, with a present expedient to meet the emergency of his condition.

The most perplexing feature in this man's present position was his recent connexion with Tyrrel; a fact that recurred to Butler with many alarming doubts. All the other circumstances accompanying Butler's condition, at this moment, were subjects of distressful uncertainty. Ignorant of the place to which he was to be taken, into whose hands he was to be delivered, how he was to be disposed of, he could only anticipate the worst. It was obvious that his journey was an expected one, and that the gang who held him were employed by persons in authority, set on, no doubt, by the agency of Tyrrel: but where was he — and who was he? — and what influence could he bring to bear against his, Butler's life, now that he had failed in his bloody purpose of lying in wait; and that it was resolved by these ruffians, who had in part only obeyed his behests, to deliver their prisoner up to the regular authorities of the British army? The mention of the name of Innis by one of the troopers was not calculated to allay his inquietude. This person he knew to have been an active confederate and eager adviser of the new court, lately established at Charleston, to promote the confiscation of the estates of the inhabitants of Carolina disaffected to the royal cause. He was, besides, a zealous Tory partisan, and, having lately joined the army, was now in command of a detachment of loyalists on the Ennoree.

Then, again, there was abundant cause of anxiety to the unfortunate officer in the question whether Robinson could be kept acquainted with his condition, or even of the place to which he might be removed — and if acquainted with these particulars, whether, in the disturbed state of the country, he could render any service. These thoughts all contributed to sink his spirits.

Notwithstanding the usual assumed levity of Curry, he had now become resentful towards Butler, and did not give himself the trouble to conceal it. His manner was quick and unaccommodating, showing his vexation at his own want of sagacity, inferred by the successful flight of Robinson. Expressions occasionally escaped him that indicated a self-reproof on this subject, though they were partially disguised by an affected undervaluing of the importance of having such a prisoner, so long as he retained the custody of the principal object of the enterprise. But the consciousness of being again baffled by a man who had once before obtained the mastery over him, roused his pride into the exhibition of a peevish and vindictive demeanor. In this temper he seconded the brutal disposition of Habershaw, and abandoned the captive officer to the coarse insults of those who exercised control over him. There was some mitigation to this annoyance, in the reserved and partial spirit in which the insurgent party of the squad manifested some slight signs of good will towards him. An instance of this spirit was afforded in a passing hint conveyed by Clopper, on one occasion when the troop had halted to water their horses. "Whatever is to come of it, after we give you up to other hands," he said, apart to Butler, "we will stick to the ground we have taken, that no harm shall be done to you in our keeping."

The day was intensely hot, and the road, over which the party travelled, rugged and fatiguing; it was, therefore, near one o'clock when they came in sight of the Tiger, a rough, bold, impetuous stream that rushed over an almost unbroken bed of rocks. On the opposite bank was Blackstocks, a rude hamlet of some two or three houses, scattered over a rugged hill-side — a place subsequently rendered famous by the gallant repulse of Tarleton by Sumpter. The troop struck into a narrow ford, and, with some scrambling amongst the rocks, succeeded in crossing the stream; they then galloped rapidly up the hill, towards a farm-house which seemed to be the principal place of resort for the people of the neighborhood. The approach of the party of cavalry drew to the door a bevy of women, children, and negroes, who stood idly gaping at the spectacle; and, in addition to these, a detachment of militia, consisting of between twenty and thirty men, were seen to turn out and form a line in front of the house. Habershaw, with an air of magnified importance, halted opposite this detachment, gave a few prompt orders to Curry in regard to the disposition of the troop, and in an authoritative tone of command, ordered the officer of the militia to detail a guard for the safe keeping of a prisoner of state. The personage addressed — a tall, ungainly, and awkward subaltern — signified his acquiescence with a bow, and immediately took possession of Butler by seizing the rein of his horse and leading him to one side, where two men, armed with rifles, placed themselves at either stirrup. Habershaw now directed his men to alight, accompanying the order with a caution that the prisoner was not to be allowed to enter the house. "The d——d rascal," he added, "shall not play the trick of his rebel associate; no more privilege of going into bar-rooms, and lounging about doors! See the man stowed away in the barn, and tell the sentinels never to take their eyes off of him — do you hear, lieutenant?"

"You may depend upon my look-out," replied the lieutenant, with a flourish of a hacked and rusty sword. "Men, march your prison straight to the barn. Have a relief, Corporal, every two hours, and towards night, set four on the watch at a time."

"Look to it, Lieutenant!" shouted Habershaw. "No words, sir: do your duty!"

And having thus given vent to his own high opinion of himself, the bulky captain withdrew into the house.

Butler was now marched into a large log barn, in one corner of which an armful of fodder, or dried blades of Indian corn, were shaken out for his bed; and this, he was told, was to be his prison until other orders awaited him. The guard, consisting of two sentinels, were stationed on the inner side of the door, having the prisoner immediately under their eye; and, this disposition being completed, the officer commanding the detachment retired to mingle with the troopers in the farm-house.

Half an hour had scarcely elapsed after the arrival of the troopers at Blackstocks before James Curry had refreshed himself with a hasty meal, and had his horse brought to the door. He seemed bound upon some urgent mission.

"Captain St. Jermyn, you say, left this at sunrise this morning?" said the dragoon, addressing the lieutenants of the militia.

"He did. He was here all day yesterday, and thought he should hear from you last night."

"What route did he take?"

"To Turnbull, at Ninety-Six."

"Is Turnbull there now, think you?"

"He is," replied the lieutenant. "They say orders have gone up from Cornwallis to the post for four light companies, and it is expected that Captain Campbell is now on his way with them towards Camden; neither Turnbull nor Cruger would leave the post."

"I have heard that this corps was marching to head-quarters. Are you sure St. Jermyn is not with Campbell?"

"He said nothing about it yesterday, but I think he wishes to join Colonel Innis with the loyalist cavalry."

"Where is Innis?" inquired Curry.

"Over on Ennoree, about two miles from Musgrove's mill."

"Humph!" said Curry thoughtfully, "I must ride to the garrison at Ninety-Six. The devil take this cantering about the country! I have had more than enough of it."

And saying this, the dragoon mounted his horse, and clapping spurs to the restive animal, was soon out of sight.

It was late in the day before the wants of Butler were attended to. He had thrown aside his coat, from the oppressive heat of the weather, and, placing it under his head for a pillow, had fallen into a sleep, from which he was awakened by a summons from one of the sentinels to partake of food. There was more kindness apparent in the demeanor of the soldier than Butler had been accustomed to meet from the persons who held him captive, and this circumstance won upon his heart and induced him to accept with courtesy the proffered attentions.

"You live in a divided country, and witness much to make a good man wish this unhappy war was at an end," said Butler, after he had eaten of the provisions placed before him.

"Indeed we do, sir," replied the soldier, "and it is enough to make a man's heart bleed to see brothers fighting against each other, and kindred that ought to hold together seeking each other's lives. Men will have, and ought to have their opinions, sir; but, it is hardly good reason for treating one another like savage Indians, because all cannot think alike."

"Do you live in this neighborhood?" inquired Butler.

"Not far away," answered the man.

"You are married?"

"Yes, and have six children."

"They should be young," said Butler, "judging by your own age."

"Thank God, sir!" exclaimed the soldier, with fervor, "they are young! And I would pray that they may never live to be old if these wars are to last. No father can count upon his own child's living in harmony with him. My boys, if they were grown enough, might be the first I should meet in battle."

"Your name, friend?" said Butler.

"Bruce," replied the other.

"A good and a brave name; a name once friendly to the liberty of his country."

"Stop, sir!" said the sentinel. "This is not the place to talk upon questions that might make us angry with each other. It is a name still friendly to the liberty of his country; that liberty that supports the king and laws, and punishes treason."

"I cannot debate with you," replied Butler; "I am your prisoner."

"I am a man," said the soldier firmly, "and would not take advantage of him that cannot take his own part; but these questions, sir, are best dropped — they have made all the provinces mad. However, I do not blame you, sir; I will not deny that there are good men on your side."

"And on yours, doubtless," returned Butler.

"We have many bad ones, sir," returned the soldier; "and as you have spoken like a well-tempered gentleman to me, I will give you a friendly hint." Here the sentinel spoke in a lowered tone. "Have your eyes about you; these men are none of the best, and would think but little of taking from you anything of value. As you slept, just now, I saw a golden trinket hanging by a ribbon in your bosom. You are a young man, sir, and a soldier, I hear; this may be some present from your lady, as I guess you have one. If others had seen it, as I saw it, you might have been the loser. That's all."

"Thank you, honest friend! from my heart, I thank you!" replied Butler eagerly. "Oh, God! that bauble is a consolation to me that in this hour I would not part with — no, no! Thank you, friend, a thousand times!"

"Have done," said the soldier, "and in future be more careful. The relief is coming this way."

And the sentinel, taking up his rifle, repaired to his post. In a few moments the guard was changed, and those lately on duty were marched to the dwelling-house.

When night came on the immediate guard around Butler's person was doubled. Some few comforts were added to his forlorn prison by the kindness of the soldier Bruce, and he was left to pass the weary hours of darkness in communion with his own thoughts, or in the enjoyment of such repose as his unhappy state of thraldom allowed. If the agitation of his spirit had permitted sleep, there were but few moments of the night when it might have been indulged. The outburts of revelry, the loud and boisterous laugh, and still louder oaths of the party who occupied the dwelling-house near at hand, showed that they had plunged into their usual debauch, and now caroused over their frequently filled cups; and the clamor that broke upon the night might have baffled the slumbers of a mind less anxious and wakeful than his own.

The party of troopers and militia sat at the door to take advantage of the coolness of the night, and as they plied the busy flagon, and with heavy draught grew more noisy, scarce a word fell from their lips that was not distinctly heard by Butler. It was with intense interest, therefore, that he listened to the conversation when it led to a topic that greatly concerned himself; and that he might not alarm the suspicion of the speakers he affected sleep.

"Sumpter has been hovering about Ninety-Six," said the lieutenant; "and if one could believe all the stories that are told about him, he must be a full cousin at least to a certain person that it wouldn't be right to mention in respectable company; for, by the accounts, he is one day on the Wateree, and the next, whoop and away! — and there he is, almost over at Augusta. It seems almost past the power of human legs for a mortal man to make such strides as they tell of him."

"Who says Sumpter is near Ninety-Six?" inquired one of the party; "I can only say, if that's true, he is a ghost — that's all. Here's Harry Turner will swear that he saw him, day before yesterday, in North Carolina, on his march towards Burk."

"Indeed did I," responded Harry, one of the militia-men.

"There is no mistake about it," interposed the lieutenant. "A vidette of Brown's came scampering through here this morning, who reported the news; and the man had good right to know, for he saw Cruger yesterday, who told him all about it, and then sent him off to Wahab's plantation, near the Catawba fords, for Hanger's rangers. It was on his way back this morning that he stopped here five minutes, only to give us warning."

"This is only some story that your drunken head has been dreaming about, Gabriel," said Habershaw. "There is not a word of truth in it; the rangers went down to Camden three days ago. Who saw the vidette besides yourself?"

"The whole detachment," replied the lieutenant. "We talked to the man and had the story from him — and a queer fellow he was — a good stout chap that liked to have been caught by a pair of reconnoitring Whigs, a few miles back between this and Pacolet; they pushed him up to the saddleflaps. But you must have seen him yourself, Captain Habershaw; for he told us you were on the road."

"From towards Pacolet!" exclaimed the captain with surprise. "We saw nobody on that road. When did the man arrive?"

"About an hour before you. He came at full speed, with his horse — a great, black, snorting beast seventeen hands high at least — all in a foam. He was first for passing by without stopping, but we challenged him and brought him short upon his haunches, and then he told us he was in a hurry, and mustn't be delayed."

"What kind of a looking man was he?" inquired Habershaw.

"A jolly fellow," replied the lieutenant: "almost as big as his horse. A good civil fellow, too, that swigs well at a canteen. He made a joke of the matter about your coming up, and called you old Cat-o'-nine tails — said that you were the cat, and your nine tag-rags were the tails — ha, ha ha!"

"Blast the bastard!" exclaimed Habershaw; "who could he be?"

"Why we asked that, but he roared out with a great haw-haw — took another drink, and said he was never christened."

"You should, as a good soldier," said Habershaw, "have made him give his name."

"I tried him again, and he would only let us have a nickname; he told us then that he was called Jack-o'-Lantern, and had a special good stomach, and that if we wanted more of him we must give him a snatch of something to eat. Well, we did so. After that, he said he must have our landlord's sword, for his own had been torn from him by the Whig troopers that pushed him so hard, and that the bill for it must be sent to Cruger. So he got the old cheese-knife that used to hang over the fire-place and strung it across his shoulder. He laughed so hard, and seemed so good-natured, that there was no doing anything with him. At last he mounted his horse again, just stooped down and whispered in my ear at parting, that he was an old friend of yours, and that you could tell us all the news, and away he went, like a mad bully, clinking it over the hill at twenty miles to the hour."

"A black horse did you say?" inquired Habershaw. "Had he a white star in the forehead, and the two hind legs white below the knee?"

"Exactly," said the lieutenant and several others of the party.

"It was Horse Shoe Robinson!" exclaimed Habershaw, "by all the black devils!"

"Horse Shoe, Horse Shoe, to be sure!" responded half a dozen voices.

"He was a famous good rider, Horse Shoe or anybody else," said the lieutenant.

"That beats all!" said one of the troopers; "the cunning old fox! He told the truth when he said you would tell the news, captain: but to think of his lies getting him past the guard, with a sword and a bellyfull into the bargain!"

"Why didn't you report instantly upon our arrival?" asked Habershaw.

"Bless you," replied the lieutenant, "I never suspicioned him, more than I did you. The fellow laughed so naturally that I would never have thought him a runaway."

"There it is," said Habershaw; "that's the want of discipline. The service will never thrive till these loggerheads are taught the rules of war."

Butler had heard enough to satisfy him on one material point, namely, that Robinson had secured his escape, and was in condition to take whatever advantage of circumstances the times might afford him. It was a consolation to him also to know that the sergeant had taken this route, as it brought him nearer to the scene in which the major himself was likely to mingle. With this dawn of comfort brightening up his doubts, he addressed himself more composedly to sleep, and before daylight, the sounds of riot having sunk into a lower and more drowsy tone, he succeeded in winning a temporary oblivion from his cares.

CHAPTER XX

> "What ho! What ho! — thy door undo:
> Art watching or asleep?"
>
> BURGER'S LEONORA.

ON the banks of the Ennoree, in a little nook of meadow, formed by the bend of the stream which, fringed with willows, swept round it almost in a semicircle, the inland border of the meadow being defined by a gently rising wall of hills covered with wood, was seated within a few paces of the water, a neat little cottage with a group of out-buildings, presenting all the conveniences of a comfortable farm. The dwelling-house itself was shaded by a cluster of trees which had been spared from the native forest, and within view were several fields of cultivated ground neatly inclosed with fences. A little lower down the stream and within a short distance of the house, partially concealed by the bank, stood a small low-browed mill, built of wood. It was near sundown, and the golden light of evening sparkled upon the shower which fell from the leaky race that conducted the water to the head gate, and no less glittered on the spray that was dashed from the large and slowly revolving wheel. The steady gush of the stream, and the monotonous clack of the machinery, aided by the occasional discordant scream of a flock of geese that frequented the border of the race, and by the gambols of a few children, who played about the confines of the mill, excited pleasant thoughts of rural business and domestic content. A rudely constructed wagon, to which were harnessed two lean horses, stood at the door of the mill, and two men, one of them advanced in years, and the other apparently just beyond the verge of boyhood, were occupied in heaping upon it a heavy load of bags of meal. The whitened habiliments of these men showed them to be the proper attendants of the place, and now engaged in their avocation. A military guard stood by the wagon, and as soon as it was filled, they were seen to put the horses in motion, and to retire by a road that crossed the stream and take the descending direction of the currant close along the opposite bank.

When this party had disappeared, the old man directed the

mill to be stopped. The gates were let down, the machinery ungeared, and, in a few moments, all was still. The millers now retired to the little habitation hard by.

"There is so much work lost," said the elder to his companion, as they approached the gate that opened into the curtilage of the dwelling. "We shall never be paid for that load. Colonel Innis doesn't care much out of whose pocket he feeds his men; and as to his orders upon Rawdon's quarter-master, why it is almost the price of blood to venture so far from home to ask for payment — to say nothing of the risk of finding the army purse as low as a poor miller's at home. I begrudge the grain, Christopher, and the work that grinds it; but there is no disputing with these whiskered footpads with bayonets in their hands — they must have it and will have it, and there's an end of it."

"Aye," replied the man addressed by the name of Christopher, "as you say, they will have it; and if they are told that a poor man's sweat has been mixed with their bread, they talk to us about the cause — the cause — the cause. I am tired of this everlasting preaching about king and country. I don't know but if I had my own way I'd take the country against the king any day. What does George the Third care for us, with a great world of water between?"

"Whisht, Christopher Shaw — whisht, boy! We have no opinions of our own; trees and walls have ears at this time. It isn't for us to be bringing blood and burning under our roof, by setting up for men who have opinions. No, no. Wait patiently; and perhaps, Christopher, it will not be long before this gay bird Cornwallis will be plucked of his feathers. The man is on his way now that, by the help of the Lord, may bring down as proud a hawk as ever flew across the water. If it should be otherwise, trust to the power above the might of armies, and wiser than the cunning of men, that, by a righteous and peaceful life, we shall make our lot an easier one than it may ever be in mingling in the strife of the evil-minded."

"It is hard, for all that — wise as it is — to be still," said Christopher, "with one's arms dangling by one's side, when one's neighbors and kinsmen are up and girding themselves for battle. It will come to that at last; fight we must. And, I don't care who knows it, I am for independence, uncle Allen."

"Your passion, boy, and warmth of temper, I doubt, outrun your discretion," said the old man. "But you speak bravely and I cannot chide you for it. For the present, at least, be temperate, and, if you can, silent. It is but unprofitable talk for persons in our condition."

The uncle and nephew now entered the house, and Allen Musgrove — for this was the person to whom I have introduced my reader — was soon seated at his family board, invoking a blessing upon his evening meal, and dispensing the cares of a quiet and peaceful household.

"I wonder Mary stays so long with her aunt," he said, as the early hour of repose drew nigh. "It is an ill place for her, wife, and not apt to please the girl with anything she may find there. Wat Adair is an irregular man, and savage as the beasts he hunts. His associates are not of the best, and but little suited to Mary's quiet temper."

The wife, a staid, motherly-looking woman of plain and placid exterior, who was busily engaged amongst a thousand scraps of coarse, homespun-cloth, which she was fashioning into a garment for some of the younger members of her family, paused from her work, upon this appeal to her, and, directing her glances above her spectacles to her husband, replied:

"Mary has been taught to perform her duties to her kinsfolk, and it isn't often that she counts whether it is pleasant to her or not. Besides, Watty, rough as he is, loves our girl; and love goes a great way to make us bear and forbear both, husband. I'll warrant our daughter comes home when she thinks it right. But it is a weary way to ride over a wild country, and more so now when Whig and Tory have distracted the land. I wish Christopher could be spared to go for her."

"He shall go to-morrow, wife," returned Allen Musgrove. "Wat Adair, love her or not, is not the man to go out of his way for a wandering girl, and would think nothing to see the child set out by herself. But come, it is Saturday night and near bedtime. Put aside your work, wife; a lesson from the Book of Truth, and prayers, and then to rest," he said, as he took down a family Bible from a shelf and spread it before him.

The old man put on a pair of glasses, which, by a spring, sustained themselves upon his nose, and with an audible and solemn voice he read a portion of scripture; then, placing himself on his knees, whilst the whole family followed his example, he poured forth a fervent and heart-inspired prayer. It was a simple and homely effusion, delivered from the suggestions of the moment, in accordance with a devout habit of thanksgiving and supplication to which he had long been accustomed. He was a Presbyterian, and had witnessed, with many a pang, the profligate contempt and even savage persecution with which his sect had been visited by many of the Tory leaders — especially by the loyalist partisan, Captain Huck, who had been recently killed in an incursion of Sumpter's at Williams's plantation, not far distant from Musgrove's present residence. It was this unsparing hostility towards his religion, and impious derision of it, that, more than any other circumstance, had begotten that secret dislike of the Tory cause which, it was known to a few, the miller entertained, although his age, situation, and, perhaps, some ancient prejudice of descent (for he was the son of an early Scotch emigrant), would rather have inclined him to take the royal side; that side which, in common belief and in appearance, he still favored.

"Thou hast bent thy bow," he said, in the warmest effusion of his prayer, "and shot thine arrows, O Lord, amongst this people; thou hast permitted the ministers of vengeance, and the seekers of blood to ride amongst us, and thy wrath hath not yet bowed the stubborn spirit of sin — but the hard hearts are given strong arms, and with curses they have smitten the people. Yet even the firebrand that it did please thee not to stay because of our sins — yea, even the firebrand that did cause conflagration along our border, until by the light the erring children of men might read in the dark night, from one end of our boundary even unto the other, the enormity of their own backslidings, and their forgetfulness of thee; that firebrand hath been thrown into the blaze which it had itself kindled, and, like a weapon of war which hath grown dull in the work of destruction, hath been cast into the place of unprofitable lumber, and hath been utterly consumed. The persecutor of the righteous and the scoffer of the word hath paid the price of blood, and hath fallen into the snares wherewith he lay in wait to ensnare the feet of the unthinking. But stay now, O Lord of Hosts, the hand of the destroyer, and let the angel of peace again spread his wing over our racked and wearied land. Take from the wicked heart his sword and shield, and make the righteous man safe beside his family hearth. Shelter the head of the wanderer, and guide in safety the hunted fugitive who flees before the man of wrath; comfort the captive in his captivity, and make all hearts in this rent and sundered province to know and bless thy mercies for ever more. In especial, we beseech thee to give the victory to him that hath right, and to 'stablish the foundations of the government in justice and truth, giving liberty of conscience and liberty of law to those who know how to use it." At this point the worship of the evening was arrested by a slight knocking at the door.

"Who goes there?" exclaimed the old man, starting from his kneeling position. "Who raps at my door?"

"A stranger, good man," replied a voice without. "A poor fellow that has been hot pressed and hard run."

"Friend or foe?" asked Allen Musgrove.

"A very worthless friend to any man at this present speaking," replied the person on the outside of the door; "and not fit to be counted a foe until he has had something to eat. If you be Allen Musgrove, open your door."

"Are you alone, or do you come with followers at your heels? My house is small and can give scant comfort to many."

"Faith, it is more than I know," responded the other; "but if I have followers it is not with my will that they shall cross your door-sill. If you be Allen Musgrove, or if you be not, open, friend. I am as harmless as a barndoor fowl."

"I do not fear you, sir," said Musgrove, opening the door; "you are welcome to all I can give you, whatever colors you serve."

"Then give us your hand," said Horse Shoe Robinson, striding into the apartment. "You are a stranger to me, but if you are Allen Musgrove, the miller, that I have hearn men speak of, you are not the person to turn your back on a fellow creature of distress. Your sarvent, mistress," he added, bowing to the dame. "Far riding and fast riding gives a sort of claim these times; so excuse me for sitting down."

"You are welcome, again; your name, sir?" said Musgrove.

"Have I guessed yours?" inquired Horse Shoe.

"You have."

"Then you must guess mine; for it isn't convenient to tell it."

"Some poor Whig soldier," said Christopher Shaw privately to Musgrove. "It isn't right to make him betray himself. You are hungry, friend," added Christopher; "and we will first get you something to eat, and then you may talk all the better for it."

"That's a good word," said Horse Shoe, "and a brave word, as things go; for it isn't every man has the courage to feed an enemy in these days, though I made the devils do it for me this morning, ha, ha, ha! Some water, Mr. Musgrove, and it will not come badly to my hand if you can tangle it somewhat."

The refreshment asked for was produced by Christopher Shaw; and Horse Shoe, taking the brimming cup in his hand, stood up;

and with a rather awkward courtesy, pledged the draught with "Your health, good mistress, and luck to the little ones! for we grown-up babies are out of the days of luck, except the luck of escaping twisted hemp, or drum-head law, which for to-night, I believe, is mine;" and he swallowed the mixture at a draught; then, with a long sigh, placed the cup upon the table and resumed his seat. "That there spirit, Mr. Musgrove," he added, "is a special good friend in need, preach against it who will!"

"You say you have ridden far to-day," remarked the miller: "you must be tired."

"I am not apt to get tired," replied the sergeant, turning his sword-belt over his head, and flinging the weapon upon a bench; "but I am often hungry."

"My wife," said Musgrove, smiling, "has taken that hint before you spoke it; she has already ordered something for you to eat."

"That's an excellent woman!" exclaimed Horse Shoe. "You see, Allen Musgrove, I don't stand much upon making myself free of your house. I have hearn of you often before I saw you, man; and I know all about you. You are obliged to keep fair weather with these Tories — who have no consideration for decent, orderly people — but your heart is with the boys that go for liberty. You see I know you, and am not afeard to trust you. Perchance, you mought have hearn tell of one Horse Shoe Robinson, who lived over here at the Waxhaws?"

"I have heard many stories about that man," replied the miller.

"Well, I won't tell you that he is in your house to-night, for fear the Tories might take you to account for harboring such a never-do-well. But you have got a poor fellow under your roof that has had a hard run to get here."

"In my house!" exclaimed Musgrove; "Horse Shoe Robinson!" and then, after a pause, he continued, "well, well, there is no rule of war that justifies a Christian in refusing aid and comfort to a houseless and hunted stranger, who comes with no thought of harm to a peaceful family hearth. I take no part in the war on either side; and, in your ear, friend Robinson, I take none *against* you or the brave men that stand by you."

"Your hand again," said Horse Shoe, reaching towards the miller. "Allen, I have come to you under a sore press of heels. An officer of the Continental army and me have been travelling through these here parts, and we have been most onaccountably ambushed by a half wild-cat, half bull-dog, known by the name of Captain Hugh Habershaw, who cotched us in the night at Grindall's ford."

"Heaven have mercy on the man who has anything to do with Hugh Habershaw!" exclaimed the miller's wife.

"Amen, mistress," responded the sergeant; "for a surlier, misbegotten piece of flesh, there's not in these wild woods, giving you the choice of bear, panther, catamount, rattlesnake, or what not. We were sot upon," continued the sergeant, "by this bully and a bevy of his braggadocios, and made prisoners; but I took a chance to slip the noose this morning, and after riding plump into a hornet's nest at Blackstock's, where I put on a new face and tricked the guard out of a dinner and this here old sword, I took a course for this mill, axing people along the road where I should find Allen Musgrove; and so, after making some roundabouts and dodging into the woods until night came on, to keep clear the Tories, here I am."

"And the officer?" said Musgrove.

"He is in the hands of the Philistines yet — most likely now at Blackstock's."

"What might be his name?"

"Major Butler — a bold, warm gentleman — that's been used to tender life and good fortune. He has lands on the sea-coast — unless that new-fangled court at Charlestown, that they call the Court of Seekerstations, has made them null and void — as they have been making the estates of better gentlemen than they could ever pretend to be; taking all the best lands, you see, Allen, to themselves, the cursed iniquiters!"

"Where did you come from with this gentleman?"

"A long way off, Mr. Musgrove — from old Virginny — but lastly from Wat Adair's."

"Wat's wife is a relation of my family."

"Then he is a filthy disgrace to all who claim kin with him, Allen Musgrove. Wat was the man who put us into the wild-cat's claws — at least, so we had good reason to think. There was a tidy, spruce, and smart little wench there — tut, man — I am talking of your own kith and kindred, for her name was Mary Musgrove."

"Our girl!" said the dame with an animated emphasis; "our own Mary; what of *her*, Mr. Horse Shoe Robinson?"

"That she is as good a child, Mistress Musgrove, as any honest parent mought wish for. She got some sort of inkling of what was contrived; and so she appeared to Major Butler in a dream — or her ghost."

"Mercy on us! the child has not been hurt?" cried the mother.

"Ondoubtedly not, ma'am," said Robinson; "but it is as true as you are there, she gave us, somehow or other, a warning that there was harm in the wind; and we took her advice, but it didn't do."

"I wish the child were home," said Musgrove. "Christopher, at day-light, boy, saddle a horse and be off to Adair's for Mary."

The nephew promised to do the errand.

"Come, Mr. Robinson, draw near the table and eat something."

"With right good heart," replied Horse Shoe; "but it's a kind of camp rule with me, before I taste food — no matter where — just to look after Captain Peter Clinch; that's my horse, friend Musgrove. So, by your leave, I'll just go take a peep to see that the Captain is sarved. A good beast is a sort of right arm in scrapish times; and as God ha'n't given them the gift of speech, we must speak for them."

"Christopher shall save you the trouble," replied Musgrove.

"A good horse never loses anything by the eye of his master," said Horse Shoe; "so, Christopher, I'll go with you."

In a short time the sergeant returned into the house, and took his seat at the table, where he fell to, at what was set before him, with a laudable dispatch.

"How far off," he inquired, "is the nearest Tory post, Mr. Musgrove?"

"Colonel Innis has some light corps stationed within two miles. If you had been a little earlier you would have found some of them at my mill."

"Innis!" repeated Horse Shoe, "I thought Floyd had these parts under command?"

"So he has," replied the miller, "but he has lately joined the garrison at Rocky Mount."

"Ha! ha! ha!" ejaculated Robinson, "that's a pot into which Sumpter will be dipping his ladle before long. All the land between Wateree and Broad belongs to Tom Sumpter, let mad-cap Tarleton do his best! We Whigs, Mr. Musgrove, have a little touch of the hobgoblin in us. We travel pretty much where we please. Now, I will tell you, friend, very plainly what I am after. I don't mean to leave these parts till I see what is to become of Major Butler. Innis and Floyd put together sha'n't hinder me from looking after a man that's under my charge. I'm an old sodger, and they can't make much out of me if they get me."

"The country is swarming with troops of one kind or another," said the miller; "and a man must have his wits about him who would get through it. You are now, Mr. Robinson, in a very dangerous quarter. The fort at Ninety-Six on one side of you, and Rocky Mount and Hanging Rock on the other — the road between the three is full of loyalists. Colonel Innis is here to keep the passage open, and, almost hourly, his men are passing. You should be careful in showing yourself in daylight. And as for your poor friend, Major Butler, there is not likely to be much good will shown towards him. I greatly fear his case is worse than it seems to you."

"There is somewhere," said Robinson, "in that book that lies open on the table — which I take to be the Bible — the story of the campaigns of King David; and as I have hearn it read by the preacher, it tells how David was pushed on all sides by flying corps of the enemy, and that, seeing he had no sword, he came across a man who gave him victuals and the sword of Goliath — as I got my dinner and a sword this morning from the tavern-keeper at Blackstock's; and then he set off on his flight to some strange place, where he feigned himself crazy and scrabbled at the gate, and let the spit run down on his beard — as I have done before now with Tarleton, Mr. Musgrove; and then King David took into a cave — which I shouldn't stand much upon doing if there was occasion; and there the King waited, until he got friends about him and was able to drub the Philistians for robbing the threshing-floors — as I make no doubt these Tories have robbed yours, Allen Musgrove. But you know all about it, seeing that you are able to read, which I am not. Now, I don't pretend to say that I nor Major Butler are as good men as David — not at all; but the cause of liberty is as good a cause as ever King David fought for, and the Lord that took his side in the cave, will take the side of the Whigs, sooner or later, and help them to beat these grinding, thieving, burning, and throat-cutting Tories. And, moreover, a brave man ought never to be cast down by such vermin; that's my religion, Mr. Musgrove, though you mought hardly expect to find much thought of such things left in a rough fellow like me, that's been hammered in these here wars like an old piece of iron that's been one while a plough coulter, and after that a gun-barrel, and finally that's been run up with others into a piece of ordnance — not to say that it moughtn't have been a horse shoe in some part of its life, ha! ha! ha! There's not likely to be much conscience or religion left after all that hammering."

" 'He shall keep the simple folk by their right,' " said Musgrove, quoting a passage from the Psalms, " 'defend the children of the poor and punish the wrong-doer.' You have finished your supper, Mr. Robinson," he continued, "and before we retire to rest you will join us in the conclusion of our family worship, which was interrupted by your coming into the house. We will sing a Psalm which has been given to us by that man whose deliverance has taught you where you are to look for yours."

"If I cannot help to make music, Allen," said Horse Shoe, "I can listen with good will."

The miller now produced a little book in black-letter, containing a familiar and ancient version of the Psalms, and the following quaint and simple lines were read by him in successive couplets, the whole family singing each distich as soon as it was given out — not excepting Horse Shoe, who, after the first couplet, having acquired some slight perception of the tune, chimed in with a voice that might have alarmed the sentinels of Innis's camp:

"A king that trusteth in his host
Shall not prevail at length;
The man that of his might doth boast
Shall fall, for all his strength.

"The troops of horsemen eke shall fail,
Their sturdy steeds shall starve:
The strength of horse shall not prevail
The rider to preserve.

"But so the eyes of God intend,
And watch to aid the just;
With such as fear him to offend,
And on his goodness trust.

"That he of death and great distress
May set their souls from dread;
And if that dearth their land oppress,
In hunger them to feed.

"Wherefore our soul doth whole depend
On God, our strength and stay;
He is our shield us to defend
And drive all darts away."

When this act of devotion was concluded the old man invoked a blessing upon his household, and gave his orders that the family should betake themselves to rest. Horse Shoe had already taken up his sword and was about retiring to a chamber, under the guidance of Christopher Shaw, when the door was suddenly thrown wide open, and in rushed Mary Musgrove. She ran up, threw herself into her father's arms, and cried out—

"Oh, how glad I am that I have reached home to-night!" then kissing both of her parents, she flung herself into a chair, saying—"I am tired—very tired. I have ridden the livelong day, alone, and frightened out of my wits."

"Not alone, my daughter!—on that weary road, and the country so troubled with ill-governed men! Why did you venture, girl? Did you not think I would send your cousin Christopher for you?"

"Oh, father," replied Mary, "there have been such doings! Ah! and here is Mr. Horse Shoe Robinson; Major Butler, where is he, sir?" she exclaimed, turning to the sergeant, who had now approached the back of her chair to offer his hand.

"Blessings on you for a wise and a brave girl!" said Robinson. "But it wouldn't do; we were ambushed, and the Major is still a prisoner."

"I feared it," said Mary, "and therefore I stole away. They are bloody-minded and wicked, father; and uncle Adair's house has been the place where mischief and murder has been talked of. Oh, I am very sick! I have had such a ride!"

"Poor wench!" said the father, taking her to his bosom. "You have not the temper nor the strength to struggle where ruthless men take up their weapons of war. What has befallen? Tell us all!"

"No, no!" interposed the mother; "no, Allen, not now. The girl must have food and sleep, and must not be wearied with questions to-night. Wait, my dear Mary, until to-morrow. She will tell us everything to-morrow."

"I must hear of Major Butler," said Mary; "I cannot sleep until I have heard all that has happened. Good Mr. Robinson, tell me everything."

In few words the sergeant unfolded to the damsel the eventful history of the last two days, during the narrative of which her cheek waxed pale, her strength failed her, and she sank almost lifeless across her father's knee.

"Give me some water," she said. "My long ride has worn me out. I ran off at daylight this morning, and have not stopped once upon the road."

A glass of milk with a slice of bread restored the maiden to her strength, and she took the first opportunity to inform the circle who surrounded her of all the incidents that had fallen under her observation at Adair's.

Her father listened with deep emotion to the tale, and during its relation clenched his teeth with anger, as he walked, to and fro, through the apartment. There was an earnest struggle in his feelings to withhold the expression of the strong execration, which the narrative brought almost to his lips, against the perfidy of his wife's kinsman. But the habitual control of his temper, which his religious habits inculcated, kept him silent; and considerations of prudence again swayed him from surrendering to the impulse, which would have led him to declare himself openly against the cause of the royal government and its supporters in the district where he lived. He cross-questioned his daughter as to many minute points of her story, but her answers were uniform and consistent, and were stamped with the most unequivocal proofs of her strict veracity. Indeed, the collateral evidences furnished by Robinson, left no doubt on the miller's mind that the whole of Mary's disclosures were the testimony of a witness whose senses could not have been disturbed by illusions, nor distempered by fear.

"It is a dreadful tale," he said, "and we must think over it more maturely. Be of good heart, my daughter, you have acted well and wisely; God will protect us from harm."

"And so it was no ghost, nor spirit," said Horse Shoe, "that the major saw in the night? But I wonder you didn't think of waking me. A word to me in the night — seeing I have sarved a good deal on outposts, and have got used to being called up — would have had me stirring in a wink. But that's part of Wat's luck, for I should most ondoubtedly have strangled the snake in his bed."

"I called you," said Mary, "as loudly as I durst, and more than once, but you slept so hard!"

"That's like me too," replied Horse Shoe. "I'm both sleepy

and watchful, according as I think there is need of my sarvices."

"Now to bed, my child," said Musgrove. "Your bed is the fittest place for your wearied body. God bless you, daughter!"

Once more the family broke up, and as Robinson left the room Mary followed him to the foot of the little stair that wound up into an attic chamber; here she detained him one moment, while she communicated to him in a half whisper,

"I have a friend, Mr. Robinson, that might help you to do something for Major Butler. His name is John Ramsay: he belongs to General Sumpter's brigade. If you would go to his father's, only six miles from here, on the upper road to Ninety-Six, you might hear where John was. But, may be, you are afraid to go so near to the fort?"

"May be so," said Robinson, with a look of comic incredulity. "I know the place, and I know the family, and, likely, John himself. It's a good thought, Mary, for I want help now, more than I ever did in my life. I'll start before daylight — for it won't do to let the sun shine upon me, with Innis's Tories so nigh. So, if I am missed to-morrow morning, let your father know how I come to be away."

"Tell John," said Mary, "I sent you to him. Mary Musgrove, remember."

"If I can't find John," replied Horse Shoe, "you're such a staunch little petticoat sodger, that I'll, perhaps, come back and enlist you. 'Tisn't everywhere that we can find such valiant wenches. I wish some of our men had a little of your courage; so, good night!"

The maiden now returned to the parlor, and Horse Shoe, under the guidance of Christopher Shaw, found a comfortable place of deposit for his hard-worked, though — as he would have Christopher believe — his unfatigued frame. The sergeant, however, was a man not born to cares, notwithstanding that his troubles were "as thick as the sparks that fly upward," and it is a trivial fact in his history, that, on the present occasion, he was not many seconds in bed before he was as sound asleep as the trapped partridges, in the fairy tale, which, the eastern chronical records, fell into a deep sleep when roasting upon the spit, and did not wake for a hundred years.

CHAPTER XXI

> "Now if you ask who gave the stroke
> I cannot tell, so mote I thrive;
> It was not given by man alive."
>
> LAY OF THE LAST MINSTREL.

It was a little before day-break on Sunday morning, the fifteenth of August (a day rendered memorable by the exploit of Sumpter, who captured, in the vicinity of Rocky Mount, a large quantity of military stores, and a numerous escort, then on their way from Ninety-Six to Camden), that James Curry was travelling in the neighborhood of the Ennoree, some four miles distant from Musgrove's mill. He had a few hours before left the garrison of Ninety-Six, and was now hieing with all haste to Blackstock's on a mission of importance. The night had been sultry, but the approach of the dawn had brought with it that refreshing coolness which is always to be remarked in the half hour that precedes the first blush of morning. The dragoon had had a weary night-ride, but the recent change of temperature had invigorated his system and given buoyancy to his spirits. This effect was exhibited in his first whistling a tune, then humming the words of a dittty, and, finally, in breaking forth into a loud full song, which, as he had a good voice and practised skill, increased in loudness as he became better pleased with the trial of his powers. The song was occasionally intermitted to give room to certain self-communings which the pastime suggested.

"You may take it for sooth, that wit without gold,"

he sang in the loudest strain, trying the words on different keys, and introducing some variations in the tune —

"Will make a bad market whenever 'tis sold."

"That's true; your poor moneyless devil, how should his wit pass current? He was a shrewd fellow that wrote it down.

Your rich man for wit, all the world over, and so the song runs: —

"'But all over the world it is well understood
That the joke of a rich man is sure to be good.'

"True, true as gospel! Give the knaves dinners, plenty of Burgundy and Port, and what signifies an empty head? Go to college, and how is it there? What is a sizer's joke? If the fellow have the wit of Diogenes, it is sheer impertinence. But let my young lord Crœsus come out with his flatulent nonsense, oh, that's the true ware for the market! James Curry, James Curry, what ought you to have been, if the supple jade fortune had done your deserts justice! Instead of a d——d dodging dragoon, obedient to the beck of every puppy who wears his majesty's epaulets; but it's no matter, that's past; the wheel has made its turn, and here I am, doing the work of the scullion, that ought to sit above the salt-cellar. Vogue la galére! We will play out the play. Meantime, I'll be merry in spite of the horoscope: come then, I like these words and the jolly knave, whoever he was, that penned them.

"'You may take it for sooth that wit without gold.'"

The singer was, at this instant, arrested at the top of his voice by a blow against the back of his head, bestowed, apparently, by some ponderous hand, that so effectually swayed him from the line of gravity, as to cause him to reel in his saddle, and, by an irrecoverable impetus, to swing round to the ground, where he alighted on his back, with the reins of his horse firmly held in his hand.

"Singing on Sunday is against the law," said a hoarse voice, that came apparently from the air, as the darkness of the hour — which was increased by an overcast and lowering sky, as well as by the thick wood through which the road ran, prevented the stricken man from discerning anything that might have done him harm, even if such thing had been bodily present. The soldier lay for a moment prostrate, bewildered by the suddenness of this mysterious visitation; and when, at length, he regained his feet, he almost fancied that he heard receding from him, at a great distance, the dull beat of a horse's foot upon the sandy road.

Curry, who as a soldier was insensible to fear, now shook in every joint, as he stood beside his horse in a state of confused and ravelled wonderment. He strained his ear to catch the sound in the direction towards which he thought he had heard the retreating footsteps, but his more deliberate attention persuaded him that he was mistaken in his first impression. Still more puzzled as he came into the possession of his faculties, of which the abruptness of the surprise had almost berefit him, he stood for some time mute; then drawing his sword with the alacrity of a man, who all at once believes himself in danger of an uplifted blow, he called out loudly,

"Speak and show yourself, if you be a man! Or if there be a party, let them come forth. Who waylays me? Remember, I warn him, in the name of the king, that I am on his majesty's errand, and that they are not far off who will punish any outrage on my person. By all the powers of Satan, the place is bewitched!" he exclaimed, after a pause. "Once more, speak; whether you are to be conjured in the name of the king or of the devil!"

All remained silent, except the leaves of the forest that fluttered in the breeze; and it was with an awkward and unacknowledged sense of faint-heartedness that Curry put up his sword and remounted into his saddle. He first moved slowly forward in continuation of his journey; and, as his thoughts still ran upon the extraordinary incident, he applied spurs to his horse's side, and gradually increased his pace from a trot to a gallop, and from that to almost high speed, until he emerged from the wood upon a track of open country. When he reached this spot the day had already appeared above the eastern horizon; and reassured, as the light waxed stronger, the dragoon, by degrees, fell into his customary travelling pace, and resumed the equanimity of his temper.

About ten o'clock in the day he reached Blackstock's, where he arrived in a heavy rain, that had been falling for the last three hours, and which had drenched him to the skin. So, rapidly dismounting and giving his horse into the charge of some of the idlers about the door, he entered the common room in which were assembled the greater part of the militia guard and of Habershaw's troopers. His first movement was to take the burly captain aside, and to communicate to him certain orders from the commanding officer at Ninety-Six, respecting the prisoner; which being done, he mingled with his usual affectedly careless and mirthful manner amongst the throng.

Butler, through the intercession of Bruce, had been indulged with some mitigation of the restraints at first imposed upon him; and he was, at this moment, availing himself of the privilege that had been allowed him, on account of the leaky condition of the barn in which he had spent the night, to take his morning meal inside of the dwelling-house. He was accordingly seated at a table, in a corner of the room, with some eatables before him in a more comfortable state of preparation than he had hitherto enjoyed. Two soldiers stood sufficiently near to render his custody effectual without much personal annoyance. As yet he had been unable to glean anything from the conversation of those around him, by which he might form the least conjecture as to his probable destiny. His intercourse with his captors was restricted to the mere supply of his immediate wants. All other communication was strictly interdicted. Even Habershaw himself seemed to be under some authoritative command, to deny himself the gratification of either exhibiting his own importance, or of wreaking his spleen upon his prisoner; and when Butler attempted to gain from Bruce some hint as to what was intended, the only answer he received was conveyed by the soldier's putting his finger on his lip.

Butler knew enough of Robinson's hardihood and venturesome disposition, to feel perfectly confident that he would make good his promise to be near him, at whatever personal hazard; and he was, therefore, in momentary expectation of receiving further intelligence from the sergeant in some of those strange, bold, and perilous forms of communication, which the character of the trusty soldier warranted him in counting upon. His knowledge that Robinson had passed by Blackstock's on the day preceding, gave him some assurance that the sergeant was in the diligent prosecution of his purpose to seek Sumpter, or some other of the partisan Whig corps in their hiding-places, and to try the hazardous experiment of his (Butler's) rescue from his present thraldom, by a vigorous incursion into the district where he was now confined. With this calculation of the course of events, he was prepared to hear, at every hour of the day, of some sudden alarm; and ready to co-operate, by seizing the first moment of confusion to snatch up a weapon, and force his way through the ranks of his guard. It was with such anticipations that now, whilst seemingly engrossed with the satisfaction of his physical wants at the table, he lent an attentive ear to the conversation which passed in the house between Curry and the company who were clustered around him. The dragoon, at first, in a light and merry vein of narrative, recounted to his hearers the singular visitation he had experienced before daybreak; and he contrived to fling over his story an additional hue of mystery, by the occasional reflections with which he seasoned it, tending to inculcate the belief to which he himself partly inclined, that the incident was brought about through the agency of some pranking and mischievous spirit, — a conclusion which, at that period, and amongst the persons to whom the adventure was related, did not require any great stretch of faith to sustain it. Some of his auditors fortified this prevailing inclination of opinion, by expressing their own conviction of the interference of malignant and supernatural influences in the concerns of mankind, and gave their personal experience of instances in which these powers were active. The conversation by degrees changed its tone from that of levity and laughter into one of grave and somewhat fearful interest, according to the increasing marvel which the several stories that were told excited in the superstitious minds of the circle; and in the same proportion that this sentiment took possession of the thoughts of the company, they became more unreserved in their language, and louder in the utterance of it, thus giving Butler the full benefit of all that was said.

"But, after all," said one of the men, "mightn't you have been asleep on your horse, James Curry, and had a sort of jogging dream, when a limb of a tree across the road, for it was a dark morning, might have caught you under the throat and flung you out of your saddle: and you, not knowing whether you was asleep or awake, for a man who is on duty, without his night's rest, sometimes can't tell the difference, thought it was some hobgoblin business?"

"No," said Curry, "that's impossible; for I was singing a song at the time, and almost at the top of my voice. I had been sleepy enough before that, just after I left Ninety-Six, near midnight, for I had ridden a long way; but as it grew towards daylight I began to rouse up, so that when this thing happened I was as much awake as I am now."

"Then it's a downright case of ghost," said the other. "It knew you was upon a wicked errand, and so that back-handed blow was a warning to you. These things are sometimes meant to be friendly; and who knows but this oversetting you in the road might have been intended to signify that you had better not meddle in cases of life and death. If you would take my advice, you would just treat this Major Butler, that you took prisoner" —

Curry looked at the speaker with a frown, as he made a motion to him to be silent. "Remember where you are, and who may hear you," he said in a cautious voice, as he glanced his eye towards Butler, who was leaning his head upon the table, as if in slumber.

"Oh, I understand," replied the soldier of the guard. "I forgot he was in the room."

"The weather holds up," said Habershaw, who now walked into the house. "The rain has slackened; and so, orderly, if you have had a bite of something to eat, the boys had better be got ready to march. We have a long way to go, and as the infantry march with us we shall get on slowly."

"I think so, noble Captain," replied Curry. "I shall be ready to join you before you get your line formed."

Orders were now issued by Habershaw, both to the troopers of his own squad and to the militia detachment, to put themselves in condition for an immediate movement. The clouds, during the last half hour, had been breaking away, and the sun soon burst forth upon the wet and glittering landscape, in all the effulgence of mid summer. During a brief interval of preparation the party of infantry and cavalry that now occupied the hamlet exhibited the bustle incident to the gathering of the corps. Some ran to one quarter for their arms, others to the stables for their horses; a cracked trumpet in the hands of a lusty performer, who here joined the troop, kept up a continual braying, and was seconded by the ceaseless beat of a slack and dull drum. There were some who, having put on their military equipments, thronged the table of the common room of the house, where spirits and water had been set out for their accommodation, and rude jokes, laughter, and oaths, were mingled together in deafening clamor.

"Move out the prisoner," shouted Habershaw; "he goes with the infantry afoot. I'll never trust another of the tribe with a horse."

"Follow, sir," said one of the sentinels near Butler's person, as he faced to the right with his musket at an "advance," and led the way to the door.

Butler rose, and, before he placed himself in the position required, asked:

"Where is it you purpose to conduct me?"

"Silence!" said Habershaw sternly. "Obey orders, sir, and march where you are directed."

Butler folded his arms and looked scornfully at the uncouth savage before him as he replied:

"I am a prisoner, sir, and therefore bound to submit to the force that constrains me. But there will be a day of reckoning, both for you and your master. It will not be the lighter to him for having hired such a ruffian to do the business in which he is ashamed to appear himself."

"Devil's leavings!" screamed Habershaw, almost choked with choler, "dare you speak to me so? By my heart, I have a mind to cleave your skull for you! My master, sir! You will find out, before long, who is master, when Hugh Habershaw has tied the knot that is to fit your neck."

"Peace, villian!" exclaimed Butler; "I cannot come too soon into the presence of those who claim to direct your motions."

Here James Curry interposed to draw off the incensed captain, and Butler, having received another order from the officer of the guard moved out upon the road and took the place that was assigned him, between two platoons of the foot soldiers.

The troopers being mounted and formed into column of march with Habershaw and his trumpeter at the head and Curry in the rear, now moved forward at a slow gait, followed by the detachment of infantry who had the prisoner under their especial charge.

It was near noon when the party took up the line of march, and they prosecuted their journey southward with such expedition as to tax Butler's powers to the utmost to keep even pace with them over roads that were in many places rendered miry by the late rain. Towards evening, however, the sun had sufficiently dried the soil to make the travel less fatiguing; and by that hour when the light of day only lingered upon the tops of the western hills, the military escort, with their prisoner, were seen passing through a defile that opened upon their view an extensive bivouac of some two or three hundred horse and foot, and occupying a space of open field, encompassed with wood and guarded in its rear by a smooth and gentle river.

The spot at which they had arrived was the camp of a partisan corps under the command of Colonel Innis. A farm-house was seen in the immediate neighborhood, which was used as the headquarters of a party of officers. Numerous horses were attached to the trees that bounded the plain, and various shelters were made in the same quarter, in the rudest form of accommodation, of branches and underwood set against ridge-poles, that were sustained by stakes, to protect the men against the weather. Groups of this irregular soldiery were scattered over the plain, a few wagons were seen collected in one direction, and, not far off, a line of fires, around which parties were engaged in cooking food. Here and there a sentinel was seen pacing his short limits, and occasionally the roll of a drum and the flourish of a fife announced some ceremony of the camp police.

The escort marched quickly across this plain until it arrived in front of the farm-house. Here a guard was drawn up to receive them; and, as soon as the usual military salute was passed and the order to "stand at ease" given, Habershaw put the detachment under the command of the lieutenant of infantry, and, accompanied by Curry, walked into the house to make his report to the commanding officer of the post.

In a few moments afterwards Colonel Innis, attended by two or three military men — some of whom wore the uniform of the British regular army — came from the house and passed hastily along the line of the escort, surveying Butler only with a rapid glance. Having regained the door, he was heard to say —

"It is very well; let the prisoner have a room above stairs. See that he wants nothing proper to his situation; and, above all, be attentive that he be kept scrupulously under the eye of his guard."

When this order was given, the Colonel retired with his attendants to his quarters, and Butler was forthwith conducted, by a file of men, up a narrow, winding stair, to a small apartment in the angle of the roof, where he was provided with a chair, a light, and a comfortable bed. His door was left open, and on the outside of it, full in his view, was posted a sentinel. He was too weary even to be troubled with the cares of his present condition; and, without waiting, therefore, for food, or seeking to inquire into whose hands he had fallen, or even to turn his thoughts upon the mysterious train of circumstances that hung over him, he flung himself upon the couch and sank into a profound and grateful sleep.

CHAPTER XXII

AN ADVENTURE WHEREIN IT IS APPARENT THAT THE ACTIONS OF REAL LIFE ARE FULL AS MARVELLOUS AS THE INVENTIONS OF ROMANCE

David Ramsay's house was situated on a by-road, between five and six miles from Musgrove's mill, and at about the distance of one mile from the principal route of travel between Ninety-Six and Blackstock's. In passing from the military post that had been established at the former place, towards the latter, Ramsay's lay off to the left, with a piece of dense wood intervening. The by-way, leading through the farm, diverged from the main road, and traversed this wood until it reached the cultivated grounds immediately around Ramsay's dwelling. In the journey from Musgrove's mill to this point of divergence, the traveller was obliged to ride some two or three miles upon the great road leading from the British garrison, a road that, at the time of my story, was much frequented by military parties, scouts, and patroles, that were concerned in keeping up the communication between the several posts which were established by the British authorities along that frontier. Amongst the whig parties, also, there were various occasions which brought them under the necessity of frequent passage through this same district, and which, therefore, furnished opportunities for collision and skirmish with the opposite forces.

It is a matter of historical notoriety, that immediately after the fall of Charleston, and the rapid subjugation of South Carolina that followed this event, there were three bold and skilful soldiers who undertook to carry on the war of resistance to the established authorities, upon a settled and digested plan of annoyance, under the most discouraging state of destitution, as regarded all the means of offence, that, perhaps, history records. It will not detract from the fame of other patriots of similar enthusiasm. and of equal bravery, to mention the names of Marion, Sumpter, and Pickens, in connexion with this plan of keeping up an apparently hopeless partisan warfare, which had the promise neither of men, money, nor arms, — and yet which was so nobly sustained, amidst accumulated discomfitures, as to lead eventually to the subversion of the "Tory ascendency" and the expulsion of the British power. According to the plan of operations concerted amongst these chieftains, Marion took the lower country under his supervision; Pickens the south-western districts, bordering upon the Savannah; and to Sumpter was allotted all that tract of country lying between the Broad and the Catawba rivers, from the angle of their junction, below Camden, up to the mountain districts of North Carolina. How faithfully these men made good their promise to the country, is not only written in authentic history, but it is also told in many a legend amongst the older inhabitants of the region that was made the theatre of action. It only concerns my story to refer to the fact, that the events which have occupied my last five or six chapters, occurred in that range more peculiarly appropriated to Sumpter, and that the high road from Blackstock's towards Ninety-six was almost as necessary for communication between Sumpter and Pickens, as between the several British garrisons.

On the morning that succeeded the night in which Horse Shoe Robinson arrived at Musgrove's, the stout and honest sergeant might have been seen, about eight o'clock, leaving the main road from Ninety-six, at the point where that leading to David Ramsay's separated from it, and cautiously urging his way into the deep forest, by the more private path into which he had entered. The knowledge that Innis was encamped along the Ennoree, within a short distance of the mill, had compelled him to make an extensive circuit to reach Ramsay's dwelling, whither he was now bent; and he had experienced considerable delay in his morning journey, by finding himself frequently in the neighborhood of small foraging parties of Tories, whose motions he was obliged to watch for fear of an encounter. He had once already been compelled to use his horse's heels in what he called "fair flight;" and once to ensconce himself, a full half hour, under cover of the thicket afforded him by a swamp. He now, therefore, according to his own phrase, "dived into the little road that scrambled down through the woods towards Ramsay's, with all his eyes about him, looking out as sharply as a fox on a foggy morning:" and with this circumspection, he was not long in arriving within view of Ramsay's house. Like a practised soldier, whom frequent frays has taught wisdom, he resolved to reconnoitre before he advanced upon a post that might be in possession of an enemy. He therefore dismounted, fastened his horse in a fence corner, where a field of corn concealed him from notice, and then stealthily crept forward until he came immediately behind one of the out-houses.

The barking of a house-dog brought out a negro boy, to whom Robinson instantly addressed the query —

" Is your master at home? "

" No, sir. He's got his horse, and gone off more than an hour ago."

" Where is your mistress? "

" Shelling beans, Sir."

" I didn't ask you," said the sergeant, " what she is doing, but where she is."

" In course, she is in the house, Sir," — replied the negro with a grin.

" Any strangers there? "

" There was plenty on 'em a little while ago, but they've been gone a good bit."

Robinson having thus satisfied himself as to the safety of his visit, directed the boy to take his horse and lead him up to the door. He then entered the dwelling.

" Mistress Ramsay," said he, walking up to the dame, who was occupied at a table, with a large trencher before her, in which she was plying that household thrift which the negro described; " luck to you, ma'am, and all your house! I hope you haven't none of these clinking and clattering bullies about you, that are as thick over this country as the frogs in the kneading troughs, that they tell of."

" Good luck, Mr. Horse Shoe Robinson," exclaimed the matron, offering the sergeant her hand. " What has brought you here? What news? Who are with you? For patience sake, tell me! "

" I am alone," said Robinson, " and a little wettish, mistress; " he added, as he took off his hat and shook the water from it: " it has just sot up a rain, and looks as if it was going to give us enough on't. You don't mind doing a little dinner-work of a Sunday, I see — shelling of beans, I s'pose, is tantamount to dragging a sheep out of a pond, as the preachers allow on the Sabbath — ha, ha! — Where's Davy? "

" He's gone over to the meeting-house on Ennoree, hoping to hear something of the army at Camden: perhaps you can tell us the news from that quarter? "

" Faith, that's a mistake, Mistress Ramsay. Though I don't doubt that they are hard upon the scratches, by this time. But, at this present speaking, I command the flying artillery. We have but one man in the corps — and that's myself; and all the guns we have got is this piece of ordnance, that hangs in this old belt by my side (pointing to his sword) — and that I captured from the enemy at Blackstock's. I was hoping I mought find John Ramsay at home — I have need of him as a recruit."

"Ah, Mr. Robinson, John has a heavy life of it over there with Sumpter. The boy is often without his natural rest, or a meal's victuals; and the general thinks so much of him, that he can't spare him to come home. I hav'n't the heart to complain, as long as John's service is of any use, but it does seem, Mr. Robinson, like needless tempting of the mercies of providence. We thought that he might have been here to-day; yet I am glad he didn't come — for he would have been certain to get into trouble. Who should come in, this morning, just after my husband had cleverly got away on his horse, but a young cock-a-whoop ensign, that belongs to Ninety-Six, and four great Scotchmen with him, all in red coats; they had been out thieving, I warrant, and were now going home again. And who but they! Here they were, swaggering all about my house — and calling for this — and calling for that — as if they owned the fee-simple of everything on the plantation. And it made my blood rise, Mr. Horse Shoe, to see them run out in the yard, and catch up my chickens and ducks, and kill as many as they could string about them — and I not daring to say a word: though I did give them a piece of my mind, too."

"Who is at home with you?" inquired the sergeant eagerly.

"Nobody but my youngest boy, Andrew," answered the dame. "And then, the filthy, toping rioters — " she continued, exalting her voice.

"What arms have you in the house?" asked Robinson, without heeding the dame's rising anger.

"We have a rifle, and a horseman's pistol that belongs to John. — They must call for drink, too, and turn my house, of a Sunday morning, into a tavern."

"They took the route towards Ninety-Six, you said, Mistress Ramsay?"

"Yes, — they went straight forward upon the road. But, look you, Mr. Horse Shoe, you're not thinking of going after them?"

"Isn't there an old field, about a mile from this, on that road?" inquired the sergeant, still intent upon his own thoughts.

"There is," replied the dame; "with the old school-house upon it."

"A lop-sided, rickety log-cabin in the middle of the field. Am I right, good woman?"

"Yes."

"And nobody lives in it? It has no door to it?"

"There ha'n't been anybody in it these seven years."

"I know the place very well," said the sergeant, thoughtfully; "there is woods just on this side of it."

"That's true," replied the dame: "but what is it you are thinking about, Mr. Robinson?"

"How long before this rain began was it that they quitted this house?"

"Not above fifteen minutes."

"Mistress Ramsay, bring me the rifle and pistol both — and the powder-horn and bullets."

"As you say, Mr. Horse Shoe," answered the dame, as she turned round to leave the room; "but I am sure I can't suspicion what you mean to do."

In a few moments the woman returned with the weapons, and gave them to the sergeant.

"Where is Andy?" asked Horse Shoe.

The hostess went to the door and called her son, and, almost immediately afterwards, a sturdy boy of about twelve or fourteen years of age entered the apartment, his clothes dripping with rain. He modestly and shyly seated himself on a chair near the door, with his soaked hat flapping down over a face full of freckles, and not less rife with the expression of an open, dauntless hardihood of character.

"How would you like a scrummage, Andy, with them Scotchmen that stole your mother's chickens this morning?" asked Horse Shoe.

"I'm agreed," replied the boy, "if you will tell me what to do."

"You are not going to take the boy out on any of your desperate projects, Mr. Horse Shoe?" said the mother, with the tears starting instantly into her eyes. "You wouldn't take such a child as that into danger?"

"Bless your soul, Mrs. Ramsay, there ar'n't no danger about it! Don't take on so. It's a thing that is either done at a blow, or not done, — and there's an end of it. I want the lad only to bring home the prisoners for me, after I have took them."

"Ah, Mr. Robinson, I have one son already in these wars — God protect him! — and you men don't know how a mother's heart yearns for her children in these times. I cannot give another," she added, as she threw her arms over the shoulders of the youth and drew him to her bosom.

"Oh! it aint nothing," said Andrew, in a sprightly tone. "It's only snapping of a pistol, mother, — pooh! If I'm not afraid, you oughtn't to be."

"I give you my honor, Mistress Ramsay," said Robinson, "that I will bring or send your son safe back in one hour; and that he sha'n't be put in any sort of danger whatsomedever: come, that's a good woman!"

"You are not deceiving me, Mr. Robinson?" asked the matron, wiping away a tear. "You wouldn't mock the sufferings of a weak woman in such a thing as this?"

"On the honesty of a sodger, ma'am," replied Horse Shoe, "the lad shall be in no danger, as I said before — whatsomedever."

"Then I will say no more," answered the mother. "But Andy, my child, be sure to let Mr. Robinson keep before you."

Horse Shoe now loaded the fire-arms, and having slung the pouch across his body, he put the pistol into the hands of the boy; then shouldering his rifle, he and his young ally left the room. Even on this occasion, serious as it might be deemed, the sergeant did not depart without giving some manifestation of that light-heartedness which no difficulties ever seemed to have the power to conquer. He thrust his head back into the room, after he had crossed the threshold, and said with an encouraging laugh, "Andy and me will teach them, Mistress Ramsay, Pat's point of war — we will *surround* the ragamuffins."

"Now, Andy, my lad," said Horse Shoe, after he had mounted Captain Peter, "you must get up behind me. Turn the lock of your pistol down," he continued, as the boy sprang upon the horse's rump, "and cover it with the flap of your jacket, to keep the rain off. It won't do to hang fire at such a time as this."

The lad did as he was directed, and Horse Shoe, having secured his rifle in the same way, put his horse up to a gallop, and took the road in the direction that had been pursued by the soldiers.

As soon as our adventurers had gained a wood, at the distance of about half a mile, the sergeant relaxed his speed, and advanced at a pace a little above a walk.

"Andy," he said, "we have got rather a ticklish sort of a job before us, so I must give you your lesson, which you will understand better by knowing something of my plan. As soon as your mother told me that these thieving villains had left her house about fifteen minutes before the rain came on, and that they had gone along upon this road, I remembered the old field up here, and the little log hut in the middle of it; and it was natural to suppose that they had just got about near that hut, when this rain came up; and then, it was the most supposable case in the world, that they would naturally go into it, as the driest place they could find. So now, you see, it's my calculation that the whole batch is there at this very point of time. We will go slowly along, until we get to the other end of this wood, in sight of the old field, and then, if there is no one on the look-out, we will open our first trench; you know what that means, Andy?"

"It means, I s'pose, that we'll go right smack at them," replied Andrew.

"Pretty exactly," said the sergeant. "But listen to me. Just at the edge of the woods you will have to get down, and put yourself behind a tree. I'll ride forward, as if I had a whole troop at my heels, and if I catch them, as I expect, they will have a little fire kindled, and, as likely as not, they'll be cooking some of your mother's fowls."

"Yes, I understand," said the boy eagerly —

"No, you don't," replied Horse Shoe, "but you will when you hear what I am going to say. If I get at them onawares, they'll be mighty apt to think they are surrounded, and will bellow, like fine fellows, for quarter. And, thereupon, Andy, I'll cry out 'stand fast,' as if I was speaking to my own men, and when you hear that, you must come up full tilt, because it will be a signal to you that the enemy has surrendered. Then it will be your business to run into the house and bring out the muskets, as quick as a rat runs through a kitchen: and when you have done that, why, all's done. But if you should hear any popping of fire-arms — that is, more than one shot, which I may chance to let off — do you take that for a bad sign, and get away as fast as you can heel it. You comprehend."

"Oh! yes," replied the lad, "and I'll do what you want, and more too, may be, Mr. Robinson."

"*Captain* Robinson, — remember, Andy, you must call me captain, in the hearing of these Scotsmen."

"I'll not forget that neither," answered Andrew.

By the time that these instructions were fully impressed upon the boy, our adventurous forlorn hope, as it may fitly be called, had arrived at the place which Horse Shoe Robinson had designated for the commencement of active operations. They had a clear view of the old field, and it afforded them a strong assurance that the enemy was exactly where they wished him to be, when they discovered smoke arising from the chimney of the hovel. Andrew was soon posted behind a tree, and Robinson only tarried a moment to make the boy repeat the signals agreed on, in order to ascertain that he had them correctly in his memory. Being satisfied from this experiment that the intelligence of his young companion might be depended upon, he galloped across the intervening space, and, in a few seconds, abruptly reined up his steed, in the very doorway of the hut. The party within was gathered around a fire at the further end, and, in the corner near the door, were four muskets thrown together against the wall. To spring from his saddle and thrust himself one pace inside of the door, was a movement which the sergeant executed in an instant, shouting at the same time —

"Halt! File off right and left to both sides of the house, and wait orders. I demand the surrender of all here," he said, as he planted himself between the party and their weapons. "I will shoot down the first man who budges a foot."

"Leap to your arms," cried the young officer who commanded the little party inside of the house. "Why do you stand?"

"I don't want to do you or your men any harm, young man," said Robinson, as he brought his rifle to a level, "but, by my father's son, I will not leave one of you to be put upon a muster-roll if you raise a hand at this moment."

Both parties now stood, for a brief space, eyeing each other in a fearful suspense, during which there was an expression of doubt and irresolution visible on the countenances of the soldiers, as they surveyed the broad proportions, and met the stern glance of the sergeant, whilst the delay, also, began to raise an apprehension in the mind of Robinson that his stratagem would be discovered.

"Shall I let loose upon them, captain?" said Andrew Ramsay, now appearing, most unexpectedly to Robinson, at the door of the hut. "Come on, boys!" he shouted, as he turned his face towards the field.

"Keep them outside of the door — stand fast," cried the doughty sergeant, with admirable promptitude, in the new and sudden posture of his affairs caused by this opportune appearance of the boy. "Sir, you see that it's not worth while fighting five to one; and I should be sorry to be the death of any of your brave fellows; so, take my advice, and surrender to the Continental Congress and this scrap of its army which I command."

During this appeal the sergeant was ably seconded by the lad outside, who was calling out first on one name, and then on another, as if in the presence of a troop. The device succeeded, and the officer within, believing the forbearance of Robinson to be real, at length said: —

"Lower your rifle, sir. In the presence of a superior force, taken by surprise, and without arms, it is my duty to save bloodshed. With the promise of fair usage, and the rights of prisoners of war, I surrender this little foraging party under my command."

"I'll make the terms agreeable," replied the sergeant. "Never doubt me, sir. Right hand file, advance, and receive the arms of the prisoners!"

"I'm here, captain," said Andrew, in a conceited tone, as if it were a mere occasion of merriment; and the lad quickly entered the house and secured the weapons, retreating with them some paces from the door.

"Now, sir," said Horse Shoe to the Ensign, "your sword, and whatever else you mought have about you of the ammunitions of war!"

The officer delivered up his sword and a pair of pocket pistols.

As Horse Shoe received these tokens of victory, he asked, with a lambent smile, and what he intended to be an elegant and condescending composure, "Your name, sir, if I mought take the freedom?"

"Ensign St. Jermyn, of his Majesty's seventy-first regiment of light infantry."

"Ensign, your sarvent," added Horse Shoe, still preserving this unusual exhibition of politeness. "You have defended your post like an old sodger, although you ha'n't much beard on your chin; but, seeing you have given up, you shall be treated like a man who has done his duty. You will walk out, now, and form yourselves in line at the door. I'll engage my men shall do you no harm; they are of a marciful breed."

When the little squad of prisoners submitted to this command, and came to the door, they were stricken with equal astonishment and mortification to find, in place of the detachment of cavalry which they expected to see, nothing but a man, a boy, and a horse. Their first emotions were expressed in curses, which were even succeeded by laughter from one or two of the number. There seemed to be a disposition on the part of some to resist the authority that now controlled them; and sundry glances were exchanged, which indicated a purpose to turn upon their captors.

The sergeant no sooner perceived this, than he halted, raised his rifle to his breast, and, at the same instant, gave Andrew Ramsay an order to retire a few paces, and to fire one of the captured pieces at the first man who opened his lips.

"By my hand," he said, "if I find any trouble in taking you, all five, safe away from this here house, I will thin your numbers with your own muskets! And that's as good as if I had sworn to it."

"You have my word, sir," said the Ensign. "Lead on."

"By your leave, my pretty gentleman, you will lead, and I'll follow," replied Horse Shoe. "It may be a new piece of drill to you; but the custom is to give the prisoners the post of honor."

"As you please, sir," answered the Ensign. "Where do you take us to?"

"You will march back by the road you came," said the sergeant.

Finding the conqueror determined to execute summary martial law upon the first who should mutiny, the prisoners submitted, and marched in double file from the hut back towards Ramsay's — Horse Shoe, with Captain Peter's bridle dangling over his arm, and his gallant young auxiliary Andrew, laden with double the burden of Robinson Crusoe (having all the fire-arms packed upon his shoulders), bringing up the rear. In this order victors and vanquished returned to David Ramsay's.

"Well, I have brought you your ducks and chickens back, mistress," said the sergeant, as he halted the prisoners at the door; "and what's more, I have brought home a young sodger that's worth his weight in gold."

"Heaven bless my child! my brave boy!" cried the mother, seizing the lad in her arms, and unheeding anything else in the present perturbation of her feelings. "I feared ill would come of it; but Heaven has preserved him. Did he behave handsomely, Mr. Robinson? But I am sure he did."

"A little more venturesome, ma'am, than I wanted him to be," replied Horse Shoe; "but he did excellent service. These are his prisoners, Mistress Ramsay; I should never have got them if it hadn't been for Andy. In these drumming and fifing times the babies suck in quarrel with their mother's milk. Show me another boy in America that's made more prisoners than there was men to fight them with, that's all!"

CHAPTER XXIII

SHOWING HOW A GOOD SOLDIER WILL TURN THE ACCIDENTS OF WAR TO THE BEST ACCOUNT. ENSIGN ST. JERMYN IN A DISAGREEABLE DILEMMA

ROBINSON having thus succeeded in his enterprise, now found himself in circumstances of peculiar perplexity in regard to the disposal of his prisoners. Here he was, in the neighborhood of the British posts — in a district of country of which the enemy might be said to have, at this moment, complete possession — (for Horse Shoe himself was almost the only belligerent in the field against them) — and, more than that, he was but a few miles' distant from a camp whose scouts had chased him almost to his present place of refuge. It was scarcely probable, therefore, that he could hope to retain his captives long under his control, or prevent the enemy from receiving intelligence of the capture. He was, however, notwithstanding these embarrassments, as usual, cheerful, confident, and self-possessed. He had no wish or motive to detain the private soldiers as prisoners of war, and would at once have dismissed them, if he could have assured himself that they would not make the earliest use of their liberty to convey information of their misadventure to the first corps of loyalists they should meet, and thus get up a hot pursuit of him through the whole district. But he had cogent and most important reasons for holding the ensign, St. Jermyn, in close custody. It occurred to him, that this officer might be used to control the procedure that should be adopted by those who meditated injury to Arthur Butler; and he, therefore, at once formed the resolution of communicating with the nearest British authorities, in order to assure them that he would retaliate upon the Ensign any pain that might be inflicted upon his late comrade. His plan was speedily formed — it was to keep his prisoners until night-fall, move off under cover of the darkness, to some remote and concealed spot with St. Jermyn, and release the others, on their parole or pledge not to take up arms until regularly exchanged.

Whilst the sergeant was deliberating over these arrangements, the prisoners were allowed to shelter themselves from the rain under a shed near the door of the dwelling, where Andrew, with all the pride and importance of his new station, marched to and fro, before them, like a trained sentinel. There was a small log building in the yard of Ramsay's mansion, which had been recently erected as a store-house, and which being well secured at the door by a padlock, Robinson determined to convert for the nonce into a prison. It contained but one room, not above twelve feet square, with an earthen floor, and received no light except such as was admitted under the door, and through a few crannies about the roof. Into this narrow apartment the soldiers were now marched; a bundle of straw was thrown upon the floor; sundry flitches of bacon, that hung upon the walls, were removed; and a few comforts, in the way of food and drink, were supplied to render the accommodation as tolerable to the inmates as was compatible with their safe custody. This being done, our friend Andrew was posted in the passage-way of the dwelling, in full view of the door of the store-house, which was carefully locked, with a musket in his hand, and with orders to make a circuit every five minutes round the little building, to guard against any attempts at escape by undermining the foundation.

As noon approached the weather began to clear up, and with the first breaking forth of the sun came David Ramsay, the proprietor of the farm which was the scene of the present operations. His recognition of Horse Shoe Robinson was accompanied by a hearty greeting, and with an expression of wonder that he should have ventured, in hostile guise, through a country so beset as this was by the forces of the enemy; but when he heard the narrative of the exploit of the morning, and saw the trophies of its success in the weapons piled against the wall, and, more especially, when he received from the lips of his wife a circumstantial account of the part which had been performed in this adventure by his son Andrew, his delight seemed almost to be absorbed by his astonishment and incredulity. The proofs, however, were all around him; and after assuring himself, by an actual inspection of the prisoners through one of the chinks of the store-house, he came into his own parlor, sat down, and laughed out-right.

Ramsay was a staunch friend of the independence of his country; and although he had not been up in arms in the cause, he gave it all the aid he could by the free expression of opinion, and by a resolute refusal to comply with the requisitions of the royalists. His eldest son had joined Sumpter, and had already been active in the field; and he himself looked, with an almost certain expectation, to see visited upon himself that proscription under which thousands were already suffering, and which he had only escaped as yet by the temporizing delays of his opponents, or by their neglect, arising out of the incessant hurry and pressure of their military operations in the organization of the new dominion which the royal forces had but lately acquired. He was a man of sturdy frame — now only in the prime of life — brave, thoughtful, and intelligent, and firmly resolved to stand by his principles through whatever adverse chances. The present aspect of affairs was, to his mind, almost decisive of his fate: the capture of these prisoners, made from information derived from his own family, and in which his own son had been a principal agent; their confinement, too, in his own house, were facts of so unequivocal a character as inevitably to draw upon him the prompt ire of the Tories, and compel him to assume the attitude and abide by the issues of a partisan. As he had faith in the justice of his quarrel, and a strong devotion to the principles upon which it was sustained, he did not hesitate in the crisis before him, but heroically determined to meet the worst that might befall. He, therefore, in the present emergency, became a useful and efficient ally to Robinson, who opened to him the full history of Butler, and the course of measures he was about to pursue for the relief of that unfortunate officer.

We must now leave the sergeant holding watch and ward over his vanquished foes, and shift our scene to Musgrove's Mill.

The family of Allen Musgrove were in a state of great disquietude. Horse Shoe Robinson had disappeared before daylight; and when the miller and his nephew left their beds, a little after the dawn, the only intelligence they had of the departure of their guest was inferred from finding the stable door open and the sergeant's horse absent. This fact was explained when Mary met them at breakfast. Horse Shoe had set out for Ramsay's to learn some tidings of John, and to enlist him in an effort to liberate Butler. He had departed under cover of darkness to avoid molestation from Innis's scouts, and she, Mary Musgrove, had placed the key of the stable, the night before, in a place where Horse Shoe might find it. Such was the extent of the maiden's information. The day passed wearily upon her hand: she was anxious to hear something of Butler — something of Horse Shoe — and something, we suppose, of John Ramsay. Frequently during the morning she and Christopher Shaw held secret conferences: they spoke in whispers: suspense, care, and doubt were pictured upon her face; and as the rain pattered against the windows she oftentimes stood before them, and looked out upon the distant road, and across the wide fields, and then upwards to the clouded sky. The sun at length appeared, and his rays seemed to shoot a glimpse of joy into the breast of the maiden, as she walked forth to note the drying of the roads, and to see the clear blue, which, in that climate, outvies the mellow and rich tints of a Tuscan heaven.

The day waxed, and the birds sang, and nature was gay, but the maiden was restless and unquiet: the day waned, and the sun rode downwards on the western slope in gorgeous beauty; but Mary was ill at ease, and thought little of the grand and glorious firmament. Her communings with Christopher Shaw, meantime, became more eager: she and her cousin were seen to wander towards the mill; then Christopher left her, and, presently, he might be discovered leading two horses, one bearing a side-saddle, down to the margin of the stream. There was a short visit to the house by the young man — a word whispered in the ear of the mother — a shake of her head, an expression of doubt, a final nod of assent, — and, in the next moment, Mary and Christopher were seen trotting off on horseback, on the road that led towards Ramsay's.

When they had ridden some two or three miles, and had entered upon the high-road between Ninety-Six and Blackstock's — somewhere near to that piece of haunted ground, where, on the morning of this very day, a goblin had struck down James Curry from his steed — they descried a military party of horse and foot slowly advancing from the direction to which they were travelling. In a few moments they met the first platoon of the cavalry, headed by a trumpeter and the unsightly captain Hugh Habershaw. They were detained at the head of this column, whilst some questions were asked respecting the object of their journey, the troops in their neighborhood, and other matters connected with the affairs of the times. Christopher's answers were prompt and satisfactory: he was only riding with his kinswoman on a visit to a neighbor; Innis's camp was not above two miles and a half away, and the country in general was quiet, as far as he had the means of knowing. The travellers were now suffered to pass on. In succession, they left behind them each platoon of threes, and then encountered the small column of march of the infantry. Mary grew pale as her eyes fell upon the form of Arthur Butler, posted in the centre of a guard. Her feeling lest he might not recognise her features, and guess something of her errand, almost overpowered her. She reined up her horse, as if to gratify an idle curiosity to see the soldiers passing, and halted in a position which compelled the ranks to file off, in order to obtain a free passage round her. Every look seemed to be turned upon her as the escort marched near her horse's head, and it was impossible to make the slightest sign to Butler without being observed. She saw him, however, lift his eyes to hers, and she distinctly perceived the flash of surprise with which it was kindled as he became aware of her features. A faint and transient smile, which had in it nothing but pain, was the only return she dared to make. An order from the van quickened the march; and the detachment moved rapidly by. As Mary still occupied the ground on which she had halted, and was gazing after the retreating corps, she saw Butler turn his face back towards her; she seized the moment to nod to him and to make a quick sign with her hand, which she intended should indicate the fact that she was now engaged in his service. She thought she perceived a response in a slight motion of Butler's head, and now resumed her journey, greatly excited by the satisfaction of having, in this accidental rencounter, obtained even this brief insight into the condition of the prisoner.

The sun was set, when Mary with her convoy, Christopher Shaw, arrived at Ramsay's. Always an acceptable guest at this house, she was now more than ever welcome. There was business to be done in which she could discharge a most important part, and the service of Christopher Shaw in reinforcing the garrison was of the greatest moment. When the intelligence regarding the movement of Butler to Innis's camp was communicated to the sergeant, it suggested a new device to his mind, which he determined instantly to adopt. Butler was at this moment, he concluded, in the hands of those who had engaged the ruffians to set upon him at Grindall's ford, and it was not improbable that he would be summarily dealt with: there was no time, therefore, to be lost. The sergeant's plan, in this new juncture, was, to compel the young ensign to address a letter to the British commandant, to inform that officer of his present imprisonment, and to add to this information the determination of his captors to put him to death, in the event of any outrage being inflicted upon Butler. This scheme was communicated to Ramsay, Shaw, and Mary. The letter was to be immediately written; Mary was to return with it to the mill, and was to contrive to have it secretly delivered, in the morning, at Innis's head-quarters; and David Ramsay himself was to escort the maiden back to her father's house, whilst Shaw was to attend the sergeant and assist him to transport the young ensign to some fit place of concealment. The private soldiers were to remain prisoners, under the guard of Andrew, until his father's return, when they were to be released on parole, as prisoners of war.

The plan being thus matured, Robinson went forthwith to the prison-house, and directed Ensign St. Jermyn to follow him into the dwelling. When the young officer arrived in the family parlor, he was ordered to take a chair near a table, upon which was placed a light, some paper, pen, and ink.

"Young man," said Robinson, "take up that pen and write as I bid you."

"To what end am I to write? I must know the purpose you design to answer, before I can put my hand to paper."

"To the end," replied Horse Shoe firmly, and with unwonted gravity, "of the settlement of your worldly affairs, if the consarns of to-morrow should bring ill luck to a friend of mine."

"I do not understand you, sir. If my life is threatened to accomplish an unrighteous purpose, it is my duty to tell you at once, that that life belongs to my king; and if his interests are to suffer by any forced act of mine, I am willing to resign it at once."

"Never was purpose more righteous, sir, in the view of God and man, than ours," said David Ramsay.

"I have a friend," added Horse Shoe, greatly excited as he spoke, "who has been foully dealt by. Some of your enlisted gangs have laid an ambuscade to trap him: villany has been used, by them that ought to be ashamed to see it thriving under their colors, to catch a gentleman who was only doing the common duties of a good sodger; and by mean bush-fighting, not by fair fields and honest blows — they have seized him and carried him to the camp of that blood-sucking Tory, Colonel Innis. I doubt more harm is meant him than falls to the share of a common prisoner of war."

"I know nothing of the person, nor of the circumstances you speak about," said the ensign.

"So much the better for you," replied the sergeant. "If your people are brave sodgers or honest men, you will not have much occasion to be afeard for yourself; but, by my right hand! if so much as one hair of Major Arthur Butler's head be hurt by Colonel Innis, or by any other man among your pillaging and brandishing bullies, I myself will drive a bullet through from one of your ears to the other. This game of war is a stiff game, young man, but we will play it out."

"Major Arthur Butler!" exclaimed the officer, with astonishment, "is he taken?"

"Ha! you've hearn of him, and know something, mayhap, of them that were on the look-out for him?"

"I cannot write," said the officer sullenly.

"No words, sir," interrupted Horse Shoe, "but obey my orders; write what I tell you, or take your choice. I will bind you hand and foot to a tree on yonder mountain, to starve till you write that letter; or to feed the wild vermin with your body, if you refuse."

The ensign looked in Robinson's face, where a frown of stern resolution brooded upon his brow, and a kindling tempest of anger showed that this was not a moment to hazard the trial of his clemency.

"What would you have the purport of my letter?" asked the officer, in a subdued voice.

"That you have got into the hands of the Whigs," replied the sergeant; "and that if so be any mischief should fall upon Major Butler, by the contrivings of your friends, you die the first minute that we hear of it."

"I have had no hand in the taking of Major Butler," said the young St. Jermyn.

"I am glad of it," answered Robinson, "for your sake. You will die with a better conscience. If you had a hand in it, young man, I wouldn't ask you to write a line to any breathing man: your brains would spatter that door-post. Take up the pen and write, or stand by the consequences."

The officer took up the pen, then, hesitating a moment, flung it down, saying:

"I will not write; do with me as you choose."

"The young man drives me to it, against my own nature," said Robinson, speaking under strong excitement. "If he will not pen that letter, then, David Ramsay, you will write to Innis, in my name, and say Galbraith Robinson has got the Ensign where no Tory foot will ever follow him, and holds him to answer the first mischief that is done to Arthur Butler. But, I swear to this sulky boy, that if that letter goes to Innis for want of a better, as I am a man and a sodger, he will never taste food or water till I hear that Major Butler is free. He shall starve in the mountain."

"Oh, God! oh, God!" ejaculated the young soldier, in bitterness of heart; and covering his face with his hands, he threw his head upon the table, where he wept tears of agony. At length, looking in the countenance of Robinson, he said: "I am young, sir — not above twenty years. I have a mother and sisters in England."

"We have no time to spare," interrupted Robinson, "much less to talk about kinsfolk. Major Butler has them that love his life better than e'er an Englishwoman loves her son. If they are brought to grief by this onnatural rascality, it matters nothing to me if every daughter and sister in England pines away of heart-sickness, for the loss of them that they love best. Take my advice, my lack-beard," added Robinson, patting him on the shoulder, "and write the letter. You have the chances of war in your favor, and may save your neck."

"I will do your bidding, sir," said the ensign, after a pause. "Under the compulsion of force, I agree to write," and he once more took up the pen.

"You speak now like a reasonable gentleman," said Horse Shoe. "I pity you, friend, and will preserve you against harm, so far as it can be done in the circumstances of the case."

The ensign then wrote a few lines, in which he communicated to Colonel Innis, or to whatever officer his letter might be delivered, the straits in which he found himself, and the resolution of his captors to hold his life forfeit upon the event of any rigors, beyond those of an ordinary prisoner of war, imposed upon Major Butler. When he had finished, he gave the paper to Robinson.

"Read it aloud Mr. Ramsay," said Horse Shoe, delivering the scrawl to his friend.

Ramsay read what was written.

"It must be wrote over again," said Horse Shoe, after he had heard the contents. "First, it must make no mention of his being only a few miles off; that must be left out. Secondly, my name needn't be told; though if the runagates knowed he was in my hands, they wouldn't think his chance any better on that account. Let him say that the Whigs have got him — that's enough. And lastly, he must write his own name in full at the bottom. And, look you, young man, don't be scrawling out the lines in such a way that your own hand-write moughtn't be known. That must speak for itself, because upon this letter depends your life. You understand?"

"Give it me," said the ensign; "I will write it as you desire."

And again the unfortunate officer applied himself to the task that was imposed upon him; and in a short time produced a letter, which, being subjected to the criticism of the bystanders, was pronounced satisfactory.

As soon as this was done, St. Jermyn was conducted into another apartment, and there confided to the guardianship of Christopher Shaw. Horse Shoe now took a light and the writing materials from the table, and repaired with David Ramsay — both of them well armed — to the store-house, where the other prisoners were confined. After they had entered and closed the door, posting Andrew with his musket on the outside, Horse Shoe addressed the men in a gay and cheerful tone:

"Come, my lads, as you are good, honest fellows, that can have no great love for these little country cabins, judging by your bad luck and oncomfortable circumstances in that one where I found you this morning, I have come to set you free. By the laws of war, you have the right, if I choose to take it, to give me your parole. So now, if you have a minute to promise me, on the honor of sodgers, not to sarve again until you are fairly exchanged, you shall all leave this before day-break. What do you say to the terms?"

"We are all agreed," replied the men, with one accord.

"Then write out something to that effect," said the sergeant to Ramsay. "You that can't scratch like scholards, stick your marks to the paper — d'ye hear?"

The parole was written out by Ramsay, and duly signed or marked by each of the four men. This being done, the sergeant informed them that, exactly at three in the morning, the door would be opened, and they would be at liberty to go where they pleased, provided they pledged themselves to visit no post of the enemy within twenty miles, nor communicate any particulars relating to their capture or detention to any British or Tory officer or soldier, within seven days. This pledge was cheerfully given, and after a few words of jocular good-nature were exchanged on both sides, Horse Shoe and his companion retired.

David Ramsay now ordered out his own and Mary Musgrove's horses, with an intention to set out immediately for the mill.

"Does Major Butler know that you are in his neighborhood?" inquired Ramsay of the sergeant, before the horses were brought to the door.

"Oh, bless you, yes," replied Horse Shoe. "I left word for him yesterday at Blackstock's, by giving the babblers there something to talk about, which I knew he would hear." And the sergeant went on to relate the particulars of his stop at that post: "And I sent him a message," continued he, "this morning, by James Curry, in the same sort of fashion. A little before daylight, I heard the devil singing one of his staves upon the road back here, so loud that he seemed to be frightened by ghosts or sperits; so I rode up fast behind him, and cuffed him out of his saddle, and then away I went like a leather-winged bat. I knowed the curmudgeon's voice, and I expect he knowed my hand, for he has felt it before. I'll be bound, he made a good story out of it; and, as such things fly, I make no doubt it wasn't long reaching the ear of the major, who would naturally think it was me, whether James told my name or not, because he knows my way. It was as good as writing a letter to the major, to signify that I was lurking about, close at hand. I never went to school, Mr. Ramsay, so I write my letters by making my mark. I can make a blow go further than a word upon occasion, and that's an old-fashioned way of telling your thoughts, that was found out before pen and ink."

"Well, Horse Shoe, you are a man after your own sort," replied Ramsay, laughing. "Come, Mary, take the letter; our horses are at the door."

"Good bye t'ye, David," said Horse Shoe, shaking Ramsay's hand; "it may be some days before we see each other again. Kit and me will be off with this young ensign before you get back. Don't forget the prisoners at three o'clock. And, a word, David — where had we best take this young sparrow, the ensign, to keep him out of the way of these fellows that are scouring the country?"

"Leave that to Christopher Shaw," replied Ramsay; "he knows every nook in the country. So, now, friend Robinson, good night, and luck go with you!"

It was a clear star-lit night, and every tree and pool sent forth a thousand notes from the busy insects and reptiles that animate the summer hours of darkness, when David Ramsay set out with Mary Musgrove for her father's house.

CHAPTER XXIV

NEW DIFFICULTIES OPEN UPON BUTLER

WITH the last notes of the reveillée everything was stirring in Innis's camp. It was a beautiful, fresh morning; a cool breeze swept across the plain, and each spray and every blade of grass sparkled with the dew; whilst above, an unclouded firmament gave promise of a rich and brilliant mid-summer's day. The surrounding forest was alive with the twittering of birds; and the neighing of horses showed that this portion of the animal creation partook of the hilarity of the season. From every little shed or woodland lair, crept forth parties of soldiers, who betook themselves to their several posts to answer at the roll-call; and by the time the sun had risen, officers, on horseback and on foot, were seen moving hurriedly across the open plain, to join the groups of infantry and cavalry, which were now forming in various quarters for the purposes of the morning drill. Companies were seen in motion, passing through the rapid evolutions of the march, the retreat, and the many exercises of service. Drums were beating, and fifes were piercing the air with their high notes, and, ever and anon, the trumpet brayed from the further extremities of the field. Picquet-guards were seen mustering on the edge of the camp — wearied and night-worn: salutes were exchanged by the small detachments on service; and, here and there, sentinels might be descried, stationed at the several outlets of the plain, and presenting their arms as an officer passed their lines.

The troops that occupied this space were mostly of the irregular kind. Some were distinguished by ill-fitted and homely uniforms; others were clad in the common dress of the country, distinguished as soldiers only by their arms and accoutrements; but amongst them was also a considerable party of British regulars, clad in the national livery of scarlet. Amongst the officers, who were in command of the subordinate departments of this mixed and particolored little army, were several who, from their costume, might be recognised as belonging to the regiments that had come from the other side of the Atlantic.

Colonel Innis himself was seen upon the parade, directing the movements of divisions that, under their proper officers, were practising the customary lessons of discipline. He was a tall, thin man, of an emaciated complexion, with a countenance of thoughtful severity. A keen black eye seemed almost to burn within its orb, and to give an expression of petulant and peevish excitability, like the querulousness of a sick man. A rather awkward and ungainly person, arrayed in a scarlet uniform that did but little credit to the tailor-craft employed in its fabrication, conveyed to the spectator the idea of a man unused to the pride of appearance that belongs to a soldier by profession; and would have suggested the conclusion, which the fact itself sustained, that the individual before him had but recently left the walks of civil life to assume a military office. His demeanour, however, showed him to be a zealous if not a skilful officer. He gave close attention to the duties of his command, and busied himself with scrupulous exactitude in enforcing the observances necessary to a rigorous system of tactics.

This officer, as we have before hinted, had been an active participator in the proceedings of the new court of sequestrations at Charleston; and had rendered himself conspicuous by the fierce and unsparing industry with which he had brought to the judgment of that tribunal, the imputed delinquencies of some of the most opulent and patriotic citizens of the province.

Amongst the cases upon which he had been called into consultation was that of Arthur Butler, whose possessions being ample, and whose position, as a rebellious belligerent, being one of "flagrant delict," there was but little repugnance, on the part of the judges and their adviser, to subject him to the severest law of confiscation. The proceedings, however, had been delayed, not from any tenderness to the proprietor, but, as it was whispered in the scandal of the day, on account of certain dissensions, amongst a few prominent servants of the British crown, as to which of them the privilege of a cheap purchase should be extended. The matter was still in suspense, with a view (as that busybody, common rumor, alleged) to regard a particular favorite of the higher powers with the rich guerdon of these good lands, in compensation for private and valuable secret services, rendered in a matter of great delicacy and hazard — no less a service than that of seducing into the arena of politics and intrigue, an opulent and authoritative gentleman of Virginia, Mr. Philip Lindsay.

In consequence of the odious nature of the duty which Colonel Innis had assumed to perform, he became peculiarly hateful to the

Whigs; and this sentiment was in no degree abated when, relinquishing his occupation as a counsellor to the court at Charleston, he accepted a commission to command a partisan corps of royalists in the upper country. He was, at the juncture in which I have exhibited him to my reader, new in his command, and had not yet "fleshed his maiden sword:" the day, however, was near at hand when his prowess was to be put to the proof.

Such was the person into whose hands Arthur Butler had now fallen.

After the morning exercises of the camp were finished, and the men were dismissed to prepare their first repast, the principal officers returned to the colonel's head-quarters in the farm-house, where, it will be remembered, Butler had been delivered by the escort that had conducted him from Blackstock's. The prisoner had slept soundly during the whole night; and now, as the breakfast hour drew nigh, he had scarcely awaked and put on his clothes, before he heard an inquiry, made by some one below, of the orderly on duty, whether the Whig officer was yet in a condition to be visited; and, in the next moment, the noise of footsteps, ascending the stair towards his chamber, prepared him to expect the entrance of the person who had asked the question.

A British officer, in full uniform, of a graceful and easy carriage, neat figure, and of a countenance that bespoke an intelligent and cultivated mind, made his appearance at the door. He was apparently of five or six and thirty years of age; and whilst he paused a moment, as with a purpose to apologize for the seeming intrusion, Butler was struck with the air of refined breeding of the individual before him.

"Major Butler, I understand, of the Continental army?" said the stranger. "The unpleasant nature of the circumstances in which you are placed, I hope will excuse the trespass I have committed upon your privacy. Captain St. Jermyn, of his Majesty's army, and lately an aide-de-camp of Lord Rawdon."

Butler bowed coldly, as he replied:

"To meet a gentleman, as your rank and name both import, is a privilege that has not been allowed me of late. Without knowing wherefore, I have been waylaid and outraged by bravoes and ruffians. You, perhaps, sir, may be able to afford me some insight into the causes of this maltreatment."

"Even if it were proper for me to hold discourse with you on such a subject, I could only speak from common report," replied the officer. "I know nothing of your seizure, except that, by the common chances of war, you have fallen into the hands of the ruling authorities of the province, and you will, doubtless, as a soldier, appreciate my motives for declining any reference to the circumstances in which you have been found. My visit is stimulated by other considerations, amongst which is foremost a desire to mitigate the peculiarly uncomfortable captivity to which I am sorry to learn you have been subjected."

"I thank you," replied Butler, "for the intention with which your good offices are proffered; but you can render me no service that I should value so much as that of informing me why I have been brought hither, at whose suggestion, and for what purpose."

"I will be plain with you, Major Butler. Your situation demands sympathy, however inexorably the present posture of our affairs may require the decrees of stern justice, in respect to yourself, to be executed. I feel for you, and would gladly aid you to any extent which my duty might allow, in averting the possible calamity that may hang over you. You are known as a gentleman of consideration and influence in the colonies. I may further add, as a brave and venturesome soldier. You are believed to have, more boldly than wisely, enterprised the accomplishment of certain schemes against the safety of his majesty's acknowledged government in this province; besides having committed other acts in violation of a faith plighted for you by those who had full authority to bind you, thus bringing yourself within the penalties appropriate to the violation of a military parole, if not within those of treason itself."

"He lies in his throat," cried Butler, "who charges me with forfeiture of plighted word or honor, in any action of my life. That I have arrayed myself against what you are pleased to term his majesty's acknowledged government in this province, I am proud to confess, here in the midst of your bands, and will confess it again at your judgment seat; but if aught be said against me that shall be intended to attaint my honor as a gentleman, I will, in the same presence and before God, throw the lie in the teeth of my accuser. Aye, and make good my word, now or hereafter, wheresoever it may be allowed me to meet the slanderer."

"I do not condemn your warmth," said St. Jermyn, calmly, "in a matter that so deeply stirs your self-esteem; and only desire now to second it in all things wherein an honorable enemy may claim the support of those who themselves value a good name. The authorities of this post have considerately resolved to give you the benefit of a court of inquiry. And I hope you will take it as it was meant, in all kindness to you, that I have come, before the communication of an official order, to apprise you that charges will be duly exhibited against you, and a trial be instantly had. If you will accept of my services, feeble and inadequate as they may be, I would gladly tender them to afford you such facilities as the pressure of the present emergency may allow."

"To be tried! when, and for what? If the charge is that I carry on open war against those who are in the habit of calling me and my compatriots rebels — I am ready to confess the charge. What need of court or trial?"

"There are graver and more serious offences than that imputed to you," said St. Jermyn.

"When am I to be informed of them, and to what do they tend?"

"You will hear them this morning; when, I am sorry to add, the nature of our military operations also enforces the necessity of your trial."

"You can be of little service, if that be true," returned Butler, thoughtfully. "My cause can only be defended by my country, long after I am made the victim of this unrighteous procedure."

"There is one alternative," said St. Jermyn, with some hesitation in his manner, "which a mature deliberation upon your relations as a subject — pardon me, for I do not deem this ill-timed rebellion to have obliterated them — may present to your mind."

"Speak it," said Butler, vehemently; "speak out the base thought that is rising to your lip, if you dare. Prisoner as I am, I will avenge the insult on the spot with the certainty of loss of life. The alternative you suggest, is to dishonor me and all who are dear to me by the foul opprobrium of treason to my country. You would have me, I suppose, renounce the cause to which I have dedicated my life, and take shelter with the recreants that have crowded under the banner of St. George?"

"Hold! remember, sir, that you are a prisoner," said St. Jermyn, with great coolness; and then after a pause, he added with a sigh: "I will not wound, by further converse, the exaggerated and delusive sense of honor which is too fatally predominant in your breast, and, as I have found it, in the breasts of many of your misguided countrymen. I came to serve you, not to excite your feelings; and I will now, even in your displeasure, serve you as far as the occasion may afford me means: I pray you, call on me without reserve. For the present, believe me, in pain and sorrow I take my leave."

With these words, the officer retired.

Butler paced to and fro through his narrow chamber for some minutes, as his mind revolved the extraordinary and unexpected disclosures which had been made to him in this short visit. A thousand conjectures rose into his thoughts as to the nature of the supposed charges that were to be brought against him. He minutely retraced all the incidents of his late adventures, to ascertain how it was possible to found upon them accusation of violated faith, or to pervert them into an imputation of treason against the present doubtful and disputed authority of the self-styled conquerors of Carolina. If his attempt to join Clarke was treason, it could be no less treason in the followers of Gates to array themselves against the royal army; and, that every prisoner hereafter taken in battle was to be deemed a traitor to the contested power of Cornwallis, seemed to be a pretension too absurd for the most inveterate partisans to assert. There was nothing in this review of his actions that the most ingenious malice could pervert into an offense punishable by the laws of war, by other rigor than such as might be inflicted upon an ordinary prisoner taken in arms. Still, there were unhappy doubts of some secret treachery that rose to his reflections: the perfidy of Adair, manifestly the effect of a bribe; the ambuscade promoted and managed by James Curry; the bloody purpose of the brutal gang who captured him, frustrated only by the accidental fray in which Blake was wounded. Then the "doubtful givings out" which fell from the lips of some of the soldiers at Blackstock's, of his case still being one of life and death; the insinuation of the savage Habershaw, at the same place, conveyed in the threat of twisted hemp; the knowledge which his present keepers affected to have of his rank and consequence, of his past life and present aims; and, above all, his being brought for immediate trial, in a matter affecting his life, before the very man, now in the capacity of a military commander, who had heretofore been active in promoting the design of confiscating his estate. All these considerations, although unconnected with any circumstance of specific offence within his knowledge, led him into the most anxious and melancholy forebodings as to the result of this day's proceedings.

"I am doomed to fall," he said, "under some secret stroke of vengeance, and my country is to have in my case another stirring appeal against the enormity of that iron rule that seeks to bow her head into the dust. So be it! The issue is in the hand of God, and my fate may turn to the account of the establishment of a nation's liberty. Oh, Mildred, I tremble to think of thee! Heaven grant, my girl, that thy fortitude may triumph over the martyrdom of him that loves thee better than his life!"

CHAPTER XXV

A TRIAL.—A GRAVE ACCUSATION THAT STILL FURTHER CONFIRMS BUTLER IN HIS BELIEF OF A SECRET ENEMY.—A SUDDEN RESPITE

BUTLER'S baggage, ever since he left Robinson's habitation on the Catawba, had been divided into two parcels, one of which he carried in a portmanteau on his own horse, and the other had been stowed away in a pair of black leather saddle-bags that were flung across Captain Peter. These latter sufficed, also, to inclose, in addition to the sergeant's own wardrobe, sundry stores of provender, which the careful appetite and soldier-like foresight of the trusty squire had, from time to time, accumulated for their comfort upon the road-side. After the escape of the sergeant, this baggage had been kept with more scrupulousness than might have been expected from the character of the freebooters into whose possession it had fallen; and now, when Butler had been surrendered up to the custody of Colonel Innis, it was restored to the prisoner without the loss of any article of value. On this morning, therefore, Butler had thrown aside the rustic dress in which he had heretofore travelled, and appeared habited as we have described him when first introduced to the reader.

After a very slight meal, which had been administered with more personal attention and consideration for his rank and condition than he was prepared to expect, an officer entered his apartment and communicated an order to him to repair to the yard in front of the quarters. Here he found a sergeant's guard mustered to receive him, and he was directed to march with them to the place that had been selected for this trial. The spot pitched upon for this purpose, was at the foot of a large mulberry that stood on the border of the plain, at a short distance from the house.

When the guard arrived with the prisoner, Colonel Innis was already seated at the head of a table, around which were placed several officers, both of the regular and militia forces. Writing materials were also arranged upon the board, and at the lower end, a few paces removed from it, stood a vacant chair. Behind this was erected a pile of drums, with one or two colours laid transversely across them. Sentinels were stationed at different points near this group, and within their lines were collected the principal officers of Innis's command. Somewhat more remote, a number of idle spectators were assembled, amongst whom might have been discerned Habershaw, Curry, and many of the heroes who had figured at Grindall's ford. Captain St. Jermyn had taken a station a little to the left of the presiding officer at the table, and in the rear of those who appeared to have the management of the approaching procedure, and now stood, with his hands folded, apparently an anxious and interested looker-on.

There was a thoughtful and even stern expression upon every face when Butler appeared — and a silence that was scarce broken by the occasional whispers in which the several individuals present communicated with each other. The guard marched the prisoner around the circle, and inducted him into the vacant chair, where he was received by a quiet and cold inclination of the head from each member of the court.

For a few moments he looked around him with a scornful gaze upon the assemblage that were to sit in judgment upon him, and bit his lip, as his frame seemed to be agitated with deep emotion: at length, when every look was bent upon him, and no one breathed a word, he rose upon his feet and addressed the company.

"I understand that I am in the presence of a military court, which has been summoned for the purpose of inquiring into certain offences, of the nature of which I have not yet had the good fortune to be informed, except in so far as I am given to infer that they purport of treason. I ask if this be true."

The presiding officer bowed his head in token of assent, and then presented a paper, which he described as containing the specification of charges.

"As an officer of the American army, and the citizen of an independent republic," continued Butler, "I protest against any accountability to this tribunal; and, with this protest, I publish my wrongs in the face of these witnesses, and declare them to arise out of facts disgraceful to the character of an honorable nation. I have been drawn by treachery into an ambuscade, overpowered by numbers, insulted and abused by ruffians. I wish I could say that these outrages were practised at the mere motion of the coarse banditti themselves who assailed me; but their manifest subserviency to a plan, the object of which was to take my life, leaves me no room to doubt that they have been in the employ and have acted under the orders of a more responsible head" —

"Keep your temper," interrupted Innis, calmly. "Something is to be allowed to the excited feelings of one suddenly arrested in the height of a bold adventure, and the court would, therefore, treat your expression of such feelings at this moment with lenity. You will, however, consult your own welfare, by giving your thoughts to the charges against you, and sparing yourself the labor of this useless vituperation. Read that paper, and speak to its contents. We will hear you patiently and impartially."

"Sir, it can avail me nothing to read it. Let it allege what it may, the trial, under present circumstances, will be but a mockery. By the chances of war, my life is in your hands; it is an idle ceremony and waste of time to call in aid the forms of justice, to do that which you have the power to do, without insulting Heaven by affecting to assume one of its attributes."

"That we pause to inquire," replied Innis, "is a boon of mercy to you. The offence of rank rebellion which you and all your fellow-madmen have confessed, by taking up arms against your king, carries with it the last degree of punishment. If, waiving our right to inflict summary pain for this transgression, we stay to hear what you can say against other and even weightier charges, you should thank us for our clemency. But this is misspending time. Read the paper to the prisoner," he added, addressing one of the officers at the table.

The paper was read aloud. It first presented a charge against the prisoner for violating the terms of the parole given at the capitulation of Charleston. The specification to support this charge was that, by the terms of the surrender, General Lincoln had engaged that the whole garrison should be surrendered as prisoners of war, and that they should not serve again until exchanged. The prisoner was described as an officer of that garrison, included in the surrender, and lately taken in the act of making war upon his majesty's subjects.

The second charge was, that the prisoner had insinuated himself, by false representations, into the territory conquered by the royal army; and that, in the quality of a spy, he had visited the family of a certain Walter Adair, with a view to obtain a knowledge of the forces, plans, movements, and designs of the various detachments engaged in his majesty's service in the neighborhood of Broad River.

And, third and last, that he, together with certain confederates, had contrived and partially attempted to execute a plan to seize upon and carry away a subject of his majesty's government, of great consideration and esteem — Mr. Philip Lindsay, namely, of the Dove Cote, in the province of Virginia. That the object of this enterprise was to possess himself of the papers as well as of the person of the said Philip Lindsay, and, by surrendering him up to the leaders of the rebel army, to bring upon him the vengeance of the rebel government, thus exposing him to confiscation of property, and even to peril of life.

Such was the general import and bearing of the accusations against the prisoner, expressed with the usual abundance of verbiage and minuteness of detail. Butler listened to them, at first, with indifference, and with a determination to meet them with inflexible silence; but, as the enunciation of them proceeded, and the extraordinary misrepresentations they contained were successively disclosed, he found his indignation rising to a height that almost mastered his discretion, and he was on the point of interrupting the court with the lie direct, and of involving himself in an act of contumacy which would have been instantly decisive of his fate. His better genius, however, prevailed, and, smothering his anger by a strong effort of self-control, he merely folded his arms and abided until the end, with a contemptuous and proud glance at his accusers.

"You have heard the allegations against you, sir," said Colonel Innis; "what say you to them?"

"What should an honorable man," replied Butler, "say to such foul aspersions? The first and second charges, sir, I pronounce to be frivolous and false. As to the last, sir, there are imputations in it that mark the agency of a concealed enemy, lost to every impulse of honor — a base and wicked liar. Confront me with that man, and let the issue stand on this — if I do not prove him to be, in the judgment of every true gentleman of your army, an atrocious and depraved slanderer, who has contrived against my life for selfish purposes, I will submit myself to whatever penalty the most exasperated of my enemies may invent. It was my purpose, sir, to remain silent, and to refuse, by any act of mine, to acknowledge the violation of the rights of war by which I have been dragged hither. Nothing could have swayed me from that determination, but the iniquitous falsehood conveyed in the last accusation."

"We cannot bandy words with one in your condition," interrupted the president of the court. "I must remind you again, that our purpose is to give you a fair trial, not to listen to ebullitions of anger. Your honor is concerned in these charges, and you will best consult your interest by a patient demeanor in your present difficulties."

"I am silent," said Butler, indignantly, taking his seat.

"Let the trial proceed," continued the president. "You will not deny," he said, after an interval of reflection, "that you are a native of Carolina?"

"I can scarcely deny that before you," replied Butler, "who, in my absence, as report says, have been busy in the investigation of my affairs."

"There are bounds, sir, to the forbearance of a court," said Innis, sternly. "I understand the taunt. Your estates have been the subject of consideration before another tribunal; and if my advice were listened to, the process relating to them would be a short one."

"You are answered," returned Butler.

"Nor can you deny that you were an officer belonging to the army under the command of General Lincoln."

Butler was silent.

"You were at Charleston during the siege?" inquired one of the court.

"In part," replied Butler. "I left it in March, the bearer of despatches to Congress."

"And you were in arms on the night of the thirteenth, at Grindall's Ford?" continued the same questioner.

"I confess it, sir."

"That's enough," interrupted Innis. "In the ninth article of the capitulation of Charleston we read: 'all civil officers, and the citizens who have borne arms *during the siege,* must be prisoners on parole.'"

"I should say," interposed St. Jermyn, who now, for the first time, opened his lips, "that the prisoner scarcely falls within that description. The words 'during the siege' would seem to point to a service which lasted to the end. They are, at least, equivocal; and I doubt Lord Cornwallis would be loath to sanction a judgment on such a ground."

Upon this ensued a consultation amongst the officers at the table, during which Butler was withdrawn to a short distance in the rear of the assemblage. Several of the unoccupied soldiers of the camp, at this stage of the trial, had crowded into the neighborhood of the court; and the sentinels, yielding to the eagerness of the common curiosity, had relaxed their guard so far as to allow the spectators to encroach beyond the lines. Among those who had thrust themselves almost up to the trial-table were a few children, male and female, bearing on their arms baskets of fruit and vegetables, which had been brought within the camp for sale. A smart-looking girl, somewhat older than the rest, seemed to have gained more favor from the crowd than her competitors, by the temptation which she presented of a rich collection of mellow apples; and perhaps her popularity was in some degree increased by the soft and pleasant-toned voice in which she recommended her wares, no less than by the ruddy, wholesome hue of her cheek, and an agreeable, laughing, blue eye, that shone forth from the shade of a deep and narrow sun-bonnet, the curtain of which fell upon her shoulders and down her back.

"Buy my apples, gentlemen," said the pretty fruit-merchant, coming up fearlessly to Colonel Innis, in the midst of the consultation.

"Three for a penny; they are very ripe and mellow, sir."

The colonel cast his eye upon the treasures of the basket, and began to select a few of the choicest fruit. Thus encouraged, the girl set her load upon the table, in the midst of the hats and swords with which it was encumbered, and very soon every other member of the court followed the example of the presiding officer, and became purchasers of the greater part of the store before them. When this traffic was concluded, the little huckster took up her burden and retired towards the group of spectators. Seeing the prisoner in this quarter, she walked up to him, curtsied, and presented him an apple, which was gratefully accepted, and the proffered return, from him, in money, refused.

When about a quarter of an hour had elapsed, Butler was resummoned to his seat, and the court again proceeded to business. The inquiry now related to the second charge — that, namely, which imputed to the prisoner the character of a spy in his visit at Adair's. To this accusation, Captain Hugh Habershaw and several of his troop were called as witnesses. The amount of testimony given by them was, that, on the eleventh of the month, they had received information that a Continental officer, whose real name and title was Major Butler, but who was travelling in disguise and under an assumed name, from the Catawba towards the Broad River, in company with a well known, stark Whig — a certain Horse Shoe Robinson — was expected in a few days to arrive at Wat Adair's. That Habershaw, hoping to intercept them, had scoured the country between the two rivers; but that the travellers had eluded the search, by taking a very circuitous and unfrequented route towards the upper part of Blair's Range and Fishing Creek. That, on the night of the twelfth, the two men arrived at Adair's, unmolested; and, on the morning of the thirteenth, some of the woodman's family had met Habershaw and apprised him of this fact; adding, further, that the prisoner had offered a bribe to Adair, to induce him to give information in regard to the loyalist troops in the neighborhood, with a view to communicate it to a certain Colonel Clarke, who had appointed to meet Butler and his companion somewhere on the upper border of the province. That, in consequence of this attempt, Adair had directed the prisoner towards Grindall's Ford; and, this intelligence being communicated to the witness, he had conducted his troop to that place, where he succeeded in arresting the prisoner and his comrade, with the loss of two men in the struggle. The narrative then went on to give the particulars of Horse Shoe's escape, and the other facts with which the reader is acquainted. This account was corroborated by several witnesses, and, amongst the rest, by Curry.

Butler heard the testimony with the most painful sensations. There was just enough of truth in it to make the tale plausible, and the falsehood related to points which, as they were affirmed upon hearsay, he could not repel by proof. There was a common expression of opinion amongst the bystanders — who in general were inclined to take the side of the prisoner in reference to the charge which was supposed to affect his life — that this accusation of Butler's acting the part of a spy was sustained by the proof. In vain did he protest against the injustice of being condemned on what was alleged to have been said by some of Adair's family; in vain did he deny that he had offered a bribe to Adair for information respecting the Tories; and equally in vain did he affirm that he had asked of Adair nothing more than the common hospitality due to a traveller, and for which he had made him a moderate requital — the only money the woodman had received from him. The current was now setting violently against him, and it seemed impossible to stem it.

"It is but due," said Captain St. Jermyn, a second time interposing in behalf of the prisoner, "to the rank and character of Major Butler, since a portion of this testimony is second-hand, to take his own examination on these alleged facts. With permission, therefore, I would ask him a few questions."

"The court will not object," said Innis, who throughout affected the air of an impartial judge.

"It is true, Major Butler, that you were at Adair's on the night of the twelfth?" said the volunteer advocate of the prisoner.

"I was, sir."

"And you made no concealment of your name or rank?"

"I will not say that," replied Butler.

"You were under a feigned name then, sir?" inquired Innis, as St. Jermyn seemed a little confounded by the answer he had received.

"I was called Mr. Butler, sir; my rank or station was not communicated."

"Your dress?"

"Was an assumed one, to avoid inquiry."

"This man, Horse Shoe Robinson," said St. Jermyn, "was known to Adair as a whig soldier?"

"Well known," replied Butler; "and I was also represented as belonging to that party. Adair himself led us to believe that he was friendly to our cause."

Here several members of the court smiled.

"Had you met any parties of loyalists," inquired Innis, "in your journey between Catawba and Broad?"

"We had — more than one."

"How did you escape them?"

"By assuming feigned characters and names."

"Your purpose was to join Clarke?"

"I am not at liberty to answer that question," replied the prisoner. "Suffice it, sir, I was travelling through this region on a mission of duty. My purpose was to act against the enemy. So far the charge is true, and only to this extent. I came with no design to pry into the condition of the royal troops; I sought only a successful passage through a contested, though sadly overpowered country."

"You offered no money to Adair," said St. Jermyn again, as if insisting on this point of exculpation, "but what you have already called a moderate requital for his entertainment?"

"None," replied the prisoner — "except," he added, "a guinea, to induce him to release, from some wicked torture, a wolf he had entrapped."

"It will not do," said Colonel Innis, shaking his head at St. Jermyn; and the same opinion was indicated in the looks of several of the court.

"I was at Walter Adair's that night, and saw the gentleman there, and heard all that was said by him; and I am sure that he offered Watty no money," said our little apple-girl, who had been listening with breathless anxiety to the whole of this examination, and who had now advanced to the table as she spoke the words. "And I can tell more about it, if I am asked."

"And who are you, my pretty maid?" inquired Colonel Innis, as he lifted the bonnet from her head and let loose a volume of flaxen curls down upon her neck.

"I am Mary Musgrove, the miller's daughter," said the damsel, with great earnestness of manner, "and Watty Adair is my uncle, by my mother's side — he married my aunt Peggy; and I was at his house when Major Butler and Mr. Horse Shoe Robinson came there."

"And what in the devil brought you here?" said Habershaw, gruffly.

"Silence!" cried Innis, impatient at the obtrusive interruption of the gross captain. "What authority have you to ask questions? Begone, sir."

The heavy bulk of Hugh Habershaw, at this order, sneaked back into the crowd.

"I came only to sell a few apples," said Mary.

"Heaven has sent that girl to the rescue of my life," said Butler, under the impulse of a feeling which he could not refrain from giving vent to in words. "Pray allow me, sir, to ask her some questions."

"It is your privilege," was the answer from two or three of the court; and the spectators pressed forward to hear the examination.

Butler carefully interrogated the maiden as to all the particulars of his visit, and she, with the most scrupulous fidelity, recounted the scenes to which she had been a witness. When she came to detail the conversation which she had overheard between Adair and Lynch, and the events that followed it, the interest of the bystanders was wound up to the highest pitch. There was a simplicity in her recital of this strange and eventful story, that gave it a force to which the most skilful eloquence might in vain aspire; and when she concluded, the court itself, prejudiced as the members were against the prisoner, could not help manifesting an emotion of satisfaction at the clear and unequivocal refutation which this plain tale inferred against the testimony of Habershaw and his confederates. Innis alone affected to treat it lightly, and endeavored in some degree to abate its edge, by suggesting doubts as to the capacity of a young girl, in circumstance so likely to confuse her, to give an exact narrative of such a complicated train of events. Every cross-examination, however, which was directed to the accuracy of the maiden's story, only resulted in producing a stronger conviction of its entire truth. This concluded the examination on the second charge.

The court now proceeded to the third and last accusation against the prisoner.

To this there was but one witness called — James Curry. In the course of the examination this man showed great address and knowledge of the world. He gave some short account of himself. He had been a man born to a better condition of life than he now enjoyed. His education had been liberal, and his associations in life extremely various. It was to be inferred from his own relation, that he had fallen into some early indiscretion which had thrown him into the lowest stations of society, and that his original delinquency had prevented him from ever rising above them. He had served for many years in the army, and was present at the surrender of Charleston, being at that period a confidential servant, or man of business, to the young Earl of Caithness, the aide-de-camp of Sir Henry Clinton. Upon the departure of that young nobleman with the rest of Sir Henry's military family, for New York, he had remained behind, and had taken a similar service to that which he had left, with another officer of some repute. "There were state reasons," he said, "why this gentleman's name could not now be communicated to the court." That, in the month of July, he had attended his master on a visit to Mr. Philip Lindsay, in Virginia; and whilst in the immediate vicinity of that gentleman's residence, at a small country tavern, he had accidentally become privy to the design of the prisoner, and the same Horse Shoe Robinson who had been mentioned before, to seize upon the person and papers of Mr. Lindsay: that these two persons had actually arrived at the tavern he spoke of to commence operations. That he had overheard them discussing the whole plan; and he had no doubt they had allies at hand to assist in the scheme, and would have proceeded that same night to put it in execution, if he had not frustrated their design at the risk of his life. That, with the view of interrupting this enterprise, he had lured Robinson, the companion of the prisoner, to walk with him at night to the margin of a small river near the tavern, where he accused him of the treacherous design which he and his comrade had in view: that, in consequence of this, Robinson had endeavored to take his life, which was only saved by a severe struggle; and that, being thus discovered in their purpose, this man, Robinson, and the prisoner had made a hasty retreat towards Gates's head-quarters.

Such was in effect the narrative of James Curry, which was solemnly given upon oath. Butler was for some moments confounded with astonishment at the audacity of this falsehood. He urged to the court the improbability of the whole story. "It would have been easy," he said, "if I had been hostile to Mr. Philip Lindsay — which, God knows, there are most cogent reasons to disprove — it would have been easy to procure his arrest without an attempt at a violent seizure by me. I had only to speak, and the whole country around him would have united in treating him as an object of suspicion, on account of his politics." He admitted that he was at Mrs. Dimock's at the time spoken of — that Robinson attended him there; but all else that had been said relating to the visit, he affirmed to be utterly false. He gave the particulars of the meeting between Horse Shoe and the witness, as he had it from Robinson; and spoke also of his knowledge of the visit of Tyrrel at the Dove Cote — "which person," he said, "he had reason to believe, came under a name not his own."

"How do you happen to be so familiar," inquired Innis, "with the affairs of Mr. Lindsay?"

"That question," replied Butler, "as it refers to matters entirely private and personal, I must decline to answer."

Curry, upon a second examination, re-affirmed all he had said before, and commented with a great deal of dexterity upon Butler's statement, particularly in reference to such parts of it as the prisoner's repeated refusal to answer had left in doubt. After a protracted examination upon this point, the trial was at length closed, and Butler was ordered back to his apartment in the farm-house.

Here he remained for the space of half an hour, an interval that was passed by him in the most distressing doubt and anxiety. The whole proceeding of the court boded ill to him. The haste of his trial, the extraordinary nature of the charges, and the general unsympathizing demeanor of the court itself, only spoke to his mind as evidences of a concealed hostility, which sought to find a plausible pretext for making him a sacrifice to some private malevolence. He was therefore prepared to expect the worst when, at the close of the half hour, St. Jermyn entered his chamber.

"I come, sir," said the officer, "to perform a melancholy duty. The court have just concluded their deliberations."

"And I am to be a sacrifice to their vengeance. Well, so be it! There was little need of deliberation in my case, and they have soon despatched it," said Butler, with a bitter spirit, as he paced up and down his narrow chamber. "What favor have these, my impartial judges, vouchsafed to me in my last moment? Shall I die as a common felon, on a gibbet, or am I to meet a soldier's doom?"

"That has been thought of," said St. Jermyn. "The commanding officer has no disposition to add unnecessary severity to your unhappy fate."

"Thank God for that! and that the files detailed for this service are to be drawn from the ranks of my enemies! I will face them as proudly as I have ever done on the field of battle. Leave me, sir; I have matters in my thought that require I should be alone."

"Your time, I fear, is brief," said St. Jermyn. "The guard is already at hand to conduct you to the court, who only stay to pass sentence. I came before to break the unhappy news to you."

"It is no news to me," interrupted Butler. "I could expect no other issue to the wicked designs by which I have been seized. This solemn show of a trial was only got up to give color to a murderous act which has been long predetermined."

At this moment, the heavy and regular tap of the drum, struck at equal intervals, and a mournful note from a fife, reached the prisoner's ear.

"I come!" exclaimed Butler. "These fellows are practising their manual for an occasion in which they appear impatient to act. One would think, Captain St. Jermyn," he added, with a smile of scorn, "that they needed but little practise to accomplish them for a ceremony which has of late, since his majesty has extended his merciful arm over this province, grown to be a familiar piece of military punctilio."

St. Jermyn hastily fled from the room, and rushing out upon the grass-plot where the guard was collected, cried out:

"Silence, you base and worthless knaves! Is it thus you would insult the sufferings of an unfortunate enemy, by drumming, under his very ear, your cursed death-notes? Strike but one note upon that drum again, and I will have you up to the halberds."

"The music did but try a flourish of the dead march," replied the sergeant of the guard; "they are a little rusty, and seeing that the Whig officer"—

"Another word, sir, and you shall be sent to the provost-marshal. Attend the prisoner."

"I am here," said Butler, who had overheard this conversation, and had already descended to the door.

With a mournful and heavy heart, though with a countenance that concealed his emotions under an air of proud defiance, he took his place in the ranks, and marched to the spot where the court were yet assembled.

"A chair for the prisoner," said some of the individuals present, with an officious alacrity to serve him.

"I would rather stand," replied Butler. "It is my pleasure to hear the behests of my enemies in the attitude a soldier would choose to meet his foe in the field."

"Mine is a painful duty, Major Butler," said Innis, rising, as he addressed the prisoner. "It is to announce to you that, after a full and most impartial trial, in which you have had the advantage of the freest examination of witnesses, and every favor accorded to you which the usages and customs of war allow, you have been found guilty of two of the charges imputed to you in the list with which you were furnished this morning. Notwithstanding the satisfactory testimony which was given in your behalf by the girl Mary Musgrove, in relation to your conduct at the house of Adair, and however disposed the court were to abandon an accusation which thus seemed to be refuted, it has occurred to them, upon subsequent reflection, that, by your own confession — given, sir, permit me to say, with the frankness of a soldier — you came into this district in disguise and under false names, and thus enabled yourself to collect information relative to the condition of the royal forces, which it was doubtless your purpose to use to our detriment. The court, for a moment, might have led you to entertain hope that they were satisfied that in this charge you had been wronged. The simple, affecting, and, no doubt, true narrative made by the miller's daughter produced a momentary sensation that was too powerful to be combated. That narrative, however, does not relieve you from the effect of your own confessions, since both may be true, and the charge still remain unimpaired against you.

"The offence of breaking your parole and infringing the terms of the capitulation of Charleston, is open to a legal doubt, and, therefore, in tenderness to you, has not been pressed; although the court think, that the very circumstance of its doubtful character should have inculcated upon you the necessity of the most scrupulous avoidance of service in the conquered province.

"The last charge against you is fully proved. Not a word of

counter evidence has been offered. Strictly speaking, by the usages of war, this would not be an offence for the notice of a military tribunal. The perpetrators of it would be liable to such vindictive measures as the policy of the conqueror might choose to adopt. That we have given you, therefore, the benefit of an inquiry, you must regard as an act of grace, springing out of our sincere desire to do you ample justice. The nature of the offence imputed and proved is such as, at this moment, every consideration of expediency demands should be visited with exemplary punishment. The friends of the royal cause, wherever they may reside, shall be protected from the wrath of the rebel government; and we have, therefore, no scruple in saying, that the attempt upon the person of Mr. Philip Lindsay requires a signal retribution. But for this last act, the court might have been induced to overlook all your other trespasses. Upon this, however, there is no hesitation.

"Such being the state of the facts ascertained by this tribunal, its function ceases with its certificate of the truth of what has been proved before it. The rest remains to me. Without the form of an investigation, I might, as the commanding officer of a corps on detached service, and by virtue of special power conferred upon me, have made up a private judgment in the case. I have forborne to do that, until, by the sanction of a verdict of my comrades, I might assure myself that I acted on the clearest proofs. These have been rendered.

"My order, therefore, is, in accordance with the clear decision of the court, — and, speaking to a soldier, I use no unnecessary phrase of condolence, — that you be shot to death. Time presses on us and forbids delay. You will be conducted to immediate execution. Major Frazer," he said, turning to one of his officers, "to your discretion I commit this unpleasant duty." Then, in a tone of private direction, he added, "Let it be done without delay; pomp and ceremony are out of place in such a matter. I wish to have it despatched at once."

"I would speak," said Butler, repressing the agitation of his feelings, and addressing Innis with a stern solemnity, "not to implore your mercy, nor to deprecate your sentence: even if I could stoop to such an act of submission, I know my appeal would reach your ears like the idle wind: but I have private affairs to speak of."

"They were better untold, sir," interrupted Innis with an affected air of indifference. "I can listen to nothing now. We have other business to think of. These last requests and settlements of private affairs are always troublesome," he muttered in a tone just audible to the officers standing near him; "they conjure up useless sympathies."

"I pray you, sir," interposed St. Jermyn.

"It is in vain, I cannot hear it," exclaimed the commander, evidently struggling to shake from his mind an uncomfortable weight. "These are woman's requests! God's mercy! How does this differ from death upon the field of battle? a soldier is always ready. Ha! What have we here?" he exclaimed, as a trooper rode up to the group. "Where are you from? What news?"

"A vidette from Rocky Mount," answered the horseman. "I am sent to inform you that, yesterday, Sumpter defeated three hundred of our people on the Catawba, and has made all that were alive, prisoners, besides capturing fifty or sixty wagons of stores which the detachment had under convoy for Camden."

The first inquiries that followed this communication related to Sumpter's position, and especially whether he was advancing towards this camp.

"He is still upon Catawba, tending northwards," replied the vidette.

"Then we are free from danger," interrupted Innis. "I am stripping the feathers from a bird to-day that is worth half of Sumpter's prize," he added, with a revengeful smile, to an officer who stood by him.

During this interval, in which the commander of the post was engaged with the vidette, the guard had conducted the prisoner back to the house, and Innis, freed from the restraint of Butler's presence, now gave way to the expression of a savage exultation at the power which the events of the morning had given him, to inflict punishment upon one that he termed an audacious rebel. "The chances jump well with us," he said, "when they enable us to season the joy of these ragged traitors, by so notable a deed as the execution of one of their shrewdest emissaries. This fellow Butler has consideration amongst them, and fortune too: at least he had it, but that has gone into better hands; and, to say truth, he has a bold and mischievous spirit. The devil has instigated him to cross our path; he shall have the devil's comfort for it. The whole party taken did you say?"

"Every man, sir," replied the vidette.

"How many men had this sulking fellow, Sumpter, at his back?"

"They say about seven hundred."

"And did the cowards strike to seven hundred rebels?"

"They were tangled with the wagons," said the soldier, "and were set on unawares, on the bank of the river, at the lower ferry."

"Aye, that's the way! An ambuscade, no doubt, — a piece of cowardly bush-fighting. Fresh men against poor devils worn down by long marching! Well, well, I have a good requital for the rascally trick. Major Butler's blood will weigh heavy in the scale, or I am mistaken! Come, gentlemen, let us to quarters — we must hold a council."

"Here is a letter," said one of the officers of the court, "which I have this moment found on the table, under my sword belt; it seems, from its address, to contain matter of moment. How it came here does not appear."

"'To Colonel Innis, or any other officer commanding a corps in his majesty's service,'" said Innis, reading the superscription; "besides, here is something significant, '*for life or death, with speed.*' What can this mean?" he added, as he broke open the paper and ran his eyes hastily over the contents. "St. George! here is something strange, gentlemen. Listen! —

"'By ill luck I have fallen into the possession of the Whigs. They have received intelligence of the capture of Major Butler, and, apprehending that some mischief might befal him, have constrained me to inform you that my life will be made answerable for any harsh treatment that he may receive at the hands of our friends. They are resolute men, and will certainly make me the victim of their retaliation.

EDGAR ST. JERMYN,
Ensign of the 71st Reg't.

P. S. For God's sake respect this paper, and be lenient to the prisoner.'"

"Treason and forgery, paltry forgery!" exclaimed Innis, with a smile of derision, as he finished reading the letter. "What ho! tell Frazer to lead out the prisoner, and despatch him without a moment's delay. So much for this shallow artifice!"

"A base forgery," said one of the officers in attendance, "and doubtless the work of the rebel major himself. He will die with this silly lie upon his conscience. St. Jermyn, here!" cried out the same officer to the captain, who was now at some distance, "here is an attempt to put a trick upon us by a counterfeit of your brother's hand, telling a most doleful and improbable falsehood. Look at it."

St. Jermyn read the letter, and suddenly turning pale, exclaimed: "Sir, this is no trick. It is my brother's own writing. He is in the custody of the Whigs! How came this here? Who brought it? When was it written? Can nobody tell me?"

"Tut, St. Jermyn!" interrupted the officer, smiling, "you surely cannot be imposed upon by such a device. Look at the scrawl again. In truth, are you sure of it, man?" he inquired with great surprise, as he perceived the increasing paleness of St. Jermyn's brow.

"My brother's life is in imminent danger," replied St. Jermyn, with intense earnestness. "Colonel Innis, as you value my happiness, I entreat you, countermand the order for the prisoner's execution. I implore you, respect this letter; it is genuine, and I dread the consequences. My poor brother, the youngest of my family, and the special darling of his parents! For heaven's sake, good colonel, pause until we learn something more of this mysterious business."

"For your sake, my friend, and until we can investigate this matter," said Innis, "let the execution be suspended."

St. Jermyn instantly hurried to the guard, to communicate the new order.

"Whence comes this missive?" demanded Innis. "It has neither date nor place described. Who brought it? Did any one see the bearer?" he asked aloud of the bystanders.

No one answered except the officer who had first discovered the paper. "I know nothing more than what you see. It was here upon the table. How long it had been there I cannot tell."

"It is strange," continued Innis. "Can this young St. Jermyn have fallen in with Sumpter? Or, after all, is it not an ingenious forgery which has deceived our friend the captain? Still, who could have brought it here?"

The letter was again examined by every individual present.

"It must be genuine," said one of the officers, shaking his head. "Captain St. Jermyn was very much in earnest, and it is not likely he could be deceived. It has been mysteriously deposited here by some agent of the Whigs. The person should be found, and compelled to give us more specific information. This matter must be looked to; the ensign, I doubt not, is in perilous circumstances."

"Let the prisoner be strictly guarded, and held to wait our future pleasure," said Innis. "I would not put in jeopardy the young ensign's life. A reward of twenty guineas shall be given to any one who brings me the bearer of this letter. And you, Lieutenant Connelly, take thirty troopers, and scour the country round to gain intelligence of this capture of Edgar St. Jermyn. Be careful to examine every man you meet, as to the presence of Whig parties in this district. Away instantly, and do not return without tidings of this singular event."

The camp, by these occurrences, was thrown into great bustle. The prisoner was securely lodged in his former quarters, and placed under a double guard; consultations were held amongst the officers; and Butler himself was strictly interrogated in regard to the appearance of this mysterious letter, of the contents of which he was yet ignorant. The examination threw no light on the affair; and, very soon afterwards, a troop of horse were seen sallying beyond the limits of the camp, under Lieutenant Connelly, to seek information of the fate of Ensign St. Jermyn.

CHAPTER XXVI

THE SERGEANT AND HIS COMRADE PROJECTS AN EXPEDITION WHICH FURNISHES THE ENSIGN AN OPPORTUNITY OF ENJOYING THE PICTURESQUE

As soon as David Ramsay had departed with the maiden for Musgrove's mill, Robinson ordered his own and Christopher Shaw's horse to be saddled, and another to be made ready for St. Jermyn. His next care was to determine upon a secure place of retreat — reflecting that the news of the capture of the ensign must soon reach the British posts, and that the country would be industriously explored with a view to his rescue. A spot known to the woodsmen of this region by the name of the Devil's Ladder, which was situated in the defile of a mountain brook that emptied into the Ennoree, occurred to Christopher Shaw as the most secret fastness within their reach. This spot lay some twenty miles westward of Ramsay's, accessible by roads but little known, and surrounded by a district which grew more wild and rugged the nearer it approached the defile.

Here it was supposed the party might arrive by daylight the next morning, and remain for a few days at small risk of discovery; and thither, accordingly, it was resolved they should repair.

This being settled, Horse Shoe now procured a supply of provisions from Mistress Ramsay, and then proceeded to arm himself with the sword and pistols of the ensign, whilst Christopher suspended across his body the sword of Goliath, as the sergeant called the brand he had snatched up at Blackstock's, and also took possession of one of the captured muskets.

"If it don't go against your conscience, Mistress Ramsay," said Horse Shoe, when the preparations for the journey were completed, "I would take it as a favor, in case any interlopers mought happen to pop in upon you, if you would just drop a hint that you have hearn that Sumpter's people had been seen about these parts. It would have an amazing good bearing on the Tories. Besides making them wary how they strayed about the woods it would be sure to put the bloodhounds on a wrong scent, if they should chance to be sarching for the young ensign. I know you women are a little ticklish about a fib, but then it's an honest trick of the war sometimes. And, to make you easy about it, it will be no more than the truth to say you did hear it — for, you obsarve, I tell you so now."

"But," replied the scrupulous matron, "if they should ask me who told me, what should I answer?"

"Why," said the sergeant, hesitating, "just out with it — tell 'em you heard it from one Horse Shoe Robinson; that'll not make the news the worse in point of credit. And be sure, good woman, above all things, to remind David, when he gets back to-night, that the rank and file, in our prison yonder, are not to be turned loose before three o'clock in the morning."

This last caution was repeated to Andy, who still performed the duty of a sentinel at the door of the out-house. All things being now arranged for their departure, Ensign St. Jermyn was brought from the chamber where he had been confined, and was invited to join the sergeant and Christopher at supper before they set out. This meal was ably and rapidly discussed by the stout yeomen, and scarcely less honored by the prisoner, whom the toils and privations of the day had brought to enjoyment of a good appetite.

With many cheering and kind expressions of encouragement from the sergeant, the young officer prepared to comply with the demands of his captors, and was soon in readiness to attend them. Robinson lifted him into his saddle with a grasp as light as if he was dealing with a boy, and then bound him by a surcingle to the horse's back, whilst he offered a good-humored apology for the rigor of this treatment.

"It is not the most comfortable way of riding, Mr. Ensign," he said, with a chuckle; "but fast bind, fast find, is a'most an excellent good rule for a traveller in the dark. I hope you don't think I take any pleasure in oncommoding you, but it is my intention to lead your horse by the rein to-night, and this friend of mine will keep in the rear. So, by way of a caution, I would just signify to you that if you should think of playing a prank you will certainly bring some trouble upon your head — as one or another of us would in that case be obliged to fire. It is nothing more than military punctilium to give you a friendly warning of this."

"You might dispense with this severity, I should think," replied the prisoner, "upon my pledge of honor that I will make no effort to escape."

"I can take no pledge in the dark," returned Horse Shoe;

"daylight mought make a difference. If we should happen to fall in with any of your gangs I'm thinking a pledge wouldn't come to much more than a cobweb when I should ax you to gallop out of the way of your own people. Flesh is weak, as the preacher says, and, to my mind, it's a little the weaker when the arm is strong or the foot swift. Temptation is at the bottom of all backsliding. No, no, Mr. Ensign, you may get away, if you can; we'll take care of you whilst we're able — that's a simple understanding."

Without further speech the party proceeded on their journey. They travelled as rapidly as was consistent with the ease of the prisoner and the nature of the ground over which they had to move. For the first eight or ten miles, their route lay across a country with but few impediments, except such as arose from the unseasonable hour of the ride. After this they found the toil and hazard of travel continually increasing. They had been retreating from the settled country towards a rough wilderness, which was penetrated only by an obscure road, so little beaten as to be scarcely discernible in the faint starlight, and which it required all Christopher's skill in woodcraft to follow. Our travellers, consequently, often lost their way, and were obliged to get down from their horses and grope about to ascertain the path. The stars had shone all night through a cloudless firmament, but the deep shade of the forest thickened around the wanderers, and it was frequently with difficulty, even, that they could discern each other's figures.

They reached at length the small stream upon whose banks, some miles above, was situated the place to which their steps were directed; and they were thus rendered more sure of their road, as they had only to follow the ascending course of the brook. The delays and impediments of the journey had nearly outrun the night, and whilst our travellers were yet some two or three miles from their destination, the first traces of morning began to appear in the east. The increasing light disclosed to them the nature of the scenery around. A limpid rivulet tumbled over a rocky channel, girt with a profusion of brush and briar, amongst which were scattered a thousand wild-flowers, that, renovated by the dew, threw forth a delicious perfume. A succession of abrupt hills, covered with the varied foliage of a rich forest growth, bounded the brook on either side. Occasional rocks jutted above the heads of the travellers as they wound along the paths, worn by the wild cattle in the bottom of the dell.

Both Robinson and Shaw had dismounted when they entered this defile, and whilst the former led the horse of the prisoner his companion preceded him to explore the doubtful traces of the road, which frequently became so obscure as to render it necessary to seek a passage in the bed of the stream. During all this progress Horse Shoe's good nature and light-heartedness were unabated. He conversed with the prisoner in the same terms of friendly familiarity that he did with Shaw, and neglected no attention that might in any degree relieve the irksomeness of St. Jermyn's necessary thraldom.

That peculiar conformation of country which had given rise to the name of the place to which they were conducting the prisoner, was now to be discerned at some little distance ahead. It presented a series of bold crags of granite intermixed with slate, in which rock piled upon rock presented a succession of shelves, each beetling over its base, and thus furnishing a shelter against the weather. Some of these were situated near the bank of the stream, projecting over the water, whilst others towered at different heights, in such a manner as to bear a resemblance to a flight of huge steps cut in the slope of the mountain, and by this likeness, doubtless, suggesting the imaginative name by which the spot was known to the few hunters to whom it was familiar. The cavern-like structure of these ledges abundantly supplied the means of concealment to both men and horses, from the casual notice of such persons as accident might have brought into this sequestered defile.

When the party arrived at the foot of the Devil's Ladder, it was with great satisfaction to all that they now made a halt. A short time was spent in selecting a spot, amongst the impending cliffs, of such a character as might afford the advantage of shelter, as well as the means of ready look-out and escape in case of discovery or pursuit. The place chosen was about half way up the hill, where the ridge of a promontory enabled the occupants to see some distance up and down the valley; whilst the crag itself contained within its recesses a chamber sufficiently large for the purpose to which it was to be applied. A natural platform, near this point, allowed sufficient space for the horses, which might be conducted there by a sideling path up the slope; at the same time, the means of retreat were furnished by the nature of the ground towards the top of the hill.

To this place of security the ensign was ordered by his guard, and, being released from his bonds, he dismounted and threw himself at length upon the mossy surface of the rock, where he lay wearied in body and dejected in mind. The horses were taken in charge by Shaw; provisions were produced, and all arrangements of caution and comfort were made for passing the next two or three days in this wild sojourn.

Here, for the present, we must leave our adventurers, to tell of other matters that are proper to be made known to the reader of this history.

In due time David Ramsay returned from Musgrove's. Precisely at three o'clock in the morning, the soldiers were released according to the terms of the parole; and my reader will, no doubt, be pleased to hear that Andy, being discharged from duty, went to bed as drowsy as e'er a man of mould after a feat of glory, and slept with a sleep altogether worthy of his heroic achievement.

The next day passed by, at Ramsay's dwelling, with a varied and fearful interest to his family. They had received intelligence, before night, of the event of Butler's trial, and had reason to rejoice that Mary Musgrove had so played her part in the delivery of the letter. They were apprised also of the reward that had been offered for the discovery of the bearer of this letter, and were informed that detachments of horse were out to scour the country in quest of the ensign. These tidings filled them with apprehension. It occurred to Ramsay that if, perchance, the released prisoners should fall in with any of the parties of the loyalists, they would of course relate their story, and thus bring down the full rancor of the Tory wrath upon his household: this would also lead with more certainty to the pursuit of Horse Shoe. There was still good reason to hope that the liberated men might not so soon be able to give the alarm; inasmuch as they were more likely to shape their course towards Fort Ninety-Six than to repair to Innis's camp, where they might be forced to do duty, as much against their inclinations as against their parole. They might even, from a natural aversion to labor, prefer loitering about the country rather than put themselves voluntarily in the way of military operations.

"Come what will of it," said Ramsay, summing up the chances for and against him; "I will be ready for the worst. Many better men have given all they had to the cause of independence, and I will not flinch from giving my share. They may burn and break down; but, thank God, I have a country — aye, and a heart and an arm to stand by it!"

On the same evening, towards sun-down, a horseman drew up his rein at Ramsay's door. He was young — in the prime of early manhood, his dress was that of a rustic, his equipment showed him to be a traveller — a weary one, from the plight of his horse, and, like most travellers of the time, well armed. He did not stand to summon any one to the door, but put his hand upon the latch with eager haste, and entered with the familiarity of one acquainted with the place. Mistress Ramsay was seated at her spinning-wheel, anxiously brooding over the tales of the day. Her husband reclined in his chair, silently and thoughtfully smoking his pipe. They both sprang up at once, as the visitor crossed the threshold, and with fervent joy greeted their son John Ramsay. The household was clamorous with the affectionate salutations of the parents, of the brothers and sisters, and of the domestics. John was the eldest of Ramsay's children, and had just reached his paternal roof after an absence of some months, during which he had been in service with Sumpter. The gathering in of the members of a family around the domestic board, in times of peril and distress, is one of the luxuries of the heart that in peace we cannot know. The arrival of John Ramsay at the present moment was a source of the liveliest happiness to his parents. They needed a cheerful as well as a resolute comforter. John had, only twenty-four hours previous, left Sumpter near Rocky Mount — immediately after the battle with the British convoy was won. He was sent with despatches to Colonel Williams, a Whig partisan of note, who was now supposed to be in the neighborhood of the Saluda. These had some reference to the military movements of the parties; and John Ramsay was permitted by Sumpter to make a short halt at his father's house.

In the first hour after his arrival, he had given to the family the history of his homeward ride. He had discovered that hostile forces — of which, until his journey was nearly finished, he heard nothing — were encamped in the neighborhood; that a court-martial had been sitting for the trial of an American officer, as a spy, and had condemned him to be shot. He had been apprised, moreover, that small parties were out, riding into every corner of the country. He himself had nearly been surprised by one of these, as he endeavored to make his way to the house of Allen Musgrove, where he had proposed to himself a visit, even before he came to his father's, but, fearing something wrong, he had fled from them, and baffled their pursuit, although they had chased him more than a mile; he had, in consequence, been deprived of the opportunity of visiting the miller.

"Although it is four months since we have seen you, John," said the dame, with a tone of affectionate chiding, "yet, you would turn aside to get under Allen Musgrove's roof, before you thought of the arms of your mother."

John's sun-burnt cheek blushed crimson red as he replied, "It was but a step out of the way, mother, and I should not have stayed long. Mr. Musgrove and his folks are safe and well, I hope, and Christopher?"

"Tut, boy! speak it out, and don't blush about it," interrupted the father briskly: "she is a good girl, and you needn't be ashamed to name her, as you ought to have done, first and before all the rest. Mary is well, John, and has just proved herself to be the best girl in the country."

This passage of mirth between the parents and their son, led to a full narrative by David Ramsay of the events which had occurred in the last two or three days, concluding with the capture of the ensign, and the retreat of Horse Shoe and Christopher Shaw to the Devil's Ladder. The communication wrought a grave and thoughtful mood on the young soldier. It presented a crisis to him for immediate action. He was wearied with a long ride, but it seemed to him to be no time for rest.

"Father," he said, after turning over in his thoughts the intelligence he had just received, "it was a brave and beautiful thing for so young a lad as Andy to do; and the taking of the ensign has served a useful purpose, but it brings this house and family into danger. And I fear for poor Mary. Christopher Shaw must get back to the mill, and quickly too. His absence will bring his uncle's family into trouble. I will take Christopher's place, and go to Horse Shoe's assistance this night. We may take the prisoner with us to Williams."

"To-night!" said the mother anxiously, "you would not leave us to-night, John?"

"Aye, to-night, wife," answered David Ramsay, "the boy is right, there is no time to spare."

"Have mercy upon us," exclaimed the dame; "to ride so far to-night, after so heavy a journey, John! — you have not strength."

"Dear mother," said John, "think that you are all in danger, and that Mary, who has behaved so well, might be suspected, and brought to harm. I must hurry forward to Colonel Williams, and this road by the Devil's Ladder is far out of my way. No, I am not so much fatigued, mother, as you suppose. I will rest for a few hours, and then try the woods. Daybreak, I warrant, shall not find me far from Horse Shoe."

John Ramsay was not above six-and-twenty. He was endued with a stout and manly frame, well adapted to hard service; and this was associated with a bold and intelligent countenance, which, notwithstanding the dint of wind and weather, was handsome. He had for a year or two past been actively engaged in the war, and his manners had, in consequence, acquired that maturity and decision which are generally found in those whose habits of life render them familiar with perils. On the present occasion he regarded the necessity of co-operation with Robinson as so urgent, that no other thought crossed his mind but that which belonged to the care of putting himself in condition to make his services effectual.

With this view he now directed his horse to be carefully tended; then, having taken a hearty meal, he retired to rest, desiring that he might be waked up at midnight, when he proposed to follow the path of Horse Shoe and his comrade.

CHAPTER XXVII

A RETREAT AFTER THE MANNER OF XENOPHON

THE next morning, a little after sunrise, as Robinson was holding the watch on the outer ledge of the rock, in a position that enabled him to survey the approaches to the spot through the valley, as well as to keep his eye upon the ensign and Christopher Shaw, who were both asleep under cover of the crag, he was startled by a distant noise of something breaking through the bushes on the margin of the brook. At first it struck him that this was caused by deer stalking up the stream; but he soon afterwards descried the head and shoulders of a man, whose motions showed him to be struggling through the thicket towards the base of the hill. This person at length reached a space of open ground, where he halted and looked anxiously around him, thus revealing his figure, as he sat on horseback, to the observation of the sergeant, who, in the meantime, had taken advantage of a low pine tree and a jutting angle of a rock to screen himself from the eager eye of the traveller — at least until he should be satisfied as to the other's character and purpose.

A loud and cheerful halloo, several times repeated by the stranger, seemed to indicate his quest of a lost companion; and this gradually drew the sergeant, with a weary motion, from his hiding-place, until assuring himself that the comer was alone, he stept out to the edge of the shelf of rock, and presenting his musket, peremptorily gave the common challenge of "Who goes there?"

"A friend to Horse Robinson," was the reply of the visitor, in whom my reader recognises John Ramsay.

Before further question might be asked and answered, John had dismounted from his horse and clambered to the platform, where he greeted the sergeant and the hastily-awakened Christopher Shaw, with a hearty shake of the hand; and then proceeded to communicate the pressing objects of his visit, and to relate all that he had learned of the recent events during his short stay at his father's house.

In the consultation that followed these disclosures, Ramsay

earnestly urged his comrades to make instant preparation to quit their present retirement, and to attempt the enterprise of conducting the prisoner to Williams, who was supposed to be advancing into the neighborhood of a well known block-house, or frontier fortification, on the Saluda, about forty miles from their present position.

The message with which Ramsay was charged from Sumpter to Williams, made it necessary that he should endeavor to reach that officer as soon as possible; and the sergeant, rejoicing in the thought of being so near a strong body of allies who might render the most essential aid to the great object of his expedition, readily concurred in the propriety of the young trooper's proposal. This enterprise was also recommended by the necessity of taking some immediate steps to preserve the custody of the ensign, whose capture had already been so serviceable to the cause of Arthur Butler. In accordance, moreover, with John Ramsay's anxious entreaty, Christopher Shaw, it was determined, should hasten back to the mill at the earliest moment.

A speedy departure was, therefore, resolved on, and accordingly all things were made ready, in the course of an hour, to commence the march. At the appointed time the ensign was directed to descend into the valley, where he was once more bound to his horse. The conferences between the sergeant and his two comrades had been held out of the hearing of the prisoner; but it was now thought advisable to make him acquainted with the late proceedings that had transpired with regard to Butler, and especially with the respite that had been given to that officer by Innis. This communication was accompanied by an intimation that he would best consult his own comfort and safety by a patient submission to the restrictions that were put upon him: inasmuch as his captors had no disposition to vex him with any other precautions than were necessary for his safe detention during the present season of peril to Butler.

With this admonition the party began their journey. The first two or three hours were occupied in returning, by the route of the valley, to the Ennoree. When they reached the river they found thmselves relieved from the toils of the narrow and rugged path by which they had threaded the wild mountain dell, and introduced into an undulating country covered with forest, and intersected by an occasional but unfrequented road leading from one settlement to another. Here Christopher Shaw was to take leave of his companions, his path lying along the bank of the

Ennoree, whilst the route to be pursued by the others crossed the river and extended thence southwards to the Saluda. The young miller turned his horse's head homewards, with some reluctance at parting with his friends in a moment of such interest, and bore with him many passages of comfort and courage to those whom he was about to rejoin — and more particularly from the sergeant to Butler, in case Christopher should have the good fortune to be able to deliver them. At the same time, Horse Shoe and John Ramsay, with the prisoner, forded the Ennoree, and plunged into the deep forest that lay upon its further bank.

For several hours they travelled with the greatest circumspection, avoiding the frequented roads and the chance of meeting such wayfarers as might be abroad on their route. It was a time of great anxiety and suspense, but the habitual indifference of military life gave an air of unconcern to the conduct of the soldiers, and scarcely affected, in any visible degree, the cheerfulness of their demeanor.

They reached, at length, the confines of a cultivated country — a region which was known to be inhabited by several Tory families. To avoid the risk of exposure to persons who might be unfriendly to their purpose, they thought it prudent to delay entering upon this open district until after sunset, that they might continue their journey through the night. The difficulty of ascertaining their road in the dark, and the danger of seeking information from the few families whose habitations occurred to their view, necessarily rendered their progress slow. The time was, therefore, passed in weary silence and persevering labor, in the anxious contemplation of the probability of encountering some of the enemy's scouts.

At the break of day they stopped to refresh themselves; and the contents of Horse Shoe's wallet, unhappily reduced to a slender supply of provisions, were distributed amongst the party. During this halt, John Ramsay commanded the ensign to exchange his dress with him; and our faithful ally was converted, by this traffic, for the nonce, into a spruce, well-looking, and gay young officer of the enemy's line.

The most hazardous portion of their journey now lay before them. They were within a few miles of the Saluda, from whence, at its nearest point, it was some six or seven more down the stream to the Block-house — the appointed rendezvous, where it was yet a matter of uncertainty whether Williams had arrived. The space between the travellers and the river was a fertile and comparatively thickly-peopled region, of which the inhabitants were almost entirely in the Tory interest. The broad day-light having overtaken them on the confines of this tract, exposed them to the greatest risk of being questioned. They had nothing left but to make a bold effort to attain the river by the shortest path; and thence to pursue the bank towards the rendezvous.

"Courage, John," said Horse Shoe, smiling at the new garb of his comrade; "you may show your pretty feathers to-day to them that are fond of looking at them. And you, my young clodpole, ride like an honest Whig, or I mought find occasion to do a discomfortable thing, by putting a bullet through and through you. Excuse the liberty, sir, for these are ticklish times; but I shall ondoubtedly be as good as my word."

Our adventurers soon resumed their journey. They had come within a mile of the Saluda without interruption, and began to exchange congratulations that the worst was passed, when they found themselves descending a sharp hill which jutted down upon an extensive piece of pasture ground. One boundary of this was watered by a brook, along whose margin a fringe of willows, intermixed with wild shrubbery of various kinds, formed a screen some ten or fifteen feet in height. As soon as this range of meadow was observed, our cautious soldiers halted upon the brow of the hill to reconnoitre; and perceiving nothing to excite their apprehension, they ventured down, upon the track of an ill-defined road, which took a direction immediately over the broadest portion of the field.

They had scarcely crossed the brook at the bottom of the hill, before they heard the remote voices of men in conversation, and the tones of a careless laugh. On looking towards the upper section of the stream, they were aware of a squad of loyalist cavalry, who came riding, in the shade of the willows, directly towards the spot where the travellers had entered upon the meadow. The party consisted of seven or eight men, who were, at this instant, not more than one hundred paces distant.

"They are upon us, sergeant!" exclaimed John Ramsay. "Make sure of the prisoner: retreat as rapidly as you can. Leave me to myself. Make for the Block-house — I will meet you there."

With these hasty intimations, he pricked his courser up to full speed, and shaped his flight directly across the open field, in full view of the enemy.

Horse Shoe, at the same moment, drew a pistol, cocked it, and throwing the rein of St. Jermyn's horse into the hands of the rider, he cried out: —

"Back across the branch and into the woods! Push for it, or you are a dead man! On, on!" he added, as he rode at high speed, immediately beside the ensign; "a stumble, or a whisper above your breath, and you get the bullet. Fly—your life is in your horse's heels!"

The resolute tone of the sergeant had its effect upon his prisoner, who yielded a ready obedience to the pressing orders, and bounded into the thicket with as much alacrity as if flying from an enemy.

Meanwhile, the troopers, struck with the earnest haste of one whose dress bespoke a British officer, speeding across the field, did not doubt that they had afforded this timely opportunity for the escape of a prisoner from the hands of the Whigs.

"Wheel up, lads," shouted the leader of the squad, "it is the ensign! Wheel up and form a platoon to cut off the pursuit. We have him safe out of their clutches!"

Impressed with the conviction that a considerable force of Whig cavalry were at hand, the troopers directed all their efforts to cover what they believed Ensign St. Jermyn's retreat, and were now seen formed into a platoon, and moving towards the middle of the plain, in such a manner as to place themselves between the fugitive and his supposed pursuers. Here they delayed a few minutes, as if expecting an attack; until finding that the object of their solicitude had safely crossed the field and plunged into the distant woods, they rode away at a rapid pace in the same direction. When they reached the further extremity of the open ground, they halted for an instant, turned their eyes back towards the spot of their first discovery, and, finding that no attempt was made to follow, gave a hearty huzza, and rode onward in search of their prize.

The stratagem had completely succeeded: Ramsay had escaped, and Horse Shoe had withdrawn his prisoner into the neighboring wood upon the hill, where he was able to observe the whole scene. After a brief interval, the sergeant resumed his journey, and, with all necessary circumspection, bent his steps towards the river, where he arrived without molestation, and thence he continued his march in the direction of the rendezvous.

John Ramsay did not stop until he had crossed the Saluda and advanced a considerable distance on the opposite bank, where, to his great joy, he was encountered by a look-out party of Williams's regiment. Our fugitive had some difficulty in making himself known to his friends, and escaping the salutation which an enemy was likely to obtain at their hands; but when he surrendered to them, and made them acquainted with the cause of his disguise, the party instantly turned about with him, and proceeded in quest of the sergeant and his prisoner.

It was not long before they fell in with the small detachment of Connelley's troopers — as the late masters of the meadow turned out to be — who were leisurely returning from their recent exploit. These, finding themselves in the presence of superior numbers, turned to flight. Not far behind them Ramsay and his new companions encountered Horse Shoe; and the whole party proceeded without delay to Williams's camp.

Colonel Williams had reached the Block-house on the preceding evening with a force of two hundred cavalry. Clarke and Shelby happened, at this juncture, to be with him; and these three gallant partisans were now anxiously employed in arranging measures for that organized resistance to the Tory Dominion which fills so striking a chapter in the history of the Southern war, and which it had been the special object of Butler's mission to promote. Horse Shoe was enabled to communicate to Williams and his confederates the general purpose of this mission, and the disasters which had befallen Butler in his attempt to reach those with whom he was to co-operate. This intelligence created a lively interest in behalf of the captive, and it was instantly determined to make some strenuous effort for his deliverance. Whilst these matters were brought into consultation by the leaders, Horse Shoe and John Ramsay mingled amongst the soldiers, in the enjoyment of that fellowship which forms the most agreeable feature in the associations of the camp.

CHAPTER XXVIII

BUTLER'S DIFFICULTIES INCREASE. — INNIS FINDS OCCASION TO THINK OF THE ADAGE — "THERE'S MANY A SLIP BETWIXT THE CUP AND THE LIP"

WHEN Arthur Butler was conducted back to his place of confinement, after his trial, orders were given that no one should be allowed to approach him, except the officer to whom was intrusted his safe custody. The intercourse of this person with him was short; and concerned only with the scant accommodation which his condition required. He was, therefore, deprived of all chance of becoming acquainted with the extraordinary events that had led to his present respite from death. In the interrogations that had, during the first moments of excitement, been put to him, in regard to the letter, he was not told its import; from what quarter it had come; nor how it affected his fate. He only knew, by the result, that it had suspended the purpose of his immediate execution; and he saw that it had produced great agitation at head-quarters. He found, moreover, that this, or some other cause, had engendered a degree of exasperation against him, that showed itself in the retrenchment of his comforts, and in the augmented rigor of his confinement.

Agitated with a thousand doubts, his mind was too busy to permit him to close his eyes during the night that followed; and in this wakeful suspense he could sometimes hear, amongst the occasional ramblers who passed under his window, an allusion, in their conversation, to a victory gained over the royal troops. Coupling this with the name of Sumpter, which was now and then uttered with some adjective of disparagement, he conjectured that Horse Shoe had probably fallen in with that partisan, and was, peradventure, leading him to this vicinity. But this conclusion was combated by the fact that there seemed to be no alarm in the camp, nor any preparations on foot either for instant battle or retreat. Then the letter — that was a mystery, altogether impenetrable. There was only one point upon which his mind could rest with satisfaction: of that he was sure — Horse Shoe was certainly at the bottom of the scheme, and was active in his behalf.

The whole of the next day passed over in the same state of uncertainty. It was observed by Butler, with some stress upon the circumstance, that Captain St. Jermyn, who had heretofore evinced a disposition to make himself busy in his behalf, had absented himself ever since the trial; and he thus felt himself cut off from the slightest exhibition of sympathy on the part of a single individual in the multitude of fellow beings near him. Indeed, there were various indications of a general personal ill-will against him. The house, in which he was confined, was so constructed that he could frequently hear such expressions, in the conferences of those who inhabited the rooms below stairs, as were uttered above the lower key of conversation, and these boded him no good. Once, during the day, Colonel Innis visited him. This officer's countenance was severe, and indicated anger. His purpose was to extort something from the prisoner in reference to his supposed knowledge of the course of operations of Sumpter, from whose camp Innis did not doubt this letter regarding St. Jermyn had come. He spoke in a short, quick, and peremptory tone:

"It may be well for you," he said, "that your friends do not too rashly brave my authority. Let me advise you to warn them that others may fall into our hands; and that if the ensign be not delivered up, there may be a dreadful retaliation."

"I know not, sir, of what or whom you speak," replied Butler; "and it is due to my honor to say, that I will not be induced, for the sake of saving my life, to interfere with any operations which the soldiers of Congress may have undertaken in the cause of the country. In this sentiment I admonish Colonel Innis that I desire to be put in possession of no facts from him that may be communicated under such an expectation. And having made this determination known to you, I will add to it that, from the same motives, I will answer no questions you can propose to me. You may spare yourself, therefore, the useless labor of this visit. My life is in your hands, and I have already experienced with what justice and clemency you will use your power when you dare."

"A more humble tone," said Innis, with a bitter smile, "I think would better suit your circumstances." And with this remark the commandant haughtily walked out of the apartment.

The next morning, whilst Butler was taking his breakfast, which had been brought to him by one of the soldiers of the guard, he heard a loud cheering from the troops that at that hour were on parade in the plain. This was followed by the discharge of a *feu de joie* from the whole line, and a flourish of drums and trumpets.

"What is that?" he inquired eagerly of the soldier, who, forgetful, in the excitement of the moment, of the order to restrain his intercourse with the prisoner, answered —

"They have just got the news from Camden: two days ago Cornwallis defeated Gates, and cut his army to pieces. The troops are rejoicing for the victory, and have just had the despatches read."

Butler heaved a deep sigh, as he said, "Then all is lost, and liberty is but a name! I feared it; God knows, I feared it."

The soldier was recalled to his duty by the sentinel at the door, and Butler was again left alone.

This was a day of crowding events. The tidings of the battle of Camden, gained on the sixteenth, and which had early this morning reached Innis, threw a spirit of the highest exultation into the camp. The event was considered decisive of the fate of the rebel power; and the most extravagant anticipations were indulged by the loyalists, in regard to the complete subjugation of the Whigs of the southern provinces. The work of confiscation was to be carried out to the most bitter extreme, and the adherents of the royal government were to grow rich upon the spoils of victory. The soldiers of Innis were permitted to give way to uncontrolled revelry; and, from the first promulgation of the news, this became a day devoted to rejoicings. Innis himself looked upon the victory at Camden with more satisfaction, as it gave him reason to believe that the sentence pronounced against Butler might be executed, without fear of vengeance threatened against the Ensign St. Jermyn. He was, however, exceedingly anxious to see this young officer released from the hands of the enemy; and had determined to respect the threat as long as there was any doubt that it might be performed. The personal consideration of Captain St. Jermyn, his station as an officer of importance, and, above all, the great influence of his family, in the esteem of the royal leaders, made it an object of deep concern to Innis to save the ensign, by the most scrupulous regard to his present difficulties. His power to do so seemed to be much increased by the late victory.

In the afternoon of the same day, further rumors were brought to Innis's camp, importing that Sumpter had been attacked on that morning upon the Catawba, by Tarleton, and completely routed. The prisoners and baggage, taken on the fifteenth, had been regained, and Sumpter was flying with the scattered remnant of his troops towards North Carolina. At the same time an order was brought to Innis to break up his camp and move northwards. This only added to the shouts and rejoicings of the troops, and drove them into deeper excesses. The war, they thought, was coming rapidly to an end, and they already anticipated this conclusion, by throwing off the irksomeness of military restraint. The officers were gathered into gossiping and convivial circles; and laughed, in unrestrained feelings of triumph, at the posture of affairs. The private soldiers, on their part, imitated their leaders, and formed themselves into knots and groups, where they caroused over their cups, danced, and sang. All was frolic and merriment.

In the midst of this festivity, a portion of Connelly's troopers, who had now been absent forty-eight hours, arrived, and made an immediate report to Innis. The purport of this was, that they had found Ensign St. Jermyn in the possession of a detachment of Whig cavalry near the Saluda: as soon as they descried him, which they did, some three hundred paces distant, knowing him by his scarlet uniform, they prepared to attack this party of Whigs; but the ensign perceiving his friends at hand, had already, by a brave effort, disentangled himself from his keepers, and taken off into the open field. The scouts, therefore, instead of attacking the Whigs, directed all their attention to secure the ensign's retreat, by holding themselves ready to check the pursuit: their manœuvre had been successful, and the prisoner was free.

"And is now with you in the camp, my brave fellows?" said Innis, with great exultation.

"Not yet," replied the sergeant of the squad. "He is upon the road, and will, no doubt, soon be here. We have not seen him since his escape. Whilst we hung back, with a view to favor his retreat, we fell in with a party that we took to be the escort that had made him prisoner; and as they outnumbered us, we thought it prudent to decline a skirmish with them. So we filed off and made our way back to head-quarters. The ensign must have been a good mile ahead of us, and as the road is hard to find, he may have lost his way. But this is certain, we saw him clear of the Whigs, with his horse's head turned towards this camp."

"Thank you, good friends," said Innis; "you have performed your duty handsomely. Go to your comrades; they have news for you, and an extra allowance to-day. Faith, Ker, this is a day for settling old accounts," he continued, as he turned and addressed an officer by his side. "Gates beaten, Sumpter beaten, and Ensign St. Jermyn delivered from captivity! That looks well! And now I have another account, which shall be settled on the nail. Stirring times, Captain St. Jermyn. I congratulate you, my friend, on your brother's safety, and mean to signalize the event as it deserves. Major Frazer, bring out your prisoner, and let him die the death punctually at sun-down — at sun-down, to the minute, major. We must get that job off our hands. To-morrow, my friends, we shall move towards Catawba, and thence to Hanging Rock. Meantime, we must sweep up our rubbish. So, major, look to your duty! It might as well have been done at first," he added, speaking to himself, as he walked away from the group of officers to look after other affairs.

The execution of Butler was now regarded as a mere matter of business, and to be despatched as one item of duty amongst the thousand others that were to be looked after in the hurry of breaking up the post. The interest of the trial had faded away by the lapse of time, and in the more predominating excitements which the absorbing character of the late events had afforded. The preparations for this ceremony were, therefore, attended with no display, and scarcely seemed to arouse inquiry amongst the soldiers of the camp. It was treated in all respects as a subordinate point of police. Ten files were detailed; one drum and fife put in requisition; and this party, attended by Frazer, and two or three officers who happened to be near at the moment, marched with a careless step to head-quarters.

The first announcement of this sudden resolve was made to the prisoner by a subaltern; who, without prelude or apology, or the least effort to mitigate the harshness of the order he bore, walked abruptly into the chamber and delivered the message of his superior.

"It is a sudden proceeding," said Butler, calmly; "but your pleasure must be obeyed."

"You have had two days to think of it," replied the officer; "it is not often so much time is allowed. Ensign St. Jermyn, sir, is safe, and that is all we waited for. We march to-morrow, and therefore have no time to lose. You are waited for below."

Butler stood a moment with his hand pressed upon his brow, and then muttered,

"It is even so; our unhappy country is lost, and the reign of blood is but begun. I would ask the poor favor of a moment's delay, and the privilege of pen, ink, and paper, whilst I write but a line to a friend."

"Impossible, sir," said the man. "Time is precious, and our orders are positive."

"This is like the rest," answered Butler; "I submit." Then buttoning his coat across his breast, he left the room with a firm and composed step.

When he reached the door the first person who met his eye was Captain St. Jermyn. There was an expression of formal gravity in the manner of this officer, as he accosted the prisoner, and lamented the rigor of the fate that awaited him. And it was somewhat with a cold and polite civility that he communicated his readiness to attend to any request which Butler, in his last moments, might wish to have performed.

Butler thanked him for his solicitude, and then said, "I asked permission to write to a friend; that has been denied. I feel reluctant to expose myself to another refusal. You have taken a slight interest in my sufferings, and I will, therefore, confide to you a simple wish, which it will not cost my persecutors much to gratify. It is that I may be taken to my grave, dressed as you see me now. I would not have my person stripped or plundered."

"If you have valuables about you, sir, trust them to my keeping; I promise you they shall be faithfully delivered according to your wish."

"What money there is about my person," replied Butler, "may be given to the soldiers who are compelled to execute this harsh and unjust sentence on my person; but I have a trinket," he said, drawing from his bosom a miniature, which was suspended by a ribbon, "it is the gift of one,"—here, for the first time, a tear started into Butler's eye, and his power of utterance failed him.

"I understand, sir," said St. Jermyn, eagerly reaching out his hand to take the picture, "I will seek the lady, at whatever hazard"—

"No," answered the unfortunate officer, "it must be buried with me. It has dwelt here," he added with emotion, as he placed his hand upon his heart, "and here it must sleep in death."

"On the honor of a soldier," said St. Jermyn, "I promise you its rest shall not be violated."

"You will attend me?"

"I will."

"Lead on," said the prisoner, stepping to the place assigned him in the ranks. "I seek no further delay."

"March down the river, half a mile below the camp," said Innis, who now came up, as the escort had begun its progress towards the place of execution. And the soldiers moved slowly, with the customary funeral observances, in a direction that led across the whole extent of the plain.

When this little detachment had disappeared on the further side of the field, a sudden commotion arose at head-quarters by the hasty arrival of a mounted patrol —

"We are followed!" cried the leading horseman, in great perturbation. "They will be here in an instant! We have been pressed by them for the last two miles."

"Of whom do you speak?" inquired Innis, eagerly.

"The enemy! the enemy!" vociferated several voices.

At the same moment a cloud of dust was seen rising above the trees, in the direction of the road leading up the Ennoree.

"To arms — to arms!" ejaculated the commander. "Gentlemen, spring to your horses, and sound the alarm through the camp — we are set upon by Sumpter — it can be no other. Curry, take a few dragoons — follow the prisoner — mount him behind one of your men, and retreat with him instantly to Blackstock's!"

Having given these hasty orders, Innis, with the several officers who happened to be at hand, ran to their horses, mounted, and pushed forward to the camp. They had scarcely left their quarters before two dragoons, in advance of a party of twenty or thirty men, rushed up to the door.

"Sarch the house!" shouted the leading soldier. "Three or four of you dismount and sarch the house! Make sure of Major Butler, if he is there! The rest of you forward with me!"

The delay before head-quarters scarcely occupied a moment, and in the meantime the number of the assailants was increased by the squadrons that poured in from the rear. These were led by a young officer of great activity and courage, who, seeing the disordered condition of the royalists, waved his sword in the air as he beckoned his men to follow him in a charge upon the camp.

The advanced party, with the two dragoons, were already on the field charging the first body that they found assembled; and, close behind them, followed Colonel Williams — the officer of whom I have spoken — with a large division of cavalry. At the same moment that Williams entered upon the plain from this quarter, a second and third corps, led respectively by Shelby and Clarke, were seen galloping upon the two flanks of the encampment.

The plain was now occupied by about two hundred Whig cavalry. The royalists, taken by surprise, over their cups it may be said, and in the midst of a riotous festival, were everywhere thrown into the wildest confusion. Such of them as succeeded in gaining their arms, took post behind the trees, and kept up an irregular fire upon the assailants. Colonel Innis had succeeded in getting together about a hundred men at a remote corner of his camp, and had now formed them into a solid column to resist the attack of the cavalry, whilst from this body he poured forth a few desultory volleys of musketry, hoping to gain time to collect the scattered forces that were in various points endeavoring to find their proper station. Horse Shoe Robinson and John Ramsay — the two foremost in the advance — were to be discovered pushing through the sundered groups of the enemy with a restless and desperate valor that nothing could withstand.

"Cut them down," cried Horse Shoe, "without marcy! remember the Waxhaws!" And he accompanied his exhortation with the most vehement and decisive action, striking down, with a huge sabre, all who opposed his way.

Meantime, Colonel Williams and his comrades charged the column formed by Innis, and, in a few moments, succeeded in riding through the array and compelling them to a total rout. Robinson and Ramsay, side by side, mingled in this charge, and were seen in the thickest of the fight. Innis, finding all efforts to maintain his ground ineffectual, turned his horse towards Musgrove's mill, and fled as fast as spur and sword could urge the animal forward. The sergeant, however, had marked him for his prize, and following as fleetly as the trusty Captain Peter was able to carry him, soon came up with the fugitive officer, and, with one broad sweep of his sword, dislodged him from his saddle and left him bleeding on the ground. Turning again towards the field, his quick eye discerned the unwieldy bulk of Hugh Habershaw. The gross captain had, in the hurry of the assault, been unable to reach his horse; and, in the first moments of danger, had taken refuge in one of the little sheds which had been constructed for the accommodation of the soldiers. As the battle waxed hot in the neighborhood of his retreat, he had crept forth from his den and was making the best of his way to an adjoining cornfield. He was bare-headed, and his bald crown, as the slanting rays of the evening sun fell upon it, glistened like a gilded globe. The well known figure no sooner occurred to the sergeant's view than he rode off in pursuit. The cornfield was bounded by a fence, and the burly braggart had just succeeded in reaching it when his enemy overtook him.

"Have mercy, good Mr. Horse Shoe, have mercy on a defenceless man!" screamed the runaway, in a voice discordant with terror, as he stopped at the fence, which he was unable to mount, and looked back upon his pursuer. "Remember the good-will I showed you when you was a prisoner! Quarter, quarter — for God's sake, quarter!"

"You get no quarter from me, you cursed blood-lapper!" exclaimed Horse Shoe, excited to a rage that seldom visited his breast; "think of Grindall's Ford!" and at the same instant he struck a heavy downward blow, with such sheer descent, that it clove the skull of the perfidious freebooter clean through to the spine. "I have sworn your death," said the sergeant, "even if I cotch you asleep in your bed, and right fairly have you earned it."

The body fell into a bed of mire, which had been the resort of the neighboring swine; and, leaving it in this foul plight, Horse Shoe hastened back to rejoin his comrades.

The battle now ended in the complete rout of the enemy. Williams's first care, after the day was won, was to collect his men and to secure his prisoners. Many of the Tories had escaped; many were killed and wounded; but of Butler no tidings could be gained; he had disappeared from the field before the fight began, and all the information that the prisoners could give was that orders had been sent to remove him from the neighborhood. Colonel Innis was badly wounded, and in no condition to speak with his conquerors; he was sent, with several other disabled officers, to head-quarters. Captain St. Jermyn had fled, with most of those who had mounted their horses before the arrival of Williams.

The day was already at its close, and order was taken to spend the night upon the field. Guards were posted, and every precaution adopted to avoid a surprise in turn from the enemy, who, it was feared, might soon rally a strong party and assail the conquerors.

The disturbed condition of the country, and the almost unanimous sentiment of the people against the Whigs, now strengthened by the late victories, prevented Williams from improving his present advantage, or even from bearing off his prisoners. Robinson and Ramsay volunteered to head a party to scour the country in quest of Butler, but the commanding officer could give no encouragement to the enterprise; it was, in his judgment, a hopeless endeavor, when the forces of the enemy were everywhere so strong. His determination, therefore, was to retreat, as soon as his men were in condition, back to his fastnesses. His few killed were buried; the wounded, of which there were not more than fifteen or twenty were taken care of, and the jaded troops were dismissed to seek refreshment amongst the abundant stores captured from the enemy. Ensign St. Jermyn was still a prisoner; and, for the sake of adding to Butler's security, Williams selected two or three other officers that had fallen into his hands to accompany him in his retreat. These arrangements all being made, the colonel and his officers retired to repose. The next morning at daylight there were no traces of the Whigs to be seen upon the plain. It was abandoned to the loyalist prisoners and their wounded comrades.

CHAPTER XXIX

WILLIAMS TAKES A FANCY TO FOREST LIFE. — HORSE SHOE AND JOHN RAMSAY CONTINUE ACTIVE IN THE SERVICE OF BUTLER. — MARY MUSGROVE BECOMES A VALUABLE AUXILIARY

WILLIAMS had commenced his retreat before the dawn, as much with a view to accomplish a large portion of his journey before the heat of the day, as to protect himself against the probable pursuit of the rallied forces of the enemy. His destination was towards the mountains on the north-western frontier. The overthrow of Gates had left a large force of Tory militia at the disposal of Cornwallis, who, it was conjectured, would use them to break up every remnant of opposition in this region. It was therefore a matter of great importance to Williams, to conduct his little force into some place of security against the attacks of the royalists.

Colonel Elijah Clarke had, ever since the fall of Charleston, been employed in keeping together the few scattered Whig families in that part of Carolina lying contiguous to the Savannah, with a view to an organized plan of resistance against the British authorities; and he had so far accomplished his purpose as to have procured some three or four hundred men, who had agreed to hold themselves in readiness to strike a blow whenever the occasion offered. These men were to be mustered at any moment by a preconcerted signal; and, in the meantime, they were instructed, by confining themselves to their dwellings, or pursuing their ordinary occupations, to keep as much as possible out of the way of the dominant authorities.

Clarke resided in Georgia, whence he had fled as soon as the royalist leader, Brown, had taken possession of Augusta; and we have already seen that a letter from Colonel Pinckney, at Charleston, which Horse Shoe Robinson had been intrusted to deliver, had summoned Arthur Butler to this frontier to aid in Clarke's enterprise.

Colonel Isaac Shelby, a resident of Washington county in Virginia, until the settlement of the southern line of the State had left him in the district at present known as Sullivan county in

Tennessee, had been an efficient auxiliary in Clarke's scheme, and was now ready to summon a respectable number of followers for the support of the war on the mountain border. He and Clarke had accidentally arrived at Williams's camp a day or two before the attack upon Innis, with a view to a consultation as to the general interests of the meditated campaign; and they had only tarried to take a part in the engagement from a natural concern for the fate of their intended comrade, Butler. Having no further motive for remaining with Williams, they were both intent upon returning to their respective duties, and, accordingly, during the retreat of the following day, they took their leave.

The vigilance with which these partisans were watched by their enemies, almost forbade the present hope of successful combination. From a consciousness of the hazard of attempting to concentrate their forces at this juncture, they had determined still to pursue their separate schemes of annoyance, until a more favorable moment for joint action should arise; and, in the interval, to hide themselves as much as possible in the forest. It was consequently in the hope of preserving his independence at least, if not of aiding Clarke, that Williams now moved with so much despatch to the mountains.

His course lay towards the head waters of the Fair Forest river, in the present region of Spartanburg. This district was inhabited only by a few hunters, and some scattered Indians of an inoffensive character; it abounded in game, and promised to afford an easy subsistence to men whose habits were simple, and who were accustomed to rely upon the chase for support. The second day brought our hardy soldiers into the sojourn they sought. It was a wilderness broken by mountains, and intersected by streams of surpassing transparency; whilst its elevated position and southern latitude conferred upon it a climate that was then, as well as now, remarked for its delicious temperature in summer, and its exemption from the rigors of winter.

The spot at which Williams rested was a sequestered valley, deep hidden in the original woods, and watered by the Fair Forest, whose stream, so near its fountain, scarcely exceeded the dimensions of a little brook. Here he determined to form a camp, to which in times of emergency he might safely retreat. With a view to render it easy of access as a rendezvous, he caused landmarks to be made, by cutting notches on the trees — or *blazing* them, in the woodman's phrase — in several directions, leading towards the principal highways that penetrated the country. The retreat thus established is familiar to the history of the war, under the name of the Fair Forest camp.

These arrangements being completed in the course of the first day after his arrival, Williams now applied himself to the adoption of measures for the safety of Arthur Butler. Amongst the spoils that had fallen into his hands, after the victory over Innis, was the document containing the proceedings of the court-martial. The perusal of this paper, together with the comments afforded by Robinson, convinced him of the malignity of the persecution which had aimed at the life of the prisoner. It occurred to him, therefore, to submit the whole proceedings to Lord Cornwallis, to whom he was persuaded, it either had been misrepresented, or, most probably, was entirely unknown. He did not doubt that an appeal to the honorable feelings of that officer, with a full disclosure of the facts, would instantly be followed by an order that should put Butler under the protection of the rules of war, and insure him all the rights that belong to a mere prisoner taken in arms in a lawful quarrel. A spirited remonstrance was accordingly prepared to this effect. It detailed the circumstances of Butler's case, which was accompanied with a copy of the proceedings of the court, and it concluded with a demand that such measures should be adopted by the head of the army, as comported with the rights of humanity and the laws of war; "a course," the writer suggested, "that he did not hesitate to believe his lordship would feel belonged both to the honor and duty of his station." This paper was consigned to the care of an officer, who was directed to proceed with it, under a flag of truce, to the head-quarters of the British commander.

Soon after this, Robinson apprised Williams that Ramsay and himself had determined to venture back towards the Ennoree, to learn something of the state of affairs in that quarter, and to apply themselves more immediately to the service of Butler. In aid of this design, the sergeant obtained a letter from Williams, the purport of which was to inform the commandant of any post of the loyalists whom it might concern, that an application had been made on Butler's behalf to Cornwallis, and that the severest retaliation would be exercised upon the prisoners in Williams's custody, for any violence that might be offered the American officer. Putting this letter in his pocket, our man of "mickle might," attended by his good and faithful ally, John Ramsay, took his leave of "The Fair Forest" towards noon of the fourth day after the battle near Musgrove's mill.

The second morning after their departure, the two companions had reached the Ennoree, not far from the habitation of David Ramsay. It was fair summer weather, and nature was as gay as in that piping time before the blast of war had blown across her fields. All things, in the course of a few days, seemed to have undergone a sudden change. The country presented no signs of strife: no bands of armed men molested the highways. An occasional husbandman was seen at his plough: the deer sprang up from the brushwood and fled into the forest, as if inviting again the pastime of the chase; and even when the two soldiers encountered a chance wayfarer upon the road, each party passed the other unquestioned — there was all the seeming quiet of a pacified country. The truth was, the war had rolled northwards — and all behind it had submitted since the disastrous fight at Camden. The lusty and hot-brained portions of the population were away with the army; and the non-combatants only, or those wearied with arms, were all that were to be seen in this region.

Horse Shoe, after riding a long time in silence, as these images of tranquillity occupied his thoughts, made a simple remark that spoke a volume of truth in a few homely words.

"This is an onnatural sort of stillness, John. Men may call this peace, but I call it fear. If there is a poor wretch of a Whig in this district, it's as good as his life is worth to own himself. How far off mought we be from your father's?"

The young trooper heaved a deep sigh. "I knew you were thinking of my poor father when you spoke your thoughts, Horse Shoe. This is a heavy day for him. But he could bear it: he's a man who thinks little of hardships. There are the helpless women, Galbraith Robinson," he continued, as he shook his head with an expression of sorrow that almost broke into tears. "Getting near home one thinks of them first. My good and kind mother — God knows how she would bear any heavy accident. I am always afraid to ask questions in these times about the family, for fear of hearing something bad. And there's little Mary Musgrove over at the mill" —

"You have good reason to be proud of that girl, John Ramsay," interrupted Robinson. "So speak out, man, and none of your stammering. Hoot! — she told me she was your sweetheart! You haven't half the tongue of that wench. Why, sir, if I was a lovable man, haw, haw! — which I'm not — I'll be cursed if I wouldn't spark that little fusee myself."

"This fence," said Ramsay, unheeding the sergeant's banter,

"belongs to our farm, and perhaps we had better let down the rails and approach the house across the field: if the Tories should be there we might find the road dangerous. This gives us a chance of retreat."

"That's both scrupulous and wise, John," replied the sergeant. "So down with the pannel: we will steal upon the good folks, if they are at home, and take them by surprise. But mind you, my lad, see that your pistols are primed; we mought onawares get into a wasp's nest."

The fence was lowered, and the horsemen cautiously entered the field. After passing a narrow dell and rising to the crest of the opposite hill, they obtained a position but a short distance in the rear of the homestead. From this point a melancholy prospect broke upon their sight. The dwelling-house had disappeared, and in its place was a heap only of smouldering ashes. A few of the upright frame-posts, scorched black, and a stone chimney with its ample fire-place, were all that remained of what, but a few days before, was the happy abode of the family of a brave and worthy man.

"My God! my thoughts were running upon this! I feared their spite would break at last upon my father's head," cried John Ramsay, as he put spurs to his horse and galloped up to the ruins: "the savages have done their worst. But my father and mother, where are they?" he exclaimed, as the tears rolled down his cheeks.

"Take heart, my brave boy!" said Robinson, in the kindliest tones. "There's a reckoning to come for all these villanies — and it will go hard with many a Tory yet before this account is settled."

"I will carry a hot hand into the first house that covers a Tory head," replied the young trooper, passionately; "this burning shall be paid with ten like it."

"All in good time, John," said Robinson coolly. "As for the burning, it is no great matter; a few good neighbors would soon set that to rights, by building your father a better house than the one he has lost. Besides, Congress will not forget a true friend when the war is well fought out. But it does go against my grain, John Ramsay, to see a parcel of cowardly runaways spitting their malice against women and children. The barn, likewise, I see is gone," continued the sergeant, looking towards another pile of the ruins a short distance off. "The villains! when there's foul work to be done, they don't go at it like apprentices. No matter

—I have made one observation: the darkest hour is just before the day, and that's a comfortable old saying."

By degrees John Ramsay fell into a calmer temper, and now began to cast about as to the course fit to be pursued in their present emergency. About a quarter of a mile distant, two or three negro cabins were visible, and he could descry a few children near the doors. With an eager haste, therefore, he and the sergeant shaped their course across the field to this spot. When they arrived within fifty paces of the nearest hovel, the door was set ajar, and a rifle, thrust through the aperture, was aimed at the visitors.

"Stand for your lives!" shouted the well known voice of David Ramsay. In the next instant the door was thrown wide open, the weapon cast aside, and the father rushed forward as he exclaimed, "Gracious God, my boy and Horse Shoe Robinson! Welcome, lads; a hundred times more welcome than when I had better shelter to give you! But the good friends of King George, you see, have been so kind as to give me a call. It is easy to tell when they take it in their head to visit a Whig."

"My mother!" exclaimed John Ramsay.

"In and see her, boy—she wants comfort from you. But, thank God! she bears this blow better than I thought she could."

Before this speech was uttered John had disappeared.

"And how came this mishap to fall upon you, David?" inquired Horse Shoe.

"I suppose some of your prisoners," replied Ramsay, "must have informed upon Andy and me: for in the retreat of Innis's runaways, a party came through my farm. They stayed only long enough to ransack the house, and to steal whatever was worth taking; and then to set fire to the dwelling and all the outbuildings. Both Andy and myself, by good luck, perhaps, were absent, or they would have made us prisoners: so they turned my wife and the children out of doors to shift for themselves, and scampered off as fast as if Williams was still at their heels. All that was left for us was to crowd into this cabin, where, considering all things, we are not so badly off. But things are taking an ill turn for the country, Horse Shoe. We are beaten on all sides."

"Not so bad, David, as to be past righting yet," replied the sergeant. "What have they done with Major Butler?"

"He was carried, as I learned, up to Blackstock's, the evening of the fight; and yesterday it was reported that a party has taken him back to Musgrove's. I believe he is now kept close prisoner in Allen's house. Christopher Shaw was here two days since, and told us that orders had come to occupy the miller's dwelling-house for that purpose."

Horse Shoe had now entered the cabin with David Ramsay, and in the course of the hour that followed, during which the family had prepared refreshment for the travellers, the sergeant had fully canvassed all the particulars necessary to be known for his future guidance. It was determined that he and John should remain in their present concealment until night, and then endeavor to reach the mill under cover of the darkness, and open some means of communication with the family of the miller.

The rest of the day was spent in anxious thought. The situation of the adventurers was one of great personal peril, as they were now immediately within the circle of operations of the enemy, and likely to be observed and challenged the first moment they ventured upon the road.

The hour of dusk had scarcely arrived before they were again mounted on horseback. They proceeded cautiously upon the road that led through the wood, until it intersected the highway; and, having attained this point, John Ramsay, who was well acquainted with every avenue through the country, now led the way, by a private and scarcely discernible path, into the adjacent forest, and thence, by a tedious and prolonged route, directed his companion to the banks of the Ennoree. This course of travel took them immediately to the plain on which Innis had been encamped — the late field of battle. All here was still and desolate. The sheds and other vestiges of the recent bivouac were yet visible, but not even the farm-house that had constitued Innis's head-quarters was reoccupied by its original inhabitants. The bat whirred over the plain, and the owl hooted from the neighboring trees. The air still bore the scent of dead bodies which had either been left exposed, or so meagrely covered with earth as to taint the breeze with noisome exhalations.

"There is a great difference, John," said Horse Shoe, who seldom let an occasion to moralize after his own fashion slip by, "there's a great difference between a hot field and a stale one. Your hot field makes a soldier, for there's a sort of a stir in it that sets the blood to running merrily through a man, and that's what I call pleasure. But when everything is festering like the inside of a hospital — or what's next door to it, a grave-yard — it is mighty apt to turn a dragoon's stomach and make a preacher of him. This here dew falls to-night like frost, and chills me to the heart, which it wouldn't do if it didn't freshen up the smell of dead men. And there's the hogs, busy as so many sextons among Innis's Tories: you may hear them grunt over their suppers. Well, there is one man among them that I'll make bold to say these swine hav'n't got the stomach to touch — that's Hugh Habershaw: he sleeps in the mud in yonder fence-corner."

"If you had done nothing else in the fight, Horse Shoe, but cleave that fellow's skull," said Ramsay, "the ride we took would have been well paid for — it was worth the trouble."

"And the rapscallionly fellow to think," added Horse Shoe, "that I was going to save him from the devil's clutches, when I had a broadsword in my hand, and his bald, greasy pate in reach. His brain had nothing in it but deceit and lies, and all sorts of cruel thoughts, enough to poison the air when I let them out. I have made an observation, John, all my life on them foul-mouthed, swilling braggers — that when there's so much cunning and blood-thirstiness, there's no room for a thimbleful of courage: their heart's in their belly, which is as much as to signify that the man's a most beastly coward. But now, it is my opinion that we had best choose a spot along the river here, and leave our horses. I think we can manœuvre better on foot: the miller's house is short of two miles, and we mought be noticed if we were to go nearer on horseback."

This proposal was adopted, and the two friends, when they had ridden a short distance below the battle ground, halted in a thicket, where they fastened their horses, and proceeded towards the mill on foot. After following the course of the stream for near half an hour, they perceived, at a distance, a light glimmering through the window of Allen Musgrove's dwelling. This induced a second pause in their march, when Ramsay suggested the propriety of his advancing alone to reconnoitre the house, and attempting to gain some speech with the inmates. He accordingly left the sergeant to amuse himself with his own thoughts.

Horse Shoe took his seat beneath a sycamore, where he waited a long time in anxious expectation of the return of his comrade. Growing uneasy, at last, at John's delay, he arose, and stole cautiously forward until he reached the mill, where he posted himself in a position from which he was able to see and hear what was going on at the miller's house. The porch was occupied by three or four persons, whose conversation, as it came to the sergeant's ear, proved them to be strangers to the family; and a ray of light from a taper within, after a while, made this more manifest, by revealing the scarlet uniform of the enemy. Horse Shoe was thus confirmed in the truth of the report that Butler had been brought to this place under a military escort. With this conviction he returned to the sycamore, where he again sat down to wait for the coming of his companion.

It was after ten o'clock, and the sergeant was casting over in his thoughts the long absence of John, when his attention was aroused by the sound of footsteps, and the next instant John Ramsay and Mary Musgrove stood beside him.

"What kept you till this time of night?" was the sergeant's accost.

"Softly, man, I have news for you," replied Ramsay. "Here is Mary herself."

"And so she is, indeed!" exclaimed the sergeant, at the same time shaking her hand, "this is my petticoat-sodger; how goes it with you, girl?"

"I have only a moment to spare," replied the maiden cheerfully, "and it is the greatest of good luck that I thought of coming out; for John gave me a signal, which I was stupid enough not to understand at first. But, after a while, I thought it could be no one but John Ramsay; and that, partly, because I expected he would be coming into the neighborhood ever since I heard of his being at his father's, after the ensign was made a prisoner."

"I went," said John Ramsay, "to the further side of the house, where I set to whistling an old-fashioned tune that Mary was acquainted with — walking away all the time in an opposite direction — as if there was nothing meant — "

"And I knew the tune, Mr. Horse Shoe," interrupted Mary, eagerly, "it was Maggie Lauder. John practised that trick once before to show me how to find my way to him. Upon that, I made an excuse to leave the room, and slipped out through the garden — and then I followed the whistling, as folks say they follow a jack-o'-lantern."

"And so, by a countermarch," continued the young dragoon, "we came round the meadow and through the woods, here."

"Now that you've got here at last," said Horse Shoe, "tell me the news."

"Major Butler is in the house," said Mary and John, both speaking at once. "He was brought there yesterday from

Blackstock's," continued the maiden. "Orders came from somebody that he was to be kept at our house, until they had fixed upon what was to be done with him. Colonel Innis was too ill to think of such matters, and has been carried out of the neighborhood — and it is thought he will die."

"How many men are there to guard the prisoner?" asked the sergeant.

"There are more than twenty, with a lieutenant from Ninety-Six, who has the charge of them."

"And how does the major bear his troubles?"

"He seems to be heavy at heart," replied the maiden. "But that may be because he is away from his friends. Though my father, who is a good judge of such things, says he suffers tribulation like a Christian. He asked me privately, if I had heard anything of you, Mr. Robinson: and when I told him what folks said about your being with the people that beat Colonel Innis, he smiled, and said if any man could get him free, it was Horse Shoe Robinson."

"Do they allow you to see him often?" inquired the sergeant.

"I have seen him only two or three times since he came to the house," answered the maiden. "But the officer that has charge of him is not contrary or ill-natured, and makes no objection to my carrying him his meals — though I am obliged to pretend to know less about Major Butler than I do, for fear they might be jealous of my talking to him."

"You can give him a letter?"

"I think I can contrive it," replied the maiden.

"Then give him this, my good girl," said Robinson, taking Williams's letter from his pocket and putting it in Mary's hand. "It is a piece of writing he can use whenever he is much pressed. It may save him from harm. Now, I want you to do something more. You must find a chance just to whisper in his ear that Horse Shoe Robinson and John Ramsay are in the neighborhood. Tell him, likewise, that Colonel Williams has sent a messenger to Lord Cornwallis to lay his case before that officer, and to get some order for his better treatment. That the doings of that rascally court-martial have been sent by the messenger, hoping that Lord Cornwallis, if he is a brave and a Christian man — as they say he is — will stop this onmerciful persecution of the major — which has no cause for it under heaven. Will you remember all this?"

"I'll try, sir," responded Mary; "and besides I will tell it to my father, who has more chance of speaking to Major Butler than I have."

"Now," said Horse Shoe, "we will be here again to-morrow night, a little earlier than this; you must meet us here. And say to the major, if he has any message for us, he may send it by you. But be cautious, Mary, how you are seen talking with the prisoner. If they suspect you it will spoil all."

"Trust to me," said the girl; "I warrant I have learned by this time how to behave myself amongst these red-coats."

"There, John," continued Horse Shoe, "I have said all I want to say, and as you, I have no doubt, have got a good deal to tell the girl, it is but fair that you should have your chance. So, do you walk back with her as far as the mill, and I'll wait here for you. But don't forget yourself by overstaying your furlough."

"I must get home as fast as possible," said Mary; "they will be looking for me."

"Away, John Ramsay — away," added Horse Shoe; "and have your eyes about you, man."

With this command John Ramsay and the miller's daughter hastily withdrew, and were soon out of the sergeant's hearing.

After an interval, which doubtless seemed short to the gallant dragoon, he returned to his comrade, and the two set out rapidly in quest of their horses; and once more having got into their saddles, they retraced their steps at a brisk speed to Ramsay's cabin.

CHAPTER XXX

All distant and faint were the sounds of the battle;
With the breezes they rise, with the breezes they fail,
Till the shout and the groan and the conflict's dread rattle,
And the chase's wild clamor come loading the gale.

THE MAID OF TORO.

IN the confusion that ensued upon the defeat of Innis, James Curry succeeded in conducting Butler from the field. His orders were to retreat with the prisoner to Blackstock's; and he had accordingly set out with about a dozen troopers, by a private path that led towards a quarter secure from the molestation of the enemy, when the attack commenced. Butler was mounted behind one of the men, and in this uneasy condition was borne along the circuitous by-way that had been chosen, without a moment's respite from the severe motion of the horse, nearly at high speed, until, having accomplished three miles of the retreat, the party arrived at the main road that extended between Innis's camp and Blackstock's. Here Curry, conceiving himself to be out of danger of pursuit, halted his men, with a purpose to remain until he could learn something of the combat. Butler was in a state of the most exciting bewilderment as to the cause of this sudden change in his affairs. No explanation was given to him by his conductors; and although, from the first, he was aware that an extraordinary emergency had arisen from some assault upon Innis's position, no one dropped a word in his hearing to give him the slightest clue to the nature of the attack. The troopers about him preserved a morose and ill-natured silence, and even manifested towards him a harsh and resentful demeanor. He heard the firing, but what troops were engaged, by whom led, or with what chances of success, were subjects of the most painfully interesting doubt. He could only conjecture that this was a surprise accomplished by the Whigs, and that the assailants must have come in sufficient force to justify the boldness of the enterprise. That Horse Shoe was connected with this irruption he felt fully assured; and from this circumstance he gathered the consolatory and cheerful prognostic of a better issue out of his afflictions than, in his late condition, seemed even remotely possible. This hope grew brighter as the din of battle brought the tidings of the day to his ear. The first few scattered shots that told of the confusion in which the combat was begun, were, after an interval, succeeded by regular volleys of musketry that indicated an orderly and marshalled resistance. Platoon after platoon fired in succession — signifying, to the practised hearing of the soldier, that infantry was receiving the attacks of cavalry, and that as yet the first had not faltered. Then the firing grew more slack, and random shots were discharged from various quarters — but amidst there were heard no embodied volleys. It was the casual and nearly overpowered resistance of flying men.

At this juncture there was a dark frown on the brow of Curry, as he looked at his comrades, and said, in a low and muttered tone, "That helter-skelter shot grates cursedly on the ear. There's ill-luck in the sound of it."

Presently a few stragglers appeared at a turn of the road, some quarter of a mile in the direction of the battle, urging their horses forward at the top of their speed. These were followed by groups both of infantry and cavalry, pressing onwards in the utmost disorder — those on horseback thrusting their way through the throng of foot-soldiers, seemingly regardless of life or limb; the wounded with their wounds bleeding afresh, or hastily bandaged with such appliances as were at hand. All hurried along amidst the oaths, remonstrances, and unheeded orders of the officers, who were endeavoring to resume their commands. It was the flight of men beset by a panic, and fearful of pursuit; and the clouds of dust raised by the press and hurry of this career almost obscured the setting sun.

During the first moments of uncertainty, Curry, no less anxiously than Butler, remained stationary by the roadside, reading the distant signs of the progress of the fight; but now, when the disastrous issue was no longer doubtful, he commanded his cavalcade to move forward, and from that moment prosecuted his journey with unabated speed until he arrived at Blackstock's.

Butler was unceremoniously marched to his former place of confinement in the barn, where a rigorous guard was set over his person. In the confusion and insubordination that prevailed amongst the crowd, that, during the night, was continually increasing in the little hamlet, the common rites of humanity towards the prisoner were forgotten, and he was left to pass the weary hours till morning, on a shock of hay, without food or other refreshment than a simple draught of water. From the unreserved murmurs of those who frequented the place, and the querulous upbraidings of the soldiery against each other, Butler was enabled to glean the principal incidents of the day. The supposed death of Innis reached him through this channel, and, what was scarcely a subject of less personal interest to him, the certain end of Hugh Habershaw. It was with a silent satisfaction at the moral or *poetical* justice — as it has been called — of the event, that he heard the comrades of the late self-conceited captain describe his death in terms of coarse and unpitying ribaldry — a retribution due to the memory of a cruel and cowardly braggart.

When the morning was fully abroad, the disarranged and broken remnants of the Tory camp began gradually to be reduced to a state of discipline. The day was spent in this occupation. Orders were every moment arriving from the higher officers of the late camp, or from the nearest British posts. Videttes bore the tidings of the different military operations from the neighborhood of the enemy. The fragments of companies were marshalled into squads and subdivisions; and, successively, one party after another was seen to leave the hamlet, and take a direction of march that led towards the main British army, or to the garrisons of the lower districts.

Towards the close of the day one detachment only was left; and Butler was given to understand that this was intrusted with his especial keeping. It was composed of a few regular soldiers of the garrison of Ninety-Six, and a small number of the country militia, — making, in all, about twenty men, commanded by Lieutenant Macdonald, of the regular army.

Butler remained in his present state of seclusion four or five days, during which he experienced much mitigation of the rigors of his captivity. Macdonald was a careful and considerate soldier, and demeaned himself towards his prisoner with such kindness as the nature of his trust allowed. He removed him into a comfortable apartment in the dwelling-house, and supplied him with the conveniences his situation required; he even made him occasional visits, which were attended with more than the mere observances of courtesy and respect, and expressed a sympathy in his sufferings.

These unexpected tones of comfort, from a quarter in which Butler had hitherto heard nothing but fierce hatred and harsh rebuke, fell gratefully upon his ear, and gave a brighter color to his hopes for the future. But he could not help observing, that no hint was dropped by Macdonald which might furnish him the slightest ground of surmise as to the vicissitudes that yet awaited him. The reported fall of Innis seemed to afford a natural foundation for the belief, that the malice of his enemies might hereafter be less active, — as he attributed much of the persecution he had suffered to the secret machinations of that individual. He no longer saw around his person those agents who first pursued him with such bitter hostility. He seemed to have fallen into entirely new combinations, and had reason to augur, from all he saw, that their purposes against him were less wicked. And first, above all other topics of consolation and comfort, was the conviction that a brave and efficient party of friends were in the field, intent upon his liberation. Still, his situation was one in which it required all his manhood to sustain himself. A young soldier of an ardent temper, and zealously bent upon active and perilous service, can ill brook the tedious, dull delays of captivity, even in its mildest form: but if this thraldom befal in a period of universal agitation, when "great events are on the gale," of which the captive is only a witness to the pervading interest they excite, without being permitted to know their import; if moreover, as in the case of Butler, an impenetrable veil of mystery hang over the purpose of his captivity, behind which the few short glimpses afforded him, open upon his view nothing but death in its most frightful forms; and if to these are added, by far the bitterest of its qualities, the anxieties, cares, and pains of a devoted, plighted lover, separated from the heart that loves him, we may well conjecture that the most gallant spirit may find in it, even amidst occasional gleams of sunshine, that sinking of hope which the philosophic king of Israel has described as making "the heart sick," — that chafing of the soul that, like the encaged eaglet, wearies and tears its wing against the bars of its prison. Even so fared it with Arthur Butler, who now found himself growing more and more into the shadow of a melancholy temper.

It was soon ascertained that Williams had abandoned the field he had won, and had retreated beyond the reach of immediate pursuit. And as the post at Musgrove's mill afforded many advantages, in reference to the means of communicating with the garrisons of the middle section of the province, and was more secure against the hazard of molestation from such parties of

Whigs as might still be out-lying, an order was sent to Macdonald to remove with his prisoner to the habitation of the miller, and there to detain him until some final step should be taken in his case.

In pursuance of this requisition. Butler was conducted, after the interval of the few days we have mentioned, to Allen Musgrove's. The old man received his guests with that submission to the domination of the military masters of the province, which he had prescribed to himself throughout the contest, — secretly rejoicing that the selection made of his house for this purpose, might put it in his power to alleviate the sufferings of a soldier, towards whose cause he felt a decided though unavowed attachment. This selection furnished evidence to the miller, that nothing had transpired to arouse the distrust of the British authorities in the loyalty of any part of his family, — and to Butler, it inferred the consolatory fact, that the zealous devotion of Mary Musgrove to his service had as yet passed without notice; whilst to the maiden herself, it was proof that her agency in the delivery of the letter, which she had so adroitly put within the reach of the officers of the court, had not even excited a suspicion against her.

The best room in the house was allotted to the prisoner; and the most sedulous attention on the part of the family, so far as it could be administered without inducing mistrust, was employed in supplying him with whatever was needful to his condition. On the part of the commanding officer, the usual precautions known to military experience for the safe keeping of a prisoner were adopted. The privates of the guard occupied the barn, whilst Macdonald and one or two subordinate officers took up their quarters in the dwelling-house: sentinels were posted at the several avenues leading to the habitation, and a sergeant had the especial care of the prisoner, who, under this supervision, was occasionally allowed the range of the garden. The usual forms of a camp police were observed with scrupulous exactness; — and the morning and the nightly drum, the parade, the changing of sentries, the ringing of ramrods in the empty barrels of the muskets, and the glitter of weapons, were strangely and curiously associated with the rural and unwarlike features of the scenery around.

CHAPTER XXXI

BUTLER FINDS A GLEAM OF SUNSHINE IN HIS DISTRESS

Allen Musgrove had heard enough of Butler's history from his daughter and from Galbraith Robinson, to feel a warm interest in that officer's safety; and now his personal acquaintance with the prisoner still further corroborated his first prepossessions. The old man took the earliest opportunity to indicate to Butler the concern he felt in his welfare. From the moderate and kindly tone of his own character, he was enabled to do this without drawing upon himself the distrust of the officer of the guard. His expressions of sympathy were regarded, by Macdonald, as the natural sentiments of a religious mind imbued with an habitual compassion for the sufferings of a fellow creature, and of one who strove to discharge the duties of a peace-maker. His visits were looked upon as those of a spiritual counsellor, whose peculiar right it was to administer consolation to the afflicted, in whatever condition; he was therefore permitted freely to commune with the prisoner, and, as it sometimes happened, alone with him in his chamber.

This privilege was now particularly useful; for Mary having, on the morning after her midnight interview with John Ramsay and Robinson, communicated to her father the incidents of that meeting, and put in his possession the letter which the sergeant had given her, and having also repeated her message to him accurately as she had received it, Musgrove took occasion, during the following day, to deliver the letter to Butler, and to make known to him all that he had heard from his daughter. This disclosure produced the most cheering effect upon Butler's spirits. It, for the first time since the commencement of his sufferings, opened to his mind a distinct view of his chance of eventual liberation. The expectation of having his case represented to Cornwallis inspired him with a strong confidence that justice would be done to him, and the covert malice of his enemies be disarmed. In this hope, it occurred to him to take some instant measures to satisfy the British commander-in-chief of the groundless character of the principal accusation brought against him by the court-martial, — that which related to the pretended design to deliver up Philip Lindsay to the wrath of the Republican government. For this purpose he resolved to make an appeal to Lindsay himself, by letter, and frankly to call upon him to put at rest this most unjust and wicked accusation. He knew that however strong Lindsay's antipathy to him might be, the high sense of honor which distinguished the father of Mildred might be confidently and successfully invoked to furnish such a statement as should entirely satisfy his accusers of the gross injustice of the charge. "I will write to him," he said, "and throw myself upon his protection. I will require of him to detail the whole history of my intercourse with his family, and to say how improbable even he must deem it, that I could be so base as to plot against his peace. And I will appeal to Mildred to fortify her father's statement, to show that this wicked accusation rests upon a story which it is impossible could be true."

Whilst Butler's thoughts were still occupied with this resolve, Mary Musgrove entered his apartment, bearing in her hands a napkin and plate which she had come to spread for his dinner, and as the maiden employed herself in arranging a small table in the middle of the room, she cast a few distrustful glances towards the sentinel who paced to and fro opposite the door, and then, seizing on a moment when the soldier had disappeared from view, she whispered to Butler —

"You have seen my father, sir?"

Butler nodded his head.

"He has told you all?"

Butler again signified a silent assent.

The tramp of the sentinel showed that he was again approaching the door; and when Mary turned her eyes in that direction, she beheld the watchful soldier halting in such a position as to enable him both to see and hear what was passing in the room. Without showing the least perturbation, or even appearing to notice the guard, she said in a gay and careless voice, — "My father and Lieutenant Macdonald, — who is a good gentleman — think it belongs to Christian people to do all the good we can for them that providence has put under us; and so, sir, I have been to gather you some blackberries, which I thought, may be, you would like, sir."

The sentinel walked away, and Mary smiled as she saw her little stratagem succeed.

"Bring me some paper," said Butler cautiously. "You are

a considerate girl," he continued, in a loud voice, "and I thank you for this good will." Then finding that the sentinel did not immediately return, he whispered — "I wish to write to Robinson — you shall take the letter and read it to him."

"I will do my best," replied the maiden; and again the sentinel interrupted the conference.

Mary, having arranged the table, left the room. In a few moments she returned, bringing with her the family Bible.

"If you would like to read, sir," she said, "here is a book that a body may look at a long time without getting tired of it. We have only got this, and the Pilgrim's Progress, and the hymn-book, in the house; but my father says this is worth all the others that ever were printed, put together; and especially, sir, when one's in distress, and away from their friends."

An expression of pleasure played across Butler's features as he took the heavy volume from the girl.

"A thousand thanks to you, my pretty maiden," he replied. "I doubt not I shall grow both wiser and better under your tutoring. This kindness almost reconciles me to my fate."

"John is doing all he can for you, and he is a good helper to Mr. Robinson," said Mary, in the same cautious whisper that she had first spoken in, as she retreated from the room. Butler opened the book, and found a sheet of paper folded away amongst the leaves; then closing it, he threw it upon his bed.

In due course of time, Mary Musgrove returned with a few dishes of food which she set out upon the table, and, in one of the successive visits which were employed in furnishing the repast, she took from beneath her apron a small ink-horn and pen, which she placed, unobserved by the sentinel, in Butler's hand. Having done this, she retired, leaving the prisoner to despatch his meal alone.

After dinner, Butler threw himself upon his bed, where he lay with the Bible opened out before him, with his back turned towards the door; and, whilst Mary Musgrove was engaged in removing the furniture of the table, he found means to write a few lines to Philip Lindsay. He took the same opportunity to pen a short letter to Mildred; and then to set down some directions for Horse Shoe Robinson, the purport of which was that the sergeant should take the two letters and depart, with all despatch, for the Dove Cote, and to put both into the hands of Mildred, with a request that she would procure him the necessary reply from her father. Horse Shoe was also directed to explain to Mildred such particulars of Butler's history as were necessary to be made known for the accomplishment of the object of the mission.

When these papers were finished they were folded up into a small compass, and in the course of the evening put into Mary's hands, with a request that she would herself read the instructions intended for the sergeant, and apprise him of their contents when she delivered the papers to him.

So far all had succeeded well, and Butler found additional reason to dispel the gloom that hung upon his spirits, in the prospect that was now opened to him of enlisting strong and authoritative friends in the scheme of his liberation.

CHAPTER XXXII

MARY MUSGROVE'S PERPLEXITIES

As a mariner who watches the heavens from the deck, and notes the first uprising of the small cloud, "no bigger than a man's hand," that to his practised eye shows the sign of tempest; and anon, as the speck quickly changes into a lurid mass, whence volume after volume of dun vapor is driven in curled billows forward, covering the broad welkin with a gloomy pall, he looks more frequently and more intently upwards, anxious to lay his vessel safe, and assure himself of his proper course to steer: so — not with the same doubt of safety, but with the same restless inspection of the heavens — did Mary watch the slow approach of night. First, she looked wistfully at the declining sun, and observed with pleasure the night-hawk begin to soar: then, through the long twilight, she noted the thickening darkness, and saw the bat take wing, and heard the frog croaking from his pool. And as the stars, one by one, broke forth upon the night, it gladdened her to think the hour of her mission was approaching, for she was troubled in her spirit and anxious to acquit herself of her charitable office; and perhaps, too, it may be told of her, without prejudice to her modest, maidenly emotions, a spur was given to her wishes by the hope of meeting John Ramsay.

For an hour after supper she paced the porch, and still looked out upon the stars, to mark the slow waxing of the night; and, now and then she walked forth as far as the mill, and lingered by the bank of the river, and again returned to ask the sentinel the hour.

"You seem disturbed, Mary," said Macdonald, playfully. "Now, I'll venture to say I can guess your thoughts: this star-gazing is a great tell-tale. You were just now thinking that, as the tug of the war is over, some lad who has borne a musket lately, will be very naturally tripping this way to-night, instead of going home to see his mother. Come — isn't that a good guess?"

"Do you know him, sir?" asked Mary, with composure.

"Aye, to be sure I do: a good, brave fellow, who eats well, drinks well, and fights well."

"All men do that now," replied the maiden; "but I am sure you are wrong, sir, if you think any such considers it worth his while to come here."

"He must come quickly, or we cannot let him in without a countersign," said the officer: "sergeant, order the tattoo to beat, it is nine o'clock. Mary, stay, I must cross-question you a little about this same gallant."

"Indeed, sir, I did but jest, and so I thought you did. My father says it is not proper I should loiter to talk with the men; good night, sir: it is our time for prayers." And with these words the young girl withdrew into the house.

In some half hour afterwards Mary escaped by another door and, taking a circuitous path through the garden, she passed behind the sentinel and sped towards the mill, intent upon keeping her appointment with the friends of Butler. As soon as she reached the river bank, she quickened her pace, and hurried with a nimble step towards the distant thicket.

"What ho! who goes there?" shouted the voice of a man from the neighborhood of the mill: "who flies so fast?"

"Faith, Tom, it must be a ghost," said a second voice, loud enough to be heard by the damsel, who now increased the speed with which she fled towards the cover.

In an instant two of the soldiers of the guard rushed upon the track of the frightened girl.

"Spare me, good sir — for pity's sake, spare me!" exclaimed the maiden, suddenly turning round upon her pursuers.

"Where away so fast?" said one of the men. "This is a strange time of night for girls to be flying into the woods. What matter have you in hand that brings you here — and what is your name?"

"I am the daughter of Allen Musgrove," replied Mary indignantly.

"Is it so?" said the first speaker; "then it is the Miller's own daughter, and we ask your pardon. We only saw you flying along the bank of the river, and not knowing what it was, why we thought it right to follow. But as it is all explained now, we will see you back to the house."

"I can find my way without help," replied the maiden.

"Now, that's not good-natured for so kind a girl as the miller's daughter ought to be," said the second soldier.

"I will see if my father can protect me," said Mary, hastening back towards the house so rapidly as almost to run. "I will know if Lieutenant Macdonald will allow me to be insulted."

With a hurried step she entered upon the porch, and, without stopping to parley with those who occupied this part of the dwelling, retired to her chamber and threw herself into a chair, where she sat for some time panting with affright. As she gradually recovered her strength, she began to turn her thoughts upon her recent discomfiture; and it was with a deep sense of chagrin and disappointment, that she reflected upon her not being able successfully to renew her enterprise on the same night. The hour of meeting had arrived; the officers of the guard were still frequenting the porch; her conduct had already excited notice, and if she wished to be in a condition to render future service, her most obvious duty was to postpone any further attempt to deliver the papers until another time. On the other hand, she had reason to fear that John Ramsay would be hovering near to ascertain the cause of her failure to meet him, and might rashly resort to the same mode of conveying a signal which he had successfully practised heretofore. This would infallibly, she believed, provoke an investigation that might entirely frustrate all their views. "But then John is a good soldier," she said, in the way of self-consolation, "and will know that the enemy is awake; because if it was not so, he would be sure I would keep my word. And if he only takes that notion into his head, he is too careful to run the chance of spoiling all by coming here."

Still, with some little mistrust as to John's soldiership when it crossed the path of his love, which naturally, she reflected, makes a man rash, she thought it best to provide against accident, by throwing herself into the company of the officers who loitered about the door in idle discourse with her father. She accordingly left her room, and, with an anxious and troubled heart, went out and seated herself quietly on the steps of the porch, where she remained for some time a silent but inattentive listener to the conversation of those around her.

As a part of that system of things by which it is contrived that the current of true love shall never run smooth, I have ever found that when it was peculiarly fitting that some grandam, uncle, cousin, father, or guest, should retire early to bed, in order that some scheme of interest to young lovers might be successfully achieved; precisely on such nights is the perversity of fate most conspicuous, in inclining the minds of such grandam, uncle, cousin, and so forth, to sit up much longer than they are wont;

thus showing that the grooves and dovetails of things in this world are not nicely fitted to the occasions of those who deal in the tender passion. And so it befel for poor Mary Musgrove this night.

The hour was now fast verging upon eleven, and she anxiously noted every sentence that was spoken, hoping it was to be the last; and then she trembled to think that John, regardless of the danger, might be lurking near, and indiscreetly expose himself. And still the talkers discoursed as if they meant to sit up all night. It was a delicious, cool hour, after a sultry day, and there was luxury in the breeze; but as the minutes were counted over by the maiden, in their slow passage, her fears increased. At length, far off, as if it were a mile away, the clear notes of one whistling an old tune were heard. Mary involuntarily started from her seat, and moved along the little pathway towards the gate, her heart beating against her bosom as if it would have "overbourne its continents." The signal notes freshened upon the air, and the tune came forth blithely and boldly, showing that the wayfarer was trudging, with a light heart, down the main road towards the mill. The party in the porch, however, were too much engrossed in their colloquy to notice the incident. The whistling came still nearer, until, at last, it seemed to be scarce a gunshot from the house. Beyond this point it did not advance; but here indicated that the person from whom it proceeded had halted. If Mary's cheek could have been brought to the light, it would have shown how the blood had deserted it from very fear: her whole frame shook with this emotion. To exhibit her unconcern, which, in truth, was most sadly affected, she mingled amongst the company in the porch, and leant against the door-post. Still the whistling continued, with no symptom of retreat, and Mary impatiently walked towards the further end of the house. "John Ramsay makes a fool of himself," she muttered peevishly. "Hasn't he the sense to see I cannot get out? What keeps the simple man dallying shilly-shally at the fence, as if he actually wanted them to take him? I don't believe in the mighty sense and wisdom of these men! If John had half an eye he would see that I couldn't get away to-night."

As the maiden grew fretful, her fears had less mastery over her; and now, taking heart of grace, she returned to the porch.

"Sergeant," said Macdonald, calling to one of his men, "take two files and patrole the road until you ascertain who that fellow is who makes himself so merry to-night. I thought it some fool," he continued, addressing himself to Allen Musgrove, "who, as the poet says, 'whistled as he went for want of thought,' but he seems to have a hankering after these premises that is not exactly to my mind. Perhaps, after all, Mary," he added privately in the maiden's ear; "it is the lad I was telling you of; and as he is a bashful youth, we will bring him in by force. You know, he can't help that; and old dad here can never blame you if I should make the fellow come to see you against your will. Sergeant, treat the man civilly, you understand."

"It is not worth your while to be sending after Adam Gordon," said Mary, with some slight confusion in her accent; "he is only half-witted; and almost the only thing he does for a living, is to come down of nights here to the mill-dam, to bob for eels. If it wasn't for that, his mother would go many a day without a meal."

"No matter, we will bring Adam in," replied the lieutenant, "and if he is good at his sport, why we will go and join him."

"He is shy of company," said Mary, still faltering in her speech, "and will not come amongst strangers."

Partly from a spirit of resignation, partly to avoid further exposure of her feelings, and in part too, perhaps, from some slight feeling of remorse, such as is natural to a virtuous and youthful mind at being obliged to practise a deceit however lawful (as I contend it was in this case), the maiden withdrew into the parlor, where, unseen by any, she offered up a short and earnest prayer for direction and forgiveness.

Meantime the patrole had set out, and, after the lapse of a short time, returned, when the officer reported that before his arrival, the person they had gone in quest of had left the place, and, in the darkness of the night, they had no clue to follow him. This was scarcely announced before the same whistle was heard, at the same remote point where it had first attracted Mary's notice.

"It is as our young mistress has said," muttered Macdonald, "some bumpkin, too shy to be caught, and not worth the catching. We have sat it out to-night long enough, friend Musgrove, so let's to bed."

In a few moments the party betook themselves to their several places of rest.

As Mary prepared herself for her couch, the anxious events of the night busied her thoughts, and the image of John Ramsay was summoned up alternately to be reproved and applauded. "If he is foolhardy," she said, as she laid her head on the pillow, "no one will say he isn't wise besides. And if he will be thrusting his head into danger, he knows right well how to get it out again. So God bless him, for a proper man as he is!" And thus, in a better temper with her lover, the maiden fell asleep.

In order to avert all suspicion of disloyalty from the miller's family, Christopher Shaw had offered his services to Macdonald, to do duty as one of the detachment, during the period of Butler's detention in the house. The offer had been accepted, and Christopher was appointed to serve in the character of a quartermaster, or purveyor for the little garrison, — a post, whose duties did not materially interfere with his daily occupation at the mill.

Mary was in the habit of communicating to Christopher all her secrets, and of enlisting his aid in her plans whenever it was necessary. And now, soon after the morning broke, the maiden arose and went to the mill, where she communicated to Christopher all the perplexities of the preceding night.

"The thing must be managed to-day," said the young man, after he had heard the whole story. "I have provisions to collect from the neighborhood; and what is to hinder you, Mary, from riding out with me, — if it should only be to buy some eggs? — and then, what is to hinder us from popping in upon David Ramsay, and there fixing the whole matter?"

"Will not the lieutenant be sending some of his own men with you?" inquired the maid.

"He doesn't suspect us," answered Christopher, as cautiously as if the walls of his mill had ears. "At any rate we can try it, you know, and if the thing should take a wrong turn, you can only stay at home; and we may, at the worst, make another venture at night."

"I have the letter in my bosom," said Mary, "and will be ready immediately after breakfast."

When the appointed time arrived, things went as favorably as Mary could have wished. Her good spirits had returned; and she plied her household duties with a happy cheerfulness in her looks that completely disarmed all suspicion. She received the banter of Macdonald, as to the cause of her restlessness on the preceding night, with perfect good nature; and when Christopher announced to the commanding officer his purpose of going out upon a purveying ride, and invited his cousin to accompany him, she accepted the proposal with such a tone of laughing pleasure, as put it on the footing of a pastime.

The horses were brought to the door, and the maiden and her escort rode cheerily forth. They were not long in accomplishing the five or six miles that brought them to David Ramsay's cabin. I need not tell the affectionate concern with which Mary Musgrove met her lover, John Ramsay; nor how she upbraided him as a silly fellow, for tramping and trudging about the mill, and whistling his signals, when he ought to have known, by her not coming to meet him, that there was good reason for it. Nor is it important to detail the circumstances of Horse Shoe's and John's fruitless expedition, and their disappointment at not seeing Mary; and how shrewdly, last night, Robinson guessed the true cause of it; and how entirely he agreed with the maiden, beforehand, in thinking John a venturesome, harebrained fool, to put himself in danger, when he might have been certain it would have ended as it did, in a run from "the rascally red coats," as John had to run, to get out of the clutches of the patrole. My story requires that I should pass these things by, and go to the business in hand.

Horse Shoe and Ramsay had grown exceedingly impatient, both because they were in hourly danger of being surprised by casual parties of the enemy, and because the time for useful action was fast gliding away. They had used every precaution to keep their visit to David Ramsay's a profound secret to the neighborhood; and had, with that object, lain perdue in one of the small cabins, from which they might watch the approach of visitors, and, if need required, secure an immediate retreat. During the day, they seldom left their concealment, confining all their out-door operations to the night.

A consultation was held in David Ramsay's cabin, — the letters were produced and delivered to Horse Shoe, and the instructions intended for him by Butler were carefully read. It was resolved that Horse Shoe should set out for the Dove Cote without delay, taking the route through the mountain country of North Carolina, as that least likely to be interrupted by the British troops. John Ramsay, for the present, was to return to the Fair Forest camp, to inform Williams of the state of affairs; and he was hereafter to act as occasion might suggest. Christopher Shaw and Mary were to attend upon Butler, and communicate whatever might transpire of interest to David Ramsay, who promised to find means of intercourse with Williams and Sumpter, as circumstances should allow.

These matters being arranged, Mary and Christopher Shaw took their leaves of Ramsay's family, and went about the ostensible object of their expedition.

Horse Shoe's plan of travel during the first and most perilous stages of his journey towards Virginia, was to avail himself of the darkness of the night; and he accordingly resolved to set out as soon as this day should draw to a close. His immediate cares were, therefore, directed to making all the necessary preparations for his departure. Captain Peter was carefully tended, and supplied with a double allowance of provender; provisions were stowed away, both for himself and his trusty beast: his pistols were put in order: his rifle cleaned out, and a supply of ammunition provided; and, finally, the letters were sewed up in a leather pouch, and buckled around his body by a strap, inside of his clothes. It was no inconsiderable item in the sergeant's preparation for his expedition, to sit down and eat a meal, which, from the quantity bestowed, and the vigor with which the assault upon it was made, might have betokened a full week's starvation.

The day waned, and the night came a welcome visitor to the sergeant; and, at that hour which old chroniclers designate as "inter canem et lupum," Captain Peter was brought to the door, ready dight for travel. Ramsay's family stood around, — and whilst Andy, with boyish affection, held Horse Shoe's rifle in his hand, the sergeant feelingly spoke the words of parting to his friends; — then, with a jaunty air of careless mirth, springing into his saddle, and receiving his trusty weapon from the young comrade of his late gallant adventure, he rode forth with as stout a heart as ever went with knight of chivalry to the field of romantic renown.

CHAPTER XXXIII

A GLANCE AT THE DOVE COTE.—THE COMPANIONSHIP OF BROTHER AND SISTER

Our story once more brings us back to the Dove Cote. During the first week that followed her interview with Arthur Butler under the Fawn's Tower, Mildred was calm and thoughtful, and even melancholy: her usual custom of exercise was foregone, and her time was passed chiefly in her chamber. By degrees, however, her firm and resolute temper predominated over the sadness of her fortunes, and she began to resume that cheerfulness which circumstances can never long subdue in a strong and disciplined mind. She had grown more than ever watchful of the public events, and sought, with an intense avidity, to obtain information in regard to the state of things in the south. She now felt herself closely allied to the cause in which Arthur Butler had embarked, and, therefore, caught up the floating rumors of the day, in what regarded the progress of the American arms in the southern expedition, with the interest of one who had a large stake depending on the issue.

She had received several letters from Butler, which detailed the progress of his journey from the Dove Cote to Gates's camp, and from thence to Horse Shoe's cottage. They were all written in the confident and even jocular tone of a light-hearted soldier who sought to amuse his mistress; and they narrated such matters of personal history as were of a character to still her fears for his safety. Their effect upon Mildred was to warm up her enthusiasm, as well as to brighten her anticipations of the future, and thus to increase the returning elasticity of her spirits. Up to this period, therefore, she grew every day more buoyant and playful in her temper, and brought herself to entertain a more sanguine reckoning of the eventual determination of affairs. She was now frequently on horseback, attended by her brother, with whom she scarcely ever failed to make a visit to the good Mistress Dimock, where she either found a letter from Butler, or heard some of the thousand tidings which report was for ever busy in propagating or exaggerating in regard to the movements of the army.

"I'll warrant you, Arthur is a man for the pen as well as for the spur and broadsword, my pretty lady," was one of the landlady's comments, as she handed to Mildred the eighth or ninth epistle that had fallen into her hands since Butler's departure; "there scarcely comes trotting by a soiled traveller with his head set northwards, but it is — 'Good woman, is this Mistress Dimock's?' and when I say, 'aye,' then 'here's a letter, madam, for you, that comes from the army:' and so, there's Arthur's own hand-writing to a great pacquet, 'for Mistress Dimock of the Rockfish inn, of Amherst,' and not even, after all, one poor line for me, but just a cover, and the inside for Miss Mildred Lindsay of the Dove Cote. Ha, ha! we old bodies are only stalking-horses in this world. But God bless him! — he is a fine and noble gentleman." And Mildred would take the pacquet and impatiently break the seal; and as she perused the close-written contents the color waxed and waned upon her cheek, and her eye would one instant sparkle with mirth, and in the next grow dim with a tear. And when she had finished reading, she would secretly press the paper to her lips, and then bestow it away in her bosom, evincing the earnest fondness of a devoted and enthusiastic nature.

Mildred and Henry were inseparable; and, in proportion as his sister's zeal and attachment to the cause of independence became more active, did Henry's inclination to become a partisan grow apace. Hers was a character to kindle the spirit of brave adventure. There was in it a quiet and unostentatious but unvarying current of resolution, that shrank before no perils. Her feelings, acute and earnest, had given all their warmth to her principles; and what she once believed her duty commanded, was pursued with the devout self-dedication of a religious obligation. To this temper, which, by some secret of its constitution, has a spell to sway the minds of mankind, there was added the grace of an exquisitely feminine address. The union of these two attributes rendered Mildred Lindsay an object of conspicuous interest in such a time as that of the revolutionary struggle. Her youth, her ready genius, her knowledge and her habits of reflection, much in advance of her years, enhanced the impression her character was adapted to produce, and brought upon her, even in her secluded position, a considerable share of public observation. It was not wonderful that a mind so organized and accomplished should have acquired an unlimited dominion over the frank, open-hearted, and brave temper of her brother, now just stepping beyond the confines of mere boyhood. Her influence over Henry was paramount and unbounded: her affections were his, her faith was his, her enthusiasm stole into and spread over his whole temper.

With these means of influence she had sedulously applied herself to infuse into Henry's mind her own sentiment in regard to the war; and this purpose had led her to interest herself in subjects and pursuits, which, in general, are very foreign from her sex. Her desire to enlist his feelings in aid of Butler, and her conviction that a time was at hand when Henry might be useful, gave rise to an eager solicitude to see him well prepared for the emergencies of the day, by that necessary mode of education which, during the period of the revolution, was common amongst the young gentlemen of the country. He was a most willing and ready pupil; and she delighted to encourage him in his inclination for military studies, however fanciful some of his conceptions in regard to them might be. She, therefore, saw, with great satisfaction, the assiduous though boyish devotion with which he set himself to gain a knowledge of matters relating to the duties of a soldier. However little this may fall within the scope of female perception in ordinary times, it will not appear so much removed from the capabilities or even the habits of the sex, when we reflect that in the convulsions of this great national struggle, when every resource of the country was drained for service, the events of the day were contemplated with no less interest by the women than by the men. The fervor with which the American women participated in the cares and sacrifices of the revolutionary war, has challenged the frequent notice and warmest praises of its chroniclers. Mildred but reflected, in this instance, the hues of the society around the Dove Cote, which consisted of many families, scattered along the country side, composed of persons of elevated character, easy circumstances, and of the staunchest Whig politics, with whom she held an uninterrupted and familiar intercourse.

Another consideration may serve to explain the somewhat masculine character of Mildred's pursuits. Her most intimate companion, at all times, and frequently for weeks together her only one, was her brother. These two had grown up together in all the confidence of childhood; and this confidence continued still unabated. Their pursuits, sports, exercises, thoughts, and habits were alike, with less of the discrimination usual between the sexes, than is to be found between individuals in larger associations. They approximated each other in temper and disposition; and

Henry might, in this regard, be said to be, without disparagement to his manly qualities, a girlish boy; and Mildred, on the other hand, with as little derogation, to be a boyish girl. This home-bred freedom of nurture produced, in its development, some grotesque results, which my reader has, doubtless, heretofore observed with a smile; and it will, likewise, serve to explain some of the peculiar forms of intercourse which may hereafter be noticed between the brother and sister.

The news of the battle of Camden had not yet reached the neighborhood of the Dove Cote; but the time drew nigh when all the country stood on tiptoe, anxious to receive tidings of that interesting event. A week had elapsed without bringing letters from Butler; and Mildred was growing uneasy at this interval of silence. There was a struggle in her mind; an unpleasant foreboding that she was almost ashamed to acknowledge, and yet which she could not subdue. The country was full of reports of the hostile operations, and a thousand surmises were entertained, which varied according to the more sanguine or desponding tempers of the persons who made them. Mildred was taught by Butler to expect defeat, yet still she hoped for victory; but the personal fate of her lover stole upon her conjectures, and she could not keep down the misgiving which affection generally exaggerates, and always renders painful. In this state of doubt, it was observable that her manners occasionally rose to a higher tone of playfulness than was natural to her; and by turns they sank to a moody silence, showing that the equipoise of the mind was disturbed, and that the scales did not hang true: it was the struggle of mental resolution with a coward heart — a heart intimidated by its affections.

Such was the state of things when, in the latter fortnight of August, the morning ushered in a day of unsurpassed beauty. The air was elastic; the cool breeze played upon the shrubbery, and stole the perfume of a thousand flowers. The birds sang with unwonted vivacity from the neighboring trees; and the sun lighted up the mountains with a golden splendor, the fast drifting clouds flinging their shadows upon the forest that clothed the hills around, and the eagle and the buzzard sailing in the highest heavens, or eddying around the beetling cliffs with a glad flight, as if rejoicing in the luxuries of the cool summer morning. Breakfast was scarcely over before Henry was seen upon the terrace, arrayed in his hunting dress. His bugle was daintily suspended by a green cord across his shoulders; it was a neat and glittering instrument, whose garniture was bedizened with the coxcombry of silken tassels, and was displayed as ostentatiously as if worn by the hero of a melodrame.

Like St. Swithin in the ballad, he had " footed thrice the wold," when he put the bugle to his mouth and " blew a recheate both loud and long."

" How now, good master Puff," said Mildred, coming up playfully to her brother, " what means this uproar? Pray you, have mercy on one's ears."

Henry turned towards his sister, without taking the bugle from his lips, and continued the blast for a full minute; then, ceasing only from want of breath, he said, with a comic earnestness —

" I'm practising my signals, sister; I can give you 'to Horse,' and 'Reveillee,' and 'Roast Beef,' like a trained trumpeter."

" Truly you are a proper man, master," replied Mildred. " But it is hardly a time," she continued, half muttering to herself, " for you and me, Henry, to wear light hearts in our bosoms."

" Why, sister," said Henry, with some astonishment in his looks, " this seems to me to be the very time to practise my signals. We are at the very tug of the war, and every man that has a sword, or bugle either, should be up and doing."

" How come on your studies, brother? " interrupted Mildred, without heeding Henry's interpretation of his duty.

" Oh, rarely! I know most of the speeches of Coriolanus all by heart: —

"'Like an eagle in a dove cote, I
Fluttered your voices in Corioli:
Alone I did it. — Boy! '"

he spouted, quoting from the play, and accompanying his recitation with some extravagant gestures.

" This is easy work, Henry," said Mildred, laughing, " there is too much of the holiday play in that. I thought you were studying some graver things, instead of these bragging heroics. You pretended to be very earnest, but a short time ago, to make a soldier of yourself."

" Well, and don't you call this soldiership? Suppose I were to pounce down upon Cornwallis — his lordship, as that fellow Tyrrel calls him — just in that same fashion. I warrant they would say there was some soldiership in it! But, sister, haven't I been studying the attack and defence of fortified places, I wonder? And what call you that? Look now, here is a regular hexagon," continued Henry, making lines upon the gravel walk with a stick, "here is the bastion, — these lines are the flank, — the face, — the gorge: here is the curtain. Now, my first parallel is around here, six hundred paces from the counterscarp. But I could have taken Charleston myself in half the time that poking fellow, Clinton, did it, if I had been there, and one of his side, which — thank my stars — I am not."

"You are entirely out of my depth, brother," interrupted Mildred.

"I know I am. How should women be expected to understand these matters? Go to your knitting, sister: you can't teach me."

"Have you studied the Military Catechism, Henry? that, you know, Baron Steuben requires of all the young officers."

"Most," replied Henry. "Not quite through it. I hate this getting prose by heart. Shakespeare is more to my mind than Baron Steuben. But I will tell you what I like, sister; I like the management of the horse. I can passage, and lunge, and change feet, and throw upon the haunches, with e'er a man in Amherst or Albemarle either, may be."

"You told me you had practised firing from your saddle."

"To be sure I did: and look here," replied the cadet, taking off his cap and showing a hole in the cloth. "Do you see that, Mildred? I flung the cap into the air, and put a ball through it before it fell — at a gallop."

"Well done, master; you come on bravely!"

"And another thing I have to tell you, which, perhaps, Mildred, you will laugh to hear: — I have taken to a rough way of sleeping. I want to harden myself; so, I fling a blanket on the floor and stretch out on it — and sleep like — "

"Like what, good brother; you are posed for a comparison."

"Like the sleeping beauty, sister."

"Ha! ha! that's a most incongruous and impertinent simile!"

"Well, like a Trojan, or a woodman, or a dragoon, or like Stephen Foster, and that is as far as sleeping can go. I have a notion of trying it in the woods one of these nights — if I can get Stephen to go along."

"Why not try it alone?"

"Why, it's a sort of an awkward thing to be entirely by one's self in the woods, the livelong night — it is lonesome, you know, sister; and, to tell the truth, I almost suspect I am a little afraid of ghosts."

"Indeed! and you a man! That's a strange fear for a young

Coriolanus. Suppose you should get into the wars, and should happen to be posted as a sentinel at some remote spot — far from your comrades; on picket, I think you call it? (Henry nodded) on a dark night, would you desert your duty for fear of a goblin?"

"I would die first, Mildred. I would stick it out, if I made an earthquake by trembling in my shoes."

Mildred laughed.

"And then if a ghost should rise up out of the ground," she continued, with a mock solemnity of manner.

"I would whistle some tune," interrupted Henry. "That's an excellent way to keep down fear."

"Shame on you, to talk of fear, brother."

"Only of ghosts, sister, not of men."

"You must cure yourself of this childish apprehension, master."

"And how shall I do so, Mildred? I have heard people say that the bravest men have been alarmed by spirits."

"You must accustom yourself to midnight hours and dark places, all alone. Our poor mother taught you this fear."

"I should think of *her,* Mildred, until my heart would burst, and my cheek grew pale as ashes," said Henry, with an earnest and solemn emphasis.

"Her spirit, could it rise, would love you, brother; it would never seek to do you harm," replied Mildred thoughtfully.

"Sister," said Henry, "you came here in sport, but you have made me very sad."

Mildred walked off a few paces and remained gazing steadfastly over the parapet. When she looked back she saw Henry approaching her.

"You stoop, brother, in your gait," she said, "that's a slovenly habit."

"It comes, sister, of my climbing these mountains so much. We mountaineers naturally get a stoop on the hill-sides. But if you think," continued Henry, reverting to the subject which had just been broken off, "it would make me bolder to watch of nights, I should not care to try it."

"I would have you," said Mildred, "walk your rounds, like a patrole, through the woods from twelve until two, every night for a week."

"Agreed, sister — rain or shine."

"And then I shall think you completely cured of this unsoldierlike infirmity, when you are able to march as far as the church, and serve one tour of duty in the grave-yard."

"By myself?" inquired Henry, with concern.

"You wouldn't have me go with you, brother?"

"I should feel very brave if you did, Mildred; for you are as brave as a general. But if Stephen Foster will keep in the neighborhood — near enough to hear my 'All's well' — I think I could stand it out."

"You must go alone," said Mildred, cheerfully, "before I shall think you fit to be promoted."

"If you say I must, sister Mildred, why, then I must: and there's an end of it. But your discipline is forty times more severe than the German Baron's at Richmond. Father looks pale this morning," continued Henry, as he turned his eyes towards the porch, where Mr. Lindsay was now seen walking forward and back, with his arm folded across his breast. "Something perpetually troubles him, Mildred. I wish that devil, Tyrrel, had been buried before he ever found his way to the Dove Cote! See he comes this way."

Both Mildred and Henry ran to meet Lindsay, and encountered him before he had advanced a dozen paces over the lawn.

"Such a day, father!" said Mildred, as she affectionately took his hand. "It is a luxury to breathe this air."

"God has given us a beautiful heaven, my children, and a rich and bountiful earth. He has filled them both with blessings. Man only mars them with his cursed passions," said Lindsay, with a sober accent.

"You have heard bad news, father?" said Henry, inquiringly; "what has happened?"

Mildred grew suddenly pale.

"We shall hear glorious news, boy, before many days," replied Lindsay; "as yet, all is uncertain. Henry, away to your sports, or to your studies. Mildred, I have something for your ear, and so, my child, walk with me a while."

Henry took his leave, looking back anxiously at his sister, whose countenance expressed painful alarm. Mildred accompanied her father slowly and silently to the small veranda that shaded the door of the gable next the terrace.

CHAPTER XXXIV

MILDRED PUT TO A SEVERE TRIAL: — HER FIRMNESS

"My mind troubles me," said Lindsay: "Mildred, hear me — and mark what I say. Our fortunes are coming to a period of deep interest: it is therefore no time to deal in evasive speeches, or to dally with coy and girlish feelings. I wish, my daughter, to be understood."

"Father, have I offended you?" inquired Mildred, struck with the painful and almost repulsive earnestness of Lindsay's manner.

"Arthur Butler has been at the Dove Cote," he said, sternly, "and you have concealed it from me. That was not like my child."

"Father!" exclaimed Mildred, bursting into tears.

"Nay — these tears shall not move me from my resolution. As a parent I had a right, Mildred, to expect obedience from you; but you saw him in the very despite of my commands: here, on the confines of the Dove Cote, you saw him."

"I did — I did."

"And you were silent, and kept your secret from your father's bosom."

"You forbade me to speak of him," replied Mildred, in a low and sobbing voice, "and banished me from your presence when I but brought his name upon my lips."

"He is a villain, daughter; a base wretch that would murder my peace, and steal my treasure from my heart."

Mildred covered her eyes with her hands, and trembled in silent agony.

"I have received letters," continued Lindsay, "that disclose to me a vile plot against my life. This same Butler — this furious and fanatic rebel — has been lurking in the neighborhood of my house, to watch my family motions, to pry into the character of my guests, to possess himself of my sacred confidences, to note the incoming and the out-going of my most attached friends, and thereupon to build an accusation of treason before this unholy and most accursed power that has usurped dominion in the land. I am to be denounced to these malignant masters, and to suffer such penalties as their passions may adjudge. And all this through the agency of a man who is cherished and applauded by my own daughter!"

"My dear father, who has thus abused your mind, and led your thoughts into a current so foreign from that calm judgment with which you have been accustomed to look upon the things of life?"

"Can you deny, Mildred, that this Butler followed Tyrrel to the Dove Cote; lay concealed here, close at hand; sought by discourse through some of his coadjutors with Tyrrel's servant, to learn the object of Tyrrel's visit; and offered gross outrage to the man when he failed to persuade him to betray his master? Can you deny this? Can you deny that he fled precipitately from his hiding-place when he could no longer conceal his purpose? — and, knowing these things, can you doubt he is a villain?"

"He is no villain, father," said Mildred, indignantly. "These are the wretched forgeries of that unworthy man who has won your confidence — a man who is no less an enemy to your happiness than he is a selfish contriver against mine. The story is not true: it is one of Tyrrel's basest falsehoods."

"And Butler was not here; you would persuade me so, Mildred?"

"He was in the neighborhood for a single night; he journeyed southwards in the course of his duty," answered Mildred, mildly.

"And had no confederates with him?"

"He was attended by a guide — only one — and hurried onwards without delay."

"And you met him on that single night — by accident, I suppose?"

"Do you doubt my truth, father?"

"Mildred, Mildred! you will break my heart. Why was he here at all — why did you meet him?"

"He came, father —" said Mildred, struggling to speak through a sudden burst of tears.

"Silence! I will hear no apology!" exclaimed Lindsay. Then relenting in an instant, he took his daughter's hand, as he said: "My child, thou art innocent in thy nature, and knowest not the evil imaginings of this world. He wickedly lied, if he told you that he came casually hither, or that his stay was circumscribed to one short night. I have proofs, full and satisfactory, that, for several days, he lay concealed in this vicinity; and, moreover, that his scheme was frustrated only by an unexpected discovery, made through the indiscretion of a drunken bully, who came linked with him in his foul embassy. It was a shameless lie, invented to impose upon your credulity, if he gave you room to believe otherwise."

"Arthur Butler scorns a falsehood, father, with the deepest scorn that belongs to a noble mind, and would resent the charge with the spirit of a valiant and virtuous man. If Mr. Tyrrel have such accusations to make, it would be fitter they should be made face to face with the man he would slander, than in my father's ear. But it is the nature of the serpent to sting in the grass, not openly to encounter his victim."

"The first duty of a trusty friend is to give warning of the approach of an enemy — and that has Tyrrel done. For this act of service does he deserve your rebuke? Could you expect aught else of an honorable gentleman? Shame on you, daughter!"

"Father, I know the tale to be wickedly, atrociously false. Arthur Butler is not your enemy. Sooner would he lay down his life than even indulge a thought of harm to you. His coming hither was not unknown to me — his delay, but one brief night; business of great moment called him hastily towards the army of the south."

"You speak like a girl, Mildred. I have, against this tale, the avowal of a loyal and brave soldier. Aye, and let me tell you — favorably as you may deem of this false and traitorous rebel — his wily arts have been foiled, and quick vengeance is now upon his path — his doom is fixed."

"For heaven's sake, father, dear father, tell me what this means. Have you heard of Arthur?" cried Mildred, in the most impassioned accents of distress, at the same time throwing her head upon Lindsay's breast. "Oh, God! have you heard aught of harm to him?"

"Girl! foolish, mad, self-willed girl!" exclaimed Lindsay, disengaging himself from his daughter, and rising from his seat and angrily striding a few paces upon the terrace. "Dare you show this contumacy to me! No, I did not mean that — have you the heart, Mildred, to indulge these passionate fervors for the man I hate more than I can hate any other living thing! He, a wretch, upon whose head I invoke nightly curses! A loathsome, abhorred image to my mind! Hear me, Mildred, and hear me, though your heart break while I utter it — May the felon's death whelm him and his name in eternal disgrace! — may his present captivity be beset with all the horrors of friendliness, unpitied — "

"His captivity, father! And has he then fallen into the hands of the enemy? Quick! tell me all! — I shall die — my life is wrapped up in his!" ejaculated Mildred, in agony, as she sprang towards her father and seized his arm, and then sank at his feet.

"For God's sake, my child!" said Lindsay, becoming alarmed at the violence of the paroxysm he had excited, and now lifting his daughter from the ground. "Mildred! — speak, girl! This emotion will drive me mad. Oh, fate, fate! — how unerringly dost thou fulfil the sad predictions of my spirit! How darkly does the curse hang upon my household! Mildred, dear daughter, pardon my rash speech. I would not harm thee, child — no, not for worlds!"

"Father, you have cruelly tortured my soul," said Mildred, reviving from the half lifeless state into which she had fallen, and which for some moments had denied her speech. "Tell me all; on my knees, father, I implore you."

"It was a hasty word, daughter," replied Lindsay, ill concealing the perturbation of his feelings; "I meant not what I said."

"Nay, dear father," said Mildred, "I am prepared to hear the worst; you spoke of Arthur's captivity."

"It was only a rumor," replied Lindsay, struck with apprehension at his daughter's earnestness, and now seeking to allay the feeling his hint had aroused in her mind; "it may be exaggerated by Tyrrel, whose letter, hastily written, mentions the fact, that Butler had been made a prisoner by some bands of Tories, amongst whom he had rashly ventured. The clemency of his king may yet win him back to his allegiance. A salutary confinement, at least, will deprive him of the power of mischief. His lands will be confiscated — and the close of the war, now fast approaching, will find him a houseless adventurer, baffled in his treason, and unpitied by all good men. This should persuade you, Mildred, to renounce your unnatural attachment, and to think no more of one whose cause heaven has never sanctioned, and whose condition in life should forbid all pretension to your regard — one, above all, repulsive even to loathing to the thoughts of your father."

"I loved him, father, in his happiest and brightest day," said Mildred, firmly; "I cannot desert him in his adversity. Oh, speak to me no more! Let me go to my chamber; I am ill and cannot bear this torrent of your displeasure."

"I will not detain you, Mildred. In sorrow and suffering, but still with a father's affection as warmly shining on you as when, in earliest infancy, I fondled thee upon my knee, I part with thee now. One kiss, girl. There, let that make peace between us.

For your sake and my own, I pledge my word never to distress you with this subject again. Destiny must have its way, and I must bide the inevitable doom."

With a heavy heart and an exhausted frame, Mildred slowly and tearfully withdrew.

Lindsay remained some time fixed upon the spot where his daughter had left him. He was like a man stupefied and astounded by a blow. His conference had ended in a manner that he had not prepared himself to expect. The imputed treachery of Butler, derived from Tyrrel's letters, had not struck alarm into the heart of Mildred, as he had supposed it could not fail to do. The wicked fabrication had only recoiled upon the inventor; and Mildred, with the resolute, confident, and unfaltering attachment of her nature, clung with a nobler devotion to her lover. To Lindsay, in whose mind no distrust of the honesty of Tyrrel could find shelter; whose prejudices and peculiar temperament came in aid of the gross and disgraceful imputation which the letters inferred, the constancy and generous fervor of his daughter towards the cause of Butler seemed to be a mad and fatal infatuation.

Ever since his first interview with Mildred on the subject of her attachment, his mind had been morbidly engrossed with the reflections to which it had given rise. There was such a steadiness of purpose apparent in her behavior, such an unchangeable resolve avowed, as seemed to him, in the circumstances of her condition, to defy and stand apart from the ordinary and natural impulses by which human conduct is regulated. He grew daily more abstracted and moody in his contemplations; and as study and thought gave a still graver complexion to his feelings, his mind fled back upon his presentiments; and that intense, scholar-like superstition, which I have heretofore described as one of the tendencies of his nature, began more actively to conjure up its phantasmagoria before his mental vision. A predominating trait of this superstition was an increasing conviction that, in Mildred's connexion with Arthur Butler, there was associated some signal doom to himself, that was to affect the fortunes of his race. It was a vague, misty, obscure consciousness of impending fate, the loss of reason or the loss of life that was to ensue upon that alliance if it should ever take place.

It was such a presentiment that now, in the solitary path of Lindsay's life, began to be magnified into a ripening certainty of ill. The needle of his mind trembled upon its pivot, and began to decline towards a fearful point; that point was — frenzy. His studies favored this apprehension — they led him into the world of visions. The circumstances of his position favored it. He was perplexed by the intrigues of politicians, against whom he had no defence in temper nor worldly skill: he was deluded by false views of events: he was embarrassed and dissatisfied with himself: above all, he was wrought upon, bewildered, and glamoured (to use a most expressive Scotch phrase) by the rememberance of a sickly dream.

Thus hunted and badgered by circumstances, he fled with avidity to the disclosures made in Tyrrel's letters, to try, as a last effort, their effect upon Mildred, hoping that the tale there told might divert her from a purpose which now fed all his melancholy.

The reader has just seen how the experiment had failed.

Lindsay retired to his study, and, through the remainder of the day, sought refuge from his meditations in the converse of his books. These mute companions, for once, failed to bring him their customary balm. His feelings had been turned, by the events of the morning, into a current that bore them impetuously along towards a dark and troubled ocean of thought; and when the shades of evening had fallen around him, he was seen pacing the terrace with a slow and measured step.

"It is plain she passionately loves Butler," he said, "in despite of all the visible influences around her. Her education, habits, affections, duty — all set in an opposing tide against this passion, and yet does it master them all. That I should be bound to mine enemy by a chain, whose strongest link is forged by my own daughter. She — Mildred! — No, no — that link was not forged by her: it hath not its shape from human workmanship. Oh, that like those inspired enthusiasts who, in times of old, — yea, and in a later day — have been able to open the Book of Destiny, and to read the passages of man's future life, I might get one glimpse of that forbidden page! — To what a charitable use might I apply the knowledge. Wise men have studied the journeyings of the stars, and have — as they deemed — discovered the secret spell by which yon shining orbs sway and compel the animal existences of this earth; even as the moon governs the flow of the ocean, or the fever of the human brain. Who shall say what is the invisible tissue — what the innumerable cords — that tie this planet and all its material natures to the millions of worlds with which it is affined? What is that mysterious thing which men call attraction, that steadies these spheres in their tangled pathways through the great void? — that urges their swift and fearful career into the track of their voyage, without the deviation of the breadth of a single hair — rolling on the same from eternity to eternity? How awfully does the thought annihilate our feeble and presumptuous philosophy! Is it, then, to excite the scorn of the wise, if we assert that some kindred power may shape out and direct the wanderings of man? — that an unseen hand may lay the threads by which this tottering creature is to travel through the labyrinth of this world; aye, and after it is done, to point out to him his course along the dark and chill valley, which the dead walk through companionless and silent? Have not men heard strange whispers in the breeze — the voice of warning? Have they not felt the fanning of the wing that bore the secret messenger through the air? Have they not seen some floating fold of the robe as it passed by? O God! — have they not seen the dead arise? What are these but the communings, the points of contact, between the earthy and spiritual worlds — the essences or intelligences that sometimes flit across the confine of our gross sphere, and speak to the children of clay? And wherefore do they speak, but that the initiated may regard the sign, and walk in safety? Or, perchance, some mischief-hatching fiend, — for such, too, are permitted to be busy to mar the good that God has made — may speak in malice to allure us from our better purpose. Aye, as aptly this, as the other. Miserable child of doubt, how art thou beset! Let the vain pedant prate of his philosophy, let the soldier boast his valor, the learned scholar his scepticism, and the worlding laugh his scorn, yet do they each and all yield homage to this belief. There comes a time of honest self-confession, of secret meditation to all, and then the boding spirit rises to his proper mastery: then does instinct smother argument: then do the darkness of the midnight hour, the howling wind, the rush of the torrent, the lonesomeness of the forest and the field, shake the strong nerves; and the feeble pigmy, man, trembles at his own imaginings."

In such a strain did Lindsay nurse his doubting superstition; and by these degrees was it that his mind soothed itself down into a calmer tone of resignation. In proportion as this fanciful and distempered philosophy inclined his reflection towards the belief of preternatural influences, it suggested excuses for Mildred's seeming contumacy, and inculcated a more indulgent sentiment of forbearance in his future intercourse with her.

Towards the confirmation of this temper an ordinary incident, which, at any other time, would have passed without comment, now contributed. A storm had arisen: the day, towards its close, had grown sultry, and had engendered one of those sudden gusts which belong to the summer in this region. It came, without premonition, in a violent tornado, that rushed through the air with the roar of a great cataract. Lindsay had scarcely time to retreat to the cover of the porch, before the heavy-charged cloud poured forth its fury in floods of rain. The incessant lightnings glittered on the descending drops, and illuminated the distant landscape with more than the brilliancy of day. The most remote peaks of the mountain were sheeted with the glare; and the torrents that leaped down the nearer hill-sides sparkled with a dazzling radiance. Peal after peal of abrupt and crashing thunder roared through the heavens, and echoed with terrific reverberations along the valleys. Lindsay gazed upon this scene, from his secure cover, with mute interest, inwardly aroused and delighted with the grand and sublime conflict of the elements, in a spot of such wild and compatible magnificence: the solemn and awful emotions excited by these phenomena were exaggerated by the peculiar mood of his mind, and now absorbed all his attention. After a brief interval, the rain ceased to fall as suddenly as it had begun; the thunder was silent, and only a few distant flashes of wide-spread light broke fitfully above the horizon. The stars soon again shone forth through a transparent and placid heaven, and the moon sailed in beauty along a cloudless sea. The frog chirped again from the trees, and the far-off owl hooted in the wood, resuming his melancholy song, that had been so briefly intermitted. The foaming river below, swollen by the recent rain, flung upwards a more lively gush from its rocky bed: the cock was heard to crow, as if a new day had burst upon his harem; and the house-dogs barked in sport as they gambolled over the wet grass.

Lindsay looked forth and spoke.

"How beautiful is the change! But a moment since, and the angry elements were convulsed with the shock of war; and now, how calm! My ancient oaks have weathered the gale, and not a branch has been torn from their hoary limbs: not the most delicate of Mildred's flowers; not the tenderest shrub has been scathed by the threatening fires of heaven! The Dove Cote and its inmates have seen the storm sweep by without a vestige of harm. Kind heaven, grant that this may be a portent of our fortune; and that, when this tempest of human passion has been spent, the Dove Cote and its inhabitants may come forth as tranquil, as safe, as happy, as now — more — yes, more happy than now! Our ways are in thy hands; and I would teach myself to submit to thy providence with patient hope. So, let it be! I am resigned."

As Lindsay still occupied his position in the porch, Stephen Foster appeared before him dripping with the rain of the late storm.

"A letter, sir," said Stephen. "I have just rode from the post-office, and was almost oversot in the gust: it catched me upon the road; and it was as much as I could do to cross the river. It's a mighty fretful piece of water after one of these here dashes."

Lindsay took the packet.

"Get your supper, good Stephen," he said. "Order lights for me in the library! Thank you — thank you!"

When Lindsay opened the letter, he found it to contain tidings of the victory of Camden, written by Tyrrel. After he had perused the contents, it was with a triumphant smile that he exclaimed, "And it is come so soon! Thank God, the omen has proved true! a calmer and a brighter hour at last opens upon us."

He left the study to communicate the news to his children, and spent the next hour with Mildred and Henry in the parlor. His feelings had risen to a happier key; and it was with some approach to cheerfulness, but little answered in the looks or feelings of his children, that he retired to his chamber at a late hour, where sleep soon came, with its sweet oblivion, to repair his exhausted spirits, and to restore him to the quiet of an easy mind.

CHAPTER XXXV

MILDRED IN GRIEF — SHE IS NEAR MAKING A DISCLOSURE — A VISITOR ARRIVES AT THE DOVE COTE

"Then in that hour remorse he felt,
And his heart told him he had dealt
Unkindly with his child."

ROGERS.

On the following day Mildred confined herself to her chamber. She had passed a sleepless night, and the morning found her a pale, anxious, and distressed watcher of the slow approach of light. Her thoughts were busy with the fate of Butler. This topic overwhelmed all other cares, and struck deep and unmitigated anguish into her mind. The hints that had been so indiscreetly dropped by her father, more than if the whole tale had been told, had worked upon her imagination, and conjured up to her apprehension the certain destruction of her lover. In her interview with Lindsay, her emotions had been controlled by the extreme difficulty of her situation. The fear of rousing in her father that deep and solemn tone of passion, which had now become the infirmity of his mind, and almost threatened to "deprive his sovereignty of reason," and of which she was painfully aware, had subdued the strength of her own feelings — so far, at least, as to inculcate a more seeming moderation than, in other circumstances, she could have exhibited. It was the struggle between filial affection and duty on the one side, and an ardent, though tremblingly acknowledged, attachment on the other. The course that she had previously determined to pursue, in reference to the many earnest and assiduous efforts of Lindsay to persuade her from her love, was steadily to persevere in the open acknowledgment of her plighted vow, and endeavor to win her father's favor by a calm and gentle expostulation; or to seek, in a respectful silence, the means of averting the occasion of that gusty and moody outbreak of temper, which the peculiar exacerbation of his mind was apt to make frequent. She would have resorted to this silence in the late communion with Lindsay, if he had not, with an unusual bitterness, denounced Arthur Butler as the author of a hateful crime; a crime which she knew had been foully insinuated against him by a man of whose subtle wickedness she was persuaded, and whom, of all other, she most heartily execrated. She was, therefore, led indignantly, though temperately, to repel the slander by which her father's hatred had been artfully envenomed. But when, in the fierce fervor of his displeasure, Lindsay had announced to her the danger that had befallen Butler, the disclosure opened to her mind a world of misery. The late silence of her lover had already alarmed her fears, and this announcement suggested the worst of the many anxious conjectures which her brooding spirit had imagined as the cause of that absence of tidings. Her emotions upon this disclosure were those of a bursting heart that dared not trust itself with words; and when her father, seeing the unlooked-for mischief he had done, sought to temper his speech, and retract some of the harshness of his communication, by an explanation, the only effect was, for the moment, to take off the edge of her keenest grief. But when she left his presence, and recovered herself sufficiently to recall all that had passed, the dreadful thought of disaster to Butler came back upon her imagination with all the horrors which a fond heart could summon around it. A weary hour was spent in sobs and tears; and it was only by the blandishments of her brother Henry's kind and earnest sympathy, when the youth found her in the parlor thus whelmed in sorrow, and by his manly and cheering reckoning of the many chances of safety that attend the footsteps of a prudent and a brave man, that she began to regain that resolute equanimity that was a natural and even predominating attribute of her character.

When Lindsay came into the parlor with the tidings of the victory at Camden, such was the state in which he found her; and whilst he announced to her that event which had given him so much joy, he was not unheedful of the pang he had previously inflicted, and now endeavored to make amends by throwing in some apparently casual, though intentional, reference to the condition of Butler, who, he doubted not, would now be disposed of on easy terms. "Perhaps," he continued, "as the war was drawing to a close, and the royal clemency had been singularly considerate of the mistaken men who had taken arms against their king, he would in a little while be discharged on his parole." This reluctant and forced crumb of comfort fell before one who had but little appetite to take it, and Mildred received it only in cold silence. Henry, however, made better use of the event, and by that assiduity which, in true and gentle friendships, never wearies, and never misses its aim, when that aim is to revive a sinking hope, succeeded in lifting both his father and sister into a kindlier climate of feeling. But solitude and her pillow ravelled all this work of charity. Fancy, that stirring tormentor of acute minds, summoned up all its phantoms to Mildred's waking fears, and the night was passed by her as by one who could not be comforted. In the morning she was ill, and therefore, as I have said, remained in her chamber.

Lindsay, ever solicitous for the happiness of his children, and keenly sensitive to whatever gave them pain, now that the turbid violence of his passion had subsided into a clearer and calmer medium, applied himself by every art which parental fondness could supply, to mitigate the suffering of his daughter. Like a man who, in a reckless and ungoverned moment, having done an injury which his heart revolts at, and having leisure to contemplate the wrong he has inflicted, hastens to administer comfort with an alacrity which even outruns the suggestions of ordinary affection, so did he now betake himself to Mildred's chamber, and, with sentiments of mixed alarm and contrition, seek her forgiveness for what he acknowledged a rash and unbecoming assault upon her feelings.

His soothing did not reach the disease. They could give her no assurance of Butler's safety; and on that point alone all her anguish turned. "My dear, dear father," she said, with a feeble and dejected voice, "how do you wrong me, by supposing I could harbor a sentiment that might cause me to doubt the love I bear you! I know and revere the purity of your nature, and need no assurance from you that your affection itself has kindled up this warmth of temper. But you have opened a fountain of bitterness upon my feelings," she added, sobbing vehemently, "in what you have divulged relating to a man you loathe, and one, dear father — take it from me now, as the expression of a sacred duty — one that I must ever love. Call it fate — call it infatuation; say that it does not befit my womanly reserve to avow it — but if misfortune and death have fallen upon the head of Arthur Butler, there is that bond between us, that I must die. Oh, father — "

As Mildred pronounced these words she had gradually raised herself into a sitting posture in her bed, and, at the conclusion, fell back exhausted upon her pillow. The enthusiasm, the violence and the intensity of her emotions had overborne her strength, and for some moments she lay incapable of speech.

"Mildred, Mildred! daughter!" exclaimed Lindsay, in alarm, "I forgive you, my child. Great heaven, if this should be too much for her sensitive nature, and she should die before my eyes! Dear Mildred," he said in a softer accent, as he kissed her pale forehead, "but look up, and never, never more will I oppose your wish."

"Father," she uttered, in a scarce audible whisper.

"Thank God, she revives! Forbear to speak, my love; that is enough. Do not exhaust your strength by another effort."

"Father!" she repeated in a firmer accent.

"There, there, my child," continued Lindsay, fanning the air before her face with his hand.

"Father," again uttered Mildred, "tell me of Arthur."

"He is safe, my love — and thou shalt yet be happy. Daughter — no more; compose yourself — nor attempt again to speak." And saying these words, Lindsay stole out of the chamber and summoned one of the domestics to administer a cordial to the exhausted patient; and then gave orders that she should be left to recruit her strength by sleep.

Mildred by degrees revived. Jaded by mental affliction, she had sunk into repose; and when another morning arrived, the lustre had returned to her eye, and her recovery was already well advanced. She did not yet venture from her chamber, but she was able to leave her bed and take the fresh air at her window.

Whilst she sat in the loose robe of an invalid, towards noon, looking out upon the green forest and smiling fields around her, with Henry close by her side, seeking to soothe and amuse her mind, they were enabled to descry a horseman, attended by a single servant, making his way up the hill from the ford, by the road that led directly to the door.

"As I live, sister," ejaculated Henry, "there is Tyrrel, covered with dust, and his horse all but worn down by travel."

"Heaven forbid that it should be Tyrrel indeed!" said Mildred, growing paler, and trembling as she spoke. "Oh, what ill fortune brings him hither?"

"I'll be bound," replied Henry, "that he comes with a whole budget of lies and foul thoughts. He has a knavish look, sister, and has been hatching mischief with every step of his horse. I, for one, will not see him; unless I can't help it. And you, sister, have an excuse to keep your room: so, he is like to have cold comfort here, with his rascally news of victory. We shall hear enough of Camden now. By-the-by, sister, I should like much to see our account of that business. I would bet it gives another face to the matter. These Tories do so bespatter his lordship with praises, and tell such improbable things about their victories! I will not see Tyrrel, that's flat."

"Nay, brother, not so fast. You must see him, for my sake. He has something to tell of Arthur. Persuade my father to ask him: tell him, if need be, that I requested this. And, Henry, if he says that Arthur is safe and well, if he has heard anything of him, knows anything of him, fly to and tell me it all. And, remember, brother," she said earnestly, "tell me all — whether it be good or bad."

"This is a new view of the case," said Henry. "Mildred, you are a wise woman, and think more ahead than I do. I did not reflect that this fellow might know something of Major Butler, though I am pretty sure he kept as clear of the major as a clean pair of heels would allow him. And, moreover, I take upon me to say, that he will bring as little good news of our Arthur in this direction, as he ever did of a good act in his life. But I will spy him out, sister, and report like a — like a — forty-two pounder, or the dispatch of a general who has won a fight. So, adieu, sister."

By the time that Henry had reached the porch, Tyrrel was already there. He had dismounted, and his weary steed stood panting on the gravel walk, while the servant stripped him of his baggage.

"Well met, good master Henry!" said Tyrrel approaching, and offering the youth his hand, "I am somewhat of a soiled traveller, you see. Is your father at home? And your sister, how is she?"

"My father is at home," replied Henry, dropping the proffered hand of the visitor, almost as soon as it had touched his own. "I will send him to you, sir."

"But you have not asked me the news, Henry," said Tyrrel, "and, seeing that I have come from the very theatre of war, I could tell you something good."

"I have heard my father speak of your good news," answered Henry, carelessly, "I do not serve under the same colors with you, sir."

And the youth left the porch to announce the arrival of the traveller to Lindsay.

"There spoke the rebel Mildred," muttered Tyrrel, as Henry left his presence.

In an instant, Lindsay hastened from the library and received his guest with a warm welcome.

The first cares of his reception, and some necessary order relating to his comfort, being despatched, Tyrrel began to disburden himself of his stock of particulars relating to the great and important movements of the opposing armies in the south. He had left Cornwallis a few days after the battle, and had travelled with post haste to Virginia, on a leave of absence. He described minutely the state of things consequent upon the recent victory; and it was with a tone of triumphant exultation that he frequently appealed to his predictions as to the course of events, when last at the Dove Cote. The conversation soon became too confidential for the presence even of Henry, who sat greedily devouring every word that fell from the lips of the narrator, and the further interview was transferred to the library.

Henry hastened back to Mildred.

"The fellow is so full of politics, sister," said the eager scout, "that he has not dropped one solitary word about Butler. He talks of the province being brought back to a sense of its duty, and public sentiment putting an end to this unnatural war, forsooth! And his majesty reaping fresh laurels on the fields of Virginia! Let his majesty put in his sickle here — he shall reap as fine a crop of briers to bind round his brow, as ever grew in a fence-corner! But Butler! Oh, no, he has nothing to say of Butler. He is a cunning man, sister, and keeps out of the major's way, take my word for that."

"Brother, get you again to my father, and say to him that I desire to know what tidings Mr. Tyrrel brings us. Say it in his ear privately, Henry."

The young emissary again took his leave, and, without apology, entered the library.

Mildred, in the meantime, restless and impatient, applied herself to the duties of the toilet, and, with the assistance of her maid, was soon in a condition to leave her chamber. She had, almost unwittingly, and in obedience to her engrossing wish to know something of Butler, made these preparations to appear in the parlor, without thinking of her repugnance to meet Tyrrel. And now, when she was on the point of going forth, her resolve changed, and she moved through the chamber like a perturbed spirit, anxiously waiting the return of Henry. She walked to the window, whence, looking out towards the terrace she perceived that her father and his guest had strolled out upon the lawn, where they were moving forward at a slow pace, whilst their gesticulations showed that they were engaged in an earnest conference.

Henry's footsteps at the same moment were heard traversing the long passage, and Mildred, no longer able to restrain her eagerness, hastily left her room and met her brother, with whom she returned to the parlor.

"My news, upon the whole, is good," said Henry, as he put his arm round Mildred's waist. "When I entered the library, and took a seat by my father, he suddenly broke up some long talk that was going on, in which he looked very grave, as if he knew what I came for — he is an excellent, kind father, sister, for all his moping and sad humors, and loves both you and me."

"He does, Henry, and we must never forget it."

"I would fight for him to the very death, Mildred. So, seeing that I looked as if you had sent me to him, he turned, in a kind of careless way, and asked Tyrrel if he had heard anything lately of Butler."

"Well — brother."

"'I scarce thought to mention it,' answered Tyrrel, 'but the man' — think of that way of speaking of Major Butler — 'the man had the temerity to push himself amongst the loyal troops, and was made a prisoner; he was suspected to be a spy, and there was, as I have understood, an idea of trying him by court-martial for it, and for other misdemeanors, of which I wrote you some particulars. I believe indeed, he was tried, and would, perhaps, have been shot."

"Oh, heaven! brother, can this be true?" exclaimed Mildred, as the color deserted her cheek.

"I give you exactly Tyrrel's words," replied Henry, "but the court were attacked, said he, by some bands of Whigs who stole a march upon them."

"And Arthur escaped? Kind heaven, I thank thee!" almost screamed Mildred, as she clasped her hands together.

"So Tyrrel thinks," continued Henry. "At all events they did not shoot him, like a pack of cowardly knaves as they were. And as some Tory prisoners were taken and dragged away by our good friend General Sumpter, who was the man, Tyrrel says, that set upon them, it is considered good policy — these were his words, sister — to spare the unnecessary effusion of blood on both sides. And then my father asked Tyrrel if Cornwallis knew of these doings, and he answered, not — that it was the indiscreet act of some mountain boys, who were in the habit of burning and slaying, against the wish of his Lordship: that the regular officers disapprove of harsh measures, and that peace now reigns all through the province."

"When they make a desert of the land, they call it peace," said Mildred thoughtfully, quoting a translation of the beautiful passage of Tacitus. "This war is a dreadful trade."

"For us, sister, who stay at home," replied Henry. "But God is good to us, and will favor the right, and will protect the brave men who draw their swords to maintain it."

"From treachery, ambuscade, and privy murder — I thank you, brother, for that word. Heaven shield us, and those we love! But these are fearful times."

CHAPTER XXXVI

CIRCUMSTANCES FAVOR TYRREL'S INFLUENCE OVER LINDSAY

THE discourse between Lindsay and Tyrrel was one of deep moment. Tyrrel had taken advantage of the pervading fervor which the late successes of the British arms had diffused amongst the adherents of the royal cause, in behalf of what was deemed their certain triumph, to urge forward his own views. This was the occasion of his present unexpected visit at the Dove Cote. His immediate aim was to plunge Lindsay into the contest, by forcing him to take some step that should so commit him, in the opinion of the republican government, as to leave him no chance to retreat, nor the means longer to enjoy the privileges of his late neutrality. He, unhappily, found Lindsay in a mood to favor this intrigue. The increasing anxieties of that gentleman's mind, his domestic griefs, his peculiar temperament, and the warmth of his political animosities, all stimulated him to the thought of some active participation in the struggle. Tyrrel had sufficient penetration to perceive that such was likely to be the current of Lindsay's feelings, and he had by frequent letters administered to this result.

There were several opulent families in the lower sections of the state, who still clung to the cause of the King, and who had been patiently awaiting the course of events, for the time when they might more boldly avow themselves. With the heads of these families Tyrrel had been in active correspondence, and it was now his design which under the sanction of the British leaders, he had already nearly matured, to bring these individuals together into a secret council, that they might act in concert, and strengthen themselves by mutual alliance. Immediately after the battle of Camden, it is known that Cornwallis had laid his plans for the invasion of North Carolina, by intrigues of the same kind: it was only extending the system a little in advance to apply it to Virginia. Arrangements had been made for this meeting of malcontents to be held at the house of a Mr. Stanhope, on one of the lower sections of the James river — a gentleman of good repute, with whom Lindsay had long been in the relations of close friendship.

"The moments are precious, and you are waited for," said Tyrrel, in the course of his conference with Lindsay; "we must strike whilst the iron is hot. Separated as our good friends are from each other, you are now in the power, and at the mercy — which is a significant phrase — of the unruly government of Congress. Your motions, therefore, should be prompt. There are seasons, in the history of every trouble, when the virtue of deliberation mainly lies in its rapidity and the boldness of its resolve. I beseech you, sir, to regard this as such a season, and to take the course which the honor of our sovereign demands, without further pause to think of consequences."

"When you were here a month ago," replied Lindsay, "I had my scruples. But things have strangely altered in that short interval. Your standard floats more bravely over the path of invasion than I had deemed it possible. You charged me then with being a laggard, and, you may remember, even impeached my loyalty."

"I did you a grievous wrong, my dear friend; and did I not know your generous nature pardoned, as soon as it was uttered, my rash and intemperate speech, it would have cost me many a pang of remorse. Even in this, good sir," said Tyrrel, smiling and laying his hand upon Lindsay's shoulder; "even in this, you see how necessary is it that we should have a wise and considerate councillor to moderate the ungoverned zeal of us younger men."

"My mind is made up," replied Lindsay. "I will attend the meeting."

"And Mildred will be removed forthwith to Charleston?" eagerly interrupted Tyrrel.

"Ah, sir, not one word of that. If I attend this meeting, it must be in secret. Nor do I yet commit myself to its resolves. I shall be a listener only. I would learn what my compatriots think, reserving to myself the right to act. Even yet, I would purchase peace with many a sacrifice. I abjure all violent measures of offence."

"I am content," answered Tyrrel, "that you should hold yourself unpledged to any measures which your gravest and severest judgment does not approve. Though I little doubt that, from all quarters, you will hear such tidings as shall convince you that the road, both of safety and honor, leads onward in this glorious enterprise. 'Tis from this nettle danger, that we pluck the flower 'safety.' Conscious of this, I would have Mildred and her brother cared for."

"Mildred can never be yours," said Lindsay musing. "There is the thought that makes me pause. I believed, and so do you, that the favor this Butler had found with her was the capricious and changeful fancy of a girl. It is the devoted passion of a woman: it has grown to be her faith, her honor, her religion."

"Butler is a fool — a doomed madman," replied Tyrrel with earnestness. "He came here with the hellish purpose to betray you; and he was silly enough to think he could do so, and still win your daughter. She should be told of this."

"She has been told of it, and she believes it not."

"Was my avouch given to her for the truth of the fact?"

"It was. And, to speak plainly to you, it has only made your name hateful to her ear."

"Then shall she have proof of it, which she cannot doubt. She shall have it in the recorded judgment of a court-martial, which has condemned him as a traitor and a spy; she shall have it in the doom of his death, and the sequestration of his estate," exclaimed Tyrrel with a bitter malignity, "proud girl!"

"Remember yourself, sir!" interrupted Lindsay, sternly. "This is not the language nor the tone fit for a father's ear, when the subject of it is his own daughter."

Tyrrel was instantly recalled to his self-possession; and with the humility which he could always assume when his own interest required it, spoke in a voice of sudden contrition.

"Why, what a fool am I to let my temper thus sway me! Humbly, most humbly, dear sir, do I entreat your forgiveness. I love your daughter, and revere the earnest enthusiasm of her nature; and, therefore, have been galled beyond my proper show of duty, to learn that she could discredit my word."

"I enjoin it upon you," said Lindsay, "that in your intercourse with my family here, you drop no word calculated to alarm my daughter for the safety of this Butler. It is a topic which distracts her, and must be avoided."

"For the present," replied Tyrrel, "as I have before told you, I think he is safe. The forfeiture of his estate is not a secret. But to business, my friend. When shall we set out?"

"To-morrow," answered Lindsay. "We must travel cautiously, and amongst our friends."

"This disguise has served me so far," said Tyrrel. "I may the better trust to it when in your company."

Mildred and Henry remained in the parlor, and were there

when Lindsay and his guest, having terminated their secret conference, returned to the house.

"Your cheek denies your customary boast of good health, Miss Lindsay," said Tyrrel, respectfully approaching the lady, and with an air that seemed to indicate his expectation of a cold reception. "It grieves me to learn that, at a time when all good men are rejoicing in the prospect of peace, you should not be in a condition to share the common pleasure."

"I think there is small occasion for rejoicing in any quarter," replied Mildred, calmly.

"Miss Lindsay would, perhaps, be interested to hear," said Tyrrel, not discomfited by the evident aversion of the lady, "that I have, within a few days past, left the head-quarters of the British army, where I was enabled to glean some particulars of a friend of hers, Major Butler, of the Continental service."

Mildred colored, as she said in a faint voice, "He is my friend."

"He has been unfortunate," continued Tyrrel, "having fallen into the hands of some of our skirmishers. But I believe I may assure Miss Lindsay that he is both safe and well. He enjoys the reputation of being a brave gentleman. I may be permitted to say, that had his destiny brought him under other colors, I should have been proud to be better known to him."

"Major Butler chooses his own colors," said Henry, interposing. "I don't think destiny had much to do with it. He took his side because they wanted men to help out a brave war."

Lindsay frowned, and strode once or twice across the apartment, during which an embarrassing silence prevailed.

"You are the same cockerel you always were, Henry," said Tyrrel, with undaunted playfulness; "always warm for the fight. But it is a Christian duty, you know, to be peace-makers in such times as these. We may trust, Miss Lindsay, that some conciliatory spirit shall arise to quell the quarrelsome humors of the people, and bring all things back to tranquillity. For myself, I devoutly wish it."

"The day for such a spirit does not seem to be at hand," said Mildred, quietly rising to withdraw.

"You are not well, my daughter," interposed Lindsay. "Mildred is but recently from a sick bed," he continued, addressing Tyrrel, in the way of apology for her marked coldness of demeanor.

"I am not well, father," replied Mildred, "I must be permitted to leave you;" and she now retired.

When Henry soon afterwards joined her, he found her agitated and excited.

"Better known to Arthur Butler!" she exclaimed, dwelling on the speech of Tyrrel. "He is better known already than he dreams of. Think, brother, of the cool hypocrisy of this bold schemer — this secret disturber of the quiet of our house — that he should dare boast to me of Arthur's bravery."

"And to talk about his colors too!" said Henry. "Did you mark, sister, how I set him down — in spite of my father's presence? And did you see how his brow blanched when I spoke my mind to him? He will find me too hot a cockerel, as he calls me, to venture upon our colors again. I hold no terms with him, sister, more than yourself."

"You will excuse me to my father, Henry, I will not go in to dinner to-day."

"I wondered," replied Henry, "that you met him at all, sister; but he took us unawares. And, truly, I don't think it would be safe to bring you near him again. So I advise you, keep your room. As for me — tut! I am not afraid to meet him. I warrant he gets his own upon occasion!"

"I entreat you, Henry," said Mildred, "to guard your temper. It would give our father pain to hear a rash speech from you. It would answer no good end."

"I will be as circumspect, Mildred, as the state of the war requires," answered Henry. "Fight when it is necessary, and be silent when we can't strike."

Henry now left his sister and went to his usual occupations.

Mildred, in accordance with the purpose expressed to her brother, did not appear at the dinner table; and the day was passed, by Lindsay and Tyrrel, in close communion over the topics connected with the object of the enterprise in which they were about to embark. Tyrrel had seen enough to convince him that he might, at least for the present, abandon all effort to win Mildred's good opinion; and his whole thoughts were now bent to bring Lindsay into such an attitude of hostility to the republican authorities as would inevitably lead to his removal from the state, and perhaps compel him to retire to England. Either of these events would operate to the advantage of the aspiring and selfish policy by which Tyrrel hoped to accomplish his object.

In the course of the evening Lindsay held a short interview with his children, in which he made known to them that affairs of importance were about to call him away, for a fortnight perhaps, from the Dove Cote. It was in vain that Mildred endeavored to turn him from his purpose, which, though undivulged to her, she conjectured to be, from its association with Tyrrel, some sinister political move, of which her father was to be the dupe.

In accordance with Lindsay's intimation, he and Tyrrel set out, at an early hour of the following day, on their journey towards the low country.

CHAPTER XXXVII

A DOMESTIC SCENE AT THE DOVE COTE

On the third morning following Lindsay's and Tyrrel's departure, the season being now about the commencement of September, Henry was seen, after an unusually early breakfast, to come forth upon the grass-plot, in front of the house, bearing in his hand a short rifle, — his customary accompaniment of the bugle being slung across his shoulders. For some moments he was occupied in examining his weapon; then leaning it against a tree that stood upon the lawn, he put the bugle to his mouth and sounded a long and clear signal-note. The first effects of this spell were to bring up Bell, Blanch, and Hylas, the three flap-eared hounds, who came frisking over the grass with many antics that might be said to resemble the bows and curtsies of the human species, and which were accompanied by the houndish salutation of deep-mouthed howls that the horn never fails to wake up in these animals.

Soon after these, came striding up the hill the long gaunt form of Stephen Foster, who, mounting the stone wall on the lower side, with one bound sprang over the thickset-hedge that begirt the terrace. He was now arrayed in a yellow hunting shirt that reached to the middle of his thigh, and which was decorated with an abundance of red fringe that bound the cape, elbows, wrists, and extremity of the skirt, and a wool hat encircled with a broad red band, in one side of which was set the national ornament of the bucktail. Around his waist was buckled a broad buckskin belt; he was armed besides with a rifle a little short of six feet in length.

Stephen Foster was one of that idle craft, who, having no particular occupation, was from this circumstance, by a contradiction in terms, usually called a man of all work. He belonged to that class of beings who are only to be found in a society where the ordinary menial employments are discharged by slaves; and was the tenant of a few acres of land, appertaining to the domain of the Dove Cote, where he professed to make his living by husbandry. But by far the greatest proportion of his revenues was derived from divers miscellaneous services, — such as driving a team of four lean horses, of which he was proprietor; hauling wood for fuel; assisting in the harvest fields; sometimes working in the garden; and, when required, riding errands — which he preferred to all other business. But labor was not Stephen's forte: it was constitutionally a part of his system to postpone matters of work for pleasure; and, if there was anything for which he was particularly famous, it was in avoiding all appearances of punctuality to irksome engagements. If he can be said to have had a calling at all, it was that of a hunter, a species of employment that possessed a wonderful charm for his fancy, and which was excellently adapted both to his physical and moral qualities. He, therefore, gave much of his time to the concerns of vert and venison; and his skill with the rifle was such that he could make sure of putting a ball through the brain of a wild pigeon as far as he was able to draw a sight. He was skilled in the habits of all the forest animals common to this part of Virginia, and accurately drew the line of distinction between vermin and game. He hunted wolves, bears, panthers (painters, in his own pronunciation), racoons, foxes, opossums, and squirrels; and trapped otter, beaver, and muskrats; moreover, he was an expert jigger and bobber of eels, and well knew the trouting streams. For these pursuits he was endowed with a patient nature that could endure a whole day and night in the woods without eating or sleeping; my authority says nothing of his forbearance in the third primary want of humanity. He was a man of fine thews and sinews, stout and brave; and withal of a generous, frank, and invariable good nature. The war had furnished occasion for such talents as he possessed; and Stephen was now meditating a bold severance from his wife and children, who had heretofore exerted such a dominion over his affections, that he had not the heart to leave them. But the present difficulties of the nation had made such a cogent appeal to his patriotism, that he had resolved to take one campaign in the field, and thus give scope to his natural love of adventure. It was now his peculiar glory, and one that wrought with a potent influence upon his self-love, that he held the post of lieutenant to the company of Amherst Rangers, a volunteer corps that had lately been organized with a view to the state of affairs in the south.

This worthy, when he had no expedition in hand, was generally to be found lounging about the mansion of the Dove Cote, in expectation of some call from Henry, between whom and himself there existed a mutual and somewhat exorbitant affection.

On his present appearance there was a broad, complacent grin on Stephen's features as he accosted the young bugleman with the interrogatory —

"What's in the wind now, Mister Henry? Arter another buck, I reckon? And an elegant morning it is for a drive! May be, the wind's just a little too fresh, 'cepting you was able to steal on the lower side of the game, and then the scent would come down like a rose. Thar's a great advantage in being down the wind, because the animal can't hear you breaking through the bushes, for the wind makes naturally such a twittering of the leaves that it deceives him, you see."

"I fancy I know a good hunting day, Lieutenant Foster," said Henry, putting his arms akimbo, "as well as you. Who told you I was going after a buck? Why, man, if that had been my drift I should have started you two hours ago. But we have other business in hand, Stephen. There is such dreadful news in the country! We shall march soon, take my word for it. I am resolved to go, Stephen, as soon as ever the Rangers set out, let my father say what he will. It is time men should take their sides — that's my opinion."

"Mister Henry, I wouldn't advise you," said Stephen, with a wise shake of the head. "Your father would grieve himself to death if you were to leave him."

"Don't believe the half of that, lieutenant. There would be a flurry for a little while, and, after that, father would see that the thing couldn't be helped, and so he would have to be satisfied. I'll steal away — that's flat."

"Well, take notice, Mister Henry," said Stephen, chuckling, "I give you my warning against it. But if you do go along with me I'll take as much care of you as if you were my own son."

"I know sister Mildred thinks," replied Henry, "it wouldn't be very wrong in me to go; and so I'll leave her to make my peace at home. Besides, I am going on her account, just to try and hear something of Major Butler."

"If that's her opinion," returned Stephen, "thar isn't much wrong about it. She is the head contriver and main privy-councillor," added Stephen, laughing, as he used these slang words, with which he was in the habit of garnishing his conversation, "of all matters that are done here in this house."

"These are your new regimentals, Stephen," said Henry, looking at Foster's dress; "you shine like a flecker on a sunny day. It will please sister to the life to see you so spruce; she's a prodigious disciplinarian, and doesn't like to see us rebels (here he put his hand to his mouth and pronounced this word with a mock circumspection), worse dressed than the rascally red-coats. When do the Rangers march, Stephen?"

"We are waiting for orders every day. We parade, you know, Mister Henry, this morning."

"You must plead off to-day," said Henry; "I called you up to tell you that sister and I were going to ride, and I wanted you to go with us. At any rate, if you must go to the troop, you can leave us on the road. You don't meet till twelve, and both sister and I want to talk to you. She commanded me to tell you this. I believe she wishes you to take a letter for her. Poor Mildred doesn't know that I am going with you; so, as to that, you needn't let on. Go, Stephen, have our horses ready as soon as you can get them. Quick, good Stephen; sister and I will wait for you on the lawn."

The lieutenant of the Rangers, having received his orders, hurried away to attend to their execution.

Mildred was already apparelled for her ride, and came at this moment from the house along the gravel walk. Her cheek, lately pale, had now begun to show the ruddy hue of health. Her full, dark-blue eye, although habitually expressive of a thoughtful temperament, frequently sparkled with the sudden flashes of a playful spirit, and oftener with the fire of an ardent resolution. Her features, marked by a well-defined outline, bore a strong resemblance to her brother's, and, when animated by the quick-speeding emotions of her mind, presented a countenance unusually gifted with the graces of external beauty. The impression which her physiognomy conveyed, was that of an impassioned and enthusiastic nature, and of a feminine courage that was sufficient for any emergency. A clear skin gave brilliancy to her complexion; and, although habits of exposure to the air had slightly impaired its lustre, the few traces which this exposure left, rather communicated the agreeable idea of a wholesome and vigorous constitution. The tones of her voice were soft and gentle, and full of harmony; and, when stimulated by her feelings, rich, deep, and commanding. Her figure, of what might be deemed a medium height in females, was neat and agile, well proportioned, and combining the flexible ease proper to her sex, with a degree of steadiness and strength that might be denominated masculine. Her movement was graceful, distinguished by a ready hand and free step; and it was impossible to look upon her most familiar bearing, without being struck by the indication which it gave of a self-possessed, fearless, and careering temper, allied to a mind raised above the multitude by a consciousness of intellectual force.

As Mildred advanced along the shaded walk, she was followed by a fantastical little attendant, whom, in the toyish freak of a solitary and luxurious life, she had trained to fill the station of a lady's page. This was a diminutive negro boy, not above ten years of age, of a delicate figure, and now gaudily bedecked in a vest of scarlet cloth, a pair of loose white linen trowsers drawn at the ankle, and red slippers. A ruffle fell over his neck, and full white sleeves were fastened with silken cords at his wrists. A scarlet velvet cap gave a finish to the apparel of this gorgeous little elf; and the dress, grotesque as it was, was not badly set off by the saucy, familiar port of the conceited menial. Whether he had been destined from his birth to this pampered station, — or, accidentally, like many of the eastern monarchs, raised to the purple, — he bore the romantic name of Endymion, and was fully as much at the call of his patroness, and as fond of sleep, as him of Mount Latmos. His business seemed to be at the present moment to acquit himself of the responsible duty of holding an ivory-mounted riding-whip in readiness for the service of his mistress.

When Mildred had crossed the lawn and arrived at the spot where Henry now stood, she was saluted by her brother, with —

"Stand, my gentle sister, you and your monkey! Ah, Mildred, you are not what you used to be; you have grown much too grave of late. Bear up, dear sister: for, after all, what is it! Why, we have been beaten, and we must fight it over again, that's all. And as to the major, your partiality magnifies his dangers. Hasn't he an arm? — yes; and hasn't he a leg? — which, in war, I hold to be just as useful sometimes."

"There is a dreadful uncertainty, brother," replied Mildred. "I dream of the worst."

"A fig for your dreams, sister Mildred! They have been all sorts of ways, and that you know. Now, I have a waking dream, and that is, that before you are twenty-four hours older you will hear of Major Butler."

"Would to heaven your dream may prove true!" replied Mildred. "But, Henry, you love me, and affection is an arrant cheat in its prophecies."

"Tush then, sister! don't talk of it. For when we know nothing, it does no good to get to fancying. These are the times to act; and perhaps I'll surprise you yet."

"With what, good brother?"

"Order arms," replied Henry, evading his sister's inquiry, and at the same time assuming a military erectness, and bringing his rifle briskly to the ground — "with the beauty of my drill, sister. It even surprises myself. You shall see me march." And here he sportively shouldered his rifle and stepped with a measured pace across the green, and then back again, whilst the saucy Endymion, presuming on his privilege, with mimic gestures, followed immediately in Henry's rear, taking large strides to keep his ground. When Henry perceived the apish minion thus upon his track he burst out into a laugh.

"You huge giant-killer, do you mock me?" he exclaimed. "Sister, I will smother your body-guard in the crown of my cap, if he isn't taught better manners."

"Henry, I cannot share your light heart with you," said Mildred sorrowfully, "mine is heavy."

"And mine is yours, sister, light or heavy; in sunshine or in storm, summer and winter, dear Mildred, it is always yours. It was a trick of mine to amuse you. And if I do not seem to feel, sister, as you do, it is because I mean to act. We men have no time for low spirits."

"Stephen Foster is here at the door with our horses, brother. Boy, give me the whip — now, away. The gay feathers of this bird," said Mildred, as the little black retired, "do not become a follower of mine."

The new aspect of affairs, since the defeat of Camden, had pressed grievously upon Mildred's spirits. The country was full of disheartening rumors, and every day added particulars that were of a nature to increase the distress. The bloody fate of the brave De Kalb, and the soldiers that fell by his side; the triumph with which Cornwallis had begun his preparations for further conquests; the destitution and disarray of the American army, now flying before its enemy; the tales of unsparing sequestration with which, in Carolina, the lands of those who still bore arms in the cause of independence, were visited; the military executions of prisoners charged with the violation of a constructive allegiance, in the conquered districts; the harsh measures which were adopted to break the heart of the rebellion, that still lingered behind the march of the victorious army; and, above all, the boastful confidence with which Cornwallis, by his proclamations, sought to open the way for his invasion of North Carolina and Virginia, by attempting to rally the liege subjects of the king under his standard: all these events came on the wings of rumor, and had lighted up a flame through the whole country. To Mildred, they all imported an ill omen as regarded the fate of Arthur Butler. Now and then, a straggling soldier of Gates's broken force arrived at the Dove Cote, where he was received with an eager hospitality, and closely questioned as to the events in which he had participated. But of Butler, not even the remotest tidings were obtained. For the present, the uncertainty of his fortune filled Mildred's thoughts with the most anxious and unhappy misgivings; and this frame of mind over-mastered all other feelings. The late visit of Tyrrel to the Dove Cote, and the abrupt departure of her father with this individual, on an unavowed expedition, were not calculated to allay her fears; and she felt herself pressed on all sides with the presages of coming misfortune. In these difficulties she did not lose her fortitude; but, like a mariner benighted in a dangerous strait, she counted over the anxious moments of her voyage, expecting, at each succeeding instant, to hear the dreadful stranding of her bark upon the unseen rock, though bravely prepared for the worst.

CHAPTER XXXVIII

AN ARRIVAL AT DOVE COTE. MILDRED RESOLVES ON A PERILOUS ADVENTURE

It was in the state of painful expectation described in the last chapter, that Mildred now rode out, daily, upon the highways, in the feeble hope of hearing something of importance from the casual wayfarers who, in the present excited condition of the country, were thronging the roads. On the morning to which our narrative refers, she had charged Henry to procure the attendance of Stephen Foster, to whom, as it was known that he was about to accompany his troop towards the scene of hostilities, she was anxious to intrust a letter for Butler, as well as to communicate to him some instructions relating to it.

Stephen was, accordingly, now in attendance. A sleek, full-blooded roan, of an active, deer-like figure, and showing by his mettlesome antics the high training of a pampered favorite, stood in the care of the groom at the door; and Mildred, aided by her brother, sprang into her saddle with the ease and confidence of one familiarized to the exploit. When mounted, she appeared to great advantage. She was an expert rider, and managed her horse with a dexterous grace. The very position of command and authority which her saddle gave her, seemed to raise her spirits into a happier elevation.

"Follow me, Mister Stephen," she said, "I have service for you. And it will not be out of the fashion of the time that a lady should be 'squired by an armed soldier. We take the road down the river. Have a care, brother, how you bound off at the start — the hill is steep, and a horse's foot is not over sure when pressed too rapidly on the descent."

The cavalcade descended the hill, crossed the ford, and then took a direction down the stream, by the road that led beneath the Fawn's Tower. Mildred sighed as she gazed around her, and saw the spot of her last meeting with Butler. The little skiff by which her lover had glided across the water, now lay upon a dry bed of rock, in the same position, perhaps, where a month ago he had left it. The summer drought had reduced the stream, and deprived the light boat (whose tackle kept it prisoner to the root of the sycamore) of the element on which it had floated. This spectacle suggested to Mildred's thoughts a melancholy image. "Even thus," she muttered to herself, "have I been left by him. He has gone to obey the calls of honor and duty, and I, fettered to my native woods, have seen the stream of happiness roll by, one while swollen to a torrent, and again dried up by the fervid heart of war, until, like this sun-withered bark, I have been left upon the shore, without one drop of that clear current on which alone I hoped to live. Come hither, Stephen," she said, as she slackened the rein of her horse: and the obedient attendant was immediately at her side.

"You set out southwards, with your comrades of the troop, in a few days?"

"Orders may come to-morrow," replied Foster.

"It is no holiday game that you are going to play," continued the lady.

"When Congress cut out this here war for us, Miss Mildred," answered the hunter, "they didn't count upon settling of it without making some tall fellows the shorter. And it is my opinion that it is a p'int of conscience that every man should take his spell of the work."

"You go to it with a good heart," said Mildred. "We women can only pray for you, lieutenant."

"I shall pull trigger with a steadier hand, ma'am, when I think that your father's daughter is praying for me."

"Stephen," continued Mildred, "you may chance to see some one whose duty may lead him further south than, perhaps, you may be required to travel: I will give you a letter to a friend of mine, who, I fear, is in distress. If such traveller be trusty and willing to do me a service, as perhaps he may for your sake, I must beg you to put the letter in his charge, and tell him to seek out Major Butler, and contrive to have it delivered to him."

"If it concerns you, Miss Mildred, I will take upon myself to hunt Major Butler, or I will make as sure of the letter reaching him as I may have a chance."

"Many thanks, Stephen. There is a purse containing some few pieces of gold for you. Do not spare the use of it to perform my wish."

Stephen looked bashfully at the lady as she held the proffered purse in her hand.

"Take it, Mr. Foster. It is money to be employed in my service, and it may stand you in good stead when better friends are absent."

The hunter uttered an awkward laugh. "If you would allow me to take the smallest piece of money, it would more than hire a man express."

"Take it all, Stephen, it is but a trifle. They call this the sinew of war," said Mildred, smiling.

"It's an utter, moral, and resolute impossibility," answered Foster, "for me to take all that money. Bless your soul, Miss Mildred my pocket ar'n't used to such company."

"Pshaw, Steve," ejaculated Henry, "you are the greenest soldier in these hills, to be playing boy about this money. Take it, man, and none of your nonsense; precious little gold you'll see before you get back!"

"Well, I'll not be ticklish about it," said Foster. "Empty the bag, Miss Mildred, into my hand."

"I mean that you shall have the purse with it," added Mildred.

"No, no; that's too valuable a piece of fine silk net-work for me."

"There again, Lieutenant Foster," said Henry; "if you were not my own superior officer, I would say you were a fool."

"Give it to me," replied Stephen, laughing, "I have heard of cheating money out of a man's pocket, but I never saw it cheated into it before."

"You shall have the letter to-morrow, Stephen," said Mildred, "and as you value your poor friend, who worked that purse with her own hands, do not fail to make an effort to learn something of Major Butler, and to have my letter delivered to him. He was made a prisoner somewhere on his way to Georgia, and I have heard escaped; but, perhaps, that's not true. You may find some one who can tell you more about him. Inquire of all you meet: and, Stephen, in my name, beg your comrades to aid you. Remember," added Mildred, with a smile, "this is a lady's secret. I am sure you will keep it."

"Most sacrilegiously and with all possible punctuation!" replied the woodsman. "And you shall hear of the Major, Miss Mildred, dead or alive."

"Oh, heaven!" exclaimed Mildred aloud; and then recollecting herself, she breathed in a whisper, "that word vibrated a note of fear. Your zeal shall have my warmest gratitude, Stephen."

By this time the party had reached the second ford, where the road recrossed the river, in the neighborhood of Mrs. Dimock's, and in a few moments they were at the door of the little inn.

A brief halt, and a few words with the good hostess, furnished Mildred neither with a letter nor with any information of moment from the quarter, where at this time the thoughts of nearly the whole of the American people were turned.

"Woful days, Miss Mildred," said the landlady, shaking her head, and wearing a face of lugubrious length, "woful indeed! nothing but hurry-skurry, and bragging and swearing. What with Gates's runaways, that — shame upon them! — come whipping post haste along the road; and messengers, dragoons, and drill sergeants, all out of breath, out of money, and out of everything but appetites; which, mercy on me! never fail in the worst of times: and what with musterings of volunteers, and drumming and fifing of it, up hill and down dale, it is as much as one can do to keep one's wits. Heaven help us, my dear! I don't know what we shall come to. But poor Arthur," she continued, in a mournful and lower key, "not a word from him. It looks awfully: I could almost sit down and weep. Nevertheless, Miss Mildred, my child, be of good cheer, God will keep his foot from the path that leads to the snares; we must all trust in His goodness."

"Alas, alas!" breathed Mildred, in an accent of sorrow. "Brother, ride forward. If a good word reaches you, Mistress Dimock, send it to me, even if it be at midnight."

Mildred pursued her ride, and Henry, seeing how much she was dejected, applied himself, with the kindest assiduity, to bring back comfort and cheerfulness to her mind. He sought to amuse her with such fragments of the gossip of the country-side as were likely to interest her patriotism; and he contrived to recall to her recollection passages in the life of Butler, which related to the perils he had heretofore encountered, and from which he had extricated himself by his address and soldiership; and Henry told these in such a way as to infer from them arguments of comfort that suited the present state of his sister's feelings. As was usual in most of the young cadet's discourses, he glided into that half-boastful and half-waggish vein in which he delighted to refer to his own pursuits and aspirations after military glory.

"A man naturally, sister," he said, erecting himself in his stirrups, and assuming the stiff carriage of a conceited young adjutant on parade, "a man naturally feels proud on horseback. It is what I call glorification, to have a noble beast under you, that you can turn and wind and check and set forward as you please, as if his limbs were your own. You feel stronger; and, in this world, I do believe a strong man is always proud. Now, I should think that a woman would feel even more so than a man; because, being weak by nature, she must grow happier to think how much muscle she can put in motion by only pulling a rein."

"There is some philosophy in that, Henry," replied Mildred.

"So there is, sister; and I tell you more, that when a person has this sort of glorification, as they call it, they always get more contented with themselves. And that's the reason, as far as I am a judge, that you always feel in better spirits when you are on horseback; and, especially, if it should be in front of a troop. Hallo, Stephen!" ejaculated Henry, taken by surprise, in the midst of his discourse, by the sight of a flock of wild turkeys that ran across the road, some hundred paces a-head. "Did you see that? Halt, man — here's game for us." And, in an instant, he sprang from his horse, which he fastened to one of the neighboring trees, and ran off with his rifle in his hand, in pursuit of the flock.

Stephen, whose instincts were those of a keen sportsman, when game was before him, did the same thing; and in a few moments Mildred found herself left entirely alone in the road, half disposed to chide and half to smile at the eager and ungallant desertion of her attendants, who were now in quick but cautious pursuit of the brood of turkeys. The speed with which these birds are accustomed to run through the woods, allured their pursuers to some distance into the depths of the forest; and Mildred patiently awaited the return of her companions on the ground where they had left her.

After five or ten minutes had elapsed, it was with a sensation of some little concern that she descried, upon the road, a stranger mounted on horseback, and coming at a brisk trot to the spot where she had halted. The appearance of the individual was that of one of the irregular soldiers who had accompanied Gates's army; his dress was rustic, and his weapon, according to the almost universal fashion of the country troops, the long rifle. The condition of his sturdy steed showed long and fatiguing service; whilst the bold and manly person of the rider left little room to suppose that he was to be classed amongst the many who had fled in panic from the field of action. As soon as the stranger became aware of the presence of the lady, he slackened his speed and approached with a respectful salutation.

"If I mought be so bold, ma'am, how far mought it be to a river they call the Rockfish?"

"It is scarce two miles away, sir," replied Mildred.

"And there, if I don't disremember," said the traveller, "is a house kept by the widow Dimock; the Blue Ball, I think?"

"There is, sir."

"And no forks in the road betwixt this and the widow's?"

"It is a plain road," replied Mildred.

"And about two miles beyont — is squire Lindsay's, at a place they call the Dove Cote?"

"Does your business take you there?" asked Mildred, with interest; "are you from the army? — whence come you?"

"Beg pardon, ma'am," replied the stranger, smiling, "but I am an old sodger, and rather warry about answering questions that consarn myself. I suppose it is likely I mought see Mr. Lindsay?"

"Pray, sir, tell me what brings you here, and who you are? I have special reasons for presuming so far upon your kindness. I myself live at the Dove Cote, and" —

"Then, mayhap, you mought have hearn of one Major Arthur Butler?"

"Oh, yes, sir, — if you have any news of him, speak it to me quickly," exclaimed Mildred, with much agitation.

"By that sparkling of your eye, ma'am, it is no fool's guess that you are the identical particular lady that I have rode nigh on to five hundred miles to see. You have hearn the Major tell of Horse Shoe Robinson?"

"And Arthur Butler."

"He is well, madam, and in good heart, excepting some trifling drawbacks that don't come to much account."

"Thank God, thank God, for this news!"

"I have brought two letters, Miss Lindsay, from the Major, for you; they will tell you, I believe, mainly, that the Major is in the hands of the Philistians," said Horse Shoe, rummaging through the plaits of his dress, and getting loose the belt and leathern pouch from which, by the help of his jack-knife, he extricated the missives; "but they leave the story to be told pretty much by me. The long and the short of it is, that the Major is a prisoner, and wants some assistance from you: but there is no danger of any harm being done him."

Mildred eagerly tore open the letters and read them; then heaving a sigh, she said, "He is closely watched, and galled with misfortune. He refers to you, Mr. Robinson, and I must beg you to tell me all."

Horse Shoe, with a cheerful and occasionally even with a laughing manner, adapted to reassure the lady and quell her fears, recounted all such particulars of Butler's adventures as were necessary to enable her to comprehend the nature of his present mission to the Dove Cote.

Before this narrative was brought to a close, Henry and Foster had returned, bringing with them a large turkey which Henry had shot, and which the young sportsman was exhibiting with ostentatious triumph.

"Huzza, here's a new turn of good luck! Horse Shoe Robinson, the brave sergeant," shouted Henry, as soon as he observed the stout figure of our old friend. "Is Major Butler here too?" he demanded, as he shook the sergeant's hand, "or have you come alone? Now, sister, you ought to be a happy woman. You bring us good news, Mr. Horse Shoe, I know you do."

"The news is better than it mought have been if the Tories had had their way," replied Horse Shoe. "But a sodger's life has both shade and sunshine in it; and the Major is now a little in the shade."

"Brother, mount quickly," said Mildred, "we have business before us. Mr. Robinson, ride beside me; I have much to say to you."

Stephen Foster, after saluting the sergeant, and reminding Mildred of his engagement to meet his troop, took his leave of the party.

The rest repaired, with as much expedition as they were able to employ, to the Dove Cote, Horse Shoe detailing to the brother and sister, as they went along, a great many particulars of the late history of Butler.

When they reached the house, orders were given for the accommodation of the sergeant; and the most sedulous attention was shown to everything that regarded his comfort. Frequent conferences were held between Mildred and Henry, and the trusty emissary. The letters were reperused, and all the circumstances that belonged to Butler's means of liberation were anxiously discussed.

"How unlucky is it," said Mildred, "that my father should be absent at such a moment as this! Arthur's appeal to him would convince him how wicked was Tyrrel's charge against his honor. And yet, in my father's late mood, the appeal might have been ineffectual: he might have refused. Sergeant, we are in great difficulties, and I know not what to do. A letter, you say, has been written to Lord Cornwallis?"

"Yes, ma'am, and by a man who sharpened his pen with his sword."

"You heard nothing of the answer of his Lordship?"

"There was not time to hear."

"Cornwallis will be prejudiced by those around him, and he will refuse," said Mildred, with an air of deep solicitude.

"Not if he be the man I take him to be, young lady," replied Horse Shoe. "The world says he is above doing a cowardly thing; and it isn't natural for one brave man to wish harm against another, except in open war."

"Did you hear of one Tyrrel, in the British camp? But how could you? — that was an assumed name."

"You mean the gentleman who was here when the major stopped at Mrs. Dimock's?" said Robinson: "that was the name the landlady spoke about — if I remember myself. I did not hear of him, ma'am, in my travels; but his servant, James Curry, I met oftener, I undertake to say, than the fellow wished. He was consarned in ambushing Major Butler and me at Grindall's Ford. It was our opinion he was hired."

"There," exclaimed Mildred, "that confirms what I guessed of Tyrrel's villany. I will go to Cornwallis myself: I will expose the whole matter to his lordship. Henry, my dear brother, it is a rash venture but I will essay it. You must accompany and protect me."

"That's a sudden thought, sister, and you may count on my hearty good will to help it along. It is a brave thought of yours, besides," said Henry, pondering over it — "and everybody will praise you for it."

Robinson listened to this resolve with an incredulous ear.

"You wouldn't venture, young madam, to trust yourself amongst such rough and unchristian people, as you would have to go among before you could see Cornwallis? in danger of being taken up by outposts and pickets, or arrested by patroles, or dragged about by dragoons and fellows that have more savagery in them than wolves. Oh, no, ma'am, you don't know what you would have to put up with; that's onpossible. Mr. Henry, here, and me can take a letter."

"I may not trust to letters, I must go myself. You will

protect me, Mr. Robinson? my brother and I will form some good excuse that shall take us through safely."

"Sartainly, ma'am, I will stand by you through all chances, if you go," replied the sergeant. "But there's not many women, with their eyes open, would set out on such a march."

"It will be easily achieved," said Mildred: "it is an honest and virtuous cause that takes me away, and I will attempt it with a valiant spirit. It cannot but come to good. My father's name will give me free passage through the enemy's lines. And you shall pass as my attendant."

"If you have a heart stout enough, ma'am, for such hard fare, I believe I mought undertake for your safe passage," answered Horse Shoe, "and it sartainly would do the major great good to hear that you was stirring in this matter."

"Sergeant, recruit yourself as long as you think necessary," said Mildred; "but if you can be ready to set out to-morrow, I should like to go then, and at an early hour."

"Don't stand upon my fatigue, young lady: I never saw the time when I wan't ready to march at the shortest warning. With your leave, I will go look after my horse, Captain Peter, I call him, ma'am. A little chance of a roll, and the privilege of a good green pasture, soon puts him in marching trim."

The sergeant now left the room.

"Sister," said Henry, "you never thought a better thought, and you never contrived a better act, than just taking this matter in hand yourself, under mine and Horse Shoe's protection. Because Horse Shoe is as brave a man as you ever fell in with, and as for me, I'll back the sergeant. We can finish the thing in two or three weeks, and then, when I see you safe home, I'll go and join the Rangers."

"It is a perilous and uncertain journey, brother, but it is my duty. I would rather fall beneath the calamities of war than longer endure my present feelings. Provide yourself, brother, with all things requisite for our journey, and give old Isaac, the gardener, notice that he must go with us. We shall set out to-morrow. I will write a letter to my father to-night explaining my purpose. And one thing, Henry; you will be careful to say nothing to any one of the route we shall travel."

"I'll take my carbine, sister," said Henry, "I can sling it with a strap. And I was thinking I had better have a broadsword."

"Leave that behind," replied Mildred, as a smile rose on her features.

"The bugle I will certainly take," added Henry; "because it might be useful in case we got separated; and I will teach you to understand my signals. Issac shall carry horse-pistols on his saddle, and the sergeant shall have a great wallet of provisions. You see I understand campaigning, Mildred. And now," added the eager young soldier, as he left the apartment, "hurra for the volunteers of the Dove Cote!"

CHAPTER XXXIX

MILDRED BEGINS HER JOURNEY

THE man who writes the history of woman's love will find himself employed in drawing out a tangled skein. It is a history of secret emotions and vivid contrasts, which may well go nigh to baffle his penetration and to puzzle his philosophy. There is in it a surface of timid and gentle bashfulness concealing an underflow of strong and heady passion: a seeming caprice that a breath may shake or a word alarm; yet, all the while, an earnest devotion of soul which, in its excited action, holds all danger cheap that crosses the path of its career. The sportive, changeful, and coward nature that dallies with affection as a jest, and wins admiration by its affrighted coyness; that flies and would be followed; that revolts and would be soothed, entreated, and on bended knee implored, before it is won; that same nature will undergo the ordeal of the burning ploughshare, take all the extremes of misery and distress, brave the fury of the elements and the wrath of man, and in every peril be a patient comforter, when the cause that moves her is the vindication of her love. Affection is to her what glory is to man, an impulse that inspires the most adventurous heroism.

There had been for some days past in Mildred's mind an anxious misgiving of misfortune to Butler, which was but ill concealed in a quiet and reserved demeanor. The argument of his safety seemed to have little to rest upon, and she could perceive that it was not believed by those who uttered it. There rose upon her thoughts imaginings or presentiments of ill, which she did not like to dwell upon, but which she could not banish. And now when Horse Shoe had told his tale, the incidents did not seem to warrant the levity with which he passed them by. She was afraid to express her doubts: and they brooded upon her mind, hatching pain and secret grief. It was almost an instinct, therefore, that directed her resolve, when she announced her determination to go in person in quest of Cornwallis, and to plead Butler's cause herself to the British general. Her soul rebelled at the gross calumny which had been invented to bring down vengeance upon Arthur's head; and she had no thought of thwarting the accuser's wickedness, but by an appeal to the highest power for that redress which an honorable soldier, in her opinion, could not refuse, even to an enemy. As to the personal hazard, inconvenience, or difficulty of her projected enterprise, no thought of either for a moment occupied her. She saw but her purpose before her, and did not pause to reckon on the means by which she was to promote it. She reflected not on the censure of the world; nor on its ridicule; nor on its want of sympathy for her feelings: she reflected only on her power to serve one dearer to her than a friend, upon her duty, and upon the agony of her doubts. If her father had been at hand she might have appealed to him, and, perhaps, have submitted to his counsel; but he was absent, she knew not where, and she was convinced that no time was to be lost. "Even now, whilst we debate," she said, "his life may be forfeited to the malice of the wicked men who have ensnared him."

Her conduct in this crisis is not to be weighed in the scale wherein the seemly and decorous observances of female propriety are ordinarily balanced. The times, the occasion, and the peculiar position of Mildred, take her case out of the pale of common events, and are entitled to another standard. She will be judged by the purity of her heart, the fervor of her attachment, and her sense of the importance of the service she was about to confer. And with the knowledge of these, I must leave her vindication to the generosity of my reader.

When the morning came and breakfast was over, the horses were brought to the door. Henry was active in all the preliminary arrangements for the journey, and now bestirred himself with an increased air of personal importance. Isaac, a grey-haired negro, of a sedate, and, like all his tribe, of an abundantly thoughtful length of visage, appeared in a suit of livery, ready booted and spurred for his journey. A large portmanteau, containing a supply of baggage for his mistress, was duly strapped behind his saddle, whilst a pair of pistols were buckled upon the pummel. Henry's horse also had all the furniture necessary to a campaign; and the young martialist himself, notwithstanding his sister's disapproval, was begirt with a sword-belt, from which depended a light sabre, with which he was in the habit of exhibiting himself in the corps of the Rangers. His bugle hung gracefully by his side, and his carbine was already provided with a strap to sling it across his back. Stephen Foster was lost in wonder at these sudden preparations, of the import of which he could gain no more intelligence from Henry than that a movement towards the army was intended, of a portentous character.

Horse Shoe sat quietly in the porch looking on with a professional unconcern, whilst his trusty Captain Peter, bearing a pair of saddle-bags, now stuffed with a plethora of provisions, slouched his head, in patient fixedness, waiting the order to move. A bevy of domestics hung around the scene of preparation, lost in conjectures as to the meaning of this strange array, and prosecuting an inquiry to satisfy themselves, with fruitless perseverance.

When Mildred appeared at the door she was habited for her journey. The housekeeper, an aged dame, stood near her.

"My travel, Mistress Morrison," she said, addressing the matron, and at the same time putting a letter into her hand, "I trust will not keep me long from home. If my father should return before I do, be careful to give him that. Mr. Foster, you will not forget your promise," she added, as she delivered the second letter, which, notwithstanding her own expedition, she had prepared for Butler, in the hope that opportunity might favor its transmission by Stephen.

"The gold," said Stephen, putting his hand in his pocket; "you will want it yourself, Miss Mildred, and I can do without it."

"Never mind that," interrupted Mildred. "Keep your promise, and I hope to be able to reward you more according to your deserts."

"Heaven and the saints protect you, Miss Mildred!" said the housekeeper, as the lady bade her farewell. "You leave us on some heavy errand. God grant that you come back with a gayer face than you take away!" Then turning up her eyes, and raising her hands, she ejaculated, "This is an awful thing, and past my understanding!"

Mildred took leave of the rest of the group around the door, and was soon in her saddle. This was a signal for the rest to mount, and as Stephen Foster delivered Henry his rifle, the latter took occasion to whisper in the hunter's ear—

"It is not unlikely, Steve, that we may meet each other again over here in Carolina; so remember to make inquiries for us as you go along, and tell the men I hope to join them before they fire one shot in spite. But mum, Steve, not a word about our route."

Stephen shook hands with his young comrade; and Henry, seeing that the rest of the party had already left the door and were some distance down the hill, called out with an elated tone of good humor — " Farewell, Mrs. Morrison, and all the rest of you! " and putting spurs to his horse galloped off to join his sister.

The route pursued by the travellers lay due south, and during the first three or four days of their journey they were still within the confines of Virginia. To travel on horseback was a customary feat, even for ladies, in those days of rough roads and scant means of locomotion: and such a cavalcade as we have described was calculated to excite no particular inquiry from the passer-by, beyond that which would now be made on the appearance of any party of pleasure upon the high-roads, in the course of a summer excursion. Mildred experienced severe fatigue in the first stages of her journey; but by degrees this wore off, and she was soon enabled to endure the long day's ride with scarcely less inconvenience than her fellow-travellers.

At that period there were but few inns in these thinly-peopled districts, and such as were already established were small and but meagrely provided. This deficiency was, in some degree, compensated by the good will with which the owners of private establishments in the country received the better class of travellers, and the ready hospitality with which they entertained them. Henry took upon himself to obtain information of the gentlemen's seats that lay near the route of his journey, and to conduct the party to them whenever his sister's comfort required better accommodation than the common inns afforded.

As our travellers had thus far kept along that range of country which lay immediately under the mountains, they were not annoyed by the intense heats which, at this season, prevailed in the lowlands. The weather, ever since their departure, had been uncommonly fine, and as is usual in this district, the month of September had brought its cool, dewy nights, whilst the early hours of the morning were even marked by a little sharpness, almost approaching to frost. The effect of this on Mildred was to recruit the weariness of travel, and better enable her to encounter the noon-tide fervors of the sun; and she had so far endured the toils of her journey with an admirable spirit. Actual trial generally results in demonstrating how much we are prone to exaggerate in advance the difficulties of any undertaking. Accordingly, Mildred's present experience strengthened her resolution to proceed, and even communicated an unexpected increase of contentment to her feelings.

On the fifth day the party crossed the river Dan, and entered the province of North Carolina. A small remnant of Gates's shattered army lay at Hillsborough, at no great distance from the frontier; and as Mildred was anxious to avoid the inquiry or molestation to be expected in passing through a military post, she resolved to travel by a lower route, and Horse Shoe, therefore, at her suggestion, directed his journey towards the little village of Tarborough.

Cornwallis, it was understood, since the battle of Camden, had removed his head-quarters into the neighborhood of the Waxhaws, some distance up the Catawba, where he was supposed to be yet stationary. The whole country in the neighborhood of either army was in a state of earnest preparation; the British commander recruiting his forces for further and immediate operations — the American endeavoring to reassemble his feeble and scattered auxiliaries for defence. At the present moment, actual hostilities between these two parties were entirely suspended, in anxious anticipation of the rapidly approaching renewal of the struggle. It was a breathing time, when the panting combatants, exhausted by battle, stood sullenly eyeing each other and making ready — the one to strike, the other to ward off another staggering blow.

The country over which Mildred was now to travel was calculated to tax her powers of endurance to the utmost. It was a dreary waste of barren wilderness, covered with an endless forest of gloomy pine, through which a heavy, sandy road crept in lurid and melancholy shade. Here and there a miserable hut occurred to view, with a few ragged inmates, surrounded by all the signs of squalid poverty. The principal population were only to be seen along the banks of the rivers which penetrated into this region, some twenty or thirty miles distant from each other. The alluvial bottoms through which these streams found a channel to the ocean, were the only tracts of land of sufficient fertility to afford support to man — all between them was a sterile and gloomy forest.

Still, these regions were not deserted. Bodies of irregular troops, ill clothed and worse armed, and generally bearing the haggard features of disease, such as mark the population of a sickly climate, were often encountered upon the road, directing their wearied march towards the head-quarters of the republican army.

The rigors of the Southern summer had not yet abated; and it was with painful steps in the deep sand, amid clouds of suffocating dust, that these little detachments prosecuted their journey.

Mildred, so far from sinking under the weariness and increasing hardships of her present toils, seemed to be endued with a capacity for sustaining them much beyond anything that could have been believed of her sex. Her courage grew with the difficulties that beset her. She looked composedly upon the obstacles before her, and encountered them, not only without a murmur, but even with a cheerfulness to which she had hitherto been a stranger. The steadiness of her onward march, her unrepining patience, and the gentle solicitude with which she turned the thoughts of her companions from herself, and forbade the supposition that her powers were over-taxed, showed how deeply her feelings were engaged in her enterprise, and how maturely her mind had taken its resolution.

"One never would have guessed," said Horse Shoe, towards the close of the second day after they had entered North Carolina, "that a lady so daintly nursed as you was at home, Mistress Mildred, could have ever borne this here roughing of it through these piney woods. But I have made one observation, Miss Lindsay, that no one can tell what they are fit for till they are tried; and on the back of that I have another, that when there's a great stir that rouses up a whole country, it don't much signify whether they are man or woman, they all get roused alike. 'Pon my word, ma'am, I have seen men — who think themselves sodgers too — that would be onwilling to trust themselves at this time o' year through such a dried up piece of pine barren as we have been travelling over for two days past."

"You remember the fable of the willow and the oak, Mr. Robinson," replied Mildred, smiling; "the storm may bring down the sturdy tree, but the supple shrub will bend before it without breaking."

"I'm not much given to religious takings-on," said the sergeant, "but sometimes a notion comes into my head that looks a little that way, and that is, when God appoints a thing to be done, he gives them that's to do it all the wherewithals. Now, as Major Butler is a good man and a brave sodger — God bless him! — it does seem right that you, Mistress Lindsay, — who, I take on me to understand enough of your consarns and his'n, without offence, to say has a leaning towards the major, — I say it does seem right and natural that you should lend a hand to help him out of tribulation; and so you see the cause being a good cause, the Lord has given you both wisdom and strength to do what is right."

"We owe, sergeant, a duty to our country; and we serve God and our country both, when we strengthen the hands of its defenders."

"That's a valiant speech, young lady, and it's a noble speech," said Horse Shoe, with an earnest emphasis. "I have often told the major that the women of this country had as honest thoughts about this here war, and was as warm for our cause as the men; and some of them, perhaps, a little warmer. They could be pitted against the women of any quarter of the aqueous globe, in bearing and forbearing both, when it is for the good of the country."

"Henry is asleep on his horse," said Mildred, looking at her brother, who now, jaded and worn with the effort of travel, was nodding and dropping his head forward, and almost losing his seat. "What, Henry, brother!" she added, loud enough to rouse up the young horseman. "My trusty cavalier, are you going to fall from your horse? Where is all that boasted glorification upon which you were disposed to be so eloquent only a week ago? I thought a man on horseback was naturally proud: I fear it was only on holiday occasions you meant, Henry. Hav'n't you a word for a sunny day and a dry journey? You lag more like a miller's boy with his bag of meal, than a young soldier setting out on his adventures."

"Ah, sister," said Henry, waking up, "this is nothing but pine — pine — and sand, without end. There is no game in the woods to keep a man on the look-out, except here and there a herd of wild hogs, that snort and run from us, like a squadron of cavalry, with their bristles set up on their backs as fierce as the back fin of a sunfish. There is not even grass to look at: you might see a black snake running half a mile amongst the trees. And then there are such great patches of burnt timber, every trunk staring right at you, as black as thunder. I'm tired of it all — I want to see the green fields again."

"And, in truth, brother, so do I: but not until we can bring merry faces to look upon them. How far are we from Tarborough?"

"We should be drawing nigh to the town," replied Horse Shoe, "for you may see that we shall soon be out of these woods, by the signs of open country ahead. The last squad of sodgers that passed us, said that when we came to the farms, we shouldn't be more than five miles from the town, and the sun isn't above an hour high."

"In the hope of being soon housed, then, Mr. Robinson, I may confess to you I am somewhat weary; but a good night's rest will put me in fair condition for to-morrow's ride again."

After the lapse of an hour, the party were safely sheltered in a tolerably comfortable inn at the village: and Mildred, aided by the sedulous care of Henry, found herself well bestowed in the best chamber of the house.

CHAPTER XL

From Tarborough our travellers continued their route towards the Pedee, by the main road which led through Cross creek, a small hamlet on Cape Fear river, near the site of the present town of Fayetteville. The general features of the country were even more forbidding than those I have already described as characteristic of this portion of North Carolina. Even to the present day, cultivation has done but little to cheer up the natural desolation of those tracts of wilderness which lie between the rivers. But at the early period to which the events I have been detailing have reference, the journey undertaken by our little caravan might be compared to that which is now frequently made through the more southern extremity of the Union, from the Atlantic to the Gulf of Mexico, an attempt seldom essayed by a female, and sufficiently trying to the hardihood of the stoutest travellers. The forethought and attention of Horse Shoe Robinson, however, contributed to alleviate the pains of the enterprise, and to enable Mildred to overcome its difficulties.

In the present alarmed and excited state of this province, the party were less liable to interruption in this secluded and destitute section of the country, than they might have been, had they chosen a lower and more populous district; and the consciousness that every day's perseverance brought them nearer to the ultimate term of their journey, gave new vigor, at least, to Mildred's capacity to endure the privations to which she was exposed. But few vestiges of the war yet occurred to their view. The great wilderness, like the great ocean, retains no traces of the passage of hostile bodies. Sometimes, indeed, the signs of a woodland encampment were visible in the midst of the forest, on the margin of some sluggish brook or around a sylvan fountain, where the impression of recent hoof-prints, the scattered fragments of brushwood cut for temporary shelter, and the still smouldering ashes of camp fires, showed that masses of men had been in motion. The deer fled, too, with a more frightened bound towards their coverts, as if lately alarmed by the pursuit of the huntsman; but the images of devastation, which are associated with the horrid front of war in the mind of all familiar with its ravage, were absent. The eternal, leafy shade high arching over the heads of the wayfarers, furnished no object for human vengeance; and it still sighed in the fanning of the breeze, as of old it sighed before man claimed dominion in the soil it sheltered. A far different scene was shortly to be looked upon by our venturesome friends.

Several days had again passed by, for the journey through the wilderness had been slowly prosecuted, when Robinson, towards the approach of evening, announced to Mildred his conjecture that they were not far off the Pedee. The banks of this river had been the scene of frequent hostilities, and the war that had been carried on here was of the most ruthless kind. The river is characterized by a broad, deep, and quiet stream, begirt with a vegetation of exceeding luxuriance. Its periodical overflow seems to have poured out upon its margin a soil of inexhaustible richness, that, for a mile or two on either side, forms a striking contrast with the low, barren sand-hills that hem in the river plain. Along this tract of level border, all the way to the Atlantic, are found, as is usually the case throughout the Carolinas, the large plantations of opulent gentlemen, who, by the cultivation of rice and cotton, turn the fertility of the soil to the best account. These possessions, presenting the most assailable points to an enemy, and, indeed, almost the only ones in which the great interests of the province might be wounded, were, during the whole of that bloody struggle which distinguished the days of the "Tory Ascendency," the constant objects of attack; and here the war was waged with a vindictive malignity, on the part of the British and Tory partisans, that is scarcely surpassed in the history of civil broils. The finest estates were sacked, the dwellings burnt, and the property destroyed with unsparing rage. The men were dragged from their houses and hung, the women and children turned without food or raiment into the wilderness, and political vengeance seemed to gorge itself to gluttony upon its own rapine.

The thoughts of Robinson had been, for some days past, running upon the probable difficulties that might attend the guise in which he was now about to return to his native province. This was a subject of some concern, since he ran a risk of being compelled either to desert his charge, or to bring his companions into jeopardy, amongst the many persons of both armies who were, at least by report, acquainted with his name and his military connexions. He had explained to Mildred the necessity of his appearing in some definite character, associated with the object of her journey, and of which, upon emergency, he might claim the benefit to retain his post near her. This matter was summarily settled by Henry.

"In general, Mr. Horse Shoe, you can call yourself Stephen Foster: you know Steve; and you can say that you are Mr. Philip Lindsay's gardener. Isaac, here, can let you enough into the craft to pass muster, if any of them should take it into their heads to examine you. Mind that, Isaac: and recollect, old fellow, you are only sister Mildred's waiting man."

"Sartainly, master," replied Isaac.

"And sergeant, I'll tell you all about Steve; so that you can get your lesson by heart. You have a wife and five children — remember that. I'll give you all their names by-and-by."

"Thanks to the marcies of God, that ar'n't my misfortune yet," said Horse Shoe, laughing; "but, Mr. Henry, I have got conscience enough now for any lie that can be invented. The major and me talked that thing over, and he's of opinion that lying, in an enemy's country, is not forbidden in the scriptures. And I have hearn the preacher say that Rahab, who was not a woman of good fame no how, yet she was excused by the Lord for telling the king of Jericho a most thumping lie, consarning her not knowing what had become of the two men that Joshua, the judge of Israel, who was a general besides, had sent into the town to reconnoitre; which was a strong case, Mister Henry, seeing that Rahab, the harlot, was a taking of sides against her own people. So, I like your plan and I'll stick by it."

This being agreed upon, it became one of the amusements of the road-side to put the sergeant through his catechism, which was designed to make him familiar with the traits of private history relating to the Dove Cote and its appurtenances, that he might thereby maintain his identity, in the event of a close investigation. Horse Shoe was but an awkward scholar in this school of disguise, and gave Henry sufficient employment to keep him in the path of probability; and, indeed, the young teacher himself found it difficult to maintain an exact verisimilitude in the part which it was his own province to play in this deception.

On the evening to which we have alluded, the sergeant, finding himself within a short distance of the district of country in which he was almost certain to encounter parties of both friends and foes, adopted a greater degree of circumspection than he had hitherto deemed it necessary to observe. His purpose was to halt upon the borders of the forest, and endeavor to obtain accurate information of the state of affairs along the river, before he entered upon this dangerous ground. Like a soldier who had a rich treasure to guard, he was determined to run no hazard that might be avoided, in the safe conduct of the lady in whose service he was enlisted. In accordance with this caution, he directed the cavalcade to move onward at a moderate walk, in order that they might not reach the limit of the woodland before the dusk of the evening; and also in the hope of finding there some habitation where they might pass the night. They had not advanced far in this manner before the sergeant descried, at some distance ahead, a small log hut standing by the road side, which, by the smoke that issued from the chimney, he perceived to be inhabited. Upon this discovery, he ordered the party to stop and await his return. Then giving spurs to his horse he galloped forward, and, after a short interval of absence, returned, made a favorable report of his reconnaissance, and conducted his companions to the house.

The little cabin to which Mildred was thus introduced was the homestead of an honest Whig soldier, by the name of Wingate, who was now in service, under the command of one of the most gallant partisans that any country ever produced, Francis Marion, then recently promoted to the rank of a brigadier. The inmates were the soldier's family, consisting of a young woman and a number of small children, all demonstrating by their appearance a condition of exceedingly limited comfort. The hut contained no more than two rooms, which exhibited but a scanty supply of the meanest furniture. The forest had been cleared for the space of a few acres around the dwelling, and these were occupied by a small garden or vegetable patch, meagrely stocked with scattered and half parched plants; and by a cornfield, along the skirts of which some lean hogs were seen groping with a felonious stealthiness. A shed, in the same inclosure, formed a rendezvous for a few half-starved cattle, that probably obtained their principal but slender support from the neighboring wood. Add to these a troop of fowls, that were now at roost upon one of the trees hard by, and we have, probably, a tolerably correct inventory of the worldly goods of this little family.

The woman of the house was kind and hospitable, and her attentions were in no small degree quickened by the application of a few pieces of money which Mildred insisted upon her receiving — much to the discomfiture of the dame's self-possession — the boon consisting of hard coin, to an amount of which, perhaps, she had never before been mistress.

Mildred was exceedingly fatigued, and it was an object of early consideration to furnish her the means of rest. Our hostess, assisted by old Isaac, and officiously but awkwardly superintended by Horse Shoe, began her preparations for supper, to the abundance of which the provident sergeant was enabled to contribute some useful elements from his wallet. In one of the apartments of the hut, a shock-bed was spread for the lady, and by the assistance of her cloak and some other commodities which had been provided as part of her travelling gear, she was supplied with a couch that formed no ill exchange for the weariness of her long-inhabited saddle. Use and necessity are kind nursing-mothers to our nature, and do not often fail to endow us with the qualities proper to the fortune they shape out for us. This was not Mildred's first experience of a homely lodging since she left the Dove Cote; and, as privation and toil have a faculty to convert the rough pallet of the peasant into a bed of down, she hailed the present prospect of rest with a contented and grateful spirit.

The supper being dispatched, our lady was left alone with her hostess, to seek the repose of which she stood so much in need.

The sergeant now set about making provision for the rest of his party. This was done by erecting a shelter beneath one of the trees of the forest, opposite to the door of the cabin. It was composed of a few boughs stacked against the trunk of the tree, sufficiently covered with leaves to turn aside any rain that might happen to fall. Under this cover Horse Shoe appointed that he and his comrades should pass the night, enjoining them to keep a regular watch for the security of the lady, whose welfare was now the object of his most sedulous attention. All these preparations were made with the exactness of military rule, and with a skill that greatly delighted Henry.

The long summer twilight had faded away. Mildred had been, from an early period, in the enjoyment of a profound slumber, and Henry and his negro ally were seated at the front of their sylvan tent. The sergeant had lighted his pipe, and now, taking his seat upon a log that lay near his post, he began to smoke in good earnest, with a mind as free from anxiety as if universal peace prevailed. In the sedate enjoyment of this luxury, he fell into a descant on matters and things, interlarded with long and strange stories of his own singular adventures, which he told to the no small edification and amusement of Henry and the negro.

The habits of the experienced soldier were curiously illustrated in the thoughtful and sober foresight with which Robinson adapted his plans to the exigencies of his condition, and then in the imperturbable light-heartedness with which, after his measures of safety were taken, he waited the progress of events. His watchfulness seemed to be an instinct, engendered by a familiarity with danger, whilst the steady and mirthful tone of his mind was an attribute that never gave way to the inroads of care. He was the same composed and self-possessed being in a besieged garrison, in the moment of a threatened escalade, as amongst his cronies by a winter fire-side.

"In this here starlight, Mister Henry," he said, after he had puffed out two or three charges of his pipe, "I can't see your eyes, but by your yawning, I judge you are a little sleepy. Take my advice and turn in. A sodger ought to snatch his rest when he can get it. I'll keep guard over our young lady; the Lord protect her, for a most an elegant and oncommon precious young creature! Fling your great coat upon the leaves, and go at it, my lad, like a good fellow."

"If I was at home, Mr. Horse Shoe, at the Dove Cote, I could sit up all night listening to your stories; but I believe I am bewitched to-night, for my eyelids, this hour past, have been snapping like rat traps. So, I'll just stretch out for an hour or so, and then get up and take my turn at the guard."

"Don't trouble your head about watching," replied Horse Shoe, "you are not old enough for that yet. At your time of life, Mr. Lindsay, a good night's rest is the best part of a ration. And to-morrow, if I'm not mistaken, you will have need of all the strength you can muster to-night. As for me, it isn't much account whether I'm asleep or awake."

"Not so fast, sergeant," rejoined the youth, "I'm an older soldier than you take me for; Stephen and I have watched many a night for racoons. No, no, I'll have my turn towards morning. So, you and Isaac take the first part of the night between you, and if anything should happen, call me; I'm one of your minute men. So good night. My horse trots harder than I thought he did."

It was not long before our boasted minute man was locked

up in a spell apparently as profound as that which the legend affirms assailed the seven sleepers: and Isaac, not even waiting for the good example of his master, had already sunk upon the ground, with that facility which distinguishes his race, the most uncaring and happiest of mortals.

CHAPTER XLI

Our fortress is the good green wood,
  Our tent the cypress tree,
We know the forest round us
  As seamen know the sea.

We know its walls of thorny vines,
  Its glades of reedy grass,
Its safe and silent islands
  Within the dark morass.

BRYANT.

THE faithful Horse Shoe being thus left to himself, replenished his pipe, and, taking his rifle in his hand, paced to and fro upon the border of the road, holding communion with his own thoughts, carefully weighing the probabilities connected with his present singular expedition, and revolving, after his own fashion, the fortunes of Arthur Butler and Mildred Lindsay.

It was within an hour of midnight, when the sergeant's meditations were interrupted by the tramp of a horse approaching the hut at a gallop. But a few moments elapsed before a traveller, who, in the star-light, Horse Shoe could discern to be armed, drew up his rein immediately at the door of the dwelling, against which he struck several blows with his weapon, calling out loudly at the same time —

"Mistress Wingate — for God's sake, open your door quickly! I have news to tell you, good woman."

"In the name of mercy! who are you?" exclaimed the voice of the dame within, whilst a note of alarm was also heard from her fellow-lodger.

"What do you mean by this racket and clatter?" demanded Horse Shoe, in the midst of the uproar, at the same time laying his hand upon the stranger's bridle rein. "What brings you here, sir? — stand back; the women in that house are under my charge, and I won't have them disturbed."

"If you are a friend to Mistress Wingate," said the horseman, sternly, "speak the word; if an enemy, I will shiver your skull with the butt of my musket."

"Don't be rash, good fellow," replied Horse Shoe; "I take it you and me are on the same side. What's afoot that you stir in such a hurry?"

"The Tories are afoot — the devil's afoot! Open, Mistress Wingate — open to Dick Peyton!"

"The Lord preserve us!" ejaculated the mistress of the hovel, as she opened the door; "Bloody Spur, is it you? What ill luck brings you here to-night?"

"A gang of Tories, Mistress Wingate, from the Black River, under that cut-throat Fanning, crossed Pedee this morning at Lowder's Lake. They have been thieving and burning as far as Waggamaw, and are now on the road home by the upper ferry. They will be along here in less than half an hour. Your husband, Bob Wingate, and myself, were sent out by General Marion this morning, to reconnoitre the roads. We fell in with the ruffians, after sun-set, below Lumberton, and have tracked them up here. Bob has got a pistol-shot through his arm. He was lucky enough, however, to escape their clutches; but believing they had a spite against him, and would ride past his house to-night, he told me to call and give you warning, and to help you to drive the cattle back into the swamp."

"How many mought there be, friend?" asked Horse Shoe, calmly.

"Between two and three hundred, at least," said the trooper; "we counted fifty in the vanguard — those that followed made a long column of march. They have stolen a good many horses and cattle, all of which are with them, and several prisoners."

"What, ho! — Isaac, Henry Lindsay; fall to, and saddle, boys," shouted Horse Shoe. "Miss Mildred, it will not do to stand. I am sorry to break in upon your rest, but you must be ready to move in a few minutes."

Everything about the hut was now in confusion. Henry and the sergeant were equipping the horses, whilst Isaac was gathering up the baggage. Bloody Spur — to adopt the rider's *nom de guerre* — had dismounted, and was busy in removing the few articles of value from the hut; the mother and children, meanwhile, were pouring forth loud lamentations.

Mildred, in the midst of this scene of uproar, hurriedly made her preparations for departure; and whilst she was yet engaged in this care, a confused murmur was heard, at some distance up the road — and the rattle of sabres, as well as the hoarse voice and abrupt laughter of men, announced that the freebooters were at no great distance from the dwelling.

"Merciful heaven!" exclaimed Mildred, giving way for the first time to her fears; "they are fast approaching, and we shall be captured."

"Sister," said Henry, with scarcely less alarm, "I will die by your side, before they shall hurt a hair of your head."

Horse Shoe, who at this moment was tightening the girths of Mildred's saddle, paused for an instant to listen, and then said:

"The wind is north-east, young lady, and the voice sounds far to-night. One could hardly expect you to be cool when one of these night-frays is coming on, but there's no occasion to be frightened. Now, ma'am, if you please, I'll heave you into your seat. There," continued the sergeant, setting Mildred upon her horse, "you have got four good legs under you, and by a fair use of them will be as safe as a crowned king. Mister Henry, mount, and ride with your sister slowly down the road, till I overtake you."

Henry obeyed the order.

"Is the portmanteau and the rest of the baggage all safe, Isaac? Don't be flurried, you old sinner, but look about you, before you start off."

"All safe," replied the negro.

"Up and follow your master, then. Hark you, Mr. Bloody Spur," said Horse Shoe, as Isaac rode off, to the trooper, who was still actively employed in turning the cattle loose from the inclosure, "what is the best road hereabouts for my squad to keep out of the way of these bullies?"

"About a mile from here, take a road that strikes into the woods, upon your right hand," answered the trooper hastily, "it will lead you up the river to the falls of Pedee. If you should meet any of Marion's men, tell them what you have seen; and say Dick Peyton will be along close after you."

"Where is Marion?" asked the sergeant, mounting his horse.

"What man that knows Frank Marion could ever answer that question?" said the trooper. "He is everywhere, friend. But you have no time to lose: be off."

As Bloody Spur said this, he disappeared, driving the cattle before him; whilst the mother, laden with an infant and as many pieces of furniture as she could carry, and followed by her terrified children, fled towards the neighboring thicket.

Horse Shoe in a few moments overtook his companions, and, urging them forward at a rapid flight, soon reached the diverging road, along which they journeyed with unabated speed for upwards of a mile.

"How do you bear it, sister?" asked Henry, with concern.

"Ah, brother, with a sore heart to be made so painfully acquainted with these frightful scenes. I lose all thought of my own annoyance, in seeing the calamities that are heaped upon the unoffending family of a man who dares to draw his sword for his country."

"Yes, ma'am," said Horse Shoe, gravely, "these incarnivorous devils have broken the rest of many a good woman in the Carolinas, before they routed you out to-night, ma'am. But it is one of God's marcies to see how you keep up under it."

"Mine's a trifling grievance, good sergeant: I lose but a little repose: that poor mother flies to save her children, uncertain, perhaps, of to-morrow's subsistence; and her husband's life is in daily peril. It is a sad lot. Yet truly," added Mildred with a sigh, "mine is scarcely better. Gracious heaven!" she exclaimed, looking behind her, "they have set fire to the dwelling!"

In the quarter to which she directed her eyes, the horizon was already illuminated with the blaze of Wingate's hut. The light grew brighter for a short interval, and brought into bold relief upon the sky, the tall, dark forms of the stately pines of which the forest was composed.

"They are fools as well as villains," said Horse Shoe, with an angry vehemence; "they have had liquor to-night, or they would hardly kindle up a blaze which should rouse every Whig on Pedee to track them like hounds. It would be sport worth riding to look at, if Marion should get a glimpse of that fire. But these wolves have grown obstropolous ever since Horatio Gates made his fox-paw at Camden."

"Oh, it is a most savage war," said Mildred, "that roots up the humble hearth, and fires the lowly roof, where none but defenceless women and children abide. I shudder to think of such wanton barbarity."

"There's the thing, Miss Lindsay, that turns all our blood bitter. Man to man is fair game, all the world over: but this ere stealing of cattle, and burning of houses, and even cutting up by the roots the plants of the 'arth, and turning of women and children naked into the swamps, in the dead of night! it's a sorry business to tell of a Christian people, and a cowardly business for a nation that's a boasting of its bravery."

The light of the conflagration had soon died away, and our wanderers pursued their solitary road in darkness, ignorant of the country through which they passed, and uncertain of the point to which they tended. A full hour had gone by in this state of suspense, and Robinson had once more resolved to make a halt, and encamp his party in the wood. Before, however, he could put his design into execution, he was unexpectedly challenged, from the road-side, with the military demand of — "Who goes there?"

"Travellers," was the reply.

"Where do you come from, and where are you going?"

"The first question I can answer," said Horse Shoe, "and that is, from Old Virginny, a fortnight ago, but, to-night, from a tolerable snug lodging, where some onmannerly fellows troubled our sleep. But as to where we're going, it's more likely you can tell that for us."

"You are saucy, sir."

"It's more than I meant to be," replied the sergeant. "May-hap you mought have hearn of a man they call Bloody Spur?"

"He has pricked your pillows for you — has he? Dick Peyton is good at that," said a second questioner.

"Aha, comrades, I understand you now," said Horse Shoe, with alacrity. "Dick Peyton and Bob Wingate both belong to your party. Am I right? We are friends to Marion."

"And therefore friends to us," said the patrole. "Your name, sir, and the number you have in company?"

"Take us to the general, and we will answer that," replied Horse Shoe. "The Tories have set upon Wingate's house and burnt it to the ground. It's like we may be able to tell something worth hearing at head-quarters. Your man Bloody Spur gave us in charge to report him, and to say that he would soon follow upon our track. I wonder that he isn't here before now."

"I will remain," said one of the soldiers to his companion; "you shall take charge of the travellers."

The trooper accordingly turned his horse's head and commanded Horse Shoe and his party to follow.

The scout conducted our adventurers along a by-road that led round the head of a marsh, and through several thickets which, in the darkness of the night, were penetrated with great difficulty; during this ride he interrogated Horse Shoe as to the events of the late inroad of the Tories. He and his comrade had been stationed upon the path where the sergeant encountered them, to direct the out-riding parties of his corps to the spot of Marion's encampment, the policy of this wary officer being to shift his station so frequently as almost equally to defy the search of friend and foe. Peyton and Wingate were both expected; and the trooper who remained behind only waited to conduct them to the commanding officer, who had, since the disappearance of daylight, formed a bivouac in this neighborhood. Marion's custom was to order his reconnoitring parties to return to him by designated roads, where videttes were directed to repair in order to inform them of his position, — a fact which, as his movements were accomplished with wonderful celerity and secresy, they were generally unable to ascertain in any other way.

At length, emerging from the thicket, and crossing what seemed, by the plash of the horse's feet, a morass, the party, under the guidance of the scout, came upon a piece of thinly-timbered woodland, which, rising by a gentle slope, furnished what might be called an island of dry ground, that seemed to be only accessible by crossing the circumjacent swamp. Upon this spot were encamped, in the rudest form of the bivouac, a party of cavalry, which might have amounted to two hundred men. Several fires, whose ruddy glare had been discerned for the last half mile of the journey, were blazing forth from different quarters of the wood, and threw a bold and sharp light upon the figures of men and horses, imparting a feature of lively, picturesque beauty to the scene. The greater portion of the soldiers were stretched beneath the trees, with no other covering than the leafy bowers above them. The horses were picketed in the neighborhood of their riders; and the confused array of saddles, sabres, muskets, rifles, and other warlike instruments, that were hung upon projecting boughs, or leant against the trunks, as they caught the flashes of the frequent fires, seemed to be magnified in number equal to the furniture of thrice the force. Sentinels were seen pacing their limits on the outskirts of this company, and small bodies of patroles on horseback moved across the encampment with the regularity of military discipline. Here and there, as if regardless of rest, or awaiting some soon-expected tour of duty, small knots of men sat together amusing themselves, by torchlight, at cards; and, more appropriately, others had extended their torpid frames in sleep upon their grassy pallets and knapsack pillows.

"We have seen war in its horrors," exclaimed Mildred, with an involuntary vivacity; "and here it is in all its romance!"

"Sister, I wish you were at home," said Henry, eagerly, "and Steve and I had the Rangers on this field to-night. I would undertake to command a picket with any man here!"

To Horse Shoe these were familiar scenes, and he could not comprehend the source of that sudden interest which had so vividly aroused the admiration of his companions; but asking the guide to conduct them immediately to General Marion, he followed the soldier across the whole extent of the bivouac, until they halted beneath a large tree, near which a few officers were assembled. One of this group was seated on the ground; and close by him, planted in the soil, a blazing pine-faggot flung a broad light upon a saddle, the flap of which the officer had converted, for the occasion, into a writing-desk.

"Make way for a squad of travellers picked up on the road to-night," said the scout in a loud voice. "They wish to see General Marion."

In a moment our party was surrounded by the officers; and Horse Shoe, unceremoniously dismounting, addressed the person nearest to him: —

"A lady, sir, from Virginia, that I started with from her father's house, to fetch to Carolina; but who has been most audaciously unhoused and unbedded in the very middle of the night by a hellish pack of Tories."

"My name is Lindsay, sir," said Henry, riding to the front; "my sister and myself were travelling south, and have been obliged to fly, to-night, before a detachment of horse-stealers."

"From Bob Wingate's," said Horse Shoe, "as I should judge, some six miles back. I want to report to General Marion: the lady, likewise, is tired, as she has good right to be."

The officer to whom this was addressed, directed a soldier to seek General Marion, and then approaching Mildred said:

"Madam, we can promise little accommodation suitable to a lady: the greenwood tree is but an uncouth resting-place: but what we can supply shall be heartily at your service."

"I feel sufficiently thankful," replied Mildred, "to know that I am in the hands of friends."

"Sister, alight," said Henry, who now stood beside her stirrup, and offered his hand: and in a moment Mildred was on her feet.

The officer then conducted her to a bank, upon which a few blankets were thrown by some of the soldiers in attendance. "If this strange place does not alarm you," he said, "you may perhaps find needful repose upon a couch even as rough as this."

"You are very kind," replied Mildred, seating herself. "Brother, do not quit my side," she added, in a low voice: "I feel foolishly afraid."

But a few moments elapsed before the light of the torches, gleaming upon his figure, disclosed to Mildred the approach of a person of short stature and delicate frame, in whose step there was a singular alertness and rapidity. He wore the blue and buff uniform of the staff, with a pair of epaulets, a buckskin belt, and broadsword. A three-cornered cocked-hat, ornamented with a buck-tail, gave a peculiar sharpness to his naturally sharp and decided features; and a pair of small, dark eyes twinkled in the firelight, from a countenance originally sallow, but now swarthy from sun and wind. There was a conspicuous alacrity and courtesy in the gay and chivalrous tone in which he accosted Mildred:

"General Marion, madam, is too happy to have his poor camp honored by the visit of a lady. They tell me that the Tories were so uncivil as to break in upon your slumbers to-night. It adds greatly to my grudge against them."

"I have ventured," said Mildred, "into the field of war, and it does not become me to complain that I have met its vicissitudes."

"Gallantly spoken, madam! May I be allowed to know to whom I am indebted for the honor of this visit?"

"My name is Lindsay, my father resides at the Dove Cote in Virginia: under the protection of my brother and a friend, I left home to travel into Carolina."

"A long journey, madam," interrupted Marion; "and you have been sadly vexed to-night, I learn. We have a rude and unquiet country."

"My sister and myself," said Henry, "counted the chances before we set out."

"I would call you but an inexperienced guide, sir," said the General, addressing Henry, and smiling.

"Oh, as to that," replied the youth, "we have an old soldier with us — Horse Shoe Robinson — hem — Stephen Foster, I meant to say."

"Horse Shoe Robinson!" exclaimed Marion, "where is he?"

"Mr. Henry Lindsay, General, and me," said the sergeant,

bluntly, " have been practising a lie to tell the Tories, in case they should take us unawares; but it sticks, you see, in both of our throats. It's the true fact that I'm Horse Shoe himself. This calling me Stephen Foster is only a hanging out of false colors for the benefit of the red-coats and Tories, upon occasion."

" Horse Shoe, good fellow, your hand," said Marion, with vivacity, " I have heard of you before. Miss Lindsay, excuse me, if you please; I have business to-night which is apt impertinently to thrust itself between us and our duty to the ladies. Richards," he continued, addressing a young officer who stood near him, " see if you can find some refreshment that would be acceptable to the lady and her brother. Horse Shoe, this way: I would speak with you."

Marion now retired towards the place where the writing materials were first noticed, and entered into an examination of the sergeant, as to the particulars of the recent attack upon Wingate's cabin.

Before Robinson had finished his narrative of the events of the night, a horseman dashed up almost at full speed to the spot where Marion stood, and, flinging himself from his saddle, whilst his horse stood panting beside him, asked for the General.

" How now, Bloody Spur! What's the news? " demanded Marion.

" The Black River hawks are flying," said the soldier.

" I have heard that already," interrupted the chieftain. " Tell me what else."

" I stayed long enough to secure Wingate's cattle, and then set out for the river to cut loose the boats at the Ferry. I did it in good time. Four files followed close upon my heels, who had been sent ahead to make sure of the means of crossing. The fellows found me after my work was done, and chased me good three miles. They will hardly venture, General, to swim the river to-night, with all the thievery they have in their hands; and I rather take it they will halt at the ferry till daylight."

" Then that's a lucky cast, Dick Peyton," exclaimed Marion. " Ho, there! Peters, wake up that snoring trumpeter. Tell him to sound 'to saddle.' Come lads, up, up. Gentlemen, to your duties! "

Forthwith the trumpet sounded, and with its notes everything asleep started erect. Troopers were seen hurrying across the ground in rapid motion: some hastily buckling on broadswords and slinging their muskets; others equipping the horses; and everywhere torches were seen passing to and fro in all the agitation of a sudden muster. As soon as Marion had set this mass in action, he repaired to Mildred, and in a manner that betokened no excitement from the general stir around him, he said —

"I owe you an apology, Miss Lindsay, for this desertion, which I am sure you will excuse when you know that it is caused by my desire to punish the varlets who were so ill-mannered as to intrude upon your slumbers. I hope, however, you will not be a loser by the withdrawal of our people, as I will take measures to put you under the protection of a good friend of mine, the widow of a worthy soldier, Mistress Rachel Markham, who lives but two miles from this, and whose hospitable mansion will afford you a shelter more congenial to your wishes than this broad canopy of ours. A guide shall be ready to conduct you."

"Your kindness, general," said Mildred, "puts me under many obligations."

"Horse Shoe shall take a line of explanation to my friend," added Marion. "And now, madam, farewell," he said, offering his hand. "And you, Master or Mister Henry, I don't know which — you seem entitled to both — good night, my brave lad: I hope, before long, to hear of your figuring as a gallant soldier of independence."

"I hope as much myself," replied Henry.

Marion withdrew, and by the time that he had prepared the letter and put it into Horse Shoe's hands, his troops were in line, waiting their order to march. The general mounted a spirited charger, and galloping to the front of his men, wheeled them into column, and, by a rapid movement, soon left Horse Shoe and his little party, attended by one trooper who had been left as a guide, the only tenants of this lately so busy scene. The change seemed almost like enchantment. The fires and many torches were yet burning, but all was still, except the distant murmur of the receding troops, which grew less and less, until, at last, there reigned the silence of the native forest.

Our travellers waited, almost without exchanging a word, absorbed in the contemplation of an incident so novel to Mildred and her brother, until the distant tramp of the cavalry could be no longer heard: then, under the direction of the guide, they set out for the residence of Mrs. Markham.

CHAPTER XLII

THE day had just begun to dawn as our party, under the guidance of Marion's soldier, were ferried across the Pedee, on the opposite bank of which river lay the estate and mansion of Mrs. Markham. The alarms and excitements of the past night had ceased to stimulate the frame of Mildred, and she now found herself sinking under the most painful weariness. Henry had actually fallen asleep as he sat upon the gunwale of the ferry-boat, and rested his head against the sergeant's shoulder: the whole party were overcome with the lassitude that is so distressing, at this hour of dawning, to all persons who have spent the night in watching; and even the sergeant himself, to the influences of fatigue and privation the most inaccessible of mortals, and, by fate or fortune, the most unmalleable — occasionally nodded his head, as if answering the calls of man's most welcome visitor. It was, therefore, with more than ordinary contentment that our travellers, when again mounted, were enabled to descry, in the first light of the morning, a group of buildings seated upon an eminence about a mile distant, on the further side of the cultivated lowland that stretched along the southern margin of the river. The guide announced that this was the point of their destination, and the intelligence encouraged the party to accelerate the speed with which they journeyed over the plain. When they arrived at the foot of the hill, the character of the spot they were approaching was more distinctly developed to their view. The mansion, encompassed by a tuft of trees that flung their broad and ancient limbs above its roof, was of the best class of private dwellings, old and stately in its aspect, and exhibiting all the appendages that characterized the seat of a wealthy proprietor. It was constructed entirely of wood, in accordance with a notion that prevailed at that period, no less than at the present, that a frame structure was best adapted to the character of the climate. It occupied the crest of a hill which commanded a view of the river with its extensive plains; whilst, in turn, it was overlooked by the adjacent tract of country bearing the name of the Cheraw Highlands.

As the party ascended this eminence, Henry, in the eager and thoughtless satisfaction of the moment, put his bugle to his mouth and continued to blow with all his might, deaf to the remonstrances of his sister, who was endeavoring to explain that there was some want of courtesy in so abrupt a challenge of the hospitality of the family. The blast was interrupted by Horse Shoe's laying his hand upon the instrument, as he gave the indiscreet bugler a short military lecture:

"You might fetch trouble upon us, Mister Henry: this here screeching of horns or trumpets is sometimes a sort of bullying of a garrison; and if an enemy should happen to be on post here — as, God knows, is likely enough in such scampering wars as these, why you have set the thing past cure: for it is cutting off all chance of escape, just as much as if the people had been ordered 'to horse.' It leaves nothing for us but to brazen it out."

An old negro was first startled by the summons, and appeared for a moment at the door of one of the out-buildings, evincing, as he looked down the road upon the approaching cavalcade, manifest signs of consternation. After a brief glance, he was seen to retreat across the yard so the door of the mansion-house, where he fell to beating at it with as much earnestness as if giving an alarm of fire, shouting at the same time, "Lord bless us, mistress! here is a whole rigiment of sodgers coming to turn everything topsy-turvy. Get up, get up — open the door!"

"Stop your bawling, you stunted black-jack!" said Robinson, who had galloped up to the spot, "and none of your lies. Is the lady of the house at home?"

A window was thrown up, at the same moment, in an upper story, and a female head, decorated with a nightcap, was thrust out, whilst a voice, tremulous with affright, inquired what was the cause of this disturbance; but before an answer could be given the head was withdrawn, and the door opening discovered a youth scarcely in appearance over sixteen, with a loose robe thrown around his person and a pistol in his hand.

"Who comes here, and with what purpose?" was the question firmly put by the young man.

"Friends," said Horse Shoe — "sent to the good lady by General Marion. Sorry, sir, to be the occasion of such a rumpus. But this here young lady has travelled all night and is 'most dead with hardships."

Mildred, who with the rest of the company had now arrived near the door, was about to speak, when the questioner retired, calling the negro after him into the house. In a moment the servant returned with Mrs. Markham's compliments to the party, and a request that they would alight.

"Then all's well," said Horse Shoe, dismounting, and immediately afterwards lifting Mildred from her saddle, "a friend in need, madam, is the greatest of God's blessings. I make no doubt you will find this as snug a nest as you ever flew into in your life."

"And, good sergeant, most specially welcome," replied Mildred, smiling in the midst of all her pain, "for in truth I never was so weary."

The guide, having now performed his duty, announced that he must return to his corps; and, after a few cheering words of kind remembrance from Mildred, coupled with a message of thanks to Marion, he wheeled about and galloped back towards the river. Mildred and Henry entered the house: and the sergeant, taking command of Isaac, followed the horses towards the stable.

The brother and sister were ushered into an ample parlor, comfortably furnished according to the fashion of the wealthier classes of that day; and, Mildred as she threw herself upon a capacious sofa, could not fail to recognize in the formal portraits that were suspended to the pannelled walls, that she was in the dwelling of a family of some pride of name and lineage.

After a short interval, the proprietress of the mansion entered the parlor. She was a lady of a kind and gentle aspect, apparently advanced beyond the middle period of life; and her features, somewhat emaciated, gave a sign of feeble health. She was attired in dishabille, hastily thrown on; and there was some expression of alarm in the unreserved and familiar manner with which she approached Mildred, and inquired into the nature of this early journey.

"I hope no unhappy accident, my dear, has driven you at this unusual hour to my poor house? You are heartily welcome. I fear to ask what has brought you."

"My brother and myself, madam," said Mildred, "have had a most adventurous night. This letter will explain. General Marion was so kind as to commit us to your hospitality."

The lady took the letter and read it.

"Miss Lindsay, my child, I am truly happy to serve you. You have had an awful night, but these times make us acquainted with strange afflictions. This young gentleman, your brother, is he your only attendant?"

Mildred began to communicate the details of her journey, when she was interrupted by her hostess.

"I will not trouble you with questions, now, my dear. You must have sleep; I dread lest your health may suffer by this harsh exposure. After you have had rest, we will talk more, and become better acquainted. Judith," continued the matron, addressing a servant maid, who had just entered the room, "attend this lady to a chamber. Mr. Henry Lindsay, I believe — so General Marion calls you — my son Alfred shall take you in charge."

With these words the good lady left the room, and in an instant after returned with the youth who had first appeared at the door. Upon being introduced by his mother to the guests, he lost no time in obeying her orders in regard to Henry, whom he had conducted out of the room at the same moment that Mildred followed the servant towards a chamber.

The entire day was spent by our party in recruiting their strength, towards which needful care the hospitable hostess contributed by the tenderest attentions. On the following morning Mildred, although refreshed by the slumbers of the long interval, still exhibited the traces of her recent fatigue; and upon the earnest recommendation of Mrs. Markham, seconded by the almost oracular authority of Horse Shoe, — for the sergeant had greatly won upon the respect of his companions by his prudence and discretion — she determined to remain another day in her present resting-place.

Mrs. Markham was the widow of a Carolina gentleman, who had borne the rank of a colonel in the Whig militia, and had been actively employed, in the earlier stages of the war, in the southern provinces. He had fallen in an unfortunate skirmish with some of Prevost's light troops, on the Savannah river, some sixteen months before; and his widow, with three daughters and no other male protector than an only son, was now, in this season of extreme peril, residing upon a large estate, which the evil fortune of the times had made the theatre of an eventful and active desultory war. She had been exposed to the most cruel exactions from the Tories, to whom her possessions were generally yielded up with a passive and helpless submission; and the firmness with which, in all her difficulties, she had adhered to the cause for which her husband fell, had gained for her the generous sympathy of the whig leaders, and more than once stimulated them to enterprises, in her behalf, that were followed by severe chastisement upon her enemies. These circumstances had given extensive notoriety to her name, and drawn largely upon her the observation of both friend and foe. To Marion, who hovered upon this border more like a goblin than a champion whose footsteps might be tracked, her protection had become a subject of peculiar interest; and the indefatigable soldier frequently started up in her neighborhood when danger was at hand, with a mysterious form of opposition that equally defied the calculations of Whigs and Tories.

The lady was still in her weeds, and grief and care had thrown a pallor upon her cheek; but the watchfulness imposed upon her by the emergencies of the day, her familiarity with alarms, and the necessity for constant foresight and decisive action, had infused a certain hardihood into her character, that is seldom believed to be, — but yet in the hour of trial unerringly exhibits itself — an attribute of the female bosom. Her manners were considerate, kind, and fraught with dignity. She was the personation of a class of matrons that — for the honor of our country and of the human race — was not small in its numbers, nor upon trial unworthy of its fame, in the sad history of the sufferings of Carolina.

The evening of the day on which Mildred arrived at the mansion brought rumors of a brilliant exploit achieved by Marion; and more circumstantial accounts on the following morning confirmed the good tidings. The alert partisan had fallen upon the track of the freebooters who had been marauding on the confines of North Carolina, and whose incursion had expelled our travellers from Wingate's cabin. Marion had overtaken them before sunrise, on the bank of the Pedee, where they had been detained by reason of Peyton's successful removal of the boats. A short but most decisive combat was the consequence, and victory, as she was wont, had seated herself upon Marion's banner. The chieftain and his followers had, as usual, disappeared, and the whole country was in a state of agitation and dread; the one side fearing a repetition of the blow in some unlooked-for quarter, the other alarmed by the expectation of quick and bloody reprisal.

These events still more contributed to fortify Mildred's resolution to remain another day under the shelter of Mrs. Markham's friendly roof, before she would venture forth in the further prosecution of her journey.

Here, for the present, we must leave her.

CHAPTER XLIII

OCCURRENCES AT MUSGROVE'S MILL

She passed by stealth the narrow door,
The postern way also,
And thought each bush her robe that tore,
The grasp of a warding foe.

JOANNA BAILLIE.

THE month of September was more than half gone. The night had just set in, and the waxing moon shone forth from a clear heaven, flinging her rays upon the rippling surface of the Ennoree and upon the glossy leaves that flickered in the wind by the banks of the stream, when Mary Musgrove, with wary and stealthy pace, glided along the path, intricate with shrubbery, that led upwards immediately upon the margin of the river. For a full half hour had she toiled along this narrow way since she had stolen past the sentinel near her father's gate. The distance was not a mile; but the anxious maiden, pursued by her own fears, had more than once, in the fancy that she was followed, stopped in her career and concealed herself in the thick copse-wood, and listened with painful intensity for the footsteps of those whom her imagination had set upon her track. There was, however, no pursuit: it was the prowling fox or the raccoon whose leap had disturbed the dry and rotten branches that lay upon the ground; and Mary smiled with faint-heartedness at the illusions of her own mind. She arrived at last beneath the brow of a crag that jutted over the stream, and in the shade of one of the angles of the rock, she discerned the figure of a man seated upon the grass. She paused with a distrustful caution, as she challenged the silent and half-concealed person.

"Hist, John! is it you? For mercy, speak! Why would you frighten me?—Me, Mary. Don't you know me?" said the maiden, as she took heart of grace and advanced near enough to put her hand upon John Ramsay's shoulder. "Powers above! the man's asleep," she added with a laugh. "Who would have thought I should have caught you napping, John, at such a time as this!"

"Why, in truth, Mary," said John Ramsay, waking up under the touch of his mistress, and rising to his feet, "I deserve to be shot for sleeping on my watch; but I have been so driven from post to pillar for this last fortnight, that it is as much as I can do to keep my eyes open when night comes on. So, Mary, you will forgive me, and more particularly when I tell you I was dreaming of you; and thought this war was at an end, and that you and I were happy in a house of our own. I have been waiting for you for upwards of an hour."

"Ah, John, I don't think I could sleep if it had been my turn to watch for you."

"There's the difference," replied John, "betwixt you women and us men; you are so full of frights and fidgetings and fancyings, that I do verily believe all the sleeping doses in the world could never make you shut your eyes when anything is going on that requires watching, whether it be for a sick friend or for a piece of scheming. Now, with us, we take a nap on a hard-trotting horse, and fall to snoring up to the very minute that the trumpet wakes us to make a charge. What news from Butler?"

"It is all fixed," answered Mary, "to our hearts' content. Lieutenant Macdonald, ever since Cornwallis's letter, allows Major Butler greater privileges; and the sentinels are not half so strict as they used to be; so that I think we may give them the slip. By the gable window that looks out from the garret room, the Major will be able to get upon the roof, and that, he thinks, is near enough to the tree for him to risk a leap into its branches; though I am almost afraid he is mistaken, for it looks awfully wide for a spring. He says if you will be ready with the horses an hour before day-light to-morrow, he will try the leap, and join you at the willows above the mill. Christopher will saddle one of the wagon-horses and lead him to the place."

"And the sentinel who keeps guard on that side?"

"Ah, John, that puzzles us," said Mary; "I'm so much afraid that you will be rash. It is in your nature to forget yourself."

"Tut, girl; don't talk of that. I'll find a way to manage the sentinel. I will steal up to him and take him unawares; and then seizing him by the throat, give him his choice of a knife in between his ribs, or a handful of guineas in his pocket."

"Hadn't we better tell him what a good man the Major is?" said Mary, alarmed at the idea of a struggle in which her lover's life might be endangered, " and try to coax him to take our side? "

" Ha, ha! " ejaculated the trooper involuntarily, " that's a very good woman's thought, but it won't hold out in a campaign. The fellow might happen to have some honesty, and then away goes our whole scheme. No, no; blows are the coin that these rascals buy their bread with, and, faith, we'll trade with them in the same article."

" But then, John, you will be in danger."

" What of that, girl? When have I been out of danger? And don't you see, Mary, what good luck I have with it? Never fear me; I will stifle the fellow in the genteelest fashion known in the wars."

" And if it must be so, John, I will say my prayers for you with more earnestness than I ever said them in my life. As my father says, the God of Israel will stand by our cause: and when He is for us, what care we who is against us? "

" You are a good girl, Mary," replied John Ramsay, smiling. " Get back to the house; let Major Butler know that you have seen me, and that I will be ready."

" He is to be at the window," said Mary, " and I am to signify to him that you are prepared, by setting up a plank against the garden fence in a place where he can see it. He is to keep a look-out from the window all night, and when the time comes you are to flash a little powder on the edge of the woods upon the hill: if he is ready then he will show his candle near the window-sill; that, he says, must be a sign for you to come on; and when he sees you he will take the leap."

" I understand it," said Ramsay. " Tell Christopher to be sure of the horse."

" I have a great deal of courage, John, when danger is far off — but when it comes near, I tremble like a poor coward," said Mary. " Does not my hand feel cold? "

" Your lips are warm, Mary," replied John, kissing her, " and your heart is warm. Now, never flag when it comes to the trial. Everything depends upon you. We shall be very happy, by-and-by, to talk this thing all over. How many soldiers are on Macdonald's guard? Have none left you since I saw you yesterday? "

" None," said Mary: " one man left the mill two days since. I think I heard them say he was going to Ninety-six, on business for the lieutenant."

" Well, well, it makes but little odds how many are there, so they but sleep soundly. Our business is more to run than to fight. Mary, my girl, step across to my father's to-morrow, and he will tell you what has become of me. We must get the Major out of this country of wolf-traps as fast as we can."

"I forgot to ask you," said the maiden, "if you had some coarse clothes ready for the Major. He must not seem to be what he is."

"Trust me for that," replied the trooper. "Christopher has given me a bundle with as fine a dusty suit in it as any miller's boy ever wore; and besides that, I have a meal bag to throw across the Major's saddle: and as for myself, Mary, there's ploughman in my very looks. We shall cheat all the Tories betwixt this and Catawba."

"Now, John, before I leave you, I have one favor to ask."

"And what is that?" inquired the generous-hearted soldier, "you know, if I can, I will grant it before it is named."

"I would ask as a favor to me," said Mary, with earnestness, "that you will not be too venturesome: the Major is a wiser man than you, so be governed by him. Remember, John, if any ill were to happen to you, it would break my heart."

"I am not so foolhardy, my girl," replied Ramsay, "but, that when there's occasion for it, I can show as clean a pair of heels as any man: and so, for your sake, you kitten," he said, as he put his hands upon her cheeks, and again snatched a kiss, "I will run to-morrow like a whole troop of devils. And now, Mary, good night, and God bless you, girl! it is time you were at home. Yet upon second thoughts, I will walk part of the way with you. So, take my arm and let us begin the retreat."

"John, I do so fear you may be hurt," said the maiden, as they pursued their way along the path, her whole thoughts being absorbed with the danger of the enterprise. "Be careful when you come near the sentinel to wait until his back is turned. This moon shines bright, and you may easily be seen."

"But look, girl, the moon has scarcely two hours yet to travel, and, from that circle round it, I shouldn't wonder if we had rain before day-light; so by the hour we have fixed for the Major's escape, it will be dark enough: therefore you may be easy on that score."

The humble and ardent lovers pursued their way towards the miller's dwelling with slow steps, intently engaged in conversing over the chances of their perilous project, until they arrived at a point beyond which it was not safe for John Ramsay to venture.

Here, after many affectionate caresses and fond adieus, they separated — the maiden to steal to her place of rest, the soldier to hasten back to his horse, that awaited him near the scene of the late meeting.

Mary soon arrived at the mill; then sauntering carelessly towards the dwelling-house, began, the better to conceal her purpose, to sing a simple air, during which she had wandered up to the garden fence, where she delayed long enough to set up the plank. The small window in the angle of the roof of the cottage looked down upon the spot where she stood; and as she cast her eyes towards this part of the building, she received a recognition from the prisoner, in a slight waving of the hand, which was sufficiently observable by the light of the taper within.

Matters having gone so far to the maiden's satisfaction, she now retreated into the house.

The reader will perceive from this narrative that Butler's fortunes had greatly improved since we last took leave of him. The messenger despatched to Cornwallis by Williams had brought back to the Fair Forest, where it will be remembered the vanquishers of Innis had retreated, a more favorable answer than even the republican leader had hoped. The British commander was not ignorant of the capture of Butler, but the circumstances of the trial had not before been communicated to him. Upon the representation of Williams, he had no hesitation to order a respite to be given to the prisoner for such reasonable time as might be necessary for further investigation. This obvious act of justice was more than, in the circumstances of the times, might have been expected from Cornwallis. The cruel and bloody policy which he adopted towards the inhabitants of the Carolinas, immediately after the battle of Camden, showed a tone of personal exacerbation that was scarcely consistent with the lenity displayed towards Butler. It is not unlikely, therefore, that the fear of retaliation upon the young St. Jermyn, of whose fate he might have been informed from officers of his own camp, might have induced him to temporize in the present case, and to grant a suspension of proceedings against the rebel prisoner. The reply to Williams's letter accordingly intimated that, for the present, Major Butler should be held in close custody as a prisoner of war, leaving the determination of the manner in which he was finally to be disposed of, a subject for future consideration.

John Ramsay, after the departure of Horse Shoe Robinson for Virginia, instead of rejoining his regiment, returned to the Fair

Forest camp, where he remained with Williams, until the answer from Cornwallis was received. The tidings of this answer he undertook to convey to Butler, and he again set out for his father's house. John felt himself now regularly enlisted in the service of the prisoner, and having found means to communicate his present employment to General Sumpter, he obtained permission to remain in it as long as his assistance was of value. The service itself was a grateful one to the young trooper: it accorded with the generosity of his character, and gratified his personal pride by the trust-worthiness which it implied: but more than this, it brought him into opportunities of frequent meeting with Mary Musgrove, who, passionately beloved by the soldier, was not less ardent than he in her efforts to promote the interest of Butler.

The state of the country did not allow John to be seen in day-time, and he and Mary had consequently appointed a place of meeting, where in the shades of night they might commune together on the important subjects of their secret conspiracy. Night after night they accordingly met at this spot, and here all their schemes were contrived. Mary sometimes came to David Ramsay's dwelling, and the old man's counsel was added to that of the lovers. Christopher Shaw and Allen Musgrove were not ignorant of what was in contemplation, but it was a piece of necessary policy that they should appear to be as little connected with the prisoner as possible. Christopher, therefore, pursued his duties as assistant-quarter-master or purveyor to the little garrison under Macdonald's command, with unabated assiduity.

The plan of Butler's escape was John Ramsay's. He had been anxiously awaiting an opportunity to attempt this enterprise for the last fortnight, but the difficulty of concerting operations with the prisoner had retarded his movement. This difficulty was at last overcome, and, for a few days past, the plan had been arranged. All that was left to be done was to appoint the hour. Christopher Shaw and Mary, alone of the miller's family, were made acquainted with the details. Christopher was to provide a horse and a suitable disguise for Butler, and these were to be ready at a tuft of willows that grew upon the edge of the river some quarter of a mile above the mill, whenever Mary should announce that John was ready to act. Ramsay's horse was to be brought to the same spot. The preparatory signals, already mentioned, were all agreed upon and understood by the parties. Butler was to escape to the roof, and thence by the boughs of a large oak that grew hard by the miller's dwelling. A sentinel was usually posted some fifty paces from this tree, and it was a matter of great perplexity to determine how his vigilance was to be defeated. This difficulty, John resolved, should be overcome by a stern measure: the man was to be silenced, if necessary, by a blow. John Ramsay was to steal upon him in the dark, and if signs of alarm were given, he was to master the sentinel in such a manner as the occasion might require, being furnished by Butler with a purse of gold, if such a form of influence might be necessary.

Such is the outline of the plan by which Butler's disenthralment was to be attempted.

Mary Musgrove, before she retired to her chamber, sought Chrisopher Shaw and made him acquainted with the appointment of the hour, and then left him to manage his own share of the enterprise. It was now near ten at night, and Christopher, who had charge of Allen Musgrove's stable, in order to avoid the suspicion of being seen stirring at a later hour, immediately set off to saddle the horse. One of the wagon team, well known in the family by the name of Wall Eye, was selected for this service, and being speedily accoutred, was conducted to the willows, where he was tied fast to a tree, to remain until the hour of need. The young miller soon returned, and it was not long afterwards that the household and its military companions were wrapt in the silence of unsuspecting repose.

Butler, at the hour of the customary visit of the watch, had gone to bed; and, feigning sickness, had been allowed to burn a light in his room during the night. His chamber door, also, by special favor, was closed; and the night advanced without suspicion or distrust from any quarter. At two o'clock the last sentinels were relieved, and the form had been gone through of inspecting the prisoner's chamber. To all outward show, Butler was asleep: the door was again shut, and all was still. The time for action now arrived. Butler rose silently from his bed, dressed himself, and, putting his shoes into his pockets, stole in his stockinged feet to the little gable window at the further end of his apartment. Here he remained, gazing out upon the night with fixed attention. The moon had set, and the sky was overcast with clouds, adding a fortunate obscurity to the natural darkness of the hour. By still greater good luck, after a few moments the wind began to rise and rain to descend. Everything seemed to favor the enterprise. The shadowy form of the sentinel, who was stationed on this side of the house, was dimly discerned by Butler through the gloom; and it was with joyful satisfaction that he could perceive the soldier, as the rain fell in larger drops, retreat some distance from his post and take shelter beneath the shrubbery that grew in the garden. At the same moment a flash upon the hill, which might have been mistaken for summer lightning, announced to him that his faithful comrade was at hand. Desirous to take advantage of the present neglect of the sentinel, and to avoid the possibility of bringing him into conflict with Ramsay, Butler hastily showed his candle at the window, then extinguished it, and throwing himself out upon the roof, scrambled towards the nearest point of the impending branches of the oak. Here, without a moment's pause, he made a fearless leap that flung him amongst the boughs. The darkness prevented him from choosing the most favorable lodgment in the tree, and he fell across a heavy limb with such force as to take away his breath — receiving, at the same time, a severe contusion in the head. For a brief space he hung almost senseless, and there was reason to apprehend that he would fall in a swoon to the ground; but the occasion braced his sinking strength, and before many minutes he revived sufficiently to make his way to the trunk, by which he descended safely to the earth. He now threw himself on his hands and feet, and crept to the garden fence. The rain still increased, and fell in a heavy shower. In another instant he surmounted the barrier, and betook himself with his utmost speed towards the mill, behind which he sought concealment and temporary rest.

"Stand," said John Ramsay, who had just reached this point on his way to the house, and now, taken by surprise, presented a pistol to Butler's breast. "One word above your breath and you die. Be silent, and here is gold for you."

"Ramsay," said Butler, in a low tone, "is it you?"

"Your name?" demanded the trooper, still presenting the pistol.

"Butler," was the reply.

"Thanks — thanks, good Major, for that word! You have been before me. I thought you would not miss this rain. Is all well?"

"Better, much better, than we could have hoped," answered Butler. "Seeing the sentinel was off his guard, I took time by the forelock, and have saved you trouble."

"For God's sake, Major, let us not delay here. Our horses are waiting for us above."

"I am ready," said Butler, having now put on his shoes. "My brave fellow, I owe you more than I can find words to utter: lead the way."

The liberated captive and his gallant comrade instantly hastened towards the horses, and mounting with a joyful alacrity, soon set forward as a gallop in the direction leading to David Ramsay's cottage. Here they arrived just as the day began to dawn.

CHAPTER XLIV

A MELANCHOLY INCIDENT

The hand of the reaper
Takes the ears that are hoary,
But the voice of the weeper
Wails manhood in glory.

SCOTT.

BRIEF time was taken by the fugitives for refreshment at David Ramsay's dwelling. Here Butler put on the disguise which Christopher Shaw had provided for him. Then arming himself with a pair of pistols which John had appropriated to his use, the trooper himself using a similar precaution, our two adventurers resumed their journey. Their first object was to gain a point, some seven or eight miles distant, in the direction of the Fair Forest, where John Ramsay had concealed a few troopers that had been furnished him by Williams, to give their aid, if necessary, in securing Butler's escape.

From this point they were to proceed, with all possible despatch, to Williams's camp. However, hazardous the experiment of attempting to traverse the country in open daylight, it was deemed still more dangerous to tarry any length of time so near the scene of their late adventure. Butler and his comrade, therefore, pushed forward with as much expedition as possible, resolved to outrun the fresh pursuit which they had reason to apprehend upon the discovery which the morning must produce at the miller's habitation.

Soon after sunrise the rain ceased to fall, the clouds dispersed, and a fresh and brilliant morning broke forth upon the heavens. The success of their late exploit had raised the spirits of the wanderers. A sense of intense delight animated Butler's feelings: a consciousness of liberty once more enjoyed, after hopes deferred and almost despairing captivity, seemed to regenerate him and make him acquainted with emotions he had never felt before. His heart was full of gratitude to his new friend Ramsay, and the expression of it was warm and sincere. Nature had never appeared so lovely to him as now: the whispers of the forest and the murmur of the clear brook fell on his enfranchised ear like the sweetest music: there was melody for him even in the screams of the jay and the harsh notes of the crow: and once when his companion had halted in sight of a buck that bounded through the wood before him, Butler, apprehensive that John was about to discharge a bullet after the forest-rover, found himself involuntarily pleading the cause of the noble animal: "Do not draw your pistol on him, Ramsay, I pray you. Let him run; it is liberty — liberty, good comrade — and that is sacred."

Before eight o'clock they had reached the rendezvous. Here they found three troopers who, although armed, were habited in the plain dress of the country, which enabled them to claim the denomination either of Whig or Tory militia, as their occasions might demand. These men had lain perdue, for some days, in the depth of the forest, impatiently awaiting for intelligence from Ramsay.

"Well, Harry Winter," said John, laughing, "what say you now? I have brought you the miller's boy at last. Have I not made my word good?"

"Truth, John," replied the trooper, "there is more stuff in you than we counted on. Macdonald must be a silly crow to let the fox steal his cheese from him so easily."

"You would have come nearer the mark, Harry, if you had called him a sleepy lout, for whilst he was nodding I took his cake off the griddle. It was fair filching by night, as the Major will tell you. But come, lads, here is no time for dallying, we mustn't have the grass growing to our horses' heels, when we have a whole pack of King George's hounds on our trail. So move, boys!" and saying these words, John led the party forward at a rapid gallop.

They had not gone far before they found themselves upon a road which led through a piece of thin wood that covered a small tract of marshy ground, the nature of which brought the party into a more compact body as they approached the narrowest point of the defile. At a short distance beyond this impediment the track became broader, where it ascended a hill thickly covered with an undergrowth of bushes.

Our friends had scarcely arrived in the narrow pass before they perceived on the hill in front of them, a company of some ten or fifteen horse, rapidly advancing towards them. In a moment all conversation was checked, and Harry Winter turning to his companions, had barely time to remark,

"I answer all questions: be silent, and if asked, swear to the truth of every word I say — steady: these fellows are Tories."

As he ceased speaking, the foremost of the strangers had already come up to them.

"Where from, and whither do you go?" asked Harry Winter, with a stern accent.

"From below Ninety-Six, and on our road to Fort Granby," replied a clownish voice.

"Peace, you knave!" interrupted one who appeared to be the leader of the party, and whose carriage and demeanor announced him to be an officer; "by what authority do you undertake to answer a challenge on the highway? Back, to your place, sir!"

The rebuked rustic hung his head, as he reined his horse back into the crowd that now thronged the road.

"As we are of the larger party," said the same person, addressing himself to Winter, "we have the right to the word. Who are you and whence come you?"

"We belong to Floyd's new draft," replied Winter with great coolness, "and left Winnsborough yesterday morning."

"And where bound?"

"To Augusta, on business with Brown."

"Ah ha!" exclaimed the officer, "Brown is pinched by the rebels. It is well you have thought of him. What have you to say to him? Do you bear despatches?"

"Your pardon, sir — that's a secret."

"You need not be afraid, good fellow, we are friends."

"I can hardly tell you the exact business," replied Winter. "You will meet Floyd himself with a hundred men, before you ride five miles. I believe we are going to reinforce the garrison."

"You will be very welcome," said the Tory officer, "Brown will give you a hearty reception, but devilish slim fare; he is surrounded with hornets."

"So much the better," replied Winter, "we have a knack at taking the sting out of the hornets, nowadays. Good morning, sir. Report us, if you please, to Colonel Floyd, when you come across him, and tell him the hour of the day when you met us."

During this short parley the two parties had become united into a common throng, completely filling up the road; and the proximity into which they were severally brought, gave rise to various inquiries after news amongst the subordinates on either side. In this press, Butler was startled to observe the eyes of an individual scanning him with a somewhat pointed scrutiny, and it was with an emotion that had well nigh betrayed him, that he recognised in this person one of Macdonald's soldiers. It was the man whom the lieutenant had despatched, a few days previous, with an errand to the post at Ninety-Six, and who was now returning with this detachment of militia. The soldier was evidently at fault, for in a moment afterwards Butler could perceive, from his expression of face, that whatever might have been his first suspicion, it was quieted by another glance. The disguise was so far effectual. But another cause of alarm arose, that for an instant brought Butler into greater jeopardy. The horse on which the messenger was mounted, was the yoke-fellow of the lean Wall-Eye, and the two beasts had been long accustomed to work side by side in the same wagon. Their mutual recognition, at this critical moment, became distressingly conspicuous. Their noses were brought in contact, and they began to whinny and paw the ground in that intelligible manner which constitutes one of the forms of expression by which this portion of the brute creation acknowledge their attachments. The presence of mind of John Ramsay saved the explosion which must soon have followed. He spurred his horse between the two noisy and restless animals, and immediately addressed a conversation to the soldier, which for the moment turned his thoughts into another channel.

By this time the conference had terminated, and the two leaders respectively directing their men to move forward, the defile was passed and each party extricated from the other. But no sooner was the separation completed than Butler's brutish steed, Wall-Eye, began to neigh with the most clamorous vociferation, whilst a response was heard in the same tones as pertinaciously reiterated from the retreating companion on the other side of the defile.

"We were in great danger from yonder Tories," said Ramsay, addressing Butler, "did you see that one of these fellows rode the mate of the beast you are on? Who could he be?"

"It was one of Macdonald's men," replied Butler, "I knew the fellow the moment we met; but, thank Heaven, this humble dress concealed me."

"Faster, Major!" cried John, "these cursed horses are calling after each other now. Pray, push forward until we get out of hearing. How unlucky that Christopher Shaw should have given you one of the wagon cattle!"

"Look back, lads!" exclaimed Winter with great earnestness, "there is something wrong, these fellows are returning. Whip and spur, or we are overtaken!"

Macdonald's soldier, it seems, having his attention drawn to the singular motions of his horse, had become suddenly confirmed in the suspicion which at the late meeting for a moment rested upon his mind, as to the identity of Butler; and having communicated his thought to the commanding officer, the whole party of the Tory militia had wheeled about to demand a further investigation: they were now some hundred paces in the rear of the fugitives, and were pressing forward at high speed, the officer in the front calling out at the same time.

"Hold! — Rein up and return! We have questions to ask. Halt, or we shall fire!"

"To it, boys!" cried Harry Winter. "Your safety is in your legs!"

And the party pricked onward as fast as they could urge their cavalry along the road. The chase continued for some half hour or more; the little escort of Butler leaving the road and plunging into the recesses of the forest. An occasional pistol-shot was fired during this retreat, but without effect on either side. The tangled character of the ground over which they passed, greatly retarded the pursuit, and before the half hour was spent none but a few of the boldest horsemen of the assailants were found persevering in the chase. Seeing their number diminished, and finding also that the horses of his own comrades were beginning to flag, John Ramsay assumed the command, and directed his party to turn about and offer battle to the pursuers. The immediate effect of this movement was to bring the assailants to a halt, which was no sooner witnessed by John, than he shouted "Charge, lads, charge, and the day is ours! Hack and hew, good fellows: down with the bloodhounds!"

This animated exhortation was followed up by a prompt onset, in which the brave trooper led the way; and such was the impetuosity of the assault that the enemy, although consisting of twice the number of those who attacked them, were forced to give ground. A sharp skirmish ensued, during which several pistol-shots were discharged on both sides, and some encounters, hand to hand, were sustained with a sturdy resolution; but, at last, our friends succeeded in turning their opponents to flight. The combat had been maintained in that pell-mell form of attack and defence, which defied compact or organized resistance; and the individuals of each party had been scattered over the wood for a considerable distance, so that when the late pursuers were compelled to retreat, each man urged his horse in such a direction as was most favorable to his escape. By degrees, Butler's few companions began to reassemble at that part of the wood where they had made their first stand.

"There is nothing like striking the first blow at the right time," said Harry Winter, as, with his hat in his hand to allow the air to cool his brow, he rode up to Butler, and halted to gain breath. "Give me a hot charge on a slow enemy, and I don't care much about two to one of odds. Thank God that business is cleanly done, and here we are all safe I hope. Where is John Ramsay?" he inquired, looking around him, and observing that their comrade was not amongst the number assembled.

"I saw him close at the heels of the runaways," said one of the men. "John has a trick of seeing a scrimmage to the end; and it is an even bet that he is now upon the trail like a fresh hound. The last I noticed of him was at the crupper of a couple of the rascals that, I'll engage, before now he has set his mark upon."

"Then we must to his assistance!" exclaimed Butler, eagerly; and without waiting for further consultation he set off at full speed, in the supposed direction of John Ramsay's pursuit. The rest followed. They had ridden some distance without being able to perceive any traces of their missing companion. Butler called aloud upon Ramsay, but there was no answer; and, for some moments, there was an anxious suspense as the party halted to listen for the sound of the footsteps of the trooper's approach. At length, a horse was seen far off in the wood, bounding over the turf at a wild and frightened pace; the saddle was empty, and the bridle-rein hung about his feet. On seeing his companions, the excited steed set up a frequent neigh, and, with head and tail erect, coursed immediately up to the group of horsemen. Here he came to a sudden halt, snorting with the terror of his late alarm. There were drops of blood upon the saddle.

"Gracious Heaven!" cried Butler, "some evil has befallen Ramsay. Scatter and search the wood."

It was with confused and melancholy earnestness that they all now continued the quest. After a painful suspense, one of the men was heard to shout to the rest that their lost comrade was found. The summons soon brought the party together. Ramsay, pale and faint, was stretched upon the grass of the forest, his bosom streaming forth a current of blood. In an instant Butler was seen stooping over him.

"Oh, this is a heavy ransom, for my deliverance!" he said

with the deepest anguish, as he raised the trooper's head and laid it on his lap, whilst the blood flowed from the wound. "Speak, dear friend, speak! Great God, I fear this blow is mortal! Some water, if it can be found — look for it, Winter; he has fainted from loss of blood."

Whilst Harry Winter went in search of the necessary refreshment, Butler tore his cravat from his neck and applied it to staunch the wound. The administration of a slight draught of water, after a short interval, sufficiently revived the disabled soldier to enable him to speak. He turned his sickly and almost quenched eye to Butler, as he said:

"I was foolish to follow so far. I have it here — here," he added in a feeble voice, as he put his hand upon his breast, "and it has done my work. I fought for you, major, because I was proud to fight for a friend; and because" — here his voice failed him, as for a moment he closed his eyes and faintly uttered — "it is all over — I am dying."

"Nay, good John," said Butler, whilst the tears ran down his cheeks; "it is not so bad as that — you are weak from bleeding — you will be better presently. Oh God! oh God!" he muttered to himself, "I would not have had this to save my own life, much less as the price of my liberty!"

"I fought for you," said the wounded man, again reviving, "because Mary wished it. This will kill Mary," he added after a pause. "She warned me not to be rash, but I could not help it. Be kind to her, Major Butler, and take care of her. Tell her I did not fear to die; but for her sake, and for the sake of my poor mother. Go to my parents; let them know I thought of them in my last thoughts."

"John! John!" exclaimed Butler, unable to give further utterance to his feelings.

The dying trooper lay for some moments silent, and his comrades stood around him in mute grief, and hung their heads to conceal their emotions from each other.

"In my pocket," said Ramsay, "is a Testament. Mary gave it to me for a keepsake. Take it out."

Butler drew forth the small volume.

"What shall I do with it?" he asked, in a mournful whisper.

"Give it to Mary, back from me. And this plait of her hair upon my wrist, major, take it and wear it on your own; it will remind you of my Mary — you will guard her from harm."

"Before God, John Ramsay," said Butler with solemn fervor,

"I promise you, that, while I live, she shall not want. Your parents, too, shall be my special care."

"Then I shall die with easier heart. Thanks, thanks — friends, farewell!" feebly ejaculated the stricken soldier, whose eye, already glazed with the pangs of death, now glanced upon the attending group, and after a brief but painful interval closed in darkness.

John Ramsay spake no more, and his short breathing showed that life was fast ebbing in its channel. The audible sobs of Butler, for some moments, were alone heard in the circle, as he sat supporting the head and grasping the hand of his brave comrade. The struggle was at last over, and the gallant spirit of the generous soldier had fled. Butler took from the wrist the bracelet of Mary's hair, which was now stained with the blood of its late owner, and, with an earnest vow to redeem his promise, drew it over his own hand.

The scene that followed this melancholy adventure was one of solemn interest. The proximity of the enemy, although defeated, rendered a delay at this spot, in the present circumstances of Butler, exceedingly hazardous; yet he could not entertain the thought of continuing his journey until he had communicated to David Ramsay the distressing tidings of his son's death. The last request of John seemed also to impose this task upon him as a sacred obligation, due to the friendship which had terminated in so disastrous an end. Butler's resolution, therefore, was soon taken. He determined immediately, at all hazards, to make his way back to Ramsay's cottage, and to endeavor to console the afflicted parents under their severe bereavement. Disdaining, in his present state of feeling, the disguise that seemed to make him almost a stranger to himself, he threw aside the miller's dress and again appeared in his true character, resolved manfully to meet what he now believed to be the almost certain result — a recapture with all its probable consequences. Some of his party, who were acquainted with the localities of their present position, suggested to him that a Whig family of the name of Drummond resided at no great distance from the scene of the late encounter, and that, by bearing the body to this place, they might secure for it a decent burial. The remains of the trooper were accordingly laid upon a rude litter, and his mourning comrades slowly and sorrowfully wended their way through the forest to the designated habitation. Here they arrived about noon, having traversed a space of more than two miles to gain this asylum.

Drummond was a woodman, and occupied a rude cabin, with a small clearing around it, in the depths of the wilderness, so remote from the highway as to promise as much security from the quest of the enemy, as might be expected from any portion of the region in which he lived. He received his guests with kindness; and as he was himself acquainted with the family of the deceased, he exhibited a lively sympathy with the mourners around the body.

When Butler now made known his purpose to set out immediately for the habitation of David Ramsay, Winter asked permission to accompany him, but the woodman interposed, and recommended that he alone should be permitted to perform that errand, leaving the others to remain with the corpse until his return.

"It is, before all others, my duty," said Butler; "and come what may, I will perform it."

"Then we will go together," added the proprietor of the cabin. "It will be wise to wait until the day is a little more spent, and return in the darkness of the night. David Ramsay will come back with us. He would like to see his son before we put him in the ground."

"That shall be as you please, friend," said Butler. "I will be under your guidance."

An hour or two before sun-down, Butler and his new companion left the cabin, and took their route across the woods towards Ramsay's dwelling, leaving the dead body in charge of the woodman's family and the three soldiers. The distance they had to travel did not exceed eight miles. The repulse of the Tory party in the skirmish of the morning seemed to have induced a belief, on the part of the enemy, that the fugitives had made a successful retreat which was now beyond pursuit, and there were, in consequence, no parties on the road to molest the travellers. Under these circumstances, it was still daylight when they came in view of David Ramsay's homestead.

CHAPTER XLV

Great agitation prevailed at Macdonald's post, when the morning disclosed the escape of Butler. The lieutenant was conscious that this mischance had exposed him to the risk of heavy censure, and, as was natural to a man who could not entirely acquit himself of some neglect in the performance of his duty, his first measures were taken in a spirit of peevish and angry severity. Small parties were sent out to explore the neighborhood, with a view to gain intelligence of the direction taken by the fugitive, with orders to bring him in dead or alive. The sentinels who were on duty during the night were arrested, and subjected to a rigid examination on the events of their watch; the several members of Musgrove's family were also interrogated as to matters touching their own connexion with the prisoner. Nothing, however, was gathered from these investigations that was calculated to cast a suspicion of connivance in Butler's liberation, upon any individual either of the garrison or of the family. It was only apparent that the prisoner had availed himself of the remissness of the guard and the darkness of the night, to make a bold descent from the window; and had succeeded by one of those lucky accidents which sometimes baffle the most cautious foresight. The nature of the attempt did not necessarily suppose the aid of an accomplice, and a faint hope was, therefore, entertained that Butler would be found still lurking in the vicinity of the post.

In the course of a few hours, the first parties that had been dispatched in the morning, returned. They could give no account of the prisoner; nor was there any light thrown upon the escape, until about the dinner hour, when a portion of the detachment which had intercepted Butler and his comrades in the morning, arrived at the mill, under the conduct of the soldier whose suspicions had led to the pursuit and skirmish which we have already described. The report of these men left Macdonald no room to doubt the identity of Butler with the person described. A further examination, at the suggestion of the soldier, showed that Wall-Eye, the wagon-horse, was missing; and it now became certain that Butler had been aided by a party of the enemy with whom he must have been in correspondence. The conclusion was, that with his means of flight there could be little doubt of his being, long before the present period of the day, out of the reach of successful pursuit. The scheme was laid to the account of Horse Shoe Robinson, whose name and adventures were already famous in this district; and it was conjectured that Sumpter was secretly posted in some neighboring fastness to give his assistance to the enterprise.

With these reflections, Macdonald felt himself obliged to submit to the exigencies of the case; a point of philosophy which he did not practise without a very visible chagrin and mortification. His men were called together, and after a short, fretful lecture on their neglect, and an injunction to a more soldier-like vigilance in future, which savored of the caution of locking the stable after the steed was stolen, they were dismissed.

About an hour before sun-down, Allen Musgrove and Mary, availing themselves of the confusion and relaxed discipline of the post, occasioned by the events of the morning, set out on horseback for David Ramsay's dwelling, whither they were led by a natural anxiety to learn something of the movements of the fugitives.

" It's a pleasure and a happiness, Allen Musgrove," said Mistress Ramsay, as the miller and his daughter sat down in the cabin, " to see you and Mary over here with us at any time, but it is specially so now when we have good news to tell. John and his friend are safe out of reach of Macdonald's men, and — God be praised! — I hope out of the way of all other harms. We have had soldiers dodging in and out through the day, but not one of them has made any guess what's gone with the major; and as for John, they don't seem to suspect him to be on the country-side. It's all Horse Shoe Robinson with them. They say that none but he could have helped to get the major away, and that General Sumpter was the instigator. Well, I'm sure they were welcome to that opinion, for it set them all to looking over towards Broad river, which is as good a direction as we could wish them to travel."

" The less you seem to know about it, with any of these inquiring parties, the better, Mistress Ramsay," said Allen Musgrove, " and I would advise you, even here amongst ourselves, to speak lower. David, what do you hear this evening? "

" Nothing concerning our runaways since they left us at daylight this morning," replied Ramsay. " I should guess them to be somewhere near upon Fair Forest by this time. You know Williams is outlying upon the upper branches of the river? It is more like hunted deer, Allen, than Christian men, that our poor fellows take to the woods now. God knows what will come of it!"

"He knows and has appointed it," said Musgrove, gravely, "and will in His own good time and with such instruments as shall faithfully work His purpose, give the victory to them that have the right. Man, woman, and child may perish, and house and home may be burnt over our heads, and the blood of brave men may make the dust of the road red; yes, and the pastures rich as if new laid with manure; but the will of God shall be done and His providence be accomplished. The cause of the just shall prevail against the unjust."

"There were no soldiers," inquired Mary, addressing David Ramsay, "that you have heard of, who followed towards Fair Forest? I should be sorry if John was to be troubled with persons going after him; because," — the maiden hesitated an instant, — "because it's unpleasant and disagreeable to be obliged to be riding off the road, through bushes and briers, to keep out of the way."

"If they were not greatly an overmatch, girl," interrupted Ramsay, "John wouldn't give himself much trouble upon that account."

"Oh, Mr. Ramsay," said Mary earnestly, "I was thinking of that. It's hard to say what John would call an overmatch: men are so headstrong and venturesome."

"That's God's own truth, Mary," interposed Mrs. Ramsay; "and what I have always been telling David and John both. But they never heed me, no more than if I was talking to the child in that cradle."

"I've told John as much myself," said Mary, blushing.

"And he would not heed you either," interrupted her father. "A soldier would have a holiday life of it, if he followed the advice of his mother or his sweetheart. Daughter, amongst friends here, you needn't blush; we know more of the secrets betwixt you and the trooper lad than you count upon. John's a clever boy, Mistress Ramsay, and I think you have reason to brag of him somewhat; and as there's particular good-will between him and my Mary, I'll not stand in the way when the war is over, if God spares us all, and Mary and the lad keep in the same mind; I'll not stand in the way of a new settlement in the neighborhood. Mary is a good daughter, well nurtured, and — I don't care to say it to her face — will make a thriving wife."

The mother smiled as she replied, "I don't pretend to know the young people's secrets, but I know this, you don't think better of Mary than John does — nor than me neither, perhaps."

The conversation was interrupted by a knocking at the door, and, in a moment afterwards, Arthur Butler and the woodman entered the apartment.

"Major Butler, as I am a living woman!" exclaimed Mrs. Ramsay.

"Our good friend himself!" ejaculated Musgrove, with surprise. "What has turned you back? And Gabriel Drummond here too! What has happened?"

"Where is my son John?" demanded Ramsay. "Are you followed?"

Butler walked up to Mrs. Ramsay, and, as a tear started to his eye, took her by the hand, and stood for a moment unable to speak.

"Oh, heaven have mercy on me!" screamed Mary Musgrove, as she threw herself upon a bed, "something dreadful has happened."

"For God's sake, speak what you have to tell!" said David Ramsay, instantly turning pale.

"John Ramsay is hurt," faintly articulated the mother, and Mary, rising from the bed, stood beside Butler with a countenance on which was seated the most agonizing attention. Andy, the hero of the exploit we have heretofore related, also pressed into the presence of the same group, and a death-like silence pervaded the whole party.

Butler, with an ineffectual effort to recover himself, turned to Drummond, making a sign to him to tell the object of their melancholy errand, and then flung himself into a chair.

"John Ramsay is dead," said the woodman, in a mournful tone. "Your son, mistress Ramsay, was shot in a fray with the bloody, villanous Tories. The heartiest curses upon them!"

"Killed, dear madam," said Butler, scarce able to articulate, "killed in my defence. Would to God the blow had fallen upon my own head!"

"Oh, no, no, no!" exclaimed the matron, as a flood of tears rolled down her cheeks, and she endeavored to wipe them away with her apron. "It isn't true. It can't be true. My poor, dear, brave boy!"

At the same instant Mary Musgrove fell insensible into the arms of her father, where it was some moments before she gave signs of animation. At length, being laid upon the bed, a deep groan escaped her, which was followed by the most piteous wailing.

The scene wrought upon the younger members of the family, who, as well as the domestics, were heard pouring forth deep and loud lamentations, accompanied with reiterated announcements of the death of the soldier.

When this first burst of the general grief was over, David Ramsay arose from his seat and walked across the room to a window, where he stood endeavoring to compose and master his feelings. At length, facing Butler, he said in a low and tranquil tone,

"John Ramsay, my son, killed, killed in a skirmish? God is my witness, I expected it! It was his failing to follow his enemy with too hot a hand; and I am to blame, perhaps, that I never checked him in that temper. But he died like a man and a soldier, Major Butler," he added, firmly.

"He died in my arms," replied Butler, "as bravely as ever soldier closed his life, his last thoughts were fixed upon his parents, and —

"Dead!" interrupted Ramsay, as if communing with himself, and regardless of Butler's words — "Dead! He fell doing his duty to his country, that's a consolation. A man cannot die better. If it please God, I hope my end may be like his. Andrew, my boy, come here. You are now my oldest living son," he said, taking the lad's hand and looking him full in the face, as he spoke with a bitter compression of his lips; "I am willing, much as I love you, that the country should have you."

"No, David, David," interrupted the mother, rousing herself from her silent grief, "we have given enough; no other child of mine shall venture in the war. John! John! John! my dear boy, my brave son! How good and kind he was to us all! And how glad he was to get home to see us; and how much we made of him!"

"Silence, wife," said David Ramsay, "this is no time to hold back from our duty. Andrew, listen to me: remember your brother has met his death fighting against these monsters, who hate the very earth that nurses liberty. You are young, boy, but you can handle a musket; we will not forget your brother's death."

"Nor the burning of a good house over your head, and a full barn, father; nor the frights they have given my poor mother."

"Nor the thousands of brave men," added the father, "who have poured out their blood to give us a land and laws of our own. My boy, we will remember these, for vengeance."

"Not for vengeance," said Allen Musgrove, "for justice, David. Your enemy should be remembered only to prevent him from doing mischief. The Lord will give him sword and buckler, spear and shield, who stands up for the true cause: and when it pleases Him to require the sacrifice of life from the faithful servant who fights the battle, he grants patience and courage to meet the trial. Your son was not the man, David, to turn his face away from the work that was before him; may God receive him and comfort his distressed family! He was an honest and brave son, David Ramsay."

"A braver soldier never buckled on broadsword, Allen Musgrove," replied the father. "Yes, I looked for this; ever since my dwelling was levelled to the ground by these firebrands, I looked for it. John's passion was up then, and I knew the thoughts that ran through his mind. Ever since that day his feelings have been most bitter; and he has flung himself amongst the Tories, making as little account of them as the mower when he puts his scythe into the grass of the meadows."

"God forgive him, David!" said Musgrove, "and strengthen you and the boy's good mother in this sharp hour of trial. They who draw the sword in passion may stand in fear of the judgment of the sword: it is a fearful thing for sinful man to shed blood for any end but that of lawful war, and at the bidding of his country. God alone is the avenger."

Mary had again raised herself from the bed, and at this moment gave vent to her feelings in a loud and bitter lamentation. "John Ramsay is dead, is dead!" she exclaimed. "I cannot believe it. He that was so true and so warm-hearted, and that everybody loved! They could not kill him! Oh, I begged him to keep his foot from danger, and he promised me, for my sake, to be careful. I loved him, father; I never told you so much before, but I am not ashamed to tell it now before everybody; I loved him better than all the world. And we had promised each other. It is so hard to lose them that we love!" she continued, sobbing violently. "He was so brave and so good, and he was so handsome, Mrs. Ramsay, and so dutiful to you and his father, coming home to see you whenever the war would let him. And he walked, and rode, and ran, and fought for his friends, and them that he cared for. He was so thoughtful for your comfort too," she added, as she threw herself on her knees and rested her head in the lap of the mother, and there paused through a long interval, during which nothing was heard but her own moans mingled with the sighs of the party, "we were to be married after this war was at an end, and thought we should live so happily: but they have murdered him! Oh they have murdered him," and with her hair thrown in disorder over her face, she again gave vent to a flood of tears.

"Mary, daughter! Shame on you, girl!" said her father. "Do you forget, in the hour of your affliction, that you have a friend who is able to comfort? There is one who can heal up your sorrows and speak peace to your troubled spirit, if you be not too proud to ask it. I have taught you, daughter, in all time of tribulation to look to Him for patience and for strength to bear adversity. Why do you neglect this refuge now?"

"Our Father," said the maiden, fervently clasping her hands and lifting up her eyes, now dim with weeping, as she appealed to God in prayer, "who art in heaven — teach us all to say thy will be done. Take — take — my dear John — Oh, my heart will burst and I shall die!" she uttered, almost overwhelmed with her emotions, as she again buried her face in Mistress Ramsay's lap — "I cannot speak!"

A silence of inexpressible agony prevailed for some moments. This was at length interrupted by the uprising of the full, clear, and firm voice of Allen Musgrove, who now broke forth from the opposite side of a room where he had kneeled before a chair, in an earnest and impressive supplication to the Deity, urged with all that eloquence which naturally flows from deeply-excited feeling. From the solemnity of the occasion, as well as from the habitually religious temper of the family assembled in the little cabin, the words of the prayer fell upon the hearts of those present with a singularly welcome effect, and, for the moment, brought tranquillity to their feelings.

When the prayer was ended, the grief of the mourners rolled back in its former flood, and burst from Mary Musgrove in the most heart-rending bitterness. Paroxysm followed paroxysm with fearful violence, and these outbreaks were responded to by the mother with scarcely less intensity. All attempts at consolation, on the part of the men, were unavailing; and it was apparent that nothing remained but to let the tide of anguish take its own course.

It was now some time after night-fall, when Butler and Drummond beckoned Allen Musgrove to leave the room. They retired into the open air in front of the house, where they were immediately joined by David Ramsay. Here Butler communicated to them the necessity of making immediate arrangements for their return to the woodman's cottage, and for the burial of the deceased trooper. His advice was adopted, and it was resolved that Musgrove and Ramsay should accompany the other two to the spot. Before the consultation was closed, Andy had come into the group, and he was now directed, with all haste, to throw a saddle upon his father's horse.

"You, Andrew, my son," said David Ramsay, "will stay at home and comfort your poor mother, and Mary. Speak to them, boy, and persuade them to give up their useless lamentations. It is the will of God, and we ought not to murmur at it."

"The burning, father," replied the boy, with a sorrowful earnestness, "and the fighting, and the frights we have had, was all nothing to this. I never felt before how terrible the war was."

Andy had now gone to equip the horse, and the men returned to the inside of the cabin, where they sat in profound silence. Butler, at length, rose from the door-sill where he had taken his seat, and crossing the room, took a position by the bed on which Mary Musgrove had thrown herself, and where she now lay uttering faint and half-smothered moans.

"I have a remembrance for you," he said, stooping down and speaking scarce above a whisper in the maiden's ear; "I promised to deliver it into your hand. God knows with what pain I perform my office! John enjoined upon me to give you this," he continued, as he presented to her the little copy of the Testament, "and to say to you that his last thoughts were given to you and his mother. He loved you, Mary, better than he loved any living creature in this world."

"He did, he did," sobbed forth the girl; "and I loved him far above family, friends, kinsfolk and all — I wish I were dead by his side."

"Take the book," said Butler, hardly able to articulate. "God for ever bless you," he added, after a pause of weeping, "and bring you comfort! I have promised John Ramsay, that neither you, nor any of his family, shall ever want the service of a friend, while I have life or means to render it. Before Heaven, that pledge shall be redeemed! Farewell, farewell! God bless you!"

As Butler uttered these words he grasped the maiden's hand and pressed it fervently to his lips; then turning to the mother, he addressed some phrase of comfort to her, and hastily left the room. Scarcely a sound was heard from any one, except the low sobbing of the exhausted weepers, and the almost convulsive kisses which

Mary imprinted upon the little book that Butler had put into her hand.

Musgrove, Ramsay, and the woodman, retired from the apartment at the same moment; and the horses being ready at the door, the retreating beat of the hoofs upon the turf gave notice to the in-dwellers that the four men had set forward on their journey.

CHAPTER XLVI

A RUSTIC FUNERAL

How glumly sounds yon dirgy song;
Night ravens flap the wing.

BURGER'S LEONORA.

BY eleven o'clock at night, Butler and the party from Ramsay's arrived at the woodman's cabin. Winter and his comrades had been busy in making preparations for the funeral. The body had been laid out upon a table, a sheet thrown over it, and a pine torch blazed from the chimney wall close by, and flung its broad, red glare over the apartment. An elderly female, the wife of the woodman, and two or three children, sat quietly in the room. The small detachment of troopers loitered around the corpse, walking with stealthy pace across the floor, and now and then adjusting such matters of detail in the arrangements for the interment as required their attention. A rude coffin, hastily constructed of such materials as were at hand, was deposited near the table. A solemn silence prevailed, which no less consisted with the gloom of the occasion than with the late hour of the night.

When the newly arrived party had dismounted and entered the apartment, a short salutation, in suppressed tones, was exchanged, and without further delay, the whole company set themselves to the melancholy duty that was before them. David Ramsay approached the body, and, turning the sheet down from the face, stood gazing on the features of his son. There was a settled frown upon his brow that contrasted signally with the composed and tranquil lineaments of the deceased. The father and son presented a strange and remarkable type of life and death — the countenance of the mourner stamped by the agitation of keen, living emotion, and the object mourned bearing the impress of a serene, placid, and passionless repose: — the one a vivid picture of misery, the other a quiet image of happy sleep. David Ramsay bent his looks upon the body for some minutes, without an endeavor to speak, and at last retreated towards the door, striking his hand upon his forehead as he breathed out the ejaculation, "My son, my son, how willingly would I change places with you this night!"

Allen Musgrove was less agitated by the spectacle, and whilst he surveyed the features of the deceased, his lips were moved with the utterance of a short and almost inaudible prayer. Then turning to Drummond, he inquired: "Has the grave been thought of? Who has attended to the preparations?"

"It has been thought of," replied the woodman; "I sent two of my people off to dig it before I went with Major Butler to see David. We have a grave-yard across in the woods, nigh a mile from this, and I thought it best that John Ramsay should be buried there."

"It was kindly thought on by you, Gabriel," replied Musgrove. "You have your father and others of your family in that spot. David Ramsay will thank you for it."

"I do, heartily," said Ramsay, "and will remember it, Gabriel, at another time."

"Let the body be lifted into the coffin," said Musgrove.

The order was promptly executed by Harry Winter and the other troopers. In a few minutes afterwards, the rough boards which had been provided to close up the box or coffin, were laid in their appropriate places, and Winter had just begun to hammer the nails into them, when from the outside of the cabin was heard a wild and piercing scream, that fell so suddenly upon the ears of those within as to cause the trooper to drop the hammer from his hand. In one moment more, Mary Musgrove rushed into the room and fell prostrate upon the floor. She was instantly followed by Andrew.

"God of heaven!" exclaimed Butler, "here is misery upon misery. This poor girl's brain is crazed by her misfortune. This is worst of all!"

"Mary, Mary, my child!" ejaculated Musgrove, as he raised his daughter into his arms. "What madness has come upon you, that you should have wandered here to-night!"

"How has this happened, Andrew?" said David Ramsay, all speaking in the same breath.

"When Mary heard," replied Andrew, in answer to his father's question, "that you had all come to Gabriel Drummond's to bury my brother, she couldn't rest content; and she prayed so pitifully to come after you, and see him before they put him in the ground, that I thought it right to tell her that I would come with her.

And if I hadn't, she would have come by herself; for she had got upon her horse before any of us were aware."

"I couldn't stay at home, father," said Mary, reviving and speaking in a firm voice. "I should have died with a broken heart. I couldn't let you come to put him in the earth without following after you. Where is he? I heard them nailing the coffin; it must be broken open for me to see him!"

These words, uttered with a bitter vehemence, were followed by a quick movement towards the coffin, which was yet unclosed; and the maiden, with more composure than her previous gestures seemed to render it possible for her to acquire, paused before the body with a look of intense sorrow, as the tears fell fast from her eyes.

"It is true — it is too true — he is dead! Oh, John, John!" she exclaimed, as she stooped down and kissed the cold lips, "I did not dream of this when we parted last night near the willows. You did not look as you do now, when I found you asleep under the rock, and when you promised me, John, that you would be careful and keep yourself from danger, if it was only to please me. We were doing our best for you then, Major Butler — and here is what it has come to. No longer than last night he made me the promise. Oh me, oh me! how wretched — how miserable I am!"

"Daughter, dear," said Allen Musgrove, "rise up and behave like a brave girl as, you know, I have often told you you were. We are born to afflictions, and young as you are, you cannot hope to be free from the common lot. You do yourself harm by this ungoverned grief. There's a good and a kind girl — sit yourself down and calm your feelings."

Musgrove took his daughter by the hand, and gently conducted her to a seat, where he continued to address her in soothing language, secretly afraid that the agony of her feelings might work some serious misfortune upon her senses.

"You are not angry with me, father, for following you to-night?" said Mary, for a moment moderating the wildness of her sorrow.

"No, child, no. I cannot be angry with you; but I fear this long night-ride may do you harm."

"I can but die, father; and I would not step aside from that."

"Recollect yourself, Mary; your Bible does not teach you to wish for death. It is sinful to rebel under the chastisements of God. Daughter, I have taught you in your day of prosperity, the lessons that were to be practised in your time of suffering and trial. Do not now turn me and my precepts to shame."

"Oh, father, forgive me. It is so hard to lose the best, the dearest!" Here Mary again gave way to emotions which could only relieve themselves in profuse tears.

In the meantime the body was removed to the outside of the cabin, and the coffin was speedily shut up and deposited upon a light wagon-frame, to which two lean horses were already harnessed, and which waited to convey its burden to the grave-yard.

"All is ready," said Winter, stepping quietly into the house, and speaking in a low tone to Musgrove. "We are waiting only for you."

"Father," said Mary, who, on hearing this communication, had sprung to her feet, "I must go with you."

"My child!"

"I came all this way through the dark woods on purpose, father — and it is my right to go with him to his grave. Pray, dear father, do not forbid me. We belonged to each other, and he would be glad to think I was the last that left him — the very last."

"The poor child takes on so," said the wife of Drummond, now for the first time interposing in the scene; "and it seems natural, Mr. Musgrove, that you shouldn't hinder her. I will go along, and maybe it will be a comfort to her, to have some woman-kind beside her. I will take her hand."

"You shall go, Mary," said her father; "but on the condition that you govern your feelings, and behave with the moderation of a Christian woman. Take courage, my child, and show your nurture."

"I will, father — I will; the worst is past, and I can walk quietly to John's grave," replied Mary, as the tears again flowed fast, and her voice was stifled with her sobs.

"It is a heavy trouble for such a young creature to bear," said Mistress Drummond, as she stood beside the maiden, waiting for this burst of grief to subside; "but this world is full of such sorrows."

Musgrove now quitted the apartment. He was followed by his daughter and the rest of the inmates, all of whom repaired to the front of the cabin, where they awaited the removal of the body.

A bundle of pine faggots had been provided, and each one of the party was supplied from them with a lighted torch. Some little delay occurred whilst Harry Winter was concluding his arrangements for the funeral.

"Take your weapons along, boys," said the trooper to his comrades, in a whisper. "John Ramsay shall have the honors of war — and mark, you are to bring up the rear — let the women walk next the wagon. Gabriel Drummond, bring your rifle along — we shall give a volley over the grave."

The woodman stepped into the cabin and returned with his firelock. All things being ready, the wagon, under the guidance of a negro who walked at the horses' heads, now moved forward. The whole party formed a procession in couples — the woodman's wife and Mary being first in the train, the children succeeding them, and the rest following in regular order.

It was an hour after midnight. The road, scarcely discernible, wound through a thick forest, and the procession moved with a slow and heavy step towards its destination. The torches lit up the darkness of the wood with a strong flame, that penetrated the mass of sombre foliage to the extent of some fifty paces around, and glared with a wild and romantic effect upon the rude coffin, the homely vehicle on which it was borne, and upon the sorrowing faces of the train that followed it. The seclusion of the region, the unwonted hour, and the strange mixture of domestic and military mourning, half rustic and half warlike, that entered into the composition of the group; and, above all, the manifestations of sincere and intense grief that were seen in every member of the train, communicated to the incident a singularly imaginative and unusual character. No words were spoken, except the few orders of the march announced by Harry Winter in a whisper; and the ear recognised, with a painful precision, the unceasing sobs of Mary Musgrove, and the deep groan that seemed, unawares, to escape now and then from some of the males of the party. The dull tramp of feet, and the rusty creak of the wagon-wheels, or the crackling of brushwood beneath them, and the monotonous clank of the chains employed in the gearing of the horses, all broke upon the stillness of the night with a more abrupt and observed distinctness, from the peculiar tone of feeling which pervaded those who were engaged in the sad offices of the scene.

In the space of half an hour, the train had emerged from the wood upon a small tract of open ground, that seemed to have been formerly cleared from the forest for the purpose of cultivation. Whatever tillage might have once existed there was now abandoned, and the space was overgrown with brambles, through which the blind road still struggled by a track that even in daylight it would have been difficult to pursue. Towards the centre of this opening grew a cluster of low cherry and peach trees, around whose roots a plentiful stock of wild scions had shot up in the absence of culture. Close in the shade of this cluster, a ragged and half-decayed paling formed a square inclosure of some ten or twelve paces broad, and a few rude posts set up within, indicated the spot to be the rustic grave-yard. Here two negroes were seen resting over a newly-dug grave.

The wagon halted within some short distance of the paling, and the coffin was now committed to the shoulders of the troopers. Following these, the whole train of mourners entered the burial-place.

My reader will readily imagine with what fresh fervor the grief of poor Mary broke forth, whilst standing on the verge of the pit in which were to be entombed the remains of one so dear to her. The solemn interval or pause which intervened between the arrival of the corpse at this spot, and its being lowered into the ground, was one that was not signalized only by the loud sorrow of her who here bore the part of chief mourner; but all, even to the negroes who stood musing over their spades, gave vent to feelings which, at such a moment, it neither belongs to humanity, nor becomes it, to resist.

The funeral service was performed by Allen Musgrove. The character of the miller, both physical and moral, impressed his present employment with singular efficacy. Though his frame bore the traces of age, it was still robust and muscular; and his bearing, erect and steadfast, denoted firmness of mind. His head, partially bald, was now uncovered; and his loose, whitened locks played in the breeze. The torches were raised above the group; and as they flared in the wind and flung their heavy volumes of smoke into the air, they threw also a blaze of light upon the venerable figure of the miller, as he poured forth an impassioned supplication to the Deity; which, according to the habit of thinking of that period, and conformably also to the tenets of the religious sect to which the speaker belonged, might be said to have expressed, in an equal degree, resignation to the will of Heaven and defiance of the power of man. Though the office at the grave was thus prolonged, it did not seem to be unexpected or wearisome to the auditory, who remained with unabated interest until they had chanted a hymn, which was given out by the miller, and sung in successive couplets. The religious observances of the place seemed to have taken a profitable hold upon the hearts of the mourners; and before the hymn was concluded, even the voice of Mary Musgrove rose with a clear cadence upon the air, and showed that the inspirations of piety had already supplanted some of the more violent paroxysms of grief.

This exercise of devotion being finished, the greater part of the company began their retreat to the woodman's cabin. Winter and his comrades remained to perform the useless and idle ceremony of discharging their pistols over the grave, and when this was accomplished they hurried forward to overtake the party in advance.

They had scarcely rejoined their companions, before the horses of the wagon were seized by an unknown hand; and the glare of the torches presented to the view of the company some fifteen or twenty files of British troopers.

" Stand, I charge you all, in the name of the king! " called out an authoritative voice from the contiguous thicket; and before another word could be uttered, the funeral train found themselves surrounded by enemies.

" Hands off! " exclaimed Butler, as a soldier had seized him by the coat. A pistol shot was heard, and Butler was seen plunging into the wood, followed by Winter and one or two others.

The fugitives were pursued by numbers of the hostile party, and in a few moments were dragged back to the lights.

" Who are you, sir? " demanded an officer, who now rode up to Butler, " that you dare to disobey a command in the name of the king? Friend or foe, you must submit to be questioned."

" We have been engaged," said Allen Musgrove, " in the peaceful and Christian duty of burying the dead. What right have you to interrupt us? "

" You take a strange hour for such a work," replied the officer, " and, by the volley fired over the grave, I doubt whether your service be so peaceful as you pretend, old man. What is he that you have laid beneath the turf to-night? "

" A soldier," replied Butler, " worthy of all the rites that belong to the sepulture of a brave man."

" And you are a comrade, I suppose? "

" I do not deny it."

" What colors do you serve? "

" Who is he that asks? "

" Captain M'Alpine of the new levies," replied the officer. " Now, sir, your name and character? you must be convinced of my right to know it."

" I have no motive for concealment," said Butler, " since I am already in your power. Myself and four comrades are strictly your prisoners; the rest of this party are inhabitants of the neighboring country, having no connexion with the war, but led hither by a simple wish to perform an office of humanity to a deceased friend. In surrendering myself and those under my command, I bespeak for the others an immunity from all vexatious detention. I am an officer of the Continental service: Butler is my name, my rank, a major of infantry."

After a few words more of explanation, the party were directed by the British officer to continue their march to Drummond's cabin, whither, in a brief space, they arrived under the escort of their captors.

A wakeful night was passed under the woodman's roof; and when morning came the circumstances of the recapture of Butler were more fully disclosed. The detachment under Captain M'Alpine were on their way to join Ferguson, who was now posted in the upper district; and being attracted by the sound of voices engaged in chanting the psalm at the funeral of John Ramsay, and still more by the discharge of the volley over the grave, they had directed their march to the spot, which they had no difficulty in reaching by the help of the torches borne by the mourners.

The detachment consisted of a company of horse numbering some fifty men, who had no scruple in seizing upon Butler and his companions as prisoners of war. It was some relief to Butler when he ascertained that his present captors were ignorant of his previous history, and were unconnected with those who had formerly held him in custody. He was also gratified with the assurance that no design was entertained to molest any others of the party, except those whom Butler himself indicated as belligerents.

Captain M'Alpine halted with his men at the woodman's cabin, until after sunrise. During this interval, Butler was enabled to prepare himself for the journey he was about to commence, and to take an affectionate leave of Musgrove and his daughter, David Ramsay, and the woodman's family.

Allen Musgrove and Mary, and their friend Ramsay, deemed it prudent to retreat with the first permission given them by the British officer; and, not long afterwards, Butler and his comrades found themselves in the escort of the Tory cavalry, bound for Ferguson's camp.

Thus, once more, was Butler doomed to feel the vexations of captivity.

CHAPTER XLVII

A COUNCIL OF WAR AT MRS. MARKHAM'S. THE SERGEANT SETS FORTH ON AN ADVENTURE

We return to Mildred Lindsay, who, comfortably sheltered under the roof of Mrs. Markham, had found herself, after the repose of forty-eight hours, almost entirely reinstated in her former strength; her thoughts were now consequently directed to the resumption of her journey. The gentle and assiduous attentions of the family whose hospitality she enjoyed, were, however, not confined to the mere restoration of her health. The peculiarity of her condition, thus thrown as she was amongst strangers, in the prosecution of an enterprise, which, though its purpose was not disclosed to her entertainer, was one manifestly of great peril, and such only as could have been induced by some urgent and imperious necessity, awakened in Mrs. Markham a lively interest towards Mildred's future progress. This interest was increased by the deportment of our heroine herself, whose mild and graceful courtesy, feminine delicacy, and gentleness of nurture, were so signally contrasted with the romantic hardihood of her present expedition. General Marion's letter, also, in the estimation of the hostess, put her under a special obligation to look after the welfare of her guest. Accordingly, now when the third morning of our travellers' sojourn had arrived, and Mildred thought of taking leave of the friendly family, the first announcement of this purpose was met by an almost positive prohibition.

"You are young, my dear," said the matron, "in your experience of the horrors of this civil war, and make a sad mistake if you think that your sex, or any sufficient reason you may have to justify you in going on, will protect you against insult, in case you should be so unfortunate as to meet parties of the enemy."

"My object, madam," replied Mildred, "is to go into the very heart of the enemy's ranks. My business is to see Lord Cornwallis himself. I shall, therefore, proceed directly to his head-quarters. That being my purpose, I shall not regret the opportunity to throw myself upon the protection of the first band of loyal troops I may meet."

"Into Lord Cornwallis's presence!" said Mrs. Markham, with an expression of wonder. "You have some very near friend who has suffered in the late battle — a prisoner, perhaps?" As this question escaped the lips of the lady, who had hitherto purposely forborne to inquire into the private history of Mildred's journey, she shook her head distrustfully, and, after some deliberation, added, "You will pardon me, my child, for what may seem to be an idle curiosity — I seek to know nothing that you may desire to keep secret — but your journey is so full of hazard to one so young and helpless as yourself, that I fear you have not wisely considered the evil chances to which you may be exposed."

"I have spent no thought upon the hazard, madam," replied Mildred. "There is no degree of danger that should outweigh my resolution. You guess truly — I have a friend who is a prisoner, and in sad jeopardy — and more than that, dear madam, I have persuaded myself that I have power to save him." A tear started in her eye as she added, "That is all I have thought of."

"Then may a kind and merciful Heaven shield you! They little know the heart-rending trials of war, who have not felt them as I have. These rude soldiers, Miss Lindsay — I shudder at the thought of your trusting your safety to them."

"My name, madam," replied Mildred, "I am ashamed to tell you, has all its associations on their side — I must trust to its power to bear me through."

"Not all, sister," interrupted Henry. "From the beginning up to this day, I can answer for myself, I have never had a thought that didn't take sides against the red-coats."

A faint smile played upon Mrs. Markham's features, as she turned to Henry and said, "You are a young rebel, and a warm one, I perceive. Such troubles as ours require grave advisers."

"My brother and myself must not be misapprehended," continued Mildred; "I alluded only to my father's influence. I have heard that he enjoys some consideration in the esteem of Lord Cornwallis, and it is upon the strength of that I have ventured. Besides, I am well attended by a careful and wise soldier, who rides as my companion and guide — one who would not quietly see me harmed."

"Let him be brought into our consultation," said Mrs. Markham. "I could not act without his advice. With your leave, I will send for him."

Henry and Alfred Markham, immediately upon this hint, went in pursuit of Horse Shoe.

When that important and trusty personage arrived in the parlor, a regular conference was opened, which, after a few discourses on the general aspect of affairs — wherein the sergeant showed an abundance of soldierly sagacity and knowledge, and a still greater share of warm and faithful concern for the welfare of the sister and brother whom he had in ward — resulted in the conclusion that measures should be taken to ascertain the state of the country around, in reference to the impression made by the late movements of Marion and his adversary; and, especially, what character of troops occupied the region over which the sergeant would be required to conduct his charge. This duty the sergeant very appropriately considered as belonging to himself, and he therefore determined forthwith to set out on a reconnoitring expedition. As we propose to bear him company, we will, for the present, leave the family in the parlor to the enjoyment of the kind communion that had already nursed up a mutual affection between the hostess and her guests.

The sergeant took his departure alone, notwithstanding the urgent importunities of Henry and his new companion, Alfred Markham, for permission to accompany him — a request that was utterly denied by the sturdy and cautious soldier.

"You are apt to talk too much, Mister Lindsay," he said, in answer to the petition of the young man, "for such a piece of business as I have in hand: for although, consarning your good sense, and valor both, considering your years, I would not be thought to speak rashly of them — but, on the contrary, to give you full praise and recommendation — yet you know you want experience and use to these double-dealings and dodgings that the war puts us to; whereupon, you mought fall to talking when it was best to be silent, and, in case of our meeting a body, to be letting out somewhat too much, which is a thing that discommodes in war more than you would believe. And besides this, Master Henry, there might be, mayhap, a scrimmage, a chase, and what not — in which consideration you would be only in my way, seeing that I should be obliged to be thinking of you when all my wits would be wanting for myself. No, no; upon no account is it reasonable that you should be along. It is your business to sarve as a body-guard to our young lady, who, I say, may God bless and take care of in this world and the next! And so, Mister Henry, you have my orders to stick to your post."

"Well, sergeant," replied Henry, "I must obey orders, and if you command me to stay behind, why I cannot choose about it. But, sergeant, let me give you a word of advice. Ride cautiously — keep your eyes to the right and left, as well as straight before you — and don't let them catch you napping."

"You studied that speech, Mr. Henry!" said Horse Shoe, laughing. "To hear you, one mought almost think you had shaved a beard from your chin before this. Look out, or your hair will turn grey from too hard thinking! and now, my long-headed fellow-soldier, good bye t'ye!"

"You are not going without your rifle, Mr. Horse Shoe?" said Henry, calling out to the sergeant, who had already trotted off some twenty paces.

"That's another consarn for you to ruminate over," replied Horse Shoe, in the same jocular mood. "Mine is a business of legs, not arms, to-day."

The sergeant was immediately after this upon the highway, moving forward with nothing, seemingly, to employ him but cheerful thoughts.

After riding for an hour upon the road that led towards Camden, he was enabled to collect from the country people a rumor that some detachments of horse were, at this time, traversing the country towards Pedee, but whether friends or enemies was not known to his informants. In following up this trail of common report, his vigilance quickened by the uncertainty of the tidings, he arrived about mid-day at a brook which, running between low but sharp hills, was crossed by the road at a point where a bold mass of rock, some twenty feet in height, jutted down with a perpendicular abruptness into the water. Here, as he stopped to survey the narrow and winding course of the stream, his eye was attracted by the projecting crag that thrust its bulk almost into the middle of the channel; and, for a moment, he indulged the speculation of a soldier, as he pondered upon the military advantages of such a post, either as a point from which to reconnoitre an enemy, or as a vantage-ground on which to dispute his passage of the ford. It not long afterwards fell to his lot to turn this observation to some account.

A mile beyond this spot, and where the road, as it yet crept through the bosom of the hills, was so obscured by forest as to afford not more than fifty paces of uninterrupted view, his quick ear was struck with sounds resembling the tramp of horses. Upon this conviction, it was but the action of an instant for him to turn aside into the woods and to take a station which might enable him to investigate the cause of his surmise, without exposing himself to the risk of detection. The noise grew louder, and what was vague conjecture soon became the certain report of his senses. At the nearest turn in the road, whilst protected by a screen of thicket, he could descry the leading platoons of a column of horse advancing at a slow gait; and upon examining his own position he became aware that, although the thicket might guard him from present observation, it would cease to do so as soon as the squadron should approach nearer to his ground. His thoughts recurred to the rock at the ford, and, with a view to avail himself of it, he forthwith commenced his retreat through the underwood that guarded the road side, as fact as Captain Peter could get over the ground. It was not long before he was removed beyond all risk of being seen by the advancing party, and he thus found himself at liberty to take the road again and retire without apprehension.

In Horse Shoe's reckoning, it was a matter of great importance that he should obtain the most accurate information regarding the troop that he had just encountered; and his present purpose was, accordingly, to post himself in a secure position upon the rock, and there maintain a close watch upon the party as they rode beneath it. The brook was gained, the ford passed, and the sergeant, after riding a short circuit towards the rear of the little promontory, dismounted from his horse, which he secured in the depths of the wood, and then clambered to the top of the precipice, where he had barely time to conceal himself amongst the crags and the thick shrubbery that shot up above them, before the headmost files of the cavalry appeared descending the opposite hill.

As the column came gradually into his view upon the road which wound down into the valley, it disclosed a troop of some twenty men, whose green uniform sufficiently indicated the presence of a part of Tarleton's command. He heard them call a halt upon the bank, and after a few moments' rest, he saw them ride into the stream, and pass in files around the base of the rock.

The passage of the brook occupied some time; for the thirsty horses were successively given a slack rein as they entered the ford, and were allowed to drink. This delay separated the platoons, and those who first passed over had advanced a considerable distance before the stragglers of the rear had quitted the stream. For some minutes that stir and noise prevailed which, in a military party, generally attends the attempt to restore order amongst confused or broken ranks. The frequent commands of officers summoning the loiterers and chiding their delay, were given from front to rear in loud tones, and the swift gallop of those who had lingered in the stream, as they obeyed the order and hastened forward to their places, sent forth a quick and spirited evidence of bustle, that broke sharply upon the silence of the surrounding forest. These indications of activity unfortunately pricked with a sudden astonishment the ear of one who has heretofore figured, not without renown, in this history — the lusty and faithful Captain Peter; who, not sufficiently alive to the distinction between friend and foe, now began to snuff, and paw the ground, and then with a long and clear note of recognition, to express his feelings of good fellowship towards the unseen strangers. Another moment, and the gay and thoughtless steed reared, plunged, broke his bridle, and bounded through the woods, with a frolicsome speed that brought him into the midst of the troop, where he wheeled up and took his place, like a disciplined charger, on the flank of one of the platoons.

This incident caused the officer in command of the party to come again to a halt, and to despatch a portion of his men to seek the owner of the horse. An eager search commenced, which was almost immediately terminated by the wary sergeant presenting himself to the view of the troop, on a prominent and exposed point of the rock, where he seemed to be busily and unconcernedly engaged with his jack-knife, in stripping the bark from the roots of a sassafras tree that grew out of one of the fissures of the cliff. Apparently, he gave no attention to the clamor around him, nor seemed to show a wish to conceal himself from notice.

"Who in the devil are you — and what are you about?" exclaimed the leading soldier, as he mounted the rock and came up immediately behind Robinson, who was still fixed with one knee upon the ground, plying his labor at the root of the tree.

"Good day, friend," said Robinson, looking up over his shoulder, "Good day! From your looks you belong to the army, and, if that's true, perhaps you mought be able to tell me how far it is from here to the river?"

"Get up on your feet," said the other, "and follow me quickly! I will take you to one who will oil the joints of your tongue for you, and put you to studying your catechism. Quick, fellow, move your heavy carcass, or, I promise you, I will prick your fat sides with my sword point."

"Anywhere you wish, sir, if you will only give me time to gather up this here bark," said the sergeant, who, hereupon, heedless of the objurgation of the trooper, deliberately untied the handkerchief from his neck, and spreading it out upon the ground, threw into it the pieces of bark he had been cutting, and then, taking it in his hand, rose and walked after the soldier.

He was conducted to the troop, who were waiting in the road the return of the men that had been despatched on this piece of service.

"Quick, quick, move yourselves! we have no time to lose," cried out the officer in command of the detachment, as Horse Shoe and his guide came in view: and then, after an interval of silence, during which the sergeant walked heavily to the spot where the troop waited for him, he added with an impatient abruptness, "Make few words of it, sir. Your name, where from, and where are you going?"

"My name, captain — if your honor is a captain, and if I miscall you, I ax your honor's pardon: my name is — is — Stephen Foster, Steve most commonly."

"Well, whence do you come?"

"From Virginny."

"Fool! why do you stop?"

"You axed, I think, where I was going? I was going to set on my horse that's broke his bridle, which I see you have cotched for me: and then back to my young mistress, sir, that was taken sick over here at a gentlewoman's house on Pedee. She thought a little sassafras tea might help her along, and I was sent out to try and get a few scrapings of the bark to take to her. I suppose I must have rode out of my way a matter of some eight or ten miles to find it, though I told her that I thought a little balm out of the garden would have done just as well. But women are women, sir, and a sick woman in particular."

"This fellow is more knave than fool, I take it, cornet," said the officer to a companion near him.

"His horse seems to have been trained to other duties than gathering herbs for ladies of delicate stomachs," replied the other.

"My horse," interrupted the sergeant, "would have broken clean off if it hadn't a been for your honor: they say he belonged to a muster in Verginny, and I was warned that he was apt to get rampagious when there was anything like a set of sodgers nigh him, and that is about the reason, I expect, why he took it into his head to fall into your company."

"Get on your beast," said the officer impatiently, "you must go with us. If upon further acquaintance I form a better opinion of you, you may go about your business."

"I am somewhat in a hurry to get back to the lady."

"Silence! Mount your horse, fall to the rear. Gilbert, attend to this fellow, he mustn't leave us," said the officer, as he delivered Horse Shoe into the charge of one of the leaders of a platoon, and then put spurs to his steed and moved to the head of the column.

It was in the afternoon when this incident occurred; and Robinson found himself, during the remainder of the day, compelled to follow the troop through a series of by-ways across the country, in a direction of which he was wholly ignorant, — being also in the same degree unacquainted with the object of the march. When the day closed they arrived at a farm-house, where it seemed to be their purpose to pass the night; and here the sergeant, towards whom no unnecessary rigor had been exercised, was freely allowed to participate in the cheer provided for the party. This rest was of short duration; for, before the coming of the allotted bed-hour, a courier arrived, bringing a despatch to the leader of the detachment, which produced an instant order to saddle and resume the march.

Once more upon the road, the sergeant became aware, as well as he was able to determine in the dark, that the party during the night were retracing their steps, and returning upon the same route which they had before travelled.

A half hour before the dawn found the troop ascending a long hill, the summit of which, as Robinson perceived from the rustling of the blades in the morning wind, was covered by a field of standing corn; and he was enabled to descry, moving athwart the starlit sky, the figures of men on horseback approaching the column. The customary challenge was given; a momentary halt ensued, and he could hear the patrole — for such they described themselves, — informing the officer of the detachment that Colonel Tarleton was close at hand expecting their arrival. This intelligence induced an increase of speed which, after a short interval, brought the night-worn squadron into the presence of nearly a whole regiment of cavalry.

The troops, thus encountered, were stationed upon the high-road where it crossed an open and uncultivated plain, the nearer extremity of which was bordered by the corn-field of which I have spoken. It was apparent that the regiment had passed the night at this place, as a number of horses were yet attached to the fence that guarded the field, and were feeding on the blades of corn that had been gathered and thrown before them. The greater part, however, were now drawn up in column of march, as if but recently arrayed to prepare for the toil of the coming day.

Robinson was conducted along the flank of the column, and thence to a spot in the neighborhood, where a party of officers assembled by a sylvan tent, constructed of the boughs of trees, showed him that he was at the headquarters of the commander of the corps. This tent was pitched upon a piece of high ground that afforded a view of the distant horizon in the east, where a faint streak of daylight lay like the traces of a far-off town in flames, against which the forms of men and horses were relieved, in bold profile, as they now moved about in the early preparations for their march.

A single faggot gleamed within the tent, and, by its ray, Horse Shoe was enabled to discern the well known figure of Tarleton, as he conferred with a company of officers around him. After the sergeant had waited a few moments, he was ordered into the presence of the group within:

"You were found yesterday," said Tarleton, "in suspicious circumstances — what is your name, fellow?"

"I am called Stephen Foster by name," replied the sergeant, "being a stranger in these parts. At home I'm a kind of a gardener to a gentleman in Virginia; and it isn't long since I sot out with his daughter to come here into Carolina. She fell sick by the way, and yesterday, whilst I was hunting up a little physic for her in the woods, a gang of your people came across me and fotch me here — and that's about all that I have got to say."

A series of questions followed, by which the sergeant was compelled to give some further account of himself, which he contrived to do with an address that left his questioners but little the wiser as to his real character; and which strongly impressed them with the conviction that the man they had to deal with was but a simple and rude clown.

"You say you don't know the name of the person at whose house you stopped?" inquired the commander.

"I disremember," replied Horse Shoe; "being, as I said, a stranger in the parts, and not liking to make too free with axing after people's names."

"A precious lout, this, you have brought me, Lieutenant Munroe," said Tarleton, addressing the officer who had hitherto had the custody of the sergeant. "You don't *disremember* the part of Virginia you lived in?" he added, pursuing his examination.

"They have given it the name of Amherst," replied Horse Shoe.

"And the father of Miss Lindsay, you say, resided there?"

"Sartainly, sir."

"There is a gentleman of that name somewhere in Virginia," said Tarleton, apart to one of his attendants, "and known as a friend to our cause, I think."

"I have heard of the family," replied the person addressed.

"What has brought the lady to Carolina?"

"Consarning some business of a friend, as I have been told," answered Horse Shoe.

"It is a strange errand for such a time, and a marvellous shrewd conductor she has chosen! I can make nothing out of this fellow. You might have saved yourself the trouble of taking charge of such a clod, lieutenant."

"My orders," replied the lieutenant, "were to arrest all suspicious persons; and I had two reasons to suspect this man. First, he was found upon a spot that couldn't have been better chosen for a look-out if he had been sent to reconnoitre us; and second, his horse showed some military training."

"But the booby himself was stupid enough," rejoined the commander, "to carry his passport in his face."

"I have a paper, sir, to that purpose," said Horse Shoe, putting his hands into his pockets, "it signifies, I was told,—for I can't read of my own accord—that I mought pass free without molestification from the sodgers of the king—this is it, I believe, sir."

"*To three suppers at the Rising Sun, four and six pence,*" said Tarleton, reading. "Tush, this is a tavern bill!"

"Ha, ha, so it is," exclaimed Robinson. "Well, I have been keeping that there paper for a week past, thinking it was my certificate—and, like a fool, I have gone and tore up the t'other.

"We are wasting time, gentlemen," said the commander. "Turn this fellow loose, and let him go his ways. But hark you, did you hear of a fight lately on Pedee, between some of our people and Marion — three days ago?"

"They talked of such a thing on the river," replied Horse Shoe.

"Well, and what was said?"

"Nothing in particular that I can bear in mind."

"Like all the rest we have tried to get out of him! You don't even know which party got the better?"

"Oh, I have hearn that, sir."

"What did you hear? speak out!"

"Shall I give you the circumlocutory account of the matter?" asked Horse Shoe, "or did you wish me to go into the particulars?"

"Any account, so that it be short."

"Then I have hearn that Marion gave the t'other side a bit of a beating."

"Aye, aye, so I suppose! Another tale of this Jack the Giant Killer! And what has become of Marion?"

"That's onbeknownst to me," replied Horse Shoe.

"Do you remember the fool we met at the Waxhaws last May?" asked one of the officers present, of another. "This fellow might pass for a full brother in blood — only I think this clown has the less wit of the two."

"As heavy a lump, certainly," replied the officer. "This, you say, is the first time you have been in Carolina?"

"To my knowledge," replied the sergeant.

"It is broad day, gentlemen," said Tarleton; "we have been squandering precious time upon an empty simpleton. Give him his beast and let him be gone. Sirrah, you are free to depart. But, look you, if I hear any reports along the road of your having seen me, or a word about my coming, I'll ferret you out and have you trussed upon a stake twenty feet long."

"Thank your honor," said Horse Shoe, as he left the tent. "I never troubles my head with things out of my line."

Then seeking his horse he leisurely rode back by the way he had come; and as soon as he found himself beyond the outposts of the corps, he urged Captain Peter to as much speed as the late arduous duties of the good beast left him power to exert.

CHAPTER XLVIII

AN INCIDENT OF THE WAR NOT UNFAMILIAR TO THE TIME

Breakfast was just over when Robinson was seen, from the windows of Mrs. Markham's parlor, pricking along the avenue that conducted to the front of the mansion; and when he drew up his horse at the door, the family were already assembled there to greet him. The plight, both of himself and of his steed, was such as to tell the best part of his story — they had travelled far and seen rough service. The rest was supplied by the sergeant himself, who, before he moved from the spot where he had dismounted, gave a narrative of his adventures, which was listened to with great anxiety by the household.

By the sergeant's reckoning, Mrs. Markham's residence could not be more than twenty miles from the place where, at daybreak, he had encountered the British partisan, whom he had left with a full conviction that the expedition then on foot was to be directed against the country lying upon the river. These tidings spread consternation throughout the mansion, and the morning was passed in all the confusion which such an alarm might be supposed to produce. The fright of the females rendered them irresolute, and incapable of attending to the most obvious precautions necessary to meet the emergency.

In this conjuncture, Robinson felt himself bound to assume the direction of affairs. At this suggestion, the plate and such other valuables as were likely to attract the cupidity of a licentious soldiery, were secreted in hiding places sufficiently secure to defy a hasty search. The family was advised to assume the appearance of as much composure as they could command; and the last and most emphatic injunction of the sergeant was, to provide an ample and various repast, in the hope that the ill-will of the visitants might be conciliated by the display of good cheer. All this was accordingly put into a train of accomplishment.

In the midst of these precautions, the fears of the inhabitants of the mansion were but too truly realized. It was scarcely noon when the long column of Tarleton's cavalry was descried descending the high hills that lay in the distance, and, soon afterwards, taking the road that led into the plantation.

Whilst the panic produced by this sight was still fresh, the sound of bugles and trumpets showed that the invaders had already turned their steps towards the dwelling, and the next view disclosed them deploying from a wood and advancing at a full trot. The quick beat of hoofs upon the soil, and the jangling sounds of sabres shaken against the flanks of the horses, struck upon the terrified ear of the proprietress of the estate like the harsh portents of impending ruin; and in the despair and agony of her distress, she retreated hastily to her chamber, whither she summoned her female domestics, and gave way to a flood of tears. She was followed by Mildred, who, touched by the pervading disquiet of the family, participated in the alarm, and found herself overcome by a terror which she had never before experienced in all the scenes which she had lately gone through. Obeying the instinct of her present fears, our heroine cowered beside her weeping friend, in the midst of the group of clamorous servants, and awaited in mute solicitude the coming events.

The cavalry had turned aside and halted in front of a barn some distance from the dwelling-house, and a small party, consisting principally of officers attended by a sergeant's guard, were immediately afterwards seen galloping up to the door. The air of exultation exhibited in their movement, their loud jocularity and frequent laughter, resembled the burst of gladsome riot with which a party of fox-hunters are wont to announce the first springing of their game, and gave evidence of the feelings of men who set little account upon the annoyance they threatened to a peaceful and unoffending household.

When the officers of the party had dismounted and entered the hall, the first person they encountered was Sergeant Robinson, who had thoughtfully posted himself in view of the door; and now, with some awkward and ungainly bows and scraping of his feet across the floor, bade them welcome.

"What," said Tarleton, who was at the head of the intruders, "have we stumbled so soon again upon our shrewd and sensible ox! Wise Master Stephen Foster, well met! So you are the gentleman-usher to your good friend, Mrs. Markham! By my faith, the old lady is likely to have the honors of her house well administered!"

"Your sarvant, sir," said Horse Shoe, again bowing and scraping his foot with a look of imperturbable gravity. "Mought

I ax your honor to stomp as lightly upon the floor as you can? My young lady is sick up stairs — and much noise is apt to flurry her narves."

"Tread daintily, gentlemen," said Tarleton, laughing, "for your gallantry's sake! A lady's nerves are as delicate as the strings of a harp, and must not be rudely struck. The damsel's page here (pointing to Horse Shoe), puts down his foot like a most considerate elephant — soft as a feather, you perceive; and I would by no means have you give so worshipful a master of courtesy cause to complain of you. As your wisdom," he added, again addressing the sergeant, "has found out, by this time, that you are in the house of Mrs. Markham, although you *disremembered* that this morning, I suppose you can tell whether she is at home?"

"I can answer you that she is at home, sir — that is, onless she has went out sence I saw her, which is not likely, sir."

"Then, present her Colonel Tarleton's respects, and say that he has come to offer his duty to her."

"I suppose by that, you are wishing to see the lady," replied the sergeant; "I'll let her know, sir."

Robinson retired for a few moments, and when he returned he announced to the commander that Mrs. Markham was not willing to come from her chamber. "But whatsomever your honor pleases to ax after, the lady promises you shall have," continued the sergeant.

"Well, that's a condescension! — a good, comfortable lady! So, gentlemen, you see we are in luck; a broad roof over head — a larder well stored, I hope — and a cellar not altogether empty, I think I may undertake to promise. Where are your waiting-men, my nimble Ganymede? You are a sluggish oaf, fellow, not to see that soldiers must have drink!"

Alfred and Henry now entered the hall, and the former approaching Tarleton, said, with a firm but respectful tone:

"My mother has before been visited by British troops, and she had so little then to thank them for, except their departure, that the fear of meeting them again has greatly alarmed her. Our family, sir, has no older man in it than myself — and out of regard to helpless women — "

"That's enough, my pert lad," interrupted Tarleton; "I have heard of your good mother before; she is somewhat over ready in her zeal in behalf of Marion's ragamuffins: and truly I think she is more squeamish than she should be at the sight of a soldier, when she could look upon such hang-gallows knaves without shuddering. You have another man in your house, I see (directing his eye towards Henry Lindsay, who had seated himself in the hall) — and full as old, I take it, as yourself."

"I wish I were a man of full age," said Henry, looking fearlessly at the British officer, and remaining fixed in his chair.

"Why so, my gay sparrow-hawk?"

"I would have disputed with you your right to enter this door."

"These young cocks are all trained to show their game," said the Colonel to one of his companons. "Well, you are a fine fellow, and I should be happy to be better acquainted with you. A little too stiff, perhaps: but you will learn better as you grow older. You should thank me for making holiday in your school to-day."

Here Robinson interposed before Henry could make the saucy reply he meditated, by announcing that the company would find some cool water and a supply of spirits in the adjoining room. "Besides," he added, "I have told the house-folks to make ready somewhat in the way of victuals, as I judged you mought be a little hungry."

"Not badly thought of, Mr. Ajax!" said one of the officers, as the party now crowded into the room.

"Don't forget Stephen Foster," whispered Robinson, by way of admonition in regard to his assumed character, as he passed by the chair where Henry was sitting. "And keep a civil tongue in your head."

Henry nodded compliance, and then, with Alfred, left the hall, whilst the sergeant repaired to the refreshment room to offer his officious attentions to the guests.

Meanwhile, the ladies still kept to their chamber, ever and anon gazing out at the window with a solicitous and unhappy interest, and occasionally receiving the highly-colored reports of the servants, who, as often as any new subject of wonder or fear occurred to them, were plying backwards and forwards between the apartment and the head of the staircase.

After an interval of half an hour, during which the uncouth din of laughter, of loud oaths, and of the careless swaggering of the party below, rose with a harsh note to the ear of the hostess and her companion, these sounds abruptly ceased, and it was evident that the visitors had quitted the house. It was with an emotion of delight that Mrs. Markham, from the window, beheld Colonel Tarleton and his comrades galloping towards the main body of his troops that awaited him near the barn; but, on repairing to the hall, this sudden gleam of satisfaction was as suddenly clouded, when the matron perceived a sentinel posted at the front door. As soon as she came within speech of this functionary, he threw up his hand to his brow, as he said: "The colonel commanded me to make his compliments to the ladies, and asks the honor of their company at dinner."

"Colonel Tarleton forgets himself," said Mrs. Markham, with a stately reserve that showed she had now dismissed her fears; "a brave soldier would hardly think it a triumph to insult unprotected females."

"He is here to speak for himself, madam," replied the sentinel, as Tarleton at this moment returned to the door.

The lady of the house, thus taken by surprise, firmly stood her ground, and awaited in silence the accost of the officer. Tarleton was somewhat disconcerted by this unexpected encounter. He had entered with a hurried step, but the moment he was aware of the presence of the dame, he halted and removed his cap from his head, as he made a low obeisance.

"I am too happy, madam," he said, "in the persuasion that you have overcome your unnecessary alarm at this visit; and feel pleased to be afforded an opportunity of making my respects in person."

"I can conceive no sufficient reason, Colonel Tarleton, why a defenceless house like mine should provoke the visit of such a host of armed men."

"Your house, madam, has some fame upon this border for good entertainment. It fell in my way, and you will excuse me for the freedom of saying, that I boast myself too much of a cavalier to pass it by unmarked by some token of my regard. Besides, I may add without meaning to be rude, our necessities in the article of forage, madam, are quite as great as General Marion's, who, I understand, does not scruple sometimes to take his contribution from you."

"I should more readily excuse your visit," replied the lady, "if you would time it when General Marion was levying his contribution. You might then adjust your right to the share you claim. This house is yours, sir; and it is not fit that I should remain to debate with you your claim to dispose of whatever you may find in it."

"Why, what a musty and wrinkled piece of insolence is here!" muttered the angry soldier, clenching his teeth under this rebuke as the matron withdrew. "Well, let the crones rail and the maidens weep their fill! the border is mine, and merrily will I hold it, and blithely will I light up the river, too, before I leave it! Curse on these free-spoken women! Who says they are defenceless with that supple weapon that God has given them? What ho, you bag of chaff — booby — Foster — I say! Look you; have you all the provisions in the house set out upon the tables — and don't spare your peach brandy, which we have already tasted — you have more of it. So let us have the best; I shall feast with a good will to-day, and I will do it plentifully, or your ears shall be cropped."

"Everything in the kitchen, sir, is going on at a gallop," said Horse Shoe; "and as for the drinkables, your honor shall command the house to the last jug."

"Then bestir yourself, for I am in no mood to tarry."

In a brief lapse of time an abundant board was spread, and the leaders of the corps, consisting of some twenty or thirty officers of all ranks, were gathered around it. A scene of uproar succeeded that resounded to the roof with the unfeeling and licentious mirth of those engaged in the carouse.

When they had eaten and drunk their fill, the greater portion of the guests were assembled at the front door. From this position there was to be seen, at no great distance, a small inclosure of not above ten feet square, constructed with a dark paling, above which a venerable willow drooped its branches. Toward this inclosure some five or six of the revellers repaired, to gratify an idle and, at present, a maudlin curiosity. When they arrived here, they leaned across the paling to read the inscription upon a stone that seemed but recently to have been placed there. It was a simple memorial of the death of Colonel Markham, of the Carolina militia, which was recorded to have taken place but eighteen months before on the Savannah river in an engagement with the troops under General Prevost. To this was added, in the spirit of the times and in accordance with the sentiments of the Whig leaders in the war of independence, a bitter expression of censure upon the barbarous disposition of the enemy, couched in homely but earnest phrase, and speaking the hate of the survivors in the same sentence that commended the virtues of the dead.

It was an unpropitious moment for such a tablet to meet the eye of those who gazed upon it; and when it was read aloud by the captain of a troop, whose natural temper, rendered savage by the rudeness of the war, was also at this moment exasperated almost to intoxication by the freedom of the table, he vented his curses in loud and coarse rage against the memory of him to whom the stone was dedicated. This fire of passion spread through the group around the tomb, and each man responded to the first execration by others still deeper and more fierce. Proclaiming the inscription to be an insult, they made an attack upon the paling, which was instantly demolished, and, seizing upon the largest stones at hand, they assailed the tablet with such effect as soon to break it in pieces; and then, with a useless malice, applied themselves to obliterating the inscription upon the fragments. Whilst engrossed with the perpetration of this sacrilege, their attention was suddenly aroused by the near report of a pistol, the ball of which, it was discovered, had struck into the trunk of the willow.

"I will kill some of the scoundrels, if I die for it!" was the exclamation heard immediately after the shot, and Alfred Markham was seen struggling with an officer who had seized him. The young man had been observed and followed, as he madly rushed from a wing of the mansion towards the burial-place, and arrested at the moment that he was levelling a second pistol.

"Henry, shoot him down!" he screamed to his companion, who was now approaching armed with his carbine.

"Let me go, sir! I will not see my father's tomb disturbed by ruffians."

"Loose your hands!" cried Henry, directing his passionate defiance to the individual who wrestled with Alfred, "loose your hands, I say, or I will fire upon you!"

"Fire at the drunken villains around my father's grave!" shouted Alfred.

"They shall have it," returned Henry, eagerly, "if it is the last shot I ever make." And with these words the youth levelled his piece at the same group which had before escaped Alfred's aim, but, luckily, the carbine snapped and missed fire. In the next instant Horse Shoe's broad hand was laid upon Henry's shoulder, as he exclaimed, "Why, Master Henry, have you lost your wits? Do you want to bring perdition and combustion both, down upon the heads of the whole house?"

"Galbraith Robinson, stand back!" ejaculated Henry. "I am not in the humor to be baulked."

"Hush — for God's sake, hush! — foolish boy," returned Robinson with real anger. "You are as fierce as a young panther—I am ashamed of you!"

By this time the whole company were assembled around the two young men, and the violent outbreak of wrath from those at whom the shot was aimed, as well as from others present, rose to a pitch which the authority of Tarleton in vain sought to control. Already, in this paroxysm of rage, one of the party, whose motions had escaped notice in the confusion of the scene, had hurried to the kitchen fire, where he had snatched up a burning brand, and hurled it into the midst of some combustibles in a narrow apartment on the ground floor.

The clamor had drawn Mrs. Markham and Mildred to the chamber window, and whilst they looked down with a frightened gaze upon the confused scene below, it was some moments before they became aware of the participation of Henry and Alfred in this sudden and angry boil. Mildred was the first to discern the two young men as they were dragged violently across the open space in front of the mansion by the crowd, and to hear the threats with which this movement was accompanied.

"Merciful Heaven!" she exclaimed, "they have laid hands upon Henry and Alfred—they will kill my brother, my dear brother!" Almost frantic at the danger that threatened Henry and his companion, she fled precipitately down the stair-case, and in a moment stood confronted with Colonel Tarleton and his soldiers.

"Never fear, sister," cried out Henry, who was already brought into the hall, as he saw Mildred descending the stairs. "Don't be alarmed for either Alfred or me. We are ready to confess what we did and why we did it—and Colonel Tarleton, if he is a true man, will not dare to say we did wrong."

"I charge you, Colonel Tarleton," said Mildred, with a firm but excited voice, "as the soldier of a Christian nation, to save the people of this house from an inhuman and most wicked outrage. I implore you as an officer who would be esteemed valiant—and as a gentleman who would fly from dishonor—to rescue your name from the disgrace of this barbarous violence. For the sake of mercy—spare us—spare us!"

As she uttered this last ejaculation her spirit yielded to the vehemence of her feelings, and she flung herself upon her knee at the feet of the commander. "Oh, sir, do not let harm fall upon my brother. I know not what he has done, but he is thoughtless and rash."

"Mildred," said Henry, immediately rushing to his sister, and lifting her from the floor, "why should you kneel before him, or any man here? This is no place for you — get back to your room." Then turning to Tarleton, he continued, "Alfred Markham and I tried to shoot down your men, because we saw them breaking the tomb. If it was to do over again our hands are ready."

"They have insulted the memory of my father," exclaimed Alfred, "trampled upon his grave, and broken the stone that covers him — I aimed to kill the drunken coward who did it. That I say, sir, to your face."

Tarleton, for a space, seemed to be bewildered by the scene. He looked around him, as if hesitating what course to pursue, and once or twice made an effort to obtain silence in the hall; but the tumult of many voices in angry contention still continued. At last he presented his hand to Mildred, and with a courteous action conducted her to a chair, then begged her to calm her fears, as he promised her that no evil should befall either of the young men whose indiscreet tempers had occasioned the present uproar.

"In God's name! have they fired the dwelling?" he exclaimed, as at this moment a volume of smoke rolled into the hall. "What ho, there! O'Neal, McPherson. Look where this smoke comes from, and instantly extinguish the fire! Stir yourselves, gentlemen. By my hilt, if any follower of mine has been so wild as to put a torch to this house, I will hang him up to the ridge-pole of the roof! Look to it — every man! Quick, quick — there is danger that the flames may get ahead."

In an instant nearly every soldier in the hall departed in obedience to this order.

"I beg, madam," Tarleton continued, "that you will dismiss your alarm, and rest upon my pledge that no inmate of this house shall be harmed. I conjecture that I have the honor to speak to Miss Lindsay — I have been informed that that lady has lately found shelter under this roof."

"It is my name, sir — and as the daughter of a friend to your quarrel, let me conjure you to see that this house is safe; I cannot speak with you until I am assured of that."

At this juncture, Mrs. Markham was observed at the head of the first flight of stairs, pale with affright, wringing her hands, and uttering loud ejaculations of terror and grief as she made her way down to the hall:

"Oh, sir," she said, as she approached the commander, "we are harmless women, and have done nothing to call down this vengeance upon us. Take what you will — but spare my roof and save my family! God will reward you even for that act of humanity to a desolate widow."

Before Tarleton could reply to the matron, a party of officers came hastily into his presence, at the head of whom was Captain O'Neal, who reported that the fire was extinguished.

"One of the mess, to-day," he said, "heated with drink and roused by the foolish temper of these hot-headed boys, threw a blazing billet into a closet. Luckily, we reached the spot before any great harm was done. The chaps should be switched, and taught better manners. It was a silly affair and might have made mischief."

"See that the offender be arrested," replied Tarleton, "I will take measures to curb this license. These meddling youngsters, too — however, I can't blame them, they had provocation, I confess — and this war gives an edge to all the metal of the country. Instead of pop-guns now every baby has his powder and ball — dismiss the boys. To your post, captain, and order every man to join his company. Now, madam," he added in a tone of conciliation to Mrs. Markham, as soon as the hall was cleared, "I am sure you will not accuse me of incivility. My people have withdrawn — the fire is extinguished — these inconsiderate lads at liberty: have I answered your wish?"

"You have won the gratitude of a mother," replied the dame, "and the respect of an enemy. I am bound to say to you, in return, that I cheerfully surrender to you whatever you may choose to take from my estate for the supply of your soldiers. Alfred, my son, give me your arm, and help me to my chamber — I am feeble and faint. I must ask your permission to withdraw," she continued, as she courtesied to Tarleton, and ascended the stairs.

"And I, too, must take my leave," said Tarleton. "But before I go I may claim the privilege of a word with Miss Lindsay. You spoke of your father, madam? and, especially, as a friend of our arms. I have been told he lives in Virginia, Philip Lindsay, the proprietor of a seat called 'The Dove Cote,' a royalist too — am I right?"

"So, my father is known, sir?"

"That name has stood you in stead to-day, madam. And this

is your brother? I should think he is hardly of your father's mind in regard to our quarrel. This way, my thoughtless young gallant! It was a wild, bold, and very conceited thing of you to be challenging my unruly dragoons — and would have been no less so, if you had had twenty score of tall fellows at your back. But it is past now, and you need not apologize for it — it showed mettle at least, and we never quarrel with a man for that. May I inquire, Miss Lindsay, in what direction you travel? for I learn you are but a sojourner here. It may be in my power to insure your safe-conduct."

"I seek your general, Lord Cornwallis, on matters of private concern," replied Mildred, "and if I might venture to ask it of Colonel Tarleton, his service in affording me an unquestioned passage, would be a favor that I should gratefully acknowledge."

"The obligation will be on my side, madam. It will be a pleasure to me to believe that I can serve a lady, much more the daughter of an honorable subject of the king. Permit me, without further parley, for time presses at this moment, to say that I will leave an escort behind me under the command of a trusty officer, who will wait your pleasure to conduct you, by the safest and easiest journey to head-quarters. Your commands, madam, shall in all respects regulate his motions. My communications with his lordship shall announce your coming. Now, Miss Lindsay, with my best wishes for your safety and success, I take my leave; and, as a parting request, I venture to hope you will do me the justice to say, that Tarleton is not such a graceless sinner as his enemies have sometimes been pleased to represent him."

These last words were accompanied by a laugh, and a somewhat bluff courtesy, as the speaker swayed his rigid and ungainly figure into a succession of awkward bows by which he retreated to the door.

"I shall be happy on all occasions," replied Mildred, whilst the soldier was thus strenuously playing off the graces of a gallant, "to do justice to the kindness which I have experienced at Colonel Tarleton's hands."

"There, Mildred," said Henry, when Tarleton had disappeared, "you see things have gone very pat for us. That comes of letting these fellows see who they have to deal with. A little powder and ball is a good letter of recommendation to the best of their gang. If my carbine hadn't missed fire to-day, Tarleton would have been short by one bottle-holder, at least, when he set out to steal liquor from the country cupboards."

"It has ended well, brother," replied Mildred, "but it does not become you to boast of what you have done. It was a rash and dangerous deed, and had nearly brought ruin upon this friendly family."

"Tut, sister! you are only a woman. You wouldn't have found the colonel so civil if we hadn't taught him to look after his men."

CHAPTER XLIX

MILDRED ARRIVES AT THE TERM OF HER JOURNEY. — THE READER IS FAVORED WITH A GLIMPSE OF A DISTINGUISHED PERSONAGE

CORNWALLIS, after the battle of Camden, turned his thoughts to the diligent prosecution of his conquests. The invasion of North Carolina and Virginia was a purpose to which he had looked, from the commencement of this campaign, and he now, accordingly, made every preparation for the speedy advance of his army. The sickness of a portion of his troops and the want of supplies rendered some delay inevitable, and this interval was employed in more fully organizing the civil government of the conquered province, and in strengthening his frontier defences, by detaching considerable parties of men towards the mountains. The largest of these detachments was sent to reinforce Ferguson, to whom had been confided the operations upon the north-western border.

The chronicles of the time inform us that the British general lay at Camden until the 8th of September, at which date he set forward towards North Carolina. His movement was slow and cautious, and for some time, his head-quarters were established at the Waxhaws, a position directly upon the border of the province about to be invaded. At this post our story now finds him, the period being somewhere about the commencement of the last quarter of the month.

A melancholy train of circumstances had followed the fight at Camden, and had embittered the feelings of the contending parties against each other to an unusual degree of exasperation. The most prominent of these topics of anger was the unjust and severe construction which the British authorities had given to the obligations which were supposed to affect such of the inhabitants of South Carolina, as had, after the capitulation of Charleston, surrendered themselves as prisoners on parole, or received protections from the new government. A proclamation, issued by Sir Henry Clinton in June, annulled the paroles, and ordered all who had obtained them to render military service, as subjects of the king. This order, which the prisoners, as well as those who had obtained protections, held to be a dissolution of their contract with the new government, was disobeyed by a large number of the inhabitants, many of whom had, immediately after the proclamation, joined the American army.

Cornwallis permitted himself, on this occasion, to be swayed by sentiments unworthy of the character generally imputed to him. Many of the liberated inhabitants were found in the ranks of Gates at Camden, and several were made prisoners on the field. These latter, by the orders of the British general, were hung almost without the form of an inquiry: and it may well be supposed that, in the heat of war and ferment of passion, such acts of rigor, defended on such light grounds, were met on the opposite side by a severe retribution.

Almost every day, during the British commander's advance, some of the luckless citizens of the province whom this harsh construction of duty affected, were brought into the camp of the invaders, and the soldiery had grown horribly familiar with the frequent military executions that ensued.

It was in the engrossment of the occupations and cares presented in this brief reference to the history of the time, that I have now to introduce my reader to Cornwallis.

He had resolved to move forward on his campaign. Orders were issued to prepare for the march, and the general had announced his determination to review the troops before they broke ground. A beautiful, bright, and cool autumnal morning shone upon the wide plain, where an army of between two and three thousand men was drawn out in line. The tents of the recent encampment had already been struck, and a long array of baggage-wagons were now upon the high-road, slowly moving to a point assigned them in the route of the march. Cornwallis, attended by a score of officers, still occupied a small farm-house which had lately been his quarters. A number of saddle-horses in the charge of their grooms, and fully equipped for service, were to be seen in the neighborhood of the door; the principal apartment of the house showed that some of the loiterers of the company were yet engaged in despatching the morning meal. The aides-de-camp were seen speeding between the army and the general, with that important and neck-endangering haste which characterizes the tribe of these functionaries; and almost momentarily a courier arrived, bearing some message of interest to the commander-in-chief.

Cornwallis himself sat in an inner room, busily engaged with one of his principal officers in inspecting some documents regarding the detail of his force. Apart from them, stood, with hat in hand and in humble silence, a young ensign of infantry.

"Your name, sir?" said Cornwallis, as he threw aside the papers which he had been perusing, and now addressed himself to the young officer.

"Ensign Talbot, of the thirty-third Foot," replied the young man: "I have come by the order of the adjutant-general to inform your lordship that I have just returned to my regiment, having lately been captured by the enemy while marching with the third convoy of the Camden prisoners to Charleston."

"Ha! you were of that party! What was the number of prisoners you had in charge?"

"One hundred and fifty, so please your lordship."

"They were captured"—

"On Santee, by the rebels Marion and Horry," interrupted the ensign. "I have been in the custody of the rebels for a week, but contrived, a few days since, to make my escape."

"Where found the rebels men to master you?"

"Even from the country through which we journeyed," replied the ensign.

"The beggarly runagates! Who can blame us, Major M'Arthur," said the general, appealing to the officer by his side, with an interest that obviously spoke the contest in his own mind in regard to the justice of the daily executions which he had sanctioned: "who can blame us for hanging up these recreants for their violated faith, with such thick perfidy before our eyes? This Santee district, to a man, had given their paroles and taken my protection: and, now, the first chance they have to play me a trick, they are up and at work, attacking our feeble escorts that should, in their sickly state, have rather looked to them for aid. I will carry out the work; by my sword, it shall go on sternly! Enough, Ensign, back to your company," he said, bowing to the young officer, who at once left the room.

"What is your lordship's pleasure regarding this Adam Cusack?" inquired M'Arthur.

"Oh, aye! I had well nigh forgotten that man. He was taken, I think, in the act of firing on a ferry-boat at Cheraw?"

"The ball passed through the hat of my Lord Dunglas," said M'Arthur.

"The lurking hound! A liege subject turning truant to his duty; e'en let him bide the fate of his brethren."

M'Arthur merely nodded his head, and Cornwallis, rising from his chair, strode a few paces backwards and forwards through the room. " I would tune my bosom to mercy," he said, at length, " and win these dog-headed rebels back to their duty to their king by kindness; but goodwill and charity towards them fall upon their breasts like water on a heated stone, which is thrown back in hisses. No, no, that day is past, and they shall feel the rod. We walk in danger whilst we leave these serpents in the grass. Order the gentlemen to horse, Major M'Arthur; we must be stirring. Let this fellow, Cusack, be dealt with like the rest. Gentlemen," added the chief, as he appeared at the door amidst the group who awaited his coming, " to your several commands! "

Captain Brodrick, the principal aide, at this moment arrested the preparations to depart, by placing in Cornwallis's hand a letter which had just been brought by a dragoon to head-quarters.

The general broke the seal, and, running his eye over the contents, said, as he handed the letter to the aide, " This is something out of the course of the campaign; a letter from a lady, now at the picquet-guard, and it seems she desires to speak with me. Who brought the billet, captain? "

" This dragoon, one of a special escort from the legion. They have in charge a party of travellers, who have journeyed hither under Tarleton's own pledge of passport."

" Captain," replied Cornwallis, " mount and seek the party. Conduct them to me without delay. What toy is this that brings a lady to my camp? "

The aide-de-camp mounted his horse, and galloped off with the dragoon. He was conducted far beyond the utmost limit of the line of soldiers, and at length arrived at a small outpost, where some fifty men were drawn up, under the command of an officer of the picquet-guard, which was about returning to join the main body of the army. Here he found Mildred and Henry Lindsay, and their two companions, Horse Shoe and old Isaac, attended by the small escort furnished by Tarleton. This party had been two days on the road from Mrs. Markham's, and had arrived the preceding night at a cottage in the neighborhood, where they had found tolerable quarters. They had advanced this morning, at an early hour, to the *corps de garde* of the picquet, where Mildred preferred remaining until Henry could despatch a note to Lord Cornwallis apprising him of their visit.

When Captain Brodrick rode up, the travellers were already

on horseback and prepared to move. The aide-de-camp respectfully saluted Miss Lindsay and her brother, and after a short parley with the officer of the escort, tendered his services to the strangers to conduct them to head-quarters.

"The general, madam," he said, "would have done himself the honor to wait on you, but presuming that you were already on your route to his quarters, where you might be better received than in the bivouac of an outpost, he is led to hope that he consults your wish and your comfort both, by inviting you to partake of such accommodation as he is able to afford you."

"My mission would idly stand on ceremony, sir," replied Mildred. "I thank Lord Cornwallis for the promptness with which he has answered my brother's message."

"We will follow you, sir," said Henry.

The party now rode on.

Their path lay along the skirts of the late encampment upon the border of an extensive plain, on the opposite side of which the army was drawn out; and it was with the exultation of a boy, that Henry, as they moved forward, looked upon the long line of troops glittering in the bright sunshine, and heard the drums rolling their spirited notes upon the air.

When they arrived at a point where the road emerged from a narrow strip of forest, they could discern, at the distance of a few hundred paces, the quarters of the commander-in-chief. Immediately on the edge of this wood, a small party of soldiers attracted the attention of the visitors by the earnest interest with which they stood around a withered tree, and gazed aloft at its sapless and huge boughs. Before anything was said, Mildred had already ridden within a few feet of the circle, where turning her eyes upwards she saw the body of a man swung in the air by a cord attached to one of the widest-spreading branches. The unfortunate being was just struggling in the paroxysms of death, as his person was swayed backwards and forwards, with a slow motion, by the breeze.

"Oh, God! what a sight is here!" exclaimed the lady. "I cannot, will not go by this spot. Henry — brother — I cannot pass."

The aide-de-camp checked his horse, and grasped her arm, before her brother could reach her, and Horse Shoe, at the same moment, sprang to the ground and seized her bridle.

"I should think it but a decent point of war to keep such sights from women's eyes," said Robinson, somewhat angrily.

"Peace, sirrah," returned the aide, "you are saucy. I trust, madam, you are not seriously ill? I knew not of this execution, or I should have spared you this unwelcome spectacle. Pray, compose yourself, and believe, madam, it was my ignorance that brought you into this difficulty."

"I will not pass it," cried Mildred wildly, as she sprang from her horse and ran some paces back towards the wood, with her hands covering her face. In a moment Henry was by her side.

"Nay, sister — dear sister," he said, "do not take it so grievously. The officer did not know of this. There now, you are better; we will mount again, and ride around this frightful place."

Mildred gradually regained her self-possession, and after a few minutes was again mounted and making a circuit through the wood to avoid this appalling spectacle.

"Who is this man?" asked Henry of the aide-de-camp, in a half whisper; "and what has he done, that they have hung him?"

"It is an every-day tale," replied the officer; "a rebel traitor, who has broken his allegiance, by taking arms against the king in his own conquered province. I keep no count of these fellows; but I believe this is a bold rebel by the name of Adam Cusack, that was caught lately at the Cheraw ferry; and our boobies must be packing him off to head-quarters for us to do their hangman's work."

"If we were to hang all of your men that we catch," replied Henry, "hemp is an article that would rise in price."

"What, sir," returned the officer, with a look of surprise, "do you class yourself with the rebels? What makes you here under Tarleton's safeguard? I thought you must needs be friends, at least, from the manner of your coming."

"We ride, sir, where we have occasion," said Henry, "and if we ride wrong now, let his lordship decide that for us, and we will return."

By this time the company had reached head-quarters, where Mildred found herself in the presence of Lord Cornwallis.

"Though on the wing, Miss Lindsay," said his lordship, as he respectfully met the lady and her brother upon the porch of the dwelling-house, "I have made it a point of duty to postpone weighty matters of business to receive your commands."

Mildred bowed her head, and after a few words of courtesy on either side, and a formal introduction of herself and her brother to the general as the children of Philip Lindsay, "a gentleman presumed to be well known to his lordship," and some expressions of surprise and concern on the part of the chief at this unexpected announcement, she begged to be permitted to converse with him in private. When, in accordance with this wish, she found herself and her brother alone with the general, in the small parlor of the house, she began, with a trembling accent and blanched cheek —

"I said, my lord, that we were the children of Philip Lindsay, of the Dove Cote, in Amherst, in the province of Virginia; and being taught to believe that my father has some interest with your lordship — "

"He is a worthy, thoughtful, and wise gentleman, of the best consideration amongst the friends of the royal cause," interrupted the earl, "so speak on, madam, and speak calmly. Take your time, your father's daughter shall not find me an unwilling listener."

"My father was away from home," interposed Henry, "and tidings came to us that a friend of ours was most wickedly defamed and belied, by a charge carried to the ears of your lordship; as we were told, that Major Arthur Butler of the Continental army who had been made a prisoner by your red-coats somehow or other — for I forget how — but the charge was that he had contrived a plan to carry off my father from the Dove Cote — if not to kill him, which was said, besides — and upon that charge, it was reported that your people were going to hang or shoot him — hang, I suppose, from what we just now saw over here in the woods — and that your lordship had given orders to have the thing put off until the major could prove the real facts of the case."

"The tale is partly true, young sir," said Cornwallis. "We have a prisoner of that name and rank."

"My sister Mildred and myself, thinking no time was to be lost, have come to say to your lordship that the whole story is a most sinful lie, hatched on purpose to make mischief, and most probably by a fellow by the name of —— "

"My brother speaks too fast," interrupted Mildred. "It deeply concerned us to do justice to a friend in this matter. If my father had been at home a letter to your lordship would have removed all doubts; but, alas! he was absent, and I knew not what to do, but to come personally before your lordship, to assure you that to the perfect knowledge of our whole family, the tale from beginning to end is a malicious fabrication. Major Butler loves my father, and would be accounted one of his nearest and dearest friends."

Cornwallis listened to this disclosure with a perplexed and bewildered conjecture, to unravel the strange riddle which it presented to his mind.

"How may I understand you, Miss Lindsay?" he said; "this Major Butler is in the service of Congress?"

"Even so. Your lordship speaks truly."

"Your father — my friend, Philip Lindsay, is a faithful and persevering loyalist."

"To the peril of his life and fortune," replied Mildred.

"And yet Butler is his friend?"

"He would be esteemed so, if it please your lordship — and, in heart and feeling, is so."

"He is related to your family, perhaps?"

"Related in affection, my lord, and plighted love," said Mildred, blushing and casting her eyes upon the ground.

"So! — Now I apprehend. And there are bonds between you?"

"I may not answer your lordship," returned the lady. "It only imports our present business to tell your lordship, that Arthur Butler never came to the Dove Cote but with the purest purpose of good to all who lodged beneath its roof. He has never come there but that I was apprised of his intent; and never thought rose in his heart that did not breathe blessings upon all that inhabit near my father. Oh, my lord, it is a base trick of an enemy to do him harm; and they have contrived this plot to impose upon your lordship's generous zeal in my father's behalf."

"It is a strange story," said Cornwallis. "And does your father know nothing of this visit? Have you, Miss Lindsay, committed yourself to all the chances of this rude war, and undertaken this long and toilsome journey, to vindicate a rebel charged with a most heinous device of perfidy? It is a deep and painful interest that could move you to this enterprise."

"My lord, my mission requires a frank confidence. I have heard my father say you had a generous and feeling heart — that you were a man to whom the king had most wisely committed his cause in this most trying war: that your soul was gifted with moderation, wisdom, forecast, firmness — and that such a spirit as yours was fit to master and command the rude natures of soldiers, and to compel them to walk in the paths of justice and mercy. All this and more have I heard my father say, and this encouraged me to seek you in your camp, and to tell you the plain and undisguised truth touching those charges against Major Butler. As Heaven above hears me, I have said nothing but the simple truth. Arthur Butler never dreamt of harm to my dear father."

"He is a brave soldier," said Henry, "and if your lordship would give him a chance, and put him before the man who invented the lie, he would make the scoundrel eat his words, and they should be handed to him on the major's sword-point."

"The gentleman is happy," said the chief, "in two such zealous friends. You have not answered me — is your father aware of this visit, Miss Lindsay?"

"He is ignorant even of the nature of the charge against Arthur Butler," replied the lady. "He was absent from the Dove Cote when the news arrived; and, fearing that delay might be disastrous, we took the matter in hand ourselves."

"You might have written."

"The subject, so please your lordship, was too near to our hearts to put it to the hazard of a letter."

"It is a warm zeal, and deserves to be requited with a life's devotion," said Cornwallis. "You insinuated, young sir, just now, that you suspected the author of this imputed slander."

"My brother is rash, and speaks hastily," interrupted Mildred.

"Whom were you about to name?" asked the general, of Henry.

"There was a man named Tyrrel," replied the youth, "that has been whispering in my father's ear somewhat concerning a proposal for my sister" (here Mildred cast a keen glance at her brother and bit her lip) "and they say, love sometimes makes men desperate, and I took a passing notion that, may be, he might have been at the bottom of it; I know nothing positively to make me think so, but only speak from what I have read in books."

Cornwallis smiled as he replied playfully: "Tush, my young philosopher, you must not take your wisdom from romances. I have heard of Tyrrel, and will stand in his surety that love has raised no devil to conjure such mischief in his breast. What will satisfy your errand hither, Miss Lindsay?"

"A word from your lordship, that no harm shall befall Arthur Butler beyond the necessary durance of a prisoner of war."

"That is granted at once," replied the general, "granted for your sake, madam, in the spirit of a cavalier who would deny no lady's request. And I rather grant it to you, because certain threats have been sent me from some of the major's partisans, holding out a determination to retaliate blood for blood. These had almost persuaded me to run, against my own will, to an extreme. I would have you let it be known, that as a free grace to a lady, I have done that which I would refuse to the broadsword bullies of the mountains. What next would you have?"

"Simply, an unmolested passage hence, beyond your lordship's posts."

"That too shall be cared for. And thus the business being done, with your leave, I will go to more unmannerly employments."

"A letter for your lordship," said an officer, who at this moment entered the door, and putting a packet into the general's hand, retired.

Cornwallis opened the letter and read it.

"Ha! by my faith, but this is a rare coincidence! This brings matter of interest to you, Miss Lindsay. My officer, Macdonald, who had Butler in custody, writes me that, two days since, his prisoner had escaped."

"Escaped!" exclaimed Mildred, forgetting in whose presence she spoke, "unhurt — uninjured. Thank Heaven for that!"

Cornwallis sat for a moment silent, as a frown grew upon his brow, and he played his foot against the floor, abstracted in thought. "These devils have allies," he muttered, "in every cabin in the country. We have treachery and deceit lurking behind every bush. We shall be poisoned in our pottage by these false and hollow knaves. If it gives you content, madam," he said, raising his voice, "that this Major Butler should abuse the kindness or clemency of his guard and fly from us at the moment we were extending a boon of mercy to him through your supplications, you may hereafter hold your honorable soldier in higher esteem for his dexterity and cunning."

"I pray your lordship to believe," said Mildred, with a deep emotion, which showed itself in the rich, full tones of her voice, "that Major Butler knows nothing of my coming hither. I speak not in his name, nor make any pledge for him. If he has escaped, it has only been from the common instinct which teaches a bird to fly abroad when it finds the door of his cake left open by the negligence of his keepers. I knew it not — nor, alas! have I heard aught of his captivity, but as I have already told your lordship. He is an honorable soldier, rich in all the virtues that may commend a man: I would your lordship knew him better and in more peaceful times."

"Well, it is but a peevish and silly boy," said Cornwallis, "who whines when his pie is stolen. The war has many reckonings to settle, and we contrive to make one day's profit pay another's loss. The account for the present is balanced; and so, Miss Lindsay, without discourtesy, I may leave you, with a fair wish for a happy and prosperous journey back to your father's roof. To the good gentleman himself, I desire to be well remembered. And to show you that this briery path of war has not quite torn away all the habiliments of gentleness from us, I think it dutiful to tell you that, as I have become the confidant of a precious love-tale, wherein I can guess some secret passage of mystery is laid which should not be divulged, I promise you to keep it faithfully between ourselves. And when I reach the Dove Cote, which, God willing, under the banners of St. George, I do propose within three months to do, we may renew our confidence, and you shall have my advice touching the management of this dainty and delicate affair. And now, God speed you with a fair ride, and good spirits to back it!"

"I am much beholden to your lordship's generosity," said Mildred, as Cornwallis rose with a sportive gallantry and betook himself to his horse.

"Come hither, Mr. Henry," he said after he had mounted, "farewell, my young cavalier. You will find a few files of men to conduct you and your party beyond our posts: and here, take this," he added, as now on horseback, he scrawled off a few lines with a pencil, upon a leaf of his pocket-book, which he delivered to the youth, "there is a passport which shall carry you safe against all intrusion from my people. Adieu!"

With this last speech the commander-in-chief put spurs to his horse, and galloped to the plain, to review his troops and commence the march by which he hoped to make good his boast of reaching the Dove Cote.

How fortune seconded his hopes may be read in the story of the war.

CHAPTER L

A BRITISH PARTISAN

As the events of this history are confined to the duration of the Tory Ascendency in South Carolina, it becomes me to prepare my reader for the conclusion to which, doubtless much to his content, he will hear that we are now hastening. We have reached a period which brings us to take notice of certain important operations that were in progress upon the frontier, and touching the details of which, to avoid prolixity, I must refer to the graver chronicles of the times. It answers my present purpose merely to apprise my reader that Colonel Clarke had lately assembled his followers and marched to Augusta, where he had made an attack upon Brown, but that almost at the moment when his dexterous and valiant adversary had fallen within his grasp, a timely succor from Fort Ninety-Six, under the command of Cruger, had forced him to abandon his ground, and retreat towards the mountain districts of North Carolina. To this, it is important to add that Ferguson had now recruited a considerable army amongst the native Tories, and had moved to the small frontier village of Gilbert-town, with a purpose to intercept Clarke, and thus place him under the disadvantage of having a foe both in front and rear.

The midnight seizure of Arthur Butler and his friends, whilst returning from Ramsay's funeral, was effected by M'Alpine, who happened at that moment to be hastening, by a forced march, with a detachment of newly-recruited cavalry from Ninety-Six, to strengthen Ferguson, and to aid in what was expected to be the certain capture of the troublesome Whig partisan.

As M'Alpine's purpose required despatch, he made but a short delay after sun-rise at Drummond's cabin, and then pushed forward with his prisoners with all possible expedition. The route of his journey diverged, almost at the spot of the capture, from the roads leading towards Musgrove's Mill, and he consequently had but little chance to fall in with parties who might communicate to him the nature of the accident which threw the prisoners into his possession; whilst the prisoners themselves were sufficiently discreet to conceal from him everything that might afford a hint of Butler's previous condition.

The road lay through a rugged wilderness, and the distance to be travelled, before the party could reach Gilbert-town, was something more than sixty miles. It was, accordingly, about the middle of the second day after leaving Drummond's habitation, before the troop arrived at the term of their journey, a period that coincided with that of Cornwallis's breaking ground from his late encampment at the Waxhaws, which we have seen in the last chapter.

Ferguson was a stout, fearless, and bluff soldier, and instigated by the most unsparing hatred against all who took up the Whig cause. He had been promoted by Earl Cornwallis to the brevet rank of lieutenant-colonel, a short time before the battle of Camden, and despatched towards this wild and mountainous border to collect together and organize the Tory inhabitants of the district. His zeal and activity, no less than his peremptory bearing, had particularly recommended him to the duty to be performed; and he is, at least, entitled to the commendation of having acquitted himself with great promptitude and efficiency in the principal objects of his appointment. He was now at the head of between eleven and twelve hundred men, of which about one hundred and fifty were regulars of the British line, the remainder consisting of the disorderly and untamed population of the frontier.

Gilbert-town was a small village, composed of a number of rather well-built and comfortable log-houses. It was situated in a mountainous but fertile district of North Carolina, about the centre of Rutherford country. And I may venture to add (which I do upon report only), that although its former name has faded from the maps of the present day, under that reprehensible indifference to ancient associations, and that pernicious love of change which have obliterated so many of the landmarks of our revolutionary history, yet this village is still a prosperous and pleasant community, known as the seat of justice to the county to which it belongs.

When the troop having charge of Butler and his companions arrived, they halted immediately in front of one of the largest buildings of the village, and in a short time the prisoners were marched into the presence of Ferguson. They were received in a common room of ample dimensions, furnished with a table upon which was seen a confused array of drinking vessels, and a number of half-emptied bottles of spirit surrounding a wooden bucket filled with water. Immediately against one of the posts of the door of the apartment, the carcass of a buck, recently shot and now stripped of its skin, hung by the tendons of the hinder feet; and a soldier was at this moment employed with his knife in the butcher-craft necessary to its preparation for the spit. Ferguson himself, conspicuous for his robust, athletic, and weather-beaten exterior, stood by apparently directing the operation. Around the room were hung the hide and antlers of former victims of the chase, intermingled with various weapons of war, military cloaks, cartridge-boxes, bridles, saddles, and other furniture denoting the habitation of a party of soldiers. There was a general air of disorder and untidiness throughout the apartment, which seemed to bespeak early and late revels, and no great observance of the thrift of even military housekeeping. This impression was heightened to the eye of the beholder, by the unchecked liberty with which men of all ranks, privates as well as officers, flung themselves, as their occasions served, into the room and made free with the contents of the flasks that were scattered over the table.

The irregular and ill-disciplined host under Ferguson's command lay in and around the village, and presented a scene of which the predominating features bore a sufficient resemblance to the economy of their leader's own quarters, to raise but an unfavorable opinion of their subordination and soldier-like demeanor: it was wild, noisy, and confused.

When M'Alpine entered the apartment, the words that fell from Ferguson showed that his mind, at the moment, was disturbed by a double solicitude — alternating between the operations performed upon the carcass of venison, and certain symptoms of uproar and disorder that manifested themselves amongst the militia without.

"Curse on these swaggering, upland bullies!" he said, whilst M'Alpine and the prisoners stood inside the room, as yet unnoticed, "I would as soon undertake to train as many wolves from the mountain, as bring these fellows into habits of discipline. Thady, you cut that haunch too low — go deep, man — a long sweep from the pommel to the cantle — it is a saddle worth riding on! By the infernal gods! if these yelping savages do not learn to keep quiet in camp, I'll make a school for them with my regulars, where they shall have good taste of the cat! nine hours' drill and all the camp duty besides! Ha, M'Alpine, is it you who have been standing here all this while? I didn't observe it, man

— my quarters are like a bar-room, and have been full of comers and goers all day. I thought you were but some of my usual free-and-easy customers. Damn them, I am sick of these gawky long-legged, half-civilized recruits! but I shall take a course with them yet. What news, old boy? What have you to tell of the rebels? Where is my pretty fellow, Clarke?"

"Clarke is still in the woods," replied M'Alpine. "It would take good hounds to track him."

"And Cruger, I hope, has nose enough to follow. So, the cunning Indian hunter will be caught at last! We have him safe now, M'Alpine. There is but one path for the fox to come out of the bush, and upon that path Patrick Ferguson has about as pretty a handful of mischievous imps as ever lapped blood. The slinking runaway never reaches the other side of the mountains while I am awake. With Cruger behind him — our line of posts upon his right — the wild mountains, as full of Cherokees as squirrels, upon his left — and these devils of mine right before him — we have him in a pretty net. Who have you here, captain?"

"Some stray rebel game, that I picked up on my road, as I came from Ninety-Six. This gentleman, I learn, is Major Butler of the Continental army, and these others, some of his party."

"So, ho, more rebels! damn it, man," exclaimed the commandant, "why do you bring them to me? What can I do with them" — then dropping his voice into a tone of confidential conference, he added, "but follow the fashion and hang them? I have got some score of prisoners already — and have been wishing that they would cut some devilish caper, that I might have an excuse for stringing them up, to get clear of them. A major in the regular Continental line, sir?" he asked, addressing himself to Butler.

Butler bowed his head.

"I thought the cuffs your people got at Camden had driven everything like a day-light soldier out of the province. We have some skulking bush-fighters left — some jack-o'-lantern devils, that live in the swamps and feed on frogs and water-snakes — Marion and Sumpter, and a few of their kidney: but you, sir, are the first regular Continental officers I have met with. What brought you so far out of your latitude?"

"I was on my way to join one," replied Butler, "that but now you seemed to think in severe straits."

"Ha! to visit Clarke, eh? Well, sir, may I be bold to ask, do you know where that worshipful gentleman is to be found?"

"I am free to answer you," said Butler, "that his position, at this moment, is entirely unknown to me. On my journey I heard the report that he had been constrained to abandon Augusta."

"Yes, and in haste, let me tell you. And marches in this direction, Major Butler, as he needs must. I shall make his acquaintance: and inasmuch as you went to seek him, you may count it a lucky accident that brought you here — you will find him all the sooner by it."

"Doubtless, sir, Colonel Clarke will feel proud to see you," returned Butler.

"Well, M'Alpine," said Ferguson, "I have my hands full of business; for I certainly have the wildest crew of devil's babies that ever stole cattle, or fired a haystack. I am obliged to coax them into discipline by a somewhat free use of this mother's milk — (pointing to the bottles) — "to which I now and then add a gentle castigation at the drum-head, and, when that doesn't serve, a dose of powder and lead, administered at ten paces from a few files of grenadiers. I have shot a brace of them, since you left me, only for impertinence to their officers! This waiting for Clarke plays the devil with us. I must be moving, and have some thought of crossing the mountains westward, and burning out the settlements. Faith! I would do it, just to keep my lads in spirits, if I thought Clarke would give me another week. How, now, Thady? — that buck should have been half roasted by this time. We shall never have dinner with your slow work. Look at that, M'Alpine, there is something to make your mouth water — an inch and a half of fat on the very ridge of the back. Give over your prisoners to the camp major — he will take care of them: and, hark you, captain," he added, beckoning his comrade aside, "if you choose, as you seem to think well of this Major Butler, you may bring him in to dinner presently, with my compliments. Now, away — I must to business."

The prisoners were conducted to a separate building, where they were put in charge of an officer, who performed the duties of provost-marshal over some twenty or more Whigs that had been captured in the late excursions of the Tories, and brought into camp for safe keeping. The place of their confinement was narrow and uncomfortable, and Butler was soon made aware that in the exchange of his prison at Musgrove's mill for his present one, he had made an unprofitable venture. His condition with Ferguson, however, was alleviated by the constantly-exciting hope that the events which were immediately in prospect might, by the chances of war, redound to his advantage.

In this situation Butler remained for several days. For although Ferguson found it necessary to keep in almost constant motion, with a view to hover about the supposed direction of Clarke's retreat, and, comformably to this purpose, to advance into South Carolina, and again to fall back towards his present position, yet he had established a guard at Gilbert-town which, during all these operations, remained stationary with the prisoners, apparently waiting some fit opportunity to march them off to Cornwallis's army, that was now making its way northwards. That opportunity did not present itself. The communications between this post and the commander-in-chief were, by a fatal error, neglected; and in a short time from the date of the present events, as will be seen in the sequel, a web was woven which was strong enough to ensnare and bind up the limbs of the giant who had, during the last five months, erected and maintained the Tory Ascendency in Carolina.

CHAPTER LI

MILDRED TURNS HER STEPS HOMEWARDS

I HAVE seen a generous and brave boy defied to some enterprise of terror, — such as, peradventure, to clamber in the dark night, alone, up many a winding bout of stair-case to the garret, — and he has undertaken the achievement, although sore afraid of goblins, and gone forth upon his adventure with a lusty step and with a bold tardiness, whistling or singing on his way — his eyes and ears all the time fearfully open to all household sights and sounds, now magnified out of their natural proportions; and when he had reached the furthest term of his travel, I have known him to turn quickly about and come down three steps at a leap, feeling all the way as if some spectre tracked his flight and hung upon his rear. Calling up such a venture to my mind, I am enabled, by comparison with the speed and anxiety of the boy, to show my reader with what emotions Mildred, her mission being done, now turned herself upon her homeward route. The excitement occasioned by her knowledge of the critical circumstances of Butler, and the pain she had suffered in the belief that upon the courageous performance of her duty depended even his life, had nerved her resolution to the perilous and hardy exploit in which we have seen her. But now, when matters had taken such a suddenly auspicious turn, and she was assured of her lover's safety, not even the abrupt joy which poured in upon her heart was sufficient to stifle her sense of uneasiness at her present exposed condition, and she eagerly prepared to betake herself back to the Dove Cote.

The scenes around her had wrought upon her nerves; and, although she was singularly fortunate in the courtesy which she had experienced from all into whose hands she had fallen, yet the rude licentiousness of the camp, and the revolting acts of barbarity which were ever present to her observation, appalled and distressed her. Besides, she now saw the fixed purpose with which Cornwallis was preparing to march forward in his course of invasion, and thought with alarm upon the probable event of soon having the theatre of war transferred to the neighborhood of her native woods.

Robinson's advice seconded her own alacrity. It was to hasten, with all despatch, in advance of the invading army; and as this body was now about taking up its line of march, no time was to be lost. Accordingly, but a brief delay took place after Cornwallis and his suite had departed from head-quarters, before our party set forward, accompanied by the small guard of cavalry that had been ordered to attend them. The troops were just wheeling into column on the ground where they had been lately reviewed, when Mildred and her attendants galloped past, and took the high road leading to the town of Charlotte, in North Carolina, towards which it was understood the invaders were about to direct their journey. In less than an hour afterwards they had left behind them the line of baggage wagons and the small military parties of the vanguard, and found themselves rapidly hastening towards a district occupied by the friends of independence.

The sergeant had now occasion for his utmost circumspection. In pursuing the destined route of the invasion, he had reason to expect an early encounter with some of the many corps of observation, which the opposite party were certain to put upon the duty of reporting the approach of their enemy. And so it fell out; for, towards the middle of the day, whilst the travellers were quietly plying their journey through the forest, the discharge of a pistol announced the presence of a hostile body of men; and almost instantly afterwards a small handful of Whig cavalry were seen hovering upon the road, at the distance of some three or four hundred paces in front. Robinson no sooner recognised this squad than he took the lady's handkerchief and hoisted it on a rod, as a flag of truce, and, at the same moment, directed the escort to retreat, apprising them that their presence was no longer necessary, as he had now an opportunity to deliver his charge into the hands of friends. The British horsemen, accordingly, took their leave; and, in the next moment, Horse Shoe surrendered to a patrole, who announced themselves to be a part of the command of Colonel Davie, of the North Carolina militia — a gallant partisan, then well known to fame, and whose after exploits fill up no inconsiderable page of American history.

It does not enter into the purpose of my story to detain my reader with a minute account of Mildred's homeward journey; but having now transferred her to the protection of a friendly banner, it will suffice to say that she arrived the same evening at

Charlotte, where she spent the night in the midst of the active, warlike preparations which were in progress to receive Cornwallis.

It was towards sunset on the following day, when, wearied with the toil of a long and rapid journey, our travellers arrived in front of a retired farm-house, on the road leading through the upper districts of North Carolina. The cultivation around this dwelling showed both good husbandry and a good soil, and there was an appearance of comfort and repose which was an unusual sight in a country so much alarmed and ravaged by war, as that over which the wayfarers had lately journeyed. The house stood some short distance apart from the road, and in the porch was seated an elderly man of a respectable appearance, to whom a young girl was, at this moment, administering a draught of water from a small, hooped, wooden vessel which she held in her hand.

"I am parched with thirst," said Mildred, "pray get me some of that water."

"The place looks so well, ma'am," replied the sergeant, "that I think we could not do better than make a stop here for the night. Good day, neighbor! What is the name of the river I see across yon field, and where mought we be, just at this time?"

"It is the Yadkin," answered the man, "and this county, I believe, is Iredell — though I speak only by guess, for I am but a stranger in these parts."

"The lady would be obligated," said Horse Shoe, "for a drop of that water; and, if it was agreeable, she mought likewise be pleased to put up here for the night."

"The people of the house are kind and worthy," replied the old man, "and not likely to refuse a favor. Mary, take a cup to the lady."

The girl obeyed; and, coming up to the party with the vessel in her hand, she suddenly started as her eye fell upon Horse Shoe, and her pale and wan countenance was seen bathed in tears.

"Mr. Robinson!" she exclaimed, with a faltering voice; "you don't know me? — me, Mary Musgrove. Father, it is our friend, Horse Shoe Robinson!" Then placing the vessel upon the ground, she ran to the sergeant's side, as he sat upon his horse, and leaning her head against his saddle, she wept bitterly, sobbing out: "It is me, Mary Musgrove. John — our John — that you loved — he is dead — he is dead!"

In an instant Allen Musgrove was at the gate, where he greeted the sergeant with the affection of an old friend.

This recognition of the miller and his daughter at once confirmed the sergeant in his determination to end his day's journey at this spot. In a few moments Mildred and her companions were introduced into the farm-house, where they were heartily welcomed by the indwellers, consisting of a sturdy, cheerful tiller of the soil, and a motherly dame, whose brood of children around her showed her to be the mistress of the family.

The scene that ensued after the party were seated in the house was, for some time, painfully affecting. Poor Mary, overcome by the associations called up to her mind at the sight of the sergeant, took a seat near him, and silently gazed in his face, visibly laboring under a strong desire to express her feelings in words, but at the same time stricken mute by the intensity of her emotions.

After a long suspense, which was broken only by her sobs, she was enabled to utter a few disjointed sentences, in which she recalled to the sergeant the friendship that had existed between him and John Ramsay; and there was something peculiarly touching in the melancholy tone with which, in accordance with the habits inculcated by her religious education, and most probably in the words of her father's frequent admonitions, she attributed the calamity that had befallen her to the kindly chastisement of heaven, to endure which she devoutly, and with a sigh that showed the bitterness of her suffering, prayed for patience and submission. Allen Musgrove, at this juncture, interposed with some topics of consolation suitable to the complexion of the maiden's mind, and soon succeeded in drying up her tears, and restoring her, at least, to the possession of a tranquil and apparently a resigned spirit.

When this was done, he gave a narrative of the events relating to the escape of Butler and his subsequent recapture at the funeral of John Ramsay, to which, it may be imagined, Mildred and Henry listened with the most absorbed attention.

This tale of the recapture of Butler, so unexpected, and communicated at a moment when Mildred's heart beat high with the joyful hopes of speedily seeing her lover again in safety, now struck upon her ear with the alarm that seizes upon a voyager who, fearing no hidden reef or unknown shoal, hears the keel of his ship in mid ocean crash against a solid rock. It seemed at once to break down the illusion which she had cherished with such fond affection. For the remainder of the evening the intercourse of the party was anxious and thoughtful, and betrayed the unhappy impression which the intelligence just communicated had made upon the feelings of Mildred and her brother. Musgrove, after the travellers had been refreshed by food, and invigorated by the kind and hearty hospitality of the good man under whose roof they were sheltered, proceeded to give the sergeant a history of what had lately befallen in the neighborhood of the Ennoree. Some days after the escape of Butler, the miller's own family had drawn upon themselves the odium of the ruling authority. His mill and his habitation had been reduced to ashes by a party of Tories who had made an incursion into this district, with no other view than to wreak their vengeance against suspected persons. In the same inroad, the family of David Ramsay had once more been assailed, and all that was spared from the first conflagration was destroyed in the second. Many other houses through this region had met the same fate. The expedition had been conducted by Wemyss, who, it is said, carried in his pocket a list of dwellings to which the torch was to be applied, and who, on accomplishing each item of his diabolical mission — so still runs the tradition — would note the consummated work by striking out the memorandum from his tablets.

In this general ravage, the desolated families fled like hunted game through the woods, and betook themselves with a disordered haste to the more friendly provinces northward. Musgrove had sent his wife and younger children, almost immediately after the assault upon him, to the care of a relative in Virginia, whither they had been conducted some days previous to the date of his present meeting with Horse Shoe by Christopher Shaw; whilst he and Mary had remained behind, for a short space, to render assistance to the family of Ramsay, to whom they felt themselves affined almost as closely as if the expected alliance by marriage had taken place. When this duty was discharged, and Ramsay's family were provided with a place of refuge, Musgrove had set forward with his daughter to rejoin his wife and children in their new asylum. It was upon this journey that they had now been accidentally overtaken by our travellers.

The disclosure of the motives of Mildred's expedition to Mary and her father, as may be supposed, warmed up their feelings to a most affectionate sympathy in her troubles. They had often heard of Butler's attachment to a lady in Virginia, and were aware of her name, from the incidents that had occurred at the trial of Butler, and from the nature of Horse Shoe's mission to Virginia. Mary had nursed in her mind a fanciful and zealous interest in behalf of the lady who was supposed to have engrossed Butler's affections, from the earnest devotion which she had witnessed in his demeanor, first at Adair's, and often afterwards during his captivity. The effect of this preconceived favor now showed itself in her behavior to Mildred; and, in the gentle play which it gave to her kindly sentiments, a most happy change was wrought in her present feelings. She at once warmly and fervently attached herself to Mildred, and won her way into our lady's esteem by the most amiable assiduities. In these offices of love, the poignancy of her own grief began to give way to the natural sweetness of her temper, and they were observed, in the same degree, to enliven Mildred's feelings. Mary hung fondly about her new acquaintance, proffered her most minute attentions of comfort, spoke often of the generous qualities of Butler, and breathed many a sincere prayer for future happiness to him and those he loved.

As Mildred pondered over the new aspect which the tidings of this evening had given to her condition, her inclination and duty both prompted her to the resolve to make an effort to join Butler, instead of returning to the Dove Cote. She was apprised by Musgrove that the prisoner had been conducted to Ferguson, who, she was told, was at this time stationed in the neighborhood of Gilbert-town, not a hundred miles from her present position. She had ventured far in his services, and she could not, now that she had so nearly approached him, consent to abandon the effort of reaching the spot of his captivity. She thought with alarm over the dangers that might await him in consequence of his previous escape, and this alarm was increased by her remembrance of the tone of bitter resentment with which Cornwallis, in a moment of unguarded feeling, had referred to the event in her late conference with that officer. Above all, it was her duty — such was her view of the matter — and whatever might befal, he was the lord of her heart, and all dangers and difficulties, now as heretofore, should be cast aside in her determination to administer to his safety or comfort. Her decision was made, and she so announced it to her companions.

Neither the sergeant nor Henry made the opposition to this resolve that might have been expected. To Horse Shoe it was a matter of indifference upon what service he might be ordered; his thoughts ran in no other current than to obey the order, and make the most thrifty and careful provision for its safe execution. To Henry that was always a pleasant suggestion which was calculated to bring him more into the field of adventure. Allen Musgrove, on this occasion, added an opinion which rather favored the enterprise.

"It was not much out of the way," he said, "to go as far as

Burk Court House, where, at least, the lady was likely to learn something of the plans of Ferguson, and she might either wait there, or take such direction afterwards as her friends should advise."

Mary begged that whatever route Mildred thought proper to pursue, she might be allowed to accompany her; and this request was so much to the liking of Mildred, that she earnestly implored the miller's consent to the plan. With some reluctance Musgrove acquiesced; and, feeling thus doubly interested in the fortunes of the party, he finally determined himself to attend them in their present enterprise.

These matters being settled, the wearied travellers parted for the night, happy, at least, in having found the weight of their personal afflictions relieved by the cheerfulness with which the burden was divided.

CHAPTER LII

SIGNS OF A GATHERING STORM. — MUSTER OF THE BACKWOODSMEN

In arms the huts and hamlets rise.
From winding glen, from upland brown,
They poured each hardy tenant down.
LADY OF THE LAKE.

IN gathering up the ends of our story, as we draw towards a conclusion, we are forced, after the fashion of a stirring drama, to a frequent change of scene. Accordingly, leaving Mildred and her friends to pursue their own way until we shall find leisure to look after their footsteps, we must introduce our reader to some new acquaintances, whose motions, it will be seen, are destined greatly to influence the interests of this history.

The time was about the second of October, when a considerable body of troops were seen marching through that district which is situated between the Allegany mountain and the head waters of Catawba, in North Carolina. This force might have numbered perhaps something over one thousand men. Its organization and general aspect were sufficiently striking to entitle it to a particular description. It consisted almost entirely of cavalry; and a spectator might have seen in the rude, weather-beaten faces, and muscular forms of the soldiers, as well as in the simplicity of their equipments, a hastily-levied band of mountaineers, whose ordinary pursuits had been familiar with the arduous toils of Indian warfare and the active labors of the chase. They were, almost without exception, arrayed in the hunting shirt — a dress so dear to the recollections of the revolution, and which, it is much to be regretted, the foppery of modern times has been allowed to displace. Their weapons in but few instances were other than the long rifle and its accompanying hunting-knife.

It was to be observed that this little army consisted of various corps, which were in general designated either by the color of the hunting-shirt, or by that of the fringe with which this cheap and simple uniform was somewhat ostentatiously garnished. Some few were clad in the plain, homespun working-dress of the time;

and, here and there, an officer might be recognised in the blue and buff cloth of the regular Continental army. The buck-tail, also, was an almost indispensable ornament of the cap, or usual round hat of the soldiers; and where this was wanting, its place was not unfrequently supplied by sprigs of green pine or holly, or other specimens of the common foliage of the country.

The men were mounted on lean, shaggy, and travel-worn horses of every variety of size, shape, and color; and their baggage consisted of nothing more cumbersome than a light wallet attached to the rear of their saddles, or of a meagrely supplied pair of saddlebags. The small party on foot were in no wise to be distinguished from the mounted men, except in the absence of horses, and in the mode of carrying their baggage, which was contained in knapsacks of deerskin strapped to their shoulders. These moved over the ground with, perhaps, even more facility than the cavalry, and appeared in no degree to regret the toil of the march, which was so far the lighter to them, as they were exempt from the solicitude which their companions suffered of providing forage for their beasts.

The officers in command of this party were young men, in whose general demeanor and bearing was to be seen that bold, enterprising, and hardy character, which at that period, even more than at present, distinguished the frontier population. The frequent expeditions against the savages, which the times had rendered familiar to them, as well as the service of the common war, in which they had all partaken, had impressed upon their exteriors the rugged lines of thoughtful soldiership.

The troops now associated, consisted of distinct bodies of volunteers, who had each assembled under their own leaders, without the requisition of the government, entirely independent of each other, and more resembling the promiscuous meeting of hunters than a regularly-organized military corps.

They had convened, about a week before the period at which I have presented them to my reader, at Wattauga, on the border of Tennessee, in pursuance of an invitation from Shelby, who was now one of the principal officers in command. He had himself embodied a force of between two and three hundred men, in his own district of the mountains; and Colonel Campbell, now also present, had repaired to the rendezvous with four hundred soldiers from the adjoining county in Virginia. These two had soon afterwards formed a junction with Colonels M'Dowell and Sevier, of North Carolina, who had thus augmented the joint force to the number which I have already mentioned as constituting the whole array. They had marched slowly and wearily from the mountains into the district of country which lay between the forks of Catawba, somewhere near to the present village of Morgantown — and might now be said to be rather hovering in the neighborhood of Ferguson, then advancing directly towards him. The force of the British partisan was, as yet, too formidable for the attack of these allies, and he was still in a position to make his way in safety to the main army under Cornwallis — at this time stationed at Charlotte, some seventy or eighty miles distant. It was both to gain increase of force, from certain auxiliaries who were yet expected to join them, as also, without exciting suspicion of their purpose, to attain a position from which Ferguson might more certainly be cut off from Cornwallis, that the mountain leaders lingered with such wily delay upon their march.

Ferguson was all intent upon Clarke — little suspecting the power which could summon up, with such incredible alacrity, an army from the woods fit to dispute his passage through any path of the country; and, profiting by this confidence of the enemy, Shelby and his associates were preparing, by secret movements, to put themselves in readiness to spring upon their quarry at the most auspicious moment. In accordance with this plan, Colonel Williams, who yet preserved his encampment on the Fair Forest, was on the alert to act against the British leader, who still marched further south — at every step lengthening the distance between himself and his commander-in-chief, and so far favoring the views of his enemy. Shelby and his comrades only tarried until their numbers should be complete, designing as speedily as possible after that to form a junction with Williams, and at once enter upon an open and hot pursuit of their adversary.

Their uncertainty in regard to the present condition of Clarke added greatly to their desire to strike, as early as possible, their meditated blow. This officer had, a few weeks before, commenced his retreat from Augusta through Ninety-Six, with some five hundred men, closely followed by Brown and Cruger, and threatened by the Indian tribes who inhabited the wilderness through which he journeyed. The perils and hardships of this retreat arose not only from the necessity Clarke was under to plunge into the inhospitable and almost unexplored wilderness of the Allegany, by a path which would effectually baffle his pursuers as well as escape the toils of Ferguson; but they were painfully enhanced by the incumbrance of a troop of women and children, who, having already felt the venegance of the savages, and fearing its further cruelties, and the scarcely less ruthless hatred of the Tories, preferred to tempt the rigors of the mountain rather than remain in their own dwellings. It is said that these terrified and helpless fugitives amounted to somewhat above three hundred individuals.

There were no incidents of the war of independence that more strikingly illustrated the heroism which grappled with the difficulties of that struggle at its gloomiest moment, than the patient and persevering gallantry of these brave wanderers and their confederates, whom we have seen lately assembled in arms. History has not yet conferred upon Clarke and his companions their merited tribute of renown. Some future chronicler will find in their exploits a captivating theme for his pen, when he tells the tale of their constancy, even in the midst of the nation's despair; until fortune, at length successfully wooed, rewarded their vigilance, bravery, and skill, by enabling them to subdue and destroy the Tory Ascendency in the south.

The enemy, swarming in all the strong places, elate with recent victory, well provided with the muniments of war, high in hope and proud of heart, hunted these scattered, destitute, and slender bands, with a keenness of scent, swiftness of foot, and exasperation of temper, that can only be compared to the avidity of the bloodhound. This eagerness of pursuit was, for the present, directed against Clarke; and it is one of the most fortunate circumstances that belong to the events I have been relating, that this purpose of waylaying our gallant partisan so completely absorbed the attention of Ferguson, as to cause him to neglect the most ordinary precautions for securing himself against the reverses of the war.

In this state of things, Shelby and his compatriots waited for the moment when they might direct their march immediately to the attack of the British soldier — their anxiety stimulated to a painful acuteness by the apprehension that Clarke might be overpowered by his enemies, or that Cornwallis might receive information of the gathering bands, and make a timely movement to reinforce or protect his outpost. It was in this moment of doubt and concern that we have chosen to present them in the course of our narrative.

The troops had halted about the middle of the day, to take some refreshment. The ground they had chosen for this purpose was a narrow valley or glen, encompassed by steep hills, between which a transparent rivulet wound its way over a rough, stony bed.

The margin of the stream was clothed with grass of the liveliest verdure, and a natural grove of huge forest trees covered the whole level space of the valley. The season was the most pleasant of the year, being at that period when, in the southern highlands, the hoar frost is first seen to sparkle on the spray at early dawn. The noon-tide sun, though not oppressively warm, was still sufficiently fervid to render the shade of the grove, and the cool mountain brook in the deep ravine, no unpleasant objects to wearied travellers. Here the whole of our little army were scattered through the wood; some intent upon refreshing their steeds in the running water, many seated beneath the trees discussing their own slender means, and not a few carelessly and idly loitering about the grounds in the enjoyment of the mere exemption from the constraint of discipline. The march of the troops on this day had not exceeded ten or twelve miles: — they might have been said to creep through the woods. Still, however, they had been in motion ever since the dawn of day; and as they measured the ground with their slow but ceaseless footfall, there was a silent disquiet and an eagerness of expectation, that were scarcely less fatiguing than more rapid and laborious operations.

"Cleveland will certainly join us," said Shelby, as, in the vacancy of the hour, he had fallen into company with his brother officers, who were now assembled on the margin of the brook. "It is time he were here. I am sick of this slow work. If we do not make our leap within the next two or three days, the game is lost."

"Keep your temper, Isaac," replied Campbell, who, being somewhat older than his comrade, assumed the freedom indicated in this reply, and now laughed as he admonished the fretful soldier. "Keep your temper! Williams is below, and on the look-out; and most usefully employed in enticing Ferguson as far out of reach of my lord Buzzard, there at Charlotte, as we could wish him. Ben Cleveland will be with us all in good time: take my word for that. You forget that he had to muster his lads from Wilkes and Surry both."

"And Brandon and Lacy are yet to join us," said M'Dowell.

"Damn it, they should be here, man!" interrupted Shelby again; "I hate this creaking of my boots upon the soft grass, as if we had come to fish for gudgeons. I am for greasing our horses' heels and putting them to service."

"You were always a hot-headed devil," interrupted Campbell, again, "and have wasted more shoe-leather than discretion in this world, by at least ten to one. You are huntsman enough to know, Isaac, that it is sometimes well to steal round the game to get the wind of them. Your headlong haste would only do us harm.

"You!" rejoined Shelby, with a laugh, excited by Campbell's face of good humor. "Verily, you are a pattern of sobriety and moderation yourself, to be preaching caution to us youngsters! All wisdom, forecast, and discretion, I suppose, have taken up their quarters in your wiry-haired noddle! How in the devil it came to pass, William, that yonder green and grey shirts should have trusted themselves with such a piece of prudence at their head, is more than I can guess."

At this moment a soldier pressed forward into the circle of officers:

"A letter for Colonel Shelby," he said, "brought by a trooper from Cleveland."

"Ah, ha! This looks well," exclaimed Shelby, as he ran his eyes over the lines. "Cleveland is but ten miles behind, and desires us to wait his coming."

"With how many men?" asked one of the party.

"The rogue has forgotten to tell. I'll warrant, with all he could find."

"With a good party, no doubt," interrupted Sevier. "I know the Whigs of Wilkes and Surry will not be backward."

"From this despatch, gentlemen, I suppose we shall rest here for the night—what say you?" was the interrogatory proposed to the group by Shelby.

The proposition was agreed to, and the several officers repaired to their commands. As soon as this order was communicated to the troops, everything assumed the bustle incident to the preparation of a temporary camp. Fires were kindled, the horses tethered, guards detailed, and shelters erected of green wood cut from the surrounding forest. In addition to this, a few cattle had been slaughtered from a small herd that had been driven in the rear of the march; and long before night came on, the scene presented a tolerably comfortable bivouac of light-hearted, laughing woodsmen, whose familiar habits at home had seasoned them to this forest-life, and gave to their present enterprise something of the zest of a pastime.

In the first intervals of leisure, parties were seen setting out into the neighboring hills in pursuit of game; and when the hour of the evening meal arrived, good store of fat bucks and wild turkeys were not wanting to flavor a repast, to which a sauce better than the wit of man ever invented, was brought by every lusty feeder of the camp.

At sun-down, a long line of woodland cavalry, in all respects armed and equipped in the same fashion with those who already occupied the valley, were seen winding down the rugged road which led from the high grounds to the camp. At the first intimation of the approach of this body, the troops below were ordered out on parade, and the new-comers were received with all the military demonstrations of respect and joy usual at the meeting of friendly bodies of soldiers. Some dozen horns of the harshest tones, and with the most ear-piercing discord, kept up an incessant braying, until the alarmed echoes were startled from a thousand points amongst the hills. In spite of the commands of officers, straggling shots of salutation were fired, and loud greetings of individual acquaintances were exchanged from either ranks, as the approaching body filed across the whole front of the drawn-up line. When this ceremony was over, Colonel Cleveland rode up to the little group of officers who awaited his report, and, after a long and hearty welcome, announced his command to consist of three hundred and fifty stout hearts, ready and tried friends to the issues of the war.

The force of the confederates, by this accession, now amounted to about fourteen hundred men. It became necessary, at this juncture, to give to these separate bands a more compact character, and with that view it was indispensable that the command of the whole should be committed to one of the present leaders. In the difficulty and delicacy of selecting an individual for this duty, the common opinion inclined to the propriety of submitting the appointment to General Gates. A messenger was accordingly despatched on that night, to repair to the American head-quarters at Hillsborough, to present this subject to the attention of the General. In the meantime, Shelby, whose claim, perhaps, to the honor of leading the expedition was most worthy of consideration, with that patriotic and noble postponement of self which occurs so frequently in the history of the men of the Revolution, himself suggested the expediency of conferring the command upon his friend Campbell, until the pleasure of Gates should be known. The suggestion was heartily adopted, and Colonel William Campbell was accordingly, from this moment, the chosen leader of our gallant and efficient little army.

On the following day the troops were in motion at an early hour — designing to advance, with a steady pace, towards Gilbert-town, and thence on the track of the enemy across the border into South Carolina. In the course of the forenoon, the vanguard were met by a small body of horsemen, whose travel-worn plight and haggard aspects showed that they had lately been engaged in severe service. They were now in quest of the very party whom they had thus fortunately encountered upon the march; and it was with a lively demonstration of joy that they now rode with the officer of the guard into the presence of Campbell and his staff. Their report announced them to be Major Chandler and Captain Johnson, of Clarke's party, who, with thirty followers, had been despatched from the western side of the Allegany, to announce to the confederated troops the complete success of that officer's endeavor to reach the settlements on the Nolachuckie and Wattauga rivers. Their tidings were immediately communicated to the army; and the deep and earnest interest which officers and men took in this agreeable intelligence, was evinced in a spontaneous acclamation and cheering from one extremity of the column to the other. The messengers proceeded to narrate the particulars of their late hazardous expedition, and fully confirmed the most painful anticipations which the listeners had previously entertained of the difficulties, toils, and sufferings incident to the enterprise. Clarke's soldiers, they further reported, were too much disabled to be in condition immediately to recross the mountain and unite in the present movement against Ferguson; but that, as soon as they should find themselves recruited by needful rest, they would lose no time in repairing to the scene of action.

Towards sunset of the succeeding day, our sturdy adventurers entered Gilbert-town. This post had been abandoned by Ferguson, and was now in the occupation of the two staunch Whig leaders, Brandon and Lacy, at the head of about three hundred men, who had repaired thither from the adjacent mountains of Rutherford, to await the arrival of Campbell and his friends. It was manifest that affairs were rapidly tending towards a crisis. Ferguson had hitherto appeared indifferent to the dangers that threatened him, and his movements indicated either a fatal contempt for his adversary, or an ignorance of the extent of his embarrassments — each equally discreditable to the high renown which has been attributed to him for careful and bold soldiership.

CHAPTER LIII

MILDRED MEETS AN AGREEABLE ADVENTURE

We left Mildred securely lodged with her new and kind-hearted friends, under the hospitable roof of the farmer, hard by the Yadkin. The reader has, doubtless, found reason in the course of this narrative to marvel much that a lady so delicately nurtured should, with so stout a spirit and with such singular devotion, have tempted so many dangers, and exposed herself to such unwonted hardships, for the sake of the man she loved. Perhaps, I might be able to clear up this matter, by referring to the extraordinary conjuncture of circumstances that surrounded her. It was no secret that she fervently, and with her whole heart, — yea even with a fanatical worship, — loved the man she sought. Her affection had been nursed in solitude, and, like a central fire, glowed with a fervid heat, unobserved at first, silent and steady: and by degrees her enthusiasm spread its coloring over the passion, and raised it into a fanciful but solemn self-dedication. This warmth of feeling might still have been witnessed only within her family precinct, had it not been that, at a most critical moment, when her father's absence from the Dove Cote left her without other resource than her own unaided counsel, she was made acquainted that her lover's life was in imminent peril, and that a word from her might perhaps avert his doom. We have seen with what anxious alacrity she set forth in that emergency upon her pilgrimage of duty; and how, as she became familiar with hardship and danger, her constancy and resolution still took a higher tone, growing more vigorous even with the impediments that lay across her path. This may seem strange to our peace-bred dames, — and little congruous with that feminine reserve and shrinkingness which we are wont to praise: but war, distress, and disaster work miracles in the female bosom, and render that virtuous and seemly, which ease and safety might repel. Nature is a wise and cunning charmer, and in affliction, makes that forwardness not unlovely, which in tranquil and happy times she would visit with her censure. If these considerations do not suffice to explain the present movements of my heroine, I must beg my reader to have patience to the end, when, peradventure, he will find a still better reason.

When morning came, Mildred was up with the first blush of light. Her thoughts had dwelt with a busy restlessness upon the late intelligence, and she had slept only in short and disturbed intervals. She was impatient to be again upon the road.

Accordingly, as soon as the preparations for their journey could be made, our party, now increased by the addition of Musgrove and his daughter, set forward on their travel towards Burk Court House.

This journey was protracted through several days. The disturbed state of the country, produced by the active hostilities which were now renewed, made it prudent for our wayfarers frequently to halt amongst the friendly inhabitants of the region through which they travelled, in order to obtain information, or wait for the passage of troops whose presence might have caused embarrassment.

The considerate kindness of Allen Musgrove, and the unwearied attentions of Mary, who, softened by her own griefs, evinced a more touching sympathy for the sufferings of Mildred, every day increased the friendship which their present companionship had engendered, and greatly beguiled the road of its tediousness and discomfort.

The journey, however, was not without its difficulties, nor altogether destitute of occurrences of interest to this history The upper districts of North Carolina present to the eye a very beautiful country, diversified by mountain and valley, and gifted in general with a rich soil. Considerable portions of this region were consequently occupied and put into cultivation at an early period of the history of the province; and, at the era of the revolution, were noted as the most desirable positions for the support of the southern armies. This circumstance had drawn the war to that quarter, and had induced a frequent struggle to retain a footing there, by each party who came into possession of it Such a state of things had now, as we have before remarked, embarrassed the progress of our friends, and had even compelled them to diverge largely from the direct route of their journey.

It happened, a few days after leaving the Yadkin, that the hour of sunset found our little troop pursuing a road through the deep and gloomy forest, which, for several miles past, had been unrelieved by any appearance of human habitation. Neither Horse Shoe nor Allen Musgrove possessed any acquaintance with the region, beyond the knowledge that they were upon what was called the upper or mountain road that extended from Virginia entirely through this section of North Carolina; and that they could not be much more than fifteen or twenty miles north of Burk Court House. Where they should rest during the night that was now at hand, was a matter that depended entirely upon chance; and stimulated by the hope of encountering some woodland cabin, they persevered in riding forward, even when the fading twilight had so obscured their path as to make it a matter of some circumspection to pick their way. Thus the night stole upon them almost unawares.

There is nothing so melancholy as the deep and lonely forest at night; and why it should be so I will not stop to inquire, but that melancholy, it seems to me, is enhanced by the chilliness of the autumnal evening. The imagination peoples the impenetrable depths of the wood with spectres, which the gibbering and shrill reptiles that inhabit these recesses seem to invest with a voice; the earth beneath the feet, carpeted with "the raven down of darkness," has an indefinite surface that causes the traveller to think of pitfalls and sudden banks, and fearful quagmires; and the grey light of the glow-worm, or the cold gleam of the rotten timber, shine up through the gloom, like some witch-taper from a haunted ground. Then, high above the head, the sombre forms of the trees nod in the night-wind, and the stars, — ineffectual to guide us on our way — are seen only in short and rapid glimpses through the foliage; all these things affect the mind with sadness, but the chattering of the teeth and the cold creep of the blood, rendered sluggish by a frosty atmosphere, make it still more sad.

Mildred and Mary Musgrove experienced a full share of these imaginings, as they now rode in the dark, side by side; and, peradventure, an occasional expression of impatience might have been heard, in whispers, between them. By degrees this feeling extended to Henry, and, in due course of time, seemed also to have reached the sergeant and the miller; for these two, as if suddenly struck with the necessity of making some provision for the night, now came to a halt, with a view to inquire into the comfort of the weaker members of the troop, and to deliberate on what was best to be done. To make a fire, erect a tent, and resort to the contents of their havresacks for supper, were the only expedients which their situation afforded; and as these arrangements were but the customary incidents of travel, in the times to which we refer, they were now resolved upon with but little sense of inconvenience or hardship. It was proper, however, that the party should encamp in some position where they might have water, and, with that object, they continued to move forward until they should find themselves in the neighborhood of a running stream — an event that, from the nature of the country, was soon likely to occur.

"There can be no moon to-night," said the sergeant, as they rode along in quest of their lodging-place, "yet yonder light would look as if she was rising. No, it can't be, for it is westward, as I judge, Allen."

"It is westward," replied Musgrove, looking towards a faint light which brought the profile of the tree-tops into relief against the horizon. "There must be fire in the woods."

The party rode on, all eyes being directed to the phenomenon pointed out by Horse Shoe. The light grew broader, and flung a lurid beam towards the zenith; and, as the travellers still came nearer, the radiance increased, and illuminated the summit of a hill, which, it was now apparent, lay between them and the light.

"We must rest here for a while," said the sergeant, reining up his horse in a dark and narrow ravine: "the fire is just across this hill in front. It would be wise to reconnoitre a little; there may be travellers camping on the t'other side, or troops for aught we know; or it may be an old fire left by the last persons who passed. You, Allen Musgrove, stay here with the women, and I will ride forward to look into the matter."

Henry accompanied the sergeant, and they both galloped up the hill. When they came to the top, a rich and strange prospect broke upon their sight. Some three and four hundred yards in advance, at the foot of the long slope of the hill, a huge volume of flame was discovered enveloping the entire trunk of a tall pine, and blazing forth with sudden flashes amongst the withered foliage. The radiance cast around from this gigantic torch penetrated the neighboring forest, and lit up the trees with a lustre more dazzling than that of day; whilst the strong shades brought into such immediate proximity with the sharp, red light, as it glanced upon every upright stem or trunk, gave a new and grotesque outline to the familiar objects of the wood. The glare fell upon the sward of the forest, and towards the rear upon a sheet of water, which showed the conflagration to have been kindled on the bank of some river. Not less conspicuous than the local features of the scene were the figures of a considerable party of soldiers passing to and fro in idle disarray through the region of the light, and a short distance from them a number of horses attached to the branches of the neighboring trees. Horse Shoe and his young companion stood gazing for some moments upon the spectacle, the sergeant in silent conjecture and perplexed thoughtfulness as to the character of the persons below, Henry intent only upon the novel and picturesque beauty of the view.

The light shone directly up the road, and fell upon the persons of our two friends, a circumstance to which the sergeant seemed to give no heed, until Henry pointed out to him a horseman, from the direction of the fire, who was now advancing towards them.

"Sergeant, turn back into the shade," cried Henry; "that man is coming after us."

"Keep your ground," replied Horse Shoe; "he has no ill-will to us. He wears the dress of an honest man and a good soldier."

"Who goes there?" called out the horseman, as he now came within speaking distance. "Stand and tell me who you are!"

"Friends to the hunting-shirt and buck-tail," replied Robinson.

"I am glad to hear you say so," rejoined the scout, as he advanced still nearer. "Where from, and in what direction do you travel?"

"That should be William Scoresby's voice, of the Amherst Rangers," shouted Henry, with animation; "as I live, it is the very man!"

"Who have we here!" returned the horseman. "Henry Lindsay! our deputy corporal! Why, man, where did you spring from?" he added, in a tone of joyful surprise, as he offered Henry his hand.

"Ho, sister Mildred — Mr. Musgrove!" exclaimed Henry, calling out at the top of his voice to his friends, who were waiting behind for intelligence. "Come up — come up! Here's good luck!"

And with a continued vociferation, he galloped back until he met his sister, and conducted her to the top of the hill, whence, following the guidance of William Scoresby, the party descended to the bivouac of the Amherst Rangers.

Henry eagerly sought out Stephen Foster, and, having brought him into the presence of Mildred, received from him a narrative of the course of events which had led to this fortunate meeting.

The Rangers had marched from Virginia a few days after Mildred had left the Dove Cote. They had fallen in with Gates's shattered army at Hillsborough, where, after tarrying almost a fortnight, they were furnished an opportunity to take some active share in the operations of the day by the enterprise of Shelby against Ferguson, the knowledge of which had reached them at Gates's headquarters, whither a messenger from Shelby had come to ask for aid. The Rangers had accordingly volunteered for this service, and, with the permission of the general, were now on their way towards Burk Court House, there hoping to receive intelligence that would enable them to join the allies.

They had for some miles been marching along the same road taken by our travellers, not more than two hours ahead of them; and having reached the Catawba near sundown, had determined to encamp there for the night. The soldiers, unaccustomed to exact discipline, had, in sport, set fire to a tall pine which some accident of the storm had killed, and produced the conflagration that had lighted Horse Shoe and his charge to the scene of the present meeting.

It may be imagined that this incident afforded great satisfaction to Mildred and her party, who were thus brought into connexion with a numerous body of friends, with whom they determined henceforth to pursue their journey. The first good result of this encounter was immediately experienced in the comfortable though rude accommodation which the prompt and united efforts of the Rangers supplied to Mildred and her friend, Mary Musgrove, in enabling them to pass a night of sound and healthful sleep.

On the following day, the Rangers and their new companions arrived at Burk Court House. They were here made acquainted with the fact that the mountain troops were at this time moving towards Gilbert-town. They accordingly, after a night's rest, resumed their march, and by a toilsome journey through a rugged mountain district, succeeded on the third evening in reaching the little village which had but a short time since been the headquarters of Ferguson and the spot of Arthur Butler's captivity.

They were now in advance of Campbell and his mountaineers; and, in waiting for these troops, they were afforded leisure to recruit themselves from the effects of their late fatigues. Good quarters were obtained for Mildred and her companions. She required repose, and profited by the present opportunity to enjoy it.

The village at this moment was full of troops. Brandon and Lacy, with their followers, whom we have referred to in the last chapter, were already there, in daily expectation of the arrival of the confederates; and amongst these men, Sergeant Robinson and his companion, the miller, found the means of relieving the tediousness of delay, to say nothing of Henry, who had now become so decidedly martial in his inclinations, that the camp was to him a scene of never-fading interest.

In two days Campbell's army entered the village, after a march of which we have already given a sketch to our reader. It was a duty of early concern, on the part of Allen Musgrove and the sergeant, to apprise him of the presence of Mildred and her brother, and to communicate to him the singular purpose of her mission. The effect of this was a visit by Campbell, Shelby, and Williams, to the lady on the evening of their arrival. The two latter of these officers had already been personally active in the behalf of Arthur Butler, and all felt the liveliest interest in his fortunes. The singular relation in which Mildred seemed to stand to the captive officer, and the extraordinary zeal which her present mission betrayed in his cause, drew forth a warm sympathy from the generous soldiers around her, and there was even a tincture of the romance of chivalry in the fervor with which, on the present visit, they pledged themselves to her service. With the delicacy that always belongs to honorable and brave hearts, they refrained from inquiry into the special inducements which could so earnestly enlist the lady in the service of their fellow-soldier, and sedulously strove to raise her spirits into a cheerful and happy tone by the hopes they were able to inspire.

CHAPTER LIV

FERGUSON ADVANCES SOUTH. — HE HAS REASON TO BECOME CIRCUMSPECT. — ARTHUR BUTLER FINDS HIMSELF RETREATING FROM HIS FRIENDS

We return for a moment to look after Butler. As near as my information enables me to speak — for I wish to be accurate in dates — it was about the 23d of September when our hero arrived at Gilbert-town, and found himself committed to the custody of Ferguson. His situation, in many respects uncomfortable, was not altogether without circumstances to alleviate the rigor of captivity. Ferguson, though a rough soldier, and animated by a zealous partisanship in the royal cause which imbued his feelings with a deep hatred of the Whigs, was also a man of education, and of a disposition to respect the claims of a gentleman fully equal to himself in rank and consideration — even when these qualities were found in an enemy. His intercourse, of late, had been almost entirely confined to the wild spirits who inhabited the frontier, and who, impelled by untamed passions, were accustomed to plunge into every excess which the license of war enabled them to practise. He had, accordingly, adapted his behavior to the complexion of this population, and maintained his authority, both over his own recruits and such of the opposite party as had fallen into his hands, by a severe, and not unfrequently by even a cruel bearing. Following the example set him by Cornwallis himself, he had more than once executed summary vengeance upon the Whigs whom the chances of war had brought into his power; or, what was equally reprehensible, had allowed the Tory bands who had enlisted under his banner, to gratify their own thirst of blood in the most revolting barbarities. Towards Butler, however, he demeaned himself with more consideration — and sometimes even extended to him such little courtesies as might be indulged without risk to the principal purpose of his safe custody. A separate room was provided for the prisoner, and he was allowed the occasional services of Harry Winter and the other companions of his late misfortune. Still, the familiar scenes of suffering and death which Butler was constrained to witness amongst his compatriots, and the consciousness of his own inability to avert these calamities, greatly weighed upon his spirits. His persuasion, too, that Ferguson was now aiding, by what seemed to be a most effectual participation, in the plan for the capture of Clarke, and his belief that this blow would sadly afflict, if not altogether dishearten the friends of independence in the South, added to his private grief. He knew nothing of the mustering of the mountaineers, and saw no hope of extrication from the difficulties that threatened to overwhelm his cause.

Such was the condition of Butler during the first four or five days of his captivity at Gilbert-town. At the end of this period, circumstances occurred to raise in his bosom the most lively excitement. Suddenly, an order was issued for the immediate movement of the army southwards — and the prisoners were directed to accompany the march. It was apparent that information of importance had been received, and that some decisive event was at hand. When, in pursuance of this command, the troops were marshalled for their journey, and Butler was stationed in the column, along with all the other prisoners of the post, he was startled to observe the dragoon, James Curry, appear in the ranks, as one regularly attached to the corps. Butler had seen nor heard nothing of this man since he had parted from him at Blackstock's after the battle of Musgrove's mill; and his conviction, that, acting under the control of some higher authority, this individual had been the principal agent in his present misfortunes, gave him a painful anxiety in regard to the future. This anxiety was far from being diminished, when he now discovered that the same person, with a party of dragoons, was specially intrusted with his guardianship. Winter and the other troopers who had, until this moment, been allowed to keep him company, were now directed to take a station amongst the common prisoners, and Butler was furnished with his horse, and commanded to submit to the particular supervision of the dragoon. These arrangements being made, the march of Ferguson commenced.

The army moved cautiously towards the upper sections of the district of Ninety-Six. It was evident to Butler, from the frequent hints dropped in conversation by the royalist officers, that Ferguson supposed himself to be getting every moment nearer to Clarke. In this state of suspense and weariness the first day's march was concluded.

The second was like the first. Ferguson still moved south,

slowly, but steadily. Every man that was met upon the road was questioned by the commanding officer, to ascertain whether there was any report of troops westward. "Had any crossed Saluda — or been heard of towards the mountains!" — was an invariable interrogatory.

None, that the person questioned knew of — was the common reply.

"Tush! the devil's in it, that we can hear nothing of the fellow!" exclaimed Ferguson, after the fifth or sixth wayfarer had been examined. "Clarke and his beggars are flesh and blood — they travel by land, and not through the air! Faith, I begin to think Cruger has saved us trouble, and has got his hand on the runaway's croup! James Curry."

The dragoon rode to the front and bowed.

"You left Fort Ninety-Six only on Wednesday?"

"I did."

"Where was Cruger then?"

"Marching towards Saluda, with Brown — following Clarke, as it was supposed — but on rather a cold scent as one of the couriers reported."

"Humph! I must get still nearer to the mountains," said Ferguson, as he clenched his teeth and seemed absorbed in thought.

In a short time after this, the column diverged from their former course by a road that led westward.

Thus ended the second day.

During the next two days, Ferguson had become manifestly more circumspect in his movement, and spent the greater portion of this interval upon a road which was said to extend from Ninety-Six, to the Allegany mountain. Here he remained, with the wariness of the tiger that prepares to spring upon his prey; and it was with a petulant temper that, after this anxious watch for forty-eight hours, he turned upon his heel and summoned his officers around him, and announced his determination to penetrate still further into the forest. Like a man perplexed and peevish with crosses, he soon changed his mind, and ordered a lieutenant of cavalry into his presence.

"Take six of your best appointed men," he said, "and send one half of them up this road towards the mountains — the other half southwards — and command them not to stop until they bring me some news of this night-hawk, Clarke. Let them be trusty men that you can depend upon. I will wait but twenty-four hours for them. Meantime," he added, turning to another officer present,

"I will send a courier after Cruger, who shall find him if he is above ground."

The following day — which brings us to the third of October — a decisive change took place in the aspect of affairs. Before either of the scouts that had been lately despatched had returned, a countryman was brought into Furguson's camp, who, being submitted to the usual minute examination, informed the questioners, that some thirty miles, in the direction of Fort Ninety-Six, he had met upon the road a large party of cavalry under the command of Colonel Williams — and that that officer had shown great anxiety to learn whether certain Whig troops had been seen near Gilbert-town. The informant added, that "Williams appeared to him to be strangely particular in his inquiries about Ferguson."

This intelligence seemed suddenly to awaken the British partisan from a dream. He was now one hundred miles south of Cornwallis; and, both east and west of the line of communication between them, it was apparent that hostile parties were assembling, with a view to some united action against him. It struck him now, for the first time, that an enemy might be thrown between the main army at Charlotte and his detachment, and thus cause him some embarrassment in his retreat — but it was still with the scorn of a presumptuous soldier that he recurred to the possibility of his being forced to fight his way.

"They are for turning the tables on me," he said, in a tone of derision, "and hope to pounce upon my back while I am taken up with this half-starved and long-legged fellow of the mountains. But I will show them who is master yet!"

In this temper he commenced his retreat, which was conducted slowly and obstinately; and it may be supposed that Butler, as he involuntarily followed the fortunes of his enemy, contemplated these movements with an anxious interest. The common report of the camp made him acquainted with the circumstances which had recommended the retreat, and he, therefore, watched the course of events in momentary expectation of some incident of great importance to himself.

At night Ferguson arrived at the Cowpens, just twenty-four hours in advance of his enemies. Whilst resting here he received intelligence of the stout array that had lately assembled at Gilbert-town, and which, he was now told, were in full pursuit of him. It was, at first, with an incredulous ear that he heard the report of the numbers of this suddenly-levied mountain-army. It seemed incredible that such a host could have been convened in such brief space and with such secret expedition; and even more unworthy of belief, that they could have been found in the wild and thinly-peopled regions of the Allegany. His doubt, however, yielded to his fear, and induced him to accelerate his pace.

His first care was to despatch, on that night, a courier to Cornwallis, to inform the general of his situation and ask for reinforcements. The letter which bore this request is still extant, and will show that even in the difficult juncture in which we have presented the writer of it, his boastful confidence had not abandoned him.

Before the succeeding dawn he was again in motion, directing his hasty march towards the Cherokee Ford of Broad river. This point he reached at sun-down. His journey had been pursued, thus far, with unremitting industry. If his motions had corresponded to his affected disesteem of his enemy, he would here have halted for rest; but, like one who flies with the superstitious dread of a goblin follower, the retreating partisan looked over his shoulder with an unquiet spirit, and made a sign to his companions still to press forward. They crossed the river at night, and did not halt again until they had traversed some six or eight miles beyond the further bank.

The anxiety, suspense, and eager expectation of Butler increased with these thickening demonstrations of the approach of a period which he foresaw must be decisive, not only of his own hopes, but, in a great degree, of the hopes of his country. The retreat of Ferguson towards King's Mountain, which now lay but a few miles in advance, was a visible and most striking type of the vanishing power which for a brief half-year had maintained its domination over the free spirits of the south, and which had aimed, by a cruel and bloody rule, to extinguish all that was generous and manly in these afflicted provinces.

Contenting myself with this rapid survey of events which, of themselves, possess an interest that would, if time and space permitted me, have justified the detail of a volume, I go back to the regular current of my story.

CHAPTER LV

THE WHIGS CONTINUE THEIR MARCH. — MILDRED IS LEFT BEHIND

THE army of mountaineers halted at Gilbert-town only until a vidette from Williams brought tidings of Ferguson's late movements. These reached Campbell early in the day succeeding his arrival at the village, and apprised him that Williams followed on the footsteps of the British partisan, and would expect to unite his force with that of the allied volunteers at the Cowpens — (a field not yet distinguished in story) — whither he expected to arrive on the following day. Campbell determined, in consequence, to hasten to this quarter.

The present position of Mildred, notwithstanding the kind sympathy with which every one regarded her, was one that wrought severely upon her feelings. She had heretofore encountered the hardships of her journey, and bore herself through the trials, so unaccustomed to her sex, with a spirit that had quailed before no obstacle. But now, finding herself in the train of an army just moving forth to meet its enemy, with all the vicissitudes and peril of battle in prospect, it was with a sinking of the heart she had not hitherto known, that she felt herself called upon to choose between the alternative of accompanying them in their march, or being left behind. To adopt the first resolve, she was painfully conscious would bring her to witness scenes, and perhaps endure privations, the very thought of which made her shudder; whilst, to remain at a distance from the theatre of events in which she was so deeply concerned, was a thought that suggested many anxious fears, not less intolerable than the untried sufferings of the campaign. She had, thus far, braved all dangers for the sake of being near to Butler; and now to hesitate or stay her step, when she had almost reached the very spot of his captivity, and when the fortunes of war might soon throw her into his actual presence, seemed to her like abandoning her duty at the most critical moment of trial. She was aware that he was in the camp of the enemy; that this enemy was likely to be overtaken and brought to combat; and it was with a magnified terror that she summoned up to her imagination the possible mischances which might befall

Arthur Butler in the infliction of some summary act of vengeance provoked by the exasperation of conflict. "I have tempted the dangers of flood and storm for him — of forest and field — noonday battle and midnight assault," she said, with an earnestness that showed she had shaken all doubts from her mind; "I have taken my vow of devotion to his safety — to be performed with such fidelity as befits the sacred bond between us. I will not blench now, in the last struggle, though perils thicken around me. I'm prepared for the worst."

Allen Musgrove, Robinson, and Henry combated this resolve with joint expostulation, urging upon Mildred the propriety of her tarrying in the village, at least until the active operations of the army were terminated — an event that might be expected in a few days. But it was not until Campbell himself remonstrated with her against the indiscretion of her purpose, and promised to afford her the means of repairing to the scene of action at any moment she might think her presence there useful, that she relinquished her determination to accompany the army on its present expedition. It was, in consequence, ultimately arranged that she should remain in the quarters provided for her in Gilbert-town, attended by the miller and his daughter, whilst a few soldiers were to be detailed as a guard for her person. With this train of attendants, she was to be left at liberty to draw as near to the centre of events as her considerate and faithful counsellor, Allen Musgrove, might deem safe.

Another source of uneasiness to her arose out of the separation which she was about to endure from the sergeant and her brother Henry. Horse Shoe, swayed by an irresistible and affectionate longing to be present at the expected passage of arms, which might so materially affect the fortunes of his captive fellow-soldier, Butler, had represented to Mildred the value of the services he might be able to render; and as the friendly solicitude of the miller and his daughter left nothing within their power to be supplied, towards the comfort and protection of the lady, she did not refuse her consent to this temporary desertion — although it naturally awakened some painful sense of bereavement, at a moment when her excited feelings most required the consolation of friends.

Henry, captivated with the prospect of military adventure, and magnified in his own esteem by the importance which Stephen Foster and the Rangers playfully assigned to his position in the ranks, had so far lost sight of the special duty he had assumed, as his sister's companion, that he now resolutely rebelled against all attempts to persuade him to remain in the village; and Mildred, at last, upon the pledge of the sergeant to keep the cadet under his own eye, reluctantly yielded to a demand which she found it almost impossible to resist.

These matters being settled, it was not long before Mildred and Mary Musgrove, seated at the window of the house which had been selected as their present abode, saw the long array of the army glide by at a brisk pace, and watched the careless and laughing faces of the soldiers, as they filed off through the only street in the village, and took the high road leading south.

The troops had been gone for several hours, and Allen Musgrove and the few soldiers who had been left behind, had scattered themselves over the village, to get rid of the tedium of idleness in the gossip of the scant population which the place afforded. Mildred had retired to a chamber, and Mary loitered from place to place like one disturbed with care. All the party felt that deep sense of loneliness which is so acutely perceptible to those who suddenly change a life of toil and incident for one of rest, while events of busy interest are in expectation.

"They are gone, ma'am," said Mary, as she now crept into Mildred's presence, after having travelled over nearly the whole village, in the state of disquietude I have described; "they are gone at least twenty miles, I should think, by this time; and I never would have believed that I could have cared so much about people I never saw before. But we are so lonesome, ma'am. And young Mister Henry Lindsay, I should say, must be getting tired by this time of day. As for the matter of that, people may get tireder by standing still than by going on."

"How far do they march to-day?" inquired Mildred; "have you heard your father say, Mary?"

"I heard him and the troopers who are here allow," replied the maiden, "that Colonel Campbell wouldn't reach Colonel Williams before to-morrow afternoon. They said it was good fifty miles' travel. They look like brave men — them that marched this morning, ma'am; for they went out with good heart. The Lord send that through Him they may be the means of deliverance to Major Butler!"

At the mention of this name, Mildred covered her face with her hands, and the tears trickled through her fingers. "The Lord send it!" she repeated, after a moment's pause. "May He, in his mercy, come to our aid!" Then uncovering her face, and dropping on her knees beside her chair, she whispered a prayer for the success of those who had lately marched forth against the enemy.

When she arose from this posture, she went to the window, and there stood gazing out upon the quiet and unfrequented street, running over in her mind the perils to which her brother as well as Butler might be exposed, and summoning to her imagination the thousand subjects of solicitude, which her present state of painful expectation might be supposed to create or recall.

"We will set forth early to-morrow," she said, addressing herself to her companion, "so tell your father, Mary. We will follow the brave friends who have left us: I cannot be content to linger behind them. I will sleep in the lowliest hovel, or in the common shelter of the woods, and share all the dangers of the march, rather than linger here in this dreadful state of doubt and silence. Tell your father to make his preparations for our departure to-morrow: tell him I cannot abide another day in this place."

"I should think we might creep near them, ma'am," replied Mary, "near enough to see and hear what was going on — which is always a great satisfaction, and not get ourselves into trouble neither. I am sure my father would be very careful of us, and keep us out of harm's way, come what would. And it is distressing to be so far off, when you don't know what's going to turn up. I will seek my father — who I believe is over yonder with the troopers at the shop, talking to the blacksmith — I will go there and try to coax him to do your bidding. I know the troopers want it more than we do, and they'll say a word to help it along."

"Say I desire to have it so, Mary. I can take no refusal. Here I will not stay longer."

Mary left the apartment, and as she descended the steps, she fell into a rumination which arrested her progress full five minutes, during which she remained mute upon the stair-case. "No wonder the poor dear lady wishes to go!" was the ejaculation which came at last sorrowfully from her heart, with a long sigh, and at the same time tears began to flow: "no wonder she wants to be near Major Butler, who loves her past the telling of it. If John Ramsay was there," she added, sobbing, "I would have followed him — followed him — yes, if I died for it."

CHAPTER LVI

AFFAIRS BEGIN TO DRAW TO A HEAD. PREPARATIONS FOR BATTLE. A PICTURE OF THE TWO ARMIES

AFTER leaving Gilbert-town, Campbell moved steadily toward the point at which he proposed to meet Williams, and by night-fall had accomplished about one half of the journey. The march furnished Henry Lindsay unalloyed pleasure. Every incident belonging to it awakened the fancies which he had indulged in reference to military life, and he was delighted in the contemplation of this actual accomplishment of some of the many dreams of glory which his boyish romance had engendered at home. Besides, being a favorite of those in command, he was allowed to ride in the ranks whenever it suited his pleasure, and to amuse himself with what subject of interest the journey afforded; whilst, at the same time, he found his personal ease so much attended to as to leave him but little room to complain of the discomfort or toil of the campaign.

The night was spent in the woods, and it was scarcely day-break, when the exhilarating though harsh clamor of the horns summoned the troops to the renewal of their journey, which was pursued until the afternoon, when, about four o'clock, they reached the border of the tract of country known as the Cowpens. Afar off, occupying a piece of elevated ground, Campbell was enabled to descry a considerable body of cavalry, whose standard, dress, and equipment, even at this distance, sufficiently made known to him their friendly character, — a fact that was immediately afterwards confirmed by the report of some videttes, who had been stationed upon the road by which Campbell advanced. A brief interval brought the two parties together, and the force of the allied bands was thus augmented by the addition of our gallant friend Williams, at the head of four hundred sturdy companions.

"Make a short speech of it," said Shelby, addressing Williams, after that officer had ridden into the circle of his comrades, and had exchanged with them a friendly greeting, "you have been busy, fellow-soldier, whilst we were waiting to see the grass grow. What has become of the runaway?"

"He left this spot but yesterday," replied Williams; "Ferguson has something of the bull-dog in him: his retreat, now that he is forced to it, is surly and slow; he stops to snarl and growl as if he defied us to follow him. If he had but stood his ground here, we should have had him in as pretty a field as one might desire. Devil thank him for his prudence! But he is now at the Cherokee Ford of Broad river — so I conjecture, by the report of my scouts — hard upon thirty miles from here, on his way towards Charlotte."

"Say you so?" exclaimed Campbell; "then, by my faith, we have no time to lose! Gentlemen, we will rest but an hour, and then to it, for a night march. Pick me out your best men and stoutest horses; leave the footmen behind, and the weakest of the cavalry. This fellow may take it into his head to show his heels. If I can but tread upon the tail of the copperhead with one foot, he will throw himself into his coil for fight, — that's the nature of the beast, — and after that, if need be, we can threaten him until all our force arrives. Shelby, look to the immediate execution of this order."

"That's glorious, sergeant," said Henry, who, with his companion, Robinson, had stolen up to the skirts of the circle of officers during this conference, and had heard Campbell's order. "I am of this party, whoever goes. Colonel Campbell," he added, with the familiarity of his privilege, "the Rangers are ready for you, at any rate."

"There's a mettlesome colt," said Campbell, laughing and speaking to the officers around him, "that bird shows fight before his spurs are grown. Pray, sir," he continued, addressing Henry, "what command have you?"

"I consider myself answerable for the second platoon of the Amherst Rangers," replied Henry, with a waggish sauciness, "and they march this night, whatever happens."

"You shall serve with me in the staff, master," said Campbell, playfully, "such fiery young blades must be looked after. Get your men ready; you shall go, I promise you."

Henry, delighted at the notice he had received, rode off with alacrity to spread the news.

The council broke up, and the earliest arrangements were set on foot to make the draught required by the general orders.

Before the day had departed, nine hundred picked men, well mounted and equipped, were seen spurring forward from the line, and taking a position in the column of march, which was now prepared to move. All the principal officers of the army accompanied this detachment, in which were to be seen the Amherst Rangers with their redoubtable recruits, Henry Lindsay and the sergeant.

It rained during the night, a circumstance that, however it increased the toils of the soldiers, but little abated their speed — and, an hour before daybreak, they had reached the destined point on Broad river: but the game had disappeared. Ferguson, as we have seen, had pushed his march on the preceding evening beyond this spot, and had taken the road, as it was reported, towards King's mountain, which was not above twelve miles distant.

A few hours were given by Campbell to the refreshment of his troops, who halted upon the bank of the river, where, having kindled their fires and opened their wallets, they soon found themselves in a condition that pleasantly contrasted with the discomforts of their ride during the night. The enemy consisted principally of infantry — and Campbell, having gained so closely upon their footsteps, felt no doubt of overtaking them in the course of the day. He, therefore, determined to allow his men full time to recruit their strength for the approaching conflict.

The rain had ceased before the dawn. The clouds had fled from the firmament before a brisk and enlivening autumnal breeze, and the sun rose with unusual splendor. It was one of those days which belong to October, clear, cool, and exhilarating — when all animal nature seems to be invigorated by breathing an atmosphere of buoyant health. For more than an hour after the sun had cast his broad beams over the landscape, the wearied encampment was seen stretched in slumber — the camp-guards only, and some occasional parties on fatigue service, were to be observed in motion. By degrees, the drowsy soldiers woke up, refreshed by the change of weather, no less than by the repose which they had snatched in the short moments of the halt. A general summons, at last, brought every one into motion. By nine o'clock of the morning, the army were in condition to prosecute their march, as little wanting in alacrity or vigor as when they first commenced their labors; and, at the hour designated, they were seen to prick forth upon their way with an elastic movement that had in it the vivacity of a holiday sport. Even our young martialist, Henry, had become so inured to the toils of the road, that now, with the aid of a sleep which Horse Shoe had affectionately guarded until the last moment — to say nothing of a good luncheon of broiled venison, which the boy discussed after he had mounted into his saddle — he might be considered the most light-hearted of the host.

Towards noon, the army reached the neighborhood of King's mountain. The scouts and parties of the advance had brought information that Ferguson had turned aside from his direct road, and taken post upon this eminence, where, it was evident, he meant to await the attack of his enemy. Campbell, therefore, lost no time in pushing forward, and was soon rewarded with a view of the object of his pursuit. Some two or three miles distant, where an opening through the forest first gave him a sight of the mass of highland, he could indistinctly discern the array of the adverse army perched on the very summit of the hill.

The mountain consists of an elongated ridge, rising out of the bosom of an uneven country, to the height of perhaps five hundred feet, and presenting a level line of summit or crest, from which the earth slopes down, at its southward termination and on each side, by an easy descent; whilst northward, it is detached from highlands of inferior elevation by a rugged valley — thus giving it the character of an insulated promontory, not exceeding half a mile in length. At the period to which our story refers, it was covered, except in a few patches of barren field or broken ground, with a growth of heavy timber, which was so far free from underwood as in no great degree to embarrass the passage of horsemen; and through this growth the eye might distinguish, at a considerable distance, the occasional masses of grey rock that were scattered in huge boulders over its summit and sides.

The adjacent region, lying south from the mountain, was partially cleared and in cultivation, presenting a limited range of open ground, over which the march of Campbell might have been revealed in frequent glimpses to the British partisan, for some three or four miles. We may suppose, therefore, that the two antagonists watched each other, during the advance of the approaching army across this district, with emotions of various and deep interest. Campbell drew at length into a ravine which, bounded by low and short hills, and shaded by detached portions of the forest, partly concealed his troops from the view of the enemy, who was now not more than half a mile distant. The gorge of this dell or narrow valley opened immediately towards the southern termination of the mountain; and the column halted a short distance within, where a bare knoll, or round, low hill, crowned with rock, jutted abruptly over the road, and constituted the only impediment that prevented each party from inspecting the array of his opponent.

It was an hour after noon, and the present halt was improved by the men in making ready for battle. Meanwhile, the chief officers met together in front, and employed their time in surveying the localities of the ground upon which they were soon to be brought to action. The knoll, I have described, furnished a favorable position for this observation, and thither they had already repaired.

I turn from the graver and more important matters which may be supposed to have occupied the thoughts of the leaders, as they were grouped together on the broad rock, to a subject which was, at this moment, brought to their notice by the unexpected appearance of two females on horseback, on the road, a full half mile in the rear of the army, and who were now approaching at a steady pace. They were attended by a man who, even thus far off, showed the sedateness of age; and, a short space behind them, rode a few files of troopers in military array.

It was with mingled feelings of surprise and admiration at the courage which could have prompted her, at such a time, to visit the army, that the party recognised Mildred Lindsay and her attendants, in the approaching cavalcade. These emotions were expressed by them in the rough and hearty phrase of their habitual and familiar intercourse.

"Let me beg, gentlemen," said Campbell, interrupting them, "that you speak kindly and considerately of yonder lady. By my honor, I have never seen man or woman with a more devoted or braver heart. Poor girl! — she has nobly followed Butler through his afflictions, and taken her share of suffering with a spirit that should bring us all to shame. Horse Shoe Robinson, who has squired her to our camp, even from her father's house, speaks of a secret between her and our captive friend, that tells plainly enough to my mind of sworn faith and long-tried love. As men and soldiers, we should reverence it. Williams, look carefully to her comfort and safety. Go, man, at once, and meet her on the road. God grant that this day may bring an end to her grief!"

Williams departed on his mission, and when he met the lady, her brother and the sergeant were already in her train.

Allen Musgrove explained the cause of this unlooked-for apparition. The party, in obedience to Mildred's urgent wish, and scarcely less to the content of all the others, had quitted their secluded position at Gilbert-town on the preceding morning; and learning in the course of the day from persons on the road, that Ferguson had moved northwards, the miller had taken a direction across the country which enabled him to intercept the army at its present post, with little more than half the travel which the circuitous route of the march had required. They had passed the night under a friendly roof some ten or twelve miles distant, and had overtaken their companions at the critical moment at which they have been introduced to view.

At Mildred's request she was conducted into the presence of Campbell, who still retained his station on the knoll. A thoughtful and amiable deference was manifested towards her by the assembled soldiers, who received her with many kind and encouraging greetings. That air of perturbation and timidity which, in spite of all efforts at self-control, the novelty of her position and the consciousness of the dreadful scene at hand had thrown over her demeanor, gradually began to give way before the assurances and sympathy of her friends; and, at length, she became sufficiently self-possessed to look around her and mark the events that were in progress.

The important moment of battle drew nigh, and the several leaders respectively took their leave of her, with an exhortation to be of good cheer, and to remain at her present post under the charge of her trusty companion, the miller, who was fully instructed by Campbell as to the course he should take for the lady's safety, in whatever emergency might arise.

Here we leave her for a moment, whilst we cast a glance at the preparations for battle.

It was three o'clock before these arrangements were completed. I have informed my reader that the mountain terminated immediately in front of the outlet from the narrow dell in which Campbell's army had halted, its breast protruding into the plain only some few hundred paces from the head of the column, whilst the valley, that forked both right and left, afforded an easy passage along the base on either side. Ferguson occupied the very summit, and now frowned upon his foe from the midst of a host confident in the strength of their position, and exasperated by the pursuit which had driven them into this fastness.

Campbell resolved to assail this post by a spirited attack, at the same moment, in front and on the two flanks. With this intent his army was divided into three equal parts. The centre was reserved to himself and Shelby; the right was assigned to Sevier and M'Dowell; the left to Cleveland and Williams. These two latter parties were to repair to their respective sides of the mountain, and the whole were to make the onset by scaling the heights as nearly as possible at the same instant.

The men, before they marched out of the ravine, had dismounted and picqueted their horses under the winding shelter of the hills; and, being now separated into detached columns formed in solid order, they were put in motion to reach their allotted posts. The Amherst Rangers were retained on horseback for such duty as might require speed, and were stationed close in the rear of Campbell's own division, which now merely marched from behind the shelter of the knoll and halted in the view of the enemy, until sufficient delay should be afforded to the flanking divisions to attain their ground.

Mildred, attended by Allen Musgrove and his daughter, still maintained her position on the knoll, and from this height surveyed the preparations for combat with a beating heart. The scene within her view was one of intense occupation. The air of stern resolve that sat upon every brow; the silent but onward movement of the masses of men advancing to conflict; the few brief and quick words of command that fell from the distance upon her ear; the sullen beat of the hoof upon the sod, as an occasional horseman sped to and fro between the more remote bodies and the centre division, which yet stood in compact phalanx immediately below her at the foot of the hill; then the breathless anxiety of her companions near at hand, and the short note of dread, and almost terror, that now and then escaped from the lips of Mary Musgrove, as the maiden looked eagerly and fearfully abroad over the plain; all these incidents wrought upon her feelings and caused her to tremble. Yet, amidst these novel emotions, she was not insensible to a certain lively and even pleasant interest, arising out of the picturesque character of the spectacle. The gay sunshine striking aslant these moving battalions, lighting up their fringed and many-colored hunting-shirts, and casting a golden hue upon their brown and weather-beaten faces, brought out into warm relief the chief characteristics of this peculiar woodland army. And Mildred sometimes forgot her fears in the fleeting inspiration of the sight, as she watched the progress of an advancing column — at one time moving in close ranks, with the serried thicket of rifles above their heads, and at another deploying into files to pass some narrow path, along which, with trailed arms and bodies bent, they sped with the pace of hunters beating the hill-side for game. The tattered and service-stricken banner that shook its folds in the wind above these detached bodies, likewise lent its charm of association to the field the silence and steadfastness of the array in which it was borne, and its constant onward motion; showing it to be encircled by strong arms and stout hearts.

Turning from these, the lady's eye was raised, with a less joyous glance, towards the position of the enemy. On the most prominent point of the mountain's crest she could descry the standard of England fluttering above a concentrated body, whose scarlet uniforms, as the sun glanced upon them through the forest, showed that here Ferguson had posted his corps of regulars, and held them ready to meet the attack of the centre division of the assailants; whilst the glittering of bayonets amidst the dark foliage, at intervals, rearward along the line of the summit, indicated that heavy detachments were stationed in this quarter to guard the flanks. The marching and countermarching of the frequent corps, from various positions on the summit; the speeding of officers on horseback, and the occasional movement of small squadrons of dragoons, who were at one moment seen struggling along the sides of the mountain, and, at another, descending towards the base or returning to the summit, disclosed the earnestness and activity of the preparation with which a courageous soldier may be supposed to make ready for his foe.

It was with a look of sorrowful concern which brought tears into her eyes, that Mildred gazed upon this host, and strained her vision in the vain endeavor to catch some evidences of the presence of Arthur Butler.

"We both look, perchance," she said to herself, "at this very instant, upon yon hateful banner — and with the same aversion: but oh, with what more painful apprehension it is my fortune to behold it! Little does he think that Mildred's eyes are turned upon it. 'Tis well he does not — his noble heart would chafe itself with ten-fold anguish at the cruel thraldom that separates us. Yes, 'tis well he does not dream that his Mildred is here to witness this dreadful struggle," she continued, musing over the subject of her grief, "it might tempt him to some rash endeavor to break his bondage. It is better as it is; the misery of the thought of our afflictions should be mine only; the brave patience of a manly soldier is his, and should not be embittered with sorrows that belong not to the perils of war."

"Sister," said Henry, who had stolen up the hill unobserved, and now stood beside Mildred, "take courage and keep a good heart! The very day I often prayed to see has come — and it has come sooner than you promised it should. Here I am in the field, amongst men, and no play-game is it, either, to keep us busy, but downright earnest battle. And then, dear sister, you are here to look on — isn't that a piece of good luck?"

"Ah, brother, I could talk to you with a boastful tongue when all around us was peace and security. I cannot exhort you now. If I dare, I would beg you to stay by my side. I have need of your comfort, and shudder with a chilly fear. Henry, that small hand of yours can do no service to-day — and in truth, I cannot bear to see you exposed to danger."

"In tears, sister! Come now, this is not like you. Hasn't Arthur fought many a day and often? And didn't you set him on, with good brave words for it?"

"I was not there to see him," interrupted Mildred.

"Well, sister, I must get to my post," said Henry. "I serve as aide-de-camp, and Horse Shoe is to help me. By-the-by, Mildred, the sergeant is uncommonly silent and busy to-day. He smells this battle like an old soldier, and I heard him give a few hints to Campbell, concerning the marching up yonder hill: — he told him the column should not display until they got near the top, as Ferguson has no cannon; and the Colonel took it very gladly. Horse Shoe, moreover, thinks we will beat them — and the men have great dependence on what he says. I shall not lose sight of him to-day."

"For Heaven's sake, Henry," exclaimed Mildred, "my dear brother, do not think of following the sergeant! I cannot part with you," she added, with great earnestness; "it is an awful time for brother and sister to separate — stay with me."

The cadet turned a look upon his sister of surprise, at the new light in which her present fears represented her.

"I thought, Mildred," he said, "you were brave. Hav'n't we come all this way from home to assist Butler? And are you now, for the first time — just when we are going to pluck him from the midst of the wolves upon that mountain — are you now to weep and play the coward, sister?"

"Go, go!" said Mildred, as she covered her eyes with her hand, "but, dear Henry, remember you have a weak arm and a slender frame, and are not expected to take upon you the duties of a man."

"Besides," said Mary Musgrove, who had been a silent and perplexed witness of this scene, and who now put in her word of counsel, out of the fulness of her heart, "besides, Mister

Henry Lindsay, what trouble would it give to Sergeant Robinson, and all the rest of them, if you should get lost scampering about the hills, and they shouldn't know where to find you? It would take up so much of their precious time in looking for you: and, I am sure, they hav'n't much to spare!"

"You are as valiant as a mouse," replied Henry, laughing, "and monstrous wise, Mary Musgrove. Do you take care of my sister, and speak a word now and then to keep up her spirits — that is, if your tongue doesn't grow too thick with fright. Your teeth chatter now. A kiss, Mildred. There: God bless you! I must get to my post."

With these words, Henry bounded off towards the valley to rejoin his comrades. Half way, he met Allen Musgrove, who was now on his return to the top of the hill, whence he had withdrawn for a brief space to hold some converse with Robinson.

"A word," said Allen to Henry, as they met; "you are but a stripling. Remember that this day's work is to be wrought by men of might — those who are keen of eye and steady of foot. In the tempest of battle your weight, Mister Henry, would be but as a feather in the gale. Yet in this fight none might be crushed whose fall would bring more anguish than yours. Let me beg you, as a rash and thoughtless youth, to think of that. The good lady, your sister — "

"I cannot stay to hear you," interrupted Henry; "the column is beginning to move."

And in a moment he was at the foot of the hill.

CHAPTER LVII

THE BATTLE OF KING'S MOUNTAIN

They closed full fast on every side,
No slackness there was found
And many a gallant gentleman
Lay gasping on the ground.

O dread! it was a grief to see,
And likewise for to hear
The cries of men lying in their gore
And scattered here and there.

CHEVY CHASE.

EVERY corps was now in motion, and the two flanking divisions were soon lost to view in the intervening forest. An incident of some interest to our story makes it necessary that we should, for a moment, follow the track of Cleveland in his march upon the left side of the mountain.

The principal road of travel northwards extended along the valley on this side; and upon this road Cleveland and Williams conducted their men, until they arrived at a point sufficiently remote to enable them, by ascending the height, to place themselves in Ferguson's rear. They had just reached this point when they encountered a picquet of the enemy, which, after a few shots, retired hastily up the mountain.

The little outpost had scarcely begun to give ground, before the leading companies of the Whigs had their attention drawn to the movements of a small party of horsemen who at that moment appeared in sight upon the road, some distance in advance. They were approaching the American column; and, as if taken by surprise at the appearance of this force, set spurs to their horses and made an effort to ride beyond the reach of Cleveland's fire, whilst they took a direction up the mountain towards Ferguson's stronghold. From the equipment of these individuals, it might have been inferred that they were two gentlemen of some distinction connected with the royal army, attended by their servants, and now about arriving, after a long journey, at the British camp. The first was habited in the uniform of an officer, was well mounted, and displayed a light and active figure, which appeared to advantage in the dexterous management of his horse. The second was a gentlemen in a plain riding costume, of slender and well-knit proportions, and manifestly older than his companion. He rode a powerful and spirited horse, with a confidence and command not inferior to those of this associates. The others in attendance, from their position in the rear, and from the heavy portmanteaus that encumbered their saddles, we might have no difficulty in conjecturing to be menials in the service of the two first.

The course taken by this party brought them obliquely across the range of the fire of the Whigs.

"It is a general officer and his aide," exclaimed one of the subalterns in the advance. "Ho there! Stand. You are my prisoners!"

"Spur, spur, and away! For God's sake, fly!" shouted the younger of the two horsemen to his companion, as he dashed the rowels into his steed and fled up the mountain. "Push for the top — one moment more and we are out of reach!"

"Stop them, at all hazards!" vociferated Cleveland, the instant his eye fell upon them. "Quick, lads — level your pieces — they are messengers from Cornwallis. Rein up, or I fire!" he called aloud after the flying cavalcade.

The appeal and the threat were unheeded. A score of men left the ranks and ran some distance up the mountain side, and their shots whistled through the forest after the fugitives. One of the attendants was seen to fall, and his horse to wheel round and run back, with a frightened pace, to the valley. The scarlet uniform of the younger horseman, conspicuous through the foliage some distance up the mountains, showed that he had escaped. His elder comrade, when the smoke cleared away, was seen also beyond the reach of Cleveland's fire; but his altered pace and his relaxed seat in his saddle, made it apparent that he had received some hurt. This was confirmed when, still nearer to the summit, the stranger was seen to fall upon his horse's neck, and thence to be lifted to the ground by three or four soldiers who had hastened to his relief.

These incidents scarcely occupied more time in their performance than I have taken in the narrative; and all reflection upon them, for the present, was lost in the uproar and commotion of the bloody scene that succeeded.

Meanwhile, Campbell and Shelby, each at the head of his men in the centre division of the army, steadily commenced the ascent of the mountain. A long interval ensued, in which nothing was heard but the tramp of the soldiers and a few words of almost whispered command, as they scaled the height; and it was not until they had nearly reached the summit that the first peal of battle broke upon the sleeping echoes of the mountain.

Campbell here deployed into line, and his men strode briskly upwards until they had come within musket-shot of the British regulars, whose sharp and prolonged volleys, at this instant, suddenly burst forth from the crest of the hill. Peal after peal rattled along the mountain side, and volumes of smoke, silvered by the light of the sun, rolled over and enveloped the combatants.

When the breeze had partially swept away this cloud, and opened glimpses of the battle behind it, the troops of Campbell were seen recoiling before an impetuous charge of the bayonet, in which Ferguson himself led the way. A sudden halt by the retreating Whigs, and a stern front steadfastly opposed to the foe, checked the ardor of his pursuit at an early moment, and, in turn, he was discovered retiring towards his original ground, hotly followed by the mountaineers. Again, the same vigorous onset from the royalists was repeated, and again the shaken bands of Campbell rallied and turned back the rush of battle towards the summit. At last, panting and spent with the severe encounter, both parties stood for a space eyeing each other with deadly rage, and waiting only to gather breath for the renewal of the strife.

At this juncture, the distant firing heard from either flank furnished evidence that Sevier and Cleveland had both come in contact with the enemy. The uprising of smoke above the trees showed the seat of the combat to be below the summit on the mountain sides, and that the enemy had there half-way met his foe; whilst the shouts of the soldiers, alternating between the parties of either army, no less distinctly proclaimed the fact that, at these remote points, the field was disputed with bloody resolution and various success.

It would overtask my poor faculty of description, to give my reader even a faint picture of this rugged battle-field. During the pause of the combatants of the centre, Campbell and Shelby were seen riding along the line, and by speech and gesture encouraging their soldiers to still more determined efforts. Little need was there for exhortation; rage seemed to have refreshed the strength of the men, who, with loud and fierce huzzas, rushed again to the encounter. They were met with a defiance not less eager than their own; and, for a time, the battle was again obscured under the thick haze engendered by the incessant discharges of fire-arms. From this gloom, a yell of triumph was sometimes heard, as momentary success inspired those who struggled within; and the frequent twinkle of polished steel glimmering through the murky atmosphere, and the occasional apparition of a speeding horseman, seen for an instant as he came into the clear light, told of the dreadful earnestness and zeal with which the unseen hosts had now joined in conflict. The impression of this contact was various. Parts of each force broke before their antagonists; and in those spots where the array of the fight might be discerned through the shade of the forest or the smoke of battle, both royalists and Whigs were found, at the same instant, to have driven back detached fragments of their opponents. Foemen were mingled hand to hand, through and among their adverse ranks; and for a time no conjecture might be indulged as to the side to which victory would turn.

The flanking detachments seemed to have fallen into the same confusion, and might have been seen retreating and advancing upon the rough slopes of the mountain, in partisan bodies, separated from their lines; thus giving to the scene an air of bloody riot, more resembling the sudden insurrection of mutineers from the same rank, than the orderly war of trained soldiers.

Through the din and disorder of this fight, it is fit that I should take time to mark the wanderings of Galbraith Robinson, whose exploits this day would not ill deserve the pen of Froissart. The doughty sergeant had, for a time, retained his post in the ranks of the Amherst Rangers, and with them had travelled towards the mountain top, close in the rear of Campbell's line. But when the troops had recoiled before the frequent charges of the royalists, finding his station, at best, but that of an inactive spectator, he made no scruple of deserting his companions and trying his fortune on the field in such form of adventure as best suited his temper. With no other weapon than his customary rifle, he stood his ground when others retreated; and saw the ebb and flow of "flight and chase" swell round him, according to the varying destiny of the day. In these difficulties, it was his good fortune to escape unhurt; a piece of luck that may, perhaps, be attributed to the coolness with which he either galloped over an adversary or around him, as the emergency rendered most advisable.

In the midst of this busy occupation, at a moment when one of the refluxes of battle brought him almost to the summit, he descried a small party of British dragoons, stationed some distance in the rear of Ferguson's line, whose detached position seemed to infer some duty unconnected with the general fight. In the midst of these, he thought he recognised the figure and dress of one familiar to his eye. The person thus singled out by the sergeant's glance stood bare-headed upon a projecting mass of rock, apparently looking with an eager gaze towards the distant combat. No sooner did the conjecture that this might be Arthur Butler flash across his thought, than he turned his steed back upon the path by which he had ascended, and rode with haste towards the Rangers.

"Stephen Foster," he said, as he galloped up to the lieutenant and drew his attention by a tap of the hand upon his shoulder, "I have business for you, man — you are but wasting your time here — pick me out a half-dozen of your best fellows and bring them with you after me. Quick — Stephen — quick!"

The lieutenant of the Rangers collected the desired party and rode after the sergeant, who now conducted this handful of men with as much rapidity as the broken character of the ground allowed, by a circuit for a considerable distance along the right side of the mountain, until they reached the top. The point at which they gained the summit brought them between Ferguson's line and the dragoons, who, it was soon perceived, were the party charged with the custody of Butler, and who had been thus detached in the rear for the more safe guardianship of the prisoner. Horse Shoe's manœuvre had completely cut them off from their friends in front, and they had no resource but to defend themselves against the threatened assault, or fly towards the parties who were at this moment engaged with the flanking divisions of the Whigs. They were taken by surprise — and Horse Shoe, perceiving the importance of an immediate attack, dashed onwards along the ridge of the mountain with precipitate speed, calling out to his companions to follow. In a moment the dragoons were engaged in a desperate pell-mell with the Rangers.

"Upon them, Stephen! Upon them bravely, my lads! Huzza for Major Butler! Fling the major across your saddle —

the first that reaches him," shouted the sergeant with a voice that was heard above all the uproar of battle. "What ho — James Curry!" he cried out, as soon as he detected the presence of his old acquaintance in the throng; "stand your ground, if you are a man!"

The person to whom this challenge was directed had made an effort to escape towards a party of his friends, whom he was about summoning to his aid; and in the attempt had already ridden some distance into the wood, whither the sergeant had eagerly followed him.

"Ah ha, old Trupenny, are you there?" exclaimed Curry, turning short upon his pursuer, and affecting to laugh as if in scorn. "Horse Shoe Robinson, well met!" he added sternly, "I have not seen a better sight to-day than that fool's head of yours upon this hill. No, not even when just now Patrick Ferguson sent your yelping curs back to hide themselves behind the trees."

"Come on, James!" cried Horse Shoe, "I have no time to talk. We have an old reckoning to settle, which, perhaps, you mought remember. I am a man of my word; and, besides, I have set my eye upon Major Butler," he added, with a tone and look that were both impressed with the fierce passion of the scene around him.

"The devil blast you, and Major Butler to boot!" exclaimed Curry, roused by Horse Shoe's air of defiance. "To it, bully! It shall be short work between us, and bloody," he shouted, as he discharged a pistol-shot at the sergeant's breast; which failing to take effect, he flung the weapon upon the ground, brandished his sword, and spurred immediately against his challenger. The sweep of the broadsword fell upon the barrel of Horse Shoe's uplifted rifle, and in the next instant the broad hand of our lusty yeoman had seized the trooper by the collar and dragged him from his horse. The two soldiers came to the ground, locked in a mutual embrace; and, for a brief moment, a desperate trial of strength was exhibited in the effort to gain their feet.

"I have you there," said Robinson, as at length, with a flushed cheek, quick breath, and blood-shot eye, he rose from the earth and shook the dragoon from him, who fell backwards on his knee. "Curse you, James Curry, for a fool and villain! You almost drive me, against my will, to the taking of your life. I don't want your blood. You are beaten, man, and must say so. I grant you quarter upon condition —"

"Look to yourself! I ask no terms from you," interrupted

Curry, as suddenly springing to his feet, he now made a second pass, which was swung with such unexpected vigor at the head of his adversary, that Horse Shoe had barely time to catch the blow, as before, upon his rifle. The broadsword was broken by the stroke, and one of the fragments of the blade struck the sergeant upon the forehead, inflicting a wound that covered his face with blood. Horse Shoe reeled a step or two from his ground, and clubbing the rifle, as it is called, by grasping the barrel towards the muzzle, he paused but an instant to dash the blood from his brow with his hand, and then, with one lusty sweep, to which his sudden anger gave both precision and energy, he brought the piece full upon the head of his foe, with such fatal effect as to bury the lock in the trooper's brain, whilst the stock was shattered into splinters. Curry, almost without a groan, fell dead across a ledge of rock at his feet.

"The grudge is done, and the fool has met his desarvings," was Horse Shoe's brief comment upon the event, as he gazed sullenly, for an instant, upon the dead corpse. He had no time to tarry. The rest of his party were still engaged with the troopers of the guard, who now struggled to preserve the custody of their prisoner. The bridle-rein of Captain Peter had been caught by one of the Rangers, and the good steed was now quickly delivered up to his master, who, flinging himself again into his saddle, rushed into the throng of combatants. The few dragoons, dispirited by the loss of their leader, and stricken with panic at this strenuous onset, turned to flight, leaving Butler in the midst of his friends.

"God bless you, major!" shouted Robinson, as he rode up to his old comrade, who, unarmed, had looked upon the struggle with an interest corresponding to the stake he had in the event. "Up, man — here, spring across the pommel. Now, boys, down the mountain, for your lives! Huzza, huzza! we have won him back!" he exclaimed, as seizing Butler's arm, he lifted him upon the neck of Captain Peter, and bounded away at full speed towards the base of the mountain, followed by Foster and his party.

The reader may imagine the poignancy of Mildred's emotions as she sat beside Allen Musgrove and his daughter on the knoll, and watched the busy and stirring scene before her. The centre division of the assailing army was immediately in her view, on the opposite face of the mountain, and no incident of the battle in this quarter escaped her notice. She could distinctly perceive the motions of the Amherst Rangers, to whom she turned her eyes with a frequent and eager glance, as the corps with which her brother Henry was associated; and when the various fortune of the fight disclosed to her the occasional retreat of her friends before the vigorous sallies of the enemy, or brought to her ear the renewed and angry volleys of musketry, she clenched Mary Musgrove's arm with a nervous grasp, and uttered short and anxious ejaculations that showed the terror of her mind.

"I see Mister Henry, yet," said Mary, as Campbell's troops rallied from the last shock, and again moved towards the summit. "I see him plainly, ma'am — for I know his green dress, and caught the glitter of his brass bugle in the sun. And there now — all is smoke again. Mercy, how stubborn are these men! And there is Mister Henry once more — near the top. He is safe, ma'am."

"How earnestly," said Mildred, unconsciously speaking aloud as she surveyed the scene, "Oh, how earnestly do I wish this battle was done! I would rather, Mr. Musgrove, be in the midst of yonder crowd of angry men, could I but have their recklessness, than here in safety, to be tortured with my present feelings."

"In God is our trust, madam," replied the miller. "His arm is abroad over the dangerous paths, for a shield and buckler to them that put their trust in him. Ha! there is Ferguson's white horse, rushing, with a dangling rein and empty saddle, down the mountain, through Campbell's ranks: the rider has fallen; and there, madam — there, look on it! — is a white flag waving in the hands of a British officer. The fight is done. Hark, our friends are cheering with a loud voice!"

"Thank Heaven — thank Heaven!" exclaimed Mildred as she sprang upon her feet; "It is even so!"

The loud huzzas of the troops rose upon the air; the firing ceased; the flag of truce fluttered in the breeze, and the confederated bands of the mountaineers, from every quarter of the late battle, were seen hurrying towards the crest of the mountain, and mingling amongst the ranks of the conquered foe. Again and again, the clamorous cheering of the victors broke forth from the mountain-top, and echoed along the neighboring valleys.

During this wild clamor and busy movement, a party of horsemen were seen, through the occasional intervals of the low wood that skirted the valley on the right, hastening from the field with an eager swiftness towards the spot where Mildred and her companions were stationed.

As they swept along the base of the mountain, and approached the knoll, they were lost to view behind the projecting angles of the low hills that formed the ravine, through which, my reader is aware, the road held its course. When they re-appeared it was in ascending the abrupt acclivity of the knoll, and within fifty paces of the party on the top of it.

It was now apparent that the approaching party consisted of Stephen Foster and three or four of the Rangers led by Horse Shoe Robinson, with Butler still seated before him, as when the sergeant first caught him up in the fight. These were at the same moment overtaken by Henry Lindsay, who had turned back from the mountain at the first announcement of victory, to bring the tidings to his sister.

Mildred's cheek grew deadly pale, and her frame shook, as the calvalcade rushed into her presence.

"There — take him!" cried Horse Shoe, with an effort to laugh, but which seemed to be half converted into a quaver by the agitation of his feelings, as, springing to the ground, he swung Butler from the horse, with scarce more effort than he would have used in handling a child; "take him, ma'am. I promised myself to-day, that I'd give him to you. And, now, you've got him. That's a good reward for all your troubles. God bless us — but I'm happy to-day!"

"MY HUSBAND! — MY DEAR HUSBAND!" were the only articulate words that escaped Mildred's lips, as she fell senseless into the arms of Arthur Butler.

CHAPTER LVIII

THE CONCLUSION

THE victory was won. In the last assault, Campbell had reached the crest of the mountain, and the loyalists had given ground with decisive indications of defeat. Ferguson, in the hopeless effort to rally his soldiers, had flung himself into their van, but a bullet at this instant reached his heart; he fell from his seat, and his white horse, which had been conspicuous in the crowd of battle, bounded wildly through the ranks of the Whigs, and made his way down the mountain side.

Campbell passed onward, driving the royalists before him. For a moment the discomfited bands hoped to join their comrades in the rear, and, by a united effort, to effect a retreat: but the parties led by Sevier and Cleveland, cheered by the shouts of their victorious companions, urged their attacks with new vigor, and won the hill in time to intercept the fugitives. All hopes of escape being thus at an end, a white flag was displayed in token of submission; and the remnant of Ferguson's late proud and boastful army, now amounting to between eight and nine hundred men, surrendered to the assailants.

It has scarcely ever happened that a battle has been fought, in which the combatants met with keener individual exasperation than in this. The mortal hatred which embittered the feelings of Whig and Tory along this border, here vented itself in the eagerness of conflict, and gave the impulse to every blow that was struck — rendering the fight, from beginning to end, relentless, vindictive, and bloody. The remembrance of the thousand cruelties practised by the royalists during the brief Tory dominion to which my narrative has been confined, was fresh in the minds of the stern and hardy men of the mountains, who had pursued their foe with such fierce animosity to this his last stage. Every one had some wrong to tell, and burned with an unquenchable rage of revenge. It was, therefore, with a yell of triumph that they saw the symbol of submission raised aloft by the enemy; and for a space, the forest rang with their loud and reiterated huzzas.

Many brave men fell on either side. Upon the slopes of the

mountain and on its summit, the bodies of the dead and dying lay scattered amongst the rocks, and the feeble groans of the wounded mingled with the fierce tones of exultation from the living. The Whigs sustained a grievous loss in Colonel Williams, who had been struck down in the moment of victory. He was young, ardent, and brave; and his many soldier-like virtues, combined with a generous and amiable temper, had rendered him a cherished favorite with the army. His death served still more to increase the exacerbation of the conquerors against the conquered.

The sun was yet an hour high when the battle was done. The Whigs were formed in two lines on the ridge of the mountain; and the prisoners, more numerous than their captors, having laid down their arms, were drawn up in detached columns on the intervening ground. There were many sullen and angry glances exchanged, during this period of suspense, between victors and vanquished; and it was with a fearful rankling of inward wrath, that many of the Whigs detected, in the columns of the prisoners, some of their bitterest persecutors.

This spirit was partially suppressed in the busy occupation that followed. Preparations were directed to be made for the night-quarters of the army; and the whole host was, accordingly, ordered to march to the valley. The surgeons of each party were already fully employed in their vocation. The bodies of the wounded were strewed around; and, for the protection of such as were not in a condition to be moved, shelters were made of the boughs of trees, and fires kindled to guard them from the early frost of the season. All the rest retired slowly to the appointed encampment.

Whilst Campbell was intent upon these cares, a messenger came to summon him to a scene of unexpected interest. He was informed that a gentleman, not attached to the army, had been dangerously wounded in the fight, and now lay at the further extremity of the mountain ridge. It was added that he earnestly desired an interview with the commanding officer. Campbell lost no time in attending to the request.

Upon repairing to the spot, his attention was drawn to a stranger who lay upon the ground. His wan and haggard cheek, and restless eye, showed that he suffered acute pain; and the blood upon his cloak, which had been spread beneath him, indicated the wound to have been received in the side. A private soldier of the British army was his only attendant. To Campbell's solicitous and kind inquiry, he announced himself, in a voice that was almost over-mastered by his bodily anguish, to be Philip Lindsay, of Virginia.

"You behold," he said, "an unhappy father in pursuit of his children." Then, after a pause, he continued, "My daughter Mildred, I have been told, is near me: I would see her, and quickly."

"God have mercy on us!" exclaimed Campbell, "is this the father of the lady who has sought my protection? Wounded too, and badly, I fear! Where is Major Butler, who was lately prisoner with Ferguson?" he said, addressing the attendant —"Go, go, sir," he added, speaking to the same person, "bring me the first surgeon you can find, and direct some three or four men from the ranks to come to your aid. Lose no time."

The soldier went instantly upon the errand, and soon returned with the desired assistance. Lindsay's wound had been already staunched, and all that remained to be done was to put him in some place of shelter and comfort. A cottage at the foot of the mountain was pointed out by Campbell; a litter was constructed, and the sick man was borne upon the shoulders of four attendants to the designated spot. Meantime, Campbell rode off to communicate the discovery he had made to Mildred and her brother.

Lindsay's story, since we last parted from him, may be briefly told. He and Tyrrel had journeyed into the low country of Virginia, to meet the friends of the royal government. These had wavered, and were not to be brought together. A delay ensued, during which Tyrrel had prevailed upon Lindsay to extend his journey into North Carolina; whence, after an ineffectual effort to bring the Tory party to some decisive step, they both returned to the Dove Cote, having been nearly three weeks absent.

Upon their arrival, the afflicting intelligence met Lindsay of the departure of Mildred and her brother for the seat of war. Mildred's letter was delivered to him; and its contents almost struck him dumb. It related the story of Arthur Butler's misfortunes, and announced, that, for nearly a year past, Mildred had been the wedded wife of the captive officer. The marriage had been solemnized in the preceding autumn, in a hasty moment, as Butler travelled south to join the army. The only witnesses were Mistress Dimock, under whose roof it had occurred, Henry Lindsay, and the clergyman. The motives that induced this marriage were explained: both Mildred and Arthur hoped, by this irremediable step, to reconcile Lindsay to the event, and to turn his mind from its unhappy broodings: the increased exasperation of his feelings, during the succeeding period, prevented the disclosure which Mildred had again and again essayed to make. The recent dangers which had beset Arthur Butler, had determined her to fly to his rescue. As HIS WIFE she felt it to be her duty, and she had, accordingly, resolved to encounter the peril of the journey.

For a day or two after the perusal of this letter, Lindsay fell into a deep melancholy. His presentiments seemed to have been fatally realized, and his hopes suddenly destroyed. From this despondency, Tyrrel's assiduous artifice aroused him. He proposed to Lindsay the pursuit of his children, in the hope of thus luring him into Cornwallis's camp, and connecting him with the fortunes of the war. The chances of life, he reasoned, were against Butler, if indeed, as Tyrrel had ground to hope, that officer were not already the victim of the snares that had been laid for him.

Upon this advice, Lindsay had set out for Cornwallis's head-quarters, where he arrived within a week after the interview of Mildred and Henry with the British chief.

Whilst he delayed here, he received the tidings that his daughter had abandoned her homeward journey, and turned aside in quest of Butler. This determined him to continue his pursuit. Tyrrel still accompanied him; and the two travellers having arrived at the moment of the attack upon King's mountain, Lindsay was persuaded by his companion to make the rash adventure which, we have already seen, had been the cause of his present misfortune.

It is not my purpose to attempt a description of the scene in the cottage, where Arthur Butler and his wife, and Henry, first saw Lindsay stretched upon a rude pallet, and suffering the anguish of a dangerous wound. It is sufficient to say that, in the midst of the deep grief of the bystanders, Lindsay was composed and tranquil, like one who thought it vain to struggle with fate. "I have foreseen this day, and felt its coming," he muttered, in a low and broken voice; "it has happened as it was ordained. I have unwisely struggled against my doom. There, take it," he added, as he stretched forth his hand to Butler, and in tones scarcely audible breathed out, "God bless you, my children! I forgive you."

During the night fever ensued, and with it came delirium. The patient acquired strength from his disease, and raved wildly, in a strain familiar to his waking superstition. The same vision of fate and destiny haunted his imagination; and he almost frightened his daughter from beside his couch, with the fervid eloquence of his madness.

The cottage was situated near half a mile from the encampment of the army. Towards daylight, Lindsay had sunk into a slumber, and the attendant surgeon began to entertain hopes that the patient might successfully struggle with his malady. Mildred and Mary Musgrove kept watch in the apartment, whilst Butler, with Horse Shoe Robinson and Allen Musgrove, remained anxiously awake in the adjoining room. Henry Lindsay, wearied with the toils of the preceding day, and old Isaac the negro, not so much from the provocation of previous labor as from constitutional torpor, lay stretched in deep sleep upon the floor.

Such was the state of things when, near sunrise, a distant murmur reached the ears of those who were awake in the cottage. These sounds attracted the notice of Horse Shoe, who immediately afterwards stole out of the apartment and repaired to the camp. During his walk thither the uproar became more distinct, and shouts were heard from a crowd of soldiers who were discovered in a confused and agitated mass in the valley, at some distance from the encampment. The sergeant hastened to this spot, and, upon his arrival, was struck with the shocking sight of the bodies of some eight or ten of the Tory prisoners suspended to the limbs of a large tree.

The repose of the night had not allayed the thirst of revenge amongst the Whigs. On the contrary, the opportunity of conference and deliberation had only given a more fatal certainty to their purpose. The recent executions which had been permitted in Cornwallis's camp, after the battle of Camden, no less than the atrocities lately practised by some of the Tories who were now amongst the captured, suggested the idea of a signal retribution. The obnoxious individuals were dragged forth from their ranks at early dawn, and summary punishment was inflicted by the excited soldiery in the manner which we have described, in spite of all remonstrance or command.

This dreadful work was still in progress when Horse Shoe arrived. The crowd were, at that moment, forcing along to the spot of execution a trembling wretch, whose gaunt form, crouching beneath the hands that held him, and pitiful supplications for mercy, announced him to the sergeant as an old acquaintance. The unfortunate man had caught a glance of Robinson, and, almost frantic with despair, sprang with a tiger's leap from the grasp of those who held him, and, in an instant, threw his arms around the sergeant's neck, where he clung with the hold of a drowning man.

"Oh save me, save me, Horse Shoe Robinson!" he exclaimed wildly. "Friend Horse Shoe, save me!"

"I am no friend of yours, Wat Adair," said Robinson, sternly.

"Speak for me — Galbraith — speak, for old acquaintance sake!"

"Hold!" said Robinson to the crowd who had gathered round to pluck the fugitive from his present refuge. "One word, friends! stand back, I have somewhat to say in this matter."

"He gave Butler into Hugh Habershaw's hands," cried out some of the crowd.

"He took the price of blood, and sold Butler's life for money — he shall die!" shouted others.

"No words!" exclaimed many, "but up with him!"

"Mr. Robinson," screamed Adair, with tears starting from his eyes, "only hear me! I was forced to take sides against Major Butler. The Tories would have burnt down my house; they suspected me, — I was obliged, — Mike Lynch was witness, — mercy, mercy!" and here the frightened culprit cried loud and bitterly.

"Friends," said Horse Shoe calmly to the multitude, "there is better game to hunt than this mountain-cat. Let me have my way."

"None has a better right than Horse Shoe Robinson," said a speaker from the group, "to say what ought to be done to Wat Adair. Speak out, Horse Shoe!"

"Speak! We leave it to you," shouted some of the leaders: and instantly the crowd fell back and formed a circle round Horse Shoe and Adair.

"I give you your choice," said the sergeant, addressing the captive, "for though your iniquities, Wat Adair, desarve that you should have been the first that was strung up to yonder tree, yet you shall have your choice, to tell us fully and truly, without holding back name of high or low, who put you on to ambush Major Arthur Butler's life at Grindall's Ford. Tell us that, to our satisfaction, and answer all other questions besides that we may ax you, and you shall have your life, taking, howsever, one hundred lashes to the back of it."

"I will confess all, before God, truly," cried Adair with eagerness. " James Curry told me of your coming, and gave me and Mike Lynch money to help Hugh Habershaw."

" James Curry had a master in the business," said Robinson: " His name? "

Adair hesitated for an instant and stammered out " Captain St. Jermyn."

" He was at your house? Speak it, man, or think of the rope! "

" He was there," said Adair.

" By my soul! Wat Adair, if you do not come out with the whole truth," said Robinson, with angry earnestness, " I take back my promise. Tell me all you know."

" Curry acted by the captain's directions," continued the woodsman, " he was well paid for it, as he told me, and would have got more, if a quarrel amongst Habershaw's people hadn't stopped them from taking Major Butler's life. So I have heard from the men myself."

" Well, sir? "

" That's all," replied Adair.

" Do you know nothing about the court-martial? " asked Robinson.

" Nothing, except that as the Major wasn't killed at the Ford, it was thought best to have a trial, wherein James Curry and Habershaw, as I was told, had agreed to swear against the Major's life."

" And were paid for it? "

" It was upon a consideration, in course," replied Adair.

" And Captain St. Jermyn contrived this? "

" It was said," answered Adair, " that the captain left it all to Curry, and rather seemed to take Major Butler's side himself at the trial. He didn't want to be known in the business! "

" Where is this Captain St. Jermyn? " demanded many voices.

This interrogatory was followed by the rush of the party towards the quarter in which the prisoners were assembled, and, after a lapse of time which seemed incredibly short for the performance of the deed, the unhappy victim of this tumultuary wrath was seen struggling in the agonies of death, as he hung from one of the boughs of the same tree which had supplied the means of the other executions.

By this time Butler and Henry Lindsay, attracted by the shouts that reached them at the cottage, had arrived at the scene of these dreadful events. Wat Adair was, at this moment, undergoing the punishment for which his first sentence was commuted.

The lashes were inflicted by a sturdy arm upon his uncovered back; and it was remarkable that the wretch who but lately had sunk, with the most slavish fear, under the threat of death, now bore his stripes with a fortitude that seemed to disdain complaint or even the confession of pain. Butler and Henry hurried with a natural disgust from this spectacle, and soon found themselves near the spot where the lifeless forms of the victims of military vengeance were suspended from the tree.

"Gracious Heaven!" exclaimed Butler, "is not that St. Jermyn? What has he done to provoke this doom?"

"It is Tyrrel!" ejaculated Henry. "Major Butler, it is Tyrrel! That face, black and horrible as it is to look at, I would know it among a thousand!"

"Indeed!" said Butler, gazing with a melancholy earnestness upon the scene, and speaking scarce above his breath, "is it so? Tyrrel and St. Jermyn the same person! This is a strange mystery."

Robinson, at this moment, approached, and, in answer to Butler's questions, told the whole story of the commotions that had just agitated the camp.

"St. Jermyn was not with Ferguson," said Butler, when the sergeant had finished his narrative. "How came he here today?"

"First or last," replied Robinson, "it is my observation, Major, that these schemers and contrivers against others' lives are sure to come to account. The devil put it into this St. Jermyn's head to make Ferguson a visit. He came yesterday with Mr. Lindsay, and got the poor gentleman his hurt. James Curry has done working for him now, Major. Master and man have travelled one road."

The scene was now closed. The business of the day called the troops to other labors. Campbell felt the necessity of an immediate retreat with his prisoners to the mountains, and his earliest orders directed the army to prepare for the march.

When Butler returned to the cottage, he found himself surrounded by a mournful group. The malady of Lindsay had unexpectedly taken a fatal turn. Mildred and Henry were seated by the couch of their father, watching in mute anguish the last ebbings of life. The dying man was composed and apparently free from pain, and the few words he spoke were of forgiveness and resignation.

In the midst of their sorrow and silence, the inmates of the dwelling had their attention awakened by the military music of the retiring army. These cheerful sounds vividly contrasted with the grief of the mourners, and told of the professional indifference of soldiers to the calamities of war. By degrees, the martial tones became more faint, as the troops receded up the valley; and before they were quite lost to the ear, Campbell and Shelby appeared at the door of the cottage to explain the urgency of their present departure, and to take a sad farewell of their friends.

Stephen Foster, with Harry Winter and a party of the Rangers, remained behind to await the movements of Butler. Horse Shoe Robinson, Allen Musgrove, and his daughter, were in constant attendance.

Here ends my story.

In a lonely thicket, close upon the margin of the little brook which waters the valley on the eastern side of King's mountain, the traveller of the present day may be shown an almost obliterated mound, and hard by he will see the fragment of a rude tombstone, on which is carved the letters P. L. This vestige marks the spot where the remains of Philip Lindsay were laid, until the restoration of peace allowed them to be transported to the Dove Cote.

There, also, in a happier day, Arthur Butler and Mildred took up their abode; and notwithstanding the fatal presentiment in regard to the fortunes of his house which had thrown so dark a color upon the life of Philip Lindsay, lived long enough after the revolution to see grow up around them a prosperous and estimable family.

Mary Musgrove, too, attended Mildred, and attained an advanced, and I hope a happy old age, at the Dove Cote.

Wat Adair, I have heard it said in Carolina, died a year after the battle of King's mountain, of a horrible distemper, supposed to have been produced by the bite of a rabid wolf. I would fain believe, for the sake of poetical justice, that this was true.

Another item of intelligence, to be found in the history of the war, may have some reference to our tale. I find that, in the summer of 1781, Colonel Butler was engaged in the pursuit of Cornwallis in his retreat from Albemarle towards Williamsburg: my inquiries do not enable me to say, with precision, whether it was our friend Arthur Butler who had met this promotion. His sufferings in the cause certainly deserved such a reward.